3-22-2022 See pg. 195 - Cabbage

GREAT RECIPES
FOR GOOD HEALTH

Beef Stew with Basil-Tomato Paste

Reader's Digest

GREAT RECIPES
FOR GOOD HEALTH

The Reader's Digest Association, Inc.
Pleasantville, New York/Montreal

GREAT RECIPES
FOR GOOD HEALTH

Editor: Inge N. Dobelis
Art Editor: Gerald Ferguson
Senior Editor: Gayla Visalli
Associate Art Editor: Colin Joh
Editorial Assistant: Theresa Lane

CONTRIBUTORS
Editors: Fred DuBose, Lea Gordon
Copy Editor: Virginia Croft
Writer: Paula Dranov
Indexer: Sydney Wolfe Cohen

Photography: William Pell
Food Styling: Betty Pell

Recipe Developers: Jo Ann Billowitz,
Georgia Downard, Sandra Gluck, Michele Scicolone

CONSULTANTS
Chief Consultant: Jean Anderson
Nutrition Consultant: Paul A. LaChance, Ph.D.
    Professor of Nutrition and Food Science
    Rutgers University

ACKNOWLEDGMENTS
Harry Hartman for photographs on cover and p. 160.
Gordon Smith for photograph on p. 152.
Villeroy & Boch Tableware Ltd. for
chinaware in photographs on pp. 76, 115, 122,
168, 195, 233.

READER'S DIGEST GENERAL BOOKS
Editor in Chief: John A. Pope, Jr.
Managing Editor: Jane Polley
Art Director: David Trooper
Group Editors: Norman B. Mack,
Susan J. Wernert,
Joseph L. Gardner (International),
Joel Musler (Art)
Chief of Research: Monica Borrowman
Copy Chief: Edward W. Atkinson
Picture Editor: Robert J. Woodward
Rights and Permissions: Pat Colomban
Head Librarian: Jo Manning

Library of Congress Cataloging in Publication Data

Great recipes for good health/Reader's digest.
    p. cm.
    Includes index.
    ISBN 0-89577-306-6
    1. Nutrition. 2. Cookery. I. Reader's Digest Association.
RA784.G75 1988   88-6733
641.5′63 — dc 19   CIP

Contents

7 Eating Well, Staying Healthy

25 Great Homemade Substitutes

37 Appetizers and Snacks

49 Soups

63 Meats

91 Poultry

117 Fish and Shellfish

131 Meatless Main Dishes

151 Pasta and Grains

173 Vegetables

205 Salads and Salad Dressings

227 Breads

241 Cooking for One or Two

255 Breakfasts and Brown Bag Lunches

267 Beverages

275 Desserts

293 Index

About This Book

In the last few years there has been a surge of interest in food and cooking, and what used to be considered "gourmet" food has become everyday fare. Side by side with this trend, a new concern about the healthfulness of the American diet has arisen, and the latest studies on nutrition now make front-page news. It is clear that Americans want to enjoy good health as much as they enjoy good food.

Fortunately, these aims are no longer considered contradictory. Healthy food need not be just bean sprouts and granola, and GREAT RECIPES FOR GOOD HEALTH proves that it can be delicious. Every recipe in the book has been carefully created not only to meet recommended guidelines that doctors and nutritionists say may add years to your life but also to let you continue enjoying one of life's great pleasures.

In all, there are more than 450 original, tempting, and delightfully varied selections ranging from meat, poultry, and fish dishes to pastas, salads, meatless main dishes, and desserts. Many are new versions of such old-time favorites as pot roast, potato salad, and Black Forest cake. Each recipe is followed by a complete nutritional analysis so that you'll know exactly how many calories you are getting, along with how much fat, cholesterol, sodium, sugar, protein, carbohydrates, and fiber. With the help of these data, plus the nutritional information in Chapter 1, you'll be able to mix and match recipes to meet your daily requirements.

Excess fat, sugar, and sodium have been implicated as major villains in the American diet. No main course in GREAT RECIPES FOR GOOD HEALTH has more than 18 grams of fat per serving—considerably less than the fat in a cup of cottage cheese. Sodium is kept to a minimum by the creative use of herbs and spices, inspired by the best of regional and international cuisines. Sugar is rarely added, except to desserts, and even there, the content is far less than that of ordinary sweets. Yet with all this, flavor is never sacrificed.

Although this book should not be used as a substitute for a physician's advice, people on restricted diets are sure to find many dishes that are within the guidelines their doctors recommend. This is especially true of recipes designated as extra low in fat, sugar, and sodium. These recipes are marked with special symbols for ease of reference.

Whether you are cooking for family, company, or just yourself, you'll find GREAT RECIPES FOR GOOD HEALTH indispensable in your kitchen. It's the book that proves you truly can combine great taste with good nutrition. To your health!

—The Editors

Eating Well, Staying Healthy

If you want to switch to a healthful diet, do you have to give up the foods you love? The recipes in this book prove that you do not, and this chapter tells you why. It explains the role of fat, cholesterol, sodium, protein, and carbohydrates in your diet, and tells you how to cook meals that are both good for you and delicious.

"You are what you eat." That old saw has never been taken more seriously than it is today. Interest in the way diet affects health is mounting higher all the time, and there is welcome evidence of a lasting shift in public taste. It's a sure sign that eating habits are changing when more and more makers of canned foods introduce products with "no salt added," and when margarine boxes trumpet "no cholesterol!" Excessive salt, cholesterol, and fat are now recognized as dietary bugbears, and the way Americans eat may never be the same again.

More dramatic evidence that Americans are changing their habits is the rate at which heart disease and stroke are steadily declining—in a nation that traditionally has had one of the highest incidences of those two problems. In the 1950s, studies linking diet to disease demonstrated that heart disease occurs most often in those affluent parts of the world where meat, eggs, and cheese are heavily consumed—and least often in poor countries where people still depend primarily on grains, fruits, and vegetables. Since then, researchers have established that switching from saturated fats like butter and lard to polyunsaturated and monounsaturated fats like corn oil and olive oil can lower the risk of stroke and heart disease. The latest findings suggest that dietary changes may actually halt the progression of heart disease and even reverse it.

Cancer, too, may be diet related in some cases. As with heart disease, there is an increased incidence of breast, colon, and prostate cancer among people whose diets are high in fat. So far, there is little scientific proof that reducing the consumption of fat will prevent cancer, but many health authorities believe that it is worth a try. And even if cutting back on fats in the diet does not help prevent cancer, it benefits health in other ways.

At the same time that people are being told to go easy on fatty foods, they are being encouraged to eat *more* whole-grain breads, cereals, and fresh fruits and vegetables in order to increase their intake of both fiber and certain vitamins and minerals. Adding fiber to the diet appears to reduce the risk of colon cancer and can relieve some common intestinal disorders.

But where does all this new awareness leave your taste buds? With the right recipes, in as good shape as they were before. Eating sensibly does not necessarily mean sticking to some rigid diet of boring "health foods." It simply means preparing dishes—quite sumptuous ones, really—with less of the fat that contributes little to your health but a lot to your waistline; with less salt and more flavor-enhancing herbs and spices; and with none of the "empty calories" that are the by-product of too much sugar. This book is designed to show you that healthy eating does not have to mean denial—that, in fact, if you follow a few simple dietary guidelines, you can still eat well, feel great, and perhaps even add years to your life.

Fat

Some fat in the diet is necessary. Besides giving substance and flavor to food, it plays a vital role in the maintenance of cell membranes and in furnishing the fatty acids that the body needs. It provides substantial energy. It also keeps the skin from drying and flaking and helps the body to absorb vitamins A, D, E, and K.

Amazingly, it takes very little dietary fat to accomplish all these tasks. A single daily tablespoon of polyunsaturated fat (the kind found in most vegetable oils) will do the trick. Despite this modest need, most people consume nearly half their daily calories as fat—considerably more than they need. Even if you cut down by eliminating butter, mayonnaise, and other obvious sources, you still may be consuming large quantities of "hidden" fat in meat, nuts, eggs, whole milk, and cheese. And the way food is prepared may add even more fat to your diet. All fried foods are extraordinarily fatty, as are many traditional and tempting sauces, gravies, pizzas, and desserts.

Compared to carbohydrates and protein, fat is a highly concentrated source of energy. A single gram contains 9 calories, compared to the 4 in both proteins and carbohydrates. No wonder cutting down on fats is so important in the battle to lose weight! And because so little fat is needed to maintain good health, there is no danger at all in limiting your intake.

Although doctors and nutritionists recommend reducing the amount of fat in the diet, no one is suggesting limiting it to a single tablespoon per day. A diet that stringent would deprive us of much of the taste and enjoyment food provides. Instead, nutritionists propose relatively modest changes aimed at bringing the amount of fat consumed down to between 20 and 30 percent of daily calories. Such an adjustment may significantly reduce the risks of both heart disease and cancer and will, without doubt, aid in weight loss.

The Cholesterol Connection

The relationship of a high-fat diet to heart disease is well known by now, as is the effect that high cholesterol has on health. But because the link between fat and cholesterol and their effects on the heart are still being clarified, the fat-cholesterol connection is less well understood.

Cholesterol is a fatty substance produced in the liver and used by the body to help build cell membranes, construct protective sheaths around nerve fibers, and produce vitamin D and certain hormones. Although the body makes most of the cholesterol in the blood, some of it also comes from animal food sources, primarily from red meat, eggs, and dairy products.

High blood levels of cholesterol are associated with an increased risk of arteriosclerosis, the "hardening of the arteries" that can lead to heart attacks and strokes. This condition is the result of years of accumulation of fat deposits along the inner walls of the arteries that supply blood to the heart and to the principal arteries surrounding it. The buildup of these deposits, called plaque, can eventually cause the arteries to narrow so severely that blood flow to the heart and other organs may be impeded. Should the flow be cut off by a blood clot that cannot slip through the narrowed passageway, a heart attack occurs.

Not all cholesterol contributes to this process. You may have heard that there is a distinction between "good" and "bad" cholesterol. Actually, this difference applies to the means by which cholesterol travels in the blood. Because it is a fat and is insoluble in blood plasma, cholesterol cannot move about alone. Instead, it is transported in an envelope of a fat-protein complex called lipoprotein. When doctors speak of "good" or "bad" cholesterol, they are referring to the type of lipoprotein in which the cholesterol travels.

The beneficial kind, high-density lipoprotein or HDL, generally removes more cholesterol than it deposits and seems to protect against arteriosclerosis by sweeping cholesterol off artery walls and herding it back to the liver. There it is processed into the intestinal tract for elimination from the body. "Bad" cholesterol travels in two packages: very low-density lipoprotein (VLDL) and low-density lipoprotein (LDL). VLDL's deposit energy-giving triglycerides in the body's cells, losing these triglycerides in the process to become LDL's. Because the main purpose of LDL's is to keep cholesterol in circulation, they do not clean up after themselves as HDL's do.

Lowering blood cholesterol is not as simple as it sounds. While it is important to reduce high levels, the ratio of HDL to LDL is also a consideration. The higher the HDL, the better. Although most people have much more LDL than HDL, diet and exercise can do much to favorably alter the ratio. As far as diet is concerned, a change for the better generally means cutting down on saturated fats and using more of the unsaturated fats—olive oil and corn oil are examples— that have been found to actually lower blood cholesterol. If blood cholesterol is elevated, lowering the intake of foods that themselves contain cholesterol, such as organ meats and egg yolks is also advisable.

Dietary Guidelines

The U.S. Department of Agriculture and the Department of Health and Human Services have issued a set of dietary guidelines to help people make healthful changes in their eating habits. They consist of the following recommendations:

Eat a variety of foods.
Make sure your daily diet comes from all four food groups:(1) fruits and vegetables; (2) whole-grain and enriched breads, cereals, and other products made from grains; (3) milk, cheese, yogurt, and other products made from milk; and (4) meats, poultry, fish, eggs, and beans and peas.

Maintain your desirable weight.
To help control overeating, eat slowly, take smaller portions, and avoid "seconds." To lose weight, eat more fruits, vegetables, and whole grains; eat less fat and sugar; drink less alcohol; and increase your physical activity.

Avoid too much sodium.
Learn to enjoy the flavors of unsalted foods. Cook without salt or with only a small amount of added salt (try flavoring foods with herbs, spices, and lemon juice). Add little or no salt to food at the table. Limit your intake of salty foods such as potato chips, pretzels, salted nuts and popcorn, condiments (soy sauce, steak sauce, garlic salt), pickled foods, cured meats, some cheese, and some canned vegetables and soups. Read food labels carefully to determine the amounts of sodium. Use lower sodium products, when available, to replace those you use that have higher sodium content.

Eat foods with adequate starch and fiber.
Choose foods that are good sources of fiber and starch, such as whole-grain breads and cereals, fruits, vegetables, and beans and peas. Substitute starchy foods for those that have large amounts of fats and sugars.

Avoid too much sugar.
Use less of all sugars and foods containing large amounts of sugars, including white sugar, brown sugar, raw sugar, honey, and syrups (examples include soft drinks, candies, cakes, and cookies). Read food labels for clues on sugar content—if the word *sugar, sucrose, glucose, maltose, dextrose, lactose,* or *fructose* appears first, then there is a large amount of sugar. Select fresh fruits or fruits processed without syrup or with light, rather than heavy, syrup.

Avoid too much fat, saturated fat, and cholesterol.
Choose lean meat, fish, poultry, and beans and peas as protein sources. Use skim or low-fat milk and milk products. Moderate your use of egg yolks and organ meats. Limit your intake of fats and oils, especially those high in saturated fat, such as butter, cream, lard, heavily hydrogenated fats (some margarines), shortenings, and foods containing palm and coconut oils. Trim fat off meats. Broil, bake, or boil rather than fry. Moderate your use of foods that contain fat, such as breaded and deep-fried foods. Read labels carefully to determine both the amount and type of fat present in foods.

If you drink alcoholic beverages, do so in moderation.
Alcoholic beverages are high in calories and low in nutrients. Pregnant women should refrain from the use of alcohol altogether, but one or two standard-size drinks daily appear to cause no harm in other healthy adults. Note that 12 ounces of regular beer, 5 ounces of wine, and 1½ ounces of distilled spirits contain about equal amounts of alcohol.

Good Fats and Bad

The various fats in your diet influence your blood cholesterol levels in different ways, depending on their source.

Saturated fats are found in meat and poultry, milk, butter, cheese, egg yolks, margarine, lard, coconut and palm oils, and most chocolate. Saturated fats prompt the liver to produce unwanted LDL and VLDL and thereby increase cholesterol levels in the blood. Unlike other fats, they solidify at room temperature.

Monounsaturated fats come from such plant sources as olives, peanuts, cashews, and avocados, and are often consumed as the olive oil and peanut oil used in cooking. These oils reduce "bad" cholesterol levels. Confirming this are studies that have shown very low rates of heart disease in Mediterranean countries where cooks use olive oil instead of butter or other animal fats.

Polyunsaturated fats come from other plant sources such as almonds, walnuts, pecans, corn, cottonseeds, safflower seeds, soybeans, and sunflower seeds. Polyunsaturated fats reduce blood cholesterol because they promote HDL transport and discourage LDL and VLDL formation.

Omega-3 fatty acids, or fish oils, are another type of fat that can help lower cholesterol. The source is fatty fish. The discovery that this fat has important health benefits was made in the course of medical observations of Eskimos in Greenland, who subsist almost entirely on a high-fat diet of seal and whale meat, fatty fish, and blubber, yet have an extraordinarily low rate of heart disease. Further studies have confirmed the Greenland findings: people who eat a lot of fish have lower cholesterol levels and therefore a lower incidence of heart disease than those whose regular diets do not include fish. The fish that provide the most Omega-3 are such fatty varieties as tuna, salmon, sardines, mackerel, sablefish, whitefish, bluefish, swordfish, rainbow trout, and herring. Omega-3 is also found in shrimp and lobster, which also contain cholesterol and were previously off-limits for people on low-cholesterol diets. It is now thought that Omega-3 cancels out the harmful effects of the cholesterol in shrimp and lobster, and so it should not hurt to indulge in these shellfish occasionally. Today most heart specialists are so convinced of the benefits of Omega-3 that they have been urging everyone to substitute fish for meat or poultry as often as possible.

As a guideline for the consumption of fats, most authorities, including the American Heart Association, suggest consuming no more than 10 percent of daily calories as saturated fat, and dividing the remaining 20 percent of calories from fat, which completes the recommended daily maximum, between monounsaturated and polyunsaturated fats.

Weight Watching

Fat in the diet affects more than cholesterol levels, of course. It affects how fat *you* are, and losing weight has become something of a national obsession, for reasons of both health and vanity.

The only reliable way to lose weight is to eat less and exercise more. Yet every year millions of Americans reject this tried-and-true method in favor of fad or crash diets that cannot possibly work because they are too strict, too bizarre, or too boring to live with for any length of time. Although these diets may seem to succeed at first, the loss is all too often only temporary. Moreover, a pattern of losing and regaining weight on a succession of diets makes each new attempt to lose more difficult than the one before. It can also increase the risk of heart disease.

There is no doubt that, for health reasons alone, many people must lose weight. Obesity carries such serious risks as high blood pressure, diabetes, and heart disease. At last count, more than 34 million Americans were so overweight that their health was considered in danger. For some, however, the risk is more serious than for others. Studies have shown that the location of fat on the body, more than the number on the scale, is the best indication of whether or not your weight is endangering your health. Risks are greatest when fat is concentrated in the abdomen, and statistics show that men with large stomachs are at highest risk. Overweight is not as serious when fat is located primarily in the hips and thighs, as it is in many women.

Establishing a realistic weight goal is not as simple as it sounds. To determine how much they should weigh, many people rely on the height/weight tables published by insurance companies. These tables are somewhat misleading, however, because the desirable weights are calculated on the basis of studies showing the weights at which persons of varying heights are most likely to live longest. They do not take into consideration a very important variable: the proportion of fat to muscle. In general, for good health, a man's body should contain between 10 and 15 percent fat; a woman's healthy range is higher, between 20 and 25 percent. Some football players and other athletes weigh much more than is desirable for their height, but their weight is not considered dangerous because the extra weight is muscle, not fat. Conversely, some people who do not appear to be heavy may actually be overweight because they are not physically fit and have a higher ratio of fat to lean muscle tissue than is deemed healthy.

Try these simple tests to see whether you are fatter, or leaner, than you think:

If you are a man, measure your waist and your chest. If you are wider at the waist, you should lose.

If you are a woman, measure your waist and your

hips. If your waist measurement is 80 percent or more of your hip measurement, you need to lose.

Pinch a fold of skin from the back of your upper arm. If it is more than an inch thick, you should lose.

Losing Weight and Staying Trim

No matter how much you have to lose, the method is the same: start cutting calories by reducing your intake of fats and sugar. If you can eliminate 500 calories per day, you will lose 1 pound per week.

Although most people want to lose more quickly, a slow steady loss that accompanies a healthful change in eating habits is much more likely to be permanent. Nutritionists and weight-loss specialists strongly discourage people from losing weight too quickly because the body responds to a major cutback in calories by slowing the rate at which it burns them. This change is an attempt to conserve fuel in order to survive what the body perceives as a famine. The metabolic slowdown makes it harder to lose weight—the body simply does not use up calories at the same rate as before. The result usually is predictable: dieters feel so discouraged that they are either unlikely to reach their goal or unable to maintain the losses already achieved.

Another important factor in losing weight is increased physical activity. This does not necessarily mean that you must undertake such strenuous exercises as running or jogging, although both are excellent ways for the healthy person to burn calories. A brisk daily half-hour walk has a similar effect, burning approximately 180 calories. Over the course of a year, that can add up to an 18-pound weight loss.

Protein

Protein—obtained from either animal or plant sources—is the centerpiece around which most American meals are built. It is composed of substances called amino acids (there are 23 of them), which are needed to maintain muscle, bone, and nerves and to renew skin and blood. Protein is indispensable to the human diet, but this does not mean that you should load up on it, as most Americans do. Your body needs a fresh supply daily, but a little protein goes a long way. Whatever is left over gets stored—as fat.

The average adult needs only .36 grams of protein per pound of ideal body weight. That comes to 54 grams a day for a 150-pound man. (There are 26 grams of protein in a 4-ounce slice of chicken breast.) Requirements are greater for young children, pregnant women, and nursing mothers.

The average American consumes far more protein than necessary. This is not particularly harmful unless weight is a problem. Because the body cannot store unused protein, amounts consumed above and beyond what you need are converted into fat. Pure protein releases only 4 calories per gram, but because many high-protein foods are fatty, they tend to be relatively high in calories.

The notion that athletes need extra protein in the form of red meat to build muscles and supply extra energy is more fiction than fact. Red meat is no better for muscle building than any other type of protein, and studies have shown that carbohydrates, not proteins, are the body's most efficient source of energy. Today athletes are far more likely to load up on carbohydrates before they compete.

Besides having the potential for adding unwanted weight, protein presents some hazards in special cases. When you consume more than you need, your body must eliminate a protein by-product, nitrogen, via the urine. This is not a problem for healthy people, but it can put a strain on weak kidneys. For this reason, people whose kidneys do not function properly are usually placed on low-protein diets.

Animal Protein versus Plant Protein

Most of the protein people consume comes from meat, eggs, and dairy products, but plant foods also provide it. With few exceptions, animal protein contains all the amino acids needed, in correct proportion, for good health; for this reason, it is regarded as *complete* protein.

Plant proteins are *incomplete,* in that none contain all the essential amino acids in the proper amounts. However, you can get plenty of high-quality, complete protein from plants by learning to combine foods that together provide all the essential amino acids. All you have to do is be sure you have the proper ratio of two "complementary" plant sources of protein in the same meal. You can accomplish this with any one of the following three combinations: (1) grains (such as wheat, cornmeal, or rice) with legumes (beans, peas, or lentils); (2) grains with dairy products (milk, eggs, yogurt, cheese); (3) legumes with seeds or nuts (sesame, pumpkin, and sunflower seeds, all nuts, and tahini). Vegetarians have learned these combinations so well that their way of eating is now considered more healthful than the average American's.

Good Foods, Bad Foods

If you want to have a more healthful diet, there are certain foods you should avoid as often as possible—and others you should eat a lot of. In some cases, you might want to use the recipes in "Great Homemade Substitutes," which starts on page 26.

Foods to Avoid

Egg yolks
Butter
Lard
Mayonnaise
Whole milk
Cream
Sour cream
Ice cream
Fruit-flavored yogurt
Sirloin, T-bone, and porterhouse steaks
Regular ground beef
Beef or pork salami
Ham
Pork spare ribs
Bacon
Chicken and turkey skin
Canned soups and broths
White bread
Processed cereals
Potato chips
Soy sauce

Foods That Are Good for You

Egg whites
Monounsaturated and polyunsaturated
   cooking oils
Skim milk
Buttermilk
Nonfat dry milk
Plain low-fat yogurt
Low-fat cottage cheese
Ice milk
Round steak
Very lean or extra lean ground beef
Light meat of chicken or turkey
Lean ground turkey
Reduced-sodium ham
Low-sodium canned soups and broths
Whole-grain bread
Whole-grain cereals
Unflavored popcorn
Brown rice
Wild rice
Reduced-sodium soy sauce

10 Steps to Lowering Cholesterol

1. Eat more fruits, vegetables, and grains—especially certain fiber-rich ones that have been shown to lower cholesterol: oatmeal and oat bran, apples, berries, citrus fruits, and dried beans and peas.
2. Eat no more than 6 ounces of meat or poultry a day, and choose only lean red meat or the light meat of poultry.
3. Avoid organ meats.
4. Eat fish at least twice a week.
5. Eat no more than two or three egg yolks a week.

6. When you eat milk products, make sure they are low-fat.
7. When you cook, use less fat. Think "bake" instead of "fry."
8. When you buy cooking oil, check to see that it is monounsaturated or polyunsaturated.
9. If you are overweight, make an effort to lose.
10. Adopt the "blue moon rule": If your favorite food is loaded with cholesterol but you can't give it up, learn to eat it only once in a blue moon.

Carbohydrates

Nutritionally speaking, certain carbohydrate-laden foods—bread, pasta, rice, potatoes, cereals, and all fruits and vegetables—are real bargains. Every calorie they provide (only 4 per gram, the same amount as protein) pays off in energy-giving nutrients. And contrary to popular opinion, carbohydrates are no more fattening than other foods.

Technically, carbohydrates are compounds of carbon, hydrogen, and oxygen in the form of certain starches and sugars. During digestion, the body converts carbohydrates into glucose, which is essential for nourishment of the brain and nervous system and which supplies us with the fuel the body needs for energy.

Complex Carbohydrates

Particularly energy-boosting are the "complex" carbohydrates found in starchy foods like grains, legumes, vegetables, and some fruits. That is why athletes and runners find it to their advantage to "load up on carbos"—often in the form of a plate of pasta—before a game or race.

Current nutritional thinking holds that most of your daily calories should come from complex carbohydrates. It is important to remember, however, that most carbohydrate-rich foods lose their nutritional punch when they are highly processed or refined. For example, white flour, which has been stripped of wheat bran and the vitamin-packed wheat germ, does not measure up nutritionally to whole wheat flour, which contains both the bran and the germ. (Although manufacturers can enrich white flour by adding vitamins, they do not restore the valuable bran; nor do they restore the vitamins to their original potency.) The same goes for other grains. In general, the closer a carbohydrate food is to its natural state, the better it is for you. For this reason, whole-grain breads and cereals, legumes, and brown rice are described as "nutrient dense" because they arrive on our plates still packed with the vitamins, minerals, fiber, and protein with which nature endowed them.

Sugar

Sugars, too, are carbohydrates. And although sugar itself is no more fattening than other carbohydrates, it is used in such quantities in most desserts and candies that it is the main cause of weight gain for most people. There are 5 tablespoons of sugar, accounting for 240 calories, in a slice of chocolate cake and 4 in a small wedge of apple pie.

Even if you avoid desserts and other sweets, you may find it hard to eliminate added sugar from your diet. Processed foods, ranging from ketchup to canned soups, are sources of hidden sugar. Other common culprits are presweetened dry cereals (many of which, by weight, are more than 40 percent sugar) and soft drinks, which contain between 2 and 3 tablespoons per can.

All told, the average American consumes about 600 sugar calories per day. If only 100 of those calories are not burned off in physical activity and instead are turned to fat, over the course of a year they will cause a weight gain of about 10 pounds.

Fiber

The same carbohydrate-rich foods that are so valuable as nutrients provide another health benefit. Your grandmother called it roughage or bulk and ate a lot more of it than you do today. Now it is called fiber—the residue of whole grains, fruits, and vegetables that the digestive enzymes in the upper intestine cannot break down and that the bacteria in the lower intestine only partially digest. Not only is fiber found in wheat and oat brans (exceptionally good sources, as countless television commercials attest), but it is also present in varying forms and amounts in all plant foods. Besides bran, good sources include such legumes as kidney and lima beans, popcorn, dried figs and prunes, apples, almonds, and peanuts. Remember that only plant foods—never animal products—contain fiber.

The public became more aware of the value of fiber after a 1970 report by a British physician who found that people whose diets include large amounts rarely suffer from cancers of the colon or rectum and have a low rate of the digestive disorders that are commonplace in our society: chronic constipation, irritable bowel syndrome (a chronic stress-related condition characterized by constipation and/or diarrhea), hemorrhoids, and hiatus hernia. Some types of fiber, particularly the kind found in beans, peas, and other legumes, seem to help control blood sugar when they are consumed as part of a diet that emphasizes complex carbohydrates.

Exactly how fiber reduces the risk of colon cancer is still something of a scientific mystery. One theory holds that by helping speed wastes through the intestines, it lessens the chances of any cancer-causing substances (carcinogens) in food from coming into contact with the surface of the colon. There is also some scientific evidence that fiber may have the ability to attach to carcinogens and sweep them out of the body.

Despite all its apparent benefits, fiber does have some drawbacks. It has a tendency to stimulate production of intestinal gas and can cause bloating and diarrhea, particularly if large amounts are added to the diet too quickly. It is better to increase your intake gradually to give your body a chance to adjust to the change. Nutritionists recommend that adults slowly work their way up to consuming between 25 and 35 grams of fiber per day.

Another potential disadvantage is that some types of fiber can attach to minerals, including calcium and iron, before they can be absorbed, thus depriving the body of vital nutrients. This should not be a problem unless you consume considerably more fiber than recommended.

On balance, however, a healthful diet should contain more fiber than most Americans now consume. You can increase your intake simply by eating more vegetables and fruits, substituting whole-grain breads for those made with refined flour, using brown rice instead of white, and consuming more corn, barley, and other grains.

Sodium

Sodium, much of which is consumed in the form of table salt, is an essential mineral. But you need very little of it—a mere 200 milligrams per day, an amount equivalent to one-tenth of a teaspoon. The recommended daily allowance (RDA) established by the government is considerably more generous—between 1,100 and 3,300 milligrams, or about ½ to 1½ teaspoons. Even if you do not sprinkle your food with table salt, you probably take in far more than the RDA through the processed foods you consume. Government surveys have found that most adults consume between 2 and 4 teaspoons of salt daily.

Excess sodium in the diet is thought to aggravate hypertension (high blood pressure), a condition affecting one in four Americans. High blood pressure often produces no symptoms but increases the risk of heart attack, stroke, and kidney disease. Not everyone with high blood pressure, however, can be helped by cutting down on salt; in some cases, drug treatment is required. And some people consume unlimited amounts of sodium without suffering ill effects. However, in view of the prevalence of high blood pressure and the seriousness of the risks to health it poses, some doctors are urging everyone to cut down on salt.

Sources Other Than Salt
The salt you add to food at the table or in cooking is not the only source of sodium. Some sodium is found in most foods, from fresh vegetables to TV dinners. Foods with the lowest concentrations are fresh, frozen, and canned fruits and fruit juices, fresh or frozen vegetables, unprocessed grains, fresh lean meats, poultry, and certain fish. Foods with the highest sodium counts include canned soups, canned fish, frozen dinners, and dehydrated mixes for soups, sauces, and salad dressings, as well as soy sauce, sauerkraut, ketchup, mustard, tartar sauce, chili sauce, dill pickles, green olives, and salted snack foods. Even over-the-counter drugs can be loaded with sodium: antacids and seltzer-type headache cures are particularly high.

Sodium is used in the processing and preserving of cured and processed meats, including hot dogs, hams, sausages, and luncheon meats, and high levels remain in the finished products. Similarly, processed cheeses, cheese foods, and cheese spreads are higher in sodium than natural cheeses.

Using Less
To cut down on salt, check product labels for ingredients containing sodium and buy fresh fruits, vegetables, and meats instead of their canned counterparts. In cooking, gradually reduce the salt you use by first cutting the amount in half. After a few weeks, when your taste has adjusted, cut the amount of salt in half again. Then keep using less until you need hardly any at all. Better still, use herbs and spices instead of salt, as the recipes in this book do, to enhance the flavor of foods (see "Flavoring with Herbs—Not Salt," page 17). And once you sit down to eat, be sure to taste your food before you salt it or douse it with ketchup or other sodium-laden condiments.

If you use one of the salt substitutes sold at supermarkets, be aware that many of them contain potassium instead of sodium. People with kidney problems of any kind should check with their doctors before using a potassium-based substitute.

Reading Food Labels

The more you learn about nutrition, the more interested you will be in reading the labels on canned and packaged foods.

By law, all food labels must list ingredients in descending order of content. Thus, on a cereal package you should expect to see the cereal grain used mentioned first. Sometimes, however, you will find sugar listed first, a sure sign that the product is full of sugar or other sweeteners that provide little or no nutrition. In addition to ingredients, labels must list any additives used as preservatives, stabilizers, or thickeners. Spices, flavorings, and dyes are not necessarily specified but may be listed simply as "spices," "artificial flavoring," or "artificial coloring."

The Big Three: Fat, Sugar, and Sodium

Be sure to distinguish between saturated fat, which can raise cholesterol levels, and unsaturated fat, which can have the opposite effect. Products containing saturated fats include butter, hydrogenated shortening, sour cream, sweet cream, whole milk, and whole-milk cheese, as well as meat and poultry products. In baked goods, especially, do not be misled by the words *vegetable oils.* These are not necessarily beneficial; following the words, in parentheses, you may see listed "palm oil and/or coconut oil"—both high in saturated fat. Look instead for products that are high in unsaturated fat, including corn, cottonseed, olive, peanut, safflower, and soybean oils.

Sugars also come in a variety of guises. Watch for the word *sugar* (as in cane, beet, or corn sugar), as well as the words *honey, molasses, dextrin, dextrose, fructose, galactose, glucose, lactose, maltose,* and *sucrose.*

When checking for a product's sodium content, be aware of the ingredients other than salt that contain sodium. Look out for baking powder or baking soda, self-rising flour, and any additive that contains the word *sodium* (including disodium, monosodium, and trisodium).

The U.S. Food and Drug Administration (FDA) requires foods making any nutritional claims (such as "dietetic" or "low calorie" or "fortified with vitamins") to carry certain nutritional information on their labels. Many manufacturers provide this information voluntarily on other products, so that today many packaged foods carry nutritional labels. The labels must specify the size of a single serving and how many calories it contains, and must list the amounts of protein, carbohydrate, and fat, and the per-serving percentage of the U.S. Recommended Daily Allowance of protein, vitamins A and C, thiamine, riboflavin, and niacin and the minerals calcium and iron. Many labels also list the sodium content (to be labeled "low sodium," a product may not contain more than 140 milligrams of sodium per serving), the grams of saturated and unsaturated fat, and the milligrams of cholesterol. Other optional information includes the percentage of the RDA per serving of vitamins D, E, B_6, folic acid, B_{12}, biotin, and pantothenic acid, and the minerals phosphorus, iodine, magnesium, zinc, and copper. Manufacturers also can choose whether to list the grams per serving of carbohydrates.

Additives

Many consumers avoid prepared foods because of concerns about the chemicals that are added to foods to preserve freshness and maintain texture, appearance, and flavor. Although the FDA regards all food additives in use as safe for human consumption, a few are controversial. These include

1. Butylated hydroxyanisole (BHA) and butylated hydroxytoluene (BHT), used to retard spoilage in cereals, baked goods, and a variety of other foods

2. Sodium nitrite, used in bacon, ham, hot dogs, and cold cuts to prevent botulism and to give them their characteristic pink color

3. Sulfites (including sulfur dioxide, sodium bisulfite, sodium sulfite, sodium metabisulfite, and potassium metabisulfite sulfur dioxide), used to maintain freshness and prevent discoloration in some beers and wines; frozen, dried, and canned potatoes; bottled and dried salad dressings; canned and dried sauces and gravies; soups; wine vinegar; and fresh seafood

4. Polysorbates 60, 65, and 80, used to prevent oils from separating in ice cream, beverages, and candy and to extend the shelf life of baked goods

5. Monosodium glutamate (MSG), used to enhance the flavor of foods

Some people have acute sensitivities to MSG and sulfites. MSG has been linked to headaches and muscle tightening (often called "Chinese restaurant syndrome" because MSG is commonly used in Chinese cooking). Sulfites seem to be a problem primarily for people with asthma. Reactions may include a wide range of allergy symptoms, such as difficulty in breathing, hives, and a runny nose. A few sulfite reactions have been fatal.

The other additives listed above have been linked in some animal studies to the development of tumors. However, the evidence is inconclusive. In the case of BHT and BHA, for instance, some studies have shown that they can cause tumors; others, that they prevent them.

Cooking the Healthful Way

Cutting down on fat, cholesterol, and salt is not merely a matter of changing what you eat but also how you prepare it—and even how you buy it. You can avoid almost half of the fat of ground beef, for example, if you buy it ground from lean cuts like round or shoulder; the leaner product is usually labeled "extra lean" or "very lean." (The recipes in this book specify "very lean," and the nutritional counts are figured accordingly.) Today animals are bred—and fed—to weigh up to 50 percent less than the livestock of 20 years ago, and the actual meat is about 10 percent leaner, but you still should be selective when buying. Choose round and tenderloin for beef steaks, and eye of round and sirloin tip for roasts; as a rule, avoid the fattiest cuts: T-bone, sirloin, porterhouse, and rib steaks, and chuck blade and sirloin roasts. Also avoid any other cuts that have too much "marbling"—the visible white flecks of fat that run through the lean.

Whatever cuts you buy—not only of beef and veal, but of also of pork and lamb—trim and discard any visible fat from the meat before you cook it. (Butchers tend to leave less fat on the meat than they used to, but you should go ahead and finish the job by removing it all.)

Poultry has considerably less fat than red meat—but only if you don't eat the skin of the chicken, turkey, or Cornish hen and only if you limit yourself to the light meat. Most of the poultry recipes in this book call for skinning the bird first and also specify breast or light meat, since dark meat has as much as twice the fat and considerably more cholesterol.

Cooking with Less Fat

Having reduced the fat content of meat by carefully selecting and preparing it for cooking, be careful not to add fat when you cook. If a recipe calls for sautéing vegetables, use nonstick cooking spray and a teaspoon or two of oil—preferably in a nonstick skillet. Instead of butter, use margarine or cooking oil consisting of monounsaturated or polyunsaturated fats. If the food is ending up as a stew or soup, make the dish ahead and let it chill in the refrigerator long enough for the fat to rise to the top and congeal; you can then remove it easily.

Preparing meat and vegetables so that they are less fatty also cuts down on cholesterol, of course, but remember that meats and oils are not the only source of fat and cholesterol. Eggs and dairy products particularly are high in cholesterol, but you can make substitutions. Whenever possible, for example, use only one yolk (the part of the egg that contains virtually all the fat and cholesterol) for every three or four egg whites. You'll be surprised how good a mostly whites omelet can taste, especially when you stir in a few chopped vegetables.

Most dairy products come in low-fat versions, and some, like cottage cheese and yogurt, are as widely available as their whole-milk counterparts. Low-fat products have significantly fewer grams of fat and less cholesterol but, in some cases, have just as many calories as whole-milk products; the difference is that the calories come from protein augmented by the addition of nonfat milk solids instead of from fat.

Use skim milk (86 calories and less than ½ gram of fat per cup) in place of whole milk (3.5 percent butterfat, 150 calories, and more than 8 grams of fat), making sure it has been fortified with the A and D vitamins that are lost when the fat is skimmed. Low-fat milk with 1 percent fat has approximately 6 times as much fat as skim milk; 2 percent low-fat milk has approximately 11 times as much.

Sour cream is particularly high in fat. Use the mock version found on page 26, or substitute plain low-fat yogurt (with only a third of the calories and a meager 7 percent of the fat); it has the same slight acidity as sour cream, and in most dishes you will hardly notice the difference.

Meatless Meals

More and more people are discovering the benefits of including an occasional meatless meal in the diet: low fat, high fiber, and less cost. And some choose to forgo meat altogether. If you decide to eat only meatless dishes, be aware that you need to balance the ingredients in a vegetarian meal carefully so that they provide a "complete" protein—that is, all 9 of the essential amino acids in the proportion that the body needs and that are present in meat, poultry, and fish. (See "Protein," page 11.) Grains and legumes complement each other in the proper ratio; so do grains and dairy products. Legumes combined with nuts or seeds also have the proper ratio. The combinations of rice and beans in South America and the Caribbean, of corn and beans in Mexico, of rice and lentils in Asia, and of yogurt and bulgur in the Middle East are good examples of how peoples in many parts of the world have learned to get the most nutritional value possible out of foods. American cooks can do the same.

Lowering Sodium

Canned and frozen foods, as well as cured meats, usually have staggeringly high salt contents; canned soups, sauce mixes, and condiments such as ketchup and soy sauce are notorious for their

(continued on page 19)

Flavoring with Herbs—Not Salt

You won't miss salt in your food if you use plenty of herbs and spices instead. Fresh herbs are readily available at most supermarkets in the summer and have a wonderful flavor. Use three times as much of a fresh herb as you would of its dried counterpart. Experiment with your own combinations of flavors, but be sure to add herbs sparingly at first; taste the dish as you cook it and add more as you like. You can also add a dash of lime or lemon juice to enliven virtually any dish. Here is a list of foods and the herbs and spices suited to them.

Beef	Allspice, basil, bay leaf, chili powder, cumin, curry powder, garlic, ginger, marjoram, oregano, thyme
Pork	Caraway seeds, chili powder, coriander, cumin, curry powder, dill, garlic, ginger, rosemary, sage, thyme
Lamb	Curry powder, dill, garlic, mint, oregano, rosemary, thyme
Veal	Bay leaf, coriander, dill, garlic, oregano, rosemary, sage, thyme
Eggs	Chili powder, chives, cumin, curry powder, savory, tarragon
Chicken and turkey	Basil, bay leaf, chives, coriander, curry powder, garlic, ginger, majoram, oregano, rosemary, sage, tarragon, thyme
Fish	Bay leaf, chives, coriander, dill, nutmeg, sage, tarragon, thyme
Shellfish	Bay leaf, basil, chervil, coriander, curry powder, cloves, dill, marjoram, oregano, tarragon, thyme
Asparagus	Basil, chives, dill, nutmeg, sesame seeds, tarragon
Beans, dried	Allspice, chili powder, coriander, cumin, garlic, marjoram, oregano, rosemary, sage, savory, tarragon, thyme
Beans, green	Basil, bay leaf, dill, garlic, marjoram, rosemary, savory, tarragon
Beans, lima	Basil, chives, dill, marjoram, sage, savory, tarragon
Beets	Allspice, caraway seeds, chives, dill, ginger, horseradish
Broccoli, cauliflower, cabbage, Brussels sprouts	Basil, caraway seeds, curry powder, garlic, ginger, marjoram, oregano, tarragon, thyme
Carrots	Caraway seeds, chives, cumin, ginger, marjoram, nutmeg, tarragon
Corn	Chives, coriander, cumin, rosemary, sage, savory, thyme
Eggplant	Allspice, basil, garlic, marjoram, oregano, sage, thyme
Mushrooms	Basil, chives, dill, garlic, marjoram, oregano, rosemary, tarragon
Peas	Basil, chives, dill, marjoram, mint, oregano, savory, tarragon
Peppers, sweet	Chives, coriander, garlic, marjoram, oregano, thyme
Potatoes	Caraway seeds, bay leaf, chives, coriander, curry powder, dill, garlic, mint, oregano, tarragon, thyme
Rice	Chives, cumin, curry powder, garlic, sage, tarragon
Spinach	Basil, garlic, nutmeg, tarragon
Squash, yellow and zucchini	Basil, chives, coriander, dill, garlic, ginger, marjoram, oregano, rosemary, savory, tarragon
Squash, winter	Allspice, cinnamon, cloves, curry powder, ginger, mace, nutmeg
Sweet potatoes	Allspice, cinnamon, cloves, ginger, nutmeg
Tomatoes	Basil, chives, coriander, dill, garlic, marjoram, oregano, rosemary, sage, savory, tarragon, thyme
Turnips	Allspice, cinnamon, ginger, nutmeg

Dining Out

You can control your intake of fat, sodium, and sugar at home, but you may have a harder time of it when dining out—especially if you grab a quick meal from a fast food outlet. Fast foods—including the hamburgers, pizzas, and tacos prepared by franchises and sold nationwide by the millions every day—can offer enough meats, fish, and salads to supply an adult's recommended daily allowance of vitamins and minerals, but they may also contain a staggering amount of fat, sodium, sugar, and calories.

The French fries at fast food outlets are often fried in saturated fat and have too much salt added; pizzas and the meats and processed cheeses used in hamburgers and tacos are high in fat; "shakes" are excessively sweet and usually have more than 350 calories. Ordering a slimmer, more healthful version of these foods—a single hamburger without the cheese or special sauce, for example—may be possible but will defeat the purpose of the "fast food fix" that most people are looking for.

Ordering food at a restaurant with table service and a full menu is another matter. Here you have some control over the amounts of fat, sodium, and sugar that arrive on your plate. For one thing, there are more items that you can choose from; for another, you can request that rich sauces or dressings be served on the side or not at all.

In restaurants, follow these rules to get the most healthful meal possible:

Start with clear soup or a seafood cocktail as a first course; avoid fried appetizers such as breaded zucchini sticks (and especially deep-fried cheese!) and those that mention cream or butter in the menu description. On salads, avoid creamy and cheese-based dressings (blue cheese and thousand island are among the highest in fat and sodium) and instead choose simple oil-and-vinegar-based ones. Better still, ask for cruets of vinegar and oil and dress the salad yourself—easy on the oil. And keep in mind that you can always order two first courses (soup and a shrimp cocktail are a popular combination) instead of a full entree.

When it comes to the main course, if you order chicken, turkey, or Cornish hen, remove the skin. Avoid duck, which virtually oozes fat. If you order red meat, forgo prime cuts and ground beef and choose only lean cuts such as flank, round, or tenderloin steaks, and round or rump roasts. Don't be afraid to ask the waiter what cut of meat is used in a roast.

Fish and shellfish are fine, as long as they are not sautéed, deep-fried, or basted with butter (some of the cholesterol content of shellfish is offset by its beneficial Omega-3 fatty acids). Ignore the tartar sauce or cocktail sauce that comes on the side; use lemon juice instead.

Ask the waiter if the vegetables come with a sauce; if they do, ask that the sauce be served separately or not at all.

Be aware that so-called diet plates are not always such a good nutritional bargain. They usually feature a ground beef patty, cottage cheese, and a salad of sorts; yet a 3-ounce patty can have as much as 19 grams of fat and even cottage cheese has 5 grams of fat per ½ cup.

When you choose from the bread basket, take your pick of sandwich bread, breadsticks, hard rolls, French and Italian breads, pita bread, wafers, and melba toast. Say no-thank-you to breads made with a lot of butter, sugar, or both: croissants, biscuits, muffins, and soft rolls.

For dessert, have as much fruit as you wish, or order a gelatin dessert, frozen fruit ice, or low-fat yogurt-based dish. Angel food cake and other sponge cakes are acceptable unless they are slathered with a sugar frosting. Whatever dessert you order, be sure to ask that whipped cream or other toppings—with the exception of plain fruit purées—be served on the side or not at all.

If you are on a low-sodium diet, remember that relish trays and antipastos are exceedingly salty: steer clear of pickled vegetables, relishes, and cured meats. And don't forget the high sodium content of mustard, Worcestershire sauce, steak sauce, salsa, barbecue sauce, and ketchup.

saltiness. Look for products that are labeled "no salt added," "low sodium," or, in the case of hams and soy sauce, "reduced sodium." You will probably find the reduced-sodium products still salty enough for your taste.

If you can rinse a canned product, do so. You will reduce the salt in canned beans, in particular, if you drain and rinse them in a colander under cool running water. Canned tuna, too, will be less salty if you rinse it, but, in this case, you will be washing away some vitamins and minerals as well.

The recipes in this book use little, if any, salt and depend on herbs and spices to enhance the flavor of the dishes. Try herbs (see page 17) to bring out the natural flavor of foods.

Experiment with different herbs and spices to see which appeal to you and your family. You will find that herbs and other flavorings can turn the simplest meal into something exotic. The following are some seasonings that are traditional in various countries. You can use them singly or in combinations of two or three to "go international" in your kitchen—without salt.

Chinese: Sesame seeds, fresh ginger, lemon rind or juice, orange rind or juice

Indian: Curry powder, fresh ginger, fresh coriander, garlic

French: Tarragon, chervil, thyme

Italian: Basil, oregano, garlic

Spanish and Portuguese: Garlic, paprika, coriander, lemon rind or juice, orange rind or juice

Greek: Lemon juice, garlic, cinnamon, rosemary, mint

German: Caraway seeds, vinegar

Scandinavian: Dill, caraway seeds, cardamom

Hungarian: Paprika and sour cream or yogurt

Middle Eastern: Sesame seeds, lemon juice, mint

Tex-Mex: Chili powder, cumin, fresh coriander, red pepper flakes

Creole: Gumbo filé powder, bay leaf, hot red pepper sauce

Hawaiian: Pineapple, soy sauce

Using Sugar

Add as little sugar as possible when you sweeten a food, and be aware that honey is not a healthful substitute. Like table sugar, it is sucrose and its nutrients are negligible. In fact, a tablespoon of honey has 18 more calories than the same amount of sugar. When you can, use fruit, puréed or mashed, to sweeten food. Stirring fresh fruit into plain low-fat yogurt, for example, makes a snack or dessert that is far more healthful than the sugar-laden fruit-flavored product sold commercially.

Retaining Vitamins

The longer you cook vegetables, the more B and C vitamins you lose to the cooking water. However long you cook them, save the water for use in soups or in gravy; in this way you will recapture at another time some of the nutrients you lost. Or you can steam vegetables in a steamer. This keeps them crisp and colorful, and fewer vitamins are lost. A third way to keep vegetables vitamin rich is to stir-fry them in a wok or large skillet. Because stir-frying involves cooking quickly over high heat, vitamins remain intact and the vegetables are exceptionally fresh tasting. Many of the recipes in this book call for sautéing vegetables in a little olive oil or vegetable oil or margarine. But if you are determined to do without oil altogether, you can braise them in chicken broth until they are tender but still crisp.

Remember that storing foods depletes their vitamin and mineral content. For this reason, do not keep leftovers in the refrigerator for more than a couple of days. If you are going to freeze a dish, do it right away, as soon as the food has cooled.

Making the Most of This Book

The 564 original recipes and variations in this book were created to convince you that cutting down on fat, salt, and sugar does not mean having to give up taste. Some of the recipes are low-calorie, low-fat (but still great-tasting) versions of everyday foods—mayonnaise, for example, or pancakes—while others, such as Pork Scaloppine with Honey Mustard or Spaghetti with Asparagus and Pecans, are imaginative new dishes that are likely to become a permanent part of your kitchen repertoire and a hit with both family and guests.

Nutrition Analyses

An important feature of the book is the nutrition analysis that follows each main recipe; it tells you just how many calories you're getting, as well as the amounts of total fat, saturated fat, cholesterol, protein, carbohydrates, sodium, added sugar, and fiber. But the figures won't mean much unless you have some idea of the minimum or maximum amounts of these nutrients that are needed to maintain good health. Here are some guidelines:

Calories: How many calories you should take in

each day depends on your size, your age and sex, and whether you are trying to maintain your weight or lose some. One way to compute your daily maximum number of calories—that is, the maximum that you can ingest without putting on weight—is by these formulas:

If you are fairly inactive during the day (if you sit behind a desk, for example), multiply your body weight by 12.

If you engage in light activity, such as housework, for most of the day, multiply by 15.

If you are moderately active (say, a food caterer or a golf pro), multiply by 20.

If you are extremely active (a construction worker who spends his spare time playing tennis), multiply by 25.

The figure you arrive at (1,560 calories for a 130-pound woman with a sedentary office job) is roughly the number of calories you need each day to maintain your body weight. If you want to lose weight, simply take in fewer calories than you need each day and your body will start burning stored fat.

Another way to estimate the calories you need is to consult the recommendations by the Food and Nutrition Board of the National Academy of Sciences—National Research Council (see box below). These approximate daily calorie intakes will meet the energy needs of average healthy people (exact intakes may vary, however, depending on weight, height, and activity level).

Daily Energy Needs

Males

Age	Calories per day
11–14	2,700
15–18	2,800
19–22	2,900
23–50	2,700
51–75	2,400
Over 75	2,050

Females

Age	Calories per day
11–14	2,200
15–18	2,100
19–22	2,100
23–50	2,000
51–75	1,800
Over 75	1,600
Pregnant	plus 300
Nursing	plus 500

Once you have decided how many calories you need each day in order either to maintain your weight or to reduce it, check the calories per serving whenever you use a recipe in this book. If you are having a relatively high-calorie main course (Savory Macaroni and Beef, for example, at 391 calories), compensate by accompanying it with a low-calorie side dish such as Braised Spinach (35 calories per serving) or a simple tossed green salad with Blue Cheese Dressing (9 calories per tablespoon of dressing).

Total fat and saturated fat: Where your calories come from is a major consideration. You can figure out their source by looking at the figures for total fat, saturated fat, protein, and carbohydrates. Each gram of fat in the dish accounts for 9 calories; each gram of protein for 4 calories; and each gram of carbohydrates also for 4. Remember that within a given day's diet, *no more than 30 percent of your calorie intake should come from total fat, and no more than 10 percent from saturated fat.* This means that a 300-calorie-per-serving dish with 15 grams of fat is on the high side; 15 grams of fat, at 9 calories each, account for 135 of the calories in the serving. That is 45 percent of the calories, or fully 1½ times the percentage you want. Likewise, if the dish has 5 grams of saturated fat, you are getting 45 calories from that source—considerably more than the 10 percent that should be your limit for the day.

Understand, however, that it is almost impossible—and certainly not necessary—for every dish to fall within these limits. Meat, by its nature, will almost always exceed the total fat recommendation per serving, as will whole milk and cheese. That is why you should "mix and match" your menus, balancing a meat or dairy-based dish with low-fat side dishes. It is not the individual dish but the total diet that counts.

Protein: Adults need about 50 grams of protein each day, depending on height and weight, and protein should be the source of approximately 15 percent of the calories you ingest. Since each gram of protein provides 4 calories, 15 grams of protein in a 400-calorie meal are ideal (60 calories = 15 percent of 400). When you figure your protein intake, remember that every 8-ounce glass of milk has 8 to 10 grams of protein and it is found in large amounts in other dairy products, too, such as cheese and eggs.

Carbohydrates: In the best of all possible diets, complex carbohydrates account for 50 to 55 percent of the caloric intake. Grains, legumes, vegetables, and some fruits provide complex carbohydrates. Sugars are also carbohydrates, but offer no real nourishment, only calories. Each gram of carbohydrate, whether complex or not, provides 4 calories; so, if you take in 1,800 calories a day, you should be eating about 250 grams of carbohydrates, which provide 1,000 of those calories.

Cholesterol: The American Heart Association recommends that cholesterol be limited to 100 milligrams for every 1,000 calories, not to exceed 300 milligrams per day. Keep in mind that a single egg has 260 milligrams—all of it in the yolk—so cooking with egg whites is preferable whenever possible. Note, however, that you cannot simply substitute egg whites for whole eggs in many recipes. You will find that the recipes in GREAT RECIPES FOR GOOD HEALTH provide a number of imaginative ways to avoid egg yolks. In any case, you should have no more than 2 or 3 yolks per week.

Added sugar: Many fruits, vegetables, and milk products contain simple sugars such as fructose, galactose, and glucose. Food is often sweetened further with sucrose, which has been refined as table sugar or brown sugar or processed as syrups, honey, or molasses. The recipes in this book keep this "added sugar" to a minimum, even in desserts. When sugar *is* added to a recipe—whether in the form of table sugar or the sugar found in products such as gingersnaps or cranberry juice cocktail—it is indicated in the nutrition analysis.

Sodium: Sodium intake should not average more than 1 milligram for each calorie ingested. Simply put, if your total daily sodium intake equals or is below your calorie intake, you are within the recommended limit. But no matter how many calories you consume, you should try not to exceed 3,000 milligrams of sodium per day.

Fiber: Adults should eat at least 25 to 35 grams of fiber per day. Remember that fiber comes only from plant sources—never from meat or dairy products. Green vegetables and peas, beans, or lentils are the most common daily source of fiber, but the recommended intake will be difficult to meet unless bran cereals or other high-fiber products are eaten every day. Fruits with skins—such as apples, prunes, and grapes—and citrus fruit pulp are also good sources.

Extra-Low Fat, Sodium, and Sugar Symbols

Each recipe is accompanied by green symbols labeled fat, sugar, and sodium. A dark green symbol indicates that the recipe is *extra* low in that nutrient. But every recipe, even though it does not rate a dark green symbol, still is low in fat, sodium, and sugar, as well as calories and cholesterol.

FAT SUGAR SODIUM   Extra Low in Fat

Different standards are set for different dishes, based on the dish's importance within the daily diet. A dish rates a symbol for extra-low fat if it falls below a certain number of grams of fat per serving:

Homemade substitutes: No fat
Appetizers: 2 grams of fat or less
Soups: 2 grams of fat or less if a first course, 12 or less if a main course
Main courses: 12 grams of fat or less
Side dishes and salads: 2 grams of fat or less
Salad dressings: No fat
Breads: No fat
Breakfast main dishes: 10 grams of fat or less
Beverages: No fat
Desserts: 2 grams of fat or less

Keep in mind that you don't have to remember these figures—the symbol does it for you.

FAT SUGAR SODIUM   Extra Low in Sodium

A dish is considered extra low in sodium if the milligrams of sodium per serving do not exceed the number of calories. For example, a 380-calorie dish must have 380 milligrams of sodium or less to qualify as extra low.

FAT SUGAR SODIUM   Extra Low in Sugar

A recipe rates an extra-low symbol for sugar if it calls for no *added* sugar. Added sugar can be table sugar or the sugar found in commercial products.

Preparation and Cooking Times

Each recipe is accompanied by an estimate of the time it takes to prepare (the cutting, chopping, and mixing) and the time it cooks on the stove top or in the oven. Keep in mind that cooks work at different rates, that ovens vary in temperature, and that it is often possible to do two things at once—let a vegetable cook while you prepare the sauce, for example. If you find that the estimates are not precisely to your speed, use them to judge the relative preparation time of one dish to another.

Halving Recipes

Most of the recipes in this book serve four people (although there is a special chapter on "Cooking for One or Two"). When a recipe can easily be halved to serve two, a notation to that effect is usually made in the note preceding the recipe. In the case where virtually all the recipes in a chapter can be halved ("Salads and Salad Dressings," for example), a notation is made in the chapter introduction.

Tips

Throughout the book you will find tips that give you information that relates to the recipes on the page. What to look for when buying ingredients, how to get the best out of them, and how to store leftovers are a few examples.

Menus for Good Health

Here are some suggested menus that have been balanced to fall within the recommended dietary guidelines. Most, with the exception of the special "Menus for One or Two," serve four people; the Spicy Ham and Vegetable Loaf meal in "Lunches and Suppers" serves 8. The nutrition analyses are for one person's complete meal.

Family Dinners

Quick Steak Pizzaiola (page 67)
Brussels Sprouts with
    Lemon Sauce (page 179)
Creamy Mashed Potatoes (page 194)
Blueberry Cobbler (page 283)

Calories	509	Carbohydrates	61 g
Total Fat	14 g	Sodium	327 mg
Saturated Fat	3 g	Added Sugar	44 Cal
Cholesterol	137 mg	Fiber	9 g
Protein	36 g		

Chicken Creole (page 107)
Stir-fried Carrots and Potatoes (page 181)
Wilted Spinach Salad (page 215)
Frozen Berry Yogurt (page 292)

Calories	550	Carbohydrates	58 g
Total Fat	17 g	Sodium	293 mg
Saturated Fat	3 g	Added Sugar	25 Cal
Cholesterol	93 mg	Fiber	9 g
Protein	44 g		

Fish Rarebit (page 121)
Country-Style Bread (page 229)
Broccoli-Stuffed Tomatoes (page 178)
Fresh Peach Ice (page 290)

Calories	506	Carbohydrates	59 g
Total Fat	13 g	Sodium	414 mg
Saturated Fat	7 g	Added Sugar	32 Cal
Cholesterol	101 mg	Fiber	4 g
Protein	39 g		

Homestyle Chicken Consommé (page 50)
Tofu Stir-fry with Rice (page 139)
Minted Cucumber Salad (page 212)
Lemon Soufflé (page 290)

Calories	429	Carbohydrates	55 g
Total Fat	15 g	Sodium	411 mg
Saturated Fat	3 g	Added Sugar	39 Cal
Cholesterol	47 mg	Fiber	2 g
Protein	23 g		

Company Dinners

Hearty Black Bean Soup (page 56)
Roast Chicken Stuffed with Rice and
    Apricots (page 92)
Tossed Romaine Lettuce and Tomato
    Salad
Vinaigrette Dressing (page 225)
Chocolate-Berry Crunch Parfait
    (page 291)

Calories	731	Carbohydrates	79 g
Total Fat	23 g	Sodium	239 mg
Saturated Fat	6 g	Added Sugar	24 Cal
Cholesterol	107 mg	Fiber	11 g
Protein	50 g		

Spinach-Stuffed Mushrooms (page 43)
California Seafood Medley (page 127)
Mixed Green Salad
Creamy Garlic Dressing (page 226)
Basic French Bread (page 228)
Lemon Angel Roll (page 278)

Calories	547	Carbohydrates	75 g
Total Fat	7 g	Sodium	572 mg
Saturated Fat	1 g	Added Sugar	103 Cal
Cholesterol	134 mg	Fiber	4 g
Protein	44 g		

Homestyle Chicken Consommé (page 50)
Zucchini, Pimiento, and Mushroom Lasagne
    (page 153)
Tossed Green Salad
Italian Dressing (pge 225)
Basic French Bread (page 228)

Calories	472	Carbohydrates	73 g
Total Fat	10 g	Sodium	347 mg
Saturated Fat	3 g	Added Sugar	0
Cholesterol	6 mg	Fiber	5 g
Protein	22 g		

Low-Calorie Dinners

Steak Parsley (page 68)
Cabbage Salad Mold (page 222)
Oven French Fries (page 196)
Chocolate Chip Meringue Drops (page 280)

Calories	360	Carbohydrates	40 g
Total Fat	12 g	Sodium	68 mg
Saturated Fat	2 g	Added Sugar	34 Cal
Cholesterol	49 mg	Fiber	3 g
Protein	24 g		

Chicken Breasts Dijon (page 106)
Baked Potato
Braised Yellow Squash, Corn, and Tomatoes
  (page 200)
Lime-Ginger Cheesecake (page 288)

Calories	387	Carbohydrates	39 g
Total Fat	10 g	Sodium	421 mg
Saturated Fat	2 g	Added Sugar	24 Cal
Cholesterol	101 mg	Fiber	4 g
Protein	38 g		

Tangy Cheese-Stuffed New Potatoes
  (page 43)
Flounder and Vegetables Sealed in Silver
  (page 120)
Green Beans with Dill (page 174)
Yogurt with Fresh Strawberries

Calories	371	Carbohydrates	45 g
Total Fat	10 g	Sodium	225 mg
Saturated Fat	1 g	Added Sugar	0
Cholesterol	69 mg	Fiber	7 g
Protein	31 g		

White Bean, Yellow Squash, and Tomato
  Stew (page 143)
Monkey Bread (page 230)
Tossed Green Salad
Vinaigrette Dressing (page 225)
Strawberries
Mock Whipped Cream (page 27)

Calories	392	Carbohydrates	65 g
Total Fat	9 g	Sodium	177 mg
Saturated Fat	1 g	Added Sugar	2 Cal
Cholesterol	0	Fiber	11 g
Protein	17 g		

Lunches and Suppers

Spicy Ham and Vegetable Loaf (page 85)
Four-Bean Salad (page 207)
Lemon Squares (page 281)

Calories	402	Carbohydrates	49 g
Total Fat	13 g	Sodium	527 mg
Saturated Fat	2 g	Added Sugar	67 Cal
Cholesterol	58 mg	Fiber	5 g
Protein	24 g		

Carrot-Apple Soup (page 56)
Chicken with Snow Peas and Peanut Sauce
  (page 95)
Monkey Bread (page 230)
Ginger-Peach Crisp (page 282)

Calories	557	Carbohydrates	68 g
Total Fat	19 g	Sodium	577 mg
Saturated Fat	4 g	Added Sugar	50 Cal
Cholesterol	62 mg	Fiber	8 g
Protein	31 g		

Cold Curried Tuna and Fruit (page 124)
Onion Flatbread (page 231)
Fresh Melon Ice (page 290)

Calories	320	Carbohydrates	47 g
Total Fat	5 g	Sodium	381 mg
Saturated Fat	0	Added Sugar	32 Cal
Cholesterol	48 mg	Fiber	1 g
Protein	25 g		

Alfredo-Style Noodles (page 161)
Greek Salad (page 217)
Fresh Fruit

Calories	434	Carbohydrates	65 g
Total Fat	10 g	Sodium	186 mg
Saturated Fat	3 g	Added Sugar	0 Cal
Cholesterol	65 mg	Fiber	3 g
Protein	17 g		

Breakfasts

Garden Vegetable Juice (page 274)
Asparagus-Mushroom Omelets (page 256)
Bran Muffins (page 240)

Calories	208	Carbohydrates	25 g
Total Fat	10 g	Sodium	243 mg
Saturated Fat	1 g	Added Sugar	12 Cal
Cholesterol	92 mg	Fiber	7 g
Protein	10 g		

1/4 Cantaloupe
Orange French Toast (page 260)
Herbal Tea (page 273)

Calories	235	Carbohydrates	43 g
Total Fat	4 g	Sodium	303 mg
Saturated Fat	1 g	Added Sugar	16 Cal
Cholesterol	2 mg	Fiber	3 g
Protein	9 g		

Orange Juice
Fruit Pancakes (page 259)
Raspberries
Reduced-Sodium Ham

Calories	332	Carbohydrates	60 g
Total Fat	9 g	Sodium	650 mg
Saturated Fat	0	Added Sugar	44 Cal
Cholesterol	22 mg	Fiber	4 g
Protein	16 g		

Menus for One or Two

Polish Sausage and Chick Pea Casserole
   (page 244)
Braised Spinach (page 199)
Make-Your-Own Chocolate Pudding
   (page 289)

Calories	530	Carbohydrates	77 g
Total Fat	16 g	Sodium	445 mg
Saturated Fat	5 g	Added Sugar	64 Cal
Cholesterol	22 mg	Fiber	12 g
Protein	26 g		

Oven-Fried Chicken (page 98)
Peas and Dumplings (page 190)
Pickled Beet Salad (page 209)
Deep-Dish Peach Pie (page 285)

Calories	636	Carbohydrates	68 g
Total Fat	16 g	Sodium	510 mg
Saturated Fat	5 g	Added Sugar	55 Cal
Cholesterol	97 mg	Fiber	7 g
Protein	44 g		

Linguine with Tuna and Peas (page 253)
Roasted Vegetable Salad (page 216)
Apple-Raisin Crisp (page 282)

Calories	579	Carbohydrates	82 g
Total Fat	18 g	Sodium	389 mg
Saturated Fat	4 g	Added Sugar	48 Cal
Cholesterol	32 mg	Fiber	5 g
Protein	26 g		

Meals-in-One

Stir-fried Lamb, Asparagus, and Sweet Red
   Pepper (page 88)
Brown Rice
No-Sugar Fruit Pudding (page 288)

Calories	560	Carbohydrates	67 g
Total Fat	19 g	Sodium	564 mg
Saturated Fat	7 g	Added Sugar	0
Cholesterol	80 mg	Fiber	8 g
Protein	30 g		

Chicken Pot Pie (page 96)
Tossed Green Salad
Ranch Dressing (page 225)
Mixed Fruit
Honey-Yogurt Dressing (page 226)

Calories	507	Carbohydrates	48 g
Total Fat	14 g	Sodium	185 mg
Saturated Fat	4 g	Added Sugar	0
Cholesterol	93 mg	Fiber	5 g
Protein	59 g		

Seafood Gumbo (page 128)
Boiled Rice
Tossed Green Salad
Italian Dressing (page 225)
Ginger-Pumpkin Chiffon Pie (page 286)

Calories	595	Carbohydrates	90 g
Total Fat	15 g	Sodium	462 mg
Saturated Fat	3 g	Added Sugar	55 Cal
Cholesterol	148 mg	Fiber	4 g
Protein	35 g		

Vegetable Curry with Yogurt Sauce
   (page 141)
Whole Wheat Pita Bread
Blueberry-Peach Tarts (page 286)

Calories	693	Carbohydrates	140 g
Total Fat	9 g	Sodium	536 mg
Saturated Fat	2 g	Added Sugar	51 Cal
Cholesterol	3 mg	Fiber	9 g
Protein	23 g		

Great Homemade Substitutes

Stock up on the substitutes in this chapter and never again feel deprived of "forbidden" foods. Start with the Savory Salt Substitute; a teaspoonful has only 1 milligram of sodium, while the same amount of salt has 2,132. Whip up a cup of Mock Mayonnaise with a mere 18 calories per tablespoon. And put up a store of condiments—ketchup, mustard, relishes—and forget about unwanted salt or sugar. Then give yourself a big pat on the back and enjoy these great-tasting recipes.

Savory Salt Substitute

Preparation: **8 min.** FAT SUGAR SODIUM

Use this all-purpose seasoning at the table in place of salt; it will stay fresh for several months. Even though some of the ingredients—sour salt, arrowroot, and powdered citrus peel—are unusual, they are readily found at most supermarkets.

1 tablespoon black pepper
1 tablespoon celery seeds
1 tablespoon onion powder
2¼ teaspoons cream of tartar
1½ teaspoons garlic powder
1½ teaspoons powdered orange peel
1½ teaspoons arrowroot
1½ teaspoons sugar
¾ teaspoon sour salt (powdered citric acid)
½ teaspoon white pepper
½ teaspoon dill weed
½ teaspoon dried thyme, crumbled
¼ teaspoon plus pinch powdered lemon peel
¼ teaspoon cayenne pepper

1. Place all the ingredients in a small electric coffee grinder, spice grinder, or blender. Grind for 10 seconds or until the mixture is fine.
2. Insert a funnel in the top of a glass salt shaker, pour the mixture into it, and tap the funnel lightly to fill the shaker. Cover the rest of the mixture tightly and store it in a cool, dark, dry place. Makes about ½ cup.

One Teaspoon:

Calories	6	Protein	0
Total Fat	0	Carbohydrates	1 g
Saturated Fat	0	Sodium	1 mg
Cholesterol	0	Added Sugar	1 Cal
		Fiber	0

Mock Mayonnaise

Preparation: **1 min.** Cooking: **1 min.** FAT SUGAR SODIUM

If you wish, add a tablespoon of low-sodium ketchup and a dash of hot sauce.

1 tablespoon cornstarch
1 cup cold water
2 tablespoons olive oil
2 tablespoons white vinegar

2 tablespoons plain low-fat yogurt
1 teaspoon prepared yellow mustard
½ teaspoon prepared horseradish

1. Place the **cornstarch** in a small saucepan, whisk in the cold **water**, and set the pan over medium heat. Cook, stirring constantly, until the mixture comes to a boil. Boil for 1 to 2 minutes or until the mixture is clear. Remove from the heat and transfer to a small bowl.
2. Whisk in the **olive oil, vinegar, yogurt, mustard,** and **horseradish.** Store tightly covered in the refrigerator for up to 2 weeks. Makes about 1 cup.

One Tablespoon:

Calories	18	Protein	0
Total Fat	2 g	Carbohydrates	1 g
Saturated Fat	0	Sodium	5 mg
Cholesterol	0	Added Sugar	0
		Fiber	0

Mock Sour Cream

Preparation: **6 min.,** plus 1 hr. refrigeration   Cooking: **5 min.** FAT SUGAR SODIUM

Buttermilk powder is available at health food stores and some supermarkets.

1 cup milk
4 teaspoons buttermilk powder
½ teaspoon unflavored gelatin
½ cup plain low-fat yogurt

1. In a medium-size heavy saucepan, whisk together the **milk** and **buttermilk powder.** Sprinkle the **gelatin** on top and let stand until the gelatin softens—about 5 minutes.
2. Set the pan over low heat and cook, uncovered, stirring occasionally, for 5 minutes or until the gelatin dissolves. Remove from the heat and whisk in the **yogurt.**
3. Transfer the mixture to a medium-size bowl, cover, and chill in the refrigerator for 1 hour or until thickened. Store tightly covered in the refrigerator for up to 5 days. Makes 1½ cups.

One Tablespoon:

Calories	11	Protein	1 g
Total Fat	0	Carbohydrates	1 g
Saturated Fat	0	Sodium	11 mg
Cholesterol	2 mg	Added Sugar	0
		Fiber	0

Mock Whipped Cream

Mock Whipped Cream

Preparation: **25 min.,** including
15 min. refrigeration

FAT SUGAR SODIUM

*Prepare this whipped cream substitute just before
serving, as the mixture deflates rather quickly. You
can speed up the process by having the ingredients
premeasured and ready to go.*

½ **cup skim milk**
½ **cup nonfat dry milk powder**
⅛ **teaspoon cream of tartar**
4 **teaspoons lemon juice**
2 **teaspoons sugar (optional)**
½ **teaspoon vanilla extract (optional)**

1. Put the **skim milk** in a small metal bowl, set in
   the freezer, and let stand just until ice
   crystals begin to form—about 15 minutes.

2. Remove from the freezer and add the **dry milk
   powder** and **cream of tartar.** With a hand
   electric mixer, whip the mixture at high speed
   until foamy.

3. Beat in 1 teaspoon of the **lemon juice** and
   continue beating until the mixture begins to
   thicken. Beat in another teaspoon of the lemon
   juice and, if desired, the **sugar,** and continue
   beating until the mixture peaks softly. Add the
   remaining 2 teaspoons lemon juice and continue
   whipping to stiff peaks. Fold in the **vanilla
   extract,** if desired, and serve immediately as a
   dessert topping. Makes 2 cups.

One Tablespoon:

Calories	5	Protein	1 g
Total Fat	0	Carbohydrates	1 g
Saturated Fat	0	Sodium	8 mg
Cholesterol	0	Added Sugar	0
		Fiber	0

Mock Crème Fraîche

Preparation: **2 min.,** plus 6 hr.
standing time

FAT SUGAR SODIUM

French cooks use the thick, slightly tart crème
fraîche *as a topping in place of sour cream. Here
is a reduced-calorie version.*

1¼ **cups evaporated skim milk**
1 **cup plain low-fat yogurt**
1½ **teaspoons lemon juice**

In a medium-size bowl, combine the ingredients,
cover, and let stand at room temperature at
least 6 hours. Refrigerate and serve well
chilled, whisking the mixture before using.
Store tightly covered in the refrigerator for up
to 5 days. Makes about 2¼ cups.

One Tablespoon:

Calories	11	Protein	1 g
Total Fat	0	Carbohydrates	1 g
Saturated Fat	0	Sodium	15 mg
Cholesterol	1 mg	Added Sugar	0
		Fiber	0

Herb Salad Dressing Mix

This low-sodium mix and the two that follow can be stored for up to six weeks. If you make salads often, double the recipe.

FAT SUGAR SODIUM

¼ cup parsley flakes
2 tablespoons each dried oregano, basil, and marjoram, crumbled
2 tablespoons sugar

1 tablespoon fennel seeds, crushed
1 tablespoon dry mustard
1½ teaspoons black pepper

Place all the ingredients in a 1-pint jar, cover tightly, and shake well to mix. Store in a cool, dark, dry place. Makes about 1 cup.

To Make Herbal Vinaigrette Dressing In a small bowl, whisk together 1 tablespoon Herb Salad Dressing Mix, ¾ cup warm water, 2½ tablespoons tarragon vinegar or white wine vinegar, 1 tablespoon olive oil, and 1 crushed clove garlic. Taste and add another ¼ to ½ teaspoon of the Herb Salad Dressing Mix if you want a stronger flavor. Let stand at room temperature at least 30 minutes before using, then whisk again. Makes about 1 cup.

Preparation: **5 min.**

One Tablespoon Mix:

Calories	13
Total Fat	0
Saturated Fat	0
Cholesterol	0
Protein	0
Carbohydrates	3 g
Sodium	1 mg
Added Sugar	6 Cal
Fiber	0

Buttermilk Salad Dressing Mix

FAT SUGAR SODIUM

2¼ cups buttermilk powder
¾ cup freeze-dried chives
¼ cup dill weed

¼ cup sugar
2 tablespoons dry mustard

Place all the ingredients in a large bowl and mix well. Transfer to a 1-quart jar, cover tightly, and store in the refrigerator. Makes about 3⅔ cups.

To Make Buttermilk Dressing In a small bowl, whisk together 5 tablespoons of the Buttermilk Salad Dressing Mix, ½ cup warm water, 2 tablespoons cider vinegar, and 1 tablespoon sour cream. Let stand at room temperature at least 30 minutes before using, then whisk again for a few seconds. Makes about 1 cup.

Preparation: **5 min.**

Five Tablespoons Mix:

Calories	113
Total Fat	2 g
Saturated Fat	1 g
Cholesterol	16 mg
Protein	8 g
Carbohydrates	16 g
Sodium	120 mg
Added Sugar	15 Cal
Fiber	0

Yogurt Salad Dressing Mix

FAT SUGAR SODIUM

¼ cup chili powder
¼ cup ground cumin

1 tablespoon ground ginger
1½ teaspoons cayenne pepper

Place all the ingredients in a ½-pint jar, cover tightly, and shake well to mix. Store in a cool, dark, dry place. Makes about ½ cup.

To Make Yogurt Dressing In a small bowl, whisk together 2 teaspoons of the Yogurt Salad Dressing Mix, ½ cup plain low-fat yogurt, 3 tablespoons water, 1 tablespoon cider vinegar, 1 tablespoon lemon juice, 1 crushed clove garlic, and 2 tablespoons minced fresh parsley. Let stand at room temperature at least 30 minutes before using, then whisk again. Makes about 1 cup.

Preparation: **5 min.**

Two Teaspoons Mix:

Calories	18
Total Fat	1 g
Saturated Fat	0
Cholesterol	0
Protein	1 g
Carbohydrates	3 g
Sodium	29 mg
Added Sugar	0
Fiber	0

Spaghetti Sauce Seasoning Mix

Preparation: **5 min.**　　FAT SUGAR SODIUM

You can cut the time it takes to make spaghetti sauce by keeping this mix on hand. And it's better for you than sodium-laden store-bought brands.

½ **cup onion flakes**
½ **cup parsley flakes**
2 **tablespoons dried oregano, crumbled**
2 **tablespoons sugar**
1 **tablespoon each dried thyme and basil, crumbled**
2 **teaspoons black pepper**
2 **teaspoons garlic flakes**
4 **large bay leaves, crumbled fine**

Place all the ingredients in a 1-pint jar, cover tightly, and shake well to mix. Store in a cool, dark, dry place for up to 2 months. Makes about 1½ cups.

To Make Spaghetti Sauce　In a medium-size heavy saucepan over moderate heat, mix together 2 cans (28 ounces each) low-sodium tomatoes, drained and chopped, 1 can (6 ounces) low-sodium tomato paste, and 1 cup water; stir in ½ cup Spaghetti Sauce Seasoning Mix. Reduce the heat and simmer, uncovered, for 20 minutes, stirring occasionally. Spoon over spaghetti or other pasta. *(Note: For Spaghetti Sauce with Meat, brown 1 pound very lean ground beef and drain off any fat before adding the other ingredients and proceeding as directed.)* Serves 4.

½ Cup Mix:

Calories	72	Protein	2 g
Total Fat	0	Carbohydrates	17 g
Saturated Fat	0	Sodium	6 mg
Cholesterol	0	Added Sugar	24 Cal
		Fiber	0

Chili Seasoning Mix

Preparation: **5 min.**　　FAT SUGAR SODIUM

The sweet green pepper flakes used here are available at most supermarkets.

1 **cup sweet green pepper flakes**
¾ **cup chili powder**
¼ **cup ground cumin**
½ **cup onion flakes**
¼ **cup parsley flakes**
1 **teaspoon garlic flakes**
½ **teaspoon red pepper flakes**

Place all the ingredients in a 1-quart jar, cover tightly, and shake well to mix. Store in a cool, dark, dry place for up to 2 months. Makes 2¾ cups.

To Make Chili con Carne　In a medium-size heavy saucepan over moderate heat, brown 1 pound very lean ground beef and drain off any fat. Add 1 can (1 pound) low-sodium tomatoes, drained and chopped, and 1 cup water or low-sodium beef broth; stir in ½ cup Chili Seasoning Mix. Reduce the heat and simmer, uncovered, for 20 minutes, stirring occasionally. Stir in 2 cups cooked and drained red kidney beans and heat through. Serves 4.

½ Cup Mix:

Calories	124	Protein	5 g
Total Fat	5 g	Carbohydrates	22 g
Saturated Fat	0	Sodium	243 mg
Cholesterol	0	Added Sugar	0
		Fiber	0

Barbecue Seasoning Mix

Preparation: **5 min.**　　FAT SUGAR SODIUM

Sprinkle this garlic-flavored mix on meat, poultry, or fish before cooking.

½ **cup garlic powder**
2 **tablespoons onion powder**
4 **teaspoons paprika**
2 **teaspoons dry mustard**
2 **teaspoons dried thyme, crumbled**
1 **teaspoon black pepper**

Place all the ingredients in a 1-pint jar, cover tightly, and shake well to mix. Sprinkle about ¼ teaspoon on each side of steaks, chops, chicken, or fish before grilling, broiling, or roasting. Store the mix in a cool, dark, dry place for up to 6 months. Makes about ¾ cup.

½ Teaspoon Mix:

Calories	5	Protein	0
Total Fat	0	Carbohydrates	1 g
Saturated Fat	0	Sodium	0
Cholesterol	0	Added Sugar	0
		Fiber	0

Tip: Dry mixes will stay even fresher if you store them, tightly covered, in the refrigerator.

Taco Seasoning Mix

Preparation: **3 min.**   FAT SUGAR SODIUM

- ½ **cup onion flakes**
- 3 **tablespoons ground cumin**
- 1½ **teaspoons chili powder**
- ½ **teaspoon cayenne pepper**
- ½ **teaspoon garlic flakes**

Place all the ingredients in a 1-pint jar, cover tightly, and shake well to mix. Use to season ground beef or beans, allowing 2 to 3 tablespoons of the mix and ½ cup water for each pound of meat or beans. Store the mix in a cool, dark, dry place for up to 2 months. Makes about ¾ cup.

2 Tablespoons Mix:

Calories	32	*Protein*	*1 g*
Total Fat	*1 g*	*Carbohydrates*	*6 g*
Saturated Fat	0	*Sodium*	*14 mg*
Cholesterol	0	*Added Sugar*	0
		Fiber	0

Seasoned Crumb Mix for Chicken or Pork

Preparation: **3 min.**   FAT SUGAR SODIUM

Vary the seasonings in this recipe according to the meat you're preparing—chicken or pork. Rosemary and thyme are especially compatible with chicken; sage and marjoram with pork.

- 2½ **cups wheat breakfast cereal flakes, crushed fine**
- 2 **tablespoons parsley flakes**
- ½ **teaspoon dried rosemary or sage, crumbled**
- ½ **teaspoon dried thyme or marjoram, crumbled**
- ½ **teaspoon grated lemon rind**

Place all the ingredients in a 1-pint jar, cover tightly, and shake well to mix. Use as a crumb coating for chicken or pork chops. The mix will keep in the refrigerator for up to 2 months. Makes about 1½ cups.

To Make Seasoned Chicken Cutlets or Pork Chops   Brush 1 pound chicken cutlets, pounded thin, or 1 pound thin pork chops with 1 tablespoon vegetable or olive oil, or dip in ½ cup skim milk or buttermilk. Place ½ cup of the Seasoned Crumb Mix in a bag, add the chicken or pork chops, one piece at a time, and shake well to coat. Bake the chicken, uncovered, about 15 minutes in a preheated 350°F oven until crusty. Bake the pork chops, uncovered, about 20 minutes in a preheated 375°F oven until cooked through. Serves 4. *(Note: For bone-in chicken pieces, use ½ cup mix for each pound of chicken, and bake for 30 minutes or until no longer pink when cut near the bone.)*

½ Cup Mix

Calories	87	*Protein*	*2 g*
Total Fat	0	*Carbohydrates*	*18 g*
Saturated Fat	0	*Sodium*	*304 mg*
Cholesterol	0	*Added Sugar*	0
		Fiber	*2 g*

Seasoned Crumb Mix for Chicken or Pork

Quick Bread Mix

Preparation: **10 min.**

Use this easy bread mix to make the three recipes that follow: Spiced Wheat Germ Muffins, Orange Quick Bread, and Apple Pancakes.

5 cups sifted all-purpose flour
¾ cup plus 3 tablespoons nonfat dry milk powder
½ cup plus 2 tablespoons sugar
2½ tablespoons baking powder
5 tablespoons unsalted margarine

1. Sift the **flour** with the **dry milk powder, sugar, and baking powder** 3 times; place in a large mixing bowl. Use a pastry blender or fork to cut in the **margarine** until the mixture has the texture of coarse meal.
2. Transfer to a ½-gallon jar, cover tightly, and store in the refrigerator for up to 1 month. Makes 7 cups.

One Cup:

Calories	476	*Protein*	*12 g*
Total Fat	*9 g*	*Carbohydrates*	*86 g*
Saturated Fat	*2 g*	*Sodium*	*508 mg*
Cholesterol	*2 mg*	*Added Sugar*	*69 Cal*
		Fiber	*3 g*

Spiced Wheat Germ Muffins

Preparation: **10 min.** Baking: **20 min.**

Nonstick cooking spray
2 cups Quick Bread Mix
2 tablespoons firmly packed dark brown sugar
2 tablespoons wheat germ
1 teaspoon ground cinnamon
½ teaspoon ground nutmeg
⅔ cup skim milk
¼ cup sour cream
1 large egg
1 teaspoon vanilla extract

1. Preheat the oven to 400°F. Using 1 large or 2 small muffin pans, lightly coat 12 2½-inch cups with the **cooking spray.** *(Note: You can omit the cooking spray and use paper cupcake liners instead.)* Set aside.

2. In a large bowl, combine the **Quick Bread Mix, brown sugar, wheat germ, cinnamon,** and **nutmeg** and set aside. In a 2-cup glass measuring cup, combine the **milk, sour cream, egg,** and **vanilla extract.** Add to the dry ingredients all at once and stir just until moistened (the batter will be lumpy). Pour into the muffin cups, filling each one no more than ⅔ full.
3. Bake for 15 to 20 minutes or until the muffins are lightly browned and springy to the touch. Serve hot. Makes 12 mufffins.

One Muffin:

Calories	117	*Protein*	*3 g*
Total Fat	*3 g*	*Carbohydrates*	*18 g*
Saturated Fat	*1 g*	*Sodium*	*101 mg*
Cholesterol	*25 mg*	*Added Sugar*	*17 Cal*
		Fiber	*0*

Orange Quick Bread

Preparation: **10 min.** Baking: **1 hr.**

Nonstick cooking spray
3 cups Quick Bread Mix
¾ cup orange juice
¼ cup sour cream
1 large egg
Grated rind of 1 large orange

1. Preheat the oven to 325°F. Lightly spray a 9¼"x 5¼"x 2¾" loaf pan with the **cooking spray** and set aside.
2. Place the **Quick Bread Mix** in a large bowl. In a 2-cup glass measuring cup, combine the **orange juice, sour cream, egg,** and **orange rind.** Add to the bread mix all at once and stir just until moistened (the batter will be lumpy). Pour the batter into the loaf pan.
3. Bake for 1 hour or until a toothpick inserted in the center of the loaf comes out clean.
4. Cool the bread upright in its pan on a wire rack for 10 minutes. Using a knife, loosen the loaf around the edges, then turn out onto the rack and cool to room temperature before cutting. Makes 1 loaf (about 18 slices).

One Slice:

Calories	96	*Protein*	*2 g*
Total Fat	*3 g*	*Carbohydrates*	*16 g*
Saturated Fat	*1 g*	*Sodium*	*90 mg*
Cholesterol	*17 mg*	*Added Sugar*	*11 Cal*
		Fiber	*0*

Mock Hollandaise Sauce

Apple Pancakes

Preparation: **5 min.** Cooking: **12 min.** FAT SUGAR SODIUM

- 2 cups Quick Bread Mix
- 1 teaspoon ground cinnamon
- 1¼ cups skim milk
- ¼ cup sour cream
- 1 large egg, separated
- ½ cup peeled, chopped apple
  Nonstick cooking spray

1. In a large bowl, combine the **Quick Bread Mix** and **cinnamon** and set aside. In a 2-cup glass measuring cup, combine the **milk, sour cream, and egg yolk.** Add to the dry ingredients all at once and stir just until moistened (the batter will be lumpy). Fold in the **apple.**

2. In a small bowl, beat the **egg white** until it holds stiff, dry peaks; fold into the batter. Do not overmix; a few small puffs of egg white should be visible in the batter.

3. Lightly coat a heavy 12-inch skillet with the **cooking spray** and set over moderate heat. Using about ¼ cup batter per pancake, pour in the batter, 2 or 3 portions at a time, and cook for 1 to 2 minutes or until bubbles form on the pancakes. Turn and brown 1 to 2 minutes more. Makes 15 pancakes.

One Pancake:

Calories	87	*Protein*	3 g
Total Fat	2 g	*Carbohydrates*	13 g
Saturated Fat	1 g	*Sodium*	85 mg
Cholesterol	21 mg	*Added Sugar*	9 Cal
		Fiber	0

Mock Hollandaise Sauce

Preparation: **10 min.** Cooking: **7 min.** FAT SUGAR SODIUM

Serve this lemony sauce with asparagus, broccoli, cauliflower, green beans, or steamed fish.

- 1 cup skim milk
- 2 teaspoons cornstarch
- 1 small egg yolk
- 1 tablespoon unsalted margarine
- 2½ tablespoons lemon juice
- ½ teaspoon Dijon or spicy brown mustard
- 1 tablespoon sour cream
- ⅛ teaspoon salt
- ⅛ teaspoon white or black pepper

1. In a small heavy saucepan over moderately low heat, whisk together the **milk, cornstarch, and egg yolk;** cook, stirring, until the mixture comes almost to a simmer and has thickened slightly—5 to 6 minutes. Remove from the heat.

2. Whisk in the **margarine, lemon juice, mustard, sour cream, salt,** and **pepper.** Serve warm. Makes about 1¼ cups.

Variation:

Mock Béarnaise Sauce Combine 3 tablespoons minced shallots or green onions, 2 teaspoons crumbled dried tarragon, ¼ cup dry white wine, and 3 tablespoons white wine vinegar in a small heavy saucepan. Set over moderately high heat and boil, uncovered, until the mixture has boiled down to 2 tablespoons— 2 to 3 minutes. Stir in 1 tablespoon cold water and set aside. Prepare the Mock Hollandaise Sauce as directed and stir in the tarragon mixture. Serve with beef or vegetables. Makes about 1¼ cups.

One Tablespoon:

Calories	16	Protein	1 g
Total Fat	1 g	Carbohydrates	1 g
Saturated Fat	0	Sodium	25 mg
Cholesterol	14 mg	Added Sugar	0
		Fiber	0

Basic White Sauce Mix

Preparation: **5 min.**   FAT SUGAR SODIUM

With this white powder, you can make gravies, sauces, and creamed soups in a jiffy (see Quick Cream of Mushroom Soup and Quick Cheese Soup in the recipe that follows).

½ **cup unsifted all-purpose flour**
1 **cup nonfat dry milk powder**

Place the ingredients in a 1-pint jar, cover tightly, and shake well to mix. Store in the refrigerator for up to 4 weeks. Use for making cream sauces and gravies as directed below. Makes about 1½ cups.

To Make Thin White Sauce or Gravy   In a small heavy saucepan, blend ¼ cup Basic White Sauce Mix with 1 cup water, low-sodium chicken broth, or low-sodium beef broth. Set over moderate heat and bring to a simmer, whisking constantly. Cook, uncovered, stirring often, until the sauce thickens—about 3 minutes. Season to taste with salt and pepper. Do not allow the sauce to boil or it may curdle. Makes about 1 cup.

To Make Medium White Sauce or Gravy   Use ⅓ cup Basic White Sauce Mix and 1 cup water, low-sodium chicken broth, or low-sodium beef broth. Proceed as directed above. Makes about 1 cup.

¼ Cup Mix:

Calories	78	Protein	5 g
Total Fat	0	Carbohydrates	14 g
Saturated Fat	0	Sodium	62 mg
Cholesterol	0	Added Sugar	0
		Fiber	0

Tip: *You can salvage a lumpy sauce by whirling it in a blender for a few seconds.*

Quick Cream of Mushroom Soup

Preparation: **5 min.** Cooking: **12 min.**   FAT SUGAR SODIUM

You can turn these soups into sauces by using ⅓ cup Basic White Sauce Mix and 1 cup broth.

⅔ **cup Basic White Sauce Mix**
3 **cups low-sodium chicken or beef broth**
1 **tablespoon unsalted margarine**
1 **medium-size yellow onion, chopped fine**
1½ **cups thinly sliced mushrooms**
   Pinch ground nutmeg
   Pinch cayenne pepper
¼ **cup half-and-half**
¼ **cup whole milk**
⅛ **teaspoon salt**
⅛ **teaspoon black pepper**

1. In a medium-size saucepan, use the **Basic White Sauce Mix** and **chicken broth** to prepare a thin white sauce as directed in the Basic White Sauce Mix recipe. Remove from the heat.

2. Melt the **margarine** in a heavy 10-inch skillet over moderate heat. Add the **onion** and **mushrooms** and cook for 6 to 8 minutes or until the mushrooms have browned and their juices have evaporated. Stir in the **nutmeg** and **cayenne pepper.**

3. Stir the mushroom mixture into the sauce, along with the **half-and-half, milk, salt,** and **pepper.** If the mixture seems too thick, thin with a little broth. Set over low heat and bring just to serving temperature, stirring often. Do not allow the soup to boil. Serves 4.

Variation:

Quick Cheese Soup   Prepare as directed, but omit the mushrooms and cook the onion with 1 clove garlic, minced, for 5 minutes. Add the onion mixture and spices to the sauce, along with 1 cup puréed cooked carrots, ½ cup grated Parmesan cheese, 2 tablespoons shredded Cheddar cheese, 1 tablespoon Dijon or spicy brown mustard, ½ cup skim milk. Proceed as directed but omit the whole milk and half-and-half.

One Serving:

Calories	134	Protein	5 g
Total Fat	6 g	Carbohydrates	15 g
Saturated Fat	2 g	Sodium	130 mg
Cholesterol	9 mg	Added Sugar	0
		Fiber	1 g

Low-Sodium Chicken Broth

Preparation: **10 min.**, plus 4 hr.   FAT SUGAR SODIUM
cooling and refrigeration   Cooking: **3 hr.**

Although you can buy low-sodium broth at the supermarket, homemade broth is better-tasting—and cheaper. Making your own also lets you vary the flavor as you like. Try adding chopped mushroom stems and a few whole cloves, or add a pinch of thyme, marjoram, or dill.

2 pounds chicken backs, wings, and necks
1 large yellow onion, chopped
3 medium-size carrots, peeled and chopped
2 large stalks celery, including tops, chopped
2 bay leaves
4 sprigs parsley
8 black peppercorns
4 quarts water

1. Place all the ingredients in a large heavy kettle or stockpot, set over high heat, and bring to a boil. Adjust the heat so that the liquid bubbles gently, then skim any scum from the surface. Cover, leaving a small crack between the kettle and the lid so that steam can escape. Simmer the broth about 3 hours or until the flavor is well developed. Remove from the heat and let cool slightly.

2. Line a large sieve with a double thickness of cheesecloth and place it over a large heatproof bowl. Strain the broth into the bowl, cover, and let cool to room temperature.

3. Place the cooled broth in the refrigerator and chill for at least 3 hours. Skim the congealed fat from the top and discard.

4. Ladle the broth into ½-pint or 1-pint plastic freezer containers to within ½ inch of the top. Snap on the lids, label and date the containers, and store in the freezer for up to 6 months. Makes 2½ to 3 quarts.

Variation:

Low-Sodium Beef Broth   Substitute 1 pound cracked beef bones (shin or marrow bones) and 1 pound boneless lean beef chuck, cut into ½-inch cubes, for the chicken.

One Cup:

Calories	30	Protein	2 g
Total Fat	1 g	Carbohydrates	2 g
Saturated Fat	0 g	Sodium	55 mg
Cholesterol	0 mg	Added Sugar	0
		Fiber	0

Three-Pepper Relish

Preparation: **15 min.**, plus 30 min.   FAT SUGAR SODIUM
marination   Cooking: **5 min.**

1 large sweet green pepper, cored, seeded, and chopped
1 large sweet red pepper, cored, seeded, and chopped
1 large sweet yellow pepper, cored, seeded, and chopped
1 small yellow onion, chopped
¼ cup white vinegar
2 tablespoons sugar
½ teaspoon celery seeds
¼ teaspoon red pepper flakes

1. Place all the ingredients in a large stainless steel saucepan and mix well. Set over moderate heat until the vinegar boils. Stir, reduce the heat to low, cover the pan, and simmer for 2 to 3 minutes or just until the peppers are tender but still crisp.

2. Remove the mixture from the heat and let stand, covered, at room temperature at least 30 minutes before serving. Or place in the refrigerator and chill overnight. Store tightly covered in the refrigerator for up to 1 week. Serve as an accompaniment to meats. Makes about 3¾ cups.

One Tablespoon:

Calories	3	Protein	0
Total Fat	0	Carbohydrates	1 g
Saturated Fat	0	Sodium	0
Cholesterol	0	Added Sugar	2 Cal
		Fiber	0

Onion Relish

Preparation: **10 min.**, plus 30 min.   FAT SUGAR SODIUM
refrigeration

These spicy marinated onion rings make a terrific relish for hamburgers.

3 small yellow onions, sliced thin and separated into rings
1 small red onion, sliced thin and separated into rings
2 tablespoons sugar
1 tablespoon balsamic or cider vinegar
1 tablespoon white vinegar
2 teaspoons Dijon or spicy brown mustard
⅛ teaspoon black pepper

Place all the ingredients in a small glass bowl. Cover and let stand at room temperature at

Three-Pepper Relish (left), *Onion Relish* (center), and *Hamburger Relish* (right)

least 30 minutes before serving. Or chill in the refrigerator overnight. Serve with grilled meats. Store tightly covered in the refrigerator for up to 1 week. Makes about 2 cups.

One Tablespoon:

Calories	*5*	*Protein*	*0*
Total Fat	*0*	*Carbohydrates*	*1 g*
Saturated Fat	*0*	*Sodium*	*10 mg*
Cholesterol	*0*	*Added Sugar*	*3 Cal*
		Fiber	*0*

Hamburger Relish

Preparation: **10 min.,** plus 30 min. standing time **FAT** **SUGAR** **SODIUM**

1 **large ripe tomato, cored, seeded, and chopped fine**
2 **tablespoons minced sweet pickle**
2 **tablespoons minced yellow onion**
2 **tablespoons minced sweet red pepper**
1 **clove garlic, minced**
1 **tablespoon cider vinegar**
1 **teaspoon sugar**
½ **teaspoon celery seeds**
½ **teaspoon Dijon or spicy brown mustard**

Place all the ingredients in a medium-size glass bowl and mix well. Cover and let stand at room temperature at least 30 minutes before serving. Or chill in the refrigerator overnight. Stir well and serve on hamburgers or as an accompaniment to meats. Store tightly covered in the refrigerator for up to 1 week. Makes about 1¼ cups.

One Tablespoon:

Calories	*5*	*Protein*	*0*
Total Fat	*0*	*Carbohydrates*	*1 g*
Saturated Fat	*0*	*Sodium*	*15 mg*
Cholesterol	*0*	*Added Sugar*	*1 Cal*
		Fiber	*0*

Salsa

Preparation: **5 min.,** plus
2 hr. refrigeration

FAT SUGAR SODIUM

This piquant sauce is at its best when tomatoes are in season. Use it on broiled fish or chicken.

- 3 medium-size ripe tomatoes (about 1 pound), peeled, cored, seeded, and chopped
- ½ small red onion, chopped
- 1 clove garlic, minced
- ½ fresh or canned jalapeño pepper, cored, seeded, and chopped fine
- 1 tablespoon red wine vinegar
- 2 teaspoons lime juice
- 2 teaspoons olive oil
- ¼ teaspoon hot red pepper sauce

1. In a medium-size bowl, mix the **tomatoes, onion, garlic,** and **jalapeño pepper.**
2. Stir in the **vinegar, lime juice, olive oil,** and **red pepper sauce.** Cover and chill in the refrigerator at least 2 hours before serving. Store tightly covered in the refrigerator for up to 1 week. Makes about 2 cups.

One Tablespoon:

Calories	6	Protein	0
Total Fat	0	Carbohydrates	1 g
Saturated Fat	0	Sodium	2 mg
Cholesterol	0	Added Sugar	0
		Fiber	0

Ketchup

Preparation: **10 min.**
Cooking: **1 hr. 10 min.** (mostly unattended)

FAT SUGAR SODIUM

By making your own ketchup, you can significantly reduce the amount of salt, as well as eliminate artificial additives. Stored tightly covered in the refrigerator, the ketchup will keep well for about two weeks.

- 6 large ripe tomatoes (about 3 pounds), peeled, cored, seeded, and chopped
- 1 medium-size yellow onion, chopped fine
- 3 tablespoons dark brown sugar
- 2 cloves garlic, minced
- 1 large bay leaf, crumbled
- ¼ teaspoon each celery seeds, ground allspice, and cinnamon
- ⅛ teaspoon ground cloves
- ⅓ cup cider vinegar

1. Place the **tomatoes** and **onion** in a large heavy saucepan. Set over moderate heat and cook, covered, stirring often, until soft—20 to 25 minutes. Remove the vegetables, then put them through a food mill back into the saucepan, discarding any solids left in the food mill.
2. Stir in the **brown sugar, garlic, bay leaf, celery seeds, allspice, cinnamon, cloves,** and **vinegar,** and bring to a boil over moderate heat; adjust the heat so that the mixture bubbles gently, then simmer, uncovered, stirring often, until it has the consistency of ketchup—35 to 40 minutes. Store tightly covered in the refrigerator. Makes about 2 cups.

One Tablespoon:

Calories	14	Protein	0
Total Fat	0	Carbohydrates	3 g
Saturated Fat	0	Sodium	4 mg
Cholesterol	0	Added Sugar	3 Cal
		Fiber	0

Dijon Mustard

Preparation: **5 min.**

This mustard and the three variations that follow are sodium-free, yet they have excellent flavor. And they are plenty hot! All are made with the dry mustard sold in small tins.

- ½ cup dry mustard
- 1 teaspoon sugar
- 4 tablespoons dry white wine
- 2 tablespoons olive oil

In a small bowl, mix together all the ingredients until well blended. Transfer to a ½-pint jar, cover tightly, and store in the refrigerator for up to 6 weeks. Makes about ⅔ cup.

Variations:

Whole-Grain Mustard   Add 2 teaspoons mustard seeds, lightly crushed.

Beer Mustard   Substitute 4 tablespoons flat beer for the white wine.

Herb Mustard   Add 2 cloves garlic, minced, and 2 teaspoons dried tarragon, crumbled.

One Tablespoon:

Calories	47	Protein	1 g
Total Fat	4 g	Carbohydrates	1 g
Saturated Fat	0	Sodium	1 g
Cholesterol	0	Added Sugar	3 Cal
		Fiber	0

Appetizers and Snacks

Shrimp cocktail is the favorite low-calorie appetizer and fresh fruit the snack par excellence. But who doesn't want a change now and then? Try Southwestern Style Guacamole with only 9 calories, 1 gram of fat, and 2 milligrams of sodium per tablespoon. Or serve guests Zucchini, Carrot, and Onion Quiche without having to worry about anyone's diet. And before you settle down to watch a movie, bake some Crispy Mushroom Chips— only 64 calories if you down the whole batch.

Sardine-Rice Bundles and *Tuna-Stuffed Cucumbers*

Hors d'oeuvres
Black Bean Dip

Preparation: **10 min.**   FAT SUGAR SODIUM

Serve this dip with rice crackers or fresh vegetables.

- **2 cups cooked and drained black beans**
- **4 teaspoons low-sodium tomato paste**
- **3 tablespoons water**
- **1 clove garlic, minced**
- **2 teaspoons lime juice**
- **½ teaspoon ground cumin**
- **2 green onions, chopped fine**
- **2 tablespoons chopped mild green chilies**

1. In a food processor or electric blender, place the **black beans, tomato paste, water, garlic, lime juice,** and **cumin** and whirl for 1 minute or until the mixture forms a smooth paste.
2. Transfer to a medium-size serving bowl and stir in the **green onions** and **green chilies.** Makes 2 cups.

Variation:

Garlicky White Bean Dip   Prepare as directed, substituting 2 cups cooked and drained white beans for the black beans. Omit the tomato paste and water and add ½ cup low-fat yogurt. Increase the garlic to 2 cloves and omit the green onions.

One Tablespoon:

Calories	16	*Protein*	*1 g*
Total Fat	0	*Carbohydrates*	*3 g*
Saturated Fat	0	*Sodium*	*6 mg*
Cholesterol	0	*Added Sugar*	*0*
		Fiber	*1 g*

Herbed Cottage Cheese Dip

Preparation: **10 min.,**   FAT SUGAR SODIUM
plus 1 hr. refrigeration

- **1 cup low-fat cottage cheese**
- **4 medium-size radishes, trimmed and chopped**
- **2 tablespoons minced fresh basil or 1 teaspoon dried basil, crumbled**
- **1 clove garlic, minced**
- **½ teaspoon grated lemon rind**

1. In an electric blender or food processor, whirl the **cottage cheese** for 15 seconds, until smooth.
2. Transfer to a small serving bowl and stir in the **radishes, basil, garlic,** and **lemon rind.** Cover and refrigerate at least 1 hour before serving. Makes 1¼ cups.

Variation:

Cottage Cheese–Chutney Dip   Prepare as directed, substituting ¼ cup chopped mango or tomato chutney for the radishes, basil, garlic, and lemon rind.

One Tablespoon:

Calories	9	*Protein*	*1 g*
Total Fat	0	*Carbohydrates*	*0*
Saturated Fat	0	*Sodium*	*46 mg*
Cholesterol	0	*Added Sugar*	*0*
		Fiber	*0*

Roasted Garlic Dip

Preparation: **2 min.**   FAT SUGAR SODIUM
Cooking: **1 hr.** (unattended)

This is a marvelous dip for carrot or zucchini sticks, broccoli florets, or strips of sweet red or green pepper.

- **1 large bulb (entire head) garlic**
- **1 cup part-skim ricotta cheese**
- **¼ teaspoon black pepper**

1. Preheat the oven to 375°F. Wrap the **garlic** in aluminum foil, set on the middle oven rack, and roast for 1 hour. Remove the garlic from the oven and cool until easy to handle.
2. Separate the garlic into cloves. Working over the container of an electric blender or food processor, pinch each garlic clove so that the roasted flesh slips out. Add the **ricotta cheese** and **pepper** to the blender and purée by whirling for 10 to 15 seconds. Transfer to a small bowl and serve. Makes about 1¼ cups.

One Tablespoon:

Calories	21	*Protein*	*2 g*
Total Fat	*1 g*	*Carbohydrates*	*1 g*
Saturated Fat	*1 g*	*Sodium*	*16 mg*
Cholesterol	*4 mg*	*Added Sugar*	*0*
		Fiber	*0*

Southwestern-Style Guacamole

Preparation: **20 min.** [FAT] [SUGAR] [SODIUM]

You can serve this spicy dish as a dip or as a first course on shredded lettuce.

- 1 small ripe avocado, peeled and pitted
- 2 tablespoons plain low-fat yogurt
- 2 medium-size ripe tomatoes, peeled, cored, seeded, and chopped
- ¼ cup minced fresh coriander or parsley
- ½ teaspoon ground coriander
- ½ small red onion, chopped fine
- 4 teaspoons lime juice
- 1 clove garlic, minced
- ½ small jalapeño pepper, seeded and chopped fine

Place the **avocado** in a large bowl and mash it with a potato masher until almost smooth, leaving a few lumps for texture. Mix in the remaining ingredients. Makes 2¼ cups.

One Tablespoon:

Calories	9	Protein	0
Total Fat	1 g	Carbohydrates	1 g
Saturated Fat	0	Sodium	2 mg
Cholesterol	0	Added Sugar	0
		Fiber	0

Tip: *If you do not plan to serve guacamole as soon as you make it, save the pit and push it into the guacamole. Cover the dish with plastic wrap and refrigerate. The pit will help keep the guacamole from discoloring.*

Potted Turkey Spread

Preparation: **5 min.,** plus 2 hr. refrigeration   Cooking: **5 min.** [FAT] [SUGAR] [SODIUM]

Serve this nippy spread on melba toast or stuffed in small celery stalks. Use leftover roast turkey or chicken in place of the ground turkey, if you like.

- ½ pound ground turkey
- 1 small yellow onion, chopped
- 2 tablespoons sweet pickle relish
- 2 tablespoons plain low-fat yogurt
- ¼ teaspoon paprika
  Pinch ground nutmeg
- ⅛ teaspoon black pepper

1. In a 10-inch nonstick skillet, brown the **turkey** over moderate heat for 5 minutes or until cooked through.
2. Transfer the turkey to a food processor or electric blender and add the **onion, relish, yogurt, paprika, nutmeg,** and **pepper.** Whirl the mixture for 15 seconds. Transfer to a small crock or bowl, cover tightly, and refrigerate at least 2 hours. Makes about 1 cup.

One Tablespoon:

Calories	27	Protein	3 g
Total Fat	1 g	Carbohydrates	1 g
Saturated Fat	0	Sodium	26 mg
Cholesterol	9 mg	Added Sugar	0
		Fiber	0

Lemony Chinese Chicken Morsels

Preparation: **15 min.,** plus 1 hr. refrigeration   Cooking: **14 min.** [FAT] [SUGAR] [SODIUM]

- ⅓ cup lemon juice
- 2 tablespoons reduced-sodium soy sauce
- 2 tablespoons Dijon or spicy brown mustard
- 1 teaspoon vegetable oil
- ⅛ teaspoon cayenne pepper
- 2 skinned and boned chicken breasts (about 1 pound), cut into ¾-inch cubes

1. In a medium-size bowl, combine the **lemon juice, soy sauce, mustard, vegetable oil,** and **cayenne pepper.** Add the **chicken** cubes and toss well to coat. Cover and refrigerate at least 1 hour, tossing occasionally.
2. Preheat the broiler and lightly grease the broiler pan rack. Place the chicken cubes on the rack about 1 inch apart and broil 4 to 5 inches from the heat for 7 minutes, brushing once with the soy sauce mixture halfway through the cooking. Turn the chicken and broil 7 minutes longer, again brushing with the soy sauce halfway through. Makes approximately 24 chicken morsels.

One Chicken Morsel:

Calories	26	Protein	4 g
Total Fat	1 g	Carbohydrates	0
Saturated Fat	0	Sodium	101 mg
Cholesterol	11 mg	Added Sugar	0
		Fiber	0

Peppery Chicken Wings

Peppery Chicken Wings

Preparation: **8 min.** Cooking: **20 min.** FAT SUGAR SODIUM

Here's an appetizer that's a big hit with guests; the blue cheese dip complements the peppery taste of the chicken.

16 **chicken wings (about 2 pounds)**
 1 **teaspoon peanut or vegetable oil**
 1 **teaspoon cayenne pepper**
 ½ **cup plain low-fat yogurt**
 ¼ **cup buttermilk**
 ¼ **cup crumbled blue cheese (1 ounce)**
 ½ **small yellow onion, grated**
 1 **teaspoon cider vinegar**

1. Preheat the broiler. Separate the **chicken wings** at the joint and remove and discard the wing tips. In a medium-size bowl, combine the **peanut oil** and **cayenne pepper;** add the chicken wings and turn until well coated.

2. Place the chicken wings on the broiler pan rack and broil about 8 inches from the heat, turning occasionally, until crisp and golden—about 20 minutes.

3. Meanwhile, prepare the dip. In a medium-size bowl, whisk together the **yogurt, buttermilk, blue cheese, onion,** and **vinegar;** transfer to a small serving bowl. Set the dip in the center of a warm large round platter and arrange the broiled chicken wings around it. Serves 8.

One Chicken Wing with Dip:

Calories	114	Protein	10 g
Total Fat	6 g	Carbohydrates	1 g
Saturated Fat	2 g	Sodium	62 mg
Cholesterol	30 mg	Added Sugar	0
		Fiber	0

Deviled Shrimp

Preparation: **15 min.** Cooking: **21 min** FAT SUGAR SODIUM

12 **black peppercorns**
12 **coriander seeds**
 4 **whole cloves**
 1 **bay leaf**
 ½ **teaspoon each red pepper flakes, mustard seeds, and crumbled dried thyme**
 1 **medium-size yellow onion, chopped**
 1 **small stalk celery, chopped**
 3 **slices lemon**
 3 **cloves garlic, sliced thin**
 2 **tablespoons white wine vinegar**
24 **large shrimp, shelled and deveined**
 2 **tablespoons lemon juice**

1 tablespoon olive oil
⅛ teaspoon cayenne pepper or to taste
Hot red pepper sauce to taste

1. Place the **peppercorns, coriander seeds, cloves, bay leaf, red pepper flakes, mustard seeds,** and **thyme** in a small piece of cheesecloth and tie securely. In a large heavy saucepan, bring 4 cups unsalted water to a boil over moderately high heat; add the **onion, celery, lemon slices, garlic, vinegar,** and bag of spices. Reduce the heat to moderate and let the mixture simmer, uncovered, for 15 minutes. Add the **shrimp** and cook, uncovered, stirring often, for 2 to 3 minutes or until they turn pink. Transfer to a large bowl and cool to room temperature. Cover and refrigerate.

2. Drain the shrimp and place in a serving dish. Add the **lemon juice, olive oil, cayenne pepper,** and **red pepper sauce,** and toss to mix. Serve with toothpicks. Serves 8 as a finger food.

One Shrimp:

Calories	24	Protein	3 g
Total Fat	1 g	Carbohydrates	1 g
Saturated Fat	0	Sodium	24 mg
Cholesterol	23 mg	Added Sugar	0
		Fiber	0

Spicy Stuffed Eggs

Preparation: **10 min.** Cooking: **14 min.**

Here's a version of deviled eggs that dispenses with most of the cholesterol-laden egg yolks.

6 hard-cooked large eggs
1 green onion, including top, chopped fine
1 tablespoon reduced-calorie mayonnaise
1 tablespoon minced parsley
2 sweet gherkin pickles, chopped fine
½ teaspoon Dijon or spicy brown mustard
⅛ teaspoon salt
⅛ teaspoon black pepper
8 sprigs parsley (optional)

1. Peel the **eggs** and halve them lengthwise, then place 1 egg yolk in a small bowl; discard the remaining yolks. With a fork, mash the yolk; then add 4 of the egg white halves and mash them. Mix in the **green onion, mayonnaise, parsley, pickles, mustard, salt,** and **pepper.**

2. Mound the mixture into the remaining egg white halves, dividing it evenly. Garnish each

half, if you like, with a **parsley sprig.** Cover loosely and refrigerate until ready to serve. Makes 8 stuffed half eggs.

One Half Egg:

Calories	26	Protein	4 g
Total Fat	1 g	Carbohydrates	3 g
Saturated Fat	0	Sodium	176 mg
Cholesterol	35 mg	Added Sugar	0
		Fiber	0

Chilled Cheese Fingers

Preparation: **2 min.** FAT SUGAR SODIUM
Cooking: **5 min.,** plus 3 hr. refrigeration

Here's an unusual and simple appetizer that can be made two or three days in advance.

Nonstick cooking spray
⅓ cup low-sodium chicken broth
1 envelope unflavored gelatin
2 cups part-skim ricotta cheese
½ cup grated Parmesan cheese
2 ounces cream cheese, softened
⅓ cup plain low-fat yogurt
3 tablespoons minced fresh basil or
   3 tablespoons minced parsley plus
   1 teaspoon dried basil, crumbled
¼ teaspoon black pepper
⅛ teaspoon salt

1. Lightly coat a nonmetallic 8″x 8″x 2″ baking pan with the **cooking spray** and set aside. Pour the **chicken broth** into a small heavy saucepan, sprinkle the **gelatin** over it, and let soften for 5 minutes. Set over very low heat and stir until the gelatin dissolves—about 5 minutes. Remove from the heat and set aside.

2. In the large bowl of an electric mixer, beat the **ricotta cheese, Parmesan cheese,** and **cream cheese** at moderate speed for 1 minute or until smooth. Beat in the **yogurt, basil, pepper,** and **salt,** then stir in the gelatin. Pour the mixture into the pan, cover, and refrigerate at least 3 hours or until set.

3. To serve, run a thin metal spatula around the edges of the cheese mixture and invert onto a large platter. Cut into 8 strips one way, then into 6 strips the opposite way, to form 48 fingers. Serves 16 as a finger food.

One Cheese Finger:

Calories	24	Protein	2 g
Total Fat	2 g	Carbohydrates	1 g
Saturated Fat	1 g	Sodium	39 mg
Cholesterol	5 mg	Added Sugar	0
		Fiber	0

Super Nachos

4 6-inch corn tortillas
1½ teaspoons vegetable oil
½ cup low-sodium tomato sauce
1 clove garlic, minced
½ teaspoon ground cumin
½ teaspoon chili powder
   Pinch each ground cinnamon
   and cloves

2 small jalapeño peppers,
   seeded and chopped fine
½ cup shredded part-skim
   mozzarella cheese (about
   2 ounces)
3 tablespoons grated Parmesan
   cheese
2 tablespoons minced parsley

Preparation:
15 min.
Cooking:
13 min.

One Nacho:

Calories	38
Total Fat	2 g
Saturated Fat	1 g
Cholesterol	3 mg
Protein	2 g
Carbohydrates	4 g
Sodium	105 mg
Added Sugar	0
Fiber	0

1. Preheat the oven to 400°F. Brush both sides of the **tortillas** with the **vegetable oil,** then quarter each tortilla, transfer to an ungreased baking sheet, and bake, uncovered, for 10 to 12 minutes or until crisp.

2. Meanwhile, in a small heavy saucepan, combine the **tomato sauce, garlic, cumin, chili powder, cinnamon,** and **cloves;** cover and bring to a boil over moderately high heat—about 1 minute. Reduce the heat so that the mixture bubbles gently, and simmer, uncovered, stirring often, for 5 minutes or until the sauce thickens slightly.

3. Top the tortillas with the tomato sauce and **jalapeño peppers,** then with the **mozzarella cheese** and **Parmesan cheese.** Bake, uncovered, for 3 minutes or until the cheeses have melted. Sprinkle with the **parsley.** Makes 16 nachos.

Super Nachos

Spinach-Stuffed Mushrooms

These mushrooms can be stuffed and refrigerated up to an hour before baking.

FAT SUGAR SODIUM

Nonstick cooking spray
½ pound fresh spinach, trimmed
12 medium-size mushrooms
(½ to ¾ pound)
1 tablespoon unsalted margarine
1 clove garlic, minced

¼ teaspoon dried oregano, crumbled
1 tablespoon lemon juice
2 tablespoons fine dry bread crumbs

1. Preheat the oven to 400°F. Lightly coat an 8″x 8″x 2″ baking pan with the **cooking spray** and set aside.
2. Wash the **spinach** and place in a medium-size heavy saucepan with just the water that clings to the leaves; cook, covered, over moderate heat for 2 to 3 minutes or until wilted. Drain and cool the spinach; then, with your hands, squeeze out the liquid. Chop fine and set aside.
3. Remove the **mushroom** stems and chop fine. In a heavy 7-inch skillet, melt the **margarine** over moderate heat. Add the **garlic** and cook for 30 seconds. Stir in the chopped mushrooms and cook for 5 minutes or until golden. Mix in the spinach and the **oregano** and cook, stirring, 1 minute longer. Stir in the **lemon juice** and remove from the heat.
4. Fill the mushroom caps with the spinach mixture, sprinkle with the **bread crumbs,** and transfer to the baking pan. Bake, uncovered, for 10 to 15 minutes or until the bread crumbs are lightly browned. Serve immediately. Serves 4.

Preparation:
20 min.
Cooking:
20 min.

One Mushroom:

Calories	*20*
Total Fat	*1 g*
Saturated Fat	*0*
Cholesterol	*0*
Protein	*1 g*
Carbohydrates	*2 g*
Sodium	*19 mg*
Added Sugar	*0*
Fiber	*1 g*

Tangy Cheese-Stuffed New Potatoes

To make this dish ahead, cover and refrigerate the stuffing but leave the potatoes uncut at room temperature until close to serving time. Then complete the recipe.

FAT SUGAR SODIUM

8 small new potatoes
(about ½ pound)
½ cup low-fat cottage cheese
2 tablespoons minced parsley
2 tablespoons minced chives or green onion tops

2 tablespoons snipped fresh dill or 1 teaspoon dill weed
¼ teaspoon black pepper
8 small sprigs dill or parsley (optional)

1. In a medium-size heavy saucepan over moderately high heat, bring to a boil enough unsalted water to cover the **potatoes.** Add the potatoes, reduce the heat to low, cover, and cook until tender—about 15 minutes. Drain.
2. Meanwhile, place the **cottage cheese** in an electric blender or food processor and whirl for 15 seconds or until smooth. Transfer to a small bowl and stir in the **parsley, chives, snipped dill,** and **pepper.**
3. When the potatoes are cool enough to handle, slice about ¼ inch off the top of each. With a small spoon or melon baller, remove 1 or 2 scoops of potato, being careful not to break the skin. Fill the potatoes with the cheese mixture and garnish, if you like, with the **dill sprigs.** Serves 4.

Preparation:
5 min.
Cooking:
18 min.

One Potato:

Calories	*34*
Total Fat	*0*
Saturated Fat	*0*
Cholesterol	*1 mg*
Protein	*2 g*
Carbohydrates	*6 g*
Sodium	*60 mg*
Added Sugar	*0*
Fiber	*1 g*

Variation:

Stuffed New Potatoes Topped with Caviar Omit the cottage cheese, parsley, and chives. Stir the snipped dill into ½ cup plain low-fat yogurt and fill the potatoes as directed. Top each with ¼ teaspoon red caviar.

First Course Appetizers

Cherry Tomatoes Stuffed with Shrimp

Preparation: **20 min.** Cooking: **5 min.** FAT SUGAR SODIUM

- **6 medium-size shrimp (about ¼ pound), shelled and deveined**
- **2 tablespoons minced parsley**
- **2 tablespoons minced fresh chives**
- **1 tablespoon lemon juice**
- **1 tablespoon olive oil**
  Pinch black pepper
- **1 pint cherry tomatoes (about 24 tomatoes)**

1. In a medium-size heavy saucepan, bring 2 cups unsalted water to a boil over moderately high heat; add the **shrimp** and cook, uncovered, for 3 minutes or until they turn pink. Drain and cool.
2. Whirl the shrimp in a food processor for 1 minute. Transfer to a small bowl and mix in the **parsley, chives, lemon juice, olive oil,** and **pepper;** cover and chill in the refrigerator.
3. To stuff the **tomatoes,** slice about ⅓ off the top of each one. With a small spoon, scoop out and discard the seeds. Fill the tomatoes with the shrimp mixture. Serves 4 to 6.

One Tomato:			
Calories	11	Protein	1 g
Total Fat	1 g	Carbohydrates	1 g
Saturated Fat	0	Sodium	7 mg
Cholesterol	8 mg	Added Sugar	0
		Fiber	0

Tuna-Stuffed Cucumbers

Preparation: **15 min.,** plus 4 hr. refrigeration FAT SUGAR SODIUM

- **1 can (6½ ounces) water-packed light tuna, drained and flaked**
- **½ cup soft whole wheat bread crumbs (1 slice)**
- **1 medium-size stalk celery, chopped fine**
- **¼ cup finely chopped sweet red pepper**
- **1 green onion, chopped fine**
- **2 tablespoons plain low-fat yogurt**
- **1 tablespoon minced parsley**
- **2 teaspoons lemon juice**
- **2 tablespoons reduced-calorie mayonnaise**
- **1½ teaspoons peanut oil**

- **1 teaspoon Dijon or spicy brown mustard**
- **¼ teaspoon dried tarragon, crumbled**
- **⅛ teaspoon black pepper**
- **4 medium-size unwaxed cucumbers**

1. In a small bowl, mix all the ingredients but the cucumbers and set aside.
2. Halve each **cucumber** crosswise. Using an apple corer or small paring knife, carefully scoop out the centers, leaving shells about ¼ inch thick. Stuff the tuna mixture into each hollowed-out cucumber half, wrap in plastic food wrap, and refrigerate at least 4 hours.
3. Cut the cucumbers into ½-inch slices. Makes 48 appetizers. Serves 8 as a first course.

One Cucumber Slice:			
Calories	12	Protein	1 g
Total Fat	0	Carbohydrates	1 g
Saturated Fat	0	Sodium	24 mg
Cholesterol	2 mg	Added Sugar	0
		Fiber	0

Sardine-Rice Bundles

Preparation: **2 min.**
Cooking: **25 min.** (mostly unattended) FAT SUGAR SODIUM

- **⅓ cup long-grain rice**
- **1 teaspoon sugar**
- **2 tablespoons white vinegar**
- **16 large romaine or spinach leaves**
- **1 can (3¾ ounces) unsalted water-packed sardines, drained well**
- **2 green onions, sliced thin**

1. In a medium-size saucepan, cook the **rice** by package directions, omitting the salt. Set aside.
2. In a small bowl, dissolve the **sugar** in the **vinegar.** Stir into the rice and cool.
3. In a large heavy saucepan, bring to a boil enough unsalted water to cover the **romaine leaves.** Add the romaine and cook for 1 minute. Drain and blot dry with paper towels.
4. Place a tablespoon of the cooked rice at the base of each leaf. Top with a piece of **sardine.** Sprinkle with the **green onions,** then tightly roll up the leaves, tucking in the sides. Serve warm or chilled. Accompany with hot mustard. Makes 16 bundles to serve 4 as a first course.

One Bundle:			
Calories	37	Protein	2 g
Total Fat	1 g	Carbohydrates	4 g
Saturated Fat	0	Sodium	11 mg
Cholesterol	0	Added Sugar	1 Cal
		Fiber	0

Cheese Blini

Cheese Blini

These thin pancakes are simple to make and can be enjoyed as a starter or as finger food for any occasion. If you like, prepare the blini in advance, stack them between sheets of wax paper, wrap, and freeze; thaw before using.

FAT SUGAR SODIUM

½ cup unsifted all-purpose flour
Pinch salt
⅔ cup low-fat (2% milk fat) milk
1 large egg white
Nonstick cooking spray

½ cup low-fat cottage cheese
2 teaspoons honey
⅛ teaspoon ground ginger
Pinch ground cinnamon

1. In a medium-size bowl, combine the **flour** and **salt.** In a small bowl, combine the **milk** and **egg white.** Make a well in the center of the flour, add the milk mixture, and stir just to combine.

2. Coat a 7-inch nonstick skillet with the **cooking spray** and set over moderately high heat. When the skillet is hot, pour in 2 tablespoons of the batter, rotating the pan to make a thin pancake. Cook for 30 seconds or until set, flip, and cook 20 to 30 seconds longer or until the blini is golden. Transfer to a plate, top with a sheet of wax paper, and repeat until all the batter is used.

3. Place the **cottage cheese, honey, ginger,** and **cinnamon** in a food processor or electric blender and whirl for 1 minute. Spread each blini with a tablespoon of the cheese mixture, fold in half, then fold in half again. Makes 8 cheese blini.

Preparation:
1 min.
Cooking:
8 min.

One Blini:

Calories	*56*
Total Fat	*1 g*
Saturated Fat	*0*
Cholesterol	*1 mg*
Protein	*4 g*
Carbohydrates	*9 g*
Sodium	*91 mg*
Added Sugar	*4 Cal*
Fiber	*0*

Spinach Soufflé Squares

This attractive appetizer can be made in advance and reheated before serving. To reheat, cover with aluminum foil and place in a 350°F oven for 10 to 15 minutes.

FAT SUGAR **SODIUM**

1 pound fresh spinach, trimmed and chopped, or 1 package (10 ounces) frozen chopped spinach, thawed
Pinch ground nutmeg
Pinch sugar
1 cup low-fat cottage cheese

2 teaspoons flour
2 tablespoons grated Parmesan cheese
1 large egg yolk
1/8 teaspoon black pepper
Pinch cayenne pepper
2 large egg whites

Preparation:
15 min.
Cooking:
25 min.
(mostly unattended)

One First-Course Serving:

Calories	92
Total Fat	2 g
Saturated Fat	1 g
Cholesterol	72 mg
Protein	13 g
Carbohydrates	6 g
Sodium	328 mg
Added Sugar	1 Cal
Fiber	3 g

1. Preheat the oven to 400°F. Line the bottom of an 8"x 8"x 2" baking pan with wax paper or baking parchment and set aside.

2. Wash the **spinach** and place in a heavy 12-inch skillet with just the water that clings to the leaves. Set over moderate heat and sprinkle with the **nutmeg** and **sugar**; cook, uncovered, stirring occasionally, until the spinach is tender—about 5 minutes. Cool to room temperature.

3. Place the **cottage cheese** in a food processor or electric blender and whirl for 30 seconds. Add the **flour, Parmesan cheese, egg yolk, black pepper,** and **cayenne pepper**, and whirl 30 seconds longer or until well blended. Transfer to a large bowl and mix in the cooled spinach.

4. In a medium-size bowl, beat the **egg whites** until they hold stiff peaks. Mix about ¼ cup of the beaten whites into the spinach mixture, then, with a rubber spatula, gently fold in the rest. Transfer the mixture to the baking pan, smoothing the top with the spatula. Bake, uncovered, for 20 minutes or until set and golden.

5. Place the pan on a wire rack and cool for 5 minutes, then invert onto a large platter. Cut into 4 pieces to serve as a first course, or in 1½-inch squares to serve as a party finger food.

Tortellini with Spinach Pesto Dip

A wonderful way to start an Italian—or any—meal is with this light finger-food pasta appetizer.

FAT SUGAR **SODIUM**

1½ tablespoons pine nuts or chopped walnuts
1 clove garlic, sliced
½ teaspoon lemon juice
1 pound fresh spinach, trimmed and chopped, or 1 package (10 ounces) frozen chopped spinach, thawed and drained

1 teaspoon olive oil
3 tablespoons grated Parmesan cheese
8 ounces tortellini

Preparation:
10 min.
Cooking:
10 min.

One Serving:

Calories	128
Total Fat	3 g
Saturated Fat	1 g
Cholesterol	1 mg
Protein	6 g
Carbohydrates	21 g
Sodium	72 mg
Added Sugar	0
Fiber	2 g

1. Place the **pine nuts, garlic, lemon juice, spinach,** and **olive oil** in an electric blender or food processor, and whirl for 1 minute. Transfer to a small bowl and mix in the **cheese**; set aside.

2. Cook the **tortellini** according to package directions, omitting the salt. Drain, rinse under cold running water, and drain again. Serve the tortellini as dippers for the spinach pesto, either on individual plates or on a large platter. Serves 8.

Zucchini, Carrot, and Onion Quiche

This savory low-fat quiche makes a nice first course for almost any meal.

½ cup long-grain rice
Nonstick cooking spray
1 cup shredded Swiss cheese (about 4 ounces)
3 large egg whites
1 medium-size yellow onion, halved and sliced thin
1 medium-size carrot, peeled and grated

1 medium-size zucchini (about ½ pound), grated
1 cup low-sodium chicken broth
¼ teaspoon dried marjoram, crumbled
1 large egg
1 cup skim milk
¼ teaspoon black pepper

FAT SUGAR SODIUM

Preparation:
10 min.
Cooking:
1 hr. 5 min.
(mostly unattended)

One Slice:

Calories	*127*
Total Fat	*4 g*
Saturated Fat	*2 g*
Cholesterol	*38 mg*
Protein	*7 g*
Carbohydrates	*15 g*
Sodium	*74 mg*
Added Sugar	*0*
Fiber	*0*

1. Cook the **rice** according to package directions, omitting the salt.

2. Preheat the oven to 350°F. Coat a 9-inch pie pan with the **cooking spray** and set aside. In a medium-size bowl, mix together the rice, 2 tablespoons of the **cheese,** and 1 **egg white.** With moistened hands, press the mixture over the bottom and sides of the pie pan. Bake, uncovered, for 5 minutes. Remove and cool upright on a wire rack while you prepare the filling.

3. In a medium-size saucepan, cook the **onion, carrot, zucchini, chicken broth,** and **marjoram,** uncovered, over moderate heat for 15 minutes. Increase the heat to high and cook, stirring, until all the liquid has evaporated and the vegetables are almost glazed—about 5 minutes. Transfer to a medium-size heatproof bowl and cool to room temperature— about 20 minutes.

4. Lightly beat together the remaining egg whites and the **egg;** mix into the cooled vegetables along with the **milk, pepper,** and remaining cheese. Pour the mixture into the pie shell and bake, uncovered, until the filling is puffed and set—about 20 minutes. Remove and cool for 15 minutes before serving. Serves 10 as a first course or 4 as a main course.

Zucchini, Carrot, and Onion Quiche

Marinated Fresh Vegetables

Preparation: **20 min.**, plus 12 hr. refrigeration

FAT SUGAR SODIUM

- ½ cup white wine vinegar
- 1 cup water
- 1 tablespoon olive oil
- 1 clove garlic, sliced thin
- ½ teaspoon paprika
- ¼ teaspoon black pepper
- 2 medium-size carrots, peeled and cut into matchstick strips
- 1 stalk celery, cut into matchstick strips
- 1 medium-size zucchini (about ½ pound), cut into matchstick strips
- 1 small sweet red pepper, cored, seeded, and cut into matchstick strips
- 1 tablespoon drained capers

In a medium-size bowl, mix the **vinegar, water, olive oil, garlic, paprika,** and **black pepper.** Add the **carrots, celery, zucchini, red pepper,** and **capers** and toss well. Cover and refrigerate overnight. Serves 4 as a first course.

One Serving:

Calories	50	Protein	1 g
Total Fat	2 g	Carbohydrates	8 g
Saturated Fat	0	Sodium	79 mg
Cholesterol	0	Added Sugar	0
		Fiber	1 g

Snacks

Crunchy Popcorn Mix

Preparation: **5 min.**

FAT SUGAR SODIUM

This is a simple but nutritious snack.

- 5 cups popped corn
- 1 cup crisp unsweetened whole-grain cereal
- ½ cup unsalted dry-roasted soybean nuts
- ½ cup raisins

In a large bowl, toss the popped **corn** with the **cereal, soybean nuts,** and **raisins.** Makes about 7 cups.

½ Cup:

Calories	57	Protein	2 g
Total Fat	1 g	Carbohydrates	10 g
Saturated Fat	0	Sodium	20 mg
Cholesterol	0	Added Sugar	0
		Fiber	1 g

Crispy Mushroom Chips

Preparation: **10 min.**
Cooking: **2½ hr.** (unattended)

FAT SUGAR SODIUM

- Nonstick cooking spray
- ½ pound large mushrooms

1. Preheat the oven to 250°F. Coat a large baking sheet with the **cooking spray** and set aside.
2. Using a sharp knife, slice the **mushrooms** very thin, then transfer to the baking sheet, arranging the slices in a single layer. Bake, uncovered, for 2½ to 3 hours or until crisp and completely dry. Makes about 2 cups.

½ Cup:

Calories	16	Protein	1 g
Total Fat	0	Carbohydrates	3 g
Saturated Fat	0	Sodium	2 mg
Cholesterol	0	Added Sugar	0
		Fiber	1 g

Chick Pea Snack

Preparation: **2 min.**
Cooking: **8 min.**

FAT SUGAR SODIUM

- 2 tablespoons sugar
- ½ teaspoon each ground cumin, chili powder, and paprika
- ¼ teaspoon ground coriander
- ⅛ teaspoon cayenne pepper
- ⅛ teaspoon salt (optional)
- 2 cups cooked and drained chick peas
- 2 teaspoons vegetable or peanut oil

1. In a large bowl, toss together the **sugar, cumin, chili powder, paprika, coriander, cayenne pepper,** and, if you like, the **salt.** Add the **chick peas** and toss well to coat.
2. Heat the **vegetable oil** in a heavy 10-inch skillet over moderately high heat about 1 minute; add the chick peas and cook, uncovered, shaking the pan frequently, until dry and crispy—about 7 minutes.
3. Using a slotted spoon, transfer the chick peas to a wire rack covered with paper towels to cool. Stored airtight, the chick peas will keep about 1 week. Makes 2¼ cups.

¼ Cup:

Calories	123	Protein	5 g
Total Fat	2 g	Carbohydrates	18 g
Saturated Fat	0	Sodium	8 mg
Cholesterol	0	Added Sugar	4 Cal
		Fiber	4 g

Soups

If you've stopped serving soups because packaged varieties have too much salt, try the recipes in this chapter. They'll enable you to reduce sodium while adding taste and nutrition. (Canned minestrone, for example, can have 910 milligrams of sodium and 3 grams of protein per serving. The minestrone here, by contrast, has only 145 milligrams of sodium and a full 12 grams of protein.) Besides comforting old-time favorites, you'll find some unusual creations like Roasted Eggplant Soup, as well as rich, creamy soups that are lower in fat and calories than you'd ever think.

Chicken Gumbo

Homestyle Chicken Consommé

Preparation: **10 min.**
Cooking: **36 min.** (mostly unattended)

FAT SUGAR SODIUM

This shortcut recipe is as good as any that Grandma ever made. Egg whites and egg shells are added to this recipe to make the broth sparkling clear.

6 cups low-sodium chicken broth
3 large egg whites, lightly beaten
3 egg shells, crushed
3 green onions, including tops, sliced thin
1 medium-size ripe tomato, cored and chopped
1 small carrot, peeled and sliced
½ cup chopped parsley
½ teaspoon each dried thyme and basil, crumbled
6 black peppercorns
1 bay leaf

1. In a large heavy saucepan, place all the ingredients and bring to a boil over moderately high heat, whisking constantly—about 6 minutes. Adjust the heat so that the mixture simmers and cook, uncovered, for 30 minutes.
2. Using a large fine sieve lined with a dampened dish towel or double thickness of dampened cheesecloth, strain the consommé into a large heatproof bowl. Skim any fat from the surface and ladle into bowls. Serves 4.

Variations:

Vegetable Consommé Prepare as directed, but transfer the strained consommé into a clean large heavy saucepan and add the following finely chopped, peeled vegetables: 1 small carrot, 1 small celery stalk, 1 small white turnip, and 1 small yellow onion. Simmer, uncovered, over low heat until the vegetables are just tender—about 5 minutes.

Consommé Madrilène Prepare as directed, but use 3 tomatoes instead of 1. Also peel, seed, and chop 2 additional medium-size ripe tomatoes. Ladle the madrilène into soup bowls and top with the chopped tomatoes, dividing the total amount evenly.

Jellied Consommé Prepare as directed, then transfer 1 cup of the broth to a small bowl, and sprinkle 1 envelope unflavored gelatin over it; let soften for 5 minutes. Bring the remaining consommé to a simmer in a clean large heavy saucepan over moderate heat. Stir in the gelatin mixture along with 2 tablespoons dry Madeira or sherry, and cook, stirring, just until the gelatin dissolves—about 2 minutes. Transfer the consommé to a large heatproof bowl, cool to room temperature, cover, and refrigerate for 2 hours or until lightly set. Beat the consommé briskly with a fork and serve in chilled bowls.

One Serving:

Calories	49	Protein	4 g
Total Fat	2 g	Carbohydrates	3 g
Saturated Fat	1 g	Sodium	82 mg
Cholesterol	0	Added Sugar	0
		Fiber	0

Chicken-Escarole Soup

Preparation: **15 min.**
Cooking: **30 min.** (mostly unattended)

FAT SUGAR SODIUM

For an even heartier soup, add a cup of cooked noodles or rice to this main course meal.

2 cups low-sodium chicken broth
2 cups water
1 skinned and boned chicken breast (about ½ pound)
2 medium-size carrots, peeled and chopped
2 medium-size stalks celery, chopped
1 medium-size yellow onion, chopped
¼ cup minced parsley
⅛ teaspoon black pepper
½ pound escarole, spinach, or Swiss chard, trimmed
1 large ripe tomato, peeled, cored, seeded, and chopped

1. In a large heavy saucepan over moderate heat, bring the **chicken broth** and **water** to a simmer. Add the **chicken, carrots, celery, onion, parsley,** and **pepper,** cover, and cook until the chicken is tender—about 20 minutes.
2. Remove the chicken and set aside. Stir the **escarole** and **tomato** into the saucepan and simmer, uncovered, for 5 to 10 minutes or until the escarole is tender.
3. When the chicken is cool enough to handle, cut it into ½-inch cubes, return it to the saucepan, and bring the soup to serving temperature—about 1 minute. Serves 4.

One Serving:

Calories	184	Protein	29 g
Total Fat	2 g	Carbohydrates	10 g
Saturated Fat	1 g	Sodium	148 mg
Cholesterol	66 mg	Added Sugar	0
		Fiber	3 g

Mulligatawny Soup

Mulligatawny is a thick curry-flavored soup of Indian origin. This hearty recipe makes a complete meal.

FAT **SUGAR** **SODIUM**

1 tablespoon unsalted margarine
1 medium-size yellow onion, chopped
1 medium-size carrot, peeled and sliced
1 medium-size tart apple, peeled, cored, and chopped
1 medium-size stalk celery, sliced
1 small sweet green pepper, cored, seeded, and chopped
2 tablespoons flour
1 tablespoon curry powder
4 cups low-sodium chicken broth

1 can (14½ ounces) low-sodium tomatoes, drained and chopped
3 whole cloves
¼ teaspoon each ground mace and nutmeg
⅛ teaspoon black pepper
1 cup cubed cooked light chicken meat
½ cup cooked rice
¼ cup plain low-fat yogurt
4 teaspoons chopped parsley (optional)

Preparation:
20 min.
Cooking:
46 min. (mostly unattended)

One Serving:

Calories	239
Total Fat	7 g
Saturated Fat	2 g
Cholesterol	32 mg
Protein	17 g
Carbohydrates	27 g
Sodium	130 mg
Added Sugar	0
Fiber	3 g

Tip: *If soup sticks to the bottom of the cooking pot, remove it from the heat and let it cool slightly. Carefully dislodge the solids with a wooden spoon.*

1. In a large heavy saucepan, melt the **margarine** over moderate heat. Add the **onion, carrot, apple, celery,** and **green pepper** and cook, uncovered, for 5 minutes or until the onion is soft. Blend in the **flour** and **curry powder** and cook, stirring, 1 minute longer.

2. Add the **chicken broth, tomatoes, cloves, mace, nutmeg,** and **black pepper**. Raise the heat to moderately high, cover, and bring to a boil. Adjust the heat so that the mixture bubbles gently, cover, and simmer for 30 minutes. Remove and discard the cloves; cool the soup for 10 minutes.

3. In an electric blender or food processor, whirl the soup in 3 batches for 20 seconds each. Return to the saucepan, add the **chicken** and **rice,** and cook, stirring, over moderate heat for 3 to 5 minutes or until the soup is heated through. Ladle into bowls, top each with 1 tablespoon of the **yogurt,** and sprinkle, if you like, with 1 teaspoon of the **parsley.** Serves 4.

Minted Chicken Soup

Preparation: **10 min.** Cooking: **16 min.** `FAT` `SUGAR` `SODIUM`

With a mixed salad and a slice of crusty bread, this soup is a complete meal.

1 **tablespoon unsalted margarine**
2 **tablespoons flour**
5 **cups low-sodium chicken broth**
1 **teaspoon grated lemon rind**
2 **tablespoons lemon juice**
1 **cup cubed cooked light chicken meat**
2 **tablespoons minced fresh mint**

1. In a large heavy saucepan, melt the **margarine** over moderate heat; then blend in the **flour** and cook, stirring, for 4 minutes. Slowly whisk in the **chicken broth,** add the **lemon rind** and **lemon juice,** and heat, stirring constantly, just to the boiling point—about 5 minutes.
2. Adjust the heat so that the mixture simmers and cook, stirring occasionally, for 5 minutes. Add the **chicken** and cook 1 minute more over low heat. Stir in the **mint.** Serves 4.

One Serving:

Calories	138	Protein	14 g
Total Fat	6 g	Carbohydrates	5 g
Saturated Fat	1 g	Sodium	95 mg
Cholesterol	30 mg	Added Sugar	0
		Fiber	0

Chicken Gumbo

Preparation: **15 min.** Cooking: **22 min.** `FAT` `SUGAR` `SODIUM`

This chicken gumbo is a meal in itself.

1 **tablespoon unsalted margarine**
1 **large yellow onion, chopped**
1 **clove garlic, minced**
½ **small sweet green pepper, cored, seeded, and chopped**
1 **medium-size stalk celery, chopped**
2 **tablespoons flour**
1 **can (1 pound) low-sodium crushed tomatoes, with their juice**
1 **cup low-sodium chicken broth**
¼ **teaspoon hot red pepper sauce**
2 **cups sliced fresh okra or 1 package (10 ounces) frozen sliced okra**
1½ **cups cubed cooked light chicken or turkey meat**
½ **teaspoon lemon juice**

1. In a large heavy saucepan, melt the **margarine** over moderate heat. Add the **onion, garlic, green pepper,** and **celery,** and cook, uncovered, for 5 minutes or until the vegetables are soft.
2. Blend in the **flour** and cook, stirring, for 3 minutes. Slowly stir in the **tomatoes** and **chicken broth,** then add the **red pepper sauce.** Cook, stirring constantly, until the mixture thickens and comes to a boil—3 to 5 minutes. Add the **okra,** return to a boil, cover, and cook 6 to 8 minutes more. Add the **chicken,** reduce the heat to low, and bring just to serving temperature, stirring occasionally—about 4 minutes. Stir in the **lemon juice.** Serves 4.

One Serving:

Calories	207	Protein	20 g
Total Fat	7 g	Carbohydrates	17 g
Saturated Fat	2 g	Sodium	92 mg
Cholesterol	47 mg	Added Sugar	0
		Fiber	4 g

Spicy Tomato-Fish Chowder

Preparation: **15 min.** Cooking: **19 min.** `FAT` `SUGAR` `SODIUM`

4 **teaspoons olive oil**
2 **cloves garlic, minced**
3 **medium-size ripe tomatoes (about 1 pound), peeled, cored, seeded, and chopped, or 1 can (1 pound) low-sodium tomatoes, chopped, with their juice**
1 **teaspoon dried basil, crumbled**
½ **teaspoon dried oregano, crumbled**
Pinch cayenne pepper
½ **cup dry white wine or chicken broth**
3 **cups water**
½ **pound cod or other white fish fillets, cut into bite-size pieces**
2 **tablespoons minced parsley**

1. In a large heavy saucepan, heat the **olive oil** over moderate heat; add the **garlic, tomatoes, basil, oregano, cayenne pepper,** and **wine,** and cook, uncovered, for 10 minutes.
2. Add the **water,** cover, and bring to a simmer—about 3 minutes. Mix in the **cod** and cook, uncovered, 5 minutes longer. Ladle into bowls and sprinkle with the **parsley.** Serves 4.

One Serving:

Calories	111	Protein	11 g
Total Fat	5 g	Carbohydrates	6 g
Saturated Fat	1 g	Sodium	41 mg
Cholesterol	24 mg	Added Sugar	0
		Fiber	1 g

Minestrone

Preparation: **20 min.**
Cooking: **50 min.** (mostly unattended)

FAT SUGAR SODIUM

This meal-in-one soup makes enough for eight servings, so refrigerate what you don't eat the first time around and serve later in the week.

4 teaspoons olive oil

2 medium-size yellow onions, chopped

4 cloves garlic, minced

2 medium-size carrots, peeled, halved lengthwise, and sliced thin

1 medium-size all-purpose potato, peeled and cut into ½-inch cubes

1 medium-size zucchini (about ½ pound), cut into ½-inch cubes

¼ cup minced fresh basil or 1 tablespoon dried basil, crumbled

1 teaspoon dried oregano, crumbled

2 large bay leaves

4 medium-size ripe tomatoes (about 1½ pounds), peeled, cored, seeded, and chopped, or 1 large can (28 ounces) crushed low-sodium tomatoes, with their juice

5 cups low-sodium chicken broth

¼ pound green beans, trimmed and cut into 1-inch pieces

4 ounces rotelle or tubular pasta

2 cups cooked and drained pinto or white kidney beans

½ cup grated Parmesan cheese

3 tablespoons minced parsley

1. In a large heavy kettle, heat the **olive oil** over low heat for 1 minute; add the **onions** and **garlic** and cook, uncovered, for 5 minutes or until soft. Raise the heat to moderate and add the **carrots, potato, zucchini, basil, oregano,** and **bay leaves.** Cook, uncovered, 5 minutes longer, stirring occasionally.

2. Add the **tomatoes** and **chicken broth,** and bring to a boil; adjust the heat so that the mixture bubbles gently and cook, uncovered, 20 minutes longer. Add the **green beans,** cover, and cook until the beans are tender but still crisp—about 10 minutes. Remove the bay leaves.

3. Meanwhile, cook the **rotelle** according to package directions, omitting the salt. Drain, then add to the soup along with the **pinto beans.** Cook 3 to 5 minutes longer, until heated through. Ladle into soup bowls and sprinkle with the **cheese** and **parsley.** Serves 8.

One Serving:

Calories	239	Protein	12 g
Total Fat	5 g	Carbohydrates	37 g
Saturated Fat	2 g	Sodium	145 mg
Cholesterol	4 mg	Added Sugar	0
		Fiber	5 g

Spicy Tomato-Fish Chowder

Garden-Fresh Vegetable Soup

Garden-Fresh Vegetable Soup

Preparation: **20 min.** Cooking: **30 min.** FAT SUGAR SODIUM

Yogurt gives this colorful soup extra bite.

　1 **tablespoon unsalted margarine**
　4 **small white onions, peeled**
　3 **tablespoons flour**
2½ **cups low-sodium chicken broth**
　1 **medium-size carrot, peeled and sliced diagonally ½ inch thick**
1½ **teaspoons dried tarragon, crumbled**
　1 **teaspoon lemon juice**
　¼ **teaspoon black pepper**
　½ **cup broccoli florets**
　½ **cup quartered small mushrooms**
　1 **small yellow squash (about ¼ pound), sliced ½ inch thick**
　½ **cup plain low-fat yogurt**

1. In a large heavy saucepan, melt the **margarine** over moderate heat. Add the whole **onions** and cook, turning frequently, for 8 to 10 minutes or until browned on all sides; transfer to a plate lined with paper towels and set aside.

2. Blend the **flour** into the saucepan drippings and cook over moderate heat, stirring, for 2 to 3 minutes. Gradually whisk in the **chicken broth** and cook, stirring constantly, until slightly thickened—about 3 minutes.

3. Add the reserved onions and the **carrot, tarragon, lemon juice,** and **pepper.** Bring to a boil, adjust the heat so that the mixture bubbles gently, cover, and cook for 8 to 10 minutes. Add the **broccoli, mushrooms,** and **squash,** cover, and cook about 5 minutes longer or until all the vegetables are tender.

4. Gradually whisk in the **yogurt** and heat for 1 to 2 minutes. Do not boil or the mixture will curdle. Serves 4.

One Serving:			
Calories	110	Protein	5 g
Total Fat	4 g	Carbohydrates	13 g
Saturated Fat	1 g	Sodium	66 mg
Cholesterol	2 mg	Added Sugar	0
		Fiber	1 g

Cream of Vegetable Soup

1 tablespoon unsalted margarine
1 large carrot, peeled and sliced thin
1 medium-size yellow onion, sliced thin
1 large all-purpose potato, peeled and sliced thin
3 cloves garlic, crushed
1 bay leaf
¼ teaspoon dried thyme, crumbled
2½ cups low-sodium chicken broth
2 cups low-fat (2% milk fat) milk
⅛ teaspoon salt
⅛ teaspoon black pepper

Preparation:
10 min.
Cooking:
49 min. (mostly unattended)

One Serving:

Calories	*161*
Total Fat	*6 g*
Saturated Fat	*2 g*
Cholesterol	*10 mg*
Protein	*7 g*
Carbohydrates	*19 g*
Sodium	*176 mg*
Added Sugar	*0*
Fiber	*1 g*

1. In a medium-size heavy saucepan over low heat, melt the **margarine.** Add the **carrot, onion, potato, garlic, bay leaf,** and **thyme,** tossing to coat the vegetables with the margarine. Stir in ½ cup of the **chicken broth,** cover, and cook for 15 minutes or until almost all the liquid has evaporated.

2. Raise the heat to moderate, stir in the remaining 2 cups chicken broth and the **milk,** and cook, uncovered, stirring occasionally, until the vegetables are very tender and the flavors well blended—about 30 minutes.

3. Cool the mixture slightly and strain it, reserving both the vegetables and the liquid. Discard the bay leaf. Place the strained vegetables and 1 cup of the broth in a food processor or electric blender and purée by whirling for 1 minute. Return the purée and reserved liquid to the saucepan. Add the **salt** and **pepper** and bring to serving temperature over moderate heat— about 3 minutes. Serves 4.

Variations:

Cream of Spinach Soup Prepare the soup as directed, but add 4 cups coarsely chopped fresh spinach or 1 package (10 ounces) thawed frozen chopped spinach to the soup about 5 minutes before you remove it from the heat to purée. When you bring the soup to serving temperature, add ⅛ teaspoon each ground nutmeg and ginger along with the salt and pepper.

Cream of Mushroom Soup Prepare the soup as directed, adding 1 cup coarsely chopped mushrooms to the melted margarine along with the other vegetables in Step 1. Before returning the puréed vegetables to the saucepan in Step 3, pour ½ cup of the reserved broth into the saucepan, add 1 cup thinly sliced mushrooms, cover, and cook over low heat just until the mushrooms are wilted—about 5 minutes. Add the puréed vegetables and remaining broth and proceed as directed.

Cream of Asparagus Soup Peel 1 pound asparagus, cutting off and reserving the tips. Cut the stems into thirds and add to the melted margarine along with the other vegetables in Step 1. Before returning the puréed vegetables to the saucepan in Step 3, pour ½ cup of the reserved broth into the saucepan, add the reserved asparagus tips, cover, and cook over low heat until they are just tender—about 5 minutes. Add the puréed vegetables and remaining broth and proceed as directed.

Cream of Watercress Soup Trim the stems from 1 medium-size bunch watercress. Prepare the soup as directed. When you bring the soup to serving temperature in Step 3, add the watercress, and heat, uncovered, over low heat, stirring occasionally, just until the watercress wilts—about 4 minutes.

Cheese Soup Omit the margarine and cook the vegetables in ½ cup of the chicken broth instead. When you bring the soup to serving temperature in Step 3, add ¼ cup shredded sharp Cheddar cheese and 1 tablespoon grated Parmesan cheese. Omit the salt and pepper, but add ⅛ teaspoon each cayenne pepper and paprika.

***Tip:** When cooking soup in an uncovered pot, remember that the wider the pot, the more quickly the soup will evaporate. If the liquid seems to be getting low, top it up occasionally.*

Hearty Black Bean Soup

Preparation: **15 min.**
Cooking: **23 min.** (mostly unattended)

[FAT] [SUGAR] [SODIUM]

- **2 teaspoons olive oil**
- **1 large yellow onion, chopped**
- **2 cloves garlic, minced**
- **½ teaspoon dried oregano, crumbled**
- **¼ teaspoon dried thyme, crumbled**
- **¼ teaspoon ground cumin**
- **⅛ teaspoon cayenne pepper**
- **1½ cups cooked and drained black beans**
- **1½ cups low-sodium chicken broth**
- **4 teaspoons chopped fresh coriander or parsley (optional)**

1. In a large heavy saucepan, heat the **olive oil** over moderate heat for 1 minute; add the **onion** and **garlic** and cook, uncovered, for 5 minutes or until the onion is soft. Stir in the **oregano, thyme, cumin,** and **cayenne pepper,** and cook, stirring, 1 minute longer.

2. Meanwhile, place half of the **black beans** in an electric blender or food processor and purée by whirling for 30 seconds. Add the bean purée, the remaining beans, and the **chicken broth** to the saucepan, reduce the heat to low, and cook, uncovered, for 15 minutes. Ladle the soup into bowls and garnish, if you like, with the **coriander.** Serves 4.

One Serving:

Calories	154	Protein	8 g
Total Fat	3 g	Carbohydrates	23 g
Saturated Fat	0	Sodium	29 mg
Cholesterol	0	Added Sugar	0
		Fiber	5 g

Carrot-Apple Soup

Preparation: **20 min.**
Cooking: **33 min.** (mostly unattended)

[FAT] [SUGAR] [SODIUM]

- **1 tablespoon unsalted margarine**
- **1 medium-size yellow onion, chopped**
- **1 medium-size stalk celery, sliced**
- **8 medium-size carrots (about 1 pound), peeled and sliced**
- **2 medium-size sweet apples, peeled, cored, and chopped**
- **5 cups low-sodium chicken broth**
- **½ teaspoon dried sage, crumbled**
- **¼ teaspoon black pepper**
- **1 bay leaf**
- **8 thin unpeeled sweet apple slices, dipped in lemon juice (optional)**

Hearty Black Bean Soup

1. In a large heavy saucepan, melt the **margarine** over moderate heat; add the **onion, celery, carrots,** and **chopped apples,** and cook, uncovered, until the onion is soft—about 5 minutes.

2. Stir in the **chicken broth, sage, pepper,** and **bay leaf,** raise the heat to moderately high, and bring to a boil—about 5 minutes. Adjust the heat so that the mixture bubbles gently, cover, and simmer for 20 minutes or until the carrots are tender. Remove and discard the bay leaf and cool the soup for 5 minutes.

3. In an electric blender or food processor, whirl the soup in 3 batches, each for 30 seconds. Return to the saucepan, cover, set over moderate heat, and bring just to serving temperature—about 2 minutes. Ladle into bowls and, if you like, float 2 **apple slices** on top of each portion. Serves 6.

One Serving:

Calories	102	Protein	3 g
Total Fat	3 g	Carbohydrates	16 g
Saturated Fat	1 g	Sodium	74 mg
Cholesterol	0	Added Sugar	0
		Fiber	3 g

Corn Chowder

Preparation: **15 min.** Cooking: **19 min.** FAT SUGAR SODIUM

1 tablespoon unsalted margarine
1 medium-size yellow onion, chopped
1 small stalk celery, chopped
¼ small sweet green pepper, cored, seeded, and chopped
1 tablespoon flour
½ teaspoon paprika
1 cup low-sodium chicken broth
2 cups fresh or frozen whole-kernel corn
1 cup skim milk
1½ teaspoons lemon juice
⅛ teaspoon black pepper

1. In a large heavy saucepan, melt the **margarine** over moderate heat. Add the **onion, celery,** and **green pepper,** and cook, uncovered, for 5 minutes or until the vegetables are soft.

2. Blend in the **flour** and **paprika,** and cook, stirring, for 3 minutes. Gradually stir in the **chicken broth** and cook, stirring constantly, until the mixture thickens and comes to a boil—3 to 5 minutes.

3. Add the **corn,** cover, and cook for 5 minutes. Stir in the **milk, lemon juice,** and **black pepper;** reduce the heat to low and heat the soup just to serving temperature—2 to 3 minutes. Do not boil or the mixture will curdle. Serves 4.

One Serving:

Calories	134	Protein	5 g
Total Fat	4 g	Carbohydrates	22 g
Saturated Fat	1 g	Sodium	55 mg
Cholesterol	1 mg	Added Sugar	0
		Fiber	2 g

Cold Cucumber Soup

Preparation: **10 min.,** FAT SUGAR SODIUM
plus 5 hr. refrigeration

Nothing is more cooling on a sultry summer day than refreshing cucumber soup.

2 medium-size cucumbers, peeled, seeded, and chopped
1 medium-size red onion, sliced thin
⅓ cup snipped fresh dill or 1½ teaspoons dill weed
2 tablespoons minced fresh mint or 2 teaspoons mint flakes
2 cups buttermilk
½ cup plain low-fat yogurt
½ cup low-sodium chicken broth
1½ tablespoons chopped walnuts
3 tablespoons red wine vinegar
¼ teaspoon salt
¼ teaspoon black pepper
⅛ teaspoon cayenne pepper

1. Place the **cucumbers, onion, dill,** and **mint** in a food processor, and whirl for 30 seconds. Add the **buttermilk, yogurt, chicken broth,** and **walnuts,** and whirl 20 seconds longer or until well blended.

2. Transfer to a medium-size bowl, stir in the **vinegar, salt, black pepper,** and **cayenne pepper,** cover, and chill in the refrigerator at least 5 hours. Serves 4.

One Serving:

Calories	114	Protein	7 g
Total Fat	4 g	Carbohydrates	14 g
Saturated Fat	1 g	Sodium	298 mg
Cholesterol	7 mg	Added Sugar	0
		Fiber	1 g

Roasted Eggplant Soup

Preparation: **10 min.**
Cooking: **46 min.** (mostly unattended)

Roasting the eggplants gives this soup a deep smoky flavor and removes any bitterness that the eggplant might have.

- 3 **small unpeeled eggplants (about 1½ pounds)**
- 1 **tablespoon olive oil**
- 1 **large yellow onion, sliced thin**
- 2 **cloves garlic, crushed**
- 1 **tablespoon minced fresh ginger or ½ teaspoon ground ginger**
- ¼ **teaspoon red pepper flakes**
- 2 **medium-size sweet red peppers, cored, seeded, and sliced thin**
- ¼ **teaspoon salt**
- 3 **cups low-sodium chicken broth**
- 4 **teaspoons red wine vinegar**
- ¼ **cup plain low-fat yogurt**

1. Preheat the oven to 375°F. With a fork, pierce the **eggplants** in several different places, then lay them on an ungreased baking sheet. Bake, uncovered, until very soft when pierced with a fork—about 40 minutes.
2. Meanwhile, in a medium-size heavy saucepan, heat the **olive oil** over low heat for 1 minute. Add the **onion, garlic, ginger,** and **red pepper flakes,** and cook, uncovered, until the onion is soft—about 10 minutes.
3. Stir in the **red peppers** and **salt,** cover, and cook for 10 minutes or until the peppers are somewhat soft. Add the **chicken broth,** raise the heat to moderate, and cook, uncovered, 20 minutes longer or until the peppers are very soft. Remove from the heat and strain, placing the liquid and solids in separate bowls.
4. When the eggplants are done and cool enough to handle, peel off and discard the skins. Halve the eggplants lengthwise; then, with a small spoon, remove and discard most of the seeds. Cut into 1-inch cubes.
5. In a food processor or electric blender, whirl the eggplant and strained solids with 1 cup of the reserved liquid for 1 minute or until the mixture is smooth. Return to the saucepan and add the remaining liquid and the **vinegar.** Cook, uncovered, over moderate heat until heated

through—about 5 minutes. Ladle into soup bowls and top each portion with a tablespoon of the **yogurt.** Serves 4.

One Serving:			
Calories	125	Protein	5 g
Total Fat	5 g	Carbohydrates	17 g
Saturated Fat	1 g	Sodium	193 mg
Cholesterol	1 mg	Added Sugar	0
		Fiber	3 g

Mushroom-Barley Soup

Preparation: **20 min.**
Cooking: **44 min.** (mostly unattended)

This nutritious soup is even more flavorful if made ahead of time and reheated just before serving.

- 2 **large yellow onions, chopped**
- 3 **medium-size carrots, peeled and sliced**
- ½ **pound mushrooms, sliced thin**
- 4 **cups low-sodium beef broth**
- ¼ **cup chopped parsley**
- ½ **cup medium-size barley**
- ¼ **teaspoon black pepper**

Place all the ingredients in a large heavy saucepan and bring to a boil over moderately high heat—about 4 minutes. Adjust the heat so that the mixture bubbles gently, and simmer, partly covered, for 40 minutes or until the barley is tender. Serves 4.

Variation:

Mushroom-Barley Soup with Sweet Red Pepper Substitute 2 medium-size stalks celery, sliced, for the carrots. Add ½ medium-size sweet red pepper, chopped, and proceed as directed.

One Serving:			
Calories	172	Protein	5 g
Total Fat	1 g	Carbohydrates	37 g
Saturated Fat	0	Sodium	30 mg
Cholesterol	0	Added Sugar	0
		Fiber	3 g

Tip: *If you make homemade beef broth to use in soups, be sure to crack the soup bones first (or have the butcher crack them for you). The broth will be thicker and more flavorful.*

Hearty French Onion Soup

½ tablespoon unsalted margarine
4 medium-size yellow onions, sliced
⅛ teaspoon sugar
2 tablespoons flour
5 cups low-sodium beef broth
½ cup dry white wine
½ teaspoon dried thyme, crumbled

1 bay leaf
¼ teaspoon black pepper
1 tablespoon brandy (optional)
4 slices toasted French bread, each about ¼ inch thick
1 clove garlic, split lengthwise
2 tablespoons grated Parmesan cheese

FAT SUGAR **SODIUM**

Preparation:
10 min.
Cooking:
50 min. (mostly unattended)

One Serving:

Calories	*129*
Total Fat	*3 g*
Saturated Fat	*1 g*
Cholesterol	*2 mg*
Protein	*4 g*
Carbohydrates	*28 g*
Sodium	*128 mg*
Added Sugar	*8 Cal*
Fiber	*1 g*

1. In a large heavy saucepan, melt the **margarine** over moderate heat; add the **onions** and cook, uncovered, until golden—8 to 10 minutes. Blend in the **sugar** and **flour** and cook, stirring, 3 minutes longer.

2. Add the **beef broth, wine, thyme, bay leaf,** and **pepper;** raise the heat to moderately high and bring to a boil, stirring constantly—about 6 minutes. Adjust the heat so that the mixture bubbles gently, and simmer, partly covered, for 30 minutes. Remove and discard the bay leaf, then stir in the **brandy,** if desired.

3. Preheat the broiler. Rub each piece of **bread** with the **garlic** and sprinkle with the **cheese.** Ladle the soup into 4 flameproof bowls and float a piece of bread, cheese side up, in each one. Place the bowls in the broiler, 4 to 6 inches from the heat, and broil until the cheese is golden brown—about 2 minutes. Serves 4.

Chive Vichyssoise

Here's a low-calorie version of the classic chilled potato soup.

1 tablespoon unsalted margarine
1 medium-size yellow onion, chopped
1 medium-size leek, chopped
1 medium-size stalk celery, chopped
2 medium-size all-purpose potatoes (about ½ pound), peeled and diced

1¾ cups low-sodium chicken broth
1 cup buttermilk
1 tablespoon minced fresh or freeze-dried chives
2 teaspoons lemon juice
¼ teaspoon hot red pepper sauce

FAT SUGAR **SODIUM**

Preparation:
15 min., plus 2 hr. refrigeration
Cooking:
32 min. (mostly unattended)

One Serving:

Calories	*124*
Total Fat	*4 g*
Saturated Fat	*1 g*
Cholesterol	*2 mg*
Protein	*5 g*
Carbohydrates	*17 g*
Sodium	*78 mg*
Added Sugar	*0*
Fiber	*1 g*

1. In a large heavy saucepan, melt the **margarine** over moderate heat. Add the **onion, leek,** and **celery,** and cook, uncovered, until the vegetables are tender—6 to 8 minutes. Add the **potatoes** and cook, stirring occasionally, 3 minutes more.

2. Stir in the **chicken broth** and bring to a boil. Adjust the heat so that the broth bubbles gently, cover, and simmer until the potatoes are tender— about 20 minutes.

3. In an electric blender or food processor, purée the soup in 2 or 3 batches, whirling each batch about 30 seconds. Stir in the **buttermilk, chives, lemon juice,** and **red pepper sauce.**

4. Cover the soup and refrigerate at least 2 hours before serving. Serves 4.

Variation:

Curried Vichyssoise   Prepare as directed, blending 2¼ teaspoons curry powder into the melted margarine. Garnish with coarsely chopped apple.

Split Pea and Potato Soup

Split Pea and Potato Soup

Preparation: **20 min.** FAT SUGAR SODIUM
Cooking: **43 min.** (mostly unattended)

For a lunch or supper that's a real treat, serve this soup with Waldorf Salad, page 221.

1 **tablespoon unsalted margarine**
1 **medium-size yellow onion, chopped**
2 **cups low-sodium beef broth**
2 **cups water**
½ **cup dried split green peas, rinsed and sorted**
2 **medium-size potatoes, peeled and quartered**
¼ **teaspoon black pepper**

1. In a large heavy saucepan, melt the **margarine** over moderate heat. Add the **onion** and cook, uncovered, until soft—about 5 minutes. Stir in the **beef broth** and **water** and bring to a boil— about 4 minutes. Add the **peas** and **potatoes;** adjust the heat so that the mixture bubbles gently, cover, and cook for 30 minutes or until the peas and potatoes are tender. Remove from the heat and cool for 10 minutes.

2. In an electric blender or food processor, purée the soup in 5 batches, whirling each batch about 15 seconds. Return to the pan, set over low heat, and bring to serving temperature, stirring often. Add the **pepper.** Serves 4.

One Serving:			
Calories	173	Protein	8 g
Total Fat	4 g	Carbohydrates	29 g
Saturated Fat	1 g	Sodium	16 mg
Cholesterol	0	Added Sugar	0
		Fiber	1 g

Potato and Kale Soup

Preparation: **20 min.** FAT SUGAR SODIUM
Cooking: **45 min.** (mostly unattended)

For a complete meal, serve this cold-weather soup with a white-meat turkey sandwich.

4 **teaspoons olive oil**
1 **medium-size yellow onion, chopped**
3 **cloves garlic, minced**
3 **medium-size all-purpose potatoes (about ¾ pound), peeled and sliced**
4 **cups water**
½ **pound kale, trimmed and shredded**
¼ **teaspoon black pepper**

1. In a large heavy saucepan, heat the **olive oil** over moderate heat for 1 minute; add the **onion** and cook, uncovered, until soft—about 5 minutes.

2. Mix in the **garlic, potatoes,** and **water;** cover, raise the heat to moderately high, and bring to a boil—about 4 minutes. Adjust the heat so that the mixture bubbles gently and cook,

uncovered, for 20 minutes or until tender.

3. Using a potato masher, carefully mash the potatoes right in the saucepan. Mix in the **kale** and **pepper,** cover, and simmer for 15 minutes or until the kale is just tender. Ladle into soup bowls. Serves 4.

One Serving:

Calories	134	Protein	3 g
Total Fat	5 g	Carbohydrates	21 g
Saturated Fat	1 g	Sodium	21 mg
Cholesterol	0	Added Sugar	0
		Fiber	4 g

Golden Butternut Squash Soup

Preparation: **15 min.**
Cooking: **36 min.** (mostly unattended)

FAT SUGAR SODIUM

1 tablespoon unsalted margarine
1 medium-size yellow onion, chopped
1 clove garlic, minced
1 small stalk celery, chopped
1 medium-size butternut squash (about 1½ pounds), peeled, seeded, and cubed
4 cups low-sodium chicken broth
½ teaspoon dried marjoram, crumbled
1 bay leaf
¼ teaspoon black pepper
1 cup buttermilk
Parsley sprigs (optional)

1. In a large heavy saucepan, melt the **margarine** over moderate heat; add the **onion, garlic,** and **celery,** and cook, uncovered, until the onion is soft—about 5 minutes.

2. Add the **squash, chicken broth, marjoram, bay leaf,** and **pepper,** raise the heat to moderately high, and bring to a boil—about 4 minutes. Adjust the heat so that the mixture bubbles gently, cover, and simmer for 20 minutes or until the squash is tender when pierced with a fork. Remove and discard the bay leaf and cool the soup for 5 minutes.

3. In an electric blender or food processor, whirl the soup in 4 batches, each for 30 seconds. Return the soup to the saucepan, stir in the **buttermilk,** set over moderate heat, and bring just to serving temperature—about 5 minutes. Do not boil or the soup will curdle. Ladle into cups and garnish each portion, if you like, with a **parsley sprig.** Serves 6.

One Serving:

Calories	103	Protein	4 g
Total Fat	3 g	Carbohydrates	16 g
Saturated Fat	1 g	Sodium	87 mg
Cholesterol	2 mg	Added Sugar	0
		Fiber	0

Yellow Squash Soup

Preparation: **10 min.**
Cooking: **39 min.** (mostly unattended)

FAT SUGAR SODIUM

The lemon and orange peels and dash of lemon juice give this soup its delightful fresh flavor.

1 tablespoon unsalted margarine
2 medium-size yellow onions, cut into ½-inch cubes
3 cloves garlic, minced
3 strips lemon peel, each about 2 inches long and ½ inch wide
3 strips orange peel, each about 2 inches long and ½ inch wide
1 bay leaf
½ teaspoon dried marjoram, crumbled
2 medium-size yellow squash (about 1 pound), cut into ½-inch cubes
3 cups low-sodium chicken broth
¼ teaspoon salt
5 teaspoons lemon juice

1. In a medium-size heavy saucepan, melt the **margarine** over low heat. Add the **onions, garlic, lemon peel, orange peel, bay leaf,** and **marjoram,** and cook, covered, until the onion is soft—about 10 minutes.

2. Mix in the **squash,** stirring to coat; add the **chicken broth** and **salt.** Raise the heat to moderately high, cover, and bring to a boil. Adjust the heat so that the mixture bubbles gently, cover, and simmer until the squash is soft when pierced with a fork—about 25 minutes.

3. Remove the soup from the heat; remove and discard the lemon and orange peels and the bay leaf. Stir in the **lemon juice** and ladle into soup bowls. Serves 4.

One Serving:

Calories	90	Protein	3 g
Total Fat	4 g	Carbohydrates	10 g
Saturated Fat	1 g	Sodium	180 mg
Cholesterol	0	Added Sugar	0
		Fiber	2 g

Refreshing Red Gazpacho

Preparation: **30 min.,**
plus 1 hr. refrigeration

FAT SUGAR SODIUM

1 small yellow onion, quartered
1 clove garlic, chopped
1 small sweet red or green pepper, cored, seeded, and chopped
½ medium-size cucumber, peeled, halved, seeded, and sliced thin
2 medium-size ripe tomatoes, peeled, cored, seeded, and chopped
1½ cups low-sodium chicken broth
2 tablespoons lemon juice
1 tablespoon olive oil
⅛ teaspoon cayenne pepper
⅛ teaspoon hot red pepper sauce
Vegetable Garnishes:
1 small sweet red or green pepper, cored, seeded, and chopped
2 green onions, including tops, sliced thin
1 medium-size ripe tomato, cored, seeded, and chopped
½ medium-size cucumber, peeled, halved, seeded, and chopped
¼ cup minced parsley or fresh basil

1. Place all the soup ingredients in an electric blender or food processor and whirl for 30 seconds or until smooth. Pour into a large bowl, cover loosely, and chill in the refrigerator at least 1 hour.

2. Before serving, add all the vegetable garnishes to the gazpacho, then ladle into 4 chilled bowls. Serves 4.

Variation:

Green Gazpacho Prepare as directed, but use the following ingredients instead of those listed in the master recipe: 1 halved garlic clove, 1 large peeled, seeded, and chopped cucumber, 2 sliced green onions, 2 tablespoons chopped parsley, ¼ teaspoon white or black pepper, 2 cups low-sodium chicken broth, 1 cup plain low-fat yogurt or 1 cup buttermilk, and 1 tablespoon white vinegar. Garnish only with 1 small cored, seeded, and chopped tomato.

One Serving:

Calories	83	Protein	3 g
Total Fat	4 g	Carbohydrates	10 g
Saturated Fat	1 g	Sodium	39 mg
Cholesterol	0	Added Sugar	0
		Fiber	2 g

Creamy Chilled Tomato Soup

Preparation: **15 min.,**
plus 2 hr. refrigeration
Cooking: **20 min.** (mostly unattended)

FAT SUGAR SODIUM

This is the ideal soup for a hot summer day—and a perfect way to enjoy your home-grown tomatoes.

1½ tablespoons unsalted margarine
1 medium-size yellow onion, chopped
1 medium-size carrot, peeled and grated
3 large ripe tomatoes (about 1½ pounds), peeled, cored, seeded, and chopped, or 2 cans (1 pound each) low-sodium crushed tomatoes, with their juice
1 cup low-sodium chicken broth
2 tablespoons minced fresh basil or ¼ teaspoon dried basil, crumbled
1 cup plain low-fat yogurt
1 teaspoon lemon juice
¼ teaspoon black pepper

1. In a large heavy saucepan, melt the **margarine** over low heat. Add the **onion** and **carrot,** and cook, uncovered, until the vegetables are soft— 5 to 8 minutes.

2. Add the **tomatoes, chicken broth,** and **basil,** and bring to a boil over moderate heat. Adjust the heat so that the mixture bubbles gently, and cook, uncovered, stirring occasionally, for 10 minutes.

3. In an electric blender or food processor, purée the soup in 3 batches, whirling each batch about 30 seconds. Stir in the **yogurt, lemon juice,** and **pepper.**

4. Cover the soup and refrigerate at least 2 hours before serving. Serves 4.

One Serving:

Calories	83	Protein	2 g
Total Fat	5 g	Carbohydrates	9 g
Saturated Fat	1 g	Sodium	35 mg
Cholesterol	0	Added Sugar	0
		Fiber	1 g

Tip: *When serving cold soups, especially jellied ones, chill the soup bowls first by placing them in the freezer for a few minutes.*

Meats

You can still sit down to steak for dinner and eat a healthy meal. Meat today is "slimmer" than it was only a few years ago. Fat and cholesterol have been reduced by selective animal breeding and processing, while the nutritional advantages of beef, pork, lamb, and veal—complete protein and a good range of minerals— remain unchanged. With the proper cuts and the right recipes, meat can be part of your everyday diet.

Easy Red and Green Pepper Steak

Yankee Pot Roast

Pot roast is better and easier to slice if prepared a day ahead. At serving time, place the sliced meat and sauce in a baking dish, cover with aluminum foil, and heat for 15 to 20 minutes in a 350°F oven.

1½ **pounds boneless bottom round roast**
¼ **teaspoon black pepper**
2 **medium-size yellow onions, sliced thin**
2 **cloves garlic, minced**
1½ **cups low-sodium beef broth**
1 **cup water**

2 **tablespoons low-sodium tomato paste**
½ **teaspoon each dried thyme, marjoram, and basil, crumbled Nonstick cooking spray**
¼ **pound mushrooms, sliced thin**
1 **tablespoon minced parsley**

1. Preheat the broiler. Season the **roast** with the **pepper.** Place the meat on the broiler pan rack and broil about 4 inches from the heat, turning until brown on all sides—about 10 minutes. Reduce the oven temperature to 325°F.

2. In a heavy 4-quart Dutch oven, combine the **onions, garlic, beef broth, water, tomato paste, thyme, marjoram,** and **basil.** Add the beef and bring to a simmer over moderate heat. Cover tightly, transfer to the oven, and cook for 2 to 2½ hours or until tender.

3. Slice the meat ¼ inch thick and arrange the slices, slightly overlapping, on a heated platter; keep warm.

4. Purée the vegetable mixture in an electric blender or food processor.

5. Lightly coat a heavy 10-inch skillet with the **cooking spray** and set over moderate heat for 30 seconds. Add the **mushrooms** and cook, stirring, for 5 minutes or until lightly browned. Stir in the puréed vegetables. Spoon the sauce over the beef and sprinkle with the **parsley.** Serve with Braised Red Cabbage with Cranberries, page 180. Serves 4.

FAT SUGAR SODIUM

Preparation:
20 min.
Cooking:
2 hr. 15 min. (mostly unattended)

One Serving:

Calories	*295*
Total Fat	*11 g*
Saturated Fat	*4 g*
Cholesterol	*100 mg*
Protein	*39 g*
Carbohydrates	*8 g*
Sodium	*110 mg*
Added Sugar	*0*
Fiber	*1 g*

Tip: Refrigerated leftover pot roast, as tasty as it is, should not be kept for more than four days.

Roast Sirloin with Black Peppercorn Crust

2 **tablespoons black peppercorns**
1 **pound boneless lean sirloin steak, 1½ inches thick, trimmed of fat**

1 **tablespoon olive or vegetable oil**
3 **green onions, chopped fine**
2 **tablespoons dry white wine**
1 **cup low-sodium beef broth**

1. Preheat the oven to 550°F. Place the **peppercorns** in the bottom of a 7-inch skillet and crush them with a small heavy saucepan. Coat both sides of the **steak** with the crushed peppercorns.

2. Set a heavy 10-inch skillet with an ovenproof handle over moderately high heat for 1 minute. Add the **olive oil** and heat until almost smoking—about 1 minute more. Add the steak, cook for 30 seconds on one side, then turn.

3. Transfer the skillet to the upper third of the oven and roast, uncovered, about 4 to 5 minutes for rare, 6 to 7 minutes for medium rare, 7 to 8 minutes for medium. Transfer the steak to a heated platter and slice thin.

4. Add the **green onions** to the skillet and cook, stirring, over moderate heat for 30 seconds. Add the **white wine** and cook, uncovered, for 1 minute. Add the **beef broth** and simmer for 2 to 3 minutes, scraping up any browned bits, until ½ cup of liquid remains. Serve the steak with the sauce and, if you like, Twice-Baked Potatoes, page 196, carrots, or lima beans. Serves 4.

FAT SUGAR SODIUM

Preparation:
10 min.
Cooking:
9 min.

One Serving:

Calories	*222*
Total Fat	*13 g*
Saturated Fat	*4 g*
Cholesterol	*68 mg*
Protein	*23 g*
Carbohydrates	*2 g*
Sodium	*65 mg*
Added Sugar	*0*
Fiber	*0*

Old German Sauerbraten

The secret of this intensely flavored pot roast is the long marination; the actual preparation time is only 15 minutes.

FAT SUGAR SODIUM

1 **large yellow onion, sliced**
²/₃ **cup white vinegar**
1¹/₃ **cups water**
½ **cup dry white wine**
1 **small carrot, peeled and sliced thin**
2 **tablespoons mixed pickling spice, tied in cheesecloth**
1 **teaspoon grated lemon rind**
¼ **teaspoon salt**
1½ **pounds boneless bottom round roast**
3 **tablespoons crumbled gingersnaps**

1. In a 4-quart flameproof enameled or glass casserole, bring the **onion, vinegar, water, wine, carrot, pickling spice, lemon rind,** and **salt** to a boil. Adjust the heat so that the mixture bubbles gently and cook, uncovered, for 5 minutes; cool to room temperature. Add the **roast,** turning to moisten evenly; cover and refrigerate for 3 days, turning the beef once or twice.

2. Preheat the broiler. Remove the beef from the marinade, pat it dry, and place in an ungreased shallow baking pan. Broil about 4 inches from the heat, turning occasionally, until brown on all sides—about 10 minutes. Reduce the oven temperature to 350°F.

3. Bring the marinade in the casserole to a simmer over moderate heat and add the beef. Cover, transfer to the oven, and cook for 2 to 2½ hours or until the beef is tender. Slice the beef ¼ inch thick and arrange the slices, slightly overlapping, on a heated platter and keep warm.

4. Remove the bay leaf, then purée the cooking liquid and the **gingersnaps** in an electric blender or food processor. Pour the sauce over the meat and serve, if you like, with Grated Zucchini Pancake, page 203. Serves 4.

Preparation:
15 min., plus 3 days' marination
Cooking:
2 hr. 15 min. (mostly unattended)

One Serving:

Calories	305
Total Fat	11 g
Saturated Fat	4 g
Cholesterol	102 mg
Protein	38 g
Carbohydrates	11 g
Sodium	270 mg
Added Sugar	11 Cal
Fiber	1 g

Tip: *Braising meats a day ahead has two advantages: Fat is easier to skim after refrigeration, and flavor improves when the meat is reheated.*

Roast Sirloin with Black Peppercorn Crust

Beef Roll with Chili Sauce

Beef Roll with Chili Sauce

FAT SUGAR SODIUM

1 **pound flank steak, about 1 inch thick, trimmed of fat**
1 **cup frozen mixed vegetables**
2 **medium-size yellow onions, chopped fine**
2 **large sweet green peppers, cored, seeded, and chopped fine**
½ **cup finely chopped celery**
1 **tablespoon dry bread crumbs**
3 **cloves garlic, minced**

¼ **teaspoon red pepper flakes**
1 **teaspoon grated lemon rind**
¼ **teaspoon black pepper**
1½ **cups low-sodium beef broth**
1 **can (8 ounces) low-sodium tomato sauce**
1½ **teaspoons chili powder**
½ **teaspoon dried oregano, crumbled**
1 **tablespoon flour**

Preparation:
15 min.
Cooking:
47 min. (mostly unattended)

One Serving:

Calories	299
Total Fat	13 g
Saturated Fat	5 g
Cholesterol	55 mg
Protein	24 g
Carbohydrates	22 g
Sodium	138 mg
Added Sugar	0
Fiber	1 g

1. Preheat the oven to 400°F. Holding a sharp knife parallel to the countertop, slice the **steak** open horizontally, to within ½ inch of the opposite side.

2. In a large heavy saucepan, cook the **mixed vegetables** and half of the **onions, green peppers,** and **celery** in a cup of boiling water for 1 minute; drain well and transfer to a bowl. Stir in the **bread crumbs,** half of the **garlic,** and all of the **red pepper flakes, lemon rind,** and **black pepper.**

3. Open the steak and flatten it out; spread the vegetable mixture over the entire surface, leaving a 1-inch border all around. Roll up the steak, beginning at a narrow end, and fasten with toothpicks at 1-inch intervals. Place the roll in an ungreased 8"x 8"x 2" baking pan and roast, uncovered, turning 2 or 3 times, for 45 minutes.

4. Meanwhile, to prepare the chili sauce, combine the remaining onions, peppers, celery, and garlic in a large saucepan. Stir in the **beef broth, tomato sauce, chili powder, oregano,** and **flour.** Place over low heat, cover, and simmer for 30 minutes. Keep the sauce warm.

5. As soon as the roll is done, transfer it to a plate and let cool for 15 minutes. Remove the toothpicks and slice the meat ½ inch thick. Serve with the chili sauce and Creamy Yogurt Coleslaw, page 210. Serves 4.

Minute Steaks with Pimientos and Mushrooms

Preparation: **25 min.**, including soaking of mushrooms   Cooking: **24 min.**   FAT SUGAR SODIUM

Minute steaks, also known as sandwich steaks, are thin, lean, and fast-cooking. If you can't find them under either name, buy a ¼-inch-thick round steak, trim it, and cut it into four pieces.

- 1 **package (1 ounce) dried shiitake mushrooms or ¼ pound fresh mushrooms, sliced thin**
- 1½ **tablespoons unsalted margarine**
- 8 **small white onions, peeled**
- 1⅓ **cups low-sodium beef broth**
- ¼ **teaspoon dried thyme, crumbled**
- 4 **minute steaks (about 4 ounces each)**
- 2 **cloves garlic, halved**
- ¼ **teaspoon black pepper**
  Nonstick cooking spray
- ⅓ **cup dry white wine**
- 1 **jar (4 ounces) sliced pimientos, drained**
- 2 **teaspoons cornstarch blended with 1 tablespoon cold water**
- 1 **teaspoon Dijon or spicy brown mustard**

1. Soften the **shiitake mushrooms** in a cup of boiling water for 15 to 20 minutes. Drain, cut off and discard the stems, then slice the caps ¼ inch thick; set aside. If you are using sliced fresh mushrooms, simply add in Step 4.

2. Meanwhile, melt ½ tablespoon of the **margarine** in a small saucepan over moderate heat; add the **onions** and cook, uncovered, for 3 minutes, stirring occasionally. Add the **beef broth** and **thyme;** cover and simmer over low heat until the onions are tender—about 10 minutes. Remove from the heat.

3. Rub the **steaks** with the **garlic** and sprinkle with the **pepper.** Coat a heavy 10-inch skillet with the **cooking spray,** add ½ tablespoon of the margarine, and melt over moderately high heat. Add 2 of the steaks and cook for 1 minute on each side; transfer to a warm

serving platter. Cook the last 2 steaks in the remaining margarine and transfer to the platter.

4. Pour any fat from the skillet, add the **wine,** and boil, uncovered, for 1 minute. Add the broth, onions, mushrooms, and **pimientos;** simmer, uncovered, for 5 minutes.

5. Blend in the **cornstarch** mixture and cook, stirring constantly, until slightly thickened—1 to 2 minutes; stir in the **mustard.** Spoon the sauce and vegetables over the steaks. Serves 4.

One Serving:

Calories	248	*Protein*	27 g
Total Fat	10 g	*Carbohydrates*	12 g
Saturated Fat	3 g	*Sodium*	108 mg
Cholesterol	65 mg	*Added Sugar*	0
		Fiber	1 g

Quick Steak Pizzaiola

Preparation: **2 min.** Cooking: **5 min.**   FAT SUGAR SODIUM

You can easily halve this dish for two.

- 1 **tablespoon olive or vegetable oil**
- 4 **minute steaks (about 4 ounces each)**
- ¼ **teaspoon salt**
- ¼ **teaspoon black pepper**
- 1½ **cups low-sodium crushed tomatoes**
- 2 **cloves garlic, minced**
- ½ **teaspoon dried oregano, crumbled**

1. In a heavy 12-inch skillet, heat the **olive oil** over moderately high heat until very hot. Sprinkle the **steaks** with the **salt** and **pepper** and cook for 30 seconds on each side; transfer to a heated platter and keep warm.

2. Add the **tomatoes, garlic,** and **oregano** to the skillet, and cook, stirring, until thick—about 4 minutes. Spoon the sauce over the steaks. Serves 4.

One Serving:

Calories	209	*Protein*	26 g
Total Fat	9 g	*Carbohydrates*	5 g
Saturated Fat	2 g	*Sodium*	211 mg
Cholesterol	66 mg	*Added Sugar*	0
		Fiber	1 g

Steak Parsley

1 tablespoon olive or vegetable oil
¾ pound minute steaks, cut into finger-size strips
¼ teaspoon black pepper

3 green onions, including tops, chopped fine
1 teaspoon grated lemon rind
⅓ cup low-sodium beef broth
3 tablespoons minced parsley

FAT **SUGAR** **SODIUM**

Preparation: **10 min.**
Cooking: **6 min.**

One Serving:

Calories	154
Total Fat	8 g
Saturated Fat	2 g
Cholesterol	49 mg
Protein	19 g
Carbohydrates	1 g
Sodium	50 mg
Added Sugar	0
Fiber	0

1. In a heavy 10-inch skillet, heat the **olive oil** over moderately high heat until very hot. Add the **steak** and cook, stirring, until no longer pink—about 1 minute. Transfer to a platter.
2. Add the **pepper, green onions, lemon rind,** and **beef broth,** and cook until the liquid has boiled down by half—about 4 to 6 minutes. Return the meat to the skillet, add the **parsley,** and toss until heated through. Serve with steamed brown rice and Broccoli-Stuffed Tomatoes, page 178. Serves 4.

Easy Red and Green Pepper Steak

1 tablespoon reduced-sodium soy sauce
1 tablespoon dry sherry
1 tablespoon white vinegar
1 teaspoon minced fresh ginger
¾ pound boneless top round steak, cut against the grain into finger-size strips
1 tablespoon peanut or corn oil
1½ teaspoons Oriental sesame or peanut oil
2 cloves garlic, minced

¼ pound mushrooms, quartered
1 small yellow onion, sliced thin
1 medium-size sweet green pepper, cored, seeded, and sliced lengthwise into strips about ¼ inch wide
1 medium-size sweet red pepper, cored, seeded, and sliced lengthwise into strips about ¼ inch wide
⅔ cup low-sodium beef broth
2 teaspoons cornstarch

FAT **SUGAR** **SODIUM**

Preparation:
20 min.
Cooking:
7 min.

One Serving:

Calories	195
Total Fat	9 g
Saturated Fat	2 g
Cholesterol	49 mg
Protein	21 g
Carbohydrates	7 g
Sodium	200 mg
Added Sugar	0
Fiber	1 g

1. In a medium-size bowl, combine the **soy sauce, sherry, vinegar,** and **ginger.** Add the **steak** and toss well to coat.
2. In a heavy 12-inch skillet, heat 1½ teaspoons of the **peanut oil** and all the **sesame oil** over moderately high heat about 1 minute. Drain the steak, reserving the marinade; add the steak to the skillet and cook, stirring once or twice, until no longer pink—about 1 minute. Using a slotted spoon, transfer the steak to a platter.
3. Add the remaining peanut oil and the **garlic, mushrooms, onion, green pepper,** and **red pepper** to the skillet, and cook, stirring, for 1 minute. Cover, reduce the heat to moderate, and cook until the vegetables are tender but still crisp—2 to 3 minutes.
4. Combine the marinade with the **beef broth** and **cornstarch;** stir into the skillet and cook, stirring, until the sauce has thickened—about 1 minute. Return the steak and any juices to the skillet; cook and stir just until heated through. Transfer to a heated platter and serve with rice. Serves 4.

Grilled Oriental Steak

FAT SUGAR SODIUM

Grilled Oriental Steak

Preparation: **10 min.**, plus overnight marination   Cooking: **9 min.**   FAT SUGAR SODIUM

The reduced-sodium soy sauce and Oriental sesame oil in this dish are available at better supermarkets and specialty food shops.

1 pound flank steak, trimmed of fat
2 tablespoons reduced-sodium soy sauce
1 tablespoon light or dark brown sugar
1 tablespoon lemon juice
2 teaspoons Dijon or spicy brown mustard
2 teaspoons minced fresh ginger
2 cloves garlic, minced
2 teaspoons Oriental sesame or peanut oil
¼ teaspoon black pepper
¼ cup dry sherry or white wine
 Nonstick cooking spray
2 tablespoons white vinegar
2 tablespoons water
1 teaspoon granulated sugar

1. Place the **steak** in a baking pan just large enough to hold it and pierce all over with a fork. In a small bowl, combine the **soy sauce, brown sugar, lemon juice, mustard, ginger, garlic, sesame oil, pepper,** and half the **sherry**; pour over the steak. Cover and refrigerate overnight, turning the steak once.
2. Remove the steak from the marinade, pat dry and score crisscross fashion. Lightly coat a heavy 10-inch skillet with the **cooking spray** and set over moderate heat about 30 seconds. Cook the steak 3 minutes on each side for rare, 2 to 3 minutes longer for medium rare or medium. Transfer to a warm platter.
3. Cool the skillet for 1 minute. Meanwhile, to prepare the glaze, combine the remaining sherry with the **vinegar, water,** and **granulated sugar** in a small bowl; add to the skillet and cook, stirring, over moderate heat until thickened—1 to 2 minutes.
4. Spoon the glaze over the steak, then slice the meat on the bias ½ inch thick. Serves 4.

One Serving:

Calories	280	Protein	22 g
Total Fat	17 g	Carbohydrates	8 g
Saturated Fat	7 g	Sodium	461 mg
Cholesterol	59 mg	Added Sugar	15 Cal
		Fiber	0

Tip: *Marinating in an acid medium, such as wine, lemon juice, or vinegar, helps to tenderize the tougher cuts of beef.*

Sliced Beef with Romaine, Cucumber, and Tomatoes

Preparation: **20 min.** Cooking: **3 min.**   FAT SUGAR SODIUM

1 small head romaine lettuce (about ½ pound), torn into bite-size pieces
1 small cucumber, peeled, seeded, and sliced
½ large red onion, sliced thin
2 medium-size tomatoes, quartered
½ cup chopped fresh coriander or parsley
¾ pound minute steaks
1 clove garlic, halved
2 teaspoons lime juice
¼ teaspoon black pepper
1 tablespoon peanut or corn oil
¼ cup low-sodium beef broth
 For the Dressing:
¼ cup lime juice
3 tablespoons low-sodium beef broth
1 tablespoon reduced-sodium soy sauce
1 clove garlic, minced
1 teaspoon minced fresh ginger
¼ teaspoon anchovy paste

1. Put the **lettuce, cucumber, onion, tomatoes,** and **coriander** in a salad bowl.
2. Rub the **steaks** all over with the **garlic, lime juice,** and **pepper.**
3. Meanwhile, to prepare the dressing, whirl the **dressing ingredients** in an electric blender for 10 to 15 seconds; set aside.
4. In a heavy 10-inch skillet, heat the **peanut oil** about 30 seconds over moderately high heat. Add the steaks and cook for 1 minute on each side; transfer to a cutting board. Add the **beef broth** to the skillet, set over moderate heat, and warm about 1 minute, scraping up any browned bits. Add to the dressing in the blender and whirl for 1 to 2 seconds.
5. Slice the steaks on the diagonal ½ inch thick; add to the salad along with the dressing, toss lightly, and serve with rice. Serves 4.

One Serving:

Calories	201	Protein	21 g
Total Fat	8 g	Carbohydrates	11 g
Saturated Fat	2 g	Sodium	214 mg
Cholesterol	49 mg	Added Sugar	0
		Fiber	1 g

Beef Stew with Basil-Tomato Paste

Preparation: **15 min.**
Cooking: **2 hr. 10 min.** (mostly unattended)

FAT SUGAR SODIUM

1 tablespoon olive oil
  Nonstick cooking spray
1 pound boneless lean chuck steak, cut into
  1½-inch cubes
¼ teaspoon black pepper
½ cup dry red wine
2 cups low-sodium beef broth
1 can (1 pound) low-sodium tomatoes, puréed
  with their juice
1 medium-size stalk celery, sliced
4 cloves garlic, minced
2 3-inch strips orange peel
½ teaspoon each fennel seeds and dried basil
  and thyme, crumbled
1 bay leaf
2 medium-size yellow onions, quartered
4 medium-size turnips, peeled and quartered
4 medium-size carrots, peeled and sliced 1
  inch thick
3 tablespoons minced fresh basil or
  2 tablespoons minced parsley plus
  1 teaspoon dried basil, crumbled
2 tablespoons low-sodium tomato paste
6 ounces fresh or thawed frozen snow peas

1. Heat the **olive oil** over moderate heat for 1
   minute in a heavy 10-inch skillet that has been
   coated with the **cooking spray.** Season the
   steak cubes with the **pepper,** add to the
   skillet, and brown for 4 to 5 minutes. Transfer
   the beef to a 4-quart Dutch oven.

2. Add the **wine** to the skillet and boil, uncovered,
   for 2 minutes, scraping up any browned bits.
   Add the **beef broth, tomatoes, celery,** half of
   the minced **garlic,** the **orange peel, fennel
   seeds, basil, thyme,** and **bay leaf,** and bring
   to a simmer, stirring. Pour all into the Dutch
   oven, cover, and simmer 1¼ hours.

3. Discard the bay leaf, then add the **onions,
   turnips,** and **carrots;** cover and simmer until
   the vegetables are tender—about 45 minutes.

4. Using a fork, mash the remaining garlic with
   the **fresh basil,** blend in the **tomato paste,**
   and set aside. Cook the **snow peas** for 1
   minute in boiling water, drain, and set aside.

5. Just before serving, stir the basil–tomato paste
   mixture into the stew along with the snow
   peas. Heat for 1 minute. Serves 4.

One Serving:

Calories	335	Protein	30 g
Total Fat	11 g	Carbohydrates	32 g
Saturated Fat	3 g	Sodium	214 mg
Cholesterol	68 mg	Added Sugar	0
		Fiber	6 g

Tip: *Use the genuine article when a recipe calls
for wine or sherry. Commercial cooking wines
contain considerably more salt.*

Mexican Sliced Steak

Preparation: **6 min.,** plus overnight
marination   Cooking: **6 min.**

FAT SUGAR SODIUM

You can roll the steak slices, or fajitas, *in flour
tortillas the Mexican way, but keep in mind that
each tortilla will add 140 calories.*

3 tablespoons lime juice
1 tablespoon olive or vegetable oil
1½ teaspoons ground cumin
½ teaspoon red pepper flakes
1 clove garlic, minced
1 pound boneless top round steak, about
  1 inch thick
1 teaspoon vegetable oil
3 green onions, sliced thin
3 tablespoons sour cream
3 tablespoons plain low-fat yogurt

1. In a small bowl, combine the **lime juice, olive
   oil,** 1 teaspoon of the **cumin,** the **red pepper
   flakes,** and **garlic.** Place the **steak** in a baking
   pan just large enough to hold it, and pierce well
   with a fork. Pour in the marinade and turn
   the steak to coat well; cover and refrigerate
   overnight, turning the steak once.

2. In a heavy 10-inch skillet, heat the **vegetable
   oil** over moderately high heat for 1 minute.
   Remove the steak from the marinade and pat it
   dry. Cook for 3 minutes on each side for rare, 2
   to 3 minutes longer for medium rare or
   medium. Slice the steak thin, transfer to a
   heated platter, and top with the **green onions.**

3. For the sauce, combine the **sour cream,
   yogurt,** and remaining cumin in a small bowl.
   Serve the steak slices with the sauce. Serves 4.

One Serving:

Calories	215	Protein	27 g
Total Fat	10 g	Carbohydrates	2 g
Saturated Fat	4 g	Sodium	74 mg
Cholesterol	70 mg	Added Sugar	0
		Fiber	0

Beef, Zucchini, and Tomato Kebabs

Preparation: **20 min.**, plus 3 hr.
marination   Cooking: **16 min.**

FAT SUGAR SODIUM

Marinating meat in yogurt makes it unusually tender. In this case, the yogurt is flavored with spices frequently used in East Indian cooking.

¼ **cup plain low-fat yogurt**
2 **tablespoons lemon juice**
2 **cloves garlic, minced**
2 **teaspoons minced fresh ginger or ¼ teaspoon ground ginger**
2 **teaspoons paprika**
½ **teaspoon each cayenne pepper, ground cardamom, cumin, and coriander**
¾ **pound boneless lean sirloin steak, cut into 12 cubes of equal size**
1 **medium-size zucchini (about ½ pound), sliced into 12 rounds about ½ inch thick**
8 **cherry tomatoes**
2 **medium-size yellow onions, quartered**

1. In an electric blender or food processor, whirl the **yogurt, lemon juice, garlic, ginger, paprika, cayenne pepper, cardamom, cumin,** and **coriander** for 10 to 15 seconds.
2. Place the **steak** cubes in a bowl, pour in the yogurt mixture, and toss well. Cover and marinate at room temperature for 3 hours or refrigerate overnight, turning once.
3. Preheat the broiler. In a medium-size saucepan, cook the **zucchini** in unsalted boiling water for 1 minute; drain.
4. Remove the beef from the marinade and thread it onto 4 lightly oiled, long metal skewers, along with the zucchini rounds, **cherry tomatoes,** and **onion** quarters. Lay on the broiler pan rack and broil 5 inches from the heat for 15 to 20 minutes, turning often.
5. When the kebabs are done, transfer them to a warm platter. Ideal companions are Cucumber-Yogurt Sauce, page 226, and Hearty Low-Calorie Lentil Stew, page 138. Serves 4.

One Serving:			
Calories	177	Protein	20 g
Total Fat	7 g	Carbohydrates	8 g
Saturated Fat	3 g	Sodium	64 mg
Cholesterol	52 mg	Added Sugar	0
		Fiber	1 g

Beef, Zucchini, and Tomato Kebabs

Picadillo Platter

Picadillo Platter

Garnishing with the cheese adds 1 gram of fat and 49 calories per serving.

¾ **pound very lean ground beef**
1 **large yellow onion, chopped**
1 **small sweet green pepper,
   cored, seeded, and chopped**
2 **cloves garlic, minced**
1½ **teaspoons chili powder**
1 **can (1 pound) low-sodium
   tomatoes, chopped, with
   ⅓ cup of their juice**
¼ **cup raisins**
2 **tablespoons cider vinegar**
2 **teaspoons low-sodium tomato
   paste**

½ **teaspoon each ground ginger
   and dried thyme, crumbled**
¼ **teaspoon black pepper**
1 **small head iceberg lettuce,
   trimmed, cored, and shredded**
½ **cup plain low-fat yogurt,
   whisked until creamy**
2 **green onions, sliced thin**
3 **medium-size radishes,
   chopped**
2 **tablespoons shredded
   Cheddar cheese (optional)**

Preparation:
15 min.
Cooking:
41 min.

One Serving:

Calories	315
Total Fat	16 g
Saturated Fat	6 g
Cholesterol	60 mg
Protein	21 g
Carbohydrates	24 g
Sodium	115 mg
Added Sugar	0
Fiber	3 g

1. Heat a heavy 10-inch skillet over moderate heat for 30 seconds. Add the
   ground beef and cook, stirring, until no longer pink—3 to 4 minutes. Push
   the meat to one side of the skillet.

2. Add the **onion** and **green pepper;** cook, stirring, about 5 minutes. Add the
   garlic and **chili powder;** cook and stir for 2 minutes more. Add the
   tomatoes, raisins, vinegar, tomato paste, ginger, thyme, and **black pepper**
   and simmer, uncovered, for 30 minutes, stirring occasionally.

3. To serve, make a bed of **lettuce** on a platter and mound the meat mixture on
   top. Spoon the **yogurt** into the center, then top with the **green onions** and
   radishes, and the **cheese,** if desired. Serves 4.

Spinach and Rice Loaf with Mushroom Sauce

Preparation: **20 min.**
Cooking: **45 min.** (mostly unattended)

`FAT` `SUGAR` `SODIUM`

¾ **pound very lean ground beef**
1 **medium-size yellow onion, chopped fine**
½ **cup cooked rice**
2 **cloves garlic, minced**
½ **10-ounce package frozen chopped spinach, thawed and drained**
2 **teaspoons Dijon or spicy brown mustard**
½ **teaspoon each dried thyme and rosemary, crumbled**
¼ **teaspoon black pepper**
   Nonstick cooking spray
   For the Mushroom Sauce:
1 **cup dry red wine**
½ **medium-size yellow onion, chopped fine**
¼ **pound mushrooms, sliced thin**
⅛ **teaspoon each dried thyme and rosemary, crumbled**
1½ **cups low-sodium beef broth**
1 **tablespoon low-sodium tomato paste**
1 **tablespoon cornstarch blended with 2 tablespoons water**

1. Preheat the oven to 350°F. In a large mixing bowl, combine the **beef, onion, rice, garlic, spinach, mustard, thyme, rosemary,** and **pepper;** pack into a 9″x 5″x 3″ loaf pan lightly coated with the **cooking spray.**
2. Bake, uncovered, for 45 minutes or until browned. Remove from the pan and drain.
3. Meanwhile, prepare the sauce. In a small heavy saucepan, combine the **wine, onion, mushrooms, thyme,** and **rosemary;** boil, uncovered, over moderately high heat until the liquid is reduced to ½ cup—3 to 5 minutes. Add the **beef broth** and **tomato paste;** cover and simmer for 30 minutes. Blend in the **cornstarch** mixture and cook, stirring, until slightly thickened—1 to 2 minutes.
4. Transfer the meat loaf to a warm serving platter; spoon some sauce over it and pass the rest. Serve with Green Beans with Dill, page 174. Serves 4.

One Serving:

Calories	251	Protein	19 g
Total Fat	11 g	Carbohydrates	18 g
Saturated Fat	4 g	Sodium	142 mg
Cholesterol	53 mg	Added Sugar	0
		Fiber	2 g

Savory Macaroni and Beef

Preparation: **12 min.**
Cooking: **45 min.** (mostly unattended)

`FAT` `SUGAR` `SODIUM`

½ **pound very lean ground beef**
¼ **teaspoon salt**
¼ **teaspoon black pepper**
1 **large yellow onion, chopped fine**
2 **cloves garlic, minced**
1 **can (1 pound) low-sodium tomatoes, puréed with their juice**
1 **tablespoon low-sodium tomato paste**
1 **teaspoon each ground cinnamon and dried basil, crumbled**
6 **ounces elbow macaroni**
1 **large egg white, lightly beaten**
1 **cup skim milk**
2 **tablespoons flour**
3 **tablespoons grated Parmesan cheese**

1. Heat a heavy 10-inch skillet over moderate heat for 30 seconds. Add the **ground beef, salt,** and **pepper;** cook, stirring, until no longer pink—3 to 4 minutes. Push the meat to one side.
2. Add the **onion** and **garlic,** cover, and cook until the onion is soft—about 3 minutes. Add the **tomatoes, tomato paste, cinnamon,** and **basil,** and stir. Simmer, uncovered, stirring occasionally, for 10 to 15 minutes or until most of the liquid has evaporated.
3. Meanwhile, preheat the oven to 400°F. Cook the **macaroni** according to package directions, omitting the salt; rinse in cold water, drain, then combine with the **egg white.** Spoon half the macaroni into a lightly oiled 8″x 8″x 2″ baking pan; top with half the meat mixture, the remaining macaroni, then the remaining meat.
4. In a small saucepan, combine the **milk** and **flour;** cook over moderate heat, whisking constantly, until thickened—3 to 4 minutes. Stir in 1 tablespoon of the **cheese** and spoon the sauce over the meat mixture.
5. Sprinkle the remaining cheese evenly on top; bake, uncovered, for 25 to 30 minutes or until golden brown. Serve with Greek Salad, page 217. Serves 4.

One Serving:

Calories	391	Protein	23 g
Total Fat	12 g	Carbohydrates	48 g
Saturated Fat	5 g	Sodium	306 mg
Cholesterol	43 mg	Added Sugar	0
		Fiber	2 g

Chili con Carne

Swedish Meatballs

½ pound very lean ground beef
¼ pound ground veal
1 medium-size yellow onion, grated and squeezed dry
⅓ cup dry bread crumbs soaked in 2 tablespoons skim milk
¼ teaspoon black pepper
¼ teaspoon ground mace
  Nonstick cooking spray

1 tablespoon unsalted margarine
¼ teaspoon dried thyme, crumbled
1 cup low-sodium beef broth
½ cup skim milk blended with 1½ tablespoons flour
1 tablespoon sour cream
1 tablespoon plain low-fat yogurt
1 tablespoon minced parsley

FAT SUGAR SODIUM

Preparation:
10 min.
Cooking:
23 min.

One Serving:

Calories	*302*
Total Fat	*16 g*
Saturated Fat	*6 g*
Cholesterol	*75 mg*
Protein	*24 g*
Carbohydrates	*13 g*
Sodium	*135 mg*
Added Sugar	*0*
Fiber	*0*

1. In a large bowl, combine the **ground beef, veal, onion, bread crumbs, pepper,** and ⅛ teaspoon of the **mace;** shape into 1½-inch balls.

2. Lightly coat a heavy 10-inch skillet with the **cooking spray;** add the **margarine** and heat for 30 seconds over moderate heat. Add the meatballs and brown, turning frequently, for 10 minutes. Drain the fat from the skillet. Add the **thyme** and the **beef broth,** cover, and simmer for 5 minutes. Transfer the meatballs to a platter.

3. Add the **milk-flour** mixture to the skillet and cook, stirring often, until thickened—about 5 minutes. Blend in the **sour cream, yogurt,** and remaining mace.

4. Return the meatballs and any accumulated juices to the skillet. Spoon the sauce over the meat and heat through—about 2 minutes. Transfer to a warm serving bowl and sprinkle with the **parsley.** Serves 4.

Tip: To squeeze grated onion dry, place in two folded paper towels and squeeze until the liquid is absorbed.

Chili con Carne

Preparation: **15 min.** Cooking: **35 min.** FAT SUGAR SODIUM

Garnish, if you like, with shredded Cheddar cheese, but keep in mind that ¼ cup increases the calories by 98 and the sodium by 176 milligrams. Leftover chili freezes well.

Nonstick cooking spray
½ **pound very lean ground beef**
½ **pound boned and skinned chicken breast, chopped fine**
1 **large yellow onion, chopped fine**
1 **medium-size sweet green pepper, cored, seeded, and chopped**
2 **cloves garlic, minced**
1 **tablespoon each chili powder and ground cumin**
1 **can (1 pound) low-sodium tomatoes, puréed with their juice**
1 **cup low-sodium beef broth**
1 **tablespoon low-sodium tomato paste**
1 **teaspoon each red pepper flakes and ground coriander**
1 **teaspoon each dried oregano and basil, crumbled**
1 **bay leaf**
1 **cup cooked and drained kidney beans**
¼ **cup shredded sharp Cheddar cheese (optional)**

1. Lightly coat a heavy 10-inch skillet with the **cooking spray** and set over moderate heat for 30 seconds. Add the **ground beef** and **chicken** breast; cook, stirring often, until no longer pink—about 4 to 5 minutes. Push the meat mixture to one side of the skillet.
2. Add the **onion, green pepper, garlic, chili powder,** and **cumin;** cover and cook until the onion is soft—about 5 minutes. Add the **tomatoes, beef broth, tomato paste, red pepper flakes, coriander, oregano, basil,** and **bay leaf;** simmer, uncovered, stirring occasionally, for 20 minutes.
3. Add the **kidney beans** and simmer, uncovered, stirring occasionally, 5 minutes longer. Discard the bay leaf, ladle into soup bowls and garnish with the **cheese,** if desired. Serve with rice. Serves 4.

One Serving:

Calories	321	Protein	30 g
Total Fat	12 g	Carbohydrates	24 g
Saturated Fat	4 g	Sodium	357 mg
Cholesterol	72 mg	Added Sugar	0
		Fiber	5 g

Hamburgers Lindstrom

Preparation: **10 min.**, plus 20 min. refrigeration Cooking: **10 min.** FAT SUGAR SODIUM

Beets, dill, and sour cream are combined in these ground beef patties of Scandinavian origin.

½ **pound very lean ground beef**
½ **cup finely chopped cooked beets**
⅓ **cup fine dry bread crumbs**
1 **large egg white**
2 **teaspoons red wine vinegar**
½ **teaspoon dill weed**
¼ **teaspoon black pepper**
1 **tablespoon unsalted margarine**
4 **teaspoons sour cream**
2 **teaspoons snipped fresh dill or minced parsley**

1. Mix the **ground beef, beets, bread crumbs, egg white, vinegar, dill weed,** and **pepper;** shape into 4 round patties and refrigerate for 20 minutes.
2. In a heavy 10-inch skillet, melt the **margarine** over moderately high heat; add the patties and cook, uncovered, for 5 minutes on each side.
3. Drain on paper towels, transfer to a warm platter, and garnish with the **sour cream** and **dill.** Serves 4.

One Serving:

Calories	188	Protein	13 g
Total Fat	11 g	Carbohydrates	8 g
Saturated Fat	4 g	Sodium	117 mg
Cholesterol	37 mg	Added Sugar	0
		Fiber	1 g

Tip: Regular ground beef has as much as 27 percent fat before cooking. The ground beef marked "lean" has about 21 percent fat, while "very lean" or "extra lean" has only 17 percent.

Loin of Pork with Vegetable Stuffing

Maple-Glazed Pork Roast

When cooking for two or three, use the leftovers to make Hot Roast Pork and Tortilla Sandwiches, page 77.

FAT SUGAR SODIUM

1 **pound boneless lean pork shoulder butt, trimmed of fat**
2 **cloves garlic, sliced thin**
2 **teaspoons lime juice**
1 **tablespoon dark rum or orange juice**
1½ **tablespoons maple syrup**
⅛ **teaspoon cayenne pepper**

1. With a paring knife, pierce the **pork** all over; insert the **garlic** slices into the gashes, then rub the **lime juice** into the pork.
2. Combine the **rum, maple syrup,** and **cayenne pepper** in a medium-size bowl. Add the pork, turning to coat well. Cover and refrigerate at least 8 hours. Turn the pork occasionally in the marinade.
3. Preheat the oven to 425°F. Lift the pork from the marinade and place on a rack in a shallow roasting pan. Roast, uncovered, brushing often with the marinade, for 20 minutes; lower the heat to 350°F and roast another 20 minutes, brushing often with the remaining marinade. Let the roast stand for 10 minutes at room temperature before slicing. Serves 4.

Preparation:
5 min., plus 8 hr. marination
Cooking:
40 min.

One Serving:

Calories	*239*
Total Fat	*14 g*
Saturated Fat	*5 g*
Cholesterol	*82 mg*
Protein	*21 g*
Carbohydrates	*6 g*
Sodium	*63 mg*
Added Sugar	*19 Cal*
Fiber	*0*

Loin of Pork with Vegetable Stuffing

Good either hot or cold, this dish can be made a day or two ahead. Use any leftovers for Cold Roast Pork with Black Beans and Fruit, page 78.

FAT SUGAR SODIUM

2 tablespoons finely chopped yellow onion

2 tablespoons finely chopped carrot

½ medium-size sweet red pepper, cored, seeded, and chopped fine

1 slice whole wheat bread, crumbled

¼ cup hot water

¼ teaspoon salt

¼ teaspoon ground ginger

⅛ teaspoon each black pepper and ground cloves

1 boneless loin of pork (1½ pounds), trimmed of fat

2 tablespoons lemon juice

Preparation:
10 min.
Cooking:
44 min. (mostly unattended)

One Serving:

Calories	332
Total Fat	18 g
Saturated Fat	6 g
Cholesterol	117 mg
Protein	36 g
Carbohydrates	5 g
Sodium	258 mg
Added Sugar	0
Fiber	1 g

1. Preheat the oven to 400°F. Put the **onion, carrot,** and **red pepper** in a small saucepan with just enough boiling water to cover; simmer over moderate heat until tender but still crisp—about 4 minutes. Drain, rinse under cold water, then drain well again; set aside.

2. In a medium-size bowl, soften the **bread** by pouring the hot **water** over it and letting it stand for 1 minute. Squeeze out all the liquid. Add the cooked vegetables to the bread along with the **salt, ginger, pepper,** and **cloves,** and mix well.

3. With a sharp knife, cut a large pocket in the middle of the loin of **pork,** taking care not to cut through the opposite end. Fill with the vegetable stuffing. Sprinkle the **lemon juice** over the pork and rub it in.

4. Place the pork in an ungreased 13″x 9″x 2″ baking pan and roast, uncovered, for 20 minutes; lower the heat to 350°F and roast 20 minutes longer.

5. Let the roast stand at room temperature for 20 minutes before serving. Cut into ⅜-inch-thick slices and serve. Serves 4.

Tip: To make sure leftover pork is at its best, store it in one piece in the refrigerator and use within four days.

Hot Roast Pork and Tortilla Sandwiches

Inspired by the Mexican turnover called quesadilla, *these easy-to-make sandwiches can be assembled hours before they're baked; just keep them refrigerated and increase the baking time by 5 to 10 minutes.*

FAT SUGAR SODIUM

8 6-inch corn tortillas
Nonstick cooking spray

1 cup shredded Monterey Jack cheese (about 4 ounces)

1 cup chopped cooked roast pork

1 jar (2 ounces) pimientos, drained and chopped

1 tablespoon trimmed, seeded, and chopped hot green chilies (or 4 tablespoons mild), fresh or canned

Preparation:
8 min.
Cooking:
10 min.

One Serving:

Calories	331
Total Fat	16 g
Saturated Fat	2 g
Cholesterol	57 mg
Protein	21 g
Carbohydrates	27 g
Sodium	286 mg
Added Sugar	0
Fiber	0

1. Preheat the oven to 400°F. Place 4 of the **tortillas** on 4 9-inch lengths of aluminum foil, the centers of which have been lightly coated with the **cooking spray.** Sprinkle each tortilla with ¼ of the **cheese, pork, pimientos,** and **green chilies.** Top with the remaining 4 tortillas.

2. Coat the centers of 4 more 9-inch lengths of aluminum foil with the cooking spray and place on top of the assembled sandwiches, sprayed sides down. Seal the 4 foil packets by rolling and crimping the edges snugly.

3. Bake for 10 minutes or until the cheese has melted. Serve individually in the foil packets, letting each person unwrap the sandwich and cut it into 4 wedges. Serves 4.

Cold Roast Pork with Black Beans and Fruit

Here is a delightful, simply made salad that is hearty enough to serve as a main dish. To make it for two, halve all of the ingredients except the green onion.

FAT SUGAR SODIUM

1 small head leaf lettuce

1 cup watercress sprigs

½ pound cooked roast pork, trimmed of fat and sliced thin

2 medium-size grapefruits, peeled, sectioned, and seeded

2 navel oranges, peeled and sectioned

1 cup cooked and drained black beans

2 cloves garlic

1 tablespoon red wine vinegar

2 teaspoons olive oil

⅛ teaspoon each cayenne pepper and ground ginger

¼ cup orange juice

1 green onion, including top, sliced thin

Preparation:
20 min.

One Serving:

Calories	317
Total Fat	10 g
Saturated Fat	3 g
Cholesterol	52 mg
Protein	23 g
Carbohydrates	35 g
Sodium	54 mg
Added Sugar	0
Fiber	4 g

1. Trim the **lettuce** and separate the leaves. Wash the lettuce and the **watercress,** pat dry, and place on a serving platter. Arrange the **pork** slices and **grapefruit** and **orange** sections attractively on top of the greens and spoon the **black beans** onto the center of the salad.

2. In an electric blender or food processor, combine the **garlic, vinegar, olive oil,** and **cayenne pepper;** blend for 10 to 15 seconds. Add the **ginger** and **orange juice** and blend for 3 to 4 seconds more.

3. Pour the dressing over the salad and top with the **green onion.** Serves 4.

Cold Roast Pork with Black Beans and Fruit

Pork with Roasted Peppers

Preparation: **7 min.** Cooking: **23 min.** FAT SUGAR SODIUM

This sauce is so good that you might want to make it without the pork to serve over pasta.

- 2 **large sweet red peppers**
  Nonstick cooking spray
- ¾ **pound boneless lean pork shoulder butt, sliced ¼ inch thick and pounded thin**
- 1 **tablespoon flour**
- 1 **medium-size yellow onion, chopped**
- 2 **cloves garlic, minced**
- 2 **cans (1 pound each) low-sodium tomatoes, drained and chopped**
- 2 **tablespoons golden raisins**
- 1 **tablespoon red wine vinegar**
- ¼ **teaspoon cayenne pepper**
- ¼ **teaspoon dried oregano, crumbled**

1. Place the **red peppers** on a broiler pan and broil 6 inches from the heat, turning 3 times or until charred all over—5 to 8 minutes.
2. While the peppers are cooking, lightly coat a heavy 10-inch skillet with the **cooking spray** and set over moderate heat about 30 seconds. Quickly coat the **pork** slices with the **flour,** then cook over moderate heat for 4 minutes on each side. Transfer the pork to a plate and set aside.
3. When the peppers are charred, transfer them to a brown paper bag, seal, and set in a bowl; this will steam them so that their skins peel off easily. When cool enough to handle, peel the peppers, reserving any juice; discard the stems and seeds. Cut the peppers lengthwise into strips about 1 inch wide and set aside.
4. In the skillet used to brown the pork slices, cook the **onion** and **garlic,** uncovered, over moderate heat until the onion is soft—about 5 minutes. Add the **tomatoes, raisins, vinegar, cayenne pepper, oregano,** and reserved red pepper juice. Cook, stirring occasionally, about 5 minutes.
5. Add the reserved pork slices and pepper strips; cook 5 minutes longer. Transfer to a heated platter and serve with pasta. Serves 4.

One Serving:

Calories	231	Protein	19 g
Total Fat	9 g	Carbohydrates	19 g
Saturated Fat	3 g	Sodium	92 mg
Cholesterol	58 mg	Added Sugar	0
		Fiber	3 g

Tip: *Another way to roast peppers is to place them directly on the burner of a gas stove over low heat. Using tongs, turn a few times until the skins are black, then flush with cold water and slip the skins off with your fingers.*

Pork Scaloppine with Honey Mustard

Preparation: **7 min.** Cooking: **9 min.** FAT SUGAR SODIUM

If you have time, bread the pork slices 20 minutes in advance and refrigerate them; this will help the breading to stick during cooking.

- 1 **tablespoon Dijon or spicy brown mustard**
- 1 **tablespoon coarse-grain or spicy brown mustard**
- 1 **tablespoon honey**
- ¾ **pound boneless lean pork shoulder butt, sliced ¼ inch thick and pounded thin**
- 1 **small egg, lightly beaten with ¾ teaspoon water**
- ½ **cup fine dry bread crumbs**
  Nonstick cooking spray
- 1 **medium-size lemon, cut into thin wedges (optional)**

1. Combine the **Dijon** and **coarse-grain mustards** with the **honey** in a small bowl. Using a pastry brush, spread the mustard-honey mixture on both sides of each **pork** slice.
2. Dip the pork in the **egg,** then in the **bread crumbs** to coat both sides.
3. Lightly coat a heavy 12-inch skillet with the **cooking spray** and set over moderate heat for 30 seconds. Add the pork and cook about 4 minutes on each side or until crisp and lightly browned. Garnish with the **lemon** wedges and serve with Sautéed Spinach with Lemon and Garlic, page 199. Serves 4.

One Serving:

Calories	230	Protein	19 g
Total Fat	10 g	Carbohydrates	14 g
Saturated Fat	3 g	Sodium	314 mg
Cholesterol	110 mg	Added Sugar	16 Cal
		Fiber	0

Pork Stir-fry with Five Vegetables

You can prepare the ingredients a few hours in advance, refrigerate them, then stir-fry for a made-in-minutes meal. For an authentic touch, use Oriental sesame oil and rice vinegar, available in specialty food shops and some supermarkets.

FAT SUGAR SODIUM

- 1 tablespoon cornstarch
- ½ cup low-sodium chicken broth
- 4 tablespoons dry sherry
- 1 teaspoon dark brown sugar
- 1½ tablespoons reduced-sodium soy sauce
- 1 teaspoon white wine vinegar or rice vinegar
- 1 tablespoon corn or Oriental sesame oil
- 1 teaspoon minced fresh ginger
- 2 cloves garlic, minced
- 1 medium-size carrot, peeled and shredded
- ½ large sweet red pepper, cored, seeded, and chopped
- ½ medium-size cucumber, peeled, seeded, and chopped
- 1 cup bean sprouts
- ⅓ cup sliced green onions
- ¾ pound boneless lean pork loin, cut into ¼"x ¼"x 2" strips

Preparation:
17 min.
Cooking:
11 min.

One Serving:

Calories	212
Total Fat	10 g
Saturated Fat	3 g
Cholesterol	54 mg
Protein	21 g
Carbohydrates	9 g
Sodium	299 mg
Added Sugar	3 Cal
Fiber	1 g

1. In a small bowl, whisk together the **cornstarch** and **chicken broth.** Mix in 2 tablespoons of the **sherry,** ½ teaspoon of the **brown sugar,** the **soy sauce, vinegar,** and 1½ teaspoons of the **corn oil;** set aside.

2. In a heavy 12-inch skillet or wok, heat the remaining corn oil over high heat about 1 minute. Add the **ginger** and **garlic** and cook, stirring, for 30 seconds. Add the **carrot, red pepper,** and remaining ½ teaspoon brown sugar and cook, stirring, for 2 minutes.

3. Add the **cucumber** and cook 1 minute longer. Add the **bean sprouts, green onions,** and remaining 2 tablespoons sherry; cook another minute, stirring. Using a slotted spoon, transfer the vegetables to a bowl and set aside.

4. Add the **pork** to the skillet and cook, stirring, over high heat until no longer pink—about 4 minutes. Add the cornstarch–chicken broth mixture along with the reserved vegetables and cook, stirring constantly, until thickened and glossy—about 1 minute. Serves 4.

Indian-Spiced Pork Chops

These broiled pork chops have the lively flavor of India. If you want to make them even more piquant, add about ¼ teaspoon cayenne pepper to the dry marinade. You can halve the recipe for two servings; use a pinch of salt.

FAT SUGAR SODIUM

- 2 bay leaves, well crumbled
- 1 teaspoon ground cumin
- ½ teaspoon each ground ginger and coriander
- ¼ teaspoon ground turmeric
- ⅛ teaspoon salt
- 8 lean rib pork chops (about 2 pounds), trimmed of fat
- 1 lime, quartered (optional)

Preparation:
4 min., plus 1 hr.
marination
Cooking
10 min.

One Serving:

Calories	298
Total Fat	17 g
Saturated Fat	6 g
Cholesterol	107 mg
Protein	33 g
Carbohydrates	1 g
Sodium	146 mg
Added Sugar	0
Fiber	0

1. In a small bowl, combine the **bay leaves, cumin, ginger, coriander, turmeric,** and **salt.** Rub the mixture on both sides of each **pork chop.** Cover and marinate at room temperature for 1 hour.

2. Preheat the broiler about 5 minutes. Place the pork chops on the broiler pan rack and broil 7 or 8 inches from the heat, turning 3 or 4 times, until golden and cooked through—about 10 minutes. Garnish with the **lime,** if desired, and accompany with Minted Cucumber Salad, page 212. Serves 4.

Mexicali Pork Chop Casserole

Mexicali Pork Chop Casserole

This dish is as colorful as it is quick and easy.

FAT SUGAR SODIUM

1 tablespoon unsalted margarine
1 large yellow onion, halved and sliced thin
½ medium-size sweet green pepper, cored, seeded, and cut into 1-inch squares
½ medium-size sweet red pepper, cored, seeded, and cut into 1-inch squares

1 can (1 pound) low-sodium tomatoes, drained and chopped
1 cup frozen whole-kernel corn, thawed and drained
¼ teaspoon dried marjoram, crumbled
4 lean rib pork chops (about 1 pound), trimmed of fat

Preparation:
5 min.
Cooking:
26 min.

One Serving:

Calories	*207*
Total Fat	*8 g*
Saturated Fat	*2 g*
Cholesterol	*36 mg*
Protein	*17 g*
Carbohydrates	*17 g*
Sodium	*47 mg*
Added Sugar	*0*
Fiber	*2 g*

1. Preheat the oven to 350°F. Melt the **margarine** in a heavy 10-inch skillet over moderate heat; add the **onion, red pepper,** and **green pepper** and cook, uncovered, about 5 minutes. Add the **tomatoes, corn,** and **marjoram;** raise the heat to high and cook, uncovered, 5 minutes longer. Transfer to an ungreased shallow 1½-quart casserole or 9-inch pie pan.

2. In the same skillet over moderate heat, cook the **pork chops** for 2 minutes on each side. Lay the chops on top of the vegetable mixture.

3. Cover with aluminum foil and bake for 12 to 15 minutes or until the pork chops are done. Serves 4.

Casserole of Pork and Red Cabbage

This casserole tastes even better if prepared a day ahead.

¾ pound boneless lean pork butt, cut into 1-inch cubes

2 tablespoons flour
Nonstick cooking spray

1 medium-size yellow onion, sliced thin

1 medium-size carrot, sliced

3 cloves garlic, minced

1 large apple, peeled, quartered, cored, and sliced thin

½ small red cabbage, cored and coarsely shredded (about 2½ cups)

3 tablespoons red wine vinegar

½ cup low-sodium chicken broth

2 bay leaves

7 allspice berries

6 black peppercorns

¼ teaspoon dried sage, crumbled

Preparation:
9 min.
Cooking:
1½ hr. (mostly unattended)

One Serving:

Calories	*214*
Total Fat	*9 g*
Saturated Fat	*3 g*
Cholesterol	*58 mg*
Protein	*18 g*
Carbohydrates	*16 g*
Sodium	*80 mg*
Added Sugar	*0*
Fiber	*2 g*

1. Coat the **pork** cubes with the **flour,** shaking off any excess. Lightly coat a heavy 6-quart Dutch oven with the **cooking spray,** set over moderate heat for 30 seconds, and add the pork; brown the pork, uncovered, on all sides—about 10 minutes. Transfer to a bowl and set aside.

2. Preheat the oven to 350°F. Add the **onion, carrot,** and **garlic** to the Dutch oven and cook, uncovered, over moderate heat until soft—about 5 minutes.

3. Add the **apple** and **cabbage,** cover, and cook 15 minutes longer or just until the cabbage is wilted.

4. Stir in the **vinegar, chicken broth, bay leaves, allspice berries, peppercorns, sage,** and the reserved pork. Cover and bake for 1 hour. Remove the bay leaves. Serve with mustard on the side. Serves 4.

Savory Broiled Pork on Skewers

This is a spicy, peanut-flavored kebab of Indonesian origin, called a satay. *Quickly broiling the pork seals in the natural juices and makes for a particularly succulent, flavorful dish.*

¼ teaspoon ground ginger

2 cloves garlic

1 small yellow onion, chopped

1 tablespoon reduced-sodium soy sauce

2 tablespoons chopped unsalted dry-roasted peanuts

1 tablespoon peanut or vegetable oil

2 teaspoons light brown sugar

2 teaspoons lime juice

¼ teaspoon each ground coriander, cumin, and cinnamon

¾ pound boneless lean pork butt, cut into ¾-inch cubes

Preparation:
7 min., plus 1 hr. marination
Cooking:
18 min.

One Serving:

Calories	*215*
Total Fat	*14 g*
Saturated Fat	*4 g*
Cholesterol	*58 mg*
Protein	*18 g*
Carbohydrates	*5 g*
Sodium	*214 mg*
Added Sugar	*6 Cal*
Fiber	*0 g*

1. Put the **ginger, garlic, onion, soy sauce, peanuts, peanut oil, brown sugar, lime juice, coriander, cumin, cinnamon,** and 2 tablespoons cold water into a food processor or electric blender. Blend for 8 to 10 seconds.

2. Pour the mixture into a medium-size mixing bowl, add the **pork,** and toss well to coat. Cover and marinate at room temperature for 1 hour.

3. Preheat the broiler. Thread the pork cubes onto 8 lightly oiled 8-inch-long skewers, making sure the cubes do not touch each other.

4. Lay the skewers on an ungreased broiler pan and brush with the marinade. Broil 7 to 8 inches from the heat, turning the skewers occasionally and brushing each time with the remaining marinade. Cook for 18 minutes or until the pork is browned and feels firm to the touch. Serve with Easy Nutted Brown Rice, page 168. Serves 4.

Casserole of Pork and Red Cabbbage

Pork Stew with Chick Peas

½ ounce dried mushrooms
½ cup warm water
Nonstick cooking spray
¾ pound boneless lean pork butt, cut into 1-inch cubes
2 tablespoons flour
1 small yellow onion, chopped
2 cloves garlic, minced
3 tablespoons Marsala, port, or other sweet red wine

½ cup low-sodium chicken broth
1 bay leaf
½ teaspoon dried rosemary, crumbled
¼ teaspoon black pepper
1 cup cooked and drained chick peas
½ pound fresh mushrooms, quartered
1 tablespoon lemon juice

FAT **SUGAR** **SODIUM**

Preparation:
7 min.
Cooking:
1 hr. 22 min. (mostly unattended)

One Serving:

Calories	270
Total Fat	10 g
Saturated Fat	3 g
Cholesterol	58 mg
Protein	23 g
Carbohydrates	23 g
Sodium	77 mg
Added Sugar	0
Fiber	4 g

1. In a small bowl, soak the **dried mushrooms** in the warm **water** about ½ hour. Remove from the soaking liquid, reserving both the mushrooms and the liquid. *(Note: If the dried mushrooms are gritty, strain the soaking liquid through a coffee filter or layered cheesecloth before setting aside.)*

2. Coat a heavy 10-inch skillet with the **cooking spray.** Coat the **pork** cubes with the **flour,** shaking off any excess, then brown on all sides over moderate heat about 10 minutes. Transfer the pork to a bowl and reserve.

3. In the same skillet, cook the **onion** and **garlic,** uncovered, over moderate heat until soft—about 5 minutes. Return the pork to the skillet and add the **Marsala, chicken broth, bay leaf, rosemary, pepper,** soaked mushrooms, and ¼ cup of the reserved liquid. Cover and simmer for 20 minutes.

4. Add the **chick peas** and simmer 35 minutes longer. Just before the end of the 35-minute cooking period, coat a heavy 7-inch skillet with the cooking spray. Add the **fresh mushrooms** and brown lightly—about 2 minutes.

5. Add the mushrooms to the pork and cook the stew 10 minutes longer. Stir in the **lemon juice.** Serves 4.

Tip: Pork is fattier than beef, veal, and lamb, but is lower in sodium than all three. Loin is the leanest of the pork cuts.

Easy Ham, Green Pea, and Noodle Casserole

Pork Balls in Tomato-Orange Sauce

Here is a good dish to make a day ahead. Serve on spaghetti or, for a low-calorie change of pace, on baked spaghetti squash.

FAT SUGAR SODIUM

1 medium-size yellow onion, chopped fine

2 cloves garlic, minced

1 cup low-sodium chicken broth

½ pound lean ground pork

¼ pound lean ground veal

2 tablespoons golden raisins

1 large egg, lightly beaten

2 tablespoons grated Parmesan cheese

1 tablespoon dry bread crumbs

1 tablespoon minced parsley

¼ teaspoon each black pepper and dried sage, crumbled

⅛ teaspoon salt

⅛ teaspoon nutmeg

1 cup canned low-sodium tomatoes, chopped, with their juice

1 cinnamon stick

3 strips orange peel, each about 2 inches long and ½ inch wide

2 tablespoons orange juice

Preparation:
8 min.
Cooking:
27 min.

One Serving:

Calories	226
Total Fat	11 g
Saturated Fat	4 g
Cholesterol	129 mg
Protein	21 g
Carbohydrates	11 g
Sodium	316 mg
Added Sugar	0
Fiber	1 g

1. In a small heavy saucepan, cook the **onion** and **garlic** in ⅓ cup of the **chicken broth,** covered, over moderately low heat until soft—about 7 minutes. Remove from the heat and let cool.

2. Using your hands, thoroughly mix the **pork, veal, raisins, egg, cheese, bread crumbs, parsley, pepper, sage, salt,** and **nutmeg** with the onion mixture in a medium-size bowl. Shape into 20 balls 1¼ inches in diameter.

3. In a heavy 12-inch skillet over moderate heat, brown the pork balls lightly on all sides—about 5 minutes.

4. Add the remaining chicken broth and the **tomatoes, cinnamon stick, orange peel,** and **orange juice.** Bring to a boil, then lower the heat and simmer, uncovered, for 10 to 12 minutes, stirring occasionally, until the pork balls are cooked through. Using a slotted spoon, transfer the pork balls to a heated platter and keep warm.

5. Raise the heat to high and boil the sauce, uncovered, until it has thickened slightly—about 5 minutes. Remove the cinnamon stick and orange peel and pour the sauce over the pork balls. Serves 4.

Tip: Instead of mincing, you can use kitchen scissors to snip parsley and other fresh herbs directly into a measuring spoon, cup, or mixing bowl.

Easy Ham, Green Pea, and Noodle Casserole

This quick, hearty dinner is ideal for preparing after work.

6 ounces broad egg noodles
4½ teaspoons flour
1 teaspoon dry mustard
¼ teaspoon dried sage, crumbled
⅛ teaspoon each ground nutmeg and black pepper
1½ cups skim milk
6 ounces reduced-sodium ham, cubed

2 cups fresh green peas, blanched, or 1 package (10 ounces) frozen peas, thawed and drained
1½ tablespoons soft white bread crumbs (1 slice without crust)
1 tablespoon unsalted margarine

Preparation:
5 min.
Cooking:
30 min. (mostly unattended)

One Serving:

Calories	338
Total Fat	8 g
Saturated Fat	1 g
Cholesterol	63 mg
Protein	20 g
Carbohydrates	47 g
Sodium	482 mg
Added Sugar	0
Fiber	3 g

1. Preheat the oven to 350°F. Cook the **noodles** according to package directions, omitting the salt.

2. Meanwhile, in a medium-size bowl, combine the **flour, mustard, sage, nutmeg,** and **pepper;** slowly whisk in the **milk** and set aside.

3. When the noodles are done, drain and combine with the **ham** and **peas;** add the milk mixture and stir well. Spoon into an ungreased shallow 1½-quart casserole; sprinkle with the **bread crumbs** and dot with the **margarine.**

4. Cover with aluminum foil and bake for 10 minutes. Remove the foil and bake 10 minutes longer or until bubbly and lightly browned. Serves 4.

Spicy Ham and Vegetable Loaf

Serve either hot or cold, or try in a sandwich. Freeze half of the loaf, if you like, to serve on another day.

Nonstick cooking spray
1 medium-size yellow onion, chopped
3 medium-size carrots, chopped fine (about 1 cup)
¾ pound mushrooms, chopped fine
¾ pound reduced-sodium ham, ground

½ pound lean ground pork
2 cups soft bread crumbs
1 cup skim milk
2 tablespoons prepared yellow mustard
½ teaspoon black pepper
¼ teaspoon dried sage, crumbled
1 teaspoon grated orange rind

Preparation:
11 min.
Cooking:
1 hr. 36 min. (mostly unattended)

One Serving:

Calories	167
Total Fat	6 g
Saturated Fat	1 g
Cholesterol	41 mg
Protein	17 g
Carbohydrates	13 g
Sodium	480 mg
Added Sugar	0
Fiber	2 g

1. Coat a heavy 10-inch skillet with the **cooking spray** and set over moderate heat about 30 seconds. Add the **onion** and cook, stirring frequently, until soft—about 5 minutes. Add the **carrots** and **mushrooms** and cook, continuing to stir, until the vegetables are soft and all the mushroom liquid has evaporated—about 25 minutes. If the vegetables start to burn, add a little water to the pan as necessary.

2. Preheat the oven to 350°F. Using your hands, thoroughly mix the **ham, pork, bread crumbs, milk, mustard, pepper, sage, orange rind,** and the cooked vegetable mixture in a large bowl.

3. Coat an 8"x 4"x 3" loaf pan with the cooking spray. Pack the ham mixture into the pan, cover with aluminum foil, and bake for 1 hour 5 minutes or until the juices run clear when the loaf is pierced with a knife.

4. Remove the loaf from the oven and cool in the pan upright on a wire rack for 10 minutes. Run a knife around the edges of the pan to loosen the loaf, pour off all the fat, then turn the loaf out onto a heated platter. Serve with Four-Bean Salad, page 207. Serves 8.

Stuffed Leg of Lamb with Orange Gravy

This leg of lamb is especially moist and easy to carve. A 7½-pound leg may yield more servings than needed, but roasting anything smaller will result in dry lamb. Simply use the leftovers for another meal.

FAT SUGAR SODIUM

1 tablespoon unsalted margarine
1 large yellow onion, chopped fine
4 cloves garlic, minced
1 pound mushrooms, chopped
1 medium-size navel orange
2 slices whole wheat bread, torn into small pieces
½ cup minced parsley
1 teaspoon dried marjoram, crumbled
½ teaspoon dried basil, crumbled
¼ teaspoon black pepper
1 leg of lamb (7½ pounds), trimmed of fat and boned
1 cup low-sodium beef broth
1 tablespoon flour

Preparation:
25 min.
Cooking:
1 hr. 25 min.
(mostly unattended)

One Serving:

Calories	*337*
Total Fat	*12 g*
Saturated Fat	*6 g*
Cholesterol	*157 mg*
Protein	*46 g*
Carbohydrates	*8 g*
Sodium	*137 mg*
Added Sugar	*0*
Fiber	*2 g*

1. Preheat the oven to 450°F. In a heavy 10-inch skillet, melt the **margarine** over moderate heat. Add the **onion** and **garlic** and cook, uncovered, for 5 minutes or until soft. Add the **mushrooms** and cook 5 minutes longer or until the mushroom juices have evaporated. Remove from the heat.

2. Grate 1 teaspoon rind from the **orange** into the pan, then peel the orange and set aside. Mix in the **bread, parsley, marjoram, basil,** and **pepper.**

3. Spread out the **lamb,** fat side down, and smooth the mushroom mixture over it, leaving ½-inch margins all around. Roll up as for a jelly roll, tying with string at 2-inch intervals.

4. Place the lamb on a rack in a shallow roasting pan and roast, uncovered, for 15 minutes. Reduce the oven temperature to 350°F, and roast another 55 minutes for rare (135°F on a meat thermometer), 1¼ hours for medium (160°F), and 1½ hours for well done (165°F). Transfer the lamb to a platter and let it stand for 20 minutes.

5. Meanwhile, skim the fat from the drippings in the roasting pan. To the remaining drippings, add ¾ cup of the **beef broth.** Set over low heat and stir, scraping up any browned bits. Blend the **flour** with the remaining broth, add to the pan, and cook, stirring, for 3 minutes or until the sauce has thickened. Remove from the heat. Chop the peeled orange and stir into the sauce.

6. Remove the strings from the lamb. Place the lamb on a heated platter, slice, and serve with the sauce. Serves 10.

Broiled Lamb Chops with Herbs

Preparation: **2 min.** Cooking: **8 min.**

This recipe is easily halved to make a quick meal for two.

FAT SUGAR SODIUM

8 loin or rib lamb chops, trimmed of fat (about 2⅔ pounds)
2 cloves garlic, cut in half
1 tablespoon olive oil
2 teaspoons dried marjoram, thyme, or tarragon, crumbled
¼ teaspoon black pepper
Lemon wedges (optional)

One Serving:

Calories	*213*
Total Fat	*12 g*
Saturated Fat	*5 g*
Cholesterol	*85 mg*
Protein	*23 g*
Carbohydrates	*1 g*
Sodium	*57 mg*
Added Sugar	*0*
Fiber	*0*

1. Preheat the broiler. Rub the **lamb chops** all over with the cut **garlic.** Brush with the **olive oil** and sprinkle with the **marjoram** and **pepper.**

2. Broil 4 to 5 inches from the heat for 4 to 5 minutes per side for medium-cooked lamb. Serve with **lemon** wedges, if desired, and Oven French Fries, page 196. Serves 4.

Stuffed Leg of Lamb with Orange Gravy

Lamb, Carrot, and Green Bean Stew

You can double the recipe for this hearty winter stew, refrigerate half of it, and enjoy it later in the week. Serve with crusty French bread.

FAT SUGAR SODIUM

2 tablespoons unsalted margarine
1 pound boneless lean lamb shoulder, cut into 1-inch cubes
4 small white onions, peeled
1 clove garlic, minced
2 cups low-sodium beef broth
1 tablespoon snipped fresh dill or 1 teaspoon dill weed

¼ teaspoon black pepper
2 medium-size carrots, peeled and cut into 1-inch cubes
2 small baking potatoes, peeled and cut into 1-inch cubes
2 tablespoons flour
1 cup fresh or frozen cut green beans

Preparation:
30 min.
Cooking:
57 min. (mostly unattended)

One Serving:

Calories	*304*
Total Fat	*15 g*
Saturated Fat	*6 g*
Cholesterol	*79 mg*
Protein	*24 g*
Carbohydrates	*19 g*
Sodium	*94 mg*
Added Sugar	*0*
Fiber	*2 g*

1. Melt the **margarine** in a large heavy saucepan over high heat. When it bubbles, add the **lamb** and stir to brown well on all sides—about 5 minutes. Using a slotted spoon, transfer the lamb to paper towels to drain.

2. Reduce the heat to moderate, add the **onions,** and brown, stirring often—about 8 minutes. During the last 2 minutes, stir in the **garlic.**

3. Add the **beef broth** to the pan and stir for 1 minute, scraping up any browned bits. Return the lamb to the pan, add the **dill** and **pepper,** cover, and simmer for 20 minutes.

4. Add the **carrots** and **potatoes** and bring to a boil. Cover, reduce the heat, and simmer for 15 minutes.

5. Blend the **flour** with enough of the hot cooking liquid to make a smooth paste, add to the lamb mixture, and cook, stirring, until slightly thickened—about 3 minutes.

6. Add the **green beans,** cover, and simmer about 5 minutes or until the beans are tender but still crisp. Serves 4.

Stir-fried Lamb, Asparagus, and Sweet Red Pepper

Preparation: **10 min.**, plus 30 min. marination   Cooking: **10 min.**   FAT SUGAR SODIUM

This dish is wonderfully quick to make, especially if you cut up the lamb and vegetables ahead of time, wrap them separately, then refrigerate until ready to use. Save the tough asparagus stem ends for soup.

2 **tablespoons minced fresh ginger or 1 teaspoon ground ginger**
2 **cloves garlic, minced**
2 **tablespoons reduced-sodium soy sauce**
2 **tablespoons dry sherry**
2 **tablespoons Oriental sesame or peanut oil**
1 **pound boneless lean lamb shoulder, cut into ¼"x ½"x 1" strips**
1 **pound asparagus, tough stems removed, or 1 package (10 ounces) frozen asparagus, cut at an angle into 1-inch lengths**
1 **medium-size Spanish onion, quartered and sliced thin**
1 **medium-size sweet red pepper, cored, seeded, and sliced lengthwise into strips about ¼ inch wide**
½ **teaspoon red pepper flakes**
1 **teaspoon cornstarch blended with ¼ cup low-sodium beef broth**

1. In a small bowl, combine the **ginger, garlic, soy sauce, sherry,** and 1 teaspoon of the **sesame oil.** Add the **lamb,** tossing it to coat with the marinade, and let stand for 30 minutes.
2. Set a wok or heavy 12-inch skillet over high heat, add 1 tablespoon of the remaining sesame oil, and heat about 1 minute or until ripples appear. Add the **asparagus** and stir-fry over high heat for 3 minutes. Add the **onion** and **sweet red pepper** and stir-fry 1 minute more. Cover and steam for 1 minute. Using a slotted spoon, transfer all the vegetables to a large platter.
3. Add the remaining 2 teaspoons sesame oil to the wok, add the lamb and all the marinade, sprinkle with the **red pepper flakes,** and stir-fry over high heat for 2 minutes. Blend in the **cornstarch−beef broth** mixture and stir until thickened and clear—about 1 minute.
4. Return the vegetables to the wok and toss lightly about 30 seconds. Serves 4.

One Serving:			
Calories	276	Protein	24 g
Total Fat	16 g	Carbohydrates	9 g
Saturated Fat	6 g	Sodium	381 mg
Cholesterol	79 mg	Added Sugar	0
		Fiber	1 g

Curried Lamb

Preparation: **20 min.** Cooking: **45 min.**   FAT SUGAR SODIUM

Serve this especially colorful curry over brown rice and garnish with shredded carrot.

1 **tablespoon unsalted margarine**
1 **pound boneless lean lamb shoulder, cut into ¾-inch cubes**
1 **medium-size yellow onion, sliced thin**
½ **small stalk celery, sliced thin**
1 **clove garlic, minced**
½ **small carrot, peeled and shredded**
¼ **cup unsweetened apple juice**
1 **tablespoon curry powder**
½ **teaspoon each ground cumin and coriander**
¼ **teaspoon ground cardamom**
⅛ **teaspoon cayenne pepper**
1 **firm cooking apple, unpeeled, cored, and cut into ¾-inch cubes**
1 **small zucchini (about ¼ pound), sliced into 1-inch rounds**
½ **cup plain low-fat yogurt**

1. Melt the **margarine** in a heavy 12-inch skillet over moderately high heat. Add the **lamb** and brown well on all sides, about 5 minutes. Using a slotted spoon, transfer the lamb to paper towels to drain.
2. Add the **onion, celery,** and **garlic** to the skillet, reduce the heat to moderate and cook, uncovered, until soft—about 5 minutes.
3. Return the lamb to the skillet and add the **carrot, apple juice, curry powder, cumin, coriander, cardamom,** and **cayenne pepper.** Cover and simmer over low heat for 30 minutes or until the lamb is tender.
4. Add the **apple** and **zucchini,** cover, and simmer until crisp-tender—about 5 minutes longer.
5. Blend in the **yogurt** and heat through; do not boil or the yogurt will curdle. Serves 4.

One Serving:			
Calories	222	Protein	25 g
Total Fat	7 g	Carbohydrates	14 g
Saturated Fat	4 g	Sodium	108 mg
Cholesterol	81 mg	Added Sugar	0
		Fiber	1 g

Veal Shanks Italian Style

This classic Milanese dish, called ossobuco, *is ideal for a dinner party because it requires virtually no last-minute attention.*

FAT SUGAR SODIUM

2 tablespoons unsalted margarine

4 veal shank crosscuts (2 to 2¼ pounds)

1 medium-size yellow onion, chopped

1 medium-size carrot, chopped

1 medium-size stalk celery, chopped

3 cloves garlic, minced

1 cup dry white wine

1 medium-size ripe tomato, peeled, cored, and chopped

1 bay leaf, crumbled

½ teaspoon each dried basil and thyme, crumbled

¼ teaspoon black pepper

2 tablespoons minced parsley

1½ teaspoons grated lemon rind

Preparation:
25 min.
Cooking:
2 hr. 15 min. (mostly unattended)

One Serving:

Calories	226
Total Fat	10 g
Saturated Fat	5 g
Cholesterol	85 mg
Protein	25 g
Carbohydrates	9 g
Sodium	105 mg
Added Sugar	0
Fiber	1 g

1. In a heavy, deep 12-inch skillet or 4-quart Dutch oven, melt 1 tablespoon of the **margarine** over high heat; when very hot, add the **veal** and brown about 2 minutes on each side. Transfer to a platter.

2. Reduce the heat to moderate; add the remaining margarine, the **onion, carrot, celery,** and half the **garlic** to the skillet, and cook, uncovered, for 5 minutes or until the onion is soft. Add the **wine** and boil, uncovered, stirring occasionally to loosen any browned bits, for 5 minutes or until the liquid has boiled down by half.

3. Return the veal and its juices to the skillet, and add the **tomato, bay leaf, basil, thyme,** and **pepper.** Cover and simmer over moderately low heat for 2 hours or until the meat is tender but not falling off the bones.

4. Meanwhile, combine the **parsley, lemon rind,** and remaining garlic. Add to the skillet just before serving. Serve with noodles or steamed rice. Serves 4.

Veal Cutlets with Lemon and Sage

FAT SUGAR SODIUM

3 tablespoons flour

¼ teaspoon white or black pepper

1 pound veal cutlets, pounded to ¼-inch thickness

2 tablespoons unsalted margarine

½ cup low-sodium beef broth

1 tablespoon lemon juice

2 teaspoons chopped fresh sage or ½ teaspoon dried sage, crumbled

½ lemon, sliced thin

Watercress or parsley (optional)

Preparation:
15 min.
Cooking:
6 min.

One Serving:

Calories	255
Total Fat	15 g
Saturated Fat	5 g
Cholesterol	81 mg
Protein	23 g
Carbohydrates	7 g
Sodium	80 mg
Added Sugar	0
Fiber	0

1. Combine the **flour** and **pepper** on a plate or in a small bowl. Lightly coat the **veal** cutlets with the mixture, shaking off any excess.

2. In a heavy 12-inch skillet, melt the **margarine** over moderately high heat; add the veal and brown about 1 minute on each side. Transfer to a platter.

3. Add the **beef broth, lemon juice,** and **sage** to the skillet, and heat about 1 minute, stirring to loosen any browned bits.

4. Return the veal to the skillet and heat to serving temperature—about 2 minutes. Transfer all to a warm platter, garnish with the **lemon** slices, and if you like, a few sprigs of **watercress** or **parsley.** Serve with rice or noodles and Braised Spinach, page 199. Serves 4.

Veal and Mushroom Paprikash with Yogurt

A stand-in for the usual sour cream, low-fat yogurt reduces the fat content of this veal favorite. The dish is even better if made one day and served the next.

FAT SUGAR SODIUM

1 tablespoon unsalted margarine
1 medium-size onion, chopped fine
1 clove garlic, minced
1 pound mushrooms, sliced thin
1 pound veal cutlets, pounded to ¼-inch thickness and cut into finger-size strips
¼ teaspoon black pepper

⅛ teaspoon each ground mace and dried thyme, crumbled
¼ cup dry white wine or vermouth
1 tablespoon paprika
½ cup plain low-fat yogurt
1 tablespoon finely chopped fresh or freeze-dried chives (optional)

Preparation:
10 min.
Cooking:
9 min.

One Serving:

Calories	265
Total Fat	13 g
Saturated Fat	5 g
Cholesterol	82 mg
Protein	27 g
Carbohydrates	11 g
Sodium	105 mg
Added Sugar	0
Fiber	3 g

1. In a heavy 10-inch skillet, melt the **margarine** over moderately high heat; add the **onion, garlic,** and **mushrooms,** and cook until the mushroom juices are released and have evaporated—5 to 6 minutes.
2. Push the mushroom mixture to one side of the skillet. Raise the heat to high, add the **veal,** and stir-fry quickly until no longer pink—1 to 2 minutes.
3. Lower the heat to moderate, add the **pepper, mace, thyme,** and **wine,** and cook, uncovered, for 2 to 3 minutes or until the liquid has evaporated.
4. In a small bowl, combine the **paprika** and **yogurt,** stir into the skillet, and heat to serving temperature—about 1 to 2 minutes. Do not allow to boil or the yogurt will curdle. *(Note: If the dish is to be reheated and served later, do not add the yogurt-paprika mixture until just before serving.)* Serve over noodles or rice, scattering the **chives** evenly on top, if desired. Spinach-Orange Salad, page 215, makes a nice accompaniment. Serves 4.

Tip: *Be careful not to overcook veal when pan-frying or it will toughen and lose its delicate flavor.*

Herbed Veal with Summer Squash

FAT SUGAR SODIUM

1 tablespoon olive or vegetable oil
½ pound small white onions, peeled
1 pound boneless lean veal shoulder, cut into 1-inch cubes
1 tablespoon flour
¼ teaspoon black pepper
⅓ cup dry white wine or low-sodium beef broth
1 cup low-sodium beef broth
1 tablespoon low-sodium tomato paste

1 teaspoon dried rosemary, crumbled
2 cloves garlic, minced
1 medium-size zucchini (about ½ pound), cut into ½"x ½"x 2" strips
1 medium-size yellow squash (about ½ pound), halved lengthwise, then cut into ½-inch slices
2 tablespoons minced parsley

Preparation:
10 min.
Cooking:
1 hr. 35 min. (mostly unattended)

One Serving:

Calories	297
Total Fat	15 g
Saturated Fat	6 g
Cholesterol	81 mg
Protein	25 g
Carbohydrates	15 g
Sodium	123 mg
Added Sugar	0
Fiber	1 g

1. In a 4-quart Dutch oven, heat the **olive oil** over moderate heat for 1 minute; add the **onions** and cook, stirring, until golden brown—about 5 minutes. Using a slotted spoon, transfer the onions to a platter.
2. Coat the **veal** with the **flour** and sprinkle with the **pepper.** Brown the meat in the casserole over moderately high heat—about 5 minutes. Add the **wine** and boil for 1 minute, then add the onions, **beef broth, tomato paste, rosemary,** and **garlic.** Simmer, covered, for 1¼ hours or until the meat is tender.
3. Add the **zucchini** and **yellow squash** and simmer, covered, for 8 to 10 minutes or until the vegetables are tender but still crisp. Just before serving, stir in the **parsley.** Serves 4.

Poultry

Poultry is more popular today than ever, and for good reason. It can be prepared in almost limitless ways, and as a bonus, the light meat of chicken and turkey is high in protein, low in fat and cholesterol. Roasted stuffed hens, delicately sauced scaloppine, savory pot pies, full-flavored stews, and fluffy soufflés are only a few of the ways to serve poultry, as you can see from the recipes in this section.

Chicken Creole

Chicken with Green Sauce

Preparation: **10 min.**
Cooking: **55 min.** (unattended)

FAT SUGAR SODIUM

Removing the skin after poaching makes this a low-fat dish. Freeze the broth for later use.

1 **medium-size lemon**
1 **whole chicken (2½ to 3 pounds)**
4 **bay leaves**
½ **teaspoon dried rosemary, crumbled**
3 **cloves garlic**
1 **large yellow onion, chopped**
2 **medium-size carrots, peeled and chopped**
8 **parsley sprigs**
For the Green Sauce:
2 **cups parsley sprigs**
2 **cloves garlic, peeled and cooked for 2 minutes in boiling water**
1 **green onion, chopped**
7 **tablespoons chicken broth (reserved from poaching the chicken)**
3 **tablespoons lemon juice**
1 **tablespoon olive oil**
⅛ **teaspoon salt**

1. Prick the **lemon** 20 times with a sharp-pronged fork, then place in the body cavity of the **chicken,** along with 2 of the **bay leaves,** ¼ teaspoon of the **rosemary,** and 2 of the **garlic** cloves. Truss the chicken and place breast side up in a heavy 6-quart Dutch oven; add the remaining bay leaves, rosemary, and garlic, along with the **onion, carrots,** and **parsley.**
2. Add cold water to cover the chicken; bring to a boil over moderate heat. Lower the heat and simmer, uncovered, for 50 minutes or until a leg moves easily in the hip socket.
3. Transfer the chicken to a platter and remove and discard the trussing strings and skin. Strain the broth, reserving 7 tablespoons.
4. To make the green sauce, blend the **parsley, garlic,** and **green onion** in an electric blender or food processor for 10 to 15 seconds. With the motor running, add the reserved **broth, lemon juice, olive oil,** and **salt;** blend 5 seconds more. Serve with the chicken. Serves 4.

One Serving:

Calories	302	Protein	35 g
Total Fat	12 g	Carbohydrates	13 g
Saturated Fat	3 g	Sodium	183 mg
Cholesterol	100 mg	Added Sugar	0
		Fiber	2 g

Roast Chicken Stuffed with Rice and Apricots

Preparation: **20 min.**
Cooking: **1 hr. 45 min.** (mostly unattended)

FAT SUGAR SODIUM

This recipe makes enough to serve eight. For four servings, halve the amount of stuffing and use the leftover chicken to make Chicken with Snow Peas and Peanut Sauce, page 95.

3½ **cups low-sodium chicken broth**
1 **large yellow onion, chopped**
1 **large stalk celery, chopped**
1¼ **cups long-grain rice**
½ **cup dried apricots, chopped**
½ **teaspoon dried thyme, crumbled**
2 **tablespoons lemon juice**
1 **whole chicken (4½ to 5 pounds)**
¼ **teaspoon black pepper**
Nonstick cooking spray

1. Preheat the oven to 375°F. In a medium-size saucepan over moderately low heat, bring 3 cups of the **chicken broth,** the **onion,** and **celery** to a simmer. Cook, covered, for 5 minutes. Stir in the **rice, apricots,** and **thyme,** and cook, covered, for 20 minutes or until all the liquid is absorbed. Stir in 1 tablespoon of the **lemon juice** and set aside.
2. Rub the **chicken** with the remaining lemon juice and **pepper,** and spoon the rice-and-apricot stuffing loosely into the body cavity. Spoon the extra stuffing into a small casserole that has been coated with the **cooking spray;** drizzle with the remaining chicken broth and cover with aluminum foil.
3. Truss the chicken, place breast side up on a greased rack in a 13"x 9"x 2" roasting pan, and roast, uncovered, for 1¼ to 1½ hours or until a leg moves easily in the hip socket. Place the casserole of extra stuffing in the oven for the final 30 minutes of roasting.
4. Remove the chicken, along with the casserole of extra stuffing, from the oven and let stand for 10 minutes. Transfer the chicken to a warm platter and remove the trussing strings. Serve with a green vegetable. Serves 8.

One Serving:

Calories	432	Protein	36 g
Total Fat	16 g	Carbohydrates	32 g
Saturated Fat	5 g	Sodium	128 mg
Cholesterol	104 mg	Added Sugar	0
		Fiber	2 g

Braised Whole Chicken with Green Onion Stuffing

Preparation: **20 min.**
Cooking: **1 hr. 17 min.** (mostly unattended)

FAT SUGAR SODIUM

This recipe is for eight servings.

- 1 whole chicken (4½ to 5 pounds)
- ½ cup finely chopped green onions
- 4 tablespoons minced fresh basil or parsley
- 1¼ teaspoons dried thyme, crumbled
- ¼ teaspoon black pepper
  Nonstick cooking spray
- 1½ teaspoons unsalted margarine
- 1 large yellow onion, chopped fine
- 1 stalk celery, chopped fine
- 3 cloves garlic, minced
- 1 large can (28 ounces) low-sodium tomatoes, puréed with their juice
- 1½ cups low-sodium chicken broth
- ¾ cup dry white wine
- 1 bay leaf
- ¼ teaspoon fennel seeds, crushed

1. Preheat the oven to 450°F. Loosen the breast skin of the **chicken** by gently running your fingertips underneath it. In a small bowl, combine the **green onions, basil,** ¾ teaspoon of the **thyme,** and half of the **pepper** and pat evenly and smoothly under the skin.

2. Truss the chicken, place in an ungreased 13″x 9″x 2″ baking pan, and roast, uncovered, for 30 minutes or until golden brown.

3. Meanwhile, coat a heavy 6-quart Dutch oven with the **cooking spray,** add the **margarine,** and melt over moderate heat. Add the **onion, celery,** and **garlic,** and cook, uncovered, until soft—about 5 minutes. Add the **tomatoes** and **chicken broth.**

4. Reduce the oven temperature to 400°F. Transfer the chicken to the Dutch oven and pour off any fat in the baking pan. Add the **wine** to the baking pan, set over moderate heat, and boil, uncovered, for 1 minute, scraping up any browned bits; pour into the Dutch oven.

5. Add the **bay leaf, fennel seeds,** and the remaining thyme and pepper. Bring to a simmer, cover, place in the oven, and cook for 40 minutes. Transfer the chicken to a warm serving platter.

6. Skim the fat from the sauce, discard the bay leaf, then blend half the sauce for 5 to 10 seconds in an electric blender or food processor. Stir the mixture back into the Dutch oven. Spoon some of the sauce around the chicken and pass the rest. Serves 8.

One Serving:

Calories	339	Protein	34 g
Total Fat	17 g	Carbohydrates	10 g
Saturated Fat	5 g	Sodium	130 mg
Cholesterol	104 mg	Added Sugar	0
		Fiber	1 g

Broiled Chicken with Vinegar and Honey

Preparation: **5 min.** Cooking: **40 min.**

FAT SUGAR SODIUM

Broiling and roasting give this chicken a crisp brown skin. It is equally good when prepared outdoors on the barbecue grill.

- 3 tablespoons cider vinegar
- 1 tablespoon honey
- 2 cloves garlic, minced
- 2 teaspoons minced fresh ginger or ½ teaspoon ground ginger
- 2 teaspoons reduced-sodium soy sauce
- 1 teaspoon Dijon or spicy brown mustard
- 1 whole chicken (2½ to 3 pounds), split lengthwise, with excess fat removed

1. Preheat the broiler. In the jar of an electric blender or food processor, blend the **vinegar, honey, garlic, ginger, soy sauce,** and **mustard** for 10 to 15 seconds.

2. Brush the **chicken** well with the sauce, reserving some of the sauce for basting. Arrange skin side down on a greased rack in a 13″x 9″x 2″ baking pan. Broil 6 inches from the heat for 10 minutes; turn the chicken and broil 10 minutes longer.

3. Transfer the chicken to the oven, lower the oven temperature to 400°F, and roast, uncovered, basting with the remaining sauce, for 20 to 25 minutes or until you can move a leg easily. If the chicken browns too quickly, cover it with aluminum foil.

4. Let the chicken stand at room temperature for 10 minutes before serving. Serves 4.

One Serving:

Calories	322	Protein	34 g
Total Fat	17 g	Carbohydrates	6 g
Saturated Fat	5 g	Sodium	242 mg
Cholesterol	110 mg	Added Sugar	0
		Fiber	0

Chicken with Snow Peas and Peanut Sauce

Brunswick Stew

This thrifty southern mainstay—a complete meal—originated with American Indian women, who used rabbit and squirrel instead of chicken. The stew can be made a day or two ahead and reheated just before serving.

FAT SUGAR SODIUM

1 whole chicken (2½ to 3 pounds), with excess fat removed
5 large sprigs parsley
6 black peppercorns
1 bay leaf, crumbled
4 cups low-sodium chicken broth or water
1½ teaspoons each ground poultry seasoning and sage
2 medium-size carrots, peeled and sliced 1 inch thick
2 large stalks celery, sliced 1 inch thick

2 medium-size all-purpose potatoes, peeled and cut into 1-inch cubes
1 can (14½ ounces) low-sodium tomatoes, with their juice
1 medium-size yellow onion, chopped
1 cup fresh or frozen lima beans
1 cup fresh or frozen whole-kernel corn
½ teaspoon black pepper

Preparation:
25 min.
Cooking:
2 hr.
(mostly unattended)

One Serving:

Calories	357
Total Fat	13 g
Saturated Fat	4 g
Cholesterol	90 mg
Protein	37 g
Carbohydrates	31 g
Sodium	216 mg
Added Sugar	0
Fiber	8 g

1. Place the **chicken** and giblets in a 6-quart Dutch oven. Tie the **parsley, peppercorns,** and **bay leaf** in cheesecloth and add to the pot along with the **chicken broth** and ½ teaspoon each of the **poultry seasoning** and **sage.**

2. Bring to a boil, then adjust the heat so that the liquid bubbles gently; cover and simmer for 1 hour or until the chicken is tender. Transfer the chicken and giblets to a platter; skim any fat from the broth.

3. Add the **carrots, celery, potatoes, tomatoes, onion, lima beans,** and another ½ teaspoon each of the poultry seasoning and sage to the pot; cover and simmer for 30 minutes, stirring occasionally.

4. Meanwhile, remove and discard the chicken skin and bones. Cut the meat and giblets into bite-size pieces, return to the pot, and add the **corn.** Simmer, covered, for 30 minutes, stirring occasionally. Stir in the **pepper** and remaining poultry seasoning and sage. Discard the cheesecloth bag. Ladle into soup bowls and serve with Old-Fashioned Cornbread, page 237, and Confetti Coleslaw, page 211. Serves 4.

Tip: The surest way to extract fat from a stew is to make the dish a day ahead and refrigerate it. The fat will rise to the top and congeal, making it easy to remove.

Chicken with Snow Peas and Peanut Sauce

½ pound fresh snow peas, ends trimmed, or 1 package (6 ounces) frozen snow peas
2 tablespoons peanut butter
2 tablespoons reduced-sodium soy sauce
2 tablespoons cider vinegar
1 teaspoon Oriental sesame or peanut oil
1½ teaspoons minced fresh ginger or ¼ teaspoon ground ginger
1 clove garlic, minced
⅛ teaspoon cayenne pepper or to taste
2 cups cooked chicken cut into matchstick strips
½ cup sliced radishes
½ cup sliced water chestnuts
2 tablespoons sliced green onion

1. In a large saucepan, cook the **snow peas** in boiling unsalted water for 3 minutes or until the peas are tender but still crisp. Drain well and arrange attractively on a medium-size platter.
2. In a large bowl, whisk the **peanut butter, soy sauce, vinegar,** and **sesame oil** until smooth. Stir in the **ginger, garlic,** and **cayenne pepper.** Add the **chicken, radishes,** and **water chestnuts;** toss lightly to mix.
3. Spoon the chicken mixture over the snow peas and sprinkle with the **green onion.** Serves 4.

FAT SUGAR SODIUM

Preparation:
10 min.
Cooking:
3 min.

One Serving:

Calories	*242*
Total Fat	*11 g*
Saturated Fat	*2 g*
Cholesterol	*62 mg*
Protein	*25 g*
Carbohydrates	*11 g*
Sodium	*410 mg*
Added Sugar	*0*
Fiber	*2 g*

Chicken Biriyani

In India, biriyani *is made for special occasions. This quick version, a one-dish meal, is the perfect way to use up leftover chicken or turkey.*

⅔ cup long-grain rice
5 cloves garlic
1 cinnamon stick
1 bay leaf
1 small yellow onion, chopped
1 tablespoon minced fresh ginger or ½ teaspoon ground ginger
1 tablespoon lemon juice
½ teaspoon each ground cumin, coriander, and turmeric
¼ teaspoon ground cinnamon
⅛ teaspoon each ground cloves, cardamom, and black pepper
1 cup plain low-fat yogurt
3 cups cubed cooked light chicken or turkey meat
2 cups shredded red cabbage
1 small tart green apple, cored and cubed but not peeled

1. Preheat the oven to 350°F. Cook the **rice** according to package directions, omitting the salt but adding 2 of the **garlic cloves,** the **cinnamon stick,** and **bay leaf.** When the rice is done, discard the garlic, cinnamon, and bay leaf.
2. Meanwhile, in an electric blender or food processor, make a paste of the **onion, ginger, lemon juice, cumin, coriander, turmeric, cinnamon, cloves, cardamom, pepper,** and remaining garlic by blending for 10 to 15 seconds.
3. Transfer the paste to a large bowl and blend in the **yogurt.** Add the **chicken,** tossing to coat well.
4. Place the rice in an ungreased shallow 1½-quart casserole, spoon the chicken mixture on top, cover, and bake for 35 minutes. Toward the end of the baking period, steam the **red cabbage** for 10 minutes over boiling water until it is tender but still crisp.
5. Cluster the red cabbage and **apple** in the center of the *biriyani.* Serve from the casserole. Serves 4.

FAT SUGAR SODIUM

Preparation:
15 min.
Cooking:
55 min. (mostly unattended)

One Serving:

Calories	*370*
Total Fat	*5 g*
Saturated Fat	*2 g*
Cholesterol	*94 mg*
Protein	*39 g*
Carbohydrates	*40 g*
Sodium	*127 mg*
Added Sugar	*0*
Fiber	*1 g*

Tip: If you don't have exotic spices on hand for Indian dishes, omit them entirely and substitute 1½ teaspoons good-quality curry powder for a recipe that serves 4.

Chicken Pot Pie

A green salad on the side makes this a complete meal.

FAT SUGAR SODIUM

1 chicken (2½ to 3 pounds), cut into serving pieces and skinned
Nonstick cooking spray
¼ pound small white onions, peeled
2 medium-size carrots, peeled and sliced
1 medium-size stalk celery, sliced
2 tablespoons flour
⅓ cup dry white wine or water
2 cups low-sodium chicken broth
1 bay leaf

½ teaspoon each dried sage and thyme, crumbled
¼ teaspoon black pepper
1 medium-size zucchini (about ½ pound), sliced
4 medium-size baking potatoes (about 1½ pounds), peeled and quartered
1 tablespoon unsalted margarine
¼ cup skim milk
⅓ cup plain low-fat yogurt
⅛ teaspoon paprika

Preparation:
15 min.
Cooking:
1 hr. 5 min. (mostly unattended)

One Serving:

Calories	387
Total Fat	14 g
Saturated Fat	4 g
Cholesterol	92 mg
Protein	36 g
Carbohydrates	34 g
Sodium	167 mg
Added Sugar	0
Fiber	3 g

1. Place the **chicken** in a heavy 6-quart Dutch oven that has been coated with the **cooking spray.** Cook over moderate heat, turning often, for 5 minutes.

2. Add the **onions, carrots,** and **celery;** cover and cook for 10 minutes. Blend in the **flour,** then add the **wine, chicken broth, bay leaf, sage, thyme,** and **pepper.** Cover and simmer for 20 minutes.

3. Lift the chicken from the pot. Remove the meat from the bones and cut into bite-size pieces. Return the chicken meat to the pot, along with the **zucchini,** then cover and simmer for 10 minutes.

4. Meanwhile, boil the **potatoes** in enough unsalted water to cover until tender—20 to 25 minutes. Drain well, then mash with the **margarine** and the **milk;** set aside.

5. Preheat the oven to 400°F. Using a slotted spoon, transfer the chicken and vegetables to a 2-quart casserole. Whisk the **yogurt** into the cooking liquid, then strain over the chicken. Spoon or pipe the mashed potatoes around the edge of the casserole. Sprinkle with the **paprika** and bake, uncovered, for 20 minutes or until bubbly. Serves 4.

Tip: To peel pearl onions, cut a ⅛-inch-deep X in the root ends with a sharp knife, then boil for about 2 minutes. The skins will slip off easily.

Chicken Pot Pie

Chicken Tetrazzini with Spaghetti Squash

1 spaghetti squash (about 3 pounds)
1 tablespoon unsalted margarine
1 medium-size yellow onion, chopped fine
1 medium-size stalk celery, sliced thin
⅛ teaspoon black pepper
3 tablespoons flour

2 cups low-sodium chicken broth
1 cup skim milk
1 bay leaf
2 tablespoons sour cream
2 tablespoons minced parsley
1 tablespoon lemon juice
2 cups cubed cooked chicken or turkey meat
2 tablespoons fine dry bread crumbs

FAT SUGAR SODIUM

Preparation:
30 min.
Cooking:
1½ hr. (mostly unattended)

One Serving:

Calories	*329*
Total Fat	*14 g*
Saturated Fat	*4 g*
Cholesterol	*67 mg*
Protein	*27 g*
Carbohydrates	*29 g*
Sodium	*196 mg*
Added Sugar	*0*
Fiber	*0*

1. Preheat the oven to 350°F. Slash the **squash** in several places with a small knife. Place the squash on an ungreased baking sheet and bake for 1 hour or until it can be pierced easily with a fork. Cool for 15 minutes.

2. Meanwhile, in a medium-size heavy saucepan, melt the **margarine** over moderate heat. Add the **onion, celery,** and **pepper,** and cook, uncovered, until the onion is soft—about 5 minutes.

3. Slowly add the **flour** to the vegetables and stir for 1 minute. Add the **chicken broth, milk,** and **bay leaf,** and cook, uncovered, over moderately low heat, stirring occasionally, for 20 minutes. Discard the bay leaf; stir in the **sour cream, parsley,** and **lemon juice,** and remove from the heat.

4. Halve the spaghetti squash lengthwise and remove the seeds. Using a fork, scrape the flesh into an ungreased shallow 1½-quart casserole, smoothing into an even layer; cover with the **chicken,** then the sauce, and top with the **bread crumbs.** Bake, uncovered, for 30 minutes or until bubbly. Serve with Green Beans and Cherry Tomatoes, page 175. Serves 4.

Tandoori Chicken

This East Indian dish requires little attention, yet is always a hit with dinner guests. Marinate the chicken overnight to prepare the next day.

½ cup plain low-fat yogurt
1 medium-size yellow onion, chopped
1 tablespoon minced fresh ginger or ¼ teaspoon ground ginger
2 cloves garlic, minced
1 tablespoon lime juice
1½ teaspoons ground coriander

½ teaspoon ground cumin
¼ teaspoon each ground cardamom and turmeric
⅛ teaspoon cayenne pepper
1 chicken (2½ to 3 pounds), quartered and skinned
Lime slices (optional)

FAT SUGAR SODIUM

Preparation:
10 min., plus 4 hr. marination
Cooking:
26 min.

One Serving:

Calories	*208*
Total Fat	*8 g*
Saturated Fat	*2 g*
Cholesterol	*91 mg*
Protein	*30 g*
Carbohydrates	*2 g*
Sodium	*99 mg*
Added Sugar	*0*
Fiber	*0*

1. In an electric blender or food processor, combine the **yogurt, onion, ginger, garlic, lime juice, coriander, cumin, cardamom, turmeric,** and **cayenne pepper;** whirl for 30 seconds. Place the **chicken** in a 13"x 9"x 2" baking pan, add the yogurt mixture, then cover and refrigerate at least 4 hours, turning occasionally.

2. Preheat the broiler and lightly grease the rack. Place the chicken on the rack and broil 7 inches from the heat for 8 minutes or until browned; turn and broil 8 minutes longer.

3. Reduce the heat to 325°F. Transfer the chicken to a greased 13"x 9"x 2" baking pan, cover with foil, and bake in the oven about 10 minutes or until the juices run clear when the chicken is pierced with a sharp knife.

4. Transfer to a warm platter and garnish, if desired, with **lime** slices. Serve with Curried Brown Rice with Apricots, page 168. Serves 4.

Oven-Fried Chicken

To halve this low-fat version of fried chicken, simply use one whole chicken breast, split, and half of the other ingredients.

FAT SUGAR SODIUM

1 **chicken (2½ to 3 pounds), cut into serving pieces and skinned**

½ **cup plain low-fat yogurt**

3 **cloves garlic, minced**

1 **teaspoon each dried thyme and marjoram, crumbled**

2 **cups very fine whole wheat bread crumbs (4 slices)**

¼ **cup minced parsley**

3 **tablespoons grated Parmesan cheese**

1 **tablespoon unsalted margarine**

Preparation:
15 min., plus 20 min. refrigeration
Cooking:
50 min. (mostly unattended)

1. Pat the **chicken** pieces dry. In a medium-size bowl, combine the **yogurt, garlic, thyme,** and **marjoram;** set aside. In a 9-inch pie pan, toss the **bread crumbs** with the **parsley** and **cheese** and set aside.

2. Dip the chicken first into the yogurt mixture, using a spoon to coat each piece completely, then roll in the crumb mixture. Place the pieces on a rack and let stand, uncovered, in the refrigerator for at least 20 minutes; this will help the breading to stick.

3. Preheat the oven to 375°F. In a heavy 12-inch nonstick skillet, heat the **margarine** over moderate heat until bubbly. Brown the chicken pieces about 5 minutes on each side, taking care not to dislodge the crumb coating.

4. As the chicken pieces brown, transfer them to a 13"x 9"x 2" baking pan lined with aluminum foil, arranging them in one layer. Bake, uncovered, for 30 minutes or until the chicken is fork-tender. Serves 4.

One Serving:

Calories	*315*
Total Fat	*12 g*
Saturated Fat	*4 g*
Cholesterol	*96 mg*
Protein	*35 g*
Carbohydrates	*12 g*
Sodium	*299 mg*
Added Sugar	*0*
Fiber	*1 g*

Tip: *To make bread crumbs, tear up bread slices and whirl the pieces in a blender.*

Chicken Fricassee

1 **tablespoon vegetable oil**

1 **chicken (2½ to 3 pounds), cut into serving pieces and skinned**

8 **small white onions, peeled**

8 **cloves garlic**

1 **cup low-sodium chicken broth**

2 **tablespoons bourbon or orange juice**

½ **teaspoon dried tarragon, crumbled**

Nonstick cooking spray

2 **medium-size carrots, peeled and sliced ½ inch thick**

6 **ounces mushrooms, quartered**

2 **teaspoons lemon juice**

¼ **teaspoon black pepper**

½ **cup plain low-fat yogurt**

FAT SUGAR SODIUM

Preparation:
15 min.
Cooking:
44 min. (mostly unattended)

1. Heat the **vegetable oil** in a heavy 12-inch skillet over moderate heat. Add the **chicken** and cook, turning occasionally, until no longer pink on the outside— about 5 minutes. Using a slotted spoon, transfer the chicken to a bowl.

2. In the same skillet, cook the **onions** and **garlic** until soft—about 5 minutes.

3. Add the **chicken broth, bourbon,** and **tarragon** to the skillet, and cook, uncovered, for 2 minutes. Return the chicken to the skillet, cover, and simmer for 10 minutes. Transfer the breasts to a platter and cook the remaining chicken 15 minutes longer or until fork-tender.

4. Meanwhile, coat a heavy 10-inch skillet with the **cooking spray** and set over moderate heat for 30 seconds; add the **carrots** and **mushrooms** and cook, uncovered, until the mushrooms are lightly colored—4 to 5 minutes.

5. Add the vegetables to the chicken mixture along with the **lemon juice, pepper,** and chicken breasts; bring just to serving temperature—about 5 minutes. Stir in the **yogurt** and heat (do not boil) 1 minute longer. Serves 4.

One Serving:

Calories	*284*
Total Fat	*13 g*
Saturated Fat	*4 g*
Cholesterol	*92 mg*
Protein	*33 g*
Carbohydrates	*12 g*
Sodium	*138 mg*
Added Sugar	*0*
Fiber	*2 g*

Oven-Fried Chicken

Chicken with Herb Dumplings

1 chicken (2½ to 3 pounds), cut into serving pieces and skinned
1 large stalk celery, sliced
1 large yellow onion, sliced
1 small carrot, peeled and sliced
2 cloves garlic, minced
4 cups low-sodium chicken broth
1 cup water
½ teaspoon each dill weed and dried thyme, crumbled
4 whole cloves

2 tablespoons cornstarch blended with ¼ cup plain low-fat yogurt
For the Dumplings:
⅔ cup sifted all-purpose flour
1¼ teaspoons baking powder
⅛ teaspoon salt
2 tablespoons snipped fresh dill or minced parsley
2 teaspoons unsalted margarine
¼ to ⅓ cup ice water

FAT SUGAR SODIUM

Preparation:
15 min.
Cooking:
55 min. (mostly unattended)

One Serving:

Calories	*352*
Total Fat	*15 g*
Saturated Fat	*5 g*
Cholesterol	*91 mg*
Protein	*36 g*
Carbohydrates	*25 g*
Sodium	*375 mg*
Added Sugar	*0*
Fiber	*1 g*

Tip: *Before cooking chicken, rinse it in cold water to reduce the bacteria. For the same reason, wash your hands, the working surface, and any utensils used with the chicken.*

1. In a heavy 6-quart Dutch oven, simmer the **chicken, celery, onion, carrot, garlic, chicken broth, water, dill weed, thyme,** and **cloves,** covered, for 30 minutes. Let stand to cool.

2. Remove the meat from the bones and cut into bite-size pieces. Strain the broth and return it to the pot. Bring to a boil over moderate heat, then remove from the heat and whisk in the **cornstarch-yogurt** mixture. Cook, stirring, for 1 minute or until slightly thickened. (Do not allow the sauce to boil or the yogurt will curdle.) Return the chicken to the pot and keep warm.

3. For the dumplings, combine the **flour, baking powder, salt,** and fresh **dill** in a medium-size bowl. Cut in the **margarine** with a pastry blender or two knives until the mixture resembles coarse meal. Stir in just enough **ice water** to make a light but workable dough. Shape into 12 balls.

4. Bring the chicken to a boil, drop in the dumplings, spacing them evenly, and lower the heat so that the broth bubbles gently. Cover and cook for 20 minutes. Ladle into soup plates, and serve with Roasted Vegetable Salad, page 216. Serves 4.

Sweet-and-Sour Apricot Chicken

2 tablespoons lemon juice
2 teaspoons olive oil
2 cloves garlic, minced
1 chicken (2½ to 3 pounds), cut into serving pieces and skinned
¼ teaspoon black pepper
8 medium-size dried apricots (about 2 ounces)

¾ cup orange juice
1 teaspoon light brown sugar
1 tablespoon cider vinegar
2 teaspoons minced fresh ginger or ¼ teaspoon ground ginger
1 teaspoon Dijon or spicy brown mustard

FAT **SUGAR** **SODIUM**

Preparation:
12 min.
Cooking:
51 min.

One Serving:

Calories	*279*
Total Fat	*10 g*
Saturated Fat	*3 g*
Cholesterol	*90 mg*
Protein	*30 g*
Carbohydrates	*16 g*
Sodium	*129 mg*
Added Sugar	*4 Cal*
Fiber	*1 g*

Tip: *If you use salt substitutes, add them just before serving a dish, since cooking can dull much of their taste.*

1. Preheat the oven to 425°F. In a small bowl, combine the **lemon juice, olive oil,** and half the **garlic.** Rub the **chicken** with this mixture and sprinkle with the **pepper.**

2. Arrange the chicken in a single layer on a greased rack in a shallow roasting pan; place in the oven and roast, uncovered, for 30 minutes.

3. Meanwhile, in a small saucepan, simmer the **apricots** in the **orange juice,** uncovered, for 10 minutes or until the apricots are tender. Stir in the **sugar, vinegar, ginger, mustard,** and remaining garlic; simmer 2 minutes longer. Whirl the mixture in an electric blender or food processor for 15 seconds.

4. Coat one side of the chicken with the apricot glaze and roast for 10 more minutes. Turn and coat the other side and roast 10 minutes longer or until the chicken is fork-tender. Raise the oven temperature to broil.

5. Transfer the chicken to the broiler and broil about 5 inches from the heat for 1 to 2 minutes or until tipped with brown. Arrange on a heated platter and serve with a green vegetable. Serves 4.

Chicken Laredo

1 chicken (2½ to 3 pounds), cut into serving pieces and skinned
2 tablespoons olive or vegetable oil
1 medium-size yellow onion, chopped fine
1 small sweet green pepper, cored, seeded, and chopped fine
1 small sweet red pepper, cored, seeded, and chopped fine
1 clove garlic, minced

2 teaspoons flour
¼ teaspoon ground cumin
1 pound ripe tomatoes, peeled, cored, and chopped, or 1 can (14½ ounces) crushed low-sodium tomatoes, with their juice
⅛ teaspoon each black pepper and cayenne pepper
1 tablespoon minced parsley

FAT **SUGAR** **SODIUM**

Preparation:
10 min.
Cooking:
52 min. (mostly unattended)

One Serving:

Calories	*285*
Total Fat	*15 g*
Saturated Fat	*3 g*
Cholesterol	*90 mg*
Protein	*31 g*
Carbohydrates	*7 g*
Sodium	*94 mg*
Added Sugar	*0*
Fiber	*1 g*

1. Preheat the broiler and lightly grease the rack. Broil the **chicken** 5 to 6 inches from the heat for 5 minutes. Turn and broil 5 minutes longer or until no longer pink on the outside.

2. Meanwhile, in a heavy 12-inch skillet, heat the **olive oil** over moderate heat for 1 minute. Add the **onion, green pepper, red pepper,** and **garlic,** and cook, uncovered, until soft—about 5 minutes. Blend in the **flour** and **cumin** and cook, stirring, for 1 minute. Add the **tomatoes, black pepper,** and **cayenne pepper** and cook for 5 minutes, stirring frequently.

3. Add the chicken legs, thighs, wings, and back to the skillet, spooning the sauce on top. Cover and simmer for 15 minutes; add the breasts and cook for another 10 minutes or until all the pieces are fork-tender. Uncover and simmer 5 minutes longer to thicken the sauce. Transfer the chicken and sauce to a warm platter and sprinkle with the **parsley.** Serves 4.

Country Captain

Here is a trimmed-down, slimmed-down version of an old southern classic.

FAT SUGAR SODIUM

1 tablespoon unsalted margarine
1 chicken (2½ to 3 pounds), cut into serving pieces and skinned
1 medium-size yellow onion, chopped fine
½ medium-size sweet green pepper, cored, seeded, and chopped fine
1 clove garlic, minced
1 tablespoon curry powder

1 can (14½ ounces) crushed low-sodium tomatoes, with their juice
1 teaspoon lemon juice
½ teaspoon dried thyme, crumbled
¼ teaspoon black pepper
⅓ cup raisins
2 tablespoons toasted slivered almonds

Preparation:
10 min.
Cooking:
50 min. (mostly unattended)

One Serving:

Calories	316
Total Fat	13 g
Saturated Fat	3 g
Cholesterol	90 mg
Protein	32 g
Carbohydrates	18 g
Sodium	105 mg
Added Sugar	0
Fiber	2 g

1. In a heavy 12-inch skillet, melt the **margarine** over moderate heat. Add the **chicken** and cook, turning occasionally, until no longer pink on the outside—about 5 minutes. Transfer to a platter.

2. Add the **onion, green pepper, garlic,** and **curry powder** to the skillet and cook, stirring frequently, until the onion is soft—about 5 minutes. Stir in the **tomatoes, lemon juice, thyme,** and **black pepper.**

3. Adjust the heat so that the mixture bubbles gently, then cook, uncovered, for 10 minutes. Return the legs, thighs, and back to the skillet, reduce the heat to low, cover, and cook for 15 minutes; add the breasts and cook for 10 minutes or until all the pieces are fork-tender. Stir in the **raisins** and cook, uncovered, 5 minutes longer. Transfer the chicken to a heated deep platter or shallow bowl and scatter the **almonds** on top. Accompany with fluffy boiled rice. Serves 4.

Country Captain

Chicken, Artichoke, and Rice Casserole

Preparation: **15 min.**
Cooking: **56 min.** (mostly unattended)

FAT SUGAR SODIUM

With a green salad on the side, this well-balanced casserole is the ideal one-dish meal for a luncheon or dinner party.

- 1 **chicken (2½ to 3 pounds), cut into serving pieces and skinned**
- ¼ **teaspoon black pepper**
   Nonstick cooking spray
- 1½ **teaspoons olive or vegetable oil**
- 1 **medium-size yellow onion, chopped fine**
- 2 **cloves garlic, minced**
- ½ **cup long-grain rice**
- ⅓ **cup dry white wine**
- ¾ **cup low-sodium chicken broth**
- 1 **teaspoon grated lemon rind**
- 1 **bay leaf**
- ½ **teaspoon each dried thyme and rosemary, crumbled**
- 1 **package (9 ounces) frozen artichoke hearts, cooked and drained**
- 1 **tablespoon minced parsley**

1. Preheat the oven to 350°F. Sprinkle the **chicken** with the **pepper.** Lightly coat a 4-quart Dutch oven with the **cooking spray,** add the **olive oil,** and set over moderate heat for 30 seconds. Add the chicken and cook, turning occasionally, until no longer pink on the outside—about 5 minutes. Transfer to a platter and set aside.

2. Add the **onion** to the casserole and cook, uncovered, until soft—about 5 minutes; stir in the **garlic** and **rice,** and cook, stirring, for 1 minute. Add the **wine, chicken broth, lemon rind, bay leaf, thyme,** and **rosemary,** and bring to a simmer.

3. Return the chicken to the Dutch oven and add the **artichoke hearts,** distributing them evenly. Cover with a piece of wax paper, then the lid. Bake for 45 to 50 minutes or until the chicken is fork-tender and the rice fluffy. Discard the bay leaf and sprinkle with the **parsley.** Serves 4.

One Serving:

Calories	341	Protein	33 g
Total Fat	11 g	Carbohydrates	28 g
Saturated Fat	3 g	Sodium	130 mg
Cholesterol	90 mg	Added Sugar	0
		Fiber	1 g

Chicken Burritos

Chicken Gardener's Style

Use any herbs you like in this recipe. Try marjoram and basil or your own favorite combination. A tossed green salad will complete the meal.

FAT SUGAR SODIUM

Nonstick cooking spray
1 chicken (2½ to 3 pounds), cut into serving pieces and skinned
8 small new potatoes, scrubbed
8 small white onions, peeled
4 medium-size carrots, peeled and cut into 3-inch pieces
1½ cups low-sodium chicken broth
½ cup dry white wine

1 tablespoon lemon juice
3 cloves garlic, minced
1 teaspoon dried oregano, crumbled
½ teaspoon dried thyme, crumbled
¼ teaspoon black pepper
2 tablespoons minced parsley

Preparation:
15 min.
Cooking:
40 min. (mostly unattended)

One Serving:

Calories	342
Total Fat	10 g
Saturated Fat	3 g
Cholesterol	90 mg
Protein	34 g
Carbohydrates	32 g
Sodium	144 mg
Added Sugar	0
Fiber	3 g

1. Preheat the oven to 500°F. Coat a 13"x 9"x 2" baking pan with the **cooking spray.** Arrange the **chicken, potatoes, onions,** and **carrots** in the pan.
2. Blend the **chicken broth, wine,** and **lemon juice** and pour over the chicken and vegetables; then sprinkle with the **garlic, oregano, thyme,** and **pepper.**
3. Bake, uncovered, for 40 to 45 minutes, turning the chicken and vegetables occasionally and basting with the pan juices until the chicken is fork-tender. If the juices evaporate too quickly during baking, add more chicken broth.
4. Transfer the chicken to a warm platter, arrange the vegetables around it, and sprinkle with the **parsley.** Serves 4.

Chicken Burritos

FAT SUGAR SODIUM

1 tablespoon corn or peanut oil
4 boned chicken thighs (about 1 pound), skinned and cut into ½-inch cubes
1 large yellow onion, chopped fine
3 cloves garlic, minced
2 tablespoons flour
2 teaspoons chili powder

1 teaspoon ground cumin
½ cup low-sodium chicken broth
1 cup buttermilk
1 can (4 ounces) chopped green chilies, drained
2 teaspoons low-sodium tomato paste
8 6-inch flour tortillas

Preparation:
6 min.
Cooking:
22 min.

One Serving:

Calories	379
Total Fat	14 g
Saturated Fat	3 g
Cholesterol	97 mg
Protein	30 g
Carbohydrates	37 g
Sodium	638 mg
Added Sugar	0
Fiber	0

Tip: *Flour tortillas have less flavor than those made from corn but are easier to fill and roll without cracking.*

1. Preheat the oven to 375°F. In a heavy 10-inch skillet, heat the **corn oil** over moderate heat for 1 minute. Add the **chicken** and cook, turning occasionally, until no longer pink on the outside—about 5 minutes. Using a slotted spoon, transfer the chicken to a bowl.
2. In the same skillet, cook the **onion** and **garlic,** uncovered, until soft—about 5 minutes. Blend in the **flour, chili powder,** and **cumin,** and cook, stirring constantly, for 2 minutes.
3. Stir in the **chicken broth, buttermilk, chilies,** and **tomato paste**. Reduce the heat to low and simmer, uncovered, for 4 to 5 minutes or until slightly thickened. Return the chicken to the skillet and stir.
4. Place a scant ½ cup of the chicken mixture on the lower third of each **tortilla** and roll it up like a cigar. Place seam side down in an ungreased 13"x 9"x 2" baking pan and drizzle any remaining filling down the center.
5. Bake, uncovered, for 5 minutes. Serves 4.

Tangy Barbecued Chicken Thighs

You can make the dish for two; use one cup of canned tomatoes and halve the other ingredients.

FAT SUGAR SODIUM

1 teaspoon olive or vegetable oil
1 medium-size yellow onion, chopped
2 cloves garlic, minced
1 can (1 pound) low-sodium tomatoes, with their juice
2 tablespoons cider vinegar

2 tablespoons dark molasses
1 tablespoon prepared yellow mustard
½ teaspoon chili powder
⅛ teaspoon cayenne pepper
8 chicken thighs (about 2 pounds), skinned

Preparation:
15 min., plus 4 hr. marination
Cooking:
56 min.

One Serving:

Calories	*242*
Total Fat	*7 g*
Saturated Fat	*2 g*
Cholesterol	*121 mg*
Protein	*30 g*
Carbohydrates	*13 g*
Sodium	*202 mg*
Added Sugar	*22 Cal*
Fiber	*1 g*

1. In a medium-size heavy saucepan, heat the **olive oil** over moderate heat for 1 minute; add the **onion** and **garlic** and cook, uncovered, until soft—about 5 minutes. Add the **tomatoes, vinegar, molasses, mustard, chili powder,** and **cayenne pepper;** simmer, uncovered, for 20 minutes or until the mixture is slightly thickened. Cool about 20 minutes, then whirl for 30 seconds in an electric blender or food processor.
2. Pour the sauce into a large, shallow enameled or glass bowl, add the **chicken** thighs, and turn well to coat. Cover and refrigerate at least 4 hours, turning the thighs occasionally.
3. Preheat the broiler and lightly grease the rack. Broil the chicken 7 to 9 inches from the heat for 15 minutes, basting occasionally with the sauce. Turn and broil 15 minutes longer, basting occasionally, until browned. Serve the chicken with rice and pass any remaining sauce. Serves 4.

Chicken with Cabbage and Apples

This is an old German dish that's equally good made with pork.

FAT SUGAR SODIUM

2 whole chicken breasts (about 2 pounds), halved and skinned
½ teaspoon black pepper
2 tablespoons unsalted margarine
2 firm cooking apples, cored and cubed but not peeled
1 small cabbage (about 1 pound), cut into thick slices (about 3 cups)

2 medium-size carrots, peeled, quartered lengthwise, then cut into 2-inch lengths
1 medium-size yellow onion, sliced
¼ cup unsweetened apple juice
1 tablespoon light brown sugar
1½ teaspoons cider vinegar
¼ teaspoon caraway seeds

Preparation:
15 min.
Cooking:
35 min.

One Serving:

Calories	*310*
Total Fat	*8 g*
Saturated Fat	*2 g*
Cholesterol	*86 mg*
Protein	*35 g*
Carbohydrates	*24 g*
Sodium	*120 mg*
Added Sugar	*9 Cal*
Fiber	*3 g*

1. Sprinkle the **chicken** breasts with the **pepper.** In a heavy 12-inch skillet, melt 1 tablespoon of the **margarine** over moderately high heat. Add the breasts and cook for 2½ minutes on each side; transfer to a platter.
2. Reduce the heat to moderate, add the **apples,** and cook, stirring frequently, until golden—about 5 minutes. Transfer to the platter with the chicken.
3. Melt the remaining margarine in the skillet and add the **cabbage, carrots,** and **onion;** cook, stirring, until tender but still crisp—about 5 minutes. Stir in the **apple juice, brown sugar, vinegar,** and **caraway seeds.**
4. Return the chicken and half of the apples to the skillet. Reduce the heat to low; cover and simmer for 20 minutes. Transfer the chicken to a warm platter, ladle the sauce over it, and garnish with the reserved apples. Serves 4.

Tip: For cooking, use firm, crisp apples such as Rome Beauty, Golden Delicious, or Winesap.

Caribbean Lime Chicken

Caribbean Lime Chicken

1 medium-size lime
2 tablespoons dark rum or orange juice
3 cloves garlic, sliced thin
2 tablespoons minced fresh ginger or ½ teaspoon ground
1 tablespoon hot red pepper sauce
2 whole chicken breasts (about 2 pounds), halved and skinned

Nonstick cooking spray
1 large yellow onion, chopped
1 can (1 pound) low-sodium tomatoes, with their juice
2 tablespoons molasses
1 cinnamon stick
1 banana, sliced and dipped in lime or lemon juice to prevent darkening (optional)

Preparation:
8 min., plus 8 hr. marination
Cooking:
36 min. (mostly unattended)

One Serving:

Calories	258
Total Fat	3 g
Saturated Fat	1 g
Cholesterol	86 mg
Protein	36 g
Carbohydrates	23 g
Sodium	221 mg
Added Sugar	22 Cal
Fiber	2 g

Tip: *Lime, lemon, and orange peels may have a residue of insecticide. Scrub them under running water before grating.*

1. Using a swivel-bladed vegetable peeler, remove the peel from half of the **lime** and set aside. Juice the lime into a shallow glass bowl.

2. Add the lime peel to the lime juice, along with the **rum, garlic, ginger,** and **red pepper sauce.** Add the **chicken,** tossing to coat well. Cover and refrigerate for 8 hours or overnight, turning the chicken in the marinade several times.

3. Lightly coat a heavy 12-inch skillet with the **cooking spray** and set over moderate heat for 30 seconds. Add the chicken, reserving the marinade, and cook about 2½ minutes on each side. Transfer to a platter.

4. In the same skillet, cook the **onion,** uncovered, over moderate heat until soft—about 5 minutes. Purée the **tomatoes** in an electric blender or food processor and add to the skillet, along with the **molasses, cinnamon stick,** reserved marinade, and chicken. Reduce the heat to low and simmer, uncovered, for 20 minutes. Transfer the chicken to a platter.

5. Raise the heat under the skillet to high and boil the sauce, uncovered, until slightly thickened—3 to 5 minutes. Return the chicken to the skillet and heat through for 2 to 3 minutes. Remove the cinnamon stick, arrange the chicken and sauce in a serving dish, and garnish with the **banana** slices, if you like. Serve with a tossed green salad. Serves 4.

Chicken Provençal

This is a colorful dish fit for a dinner party. If you want to reduce the salt and fat further, omit the olives.

FAT SUGAR SODIUM

2 whole chicken breasts (about 2 pounds), halved and skinned
Nonstick cooking spray
1 tablespoon olive or vegetable oil
1 large yellow onion, chopped
4 cloves garlic, sliced thin
1 medium-size sweet red pepper, cored, seeded, and cut into 1-inch squares
1 medium-size zucchini (about ½ pound), halved lengthwise and sliced ¼ inch thick

1 small eggplant (about ½ pound), sliced ¼ inch thick and cut into wedges
1 large can (28 ounces) low-sodium tomatoes, drained and chopped
¼ teaspoon each dried basil, thyme, and oregano, crumbled
10 jumbo pitted ripe olives, halved
2 tablespoons minced parsley

Preparation:
11 min.
Cooking:
45 min.

One Serving:

Calories	271
Total Fat	5 g
Saturated Fat	1 g
Cholesterol	86 mg
Protein	38 g
Carbohydrates	19 g
Sodium	221 mg
Added Sugar	0
Fiber	3 g

1. Brown the **chicken** breasts over moderate heat in a heavy 12-inch skillet that has been lightly coated with the **cooking spray**—about 5 minutes on each side. Transfer to a large bowl and set aside.

2. Add the **olive oil, onion,** and **garlic** to the skillet and cook, uncovered, for 5 minutes, stirring occasionally. Add the **red pepper** and cook for 5 minutes, then add the **zucchini** and cook 5 minutes longer. Transfer the vegetables to the bowl with the chicken. Raise the heat to moderately high and cook the **eggplant** for 5 to 7 minutes, stirring occasionally, until golden.

3. Return the chicken and vegetables to the skillet and add the **tomatoes, basil, thyme, oregano,** and **olives.** Lower the heat to moderate, cover, and cook for 15 minutes or until the chicken is no longer pink near the bone. Transfer to a heated platter, sprinkle with the **parsley,** and serve with Wilted Spinach Salad, page 215. Serves 4.

Tip: Before freezing uncooked poultry, remove from the store package, rinse under cold water, and rewrap with your own plastic wrap. This eliminates bacteria that may have accumulated between processing and purchase.

Chicken Breasts Dijon

To make this dish for two, halve all the ingredients except the bread crumbs.

FAT SUGAR SODIUM

2 whole chicken breasts (about 2 pounds), halved and skinned
2 tablespoons Dijon or spicy brown mustard
1 teaspoon lemon juice

¼ teaspoon black pepper
2 green onions, chopped fine
½ cup soft white bread crumbs (1 slice)

Preparation:
10 min.
Cooking:
14 min.

One Serving:

Calories	152
Total Fat	2 g
Saturated Fat	0
Cholesterol	66 mg
Protein	27 g
Carbohydrates	5 g
Sodium	325 mg
Added Sugar	0
Fiber	0

1. Preheat the broiler and lightly grease the rack. Broil the **chicken** breasts 5 to 6 inches from the heat for 5 minutes; turn and broil 5 minutes longer.

2. Meanwhile, combine the **mustard, lemon juice, pepper,** and **green onions.** Coat the broiled chicken breasts all over with the mixture, place them back on the broiler rack, and sprinkle lightly with half of the **bread crumbs.** Broil for 2 minutes or until the crumbs are brown.

3. Turn the breasts, sprinkle with the remaining crumbs, and brown about 2 minutes longer or until the meat is no longer pink when cut at the center. *(Note: If the chicken browns too quickly, move it farther from the heat.)* Serves 4.

Chicken Provençal

Chicken Creole

2 tablespoons unsalted margarine
1 medium-size yellow onion, chopped
1 medium-size sweet green pepper, cored, seeded, and chopped
1 large stalk celery, chopped
2 cloves garlic, minced
2 whole chicken breasts (about 2 pounds), halved and skinned
1 teaspoon paprika

¼ teaspoon cayenne pepper
1 can (1 pound) low-sodium stewed tomatoes
1 teaspoon dried rosemary, crumbled
½ teaspoon dried marjoram, crumbled
1 bay leaf
1 tablespoon flour blended with ¼ cup low-sodium chicken broth or water

FAT SUGAR SODIUM

Preparation:
10 min.
Cooking:
36 min.

One Serving:

Calories	276
Total Fat	8 g
Saturated Fat	2 g
Cholesterol	86 mg
Protein	36 g
Carbohydrates	15 g
Sodium	122 mg
Added Sugar	0
Fiber	1 g

1. In a heavy 12-inch skillet, melt 1 tablespoon of the **margarine** over moderate heat. Add the **onion, green pepper, celery,** and **garlic,** and cook, uncovered, until the onion is soft—about 5 minutes. Transfer to a small dish.
2. Raise the heat under the skillet to moderately high and add the remaining margarine. While it melts, sprinkle the **chicken** breasts all over with the **paprika** and **cayenne pepper.** Add the chicken to the skillet and cook about 5 minutes, turning occasionally.
3. Add half of the cooked vegetables to the skillet along with the **tomatoes, rosemary, marjoram,** and **bay leaf;** reduce the heat, cover, and simmer for 20 minutes or until the chicken is fork-tender.
4. Whisk in the **flour–chicken broth** mixture and cook, stirring constantly, until the sauce has thickened—about 3 minutes. Return the remaining vegetables to the skillet and heat for 3 minutes. Discard the bay leaf. Serve with fluffy boiled rice and steamed okra. Serves 4.

Tip: Dark meat is fattier than white meat: Ounce for ounce, drumsticks have more than twice the fat of chicken breasts.

107

Chicken Breasts with Lemon and Capers

Chicken Breasts with Lemon and Capers

Capers give this quick, simple dish a continental flair.

FAT SUGAR SODIUM

¼ **cup flour**
¼ **teaspoon black pepper**
½ **teaspoon paprika**
 2 **skinned and boned chicken breasts (about 1 pound), halved and pounded to ¼-inch thickness**

 5 **teaspoons corn oil**
¼ **cup low-sodium chicken broth**
 2 **tablespoons lemon juice**
 2 **tablespoons capers, drained**

Preparation:
10 min.
Cooking:
8 min.

One Serving:

Calories	*208*
Total Fat	*7 g*
Saturated Fat	*1 g*
Cholesterol	*66 mg*
Protein	*27 g*
Carbohydrates	*7 g*
Sodium	*189 mg*
Added Sugar	*0*
Fiber	*0*

1. Combine the **flour, pepper,** and **paprika** on a plate. Press the **chicken** breasts into the mixture, coating them evenly all over and shaking off any excess.

2. In a heavy 10-inch skillet, heat the **corn oil** over moderately high heat for 1 minute. Add the breasts and cook about 3 minutes on each side; do not overcook. Transfer the breasts to a heated platter.

3. Add the **chicken broth** to the skillet, scraping up any browned bits on the bottom. Stir in the **lemon juice** and **capers** and heat through. Pour the sauce over the breasts and serve with Braised Spinach, page 199. Serves 4.

Chicken and Mushrooms in Foil

Take these silver packets straight from the oven to the table so that guests can open their own. The mushroom mixture can be made in advance.

FAT SUGAR SODIUM

½ pound mushrooms, chopped fine

3 green onions, chopped fine

3 cloves garlic, minced

¼ teaspoon each dried thyme and marjoram, crumbled

3 tablespoons dry red wine

¼ cup low-sodium chicken broth

2 teaspoons lemon juice
Nonstick cooking spray

2 skinned and boned chicken breasts (about 1 pound), halved

4 thin slices reduced-sodium ham (about ¼ pound)

Preparation:
6 min.
Cooking:
30 min.

One Serving:

Calories	183
Total Fat	3 g
Saturated Fat	0
Cholesterol	80 mg
Protein	33 g
Carbohydrates	5 g
Sodium	302 mg
Added Sugar	0
Fiber	2 g

1. Set a heavy nonstick 7-inch skillet over low heat about 30 seconds. Add the **mushrooms, green onions,** and **garlic;** cover and cook for 10 minutes or until the mushrooms have released their juices. Mix in the **thyme** and **marjoram.**

2. Raise the heat to moderate, add the **wine,** and cook, uncovered, for 5 minutes. Add the **chicken broth** and cook 5 minutes longer or until almost all the liquid has evaporated. Transfer the mushroom mixture to a bowl. When the mixture has cooled slightly, stir in the **lemon juice.**

3. Preheat the oven to 350°F. Lightly coat 4 sheets of aluminum foil, each 10 inches long, with the **cooking spray.** Lay 1 piece of the **chicken** on each piece of foil, spoon on ¼ of the mushroom mixture, and top with 1 **ham** slice. Fold the foil over and crimp tightly to seal.

4. Place the packets on a baking sheet and bake for 10 minutes or until the chicken is done. Serve with Herbed Creamed Onions, page 189. Serves 4.

Chicken with Fresh Tomato Sauce

You can use turkey cutlets or fish fillets in place of the chicken and grill rather than broil them. This recipe is easily halved to serve two; use two small tomatoes.

FAT SUGAR SODIUM

3 medium-size ripe tomatoes, cored and chopped

4 green onions, chopped fine

¼ cup chopped fresh coriander or parsley

2 tablespoons olive or vegetable oil

1 teaspoon lime or lemon juice

¼ teaspoon ground cumin

1 teaspoon minced green chili, fresh or canned (optional)

2 skinned and boned chicken breasts (about 1 pound), halved and pounded to ¼-inch thickness

⅛ teaspoon black pepper
Coriander or parsley sprigs

Preparation:
10 min.
Cooking:
6 min.

One Serving:

Calories	207
Total Fat	8 g
Saturated Fat	1 g
Cholesterol	66 mg
Protein	27 g
Carbohydrates	5 g
Sodium	82 mg
Added Sugar	0
Fiber	1 g

1. Preheat the broiler and lightly grease the rack. In a small bowl, combine the **tomatoes, green onions, coriander,** 1 tablespoon of the **olive oil,** the **lime juice, cumin,** and, if you like, the **chili.** Set aside.

2. Brush both sides of each **chicken** breast with the remaining olive oil, then sprinkle with the **pepper.**

3. Broil the chicken 4 to 5 inches from the heat for 3 minutes or until lightly browned. Turn and broil 3 minutes more or until no longer pink when cut near the center.

4. Arrange the chicken on a small heated platter, ladle the sauce to one side, and garnish with the **coriander sprigs.** Serves 4.

Cheese-Stuffed Chicken Kiev

Here is a reduced-calorie version of the Russian classic.

FAT SUGAR SODIUM

2 **skinned and boned chicken breasts (about 1 pound), halved and pounded to ¼-inch thickness**
¼ **teaspoon black pepper**
2 **cloves garlic, minced**
8 **teaspoons minced fresh or freeze-dried chives**
4 **strips part-skim mozzarella cheese, each about 1"x ½"x ½" (about 2 ounces)**

1 **large egg white**
1 **tablespoon skim milk**
1 **tablespoon water**
¼ **cup unsifted flour**
⅓ **cup fine dry bread crumbs**
1 **tablespoon unsalted margarine**

Preparation:
10 min., plus 20 min. refrigeration
Cooking:
25 min.

One Serving:

Calories	*259*
Total Fat	*8 g*
Saturated Fat	*3 g*
Cholesterol	*77 mg*
Protein	*32 g*
Carbohydrates	*13 g*
Sodium	*203 mg*
Added Sugar	*0*
Fiber	*0*

Tip: *The chicken cutlets sold at the supermarket are breast fillets that usually measure no more than ¼ inch in thickness.*

1. Sprinkle the **chicken** breasts with the **pepper, garlic,** and half of the **chives.** Lay 1 strip of **cheese** in the center of each chicken breast, fold the ends over, then roll up as for a jelly roll and fasten with toothpicks.
2. In a pie pan, whisk the **egg white, milk,** and **water** together. Place the **flour** and **bread crumbs** on separate plates. Dip the chicken rolls in the flour, then in the egg mixture, then in the crumbs to coat evenly. Arrange on a rack and refrigerate, uncovered, at least 20 minutes.
3. Preheat the oven to 350°F. In a heavy 10-inch skillet, melt the **margarine** over moderately high heat, add the chicken rolls, and brown on all sides, turning carefully—about 10 minutes. Transfer to an ungreased 8"x 8"x 2" baking pan and bake, uncovered, for 15 to 20 minutes.
4. Transfer the chicken to a heated platter and sprinkle with the remaining chives. Accompany with Kasha with Vegetables, page 171. Serves 4.

Chicken Breasts Parmesan

Chilling the breaded chicken breasts beforehand makes them easier to brown. To make for two, halve all the ingredients except the olive oil.

FAT SUGAR SODIUM

⅓ **cup fine dry bread crumbs**
1 **tablespoon minced parsley**
3 **tablespoons grated Parmesan cheese**
2 **large egg whites**
2 **teaspoons water**

2 **skinned and boned chicken breasts (about 1 pound), halved and pounded to ¼-inch thickness**
1 **tablespoon olive oil**
1 **lemon, quartered lengthwise**

Preparation:
4 min.
Cooking:
7 min.

One Serving:

Calories	*218*
Total Fat	*6 g*
Saturated Fat	*2 g*
Cholesterol	*69 mg*
Protein	*31 g*
Carbohydrates	*9 g*
Sodium	*231 mg*
Added Sugar	*0*
Fiber	*0*

1. Combine the **bread crumbs** and **parsley** on a plate. Place the **cheese** on another plate. In a small bowl, lightly beat the **egg whites** with the **water.**
2. Dip the **chicken** breasts into the cheese, then into the egg whites, then into the crumb mixture, coating both sides evenly. Lay them on a rack and refrigerate, uncovered, for 20 minutes.
3. Heat the **olive oil** in a heavy 10-inch skillet over moderately high heat for 1 minute; add the chicken and brown about 3 minutes on each side or until no longer pink when cut near the center.
4. Transfer the chicken to a warm platter, garnish with the **lemon** quarters, and serve. Accompany, if you like, with Carrots Glazed with Orange and Ginger, page 181, and Creamy Mashed Potatoes, page 194. Serves 4.

Glazed Turkey Breast with Sweet Potato Stuffing

Look for a turkey breast that is not "prebasted," since the basting ingredients often include saturated fats and add unnecessary calories.

FAT SUGAR SODIUM

3 **large sweet potatoes (about 2 pounds), peeled and cut into 2-inch pieces**
  Grated rind and juice of 1 large orange
2 **tablespoons unsalted margarine**
1 **large yellow onion, chopped**
1 **medium-size carrot, peeled and chopped**

1 **medium-size stalk celery, chopped**
½ **cup peeled and chopped parsnip**
1 **teaspoon dried sage, crumbled**
1 **fresh turkey breast (about 5 pounds)**
  Nonstick cooking spray

Preparation:
20 min.
Cooking:
1½ hr. (mostly unattended)

One Serving:

Calories	323
Total Fat	7 g
Saturated Fat	2 g
Cholesterol	95 mg
Protein	43 g
Carbohydrates	21 g
Sodium	109 mg
Added Sugar	0
Fiber	2 g

1. Preheat the oven to 450°F. Place the **sweet potatoes** in a medium-size saucepan, cover with boiling unsalted water, and cook, covered, for 15 minutes or until tender when pierced with a knife. Drain well and mash. Stir in the grated **orange rind.**

2. Meanwhile, melt 1 tablespoon of the **margarine** in a 10-inch skillet over moderate heat. Add the **onion, carrot, celery,** and **parsnip,** and cook for 10 minutes, stirring frequently. Add the **sage.** Blend the mixture into the mashed sweet potatoes. Let the mixture cool slightly, then spoon it into both cavities of the **turkey** breast. Secure the neck skin with toothpicks.

3. Lightly coat a 13"x 9"x 2" baking pan with the **cooking spray.** Place the turkey breast in the pan and rub the skin with the remaining margarine. Insert a meat thermometer into the thickest part and roast for 30 minutes. Reduce the oven temperature to 375°F and roast, basting occasionally with the orange juice, for 45 more minutes or until the thermometer registers 180°F. If the turkey browns too quickly, cover it loosely with aluminum foil.

4. Remove from the oven and let stand at room temperature for 10 minutes before carving. Serve with steamed Brussels sprouts or broccoli. Serves 10.

Tip: *Defrost a frozen turkey in the refrigerator—not on the kitchen counter. It will retain its juices and be more succulent when cooked.*

Glazed Turkey Breast with Sweet Potato Stuffing

Turkey-Vegetable Soufflé

Here is a novel way to use leftover Thanksgiving turkey.

FAT SUGAR SODIUM

1 cup skim milk
3 tablespoons flour
1 small yellow onion
2 whole cloves
1 bay leaf
¼ teaspoon each ground sage and paprika
¼ teaspoon hot red pepper sauce
¼ teaspoon salt

⅛ teaspoon ground nutmeg
2 large eggs, separated, plus 3 large egg whites
¾ cup finely chopped cooked turkey
¼ cup finely chopped cooked carrot
¼ cup frozen tiny peas
Nonstick cooking spray

Preparation:
5 min.
Cooking:
30 min.

One Serving:

Calories	158
Total Fat	5 g
Saturated Fat	1 g
Cholesterol	158 mg
Protein	17 g
Carbohydrates	11 g
Sodium	289 mg
Added Sugar	0
Fiber	0

1. Preheat the oven to 400°F. In a medium-size heavy saucepan over low heat, whisk the **milk** into the **flour.** Stud the **onion** with the **cloves** and add to the pan along with the **bay leaf.** Cook, stirring, until quite thick—about 5 minutes. Remove from the heat and discard the onion, cloves, and bay leaf. Stir in the **sage, paprika, red pepper sauce, salt,** and **nutmeg;** set aside.

2. In a large bowl, whisk the **egg yolks** just until blended. Quickly stir in a little of the hot milk mixture, then stir all back into the saucepan. Stir in the **turkey, carrot,** and **peas.**

3. Beat the **egg whites** until stiff but not dry. Gently fold into the turkey-vegetable mixture.

4. Lightly coat a 1½-quart soufflé dish with the **cooking spray.** Pour in the turkey mixture and bake, uncovered, about 25 minutes or until puffy and golden. Serve immediately, before the soufflé has a chance to fall. A crisp green salad makes a good accompaniment. Serves 4.

Turkey Slices with Ham

In Italy, this recipe is made with veal scaloppine and called saltimbocca *("jump in the mouth"). This variation uses turkey, but chicken can be used as well. To make for two, halve all the ingredients except the olive oil.*

FAT SUGAR SODIUM

4 turkey breast cutlets (about 1 pound), each about ¼ inch thick
¼ teaspoon black pepper
1 teaspoon dried sage, crumbled
4 thin slices reduced-sodium ham (about ¼ pound)

1 tablespoon unsalted margarine
1 tablespoon olive oil
⅓ cup dry white wine or low-sodium chicken broth

Preparation:
5 min.
Cooking:
13 min.

One Serving:

Calories	224
Total Fat	9 g
Saturated Fat	2 g
Cholesterol	84 mg
Protein	32 g
Carbohydrates	2 g
Sodium	298 mg
Added Sugar	0
Fiber	0

1. Sprinkle the **turkey** cutlets with the **pepper** and **sage.** Cut the **ham** to fit the turkey slices, place on top, and secure with 2 toothpicks laid flat against the ham and threaded through.

2. Melt the **margarine** with the **olive oil** in a heavy 10-inch skillet over moderate heat. Brown the turkey-ham slices in 2 batches, about 3 minutes on each side; transfer to a heated platter and keep warm.

3. Add the **wine** to the skillet, raise the heat to high, and boil down slightly for 1 to 2 minutes, stirring constantly. Spoon the sauce over the turkey-ham slices and serve with Rice and Green Peas, page 166. Serves 4.

Turkey-Vegetable Soufflé

Turkey Scaloppine with Sherried Cream

An elegant sauce of sour cream, yogurt, mustard, and sherry is quickly and easily prepared, yet has the style of a more complicated creation.

FAT SUGAR SODIUM

3 tablespoons flour
¼ teaspoon each dried rosemary and thyme, crumbled
⅛ teaspoon black pepper
4 turkey breast cutlets (about 1 pound), each about ¼ inch thick
Nonstick cooking spray
1 tablespoon unsalted margarine

¼ cup dry sherry
⅓ cup low-sodium chicken broth
½ teaspoon cornstarch blended with ¼ cup each plain low-fat yogurt and sour cream
1 teaspoon Dijon or spicy brown mustard
1 tablespoon minced parsley

Preparation:
10 min.
Cooking:
7 min.

One Serving:

Calories	228
Total Fat	8 g
Saturated Fat	3 g
Cholesterol	78 mg
Protein	29 g
Carbohydrates	8 g
Sodium	136 mg
Added Sugar	0
Fiber	0

1. Combine the **flour, rosemary, thyme,** and **pepper** on a plate. Press the **turkey** cutlets into the mixture, coating them evenly all over and shaking off any excess.

2. Coat a heavy 10-inch skillet with the **cooking spray,** add the **margarine,** and set over moderately high heat about 30 seconds. Add the turkey cutlets and brown about 2 minutes on each side, then transfer to a heated platter and keep warm.

3. Pour off any drippings from the skillet, add the **sherry,** and boil, uncovered, for 30 seconds. Add the **chicken broth, cornstarch** mixture, and **mustard,** and cook, stirring, for 2 to 3 minutes or until the sauce is slightly thick.

4. Spoon the sauce over the turkey cutlets and sprinkle with the **parsley.** Serve with pasta. Serves 4.

Tarragon Turkey Loaf

Preparation: **20 min.**
Cooking: **45 min.** (mostly unattended)

FAT **SUGAR** **SODIUM**

2 **teaspoons unsalted margarine**
1 **medium-size yellow onion, chopped fine**
1 **large stalk celery, chopped fine**
1 **pound ground turkey**
⅓ **cup chopped parsley**
¼ **cup fine dry bread crumbs**
¼ **cup skim milk**
1 **large egg white**
½ **teaspoon dried tarragon, crumbled**
¼ **teaspoon each black pepper and nutmeg**
 Nonstick cooking spray
 For the Mushroom Sauce:
2 **teaspoons unsalted margarine**
1 **cup chopped mushrooms**
2 **tablespoons flour**
1 **cup low-sodium chicken broth**
⅛ **teaspoon each ground nutmeg, salt, black pepper, and dried tarragon, crumbled**

1. Preheat the oven to 350°F. In a heavy 7-inch nonstick skillet or medium-size saucepan, melt the **margarine** over moderate heat; add the **onion** and **celery**, and cook, uncovered, until the onion is soft—about 5 minutes.

2. Meanwhile, in a large bowl, combine the **turkey, parsley, bread crumbs, milk, egg white, tarragon, pepper,** and **nutmeg.** Add the onion and celery and mix well.

3. Lightly coat a 7½"x 3¾"x 2" loaf pan with the **cooking spray.** Press the turkey mixture into the pan and bake for 40 to 45 minutes or until lightly browned and firm to the touch. Cool in the pan for 15 minutes. Using 2 spatulas, transfer the loaf to a heated platter.

4. Meanwhile, prepare the sauce. In the same skillet or saucepan, melt the **margarine** over moderate heat. Add the **mushrooms** and cook for 3 to 5 minutes, stirring occasionally.

5. Remove from the heat and blend in the **flour, chicken broth, nutmeg, salt, pepper,** and **tarragon;** return to the heat and cook about 5 minutes, stirring, until thick.

6. Ladle some sauce over the loaf and serve the rest at the table. Serves 4.

One Serving:

Calories	297	Protein	24 g
Total Fat	17 g	Carbohydrates	12 g
Saturated Fat	6 g	Sodium	266 mg
Cholesterol	77 mg	Added Sugar	0
		Fiber	1 g

Turkey-Sour Cream Patties

Preparation: **5 min.,** plus 20 min. refrigeration   Cooking: **10 min.**

FAT **SUGAR** **SODIUM**

Ground turkey, both frozen and fresh, is available at most supermarkets. Frozen turkey may not hold together as well as fresh. If you use it, add the milk 1 tablespoon at a time, so that the mixture doesn't become too loose.

1 **pound lean ground turkey**
1 **cup soft white bread crumbs (2 slices)**
3 **tablespoons sour cream**
⅓ **cup skim milk**
¼ **teaspoon black pepper**
⅛ **teaspoon ground nutmeg**
 Nonstick cooking spray
1 **tablespoon unsalted margarine**

1. In a medium-size bowl, mix the **turkey,** ½ cup of the **bread crumbs,** the **sour cream, milk, pepper,** and **nutmeg;** shape into 4 flat patties. Coat on both sides with the remaining crumbs, set on a rack, and refrigerate, uncovered, for 20 minutes.

2. Lightly coat a heavy 10-inch skillet with the

Tarragon Turkey Loaf

cooking spray, add the **margarine,** and set over moderate heat about 30 seconds. Add the patties and brown for 5 minutes on each side. Transfer to a heated platter. Serves 4.

One Serving:

Calories	265	Protein	22 g
Total Fat	16 g	Carbohydrates	7 g
Saturated Fat	6 g	Sodium	162 mg
Cholesterol	77 mg	Added Sugar	0
		Fiber	0

Turkey Balsamico

Preparation: **5 min.** Cooking: **11 min.** FAT SUGAR SODIUM

Balsamic vinegar is a mellow wine vinegar made in Italy. Most supermarkets stock it now, but if you're unable to find it, substitute red wine vinegar.

 2 **tablespoons flour**
 ⅛ **teaspoon black pepper**
 4 **turkey breast cutlets (about 1 pound), each about ¼ inch thick**
 3 **tablespoons olive oil**
 2 **large sweet red peppers, cored, seeded, and sliced into 1-inch rings**
 3 **cloves garlic, minced**
 ¼ **cup chopped fresh basil or 1 teaspoon dried basil, crumbled**
 2 **tablespoons balsamic or red wine vinegar**

1. Combine the **flour** and **pepper** on a plate and press the **turkey** cutlets into the mixture, coating them evenly all over and shaking off any excess.
2. In a heavy 12-inch skillet, heat 2 tablespoons of the **olive oil** for 1 minute over moderate heat. Add the turkey and brown for 2 minutes on each side; transfer to a heated platter.
3. Add the remaining tablespoon of oil to the skillet along with the **red peppers** and the **garlic.** Reduce the heat to low, cover, and cook for 5 minutes, stirring occasionally, until the peppers are tender.
4. Add the **basil** and **vinegar;** return the turkey to the skillet, raise the heat to moderate, and cook, stirring, 2 minutes longer. Transfer to a heated platter and serve. Serves 4.

One Serving:

Calories	250	Protein	28 g
Total Fat	12 g	Carbohydrates	7 g
Saturated Fat	2 g	Sodium	78 mg
Cholesterol	70 mg	Added Sugar	0
		Fiber	1 g

Broiled Garlic-Stuffed Cornish Game Hens

Preparation: **9 min.**, plus 2 hr. FAT SUGAR SODIUM
marination Cooking: **45 min.** (mostly unattended)

Be creative when you cook these hens, adding fresh basil if you have it, or chili peppers if you like things hot. The marinade keeps well in the refrigerator and can also be used with chicken or fish.

 2 **Cornish hens** (1 to 1½ pounds each), split open but not halved
 ⅓ cup **red wine vinegar**
 1 tablespoon **olive oil**
 1 **bay leaf**, crumbled
 ½ teaspoon each dried **thyme** and **rosemary**, crumbled
 ¼ teaspoon black **pepper**
 4 strips **orange peel**, each about 2 inches long and ½ inch wide
 2 bulbs (whole heads) **garlic**

1. Place the **hens** in a large, shallow glass or earthenware dish. Combine the **vinegar, olive oil, bay leaf, thyme, rosemary, pepper,** and **orange peel,** and pour the mixture over the hens. Cover and refrigerate for 2 to 4 hours, turning the hens every hour.
2. Meanwhile, preheat the oven to 400°F. Wrap each bulb of **garlic** snugly in aluminum foil and bake 25 minutes or until soft. Remove from the oven and cool until easy to handle. Separate the garlic bulbs into cloves, squeeze out the soft pulp, and mash it.
3. Preheat the broiler. Remove the hens from the marinade. Using your fingers, carefully loosen (but do not remove) the skin from the breasts; spread the garlic pulp underneath the skin, dividing the total amount evenly.
4. Place the hens skin side down on the broiler pan rack and broil 7 to 8 inches from the heat for 10 to 12 minutes; turn and broil 10 to 12 minutes longer or until nicely browned.
5. Halve the hens, transfer to a warm platter, and serve with Braised Eggplant, Zucchini, and Tomatoes, page 186. Serves 4.

One Serving:

Calories	281	Protein	28 g
Total Fat	15 g	Carbohydrates	6 g
Saturated Fat	4 g	Sodium	86 mg
Cholesterol	88 mg	Added Sugar	0
		Fiber	0

Cornish Game Hens with Wild Rice-Apple Stuffing

Preparation: **15 min.** Cooking: **56 min.** FAT SUGAR SODIUM

 1 tablespoon unsalted **margarine**
 1 large yellow **onion**, chopped
 1 large stalk **celery**, chopped
 1 large **apple**, peeled, cored, and chopped
 ½ teaspoon each dried **sage** and **marjoram**, crumbled
 ¼ teaspoon black **pepper**
 ¾ cup long-grain and wild **rice** mixture, cooked by package directions but with seasoning packet omitted
 ¾ cup low-sodium **chicken broth**
 ½ cup apple **cider**
 ¼ cup dry white **wine**
 2 **Cornish hens** (1 to 1½ pounds each), skinned
 2 teaspoons **cornstarch** blended with ¼ cup plain low-fat **yogurt**

1. Preheat the oven to 375°F. Melt the **margarine** in a heavy 4-quart Dutch oven over moderate heat. Add the **onion, celery, apple, sage, marjoram,** and **pepper.** Cover and cook, stirring occasionally, until soft—about 5 minutes. Transfer half the mixture to a bowl and stir the cooked **rice** into it; cool.
2. Add the **chicken broth, cider,** and **wine** to the remaining mixture in the Dutch oven and simmer over low heat for 1 minute.
3. Stuff the **hens** with the rice mixture, then truss them and place in the Dutch oven. Baste them with some of the liquid, cover, and place in the oven; cook for 30 to 35 minutes or until fork-tender. Transfer the hens to a heated platter and keep warm.
4. Bring the vegetables in the Dutch oven to a simmer over moderate heat, and whisk in the **cornstarch-yogurt** mixture. Stir for 1 to 2 minutes or until slightly thickened (do not boil or the sauce will curdle). Remove from the heat.
5. Halve the hens and smother with the sauce. Serves 4.

One Serving:

Calories	336	Protein	28 g
Total Fat	9 g	Carbohydrates	38 g
Saturated Fat	2 g	Sodium	103 mg
Cholesterol	69 mg	Added Sugar	0
		Fiber	1 g

Fish and Shellfish

Fish and shellfish may be expensive, but you get your dollar's worth in terms of health—high protein and low fat. Moreover, today we know that many kinds of fish contain oils that actually reduce the risk of heart disease. In fact, nutritionists recommend eating fish at least twice a week. In the pages that follow, you'll find a number of ways to prepare this remarkable food, from homey Deviled Tuna Pot Pie to a novel Cold Spiced Shrimp.

California Seafood Medley

Wine-Poached Bluefish with Onion and Dill

Wine-Poached Bluefish with Onion and Dill

FAT SUGAR SODIUM

1 **bluefish (3 pounds), scaled and cleaned**

1 **medium-size yellow onion, chopped fine**

6 **large sprigs parsley**

4 **large sprigs dill or 1 teaspoon dill weed**

2 **cups dry white wine**

1 **tablespoon unsalted margarine**

2 **tablespoons flour**

¼ **teaspoon white or black pepper**

¼ **cup sour cream**

Lemon slices (optional)

Dill or parsley sprigs (optional)

Preparation:
10 min.
Cooking:
39 min. (mostly unattended)

One Serving:

Calories	304
Total Fat	12 g
Saturated Fat	4 g
Cholesterol	102 mg
Protein	37 g
Carbohydrates	11 g
Sodium	144 mg
Added Sugar	0
Fiber	0

1. Preheat the oven to 350°F. Lay the **bluefish** on a greased rack set in a 13"x 9"x 2" baking pan. Fill the fish cavity with half of the **onion, parsley,** and **dill.** Layer the remaining onion, parsley, and dill on top of the fish. Pour in the **wine** and cover the pan snugly with aluminum foil.

2. Bake the fish for 35 to 40 minutes or until it flakes when tested with a fork. Transfer to a heated platter, taking care not to dislodge the herbs on top.

3. Remove the parsley and dill from the fish cavity. In an electric blender or food processor, purée the herbs with 1 cup of the poaching liquid.

4. In a small heavy saucepan, melt the **margarine** over moderate heat. Blend in the **flour,** add the herb-wine mixture and cook, stirring constantly, for 3 minutes or until thickened. Whisk in the **sour cream** and heat 1 to 2 minutes longer (do not boil or the sauce will curdle).

5. Garnish the fish with **lemon** slices and sprigs of **dill** or parsley, if you like. Pass the sauce separately. Serves 4.

Lemony Baked Stuffed Whiting

This dish is a good candidate for cooking outdoors on the grill. Instead of using a baking pan, seal the fish in heavy-duty aluminum foil and cook for 30 minutes over medium-hot coals.

FAT SUGAR SODIUM

1 tablespoon unsalted margarine
2 medium-size yellow onions, chopped fine
1 clove garlic, minced
½ cup fine dry bread crumbs
2 tablespoons minced parsley

1 teaspoon grated lemon rind
¼ teaspoon black pepper
4 whole whiting or perch (about 8 ounces each), scaled and cleaned
⅓ cup dry white wine

Preparation:
15 min.
Cooking:
35 min. (mostly unattended)

One Serving:

Calories	261
Total Fat	4 g
Saturated Fat	1 g
Cholesterol	125 mg
Protein	40 g
Carbohydrates	13 g
Sodium	263 mg
Added Sugar	0
Fiber	0

1. Preheat the oven to 400°F. In a heavy 10-inch skillet, melt the **margarine** over moderate heat; add the **onions** and cook, uncovered, until soft—about 5 minutes. Remove the skillet from the heat.

2. Transfer half of the onion to a bowl; add the **garlic, bread crumbs, parsley, lemon rind,** and **pepper,** and toss lightly to mix.

3. Stuff each **whiting** with ¼ of the mixture and close it with toothpicks.

4. Sprinkle half of the remaining onion over a lightly greased 13"x 9"x 2" baking pan; arrange the fish on top in a single layer and scatter the rest of the onion over them. Pour in the **wine,** then cover the pan snugly with aluminum foil. Bake for 30 minutes or until the fish flakes easily when tested with a fork. Serves 4.

Salmon with Cucumber-Dill Sauce

A tart and refreshing cucumber-dill sauce is perfect with delicate salmon.

FAT SUGAR SODIUM

2 pounds center-cut salmon, in one piece
1 small cucumber, peeled, seeded, and chopped
½ cup plain low-fat yogurt
2 teaspoons snipped fresh dill or ½ teaspoon dill weed

1 teaspoon skim milk or water
½ teaspoon sugar
½ teaspoon prepared yellow mustard
⅛ teaspoon salt
⅛ teaspoon white or black pepper

Preparation:
10 min.
Cooking:
30 min. (mostly unattended)

One Serving:

Calories	307
Total Fat	18 g
Saturated Fat	5 g
Cholesterol	53 mg
Protein	31 g
Carbohydrates	3 g
Sodium	165 mg
Added Sugar	0
Fiber	0

1. Preheat the oven to 350°F. Place the **salmon** on a sheet of aluminum foil just large enough to hold it comfortably, then set it on a rack in an 8"x 8"x 2" baking pan. Pour cold water into the pan to a depth of 1 inch and cover the pan snugly with aluminum foil. Bake the salmon for 30 minutes or until it flakes when tested with a fork.

2. Meanwhile, in a small bowl, combine the **cucumber, yogurt, dill, milk, sugar, mustard, salt,** and **pepper.** Cover and refrigerate until ready to serve with the fish.

3. Carefully peel away the salmon skin and discard it, then ease the fish onto a small heated platter. Holding a small knife flat, cut along the central backbone; lift off the top half of the salmon, gently pull out and discard the backbone, then replace the top half. Serve with the sauce and Celery and Artichoke Hearts in Cheese Sauce, page 184 Serves 6.

Broiled Salmon with Sweet Red Pepper Sauce

Red with orange, sweet with briny—the colors and tastes of this dish make for memorable dining. The sauce is also good with broiled meats or poultry.

FAT SUGAR SODIUM

2 medium-size sweet red peppers
2 cloves garlic, unpeeled
2 teaspoons red wine vinegar
1 teaspoon olive or vegetable oil
4 salmon fillets (about 4 ounces each)

1. Preheat the broiler. On a broiler pan set 6 inches from the heat, broil the **red peppers,** turning occasionally, until charred all over—5 to 8 minutes. Transfer the peppers to a brown paper bag; seal the bag, set it in a bowl, and cool for 10 minutes. The peppers will steam so that their skins peel off easily.
2. Meanwhile, lower the oven temperature to 400°F. Wrap the **garlic** cloves in aluminum foil and roast until soft—about 5 minutes; peel and set aside. Raise the heat again to broil.
3. When the peppers are cool enough to handle, peel them over a bowl to catch any juice; discard the stems and seeds. In an electric blender or food processor, purée the peppers and their juice with the garlic, **vinegar,** and **olive oil.** Set aside.
4. On a broiler pan rack set 8 inches from the heat, broil the **salmon** for 2 to 3 minutes; turn and broil another 2 to 3 minutes or until opaque when tested with a fork in the center. Transfer the salmon to a warm platter and spoon 2 generous tablespoons of the sauce down the center of each fillet, smoothing into a broad ribbon. Serves 4.

Preparation:
6 min.
Cooking:
14 min.

One Serving:

Calories	*268*
Total Fat	*16 g*
Saturated Fat	*5 g*
Cholesterol	*44 mg*
Protein	*26 g*
Carbohydrates	*3 g*
Sodium	*86 mg*
Added Sugar	*0*
Fiber	*0*

Flounder and Vegetables Sealed in Silver

The fish packets can be prepared early in the day and cooked later.

FAT SUGAR SODIUM

1½ tablespoons unsalted margarine
1 teaspoon minced fresh or freeze-dried chives
1 teaspoon lemon juice
⅛ teaspoon paprika
1 large carrot, peeled and cut into matchstick strips
1 large leek, trimmed, washed, and cut into matchstick strips
2 large mushrooms, sliced thin
4 flounder, sole, or other white fish fillets (about 5 ounces each)
Nonstick cooking spray
4 thin slices lemon

1. Preheat the oven to 400°F. In a small bowl, combine the **margarine, chives, lemon juice,** and **paprika** and set aside.
2. In a medium-size saucepan, cook the **carrot, leek,** and **mushrooms** for 1 minute in boiling unsalted water. Drain and set aside.
3. Cut 4 sheets of aluminum foil large enough to enclose the **flounder** fillets and lightly coat with the **cooking spray.** Lay a fillet in the center of each sheet, arrange ¼ of the carrots, leeks, and mushrooms on top of each fillet, then top with ¼ of the margarine mixture and a slice of **lemon.** Fold the foil over and crimp the edges to seal.
4. Place the packets on a baking sheet and bake for 7 to 8 minutes. Transfer the packets to dinner plates and let the diners open their own. Serve with Rice with Lemon and Dill, page 166. Serves 4.

Preparation:
12 min.
Cooking:
8 min.

One Serving:

Calories	*175*
Total Fat	*7 g*
Saturated Fat	*1 g*
Cholesterol	*65 mg*
Protein	*23 g*
Carbohydrates	*7 g*
Sodium	*116 mg*
Added Sugar	*0*
Fiber	*1 g*

Broiled Salmon with Sweet Red Pepper Sauce

Fish Rarebit

This rarebit is lower in calories, fat, and cholesterol than the classic version (the calorie-laden alcohol in the beer boils away during the cooking). Frozen fish that has been thawed can be substituted for fresh.

FAT **SUGAR** SODIUM

2½ tablespoons flour
¾ teaspoon dry mustard
¼ teaspoon black pepper
⅔ cup beer
1 teaspoon Worcestershire sauce

1 cup shredded Cheddar cheese (about 4 ounces)
1 pound haddock, scrod, or ocean perch fillets, cut into 1-inch pieces

1. Preheat the oven to 375°F. In a large bowl, combine the **flour, mustard,** and **pepper.** Whisk in the **beer** and **Worcestershire sauce,** then stir in the **cheese.** Add the **haddock,** tossing well to coat; pour all into an ungreased 9-inch pie pan.

2. Cover with aluminum foil and bake for 10 minutes; uncover and bake 5 minutes longer or until the sauce is bubbly and the fish is cooked through. Ladle the rarebit over whole wheat toast or brown rice. Serves 4.

Preparation:
5 min.
Cooking:
15 min.

One Serving:

Calories	*231*
Total Fat	*10 g*
Saturated Fat	*6 g*
Cholesterol	*98 mg*
Protein	*29 g*
Carbohydrates	*6 g*
Sodium	*262 mg*
Added Sugar	*0*
Fiber	*0*

121

Stuffed Fish Fillets with Nutmeg Sauce

Sesame Sole

This is especially good for a quick after-work meal. You can easily halve the ingredients to serve two.

¼ **cup buttermilk**

4 **sole, flounder, or other white fish fillets (about 5 ounces each)**

2 **teaspoons Dijon or spicy brown mustard**

2 **teaspoons low-sodium tomato paste**

½ **teaspoon dried tarragon, crumbled**

2 **tablespoons flour**

3½ **tablespoons sesame seeds**

4 **teaspoons vegetable oil**
Lemon slices (optional)

Preparation:
6 min., plus 30 min. refrigeration
Cooking:
3 min.

One Serving:

Calories	*226*
Total Fat	*11 g*
Saturated Fat	*1 g*
Cholesterol	*68 mg*
Protein	*25 g*
Carbohydrates	*7 g*
Sodium	*243 mg*
Added Sugar	*0*
Fiber	*0*

1. Pour the **buttermilk** in a shallow dish and dip the **sole** fillets in it, coating well all over. Lay the fillets on a platter. Combine the **mustard, tomato paste,** and **tarragon,** and spread on both sides of the fillets.

2. Combine the **flour** and **sesame seeds** in a pie pan and press the fillets into the mixture to coat all over. Place the fillets on a rack and refrigerate, uncovered, for 30 minutes to make the coating stick.

3. In a heavy 12-inch skillet, heat the **vegetable oil** over moderately high heat. Add the sole and cook until golden—about 1½ minutes on each side. If the sesame seeds brown too quickly, lower the heat. Transfer the sole to a heated platter and garnish, if you like, with the **lemon** slices. Serves 4.

Stuffed Fish Fillets with Nutmeg Sauce

2 tablespoons unsalted margarine
1 green onion, chopped
1/3 cup coarsely grated carrot
1/2 cup cooked brown rice
1 teaspoon grated lemon rind
1 teaspoon lemon juice
1/2 teaspoon ground nutmeg
1/4 teaspoon black pepper
1/8 teaspoon salt

4 small flounder, sole, or other white fish fillets (about 5 ounces each)
4 teaspoons flour
3/4 cup low-sodium chicken broth
1/8 teaspoon white or black pepper
1/4 cup dry white wine or low-sodium chicken broth
1 tablespoon minced parsley
Lemon wedges (optional)

FAT SUGAR SODIUM

Preparation:
45 min.
Cooking:
33 min.

One Serving:

Calories	*240*
Total Fat	*8 g*
Saturated Fat	*2 g*
Cholesterol	*65 mg*
Protein	*24 g*
Carbohydrates	*11 g*
Sodium	*187 mg*
Added Sugar	*0*
Fiber	*0*

Tip: *Fresh fish deteriorates rapidly. Never keep it in the refrigerator for more than a day. Better still, cook it within a few hours of buying it.*

1. Preheat the oven to 350°F. In a heavy 10-inch skillet, melt half of the **margarine** over moderate heat; add the **green onion** and **carrot** and cook until just tender—3 to 5 minutes. Stir in the **rice** and half of the **lemon rind, lemon juice, nutmeg,** and **black pepper;** add the **salt.**

2. Sprinkle the **flounder** fillets with the remaining 1/8 teaspoon black pepper. Place 1/4 of the rice mixture on half of each fillet and gently pack to compress, leaving about a 1/4-inch margin on 3 edges. Fold the other half of the fillet over the filling and carefully pin the two ends together with a wooden toothpick, pushing in any loose filling.

3. Bake the fish in a lightly greased 8"x 8"x 2" baking pan for 25 to 30 minutes or until the fish flakes when tested with a fork.

4. Meanwhile, prepare the sauce. Melt the remaining margarine in a small heavy saucepan over moderate heat. Blend in the **flour** and cook, stirring, for 3 to 5 minutes. Add the **chicken broth** and the remaining lemon rind, lemon juice, and nutmeg, then the **white pepper;** cook, stirring constantly, until thickened and smooth—about 5 minutes. Stir in the **wine** and **parsley.**

5. Transfer the fish to a warm platter and garnish with **lemon** wedges, if desired. Serve with the sauce. Serves 4.

Gingery Grilled Swordfish Steaks

2 tablespoons olive or vegetable oil
2 tablespoons lemon juice
1 tablespoon dry sherry or water
2 teaspoons reduced-sodium soy sauce
2 cloves garlic, minced

2 teaspoons minced fresh ginger or 1/4 teaspoon ground ginger
1 teaspoon grated lemon rind
1/4 teaspoon black pepper
4 swordfish, tuna, or shark steaks (about 4 ounces each)
Nonstick cooking spray

FAT SUGAR SODIUM

Preparation:
10 min., plus 2 hr. marination
Cooking:
6 min.

One Serving:

Calories	*191*
Total Fat	*11 g*
Saturated Fat	*2 g*
Cholesterol	*57 mg*
Protein	*20 g*
Carbohydrates	*2 g*
Sodium	*159 mg*
Added Sugar	*0*
Fiber	*0*

1. Combine the **olive oil, lemon juice, sherry, soy sauce, garlic, ginger, lemon rind,** and **pepper** and set aside.

2. Lay the **swordfish** steaks in a shallow baking pan just large enough to hold them, pour on the marinade, and turn the steaks to coat well. Cover and refrigerate for 2 hours.

3. Lightly coat a heavy 12-inch skillet with the **cooking spray** and set over moderately high heat for 30 seconds. Add the swordfish steaks and cook, uncovered, for 3 minutes on each side or until springy-firm. Transfer the swordfish to a heated platter and serve. Serves 4.

Broiled Salmon Steaks with Radish-Yogurt Sauce

Preparation: **4 min.** Cooking: **4 min.** `FAT` `SUGAR` `SODIUM`

The pungency of the sauce is a fine complement to the richness of salmon. This recipe can easily be halved to serve two.

- 2 **cups plain low-fat yogurt**
- 3 **green onions, chopped fine**
- 1 **bunch radishes (about 10 small), trimmed and chopped**
- 3 **tablespoons prepared horseradish**
- ¼ **teaspoon each ground cumin and black pepper**
- 2 **teaspoons lemon juice**
- 2 **teaspoons olive or vegetable oil**
- 4 **salmon, swordfish, or halibut steaks (about 4 ounces each)**
  Lemon wedges (optional)

1. Preheat the broiler and lightly grease the broiler pan rack. In a medium-size bowl, combine the **yogurt, green onions, radishes, horseradish, cumin,** and ⅛ teaspoon of the **pepper;** mix well and set aside.
2. Combine the **lemon juice, olive oil,** and remaining pepper and brush the mixture over both sides of the **salmon** steaks. Place the steaks on the broiler pan rack and broil 4 to 5 inches from the heat for 2 to 3 minutes on each side or until the salmon is opaque when cut near the center.
3. Serve on warm plates, garnished with the **lemon** wedges, if you like, and with the sauce spooned to one side. Serves 4.

One Serving:

Calories	306	Protein	28 g
Total Fat	17 g	Carbohydrates	10 g
Saturated Fat	5 g	Sodium	163 mg
Cholesterol	44 mg	Added Sugar	0
		Fiber	1 g

Tip: *Salmon has an exceptionally high amount of Omega-3 fish oil, the substance that has been shown to reduce cholesterol levels in the body. Red salmon has more than pink.*

Cold Curried Tuna and Fruit

Preparation: **30 min.** `FAT` `SUGAR` `SODIUM`

Here is a perfect luncheon dish for a hot summer day. Chilling it in the refrigerator for a few hours allows the flavors to blend.

- ½ **cup plain low-fat yogurt**
- 1 **tablespoon curry powder**
- ¼ **teaspoon each ground cumin and coriander**
- ⅛ **teaspoon ground cardamom**
- ⅛ **teaspoon sugar**
- 2 **cans (6½ ounces each) water-packed light tuna, drained and flaked**
- 1 **large orange, peeled and sectioned, with sections cut into thirds**
- 1 **cup fresh or drained juice-packed pineapple chunks**
- ½ **cup seedless green grapes, halved**
- ½ **cup seedless red grapes, halved**
- ½ **cup sliced water chestnuts**
- 12 **large lettuce leaves, such as romaine**

1. In a large bowl, combine the **yogurt, curry powder, cumin, coriander, cardamom,** and **sugar;** blend until smooth.
2. Add the **tuna, orange, pineapple, green grapes, red grapes,** and **water chestnuts.** Toss together gently until the fruits are well coated with the dressing. Chill in the refrigerator for at least 4 hours.
3. Arrange the **lettuce** leaves on individual salad plates and spoon the tuna and fruit mixture on top. Serve with crusty dark rolls. Serves 4.

One Serving:

Calories	197	Protein	23 g
Total Fat	2 g	Carbohydrates	24 g
Saturated Fat	0	Sodium	343 mg
Cholesterol	48 mg	Added Sugar	0
		Fiber	1 g

Deviled Tuna Pot Pie

Preparation: **15 min.** Cooking: **18 min.** FAT SUGAR SODIUM

- 1 **tablespoon unsalted margarine**
- 1 **medium-size yellow onion, chopped fine**
- 2 **cloves garlic, minced**
- 1 **large stalk celery, sliced thin**
- 1 **cup fresh or frozen whole-kernel corn**
- 1 **jar (4 ounces) pimientos, drained and chopped fine**
- ¼ **teaspoon black pepper**
- 4 **teaspoons flour**
- 1 **cup low-sodium chicken broth**
- ½ **cup skim milk**
- 2 **tablespoons grated Parmesan cheese**
- 2 **teaspoons Dijon or spicy brown mustard**
- 2 **teaspoons lemon juice**
- 2 **cans (6½ ounces each) water-packed light tuna, drained and flaked**
- 4 **refrigerator buttermilk biscuits, halved horizontally and slightly flattened**
- ⅛ **teaspoon paprika**

1. Preheat the oven to 450°F. In a medium-size heavy saucepan, melt the **margarine** over moderate heat; add the **onion, garlic, celery, corn, pimientos,** and **black pepper,** and cook, covered, for 5 minutes or until the onion is soft.

2. Blend in the **flour,** then the **chicken broth** and **milk,** and cook, stirring constantly, until the mixture has thickened—about 3 minutes. Add the **cheese, mustard,** and **lemon juice.** Remove from the heat; fold in the **tuna.**

3. Transfer all to an ungreased shallow 5- or 6-cup casserole. Arrange the **biscuits** on top, sprinkle with the **paprika,** and bake, uncovered, about 10 minutes or until the biscuits are golden. Serves 4.

One Serving:			
Calories	*284*	*Protein*	*27 g*
Total Fat	*8 g*	*Carbohydrates*	*23 g*
Saturated Fat	*1 g*	*Sodium*	*738 mg*
Cholesterol	*49 mg*	*Added Sugar*	*0*
		Fiber	*1 g*

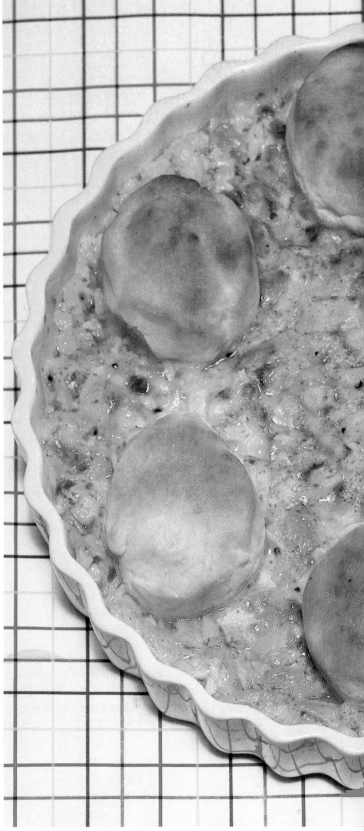

Deviled Tuna Pot Pie

Baked Tuna-Stuffed Tomatoes

4 medium-size firm, ripe
tomatoes
2 teaspoons lemon juice
1 tablespoon unsalted margarine
1 small yellow onion, chopped
1 medium-size carrot, peeled
and chopped fine
1 tablespoon flour

1 cup skim milk
1 can (6½ ounces) water-packed
light tuna, drained and flaked
1 teaspoon capers, chopped fine
¼ teaspoon black pepper
3 tablespoons fine dry bread
crumbs
½ cup shredded Monterey Jack
cheese (about 2 ounces)

FAT SUGAR SODIUM

Preparation:
25 min.
Cooking:
26 min. (mostly
unattended)

One Serving:

Calories	*191*
Total Fat	*8 g*
Saturated Fat	*1 g*
Cholesterol	*37 mg*
Protein	*17 g*
Carbohydrates	*13 g*
Sodium	*330 mg*
Added Sugar	*0*
Fiber	*1 g*

1. Preheat the oven to 350°F. Core the **tomatoes** and hollow them out, leaving shells ¼ to ½ inch thick. Sprinkle the insides of the tomatoes with the **lemon juice,** then drain them upside down on paper towels for 10 minutes.
2. In a medium-size heavy saucepan, melt the **margarine** over moderate heat; add the **onion** and **carrot** and cook, uncovered, until soft—about 5 minutes. Blend in the **flour** and cook, stirring, for 1 minute. Add the **milk** and cook, stirring constantly, until thickened—about 3 minutes.
3. In a medium-size bowl, combine the sauce with the **tuna, capers, pepper,** 2 tablespoons **bread crumbs,** and all but 1 tablespoon of the **cheese.**
4. Spoon the mixture into the tomatoes and set them in an ungreased baking pan just large enough to hold them. Sprinkle the tops with the remaining bread crumbs and cheese; bake, uncovered, for 15 minutes or until heated through. Raise the oven temperature to broil and broil the tomatoes about 6 inches from the heat for 1 minute or until tipped with brown. Serves 4.

Savory Salmon Patties

You can prepare the patties and store them in the refrigerator several hours before cooking. Since the recipe includes mashed potatoes, it's often a good choice for using up leftovers.

2 cans (6½ ounces each)
salmon, drained and flaked
1 cup mashed potatoes
2 tablespoons plain low-fat
yogurt
2 tablespoons prepared yellow
mustard
1 large egg white

1 medium-size carrot, peeled
and chopped fine
1 large yellow onion, chopped
fine
½ teaspoon paprika
1 tablespoon lemon juice
½ cup fine dry bread crumbs
1½ tablespoons corn oil

FAT SUGAR SODIUM

Preparation:
7 min.
Cooking:
7 min.

One Serving:

Calories	*310*
Total Fat	*13 g*
Saturated Fat	*2 g*
Cholesterol	*33 mg*
Protein	*23 g*
Carbohydrates	*23 g*
Sodium	*727 mg*
Added Sugar	*0*
Fiber	*1 g*

1. In a medium-size bowl, combine the **salmon, potatoes, yogurt, mustard, egg white, carrot, onion, paprika,** and **lemon juice;** shape into 8 patties.
2. Put the **bread crumbs** on a plate and coat the patties with the crumbs.
3. In a heavy 12-inch skillet, heat the **corn oil** over moderate heat for 1 minute; add the patties and cook about 3 minutes on each side or until golden brown. Transfer to a heated platter. Serves 4.

Salmon Loaf with Green Pea Sauce

FAT SUGAR SODIUM

Preparation: **15 min.**
Cooking: **55 min.** (mostly unattended)

- 2 tablespoons unsalted margarine
- 1 small yellow onion, chopped fine
- 1 medium-size stalk celery, chopped fine
- 3 tablespoons flour
- ½ cup skim milk
- 2 cans (6½ ounces each) salmon, drained and flaked
- ¼ cup fine dry bread crumbs
- 1 large egg white, slightly beaten
- 2 teaspoons dill weed
- 4 teaspoons lemon juice
- ¼ teaspoon black pepper
- 1 cup low-sodium chicken broth
- ⅛ teaspoon white or black pepper
- ½ cup cooked green peas

1. Preheat the oven to 350°F. In a medium-size saucepan, melt 1 tablespoon of the **margarine** over moderate heat; add the **onion** and **celery**, and cook, uncovered, until soft—about 5 minutes. Blend in 1 tablespoon of the **flour**, add the **milk**, and cook, stirring, for 3 to 5 minutes or until the sauce has thickened.

2. Remove from the heat and stir in the **salmon, bread crumbs, egg white,** half of the **dill weed** and **lemon juice,** and the **black pepper.**

3. Turn all into a lightly greased 7½"x 3¾"x 2" loaf pan and bake, uncovered, for 40 to 45 minutes or until lightly browned. Cool upright on a wire rack for 15 minutes.

4. Meanwhile, melt the remaining tablespoon of margarine in a small heavy saucepan over moderate heat. Blend in the remaining 2 tablespoons of flour and cook, stirring, for 3 to 5 minutes. Stir in the **chicken broth** and remaining dill weed and cook, stirring constantly, until thickened—3 to 5 minutes. Mix in the remaining lemon juice, the **white pepper,** and the **peas;** cover and keep warm.

5. When the loaf has cooled, invert it onto a warm platter and serve. Pass the sauce separately. Serves 4.

One Serving:

Calories	268	Protein	24 g
Total Fat	13 g	Carbohydrates	15 g
Saturated Fat	3 g	Sodium	475 mg
Cholesterol	33 mg	Added Sugar	0
		Fiber	1 g

California Seafood Medley

FAT SUGAR SODIUM

Preparation: **15 min.**
Cooking: **56 min.** (mostly unattended)

Often called cioppino, *this famous American dish originated on San Francisco's Fisherman's Wharf, where it was made of whatever seafood was available.*

- 1 tablespoon olive or vegetable oil
- 1 large yellow onion, chopped
- 3 cloves garlic, minced
- 1 medium-size sweet green pepper, cored, seeded, and sliced lengthwise into strips about ¼ inch wide
- 1 can (1 pound) low-sodium crushed tomatoes, with their juice
- 1½ cups low-sodium chicken broth
- ½ cup dry white wine
- ½ cup bottled clam juice
- ½ teaspoon each dried basil, thyme, and oregano, crumbled
- ½ teaspoon red pepper flakes
- 1 bay leaf
- 8 clams or mussels in the shell, scrubbed
- ½ pound haddock, halibut, or cod fillets, cut into 1½-inch pieces
- ¼ pound sea scallops, cut up
- ½ pound shrimp, shelled and deveined
- 3 tablespoons minced fresh basil or parsley

1. In a 4-quart Dutch oven, heat the **olive oil** over moderate heat for 1 minute; add the **onion, garlic,** and **green pepper,** and cook, stirring, until the onion is golden—about 7 minutes.

2. Add the **tomatoes, chicken broth, wine, clam juice, dried basil, thyme, oregano, red pepper flakes,** and **bay leaf;** cover and simmer for 45 minutes.

3. Add the **clams,** bring to a simmer, then add the **haddock, scallops,** and **shrimp.** Simmer, uncovered, stirring often, for 3 to 5 minutes or until the clams open. Discard the bay leaf and any clams that do not open. Ladle into heated bowls and sprinkle with the **fresh basil.** Serves 4.

One Serving:

Calories	241	Protein	33 g
Total Fat	6 g	Carbohydrates	13 g
Saturated Fat	1 g	Sodium	377 mg
Cholesterol	131 mg	Added Sugar	0
		Fiber	2 g

Scallops Marinated in Orange and Fennel

Seafood Gumbo

You can substitute other shellfish or cut-up fish fillets for the oysters and shrimp.

2 tablespoons unsalted margarine
2 medium-size yellow onions, chopped
1 clove garlic, minced
1 small sweet green pepper, cored, seeded, and chopped
1 medium-size stalk celery, chopped
2 tablespoons flour
3 cups low-sodium chicken broth
1 can (1 pound) low-sodium tomatoes, chopped, with their juice
½ cup chopped reduced-sodium ham (about 3 ounces)
1 bay leaf
¼ teaspoon hot red pepper sauce
½ pound fresh okra, trimmed and sliced, or 1 package (10 ounces) frozen sliced okra
1 cup long-grain rice
½ pound medium-size shrimp, shelled and deveined
½ pound fresh, canned, or frozen and thawed crabmeat, bits of shell and cartilage removed
1 dozen shucked oysters

Preparation:
20 min.
Cooking:
1 hr. 15 min. (mostly unattended)

One Serving:

Calories	313
Total Fat	11 g
Saturated Fat	2 g
Cholesterol	110 mg
Protein	23 g
Carbohydrates	37 g
Sodium	325 mg
Added Sugar	0
Fiber	3 g

1. In a heavy 4-quart Dutch oven, melt the **margarine** over moderate heat; add the **onions** and cook, uncovered, for 5 minutes. Mix in the **garlic, green pepper,** and **celery,** and cook, stirring often, for another 5 minutes. Add the **flour** and cook, stirring, for 1 minute.

2. Stir in the **chicken broth, tomatoes, ham, bay leaf,** and **red pepper sauce.** Bring to a simmer, cover partially, and cook for 30 minutes. Add the **okra** and cook, covered, another 30 minutes.

3. While the okra is cooking, prepare the **rice** according to package directions, omitting the salt. Set aside.

4. Add the **shrimp** and **crabmeat** to the gumbo. Cook, uncovered, until the shrimp are pink—about 2 minutes. Add the **oysters** and cook 1 minute longer. Remove the bay leaf. Ladle into bowls, and top each serving with a scoop of rice. Serves 6.

Tip: Lump crabmeat is preferable for salads and casseroles when you want the choice, large chunks to show. But for soups and stews, buy the cheaper flake type.

Scallops Marinated in Orange and Fennel

Preparation: **10 min.**, plus 4 hr. marination   Cooking: **5 min.**   FAT SUGAR SODIUM

Here is a wonderful make-ahead dish; the scallops may be marinated overnight, and cooking time is just 5 minutes.

¼ cup olive or vegetable oil
2 tablespoons lemon juice
2 tablespoons minced parsley
½ teaspoon fennel seeds, crushed
1 clove garlic, minced
  Grated rind of 1 small orange
1 pound sea scallops
1 medium-size zucchini, sliced ¼ inch thick (about ½ pound)
1 medium-size red onion, quartered, then cut into small wedges

1. In a medium-size shallow bowl, whisk together the **olive oil, lemon juice, parsley, fennel seeds, garlic,** and **orange rind.** Add the **scallops** and toss well; cover and refrigerate at least 4 hours or overnight.
2. Preheat the broiler. Thread the scallops onto 4 lightly greased, long metal skewers, alternating with the **zucchini** and **onion.**
3. Lay the skewers on the broiler pan rack and broil 4 to 5 inches from the heat, turning once or twice, until the scallops are just opaque—about 5 minutes. Transfer to heated dinner plates and serve with Easy Nutted Brown Rice, page 168. Serves 4.

One Serving:

Calories	244	Protein	21 g
Total Fat	15 g	Carbohydrates	7 g
Saturated Fat	2 g	Sodium	188 mg
Cholesterol	42 mg	Added Sugar	0
		Fiber	1 g

Tip: *To avoid confusing the two sizes of scallops, just remember that as the sea is larger than the bay, so are sea scallops larger than bay scallops.*

Deviled Crab

Preparation: **20 min.** Cooking: **17 min.**   FAT SUGAR SODIUM

2 tablespoons unsalted margarine
3 green onions, chopped fine
1 medium-size stalk celery, chopped fine
1 tablespoon flour
⅔ cup skim milk
2 teaspoons Dijon or spicy brown mustard
1 teaspoon lemon juice
⅛ teaspoon cayenne pepper
1 pound fresh, canned, or frozen and thawed crabmeat, bits of shell and cartilage removed
1 tablespoon chopped parsley
¼ cup fine dry bread crumbs
  Lemon peel (optional)

1. Preheat the broiler. In a medium-size heavy saucepan, melt 1 tablespoon of the **margarine** over moderate heat; add the **green onions** and **celery** and cook until just tender—about 5 minutes. Blend in the **flour** and cook 3 minutes more. Add the **milk** and cook, stirring constantly, until the mixture is thick and smooth—about 5 minutes.
2. Remove from the heat and blend in the **mustard, lemon juice,** and **cayenne pepper.** Stir in the **crabmeat** and **parsley;** set aside.
3. Melt the remaining margarine in a small saucepan over moderate heat, stir in the **bread crumbs,** and set aside.
4. Spoon equal amounts of the crab mixture into 4 lightly greased scallop shells or individual baking dishes. Sprinkle with equal amounts of the crumb mixture.
5. Broil 7 to 9 inches from the heat until browned—about 3 to 4 minutes. Garnish with strips of **lemon peel,** if desired. Serves 4.

One Serving:

Calories	210	Protein	22 g
Total Fat	8 g	Carbohydrates	10 g
Saturated Fat	1 g	Sodium	390 mg
Cholesterol	115 mg	Added Sugar	0
		Fiber	1 g

Cold Spiced Shrimp

Preparation: **10 min.,**
plus 4 hr. marination
Cooking: **10 min.**

Because it can be prepared well in advance, this makes a terrific party dish. Present the shrimp as a main course, or serve them on toothpicks as an appetizer.

2 **tablespoons vegetable oil**
1 **pound medium-size shrimp, shelled and deveined**
2 **green onions, chopped, with tops reserved**
2 **thin slices fresh ginger or ¼ teaspoon ground ginger**
¾ **cup low-sodium chicken broth**
3 **tablespoons low-sodium ketchup**
2 **tablespoons cider vinegar**
2 **tablespoons dry sherry or white wine**
1 **teaspoon sugar**
⅛ **teaspoon cayenne pepper**
8 **iceberg or Boston lettuce leaves**

1. In a heavy 10-inch skillet, heat 1 tablespoon of the **vegetable oil** over moderately high heat for 1 minute. Add the **shrimp** and stir-fry for 2 minutes; transfer to a platter.

2. Add the remaining oil to the skillet, then the **green onions** and the **ginger;** stir-fry about 30 seconds. Add the **chicken broth, ketchup, vinegar, sherry, sugar,** and **cayenne pepper;** simmer and stir for 3 minutes or until the sauce has thickened.

3. Return the shrimp to the skillet and cook, stirring, 3 minutes longer. Pour all into a bowl; cover and refrigerate for 4 hours.

4. When ready to serve, arrange the **lettuce** leaves on a platter and mound the shrimp on top. Chop the reserved green onion tops and sprinkle over the shrimp. Accompany with Roasted Vegetable Salad, page 216. Serves 4 as a main course.

One Serving:

Calories	199	Protein	25 g
Total Fat	10 g	Carbohydrates	4 g
Saturated Fat	2 g	Sodium	250 mg
Cholesterol	161 mg	Added Sugar	4 Cal
		Fiber	1 g

Stir-fried Lobster, Mushrooms, and Snow Peas

Preparation: **10 min.** Cooking: **10 min.**

¼ **cup medium-dry sherry or low-sodium chicken broth**
2 **tablespoons reduced-sodium soy sauce**
1 **tablespoon cornstarch**
⅛ **teaspoon red pepper flakes**
1 **tablespoon olive oil**
1 **1-inch cube fresh ginger, peeled and cut into matchstick strips**
½ **medium-size sweet red pepper, cored, seeded, and cut into 1-inch squares**
¼ **pound fresh snow peas, trimmed and strings removed, or 1 package (6 ounces) frozen snow peas, thawed**
¼ **pound small mushrooms, halved**
½ **cup sliced water chestnuts**
1 **pound lobster meat, cut into 1-inch cubes**

1. In a small bowl, whisk together the **sherry, soy sauce, cornstarch,** and **red pepper flakes;** set aside.

2. In a heavy 10-inch skillet, heat the **olive oil** over moderately high heat for 1 minute; add the **ginger** and cook for 3 to 4 minutes or until lightly golden. Transfer to a small plate.

3. Add the **red pepper** to the skillet and stir-fry for 2 minutes; add the **snow peas, mushrooms,** and **water chestnuts,** and stir-fry 2 minutes longer or until tender but still crisp.

4. Stir in the sherry mixture along with the **lobster** and ginger. Cook, stirring constantly, for 2 to 3 minutes or until slightly thickened. Serve with rice. Serves 4.

One Serving:

Calories	194	Protein	23 g
Total Fat	5 g	Carbohydrates	12 g
Saturated Fat	0	Sodium	547 mg
Cholesterol	96 mg	Added Sugar	0
		Fiber	1 g

Meatless Main Dishes

The "light" trend in cooking reminds us that we don't have to think of meat, chicken, or fish as the centerpiece of a meal. Meatless main dishes can be just as satisfying—and often more imaginative—than their heavier counterparts. As long as they have a good balance of beans, peas, or other legumes to grains such as wheat, corn, or barley, they can provide protein as complete as that found in meat—and at lower cost. In this section you'll find some appetizing examples: casseroles, stews, stir-fries, soufflés, pizzas, and sandwiches—all meatless and all surprisingly hearty.

Hearty Low-Calorie Lentil Stew

Cabbage-Noodle Casserole

4 ounces medium-size egg
  noodles
1 tablespoon unsalted margarine
1 medium-size yellow onion,
  sliced
1 small head cabbage (about
  1 pound), cored and sliced
  ¼ inch thick
1 teaspoon caraway seeds
½ teaspoon celery seeds
⅓ cup dry white wine or water

2 cups low-sodium chicken broth
2 tablespoons flour
½ cup plain low-fat yogurt
2 tablespoons sour cream
2 tablespoons cider vinegar
2 tablespoons grated Parmesan
  cheese
2 tablespoons fine dry bread
  crumbs
¼ cup slivered almonds

FAT SUGAR SODIUM

Preparation:
10 min.
Cooking:
49 min. (mostly
unattended)

One Serving:

Calories	308
Total Fat	14 g
Saturated Fat	4 g
Cholesterol	34 mg
Protein	12 g
Carbohydrates	39 g
Sodium	143 mg
Added Sugar	0
Fiber	2 g

1. Preheat the oven to 375°F. Cook the **noodles** according to package
   directions, omitting the salt. Drain and set aside.
2. Meanwhile, in a large heavy saucepan, melt the **margarine** over moderate
   heat; add the **onion** and cook, uncovered, until soft—about 5 minutes. Add
   the **cabbage, caraway seeds,** and **celery seeds,** and cook for 1 minute. Add
   the **wine,** cover, and simmer 10 minutes or until the cabbage is tender.
3. In a small bowl, whisk together the **chicken broth** and **flour.** Add to the
   cabbage, reduce the heat to moderately low, and cook, stirring, for 2 to
   3 minutes or until the mixture has thickened slightly. Mix in the **yogurt,**
   sour cream, and **vinegar.** Stir in the noodles.
4. Spoon the mixture into an ungreased shallow 1½-quart casserole, sprinkle
   with the **cheese** and **bread crumbs,** and bake, uncovered, for 20 minutes.
   Sprinkle the **almonds** on top of the casserole and bake, uncovered, 10 to 15
   minutes longer or until bubbling and browned on top. Serves 4.

Baked Beans on Dark Bread

2 tablespoons peanut or corn oil
2 medium-size yellow onions,
  chopped fine
4 cloves garlic, minced
1 small sweet red or green pepper,
  cored, seeded, and chopped fine
2 medium-size carrots, peeled
  and chopped fine
1 tablespoon minced fresh ginger
  or ¼ teaspoon ground ginger
½ teaspoon red pepper flakes

2 cups cooked and drained pinto
  beans
¼ cup molasses
2 teaspoons dry mustard
1 tablespoon red wine vinegar
2 teaspoons low-sodium tomato paste
¾ teaspoon dried thyme, crumbled
2 strips orange peel, each about 2
  inches long and ½ inch wide
4 slices dark bread, such as
  pumpernickel

FAT SUGAR SODIUM

Preparation:
20 min.
Cooking:
3 hr. 1 min. (mostly
unattended)

One Serving:

Calories	393
Total Fat	8 g
Saturated Fat	1 g
Cholesterol	0
Protein	14 g
Carbohydrates	69 g
Sodium	208 mg
Added Sugar	46 Cal
Fiber	9 g

1. Preheat the oven to 325°F. In a heavy 4-quart Dutch oven, heat the **peanut**
   oil over moderately low heat for 1 minute; add the **onions, garlic, red**
   pepper, carrots, ginger, and **red pepper flakes,** and cook, covered, for 30
   minutes or until the vegetables are soft.
2. Stir the **pinto beans, molasses, mustard, vinegar, tomato paste,** and **thyme**
   into the vegetables along with the **orange peel.** Add enough water to cover.
3. Cover the Dutch oven, place in the oven, and bake for 1½ hours. Add more
   water if beans appear dry and cook 1 hour longer. Remove the orange peel
   and spoon the beans over the **bread.** Serves 4.

Cabbage-Noodle Casserole

Barley-Vegetable Loaf with Yogurt-Dill Sauce

This savory loaf will serve four as a main course or eight as an appetizer; the barley may be cooked a day in advance.

FAT SUGAR SODIUM

Nonstick cooking spray
½ cup medium-size barley
1 tablespoon unsalted margarine
1 medium-size yellow onion, chopped fine
¼ pound mushrooms, chopped fine
2 medium-size zucchini (about ½ pound each), shredded
2 medium-size carrots, peeled and shredded

¾ cup shredded Cheddar cheese (about 3 ounces)
4 large egg whites
¼ cup snipped fresh dill or 1 teaspoon dill weed
½ teaspoon dried thyme, crumbled
¾ teaspoon grated lemon rind
½ cup plain low-fat yogurt

Preparation:
20 min.
Cooking:
1 hr. 50 min. (mostly unattended)

One Serving:

Calories	280
Total Fat	11 g
Saturated Fat	5 g
Cholesterol	25 mg
Protein	14 g
Carbohydrates	32 g
Sodium	221 mg
Added Sugar	0
Fiber	2 g

1. Preheat the oven to 350°F. Coat an 8½"x 4½"x 2½" loaf pan with the **cooking spray** and set aside.

2. Cook the **barley** according to package directions, omitting the salt, until tender—about 40 minutes. Drain well and set aside.

3. Meanwhile, in a heavy 10-inch skillet, melt the **margarine** over moderate heat; add the **onion, mushrooms, zucchini,** and **carrots,** and cook, stirring often, until the onion is soft—about 5 minutes.

4. Transfer the vegetable mixture to a large bowl and mix in the barley, **cheese, egg whites,** half the **dill,** the **thyme,** and the **lemon rind.** Spoon the mixture into the loaf pan; rap the pan lightly on the counter to make the loaf more compact and to release any air bubbles.

5. Cover with aluminum foil and bake for 45 minutes; uncover and bake 25 minutes more or until the loaf is brown and shrinks from the sides of the pan. Cool upright on a wire rack until the loaf is room temperature.

6. Meanwhile, combine the remaining dill with the **yogurt.** To serve, ease the loaf onto a platter and spoon the yogurt sauce on top. Serves 4.

Tip: A foolproof way to separate an egg white from the yolk is to break the egg gently into a narrow-necked funnel. The white will slip through, while the yolk remains.

Artichoke-Stuffed Peppers with Lemon Sauce

4 medium-size sweet green peppers, cored and seeded

4 ounces orzo or small elbow macaroni

1 package (9 ounces) frozen artichoke hearts

2 green onions, chopped fine

2 tablespoons snipped fresh dill or minced parsley

4 ounces feta cheese, rinsed well and crumbled

¾ cup low-sodium chicken broth

1 large egg

2 tablespoons lemon juice

⅛ teaspoon black pepper

FAT **SUGAR** **SODIUM**

Preparation:
15 min.
Cooking:
46 min. (mostly unattended)

One Serving:

Calories	*250*
Total Fat	*9 g*
Saturated Fat	*5 g*
Cholesterol	*94 mg*
Protein	*12 g*
Carbohydrates	*33 g*
Sodium	*378 mg*
Added Sugar	*0*
Fiber	*2 g*

1. Preheat the oven to 375°F. In a large saucepan, cook the **green peppers,** uncovered, in boiling unsalted water for 4 minutes. Drain upside down on paper towels.

2. Cook the **orzo** and **artichoke hearts** according to package directions, omitting the salt, and drain well. In a medium-size bowl, combine the orzo and artichoke hearts with the **green onions, dill,** and half the **cheese.**

3. In a small saucepan over moderate heat, bring the **chicken broth** to a simmer—about 3 minutes. In an electric blender or food processor, blend the **egg** and **lemon juice** by whirling for 5 seconds. With the motor still on, add ⅓ cup of the chicken broth and the **black pepper.** Pour the sauce over the orzo and artichokes and toss.

4. Set the peppers in an ungreased 8"x 8"x 2" baking pan; fill with the orzo, top with the remaining cheese, and pour the rest of the broth around them.

5. Bake, uncovered, for 30 minutes. Spoon the broth over the peppers. Serves 4.

Eggplant Lasagne

2 tablespoons lemon juice

1 tablespoon olive oil

1 medium-size eggplant (about 1 pound), unpeeled, halved lengthwise, and sliced ¼ inch thick

2 cans (8 ounces each) low-sodium tomato sauce

1 can (14½ ounces) low-sodium tomatoes, drained and chopped

2 cloves garlic, minced

¼ teaspoon each red pepper flakes, dried oregano, and dried basil, crumbled

⅓ cup fine dry bread crumbs

¼ cup grated Parmesan cheese

½ cup part-skim ricotta cheese

¼ cup shredded part-skim mozzarella cheese (about 1 ounce)

FAT **SUGAR** **SODIUM**

Preparation:
20 min.
Cooking:
51 min. (mostly unattended)

One Serving:

Calories	*240*
Total Fat	*10 g*
Saturated Fat	*4 g*
Cholesterol	*18 mg*
Protein	*12 g*
Carbohydrates	*29 g*
Sodium	*270 mg*
Added Sugar	*0*
Fiber	*3 g*

1. Preheat the broiler. In a small bowl, combine the **lemon juice** and **olive oil.** Brush the **eggplant** slices with the mixture and arrange in a single layer on a nonstick baking sheet; broil 5 to 6 inches from the heat for 2½ minutes on each side or until golden brown.

2. Reduce the oven temperature to 350°F. In a medium-size bowl, mix together the **tomato sauce, tomatoes, garlic, red pepper flakes, oregano,** and **basil.** In a small bowl, combine the **bread crumbs** and **Parmesan cheese.**

3. Spoon ⅓ of the tomato sauce into a deep flameproof 1½-quart casserole, sprinkle with ⅓ of the bread crumb mixture, and cover with a layer of eggplant. Spread ½ of the **ricotta cheese** over the eggplant and continue to layer in the same order, ending with the tomato sauce. Scatter the **mozzarella cheese** over the top and bake for 45 minutes or until bubbling.

4. Increase the heat to broil and place the casserole in the broiler 5 to 6 inches from the heat. Broil for 1 minute or until the casserole is golden. Serves 4.

Spinach Crêpes with Tomato Sauce

You may assemble these thin pancakes several hours before baking or prepare the entire dish ahead and refrigerate or freeze it.

¾ cup sifted all-purpose flour
1 cup skim milk
1 tablespoon vegetable oil
1 large egg
2 large egg whites
¾ pound fresh spinach, cooked, chopped, and drained, or
1 package (10 ounces) frozen chopped spinach, thawed and drained

1½ cups low-fat cottage cheese
¼ cup grated Parmesan cheese
⅛ teaspoon ground nutmeg
⅛ teaspoon black pepper
1 can (1 pound) low-sodium tomatoes, chopped, with their juice
1 tablespoon unsalted margarine
½ teaspoon dried basil, crumbled

Preparation:
20 min., plus 2 hr. refrigeration
Cooking:
28 min.

One Serving:

Calories	310
Total Fat	11 g
Saturated Fat	3 g
Cholesterol	77 mg
Protein	24 g
Carbohydrates	30 g
Sodium	594 mg
Added Sugar	0
Fiber	3 g

Tip: A Parmesan cheese grater is much easier to clean if you spray it with a little nonstick cooking spray before each use.

1. To prepare the batter for 12 crêpes, place the **flour, milk, vegetable oil, egg,** 1 **egg white,** and ⅓ of the **spinach** in an electric blender or food processor. Blend for 10 to 20 seconds. Cover and refrigerate the batter for 2 hours. Cover and refrigerate the remaining spinach.

2. Lightly grease a 7-inch skillet and set over moderate heat for 30 seconds. Pour in 3 tablespoons of the batter, rotating the pan to spread it evenly. Cook the crêpe until the edges are brown and crisp—about 30 seconds. With a spatula, gently loosen it and turn it over. Cook 10 seconds longer or until it is light brown on the underside. Transfer to a large plate. Cook the remaining batter in the same way, stacking the crêpes as they are done. *(Note: Here you may refrigerate or freeze the crêpes for later use.)*

3. Preheat the oven to 350°F. In a medium-size bowl, combine the remaining spinach with the remaining egg white and the **cottage cheese, Parmesan cheese, nutmeg,** and **pepper.**

4. To assemble, spoon a scant ¼ cup of the filling down the center of each crêpe, then roll it up. Place the crêpes seam side down, side by side, in a lightly greased 13"x 9"x 2" baking pan and bake, uncovered, for 20 minutes.

5. Meanwhile, in a medium-size saucepan, simmer the **tomatoes, margarine,** and **basil** over moderate heat for 20 minutes or until thickened. Just before serving, spoon the sauce over the crêpes. Serves 4.

Eggplant Lasagne

Seven-Vegetable Casserole with Couscous Crust

Spinach Ring with White Bean Sauce

2 pounds fresh spinach, trimmed and chopped, or 2 packages (10 ounces each) frozen chopped spinach, thawed and drained

4 teaspoons olive oil

2 tablespoons flour

¾ cup skim milk

¼ cup grated Parmesan cheese

1 large egg yolk

Nonstick cooking spray

2 large egg whites

1½ cups cooked and drained white beans

¾ cup water

2 tablespoons plain low-fat yogurt

1 tablespoon lemon juice

¼ teaspoon salt

⅛ teaspoon cayenne pepper

Preparation:
10 min.
Cooking:
36 min. (mostly unattended)

One Serving:

Calories	233
Total Fat	9 g
Saturated Fat	2 g
Cholesterol	74 mg
Protein	16 g
Carbohydrates	25 g
Sodium	382 mg
Added Sugar	0
Fiber	5 g

1. Preheat the oven to 350°F. In a heavy 10-inch skillet over moderate heat, cook the **spinach,** covered, in 2 teaspoons of the **olive oil** for 2 minutes. Uncover and cook, stirring, until the spinach is completely dry—about 2 minutes. Set aside.

2. In a medium-size saucepan over moderate heat, whisk the **flour** into the **milk** and cook, stirring, until thickened—about 4 minutes. Remove the sauce from the heat and blend in the **cheese, egg yolk,** and spinach.

3. Coat a 1-quart ring mold with the **cooking spray** and set aside. In a medium-size bowl, beat the **egg whites** until stiff but not dry. Stir about ¼ of the whites into the spinach mixture, then gently fold in the remainder. Spoon the mixture into the mold and smooth the top with a spatula.

4. Bake, uncovered, for 25 minutes or until firm to the touch; cool the mold upright on a wire rack for 5 minutes. Using a small knife, gently loosen the spinach ring around the edges, and carefully invert it onto a platter.

5. In a food processor or electric blender, purée the **white beans** with the remaining olive oil and the **water, yogurt, lemon juice, salt,** and **cayenne pepper** by whirling for 15 seconds. In a small saucepan, warm the sauce over low heat for 3 to 5 minutes and pour over the spinach ring. Serves 4.

Tip: *Don't feel wasteful when you throw out extra egg yolks. Most of the egg's nutrition, including a high protein content, is in the white; the yolk contains mostly fat and cholesterol.*

Seven-Vegetable Casserole with Couscous Crust

Preparation: **20 min.**
Cooking: **1 hr. 21 min.** (mostly unattended)   FAT SUGAR SODIUM

1½ cups low-sodium chicken broth
 1 cup couscous or yellow cornmeal
 1 can (1 pound) low-sodium tomatoes, chopped, with their juice
 1 medium-size yellow onion, sliced thin
 4 medium-size mushrooms, sliced thin
 1 small sweet red or green pepper, cored, seeded, and sliced lengthwise into strips about ¼ inch wide
 1 medium-size yellow squash (about ½ pound), sliced thin
 2 medium-size carrots, peeled and sliced thin
 1 cup small broccoli florets
 ½ cup cooked and drained chick peas
1½ teaspoons dried basil, crumbled
 ¼ teaspoon black pepper

1. Preheat the oven to 350°F. In a medium-size heavy saucepan over moderately high heat, bring the **chicken broth** to a boil—about 5 minutes. Remove the saucepan from the heat, add the **couscous,** and stir constantly with a fork or whisk until the mixture is thick—about 5 minutes.

2. Grease a round 2-quart casserole and spoon the couscous into it. Using a large serving spoon or wet hands, push and flatten the couscous up the sides to within ½ inch of the rim. Set aside.

3. In a medium-size saucepan over moderately low heat, bring the **tomatoes** to a simmer— about 6 minutes. Add the **onion, mushrooms, red pepper, yellow squash, carrots, broccoli, chick peas, basil,** and **black pepper.** Cover and simmer for 5 minutes or until the vegetables are tender but still crisp.

4. Spoon the vegetables into the casserole, cover with aluminum foil, and bake for 1 hour. Serve directly from the dish, or cool for 15 minutes, gently loosen the crust with a thin metal spatula, and invert onto a platter. Serves 4.

One Serving:

Calories	292	*Protein*	13 g
Total Fat	3 g	*Carbohydrates*	49 g
Saturated Fat	2 g	*Sodium*	59 mg
Cholesterol	0	*Added Sugar*	0
		Fiber	4 g

Zucchini Filled with Spinach and Ricotta

Preparation: **20 min.** Cooking: **34 min.**   FAT SUGAR SODIUM

You can halve this recipe to serve two; use a small egg.

 4 medium-size zucchini (about 2 pounds)
 2 teaspoons olive oil
 1 medium-size yellow onion, chopped fine
 4 cloves garlic, minced
 1 pound fresh spinach, trimmed and chopped, or 1 package (10 ounces) frozen chopped spinach, thawed and drained
 ¼ teaspoon black pepper
 ⅛ teaspoon ground nutmeg
 1 cup part-skim ricotta cheese
 ¼ cup grated Parmesan cheese
 1 large egg
 2 tablespoons raisins
 1 tablespoon chopped walnuts

1. Cut the **zucchini** in half lengthwise. Using a spoon, scoop out the flesh, leaving shells about ¼ inch thick. Place the shells in a medium-size saucepan with enough boiling water to cover. Cook for 4 minutes or until just tender. Drain, rinse under cold running water to stop further cooking, drain again, and set aside.

2. In a heavy 10-inch skillet, heat the **olive oil** over moderate heat for 1 minute; add the **onion** and **garlic** and cook, uncovered, until the onion is soft—about 5 minutes. Add the **spinach, pepper,** and **nutmeg** and cook, covered, for 2 minutes; uncover and cook 2 minutes longer or until the spinach is dry.

3. Remove the spinach mixture from the heat, cool for 10 minutes, then stir in the **ricotta cheese, Parmesan cheese, egg, raisins,** and **walnuts.**

4. Preheat the oven to 350°F. In an ungreased 13"x 9"x 2" baking pan, place the zucchini shells side by side and fill with the spinach mixture. Bake, uncovered, for 20 minutes or until the filling has set. Serves 4.

One Serving:

Calories	212	*Protein*	15 g
Total Fat	12 g	*Carbohydrates*	15 g
Saturated Fat	5 g	*Sodium*	237 mg
Cholesterol	92 mg	*Added Sugar*	0
		Fiber	3 g

Black Beans and Rice

1 tablespoon vegetable oil
1 medium-size yellow onion, chopped fine
1 small sweet red pepper, cored, seeded, and chopped fine
2 cloves garlic, minced
1¾ cups cooked and drained black beans
½ cup long-grain rice

1½ cups low-sodium chicken broth
¼ teaspoon red pepper flakes
¼ teaspoon dried thyme, crumbled
1 bay leaf
½ cup shredded Cheddar cheese (about 2 ounces)

FAT SUGAR SODIUM

Preparation:
15 min.
Cooking:
26 min. (mostly unattended)

One Serving:

Calories	321
Total Fat	11 g
Saturated Fat	3 g
Cholesterol	7 mg
Protein	14 g
Carbohydrates	45 g
Sodium	99 mg
Added Sugar	0
Fiber	6 g

1. In a large heavy saucepan, heat the **vegetable oil** over moderate heat for 1 minute; add the **onion** and **red pepper** and cook, stirring, for 5 minutes or until the onion is soft.
2. Add the **garlic, black beans, rice, chicken broth, red pepper flakes, thyme,** and **bay leaf,** and bring to a boil. Adjust the heat so that the mixture bubbles gently. Cover and simmer for 20 minutes or until the rice is tender.
3. Remove the bay leaf, spoon the rice and beans onto 4 heated plates, and sprinkle each portion with the **cheese.** Serves 4.

Hearty Low-Calorie Lentil Stew

The recipe for this nourishing stew makes enough for two meals. Freeze or refrigerate half to serve another day. Serving the stew with white or brown rice will increase the amount of protein by more than 3 grams per serving.

1 cup dried lentils, rinsed and sorted
4 cups low-sodium beef broth or water
1 medium-size yellow onion, chopped
2 cloves garlic, minced
2 large stalks celery, diced
4 medium-size carrots, peeled and cut into 1-inch lengths
2 cans (1 pound each) low-sodium tomatoes, chopped, with their juice

1 teaspoon dried rosemary, crumbled
¼ teaspoon black pepper
8 small white onions, peeled
2 tablespoons unsalted margarine
¼ pound small mushrooms, halved
4 medium-size all-purpose potatoes (about 1 pound), peeled and cut into 1-inch cubes

FAT SUGAR SODIUM

Preparation:
20 min.
Cooking:
1 hr. 7 min. (mostly unattended)

One Serving:

Calories	204
Total Fat	4 g
Saturated Fat	1 g
Cholesterol	0
Protein	9 g
Carbohydrates	35 g
Sodium	52 mg
Added Sugar	0
Fiber	3 g

1. In a 6-quart Dutch oven over moderate heat, bring the **lentils, beef broth, yellow onion, garlic, celery,** half the **carrots,** and the **tomatoes, rosemary,** and **pepper** to a simmer. Adjust the heat so that the mixture bubbles slowly, cover, and cook for 35 minutes.
2. Meanwhile, in a heavy 12-inch heavy skillet over moderately high heat, cook the remaining carrots and the **white onions,** uncovered, in the **margarine** for 5 to 8 minutes or until lightly browned. Add the **mushrooms** and cook, stirring, for 2 to 3 minutes.
3. Add the **potatoes** and the skillet vegetables to the Dutch oven, cover, and simmer 20 to 25 minutes longer or until the lentils and potatoes are tender. Serve with white or brown rice. Serves 8.

Tofu Stir-fry with Rice

Preparation: **20 min.** Cooking: **20 min.** FAT SUGAR SODIUM

Tofu, or soybean curd, is a popular vegetable cheese.

- 1 **cup long-grain rice**
- 1 **teaspoon sesame seeds**
- 1 **tablespoon peanut or vegetable oil**
- 2 **teaspoons minced ginger or ¼ teaspoon ground ginger**
- 2 **cloves garlic, minced**
- 1 **medium-size yellow onion, sliced ¼ inch thick**
- 1 **medium-size stalk celery, cut into matchstick strips**
- 2 **medium-size carrots, peeled and cut into matchstick strips**
- 1 **medium-size zucchini (about ½ pound), sliced ¼ inch thick**
- 1 **pound firm tofu, cut into 1-inch cubes**
- ¾ **cup low-sodium chicken broth**
- 1 **tablespoon reduced-sodium soy sauce**
- 1 **tablespoon dry sherry or white wine**
- 2 **teaspoons cornstarch**
- 1 **teaspoon Oriental sesame or peanut oil**

1. Preheat the oven to 325°F. Cook the **rice** according to package directions; omit the salt.

2. Meanwhile, to toast the **sesame seeds,** spread them out in a pie pan and bake, uncovered, shaking the pan frequently, until the seeds are golden—about 10 minutes. Set aside.

3. In a heavy 10-inch skillet, heat the **peanut oil** over moderately high heat for 1 minute. Add the **ginger** and **garlic** and stir-fry for 30 seconds. Stir in the **onion, celery,** and **carrots,** and stir-fry for 1 minute. Add the **zucchini, tofu,** ½ cup of the **chicken broth,** and the **soy sauce.** Cover and simmer until the vegetables are tender. Using a slotted spoon, transfer the mixture to a bowl; cover with aluminum foil and keep warm.

4. In a small bowl, combine the remaining chicken broth with the **sherry, cornstarch,** and **sesame oil.** Add to the skillet and cook, stirring, over moderate heat until thick—about 3 minutes.

5. To serve, spoon the rice onto a platter; top with the vegetables, drizzle the sauce over all, and sprinkle with the sesame seeds. Serves 4.

One Serving:			
Calories	*262*	*Protein*	*14 g*
Total Fat	*11 g*	*Carbohydrates*	*32 g*
Saturated Fat	*2 g*	*Sodium*	*194 mg*
Cholesterol	*0*	*Added Sugar*	*0*
		Fiber	*1 g*

Tofu Stir-fry with Rice

Spaghetti Squash Italian Style

1 large spaghetti squash (about 4 pounds)

1 tablespoon olive oil

1 medium-size yellow onion, chopped fine

¾ pound mushrooms, sliced

⅓ cup dry white wine or water

2 cans (8 ounces each) low-sodium tomato sauce

1 can (1 pound) low-sodium tomatoes, puréed with their juice

2 cloves garlic, minced

¼ teaspoon each dried basil, rosemary, and thyme, crumbled

¼ teaspoon black pepper

3 medium-size carrots, peeled and sliced

2½ cups broccoli florets

1 small zucchini (about ¼ pound), sliced

¼ cup grated Parmesan cheese

2 tablespoons minced parsley

1 tablespoon unsalted sunflower seeds, toasted

Preparation:
20 min.
Cooking:
1 hr. (mostly unattended)

One Serving:

Calories	345
Total Fat	13 g
Saturated Fat	2 g
Cholesterol	3 mg
Protein	13 g
Carbohydrates	54 g
Sodium	226 mg
Added Sugar	0
Fiber	3 g

1. Preheat the oven to 350°F. Pierce the **squash** in several places with a small knife, set it on a baking sheet, and bake for 1 to 1¼ hours or until you can pierce it easily with a fork.

2. Meanwhile, heat the **olive oil** in a medium-size saucepan over moderate heat for 1 minute. Add the **onion** and cook, uncovered, until soft—about 5 minutes. Add the **mushrooms** and **wine** and cook, covered, for 3 minutes. Mix in the **tomato sauce, tomatoes, garlic, basil, rosemary, thyme,** and **pepper,** and simmer, covered, for 3 minutes. Add the **carrots** and simmer 3 minutes more. Mix in the **broccoli** and cook for another 3 minutes. Stir in the **zucchini** and cook for 2 minutes or until tender but crisp.

3. When the squash is done, let it cool for 15 minutes, then halve it lengthwise and remove the seeds. Using a fork, scrape the flesh onto a platter. Warm up the vegetable mixture if necessary and spoon it over the squash. Sprinkle with the **cheese, parsley,** and **sunflower seeds.** Serves 4.

Tip: *Parsley will stay fresh for up to two weeks if you wash and dry it thoroughly, then store it in a screw-top jar in the refrigerator.*

Spaghetti Squash Italian Style

Vegetarian Chili with Rice

With a green salad, this chili provides a complete protein-rich meal.

1 tablespoon vegetable oil
1 large yellow onion, chopped
1 medium-size carrot, peeled and chopped
3 cloves garlic, minced
1 medium-size sweet green pepper, cored, seeded, and chopped
½ cup dried lentils, rinsed and sorted
2 teaspoons chili powder or to taste
1 teaspoon ground cumin
1 bay leaf
⅛ teaspoon cayenne pepper
1 can (1 pound) low-sodium tomatoes, chopped, with their juice
½ cup cooked and drained chick peas
½ cup cooked and drained black beans
½ cup cooked and drained pinto beans
¾ cup long-grain rice

Preparation:
15 min.
Cooking:
51 min. (mostly unattended)

One Serving:

Calories	*411*
Total Fat	*5 g*
Saturated Fat	*1 g*
Cholesterol	*0*
Protein	*17 g*
Carbohydrates	*75 g*
Sodium	*52 mg*
Added Sugar	*0*
Fiber	*7 g*

1. In a heavy 6-quart Dutch oven, heat the **vegetable oil** over moderately low heat for 1 minute; add the **onion, carrot, garlic,** and **green pepper,** and cook, covered, for 10 minutes or until the vegetables are soft.
2. Add the **lentils, chili powder, cumin, bay leaf, cayenne pepper,** and **tomatoes,** along with a small amount of water if the mixture appears thick. Cover and simmer for 10 minutes. Add the **chick peas, black beans,** and **pinto beans,** cover, and simmer for 30 minutes or until the lentils are tender.
3. Before the chili is done, cook the **rice** following package directions, omitting the salt. Ladle the chili over it and serve with a green salad. Serves 4.

Vegetable Curry with Yogurt Sauce

With its refreshing yogurt sauce, this mild Indian curry is a tasty one-dish meal.

1 tablespoon unsalted margarine
1 large yellow onion, chopped fine
2 cloves garlic, minced
2 teaspoons curry powder
½ teaspoon ground cinnamon
2 cups low-sodium chicken broth
½ cup long-grain rice
1 medium-size ripe tomato, cored and chopped
2 medium-size carrots, peeled and diced
1 cup cooked and drained chick peas
½ cup raisins
1½ cups tiny cauliflower florets
1 cup fresh or frozen green peas
1 cup plain low-fat yogurt
½ cup grated cucumber
⅛ teaspoon black pepper
2 teaspoons lemon juice
2 tablespoons minced parsley

Preparation:
20 min.
Cooking:
40 min. (mostly unattended)

One Serving:

Calories	*373*
Total Fat	*8 g*
Saturated Fat	*2 g*
Cholesterol	*3 mg*
Protein	*15 g*
Carbohydrates	*68 g*
Sodium	*99 mg*
Added Sugar	*0*
Fiber	*8 g*

1. In a large heavy saucepan, melt the **margarine** over moderate heat; add the **onion** and cook, uncovered, for 5 minutes or until soft. Add the **garlic, curry powder,** and **cinnamon,** and cook 2 minutes more, stirring often.
2. Stir in the **chicken broth, rice, tomato,** and **carrots,** and bring to a simmer. Add the **chick peas** and **raisins,** cover, and simmer for 20 minutes. Add the **cauliflower** and **peas,** cover again, and cook 10 minutes longer.
3. Meanwhile, prepare the yogurt sauce. In a small bowl, combine the **yogurt, cucumber,** and **pepper** and set aside.
4. Stir the **lemon juice** into the curry and spoon the curry onto a platter. Garnish with the **parsley.** Serve the sauce in a separate bowl. Serves 4.

Vegetable Lo Mein

Preparation: **20 min.** Cooking: **15 min.** `FAT` `SUGAR` `SODIUM`

4 ounces Oriental egg noodles or thin egg
   noodles
1 tablespoon peanut or vegetable oil
3 green onions, chopped fine, with tops sliced
   and reserved
2 cloves garlic, minced
1 teaspoon minced fresh ginger or
   ¼ teaspoon ground ginger
2 medium-size stalks celery, sliced thin
2 medium-size carrots, peeled and sliced thin
¼ pound mushrooms, sliced thin
1 cup low-sodium chicken broth or water
2 cups broccoli florets
1 tablespoon cornstarch
1 tablespoon low-sodium soy sauce
1 tablespoon dry sherry
1 teaspoon Oriental sesame or peanut oil
½ teaspoon sugar
½ pound firm tofu, cut into ¾-inch cubes

1. Cook the **noodles** according to package
directions, omitting the salt; drain and set aside.
2. Meanwhile, in a heavy 12-inch skillet, heat the
peanut oil over moderately high heat for
1 minute. Add the **green onions, garlic,** and
ginger, and cook, stirring, for 30 seconds. Add
the **celery, carrots,** and **mushrooms,** and stir-
fry 2 minutes longer. Stir in ½ cup of the
chicken broth, cover, and simmer for
3 minutes. Add the **broccoli,** cover, and simmer
for 2 minutes.
3. In a small bowl, combine the remaining chicken
broth with the **cornstarch, soy sauce,**
sherry, sesame oil, and **sugar.** Add to the
skillet and cook, stirring constantly, over
moderate heat until thick—about 4 minutes.
Add the noodles and **tofu,** cover, and simmer
for 2 minutes or until the tofu is heated
through. Transfer the vegetables to a platter,
toss gently, and sprinkle with the sliced green
onion tops. Serves 4.

One Serving:

Calories	260	*Protein*	*12 g*
Total Fat	*10 g*	*Carbohydrates*	*35 g*
Saturated Fat	*2 g*	*Sodium*	*217 mg*
Cholesterol	*27 mg*	*Added Sugar*	*2 Cal*
		Fiber	*2 g*

Sweet and Spicy Vegetable Stew

Preparation: **20 min.** `FAT` `SUGAR` `SODIUM`
Cooking: **1 hr.** (mostly unattended)

3 cups cauliflower florets (about ½ large head)
1 tablespoon olive oil
1 small yellow onion, chopped fine
3 cloves garlic, minced
1 large can (35 ounces) low-sodium
   tomatoes, drained and chopped
1 cinnamon stick
¾ teaspoon each ground turmeric and ginger
½ teaspoon each paprika and black pepper
1 medium-size sweet red pepper, cored,
   seeded, and cut into 1-inch pieces
1 medium-size carrot, peeled, halved
   lengthwise, and sliced thin
5 pitted prunes, chopped
1 cup cold water
1 cup fresh green beans, trimmed and
   snapped in half
1 cup cooked and drained chick peas
1½ cups boiling water
1 cup couscous or long-grain rice

1. In a large saucepan, cook the **cauliflower** in
boiling unsalted water for 4 minutes or until
just tender; drain and set aside.
2. In a heavy 12-inch skillet, heat the **olive oil**
over moderate heat for 1 minute; add the **onion**
and **garlic** and cook, uncovered, until the onion
is soft—about 5 minutes. Add the **tomatoes,**
cinnamon stick, turmeric, ginger, paprika,
and **black pepper;** cover and cook for 10
minutes. Stir in the **red pepper, carrot, prunes,**
and ½ cup **cold water;** cover and cook
15 minutes longer. Add the **green beans,**
cauliflower, and another ½ cup cold water, and
cook, covered, for 20 minutes. Stir in the **chick**
peas and cook, covered, for 5 minutes.
3. As soon as the chick peas are added to the
skillet, pour the boiling **water** over the
couscous, cover, and let stand 5 minutes. Fluff
the couscous with a fork; mound on a platter.
Remove the cinnamon stick from the stew and
ladle the stew on top of the couscous. Serves 4.

One Serving:

Calories	403	*Protein*	*15 g*
Total Fat	*5 g*	*Carbohydrates*	*68 g*
Saturated Fat	*1 g*	*Sodium*	*58 mg*
Cholesterol	*0*	*Added Sugar*	*0*
		Fiber	*8 g*

Spanish-Style Vegetable Casserole

With its colorful vegetables, this zesty and simple Spanish-style meal can be made ahead and served as festive fare for a party.

FAT SUGAR SODIUM

1 tablespoon olive oil
1 medium-size yellow onion, chopped
1 clove garlic, minced
1 medium-size tomato, cored and chopped
1 medium-size sweet red or green pepper, cored, seeded, and chopped
1 small all-purpose potato, peeled and diced

½ teaspoon paprika
¼ teaspoon cayenne pepper
1 cup long-grain rice
2 cups low-sodium chicken broth
1 medium-size zucchini (about ½ pound), quartered lengthwise and cut into 3-inch pieces
2 medium-size carrots, peeled, halved lengthwise, and cut into 3-inch pieces
2 cups fresh or frozen green peas

Preparation:
20 min.
Cooking:
32 min. (mostly unattended)

One Serving:

Calories	*353*
Total Fat	*7 g*
Saturated Fat	*1 g*
Cholesterol	*0*
Protein	*12 g*
Carbohydrates	*67 g*
Sodium	*53 mg*
Added Sugar	*0*
Fiber	*4 g*

1. In a large heavy saucepan, heat the **olive oil** over moderate heat for 1 minute. Add the **onion** and **garlic** and cook, stirring, for 1 minute. Mix in the **tomato** and **red pepper** and cook another 3 minutes. Add the **potato, paprika,** and **cayenne pepper,** and cook 2 minutes longer.
2. Stir in the **rice** and **chicken broth** and bring to a boil; adjust the heat so that the mixture bubbles gently. Cover and simmer for 15 minutes or until most of the liquid is absorbed. Stir in the **zucchini, carrots,** and **peas,** cover again, and cook for 10 minutes.
3. To serve, spoon the mixture onto a large heated platter. Serves 4.

White Bean, Yellow Squash, and Tomato Stew

This hearty main dish tastes even better if made a day in advance. It is equally good made with Great Northern beans or the smaller navy beans.

FAT SUGAR SODIUM

1 tablespoon olive oil
2 large yellow onions, chopped
2 cloves garlic, minced
2 large stalks celery, chopped fine
1 can (1 pound) low-sodium tomatoes, chopped, with their juice
1 medium-size yellow squash (about ½ pound), sliced thin
1 cup fresh or frozen lima beans
½ cup dry white wine or low-sodium chicken broth

1 bay leaf
¾ teaspoon each dried thyme, basil, and marjoram, crumbled
¼ teaspoon black pepper
⅛ teaspoon cayenne pepper
2 cups cooked and drained white beans
1 teaspoon lemon juice
2 tablespoons minced parsley

Preparation:
15 min.
Cooking:
21 min.

One Serving:

Calories	*257*
Total Fat	*5 g*
Saturated Fat	*1 g*
Cholesterol	*0*
Protein	*13 g*
Carbohydrates	*44 g*
Sodium	*72 mg*
Added Sugar	*0*
Fiber	*9 g*

1. In a heavy 6-quart Dutch oven, heat the **olive oil** over moderate heat for 1 minute; add the **onions, garlic,** and **celery,** and cook, uncovered, until the onion and celery are soft—5 to 8 minutes.
2. Add the **tomatoes, yellow squash, lima beans, wine, bay leaf, thyme, basil, marjoram, black pepper,** and **cayenne pepper** and simmer, uncovered, for 10 to 15 minutes.
3. Add the **white beans,** stir, and simmer 5 minutes more.
4. Stir in the **lemon juice** and **parsley** and serve. A crisp salad of tossed greens makes a nice accompaniment. Serves 4.

Tip: Cooking dried beans at home is worth the small amount of trouble. Canned beans, though convenient, may contain 40 times as much sodium.

Zesty Cheese Enchiladas

Broccoli-Cheddar Soufflé

½ tablespoon unsalted margarine
3 tablespoons flour
1 cup skim milk
1 large egg yolk
¾ cup shredded Cheddar cheese
(about 3 ounces)

1 cup chopped cooked broccoli
⅛ teaspoon cayenne pepper
6 large egg whites

1. Preheat the oven to 400°F. Coat the inside of a 1½-quart soufflé dish with the **margarine.**
2. In a large heavy saucepan, whisk together the **flour** and **milk;** bring to a simmer over moderately low heat and continue whisking for 2 minutes.
3. Remove the saucepan from the heat; immediately whisk in the **egg yolk,** and stir in the **cheese, broccoli,** and **cayenne pepper.**
4. In a large bowl, beat the **egg whites** until stiff but not dry. Stir ¼ of the whites into the cheese mixture, and gently but thoroughly fold in the remaining whites. Spoon the mixture into the soufflé dish and bake for 30 to 35 minutes or until golden brown. Serves 4.

Preparation:
10 min.
Cooking:
32 min. (mostly unattended)

One Serving:

Calories	*229*
Total Fat	*14 g*
Saturated Fat	*5 g*
Cholesterol	*86 mg*
Protein	*16 g*
Carbohydrates	*7 g*
Sodium	*254 mg*
Added Sugar	*0*
Fiber	*1 g*

Zesty Cheese Enchiladas

Commercial corn tortillas are difficult to roll in traditional enchilada style; this recipes calls for simply folding them. You can halve this recipe to serve two.

8 6-inch corn tortillas
1 cup part-skim ricotta cheese
2 green onions, chopped
1 tablespoon chopped fresh coriander or ½ teaspoon ground coriander
¾ teaspoon ground cumin

½ teaspoon chili powder
⅛ teaspoon cayenne pepper
2 teaspoons lemon juice
1 cup shredded part-skim mozzarella cheese (about 4 ounces)

Preparation:
15 min.
Cooking:
35 min. (mostly unattended)

One Serving:

Calories	304
Total Fat	13 g
Saturated Fat	7 g
Cholesterol	41 mg
Protein	17 g
Carbohydrates	30 g
Sodium	293 mg
Added Sugar	0
Fiber	0

1. Preheat the oven to 350°F. Wrap the **tortillas** in aluminum foil and heat in the oven for 10 minutes or until warm, soft, and pliable. Remove the tortillas from the oven and set aside; raise the oven temperature to 375°F.

2. In a small bowl, mix together the **ricotta cheese, green onions, coriander, cumin, chili powder, cayenne pepper,** and **lemon juice** and set aside.

3. To assemble the enchiladas, spread 2 tablespoons of the cheese mixture in the center of a tortilla and fold one side over the filling. Fill and fold the remaining tortillas in the same fashion. Using a pancake turner or wide spatula, gently lift and arrange the enchiladas in two rows, slightly overlapping, in a lightly greased 9"x 9"x 2" baking pan.

4. Cover with aluminum foil and bake for 20 minutes; uncover, sprinkle the enchiladas with the **mozzarella cheese,** and bake 5 minutes longer to melt the cheese. Using a pancake turner, carefully remove the enchiladas from the baking pan and serve directly on plates. Serves 4.

Easy Cheese and Potato Pie

Here is a flavorful main-course pie that can be made ahead and baked later.

5 medium-size all-purpose potatoes (about 1¼ pounds), peeled
1½ cups low-sodium, low-fat cottage cheese
1 large egg
¼ teaspoon black pepper

Nonstick cooking spray
2 green onions, including tops, chopped
1 cup shredded Cheddar cheese (about 4 ounces)

Preparation:
15 min.
Cooking:
50 min. (mostly unattended)

One Serving:

Calories	273
Total Fat	10 g
Saturated Fat	7 g
Cholesterol	102 mg
Protein	20 g
Carbohydrates	22 g
Sodium	207 mg
Added Sugar	0
Fiber	2 g

1. In a medium-size saucepan, place the **potatoes** in enough water to cover and cook, covered, for 20 to 25 minutes or until tender. Drain and slice thin.

2. Preheat the oven to 375°F. In an electric blender or food processor, combine the **cottage cheese, egg,** and **pepper** by whirling for 8 to 10 seconds.

3. Coat a shallow 9-inch casserole or pie pan with the **cooking spray.** Place ⅓ of the potatoes in a single layer in the casserole, spread with ½ of the cottage cheese mixture, and sprinkle with ⅓ of the **green onions** and **Cheddar cheese.** Add another ⅓ of the potatoes and spread with the remaining cottage cheese mixture. Top with the remaining potatoes and sprinkle with the remaining green onions and Cheddar cheese.

4. Bake, uncovered, for 30 to 40 minutes or until golden. Serves 4.

Mexican Corn and Cheese Pudding

3 cups skim milk
¾ cup yellow cornmeal
1⅓ cups fresh corn or 1 can (8¾ ounces) low-sodium whole-kernel corn, drained
½ cup shredded fontina cheese (about 2 ounces)
½ cup shredded Monterey Jack cheese (about 2 ounces)

2 tablespoons plain low-fat yogurt
1 can (4 ounces) chopped green chilies, drained
¼ teaspoon salt
¼ teaspoon black pepper
⅛ teaspoon cayenne pepper

FAT **SUGAR** SODIUM

Preparation:
6 min.
Cooking:
28 min. (mostly unattended)

One Serving:

Calories	*322*
Total Fat	*10 g*
Saturated Fat	*3 g*
Cholesterol	*33 mg*
Protein	*18 g*
Carbohydrates	*41 g*
Sodium	*493 mg*
Added Sugar	*0*
Fiber	*1 g*

1. Preheat the oven to 350°F. In a small bowl, whisk 1 cup of the **milk** into the **cornmeal** and set aside. In a medium-size heavy saucepan over moderate heat, bring the remaining milk to a simmer—about 3 minutes. Whisk in the cornmeal mixture and cook, stirring, for 5 to 7 minutes or until thickened.

2. Remove the mixture from the heat and stir in the **corn, fontina cheese,** half the **Monterey Jack cheese,** the **yogurt, green chilies, salt, black pepper,** and **cayenne pepper.**

3. Spoon the mixture into an ungreased 1½-quart casserole and sprinkle with the rest of the Monterey Jack. Bake, uncovered, for 20 minutes or until the pudding has set and the top is golden brown. Serves 4.

Two-Cheese Casserole

Here is a simple make-ahead casserole that is ideal for brunch.

1 tablespoon unsalted margarine
1 small yellow onion, chopped
1 small stalk celery, chopped
½ small sweet green pepper, cored, seeded, and chopped
Nonstick cooking spray
8 slices day-old whole wheat bread, cut in half diagonally
¼ cup shredded low-sodium Swiss cheese (about 1 ounce)

¼ cup grated Parmesan cheese
1 large egg
2 large egg whites
1½ cups skim milk
¾ teaspoon prepared yellow mustard
¾ teaspoon paprika
⅛ teaspoon cayenne pepper

FAT **SUGAR** SODIUM

Preparation:
20 min., plus 1 hr. refrigeration
Cooking:
46 min. (mostly unattended)

One Serving:

Calories	*256*
Total Fat	*10 g*
Saturated Fat	*2 g*
Cholesterol	*76 mg*
Protein	*16 g*
Carbohydrates	*29 g*
Sodium	*447 mg*
Added Sugar	*0*
Fiber	*3 g*

1. In a heavy 7-inch skillet, melt the **margarine** over moderate heat; add the **onion, celery,** and **green pepper,** and cook until the onion is soft—about 5 minutes.

2. Meanwhile, lightly coat an 8″x 8″x 2″ baking pan with the **cooking spray** and arrange the **bread,** overlapping the slices, in the bottom.

3. Spoon the vegetable mixture evenly over the bread. Sprinkle with the **Swiss cheese** and **Parmesan cheese.**

4. In a small bowl, lightly whisk the **egg** and **egg whites** together; blend in the **milk, mustard, paprika,** and **cayenne pepper.** Pour the egg mixture evenly over the bread slices. Cover the casserole with plastic wrap or aluminum foil and refrigerate for 1 to 3 hours.

5. Preheat the oven to 325°F. Remove the casserole from the refrigerator, uncover it, and let it stand for 15 minutes. Bake for 40 minutes or until lightly browned and set like a custard. Serves 4.

Zucchini Frittata

Zucchini Frittata

FAT SUGAR SODIUM

1 tablespoon olive oil

6 green onions, including tops, chopped fine

2 cloves garlic, minced

1 medium-size zucchini (about ½ pound), halved lengthwise and cut into ¼-inch slices

1 can (1 pound) low-sodium tomatoes, drained and chopped

¼ teaspoon each dried basil and thyme, crumbled

⅛ teaspoon black pepper

1 large egg

3 large egg whites

1 cup shredded part-skim mozzarella cheese (about 4 ounces)

Preparation:
15 min.
Cooking:
16 min.

One Serving:

Calories	173
Total Fat	10 g
Saturated Fat	4 g
Cholesterol	85 mg
Protein	13 g
Carbohydrates	10 g
Sodium	202 mg
Added Sugar	0
Fiber	2 g

1. Preheat the oven to 350°F. In a nonstick 10-inch skillet with an ovenproof handle, heat the **olive oil** over moderate heat for 1 minute. Add the **green onions** and cook, uncovered, until soft—about 5 minutes. Add the **garlic, zucchini, tomatoes, basil, thyme,** and **pepper** and cook, covered, until the zucchini is just tender—about 3 minutes.

2. In a small bowl, whisk together the **egg** and **egg whites;** blend into the vegetable mixture in the skillet and sprinkle with the **cheese.**

3. Place the skillet in the oven and bake the frittata, uncovered, until just set—about 5 minutes. Raise the oven temperature to broil and place the skillet in the broiler 5 to 6 inches from the heat; broil for 2 to 3 minutes or until the frittata is golden. Serve with a tossed green salad, carrots, or fresh strawberries. Serves 4.

Welsh Rarebit

1 cup skim milk
1 tablespoon flour
1 teaspoon Dijon or spicy brown
   mustard
½ teaspoon Worcestershire
   sauce
3 drops hot red pepper sauce or
   to taste

1 cup shredded Cheddar cheese
   (about 4 ounces)
6 slices whole wheat toast, cut
   in half diagonally
Paprika to taste

FAT SUGAR SODIUM

Preparation:
10 min.
Cooking:
11 min.

One Serving:

Calories	*227*
Total Fat	*11 g*
Saturated Fat	*6 g*
Cholesterol	*32 mg*
Protein	*13 g*
Carbohydrates	*21 g*
Sodium	*432 mg*
Added Sugar	*0*
Fiber	*0*

1. In a small heavy saucepan over moderately low heat, whisk together the
   milk, flour, mustard, Worcestershire sauce, and **red pepper sauce,** and
   heat the mixture until it bubbles gently; let it simmer for 4 minutes,
   whisking constantly.
2. Whisk in the **cheese,** a little at a time, and cook the sauce over moderately
   low heat (do not let it boil) for 4 minutes or until it is smooth.
3. Divide the **toast** among 4 plates and spoon the rarebit over each portion.
   Sprinkle with **paprika.** Serves 4.

Chick Pea Patties in Pita Pockets

This Mideastern meal, called falafel, *is quick and filling as well as nutritious.*

1 tablespoon sesame seeds
1½ cups cooked and drained
   chick peas
1 teaspoon ground cumin
1 teaspoon ground coriander
2 cloves garlic, halved
⅛ teaspoon cayenne pepper
2 teaspoons peanut oil
3 tablespoons lemon juice

Nonstick cooking spray
¾ cup plain low-fat yogurt
1 tablespoon olive oil
1 medium-size head Boston
   lettuce, roughly torn (about
   4 cups)
3 medium-size ripe tomatoes
   (about 1 pound), cored and
   cubed
4 whole wheat pita pockets

FAT SUGAR SODIUM

Preparation:
8 min.
Cooking:
10 min.

One Serving:

Calories	*406*
Total Fat	*10 g*
Saturated Fat	*2 g*
Cholesterol	*3 mg*
Protein	*17 g*
Carbohydrates	*65 g*
Sodium	*419 mg*
Added Sugar	*0*
Fiber	*7 g*

1. Preheat the oven to 325°F. Bake the **sesame seeds** in a pie pan, uncovered,
   shaking often, until the seeds are golden—about 10 minutes. Set aside.
2. In an electric blender or food processor, blend the **chick peas, cumin,
   coriander, garlic, cayenne pepper, peanut oil,** and 2 tablespoons of the
   lemon juice for 30 seconds or until smooth; if the mixture is dry, add a
   little water. Shape into 8 patties. Coat a heavy 10-inch skillet with the
   cooking spray; heat over moderate heat for 30 seconds, add the patties, and
   brown for 4 minutes on each side.
3. Meanwhile, in a large bowl, whisk together the **yogurt, olive oil,** sesame
   seeds, and remaining lemon juice. Measure and set aside ¼ cup. Add the
   lettuce and **tomatoes** to the remaining yogurt dressing and toss well to mix.
4. To serve, fill each **pita pocket** with 2 patties and ¼ of the salad mixture.
   Drizzle 1 tablespoon of the reserved dressing into each pocket. Serves 4.

Cornmeal Pizza with Pink Beans

Cornmeal Pizza with Pink Beans

1 cup yellow cornmeal
1⅓ cups cold water
¼ cup plus 2 tablespoons grated Parmesan cheese
1 tablespoon olive oil
1 medium-size yellow onion, sliced thin
1 clove garlic, minced
1 small sweet green pepper, cored, seeded, and sliced lengthwise into strips about ¼ inch wide

4 medium-size mushrooms, sliced thin
¾ teaspoon each dried basil and oregano, crumbled
⅛ teaspoon black pepper
⅔ cup cooked and drained pink, pinto, or red beans
1 cup coarsely shredded part-skim mozzarella cheese (about 4 ounces)
1 can (8 ounces) low-sodium tomato sauce

Preparation:
20 min.
Cooking:
31 min. (mostly unattended)

One Serving:

Calories	346
Total Fat	11 g
Saturated Fat	5 g
Cholesterol	22 mg
Protein	14 g
Carbohydrates	45 g
Sodium	288 mg
Added Sugar	0
Fiber	3 g

Tip: *The drier mushrooms are kept, the fresher they will stay. Never wash them until just before use.*

1. Preheat the oven to 375°F. In a small bowl, mix the **cornmeal** with ⅔ cup of the cold **water**; in a small heavy saucepan, bring the other ⅔ cup water to a boil. Gradually add the cornmeal mixture to the boiling water, whisking constantly with a fork until it is thick—about 5 minutes. Remove from the heat and stir in 2 tablespoons of the **Parmesan cheese.** With wet hands, pat the cornmeal mixture evenly onto a 12-inch pizza pan or a lightly greased baking sheet.

2. Bake the cornmeal crust, uncovered, for 15 minutes or until it is just golden.

3. Meanwhile, in a heavy 10-inch skillet, heat the **olive oil** over moderate heat for 1 minute; add the **onion, garlic,** and **green pepper,** and cook, uncovered, for 3 minutes. Add the **mushrooms, basil, oregano,** and **black pepper,** and cook, covered, for 5 minutes. Stir in the **beans** and set aside.

4. After removing the crust from the oven, reduce the temperature to 350°F. Sprinkle half the **mozzarella cheese** and half the remaining Parmesan cheese over the crust. Spoon the bean mixture on top, pour the **tomato sauce** evenly over it, and scatter the rest of the cheeses on top.

5. Bake, uncovered, for 10 to 15 minutes or until the cheese has melted. Cut into wedges. Serves 4.

Hot Vegetable Hero

1 loaf (8 ounces) French or
   Italian bread
1 tablespoon olive oil
1 large yellow onion, sliced thin
2 medium-size carrots, peeled
   and sliced thin
½ medium-size sweet red pepper,
   cored, seeded, and sliced thin

1 medium-size zucchini (about
   ½ pound), sliced thin
1 can (8 ounces) low-sodium
   tomato sauce
¾ teaspoon dried oregano
¼ teaspoon black pepper
¼ pound sliced low-sodium
   Muenster cheese

FAT **SUGAR** **SODIUM**

Preparation:
10 min.
Cooking:
18 min.

One Serving:

Calories	*364*
Total Fat	*14 g*
Saturated Fat	*1 g*
Cholesterol	*2 mg*
Protein	*14 g*
Carbohydrates	*45 g*
Sodium	*431 mg*
Added Sugar	*0*
Fiber	*1 g*

1. Preheat the broiler. Slice the **bread** in half lengthwise and scoop out and discard the soft center. Place the halves, cut side up, on a baking sheet and broil 4 inches from the heat for 1 minute or until lightly toasted. Set aside.

2. In a heavy 10-inch skillet, heat the **olive oil** over moderate heat for 1 minute; add the **onion** and cook, uncovered, for 5 minutes or until soft. Stir in the **carrots, red pepper,** and **zucchini,** and cook, covered, for 8 to 10 minutes or until the carrots are tender. Add the **tomato sauce, oregano,** and **black pepper,** and simmer, uncovered, for 2 minutes.

3. Spoon the vegetable mixture into the bottom half of the bread, top with the **cheese,** and place in the broiler 4 inches from the heat. Broil for 1 minute or until the cheese has melted. Transfer to a cutting board and top with the toasted upper half. Cut into 4 sandwiches. Serves 4.

Whole Wheat Pizza with Green Peppers

1 package (¼ ounce) quick-rise
   or regular active dry yeast
½ cup warm water
⅔ cup sifted all-purpose flour
⅔ cup unsifted whole wheat flour
3 tablespoons olive oil
   Nonstick cooking spray
1 small sweet green pepper,
   cored, seeded, and sliced
   lengthwise into strips about
   ¼ inch wide

1 can (1 pound) low-sodium
   tomatoes, drained and chopped
2 cloves garlic, minced
1 teaspoon dried oregano,
   crumbled
⅛ teaspoon red pepper flakes
1 cup shredded part-skim
   mozzarella cheese (about
   4 ounces)

FAT **SUGAR** **SODIUM**

Preparation:
1 hr., including
dough-rising time
Cooking:
28 min.

One Serving:

Calories	*338*
Total Fat	*15 g*
Saturated Fat	*2 g*
Cholesterol	*4 mg*
Protein	*14 g*
Carbohydrates	*37 g*
Sodium	*51 mg*
Added Sugar	*0*
Fiber	*4 g*

Tip: Unlike white flour, whole wheat flour becomes rancid when kept for more than a few weeks. Store it in a capped jar in the refrigerator.

1. In a large mixing bowl, combine the **yeast** and **water** according to package directions. Mix in the **all-purpose flour** and **whole wheat flour** and 2 tablespoons of the **olive oil.** Place the dough on a floured surface and knead until smooth and elastic. Coat a large bowl with the **cooking spray;** shape the dough into a ball, place in the bowl, and cover with plastic wrap. Let the dough rise in a warm place for 45 minutes or until it has doubled.

2. Meanwhile, in a heavy 10-inch skillet, heat the remaining olive oil over moderately low heat; add the **green pepper** and cook, stirring, for 5 minutes. Add the **tomatoes, garlic, oregano,** and **red pepper flakes** and simmer, uncovered, for 10 minutes or until slightly thickened; set aside.

3. Preheat the oven to 450°F. Coat a 14-inch pizza pan or baking sheet with the cooking spray; place the dough in the middle of the pan and pat it out evenly to fit. Spread the sauce over the dough, leaving a ¾-inch border. Sprinkle the **cheese** over the top. Bake on the lowest shelf of the oven for 12 to 15 minutes or until the crust is crisp. Serves 4.

Pasta and Grains

Grains, including the wheat in pasta, are among the best providers of protein, fiber, and energy-giving complex carbohydrates. They are also many families' favorite food. And when eaten as a main course, they are as satisfying as meat. Most of the recipes in this section—from Crab and Pasta Salad to Jambalaya—are hearty enough to serve as a meal's main dish. Those that are better used as side dishes, such as Homemade German Noodles, are identified in the recipe introductions.

Spaghetti with Asparagus and Pecans

Spicy Lasagne Roll-ups

Preparation: **25 min.** Cooking: **59 min.** FAT SUGAR SODIUM

Make this attractive dish one day and bake it the next, or double the recipe and freeze half. Serve with crusty whole wheat bread and a tossed salad.

- 1 **tablespoon olive oil**
- 1 **large yellow onion, chopped fine**
- 1 **teaspoon dried basil, crumbled**
- ½ **teaspoon dried marjoram, crumbled**
- 1 **bay leaf, crumbled**
- 2 **cloves garlic, minced**
- ¾ **teaspoon black pepper**
- ½ **skinned and boned chicken breast (about 4 ounces), chopped fine**
- 1 **can (1 pound) low-sodium tomatoes, chopped, with their juice**
- 2 **tablespoons low-sodium tomato paste**
- 8 **ruffle-edge lasagne noodles (about 4 ounces)**
- ½ **cup grated Parmesan cheese**
- 1 **cup part-skim ricotta cheese**
- ½ **pound fresh spinach, trimmed and chopped, or ½ 10-ounce package frozen chopped spinach, thawed and drained**
- ¼ **teaspoon ground mace or nutmeg**
- ¼ **teaspoon cream of tartar**

1. Heat the **olive oil** in a heavy 10-inch skillet over moderate heat for 1 minute. Add the **onion, basil, marjoram, bay leaf,** half the **garlic,** and ¼ teaspoon of the **pepper;** cook, uncovered, until the onion is soft—about 5 minutes. Remove 2 tablespoons of the mixture from the skillet and set aside.

2. Add the chopped **chicken** to the skillet and cook, stirring, for 3 minutes. Reduce the heat to low, add the **tomatoes** and **tomato paste,** and cook, uncovered, for 20 minutes, stirring occasionally. Set aside.

3. Meanwhile, cook the **lasagne** noodles according to package directions, omitting the salt. Rinse with cold water and drain.

4. Preheat the oven to 375°F. To prepare the filling, combine 5 tablespoons of the **Parmesan cheese** in a medium-size bowl with the **ricotta cheese, spinach, mace, cream of tartar,** the remaining garlic and pepper, and the reserved onion mixture. Mix well.

5. Spoon half the tomato sauce into an ungreased 9″x 9″x 2″ baking pan. Spread 3 tablespoons of the cheese filling on each noodle, roll up as for a jelly roll, and place seam side down in the pan. Repeat until all the noodles are used. Top with the remaining sauce.

Spicy Lasagne Roll-ups

6. Cover with aluminum foil and bake for 25 minutes. Uncover, sprinkle the remaining Parmesan cheese on top, and bake, uncovered, 5 minutes longer. Serves 4.

One Serving:			
Calories	357	Protein	25 g
Total Fat	13 g	Carbohydrates	37 g
Saturated Fat	6 g	Sodium	348 mg
Cholesterol	43 mg	Added Sugar	0
		Fiber	0

Zucchini, Mushroom, and Pimiento Lasagne

Preparation: **17 min.** FAT SUGAR SODIUM
Cooking: **1 hr. 11 min.** (mostly unattended)

You can make this one day and bake it the next.

- 2 **bulbs (entire heads) garlic**
- 4 **ounces lasagne noodles**
- 1 **tablespoon olive oil**
- 1 **medium-size yellow onion, chopped**
- 1 **medium-size zucchini (about ½ pound), halved lengthwise and sliced thin**
- ½ **pound mushrooms, sliced thin**
- 1 **cup fresh or frozen green peas**
- 2 **teaspoons lemon juice**
- ¼ **teaspoon black pepper**
- 1 **jar (4 ounces) pimientos, drained and sliced lengthwise into ½-inch strips**
- 1½ **cups skim milk**
- 2½ **tablespoons flour**
- ½ **teaspoon dried oregano, crumbled**
- ¼ **cup grated Parmesan cheese**

1. Preheat the oven to 375°F. Wrap each unpeeled **garlic** bulb in aluminum foil, set in the oven, and roast for 20 minutes. Cool in the foil until easy to handle, then pull off the garlic cloves one by one and pinch, squeezing the flesh into a small bowl; mash the garlic and set aside.

2. Cook the **lasagne** noodles according to package directions, omitting the salt. Rinse with cold water and drain.

3. Meanwhile, heat the **olive oil** in a heavy 10-inch skillet over moderate heat for 1 minute; add the **onion** and **zucchini** and cook, uncovered, until soft—about 5 minutes. Add the **mushrooms** and cook, uncovered, 3 minutes longer; add the **peas** and cook 3 more minutes. Stir in the **lemon juice, pepper,** and **pimiento** and remove from the heat.

4. In a small saucepan, whisk the **milk** into the **flour;** set over moderately low heat and cook, stirring, for 4 minutes or until thickened. Mix in the **oregano, cheese,** and reserved garlic. Measure out ½ cup of the sauce and reserve. Combine the rest with the zucchini mixture.

5. To assemble the lasagne, line the bottom of an ungreased 8"x 8"x 2" baking pan with the cooked lasagne noodles, cutting them to fit and reserving the scraps. Spread half the zucchini mixture over the noodles, add a second layer of noodles, spread with the remaining zucchini mixture, then top with the noodle scraps. Finally,

smooth the reserved sauce evenly over all.

6. Cover with aluminum foil and bake 20 minutes; uncover and bake 15 more minutes. Serves 4.

One Serving:

Calories	310	Protein	15 g
Total Fat	6 g	Carbohydrates	50 g
Saturated Fat	2 g	Sodium	159 mg
Cholesterol	6 mg	Added Sugar	0
		Fiber	4 g

Cannelloni with Ricotta and Peas

Preparation: **15 min.** FAT SUGAR SODIUM
Cooking: **40 min.** (mostly unattended)

- 12 **cannelloni shells or 8 manicotti shells**
- ¼ **cup fresh or frozen green peas**
- 1 **cup part-skim ricotta cheese**
- 2 **tablespoons golden raisins**
- 1 **large egg**
- 1 **large egg white**
- 3 **medium-size ripe tomatoes, peeled, cored, and chopped, or 1 can (1 pound) low-sodium tomatoes, drained and chopped**
- 3 **tablespoons minced fresh mint or parsley**
- ½ **teaspoon black pepper**
- 2 **tablespoons low-sodium tomato paste**

1. Preheat the oven to 350°F. Cook the **cannelloni** shells in boiling unsalted water for 6 minutes or until partially softened. Drain and set aside.

2. Bring an inch of water to a boil in a small saucepan, add the **peas,** and cook for 2 minutes. Drain. In a medium-size bowl, combine the peas, **cheese, raisins, egg, egg white,** ⅓ cup of the **tomatoes,** 1½ tablespoons of the **mint,** and ¼ teaspoon of the **pepper,** and mix well. Fill the cannelloni shells with the mixture.

3. Combine the remaining tomatoes, mint, and pepper with the **tomato paste** in a small bowl; mix well. Pour ¾ cup of the mixture into the bottom of an ungreased 8"x 8"x 2" baking pan and place the filled pasta shells on top. Pour the remaining mixture over all. Cover with aluminum foil and bake for 20 minutes. Uncover and bake 10 minutes longer. Serves 4.

One Serving:

Calories	277	Protein	15 g
Total Fat	7 g	Carbohydrates	40 g
Saturated Fat	3 g	Sodium	114 mg
Cholesterol	86 mg	Added Sugar	0
		Fiber	2 g

Fisherman's Baked Shells

1 tablespoon olive oil
1 large yellow onion, chopped
1 clove garlic, minced
1 medium-size carrot, peeled and chopped fine
1 medium-size stalk celery, chopped fine
1 small sweet red pepper, cored, seeded, and chopped fine
½ teaspoon each dried basil, marjoram, and rosemary, crumbled
¼ teaspoon black pepper

½ cup dry white wine
2 tablespoons flour
1¾ cups low-sodium chicken broth
6 ounces medium-size pasta shells
1 can (6½ ounces) water-packed light tuna, drained and flaked
3 tablespoons grated Parmesan cheese
1 tablespoon lemon juice
¼ cup minced parsley

FAT **SUGAR** **SODIUM**

Preparation:
10 min.
Cooking:
40 min.

One Serving:

Calories	310
Total Fat	8 g
Saturated Fat	2 g
Cholesterol	26 mg
Protein	19 g
Carbohydrates	44 g
Sodium	272 mg
Added Sugar	0
Fiber	2 g

1. Heat the **olive oil** in a heavy 12-inch skillet over moderate heat for 1 minute. Add the **onion, garlic, carrot, celery, red pepper, basil, marjoram, rosemary,** and **black pepper.** Cook, uncovered, stirring occasionally, until the vegetables are soft—5 to 8 minutes.

2. Add the **wine** to the skillet and boil, uncovered, for 3 minutes. Place the **flour** in a small bowl and add enough of the **chicken broth,** a tablespoon at a time, to make a smooth paste. Blend in the rest of the chicken broth and add the mixture to the skillet. Cook, stirring constantly, until slightly thickened—about 3 minutes. Lower the heat so that the mixture bubbles gently, cover, and simmer for 8 minutes or until the sauce has thickened.

3. Meanwhile, preheat the oven to 350°F. Cook the **pasta shells** according to package directions, omitting the salt. Drain well and place in an ungreased 2½-quart casserole. Add the **tuna** but do not mix.

4. Stir the **cheese, lemon juice,** and half the **parsley** into the sauce. Pour over the tuna and pasta shells and toss well to mix. Cover and bake for 20 minutes. Sprinkle with the remaining parsley and serve. Serves 4.

Tip: Water-packed tuna not only tastes better than tuna packed in oil, but also has less than a gram of fat per can. Oil-packed tuna has as many as 20 grams of fat per can and almost twice the calories.

Macaroni with Chick Peas and Tomatoes

Baked Ziti with Mozzarella

With a green salad, this is a satisfying and nutritious main course.

FAT SUGAR SODIUM

1 can (1 pound) low-sodium tomatoes, with their juice
1 tablespoon olive oil
1 medium-size yellow onion, chopped fine
1 can (8 ounces) low-sodium tomato sauce
3 cloves garlic, minced
½ teaspoon dried oregano, crumbled

1 teaspoon dried basil, crumbled
¼ teaspoon fennel seeds, crushed
⅛ teaspoon black pepper
8 ounces ziti or rigatoni
1 cup shredded part-skim mozzarella cheese (about 4 ounces)
2 tablespoons grated Parmesan cheese

Preparation: **20 min.**
Cooking: **45 min.** (mostly unattended)

One Serving:

Calories	376
Total Fat	9 g
Saturated Fat	4 g
Cholesterol	18 mg
Protein	17 g
Carbohydrates	55 g
Sodium	208 mg
Added Sugar	0
Fiber	3 g

1. Preheat the oven to 375°F. In an electric blender or food processor, purée the **tomatoes** for 10 to 15 seconds. Set aside.

2. Heat the **olive oil** in a heavy 10-inch skillet over moderate heat for 1 minute; add the **onion** and cook, uncovered, until soft—about 5 minutes. Add the tomatoes, **tomato sauce, garlic, oregano, basil, fennel seeds,** and **pepper;** bring to a boil, reduce the heat to low, and simmer, uncovered, for 10 minutes, stirring often, until the sauce has thickened slightly.

3. Meanwhile, cook the **ziti** according to package directions, omitting the salt. Rinse with cold water, drain well, and place in an ungreased shallow 1½-quart casserole. Cover with the sauce and sprinkle with the **mozzarella** and **Parmesan cheeses.**

4. Bake, uncovered, for 30 to 35 minutes or until bubbly and golden. Let stand for 5 minutes before serving. Serves 4.

Tip: To crush fennel seeds and release their aroma, place in a piece of plastic wrap and pound with a rolling pin or bottle.

Macaroni with Chick Peas and Tomatoes

Canned chick peas usually contain a lot of salt. If you can't find a low-sodium brand, cook dried chick peas according to package directions. To make this dish for two, use 1 cup tomatoes and halve the remaining ingredients.

FAT SUGAR SODIUM

1 tablespoon olive oil
1 clove garlic, minced
1 can (1 pound) low-sodium tomatoes, chopped, with their juice
2 tablespoons minced parsley
½ teaspoon each dried basil and oregano, crumbled

¼ teaspoon black pepper
1 cup cooked and drained chick peas
8 ounces elbow macaroni, ditalini, or small pasta shells

Preparation: **5 min.**
Cooking: **24 min.**

One Serving:

Calories	339
Total Fat	5 g
Saturated Fat	1 g
Cholesterol	0
Protein	12 g
Carbohydrates	61 g
Sodium	22 mg
Added Sugar	0
Fiber	5 g

1. Heat the **olive oil** in a medium-size heavy saucepan over moderate heat for 30 seconds; add the **garlic** and cook, stirring, for 30 seconds. Mix in the **tomatoes, parsley, basil, oregano,** and **pepper;** bring to a boil, lower the heat so that the mixture bubbles gently, then simmer, uncovered, for 10 minutes or until slightly thickened.

2. Stir in the **chick peas** and simmer, uncovered, 10 minutes longer.

3. Meanwhile, cook the **macaroni** according to package directions, omitting the salt; drain well and transfer to a heated bowl. Pour the chick pea mixture over all and toss well. Serves 4.

Baked Macaroni and Cheese

Preparation: **5 min.**
Cooking: **40 min.** (mostly unattended)

FAT SUGAR SODIUM

You can vary this dish by stirring in minced green onions or pimientos.

- 6 ounces elbow or other small macaroni
- 1 tablespoon unsalted margarine
- 1 teaspoon dried marjoram, crumbled
- ½ teaspoon dried thyme, crumbled
  Pinch ground nutmeg
  Pinch paprika
- 3 tablespoons flour
- 2 cups skim milk
- 1 tablespoon Dijon or spicy brown mustard
- ½ cup grated Parmesan cheese
- 1 cup low-fat cottage cheese

1. Preheat the oven to 350°F. Cook the **macaroni** according to package directions, omitting the salt; rinse with cold water and drain well.

2. Meanwhile, melt the **margarine** in a small heavy saucepan over moderate heat; add the **marjoram, thyme, nutmeg,** and **paprika,** and cook, stirring, for 1 minute. Remove from the heat and set aside.

3. In a small bowl, whisk the **flour** with ¼ cup of the **milk.** Add another ¼ cup milk and whisk until blended. Pour the mixture into the saucepan with the margarine and herbs, set over moderate heat, and add the rest of the milk in a steady stream, whisking constantly. Bring to a simmer and cook, stirring constantly, for 2 minutes or until slightly thickened. Remove from the heat and stir in the **mustard** and all but 2 tablespoons of the **Parmesan cheese.**

4. Stir the sauce into the macaroni and mix well. Add the **cottage cheese** and mix well again. Spoon into an ungreased 8"x 8"x 2" baking pan and sprinkle with the remaining 2 tablespoons of Parmesan cheese. Bake, uncovered, for 30 minutes or until bubbly and golden. Serve with a green salad. Serves 4.

One Serving:

Calories	308	Protein	15 g
Total Fat	14 g	Carbohydrates	30 g
Saturated Fat	6 g	Sodium	122 mg
Cholesterol	28 mg	Added Sugar	0
		Fiber	1 g

Linguine with White Clam Sauce

Preparation: **10 min.** Cooking: **14 min.**

FAT SUGAR SODIUM

The sauce can be made in advance and gently reheated just before serving.

- 8 ounces linguine or spaghetti
- 1½ tablespoons olive oil
- ½ small yellow onion, chopped fine
- 6 cloves garlic, minced
- 2 tablespoons flour
- ¼ cup dry white wine
- ¼ cup clam juice or low-sodium chicken broth
- 1 cup low-sodium chicken broth
- 1 can (6½ ounces) minced clams, drained, rinsed well, and drained again
- ¼ cup grated Parmesan cheese
- 2 tablespoons minced parsley

1. Cook the **linguine** according to package directions, omitting the salt. Rinse with cold water, drain, and set aside.

2. Meanwhile, heat the **olive oil** in a heavy 10-inch skillet over moderate heat for 1 minute; add the **onion** and **garlic** and cook, uncovered, until the onion is soft—about 5 minutes. Blend in the **flour** and cook, stirring constantly, for 1 minute. Add the **wine** and cook for 2 minutes, stirring constantly. Add the **clam juice** and **chicken broth** and cook, stirring, 4 minutes longer. Stir in the **clams** and **cheese.**

3. Add the reserved linguine and cook 1 minute longer, tossing well until heated through. Mix in the **parsley** and serve with a tossed green salad and crusty bread. Serves 4.

Variation:

Linguine with Red Clam Sauce Omit the flour. In Step 2, add 1 cup drained and chopped canned low-sodium tomatoes along with the clam juice and chicken broth. Cook and stir for 6 minutes or until slightly thickened, then proceed with the recipe as directed.

One Serving:

Calories	337	Protein	15 g
Total Fat	8 g	Carbohydrates	49 g
Saturated Fat	2 g	Sodium	199 mg
Cholesterol	20 mg	Added Sugar	0
		Fiber	2 g

Linguine with Tuna-Caper Sauce

Preparation: **5 min.** Cooking: **14 min.** FAT SUGAR SODIUM

Make this dish less spicy, if you wish, by omitting the red pepper flakes. To make for two, use 1 cup canned tomatoes and a 3½-ounce can of tuna.

1 tablespoon olive oil
1 clove garlic, minced
1 can (1 pound) low-sodium crushed tomatoes, with their juice
1 teaspoon dried oregano, crumbled
¼ teaspoon red pepper flakes
1 can (6½ ounces) water-packed light tuna, drained and flaked
2 tablespoons capers, chopped
2 tablespoons minced parsley
6 ounces linguine or spaghetti

1. In a heavy 10-inch skillet, heat the **olive oil** over moderate heat for 30 seconds; add the **garlic** and cook for 30 seconds. Stir in the **tomatoes, oregano,** and **red pepper flakes.** Bring to a boil, then lower the heat until the mixture barely bubbles; simmer, uncovered, for 7 to 8 minutes or until slightly thickened.
2. Stir in the **tuna, capers,** and **parsley,** and simmer 5 minutes longer.
3. Meanwhile, cook the **linguine** according to package directions, omitting the salt; drain well and transfer to a heated bowl. Pour the tuna sauce over the pasta and toss well. Serves 4.

Variation:

Linguine with Shrimp-Caper Sauce   Substitute ¾ cup chopped cooked shrimp for the tuna. Vary the flavor, if you like, by substituting minced fresh basil (or 1 teaspoon dried basil) for the parsley, and 1 teaspoon marjoram for the oregano.

One Serving:			
		Protein	17 g
Calories	256	Carbohydrates	38 g
Total Fat	5 g	Sodium	285 mg
Saturated Fat	0	Added Sugar	0
Cholesterol	23 mg	Fiber	3 g

Tip: *You can double the storage life of capers by pouring the liquid from the jar and replacing it with undiluted white vinegar.*

Pasta with Spinach Sauce

Preparation: **20 min.** Cooking: **13 min.** FAT SUGAR SODIUM

Here is a different twist on the classic Italian sauce known as pesto.

8 ounces spaghetti or linguine
1 tablespoon olive oil
1 small yellow onion, chopped fine
2 cloves garlic, minced
1 pound fresh spinach, trimmed and chopped, or 1 package (10 ounces) frozen chopped spinach, thawed and well drained
½ cup skim milk
½ cup low-sodium chicken broth
¼ cup grated Parmesan cheese
¼ teaspoon black pepper

1. In a large kettle, cook the **spaghetti** according to package directions, omitting the salt.
2. While the spaghetti is cooking, heat the **olive oil** in a small heavy saucepan over moderate heat for 1 minute; add the **onion** and **garlic** and cook, uncovered, until the onion is soft—about 5 minutes. Add the **spinach, milk, chicken broth, cheese,** and **pepper.** Bring the mixture to a boil; reduce the heat and simmer, uncovered, for 3 minutes or until the sauce thickens slightly.
3. Pour the sauce into an electric blender or food processor and whirl until the mixture is puréed. Pour the sauce back into the saucepan and reheat over moderate heat until the mixture starts to simmer—about 1 minute.
4. Drain the spaghetti and return it to the kettle. Add the spinach mixture and toss well with two forks to mix. Transfer to a heated platter and serve. Serves 4.

Variation:

Pasta with Broccoli Sauce   Substitute 2 cups chopped broccoli florets or 1 10-ounce package frozen broccoli, chopped, for the spinach. Purée in Step 3, as directed.

One Serving:			
		Protein	12 g
Calories	295	Carbohydrates	48 g
Total Fat	6 g	Sodium	162 mg
Saturated Fat	1 g	Added Sugar	0
Cholesterol	5 mg	Fiber	4 g

Pasta, Cheese, and Tomato Pie

Spaghetti with Asparagus and Pecans

You can easily halve this recipe to serve two.

FAT SUGAR SODIUM

2 tablespoons chopped pecans
8 ounces spaghetti
¾ pound asparagus, tough stems removed, or 1 package (10 ounces) frozen asparagus, cut into 1½-inch lengths
1 clove garlic, crushed
1 tablespoon unsalted margarine
¼ pound mushrooms, sliced thin

1 tablespoon minced fresh or freeze-dried chives
2 teaspoons lemon juice
¼ teaspoon salt
¼ teaspoon black pepper
3 tablespoons plain low-fat yogurt

Preparation:
7 min.
Cooking:
17 min.

One Serving:

Calories	285
Total Fat	6 g
Saturated Fat	1 g
Cholesterol	1 mg
Protein	10 g
Carbohydrates	47 g
Sodium	146 mg
Added Sugar	0
Fiber	3 g

1. Preheat the oven to 350°F. Place the **pecans** on a baking sheet and toast until crisp and somewhat darker—about 7 minutes. Set aside.

2. Meanwhile, cook the **spaghetti** according to package directions, omitting the salt. Drain, reserving ¼ cup of the cooking water. Rinse and set aside. At the same time, add the **asparagus** to a large saucepan of boiling unsalted water and cook until tender but still crisp—about 2 minutes. Set aside.

3. Rub a heavy 12-inch skillet with the **garlic,** then melt the **margarine** in the skillet over moderately high heat. Add the **mushrooms** and cook, stirring frequently, for 5 minutes. Add the cooked spaghetti, asparagus, and reserved cooking water, along with the **chives, lemon juice, salt,** and **pepper.** Toss well with two serving forks. Add the **yogurt** and pecans and cook, tossing, until heated through—2 to 3 minutes longer. Serves 4.

Pasta, Cheese, and Tomato Pie

Preparation: **15 min.**   FAT SUGAR SODIUM
Cooking: **1 hr.** (mostly unattended)

- **8 ounces linguine**
- **1 tablespoon olive oil**
- **1 medium-size yellow onion, chopped fine**
- **3 cloves garlic, minced**
- **¼ cup minced parsley**
- **1 tablespoon lemon juice**
- **1½ teaspoons dried oregano, crumbled**
- **1 teaspoon dried basil, crumbled**
- **¼ teaspoon white or black pepper**
- **½ cup part-skim ricotta cheese**
- **1 large egg white**
- **¼ cup grated Parmesan cheese**
- **2 medium-size ripe tomatoes (about 10 ounces), cored and sliced thin**
- **¼ cup shredded part-skim mozzarella cheese (about 1 ounce)**

1. Preheat the oven to 375°F. Lightly grease and flour an 8-inch springform pan and set aside.
2. Cook the **linguine** according to package directions, omitting the salt. Drain, rinse under cold running water, and drain again. Return to the cooking pot and set aside.
3. Meanwhile, heat the **olive oil** in a heavy 7-inch skillet over moderate heat for 1 minute. Add the **onion** and **garlic** and cook, uncovered, until the onion is soft—about 5 minutes. Add to the linguine along with the **parsley, lemon juice,** 1 teaspoon of the **oregano,** ½ teaspoon of the **basil,** and the **pepper;** toss well. In a small bowl, combine the **ricotta cheese, egg white,** 2 tablespoons of the **Parmesan cheese,** and the remaining ½ teaspoon of oregano and basil; add to the linguine and toss well.
4. Turn half the linguine-cheese mixture into the prepared pan and press lightly over the bottom. Arrange half the **tomato** slices on top and sprinkle with half the **mozzarella cheese;** repeat the layers, using the remaining linguine, tomatoes, and mozzarella. Sprinkle the remaining Parmesan cheese on top.
5. Cover with aluminum foil and bake for 40 minutes or until set; remove the foil and bake 5 minutes longer. Cool for 10 minutes, then gently loosen the pie around the edges with a thin-bladed knife, remove the springform pan sides, and cut the pie into 8 wedges. Serves 4.

One Serving:			
Calories	353	Protein	16 g
Total Fat	9 g	Carbohydrates	51 g
Saturated Fat	4 g	Sodium	186 mg
Cholesterol	18 mg	Added Sugar	0
		Fiber	3 g

Spaghetti with Meat and Tomato Sauce

Preparation: **10 min.**   FAT SUGAR SODIUM
Cooking: **1 hr. 9 min.** (mostly unattended)

This chunky pasta sauce is a good way to stretch a small amount of ground beef. The recipe makes twice as much sauce as needed; freeze the extra sauce for another meal. The 8 ounces of spaghetti serves four.

- **1 tablespoon olive oil**
- **1 medium-size yellow onion, chopped fine**
- **1 medium-size carrot, peeled and chopped fine**
- **1 small stalk celery, chopped fine**
- **2 cloves garlic, minced**
- **½ pound very lean ground beef**
- **3 cans (1 pound each) low-sodium tomatoes, chopped, with their juice**
- **2 tablespoons minced fresh basil or 1 teaspoon dried basil, crumbled**
- **¼ teaspoon black pepper**
- **8 ounces thin spaghetti**

1. In a large saucepan, heat the **olive oil** for 1 minute over moderate heat. Add the **onion, carrot, celery,** and **garlic,** and cook, stirring frequently, until the onion is soft—about 5 minutes.
2. Add the **ground beef** and cook, stirring, until browned—3 to 5 minutes. Add the **tomatoes, basil,** and **pepper,** reduce the heat to low, and simmer, uncovered, stirring occasionally, for 1 hour or until thickened.
3. When the sauce has only about 10 minutes longer to simmer, cook the **spaghetti** according to package directions, omitting the salt; drain well and place in a large bowl. Add half the sauce and toss well. Freeze or refrigerate the remaining sauce to serve another day. Serves 4.

One Serving:			
Calories	352	Protein	14 g
Total Fat	10 g	Carbohydrates	52 g
Saturated Fat	2 g	Sodium	51 mg
Cholesterol	10 mg	Added Sugar	0
		Fiber	4 g

Pasta with Broccoli in Sweet Tomato Sauce

Pasta with Broccoli in Sweet Tomato Sauce

When halving this recipe for two, use a 14½-ounce can of tomatoes.

FAT SUGAR SODIUM

4 cups broccoli florets
(1 medium-size head)

1 tablespoon olive oil

2 cloves garlic, minced

4 large ripe tomatoes (about
2 pounds), peeled, cored, and
chopped, or 1 large can (28
ounces) low-sodium tomatoes,
chopped, with their juice

2 tablespoons golden raisins,
chopped

⅛ teaspoon cayenne pepper

1½ tablespoons whole pine nuts
or chopped almonds

6 ounces spaghetti or
linguine

2 tablespoons minced parsley

Preparation:
10 min.
Cooking:
26 min.

One Serving:

Calories	300
Total Fat	6 g
Saturated Fat	1 g
Cholesterol	0
Protein	13 g
Carbohydrates	53 g
Sodium	50 mg
Added Sugar	0
Fiber	3 g

1. In a large saucepan, cook the **broccoli** in enough boiling unsalted water to cover until just tender—2 to 3 minutes. Rinse under cold running water, drain, and set aside.

2. In another large saucepan, heat the **olive oil** over moderately low heat for 30 seconds; add the **garlic** and cook, uncovered, until golden—about 3 minutes. Add the **tomatoes, raisins,** and **cayenne pepper,** and simmer, uncovered, for 15 minutes. Add the **pine nuts** and simmer 5 minutes longer.

3. Meanwhile, cook the **spaghetti** according to package directions, omitting the salt. Drain well and place in a large heated serving bowl.

4. Add the cooked broccoli to the warm tomato sauce, tossing to heat through. Pour over the pasta and sprinkle with the **parsley.** Serves 4.

Fusilli with Parsley-Mushroom Sauce

Fusilli *resembles long strands of spaghetti twisted like a corkscrew. Shorter, thicker corkscrew pasta is also known as* rotelle *(wheels).*

½ cup plain low-fat yogurt
¼ cup grated Parmesan cheese
¼ cup minced parsley
2 tablespoons sour cream
⅛ teaspoon black pepper
8 ounces fusilli, rotelle, or spaghetti

1 tablespoon olive oil
6 ounces mushrooms, sliced thin
1 medium-size yellow onion, chopped
2 cloves garlic, minced
¼ cup dry white wine
Parsley sprigs (optional)

FAT **SUGAR** **SODIUM**

Preparation:
30 min.
Cooking:
12 min.

One Serving:

Calories	319
Total Fat	*8 g*
Saturated Fat	*3 g*
Cholesterol	*9 mg*
Protein	*12 g*
Carbohydrates	*50 g*
Sodium	*122 mg*
Added Sugar	*0*
Fiber	*3 g*

1. In a small bowl, combine the **yogurt, cheese, parsley, sour cream,** and **pepper;** cover and refrigerate.

2. In a large kettle, cook the **fusilli** according to package directions, omitting the salt.

3. Meanwhile, heat the **olive oil** in a heavy 7-inch skillet over moderately high heat for 1 minute. Add the **mushrooms, onion,** and **garlic** and cook, stirring occasionally, for 5 to 7 minutes or until the onion is soft.

4. Add the **wine** to the mushroom mixture and cook for 1 to 2 minutes or until most of the liquid is absorbed. Add the yogurt-cheese mixture and heat through; do not boil or the sauce will curdle.

5. Drain the fusilli and return it to the kettle. Add the mushroom mixture and toss well with two forks to mix. Transfer the fusilli to a heated platter and garnish with **parsley sprigs,** if desired. Serves 4.

Alfredo-Style Noodles

This version has far fewer calories than the butter- and cream-laden classic, but still is rich and satisfying.

8 ounces broad egg noodles
¼ cup part-skim ricotta cheese
¼ cup plain low-fat yogurt

¼ cup grated Parmesan cheese
1 tablespoon unsalted margarine
¼ teaspoon black pepper

FAT **SUGAR** **SODIUM**

Preparation:
3 min.
Cooking:
8 min.

One Serving:

Calories	299
Total Fat	*8 g*
Saturated Fat	*3 g*
Cholesterol	*63 mg*
Protein	*12 g*
Carbohydrates	*43 g*
Sodium	*125 mg*
Added Sugar	*0*
Fiber	*0*

1. Cook the **noodles** according to package directions, omitting the salt. Drain well and return to the cooking pot.

2. Add the **ricotta cheese, yogurt, Parmesan cheese, margarine,** and **pepper,** and toss well to mix. Transfer to a warm platter and serve with a cooked green vegetable or Marinated Vegetable Salad, page 216. Serves 4.

Variations:

Noodles with Mushrooms Melt the margarine in a heavy 10-inch skillet over moderate heat. Add 1½ cups sliced mushrooms and cook, stirring, for 3 to 5 minutes. Toss with the noodles and the remaining ingredients.

Noodles with Onion and Garlic Melt the margarine in a heavy 7-inch skillet over moderate heat. Add 1 large yellow onion, sliced, and 1 clove garlic, minced. Cook, uncovered, until the onion is soft—about 5 minutes. Toss with the noodles and the remaining ingredients.

Crab and Pasta Salad

6 ounces vermicelli or other thin pasta

2 tablespoons Oriental sesame or peanut oil

1 medium-size sweet red or green pepper, cored, seeded, and cut into matchstick strips

2 cloves garlic, minced

3 green onions, sliced thin

6 ounces fresh, thawed frozen, or canned crabmeat, picked over for bits of shell and cartilage

1 small head romaine or other lettuce (about ½ pound), torn into bite-size pieces

2 tablespoons reduced-sodium soy sauce

2 tablespoons red wine vinegar

1 tablespoon medium-dry sherry or white wine

½ teaspoon sugar

⅛ teaspoon cayenne pepper

FAT SUGAR SODIUM

Preparation:
6 min.
Cooking:
10 min.

One Serving:

Calories	289
Total Fat	9 g
Saturated Fat	1 g
Cholesterol	43 mg
Protein	14 g
Carbohydrates	37 g
Sodium	399 mg
Added Sugar	2 Cal
Fiber	2 g

1. Cook the **vermicelli** according to package directions, omitting the salt. Drain and transfer to a serving bowl.

2. Meanwhile, heat 1 tablespoon of the **sesame oil** in a heavy 10-inch skillet over moderately high heat for 1 minute; add the **red pepper** and **garlic** and stir-fry just until limp—about 3 minutes. Add the **green onions** and stir-fry 30 seconds longer.

3. Combine the vermicelli, red pepper–green onion mixture, **crabmeat,** and **lettuce** in a large bowl. In a small bowl, whisk together the remaining sesame oil and the **soy sauce, vinegar, sherry, sugar,** and **cayenne pepper.** Pour over the pasta mixture, tossing gently to mix. Serves 4.

Crab and Pasta Salad

Sesame Noodles

This and the two variations that follow make tasty side dishes.

FAT SUGAR SODIUM

3 ounces vermicelli, capellini, or other thin pasta	**2 tablespoons unsalted margarine**
1½ tablespoons sesame seeds	**⅛ teaspoon salt**

1. Cook the **vermicelli** according to package directions, omitting the salt. Drain and transfer to a heated serving bowl.
2. While the pasta is cooking, toast the **sesame seeds** in a 7-inch skillet over moderately low heat, stirring, until they begin to turn an amber color—about 2 minutes. Add the **margarine,** swirling the skillet until the margarine melts.
3. Pour the sesame seeds and margarine over the vermicelli, add the **salt,** and toss until each strand is coated. Serves 4.

Variations:

Poppy Seed Noodles   Prepare as above, substituting 1½ tablespoons untoasted poppy seeds for the sesame seeds.

Herbed Noodles   Prepare as above, substituting 1 tablespoon each minced fresh basil, parsley, and chives for the sesame seeds. *(Note: If fresh basil is not available, substitute 1 teaspoon dried basil. Frozen or freeze-dried chives can be used in place of the fresh.)*

Preparation:
1 min.
Cooking:
10 min.

One Serving:

Calories	148
Total Fat	8 g
Saturated Fat	2 g
Cholesterol	0
Protein	2 g
Carbohydrates	17 g
Sodium	70 mg
Added Sugar	0
Fiber	1 g

Homemade German Noodles

These noodles are called spätzle *in Germany. Serve them instead of rice or potatoes.*

FAT SUGAR SODIUM

1½ cups sifted all-purpose flour	**1 large egg**
¼ teaspoon ground nutmeg	**1 tablespoon unsalted margarine**
⅓ cup skim milk	**⅛ teaspoon black pepper**
¼ cup cold water	

1. In a mixing bowl, combine the **flour** and **nutmeg.** In a measuring cup, whisk together the **milk, water,** and **egg;** add to the flour and stir with a wooden spoon to form a soft dough.
2. In a large heavy saucepan, bring 3 quarts water to a boil over high heat. Working quickly with your hands, press the dough, about 3 tablespoons at a time, through a large-holed colander or coarse grater directly into the boiling water.
3. Cook, stirring often, for 6 to 8 minutes or until the noodles are firm and no raw flour taste remains. Drain well.
4. Transfer the noodles to a heated platter, add the **margarine** and **pepper,** and toss well. Serves 6.

Variations:

Green German Noodles   Add 2 tablespoons finely minced parsley, basil, tarragon, or chives to the batter and mix well.

German Noodles with Bread Crumbs   Melt 1½ teaspoons margarine in a heavy 7-inch skillet over low heat. Add ⅓ cup fine dry bread crumbs and stir until the crumbs are golden. Sprinkle over the cooked noodles.

Preparation:
10 min.
Cooking:
9 min.

One Serving:

Calories	140
Total Fat	3 g
Saturated Fat	1 g
Cholesterol	46 mg
Protein	4 g
Carbohydrates	23 g
Sodium	19 mg
Added Sugar	0
Fiber	1 g

Noodles and Rice

Preparation: **5 min.**   FAT SUGAR SODIUM
Cooking: **24 min.** (mostly unattended)

Here is a side dish that is an interesting change from plain rice. Vary by stirring in chopped fresh chives or other herbs before serving.

1 tablespoon unsalted margarine
⅓ cup thin egg noodles
½ cup long-grain rice
1¼ cups low-sodium chicken broth
⅛ teaspoon black pepper

1. In a medium-size heavy saucepan, melt the **margarine** over moderate heat. Add the **noodles** and cook, stirring, until golden—1 to 2 minutes. Add the **rice** and cook, stirring, about 3 minutes more.

2. Add the **chicken broth** and **pepper,** bring the mixture to a boil, and lower the heat to a simmer. Cover and simmer for 20 minutes or until the rice is tender. Serves 4.

One Serving:

Calories	143	Protein	3 g
Total Fat	4 g	Carbohydrates	24 g
Saturated Fat	1 g	Sodium	17 mg
Cholesterol	6 mg	Added Sugar	0
		Fiber	0

Italian-Style Rice and Beans

Preparation: **10 min.** Cooking: **26 min.**   FAT SUGAR SODIUM

⅔ cup long-grain rice (or 1½ cups leftover cooked rice)
1 tablespoon olive oil
1 large yellow onion, chopped
2 cloves garlic, minced
3 medium-size ripe tomatoes (about 1 pound), peeled, cored, and chopped, or 1 can (1 pound) low-sodium tomatoes, drained and chopped
2 medium-size carrots, peeled and chopped
1 large stalk celery, chopped
1 tablespoon minced fresh basil or 1 teaspoon dried basil, crumbled
1 teaspoon dried oregano, crumbled
¼ teaspoon black pepper
2 cups cooked and drained kidney beans
¼ cup grated Parmesan cheese

1. Cook the **rice** according to package directions, omitting the salt. Set aside.

2. Meanwhile, heat the olive oil in a heavy 12-inch skillet over moderate heat for 1 minute; add the **onion** and **garlic** and cook, uncovered, until the onion is soft—about 5 minutes. Add the **tomatoes, carrots, celery, basil, oregano,** and **pepper** and bring to a boil; cover, reduce the heat, and simmer for 15 minutes. Stir in the **kidney beans,** cover, and cook 5 minutes longer.

3. Stir in the cooked rice, transfer to a warm serving bowl, and sprinkle with the **cheese.** Serve with a tossed green salad. Serves 4.

One Serving:

Calories	332	Protein	13 g
Total Fat	6 g	Carbohydrates	58 g
Saturated Fat	2 g	Sodium	128 mg
Cholesterol	4 mg	Added Sugar	0
		Fiber	2 g

Jambalaya

Preparation: **20 min.** Cooking: **29 min.**   FAT SUGAR SODIUM

1 tablespoon olive oil
1 small sweet green pepper, cored, seeded, and chopped
1 medium-size stalk celery, sliced thin
1 small yellow onion, chopped
1 clove garlic, minced
¾ cup long-grain rice
1 can (1 pound) low-sodium tomatoes, chopped, with their juice
1 cup low-sodium chicken broth
¼ teaspoon dried thyme, crumbled
⅛ teaspoon each ground allspice, cloves, and cayenne pepper
2 cups cubed cooked light chicken or turkey meat

1. Heat the **olive oil** in a large saucepan over medium heat for 1 minute. Add the **green pepper, celery, onion,** and **garlic,** and cook, stirring frequently, until the onion is soft—about 5 minutes. Add the **rice** and cook, stirring occasionally, 3 minutes longer or until the rice is golden.

2. Add the **tomatoes, chicken broth, thyme, allspice, cloves,** and **cayenne pepper.** Bring to a boil, reduce the heat, and simmer, uncovered, for 15 minutes. Add the **chicken** and cook 5 minutes longer or until the rice is tender. Serves 4.

One Serving:

Calories	329	Protein	24 g
Total Fat	9 g	Carbohydrates	36 g
Saturated Fat	2 g	Sodium	96 mg
Cholesterol	62 mg	Added Sugar	0
		Fiber	1 g

Tip: *White rice that is called "converted" is more nutritious than ordinary white rice. Because it is parboiled before its nutrient-rich bran is removed, some of the bran's vitamins and minerals are absorbed by the white grain.*

Spinach-Rice Mold

Preparation: **10 min.** Cooking: **20 min.** FAT SUGAR SODIUM

When the center of this attractive mold is filled with a creamed dish such as Fish Rarebit, page 121, it serves four as a complete meal.

1 **cup long-grain rice**
1 **pound fresh spinach, trimmed, or 1 package (10 ounces) frozen chopped spinach**
½ **cup finely chopped water chestnuts**
5 **teaspoons lemon juice**
¼ **teaspoon white or black pepper**
⅛ **teaspoon salt**

1. In a small saucepan, cook the **rice** according to package directions, omitting the salt.
2. Meanwhile, wash the spinach and place it in a medium-size saucepan with just the water that clings to the leaves. Cook, covered, over moderately low heat until the spinach is just limp—about 5 minutes. Remove from the pan, press the spinach as dry as possible, and chop.
3. In a large bowl, combine the rice, spinach, **water chestnuts, lemon juice, pepper,** and **salt.** Spoon the mixture into a lightly greased 1-quart ring mold and pack lightly. Let stand 1 minute, then invert onto a warm serving platter. Serves 6.

Variation:

Parsley-Rice Ring Substitute 1½ cups finely chopped parsley or watercress for the spinach and mix, uncooked, with the cooked rice and other ingredients. Spoon into the mold as directed.

One Serving:

Calories	141	Protein	4 g
Total Fat	0	Carbohydrates	31 g
Saturated Fat	0	Sodium	85 mg
Cholesterol	0	Added Sugar	0
		Fiber	1 g

Spinach-Rice Mold

Rice with Lemon and Dill

Preparation: **5 min.**
Cooking: **27 min.** (mostly unattended)

FAT SUGAR SODIUM

Dill and lemon make this perfect with fish.

2 **teaspoons unsalted margarine**
1 **medium-size yellow onion, chopped fine**
¾ **cup long-grain rice**
1¼ **cups low-sodium chicken broth**
1 **tablespoon grated lemon rind**
1 **tablespoon lemon juice**
¼ **teaspoon dried thyme, crumbled**
⅛ **teaspoon black pepper**
1 **bay leaf**
2 **tablespoons snipped fresh dill**

1. Preheat the oven to 350°F. In a medium-size heavy saucepan with an ovenproof handle, melt the **margarine** over moderate heat; add the **onion** and cook, uncovered, until soft— about 5 minutes. Mix in the **rice, chicken broth, lemon rind, lemon juice, thyme, pepper,** and **bay leaf,** and bring to a simmer.
2. Cover the pan with a piece of wax paper, then the lid; transfer to the oven and bake for 20 minutes or until the rice is tender.
3. Remove the bay leaf and add the **dill.** Serves 4.

One Serving:

Calories	167	Protein	4 g
Total Fat	4 g	Carbohydrates	32 g
Saturated Fat	1 g	Sodium	19 mg
Cholesterol	0	Added Sugar	0
		Fiber	1 g

Rice and Green Peas

Preparation: **5 min.** Cooking: **20 min.**

FAT SUGAR SODIUM

This side dish is known in Italy as Risi e Bisi.

2 **cups low-sodium chicken broth**
2 **teaspoons unsalted margarine**
1 **medium-size yellow onion, chopped fine**
⅔ **cup long-grain rice**
½ **cup fresh or frozen green peas**
1 **tablespoon grated Parmesan cheese**
⅛ **teaspoon black pepper**

1. Heat the **chicken broth** in a small saucepan. Melt half the **margarine** in a heavy 10-inch skillet over moderate heat; add the **onion** and cook, uncovered, until soft—about 5 minutes.

2. Add the **rice** and **peas** and cook, stirring, 2 minutes longer. Add ½ cup of the hot chicken broth, reduce the heat to moderately low, and stir until almost all the liquid is absorbed— about 3 minutes. Add the remaining chicken broth, ½ cup at a time, stirring after each addition until the liquid is absorbed.
3. When the rice is tender, remove from the heat and stir in the **cheese, pepper,** and remaining margarine. Serves 4.

One Serving:

Calories	174	Protein	5 g
Total Fat	3 g	Carbohydrates	31 g
Saturated Fat	1 g	Sodium	51 mg
Cholesterol	2 mg	Added Sugar	0
		Fiber	1 g

Brown Rice with Poppy Seed Sauce

Preparation: **5 min.**
Cooking: **55 min.** (mostly unattended)

FAT SUGAR SODIUM

Here is an unusual accompaniment for beef.

¾ **cup brown rice**
2¼ **cups water or low-sodium chicken broth**
2 **tablespoons plain low-fat yogurt**
2 **tablespoons sour cream**
1 **tablespoon lemon juice**
1½ **teaspoons poppy seeds**
⅛ **teaspoon white or black pepper**
⅛ **teaspoon salt**

1. Preheat the oven to 350°F. Spread the **rice** in a single layer in a pie pan. Set the pan, uncovered, in the oven and toast the rice for 8 to 10 minutes, stirring occasionally, until golden.
2. Bring the **water** to a boil in a medium-size saucepan over high heat. Stir in the toasted rice, adjust the heat so that the liquid bubbles gently, cover, and cook for 45 minutes or until all the liquid is absorbed and the rice is tender.
3. In a small bowl, combine the **yogurt, sour cream, lemon juice, poppy seeds, pepper,** and **salt.** Stir into the cooked rice and mix well. Serves 4.

One Serving:

Calories	152	Protein	3 g
Total Fat	6 g	Carbohydrates	28 g
Saturated Fat	2 g	Sodium	82 mg
Cholesterol	4 mg	Added Sugar	0
		Fiber	3 g

Brown Rice with Asparagus and Egg

Brown Rice with Asparagus and Egg

For a healthful meal, serve with Citrus and Watercress Salad, page 221.

FAT SUGAR SODIUM

1 cup brown rice

1 large egg

1 large egg white

1 tablespoon water

¼ teaspoon sugar

2¼ teaspoons reduced-sodium soy sauce

Nonstick cooking spray

⅓ pound asparagus, tough stems removed, cut into 1½-inch lengths

¼ pound fresh snow peas, trimmed, or ½ 6-ounce package frozen snow peas

1 tablespoon peanut or corn oil

4 cloves garlic, minced

1 tablespoon minced fresh ginger or ½ teaspoon ground ginger

1 medium-size sweet red pepper, cored, seeded, and chopped

1 medium-size carrot, peeled and coarsely grated

2 green onions, including tops, sliced thin

8 unsalted roasted cashews or peanuts, chopped

2 teaspoons white wine vinegar

Preparation:
11 min.
Cooking:
55 min. (mostly unattended)

One Serving:

Calories	*280*
Total Fat	*8 g*
Saturated Fat	*1 g*
Cholesterol	*69 mg*
Protein	*8 g*
Carbohydrates	*45 g*
Sodium	*158 mg*
Added Sugar	*0*
Fiber	*5 g*

1. Cook the **rice** according to package directions, omitting the salt, then chill in the freezer about 20 minutes.

2. While the rice is being chilled, prepare an omelet. In a small bowl, beat the **egg** and **egg white** with the **water, sugar,** and ¼ teaspoon of the **soy sauce.** Coat a heavy 7-inch skillet with the **cooking spray,** set over moderate heat for 30 seconds, and add the egg mixture. As the eggs begin to cook around the edges, push the cooked portions toward the center until the omelet has set—about 2 minutes. Turn onto a plate, cool slightly, and slice into strips about ¾ inch wide. Set aside.

3. In a large saucepan of boiling unsalted water, cook the **asparagus** and **snow peas,** uncovered, for 30 seconds. Rinse well under cold running water to stop the cooking; drain and set aside.

4. Heat the **peanut oil** in a heavy 12-inch skillet or wok over moderately high heat for 1 minute; add the **garlic** and **ginger** and cook, stirring, until golden—about 2 minutes. Add the cooked rice, **red pepper,** and **carrot,** and stir for 4 minutes. Add the omelet slices, asparagus, snow peas, **green onions,** and **cashews,** and stir 2 minutes longer. Add the remaining soy sauce and the **vinegar,** stir to mix well, and serve. Serves 4.

Curried Brown Rice with Apricots

Preparation: **20 min.** FAT SUGAR SODIUM
Cooking: **1 hr.** (mostly unattended)

Serve this side dish with chicken, turkey, or lamb.

1 **tablespoon unsalted margarine**
1 **medium-size yellow onion, chopped fine**
1 **clove garlic, minced**
2 **tablespoons finely chopped dried apricots**
1 **teaspoon light brown sugar**
2 **teaspoons curry powder**
¾ **cup brown rice**
2 **cups water**
2 **tablespoons lemon juice**
¼ **teaspoon black pepper**
¼ **teaspoon dried thyme, crumbled**

1. Preheat the oven to 400°F. Melt the **margarine** in a 1-quart flameproof casserole set over moderate heat. Add the **onion** and **garlic** and cook, uncovered, until the onion is soft—about 5 minutes. Add the **apricots** and cook, stirring occasionally, 3 minutes longer.

2. Reduce the heat to moderately low, stir in the **brown sugar** and **curry powder,** and cook, stirring, until the sugar has caramelized—3 to 5 minutes. Add the **rice** and cook, stirring, for 3 to 5 minutes or until golden. Meanwhile, bring the **water** to a boil in a small saucepan and add to the casserole along with the **lemon juice, pepper,** and **thyme.**

3. Cover, transfer to the oven, and bake for 45 to 50 minutes or until all the liquid is absorbed and the rice is tender. Serves 4.

One Serving:			
Calories	178	Protein	3 g
Total Fat	4 g	Carbohydrates	33 g
Saturated Fat	1 g	Sodium	7 mg
Cholesterol	0	Added Sugar	8 Cal
		Fiber	3

Easy Nutted Brown Rice

Preparation: **5 min.** FAT SUGAR SODIUM
Cooking: **47 min.** (mostly unattended)

Here is a rice side dish with a difference—and it's simple to prepare.

1⅓ **cups low-sodium chicken broth or water**
½ **cup brown rice**
⅛ **teaspoon black pepper**
2 **tablespoons chopped pecans or walnuts**
1½ **teaspoons unsalted margarine**

1. In a medium-size heavy saucepan over moderately high heat, bring the **chicken broth** to a boil. Stir in the **rice** and **pepper,** then reduce the heat so that the broth bubbles gently. Cover and cook for 45 minutes or until the rice is tender.

2. Stir in the **pecans** and **margarine** and serve. Serves 4.

One Serving:			
Calories	153	Protein	3 g
Total Fat	7 g	Carbohydrates	20 g
Saturated Fat	1 g	Sodium	19 mg
Cholesterol	0	Added Sugar	0
		Fiber	2 g

Wild Rice and Carrot Loaf

Preparation: **15 min.**
Cooking: **1 hr. 23 min.** (mostly unattended)

FAT SUGAR SODIUM

This recipe serves eight as a side dish; a smaller loaf would not be as moist and succulent. Just freeze or refrigerate any leftovers to serve another day. If you use a long-grain and wild rice mixture, be sure to omit the seasoning packet.

3 cups low-sodium beef broth or water
½ cup brown rice
½ cup wild rice or long-grain and wild rice mixture
2 tablespoons unsalted margarine
1 large yellow onion, chopped fine
2 medium-size stalks celery, chopped fine
4 medium-size carrots, peeled and grated
⅓ cup minced parsley
2 large egg whites, slightly beaten
2 teaspoons ground cumin
¼ teaspoon black pepper

1. Preheat the oven to 350°F. Bring the **beef broth** to a boil in a large heavy saucepan over moderate heat. Stir in the **brown rice** and **wild rice,** return to a boil, then adjust the heat so that the broth barely bubbles; cook, uncovered, for 15 minutes or until almost all the broth is absorbed. Turn the heat to low, cover, and cook for 5 minutes more.

2. Meanwhile, melt the **margarine** in a heavy 10-inch skillet over moderate heat; add the **onion, celery,** and **carrots** and cook, uncovered, until the vegetables are soft—5 to 8 minutes.

3. Stir the vegetables into the rice along with the **parsley, egg whites, cumin,** and **pepper.**

4. Turn all into a lightly greased 9¼"x 5¼"x 2¾" loaf pan and bake, uncovered, for 1 hour or until the loaf is browned and firm to the touch.

5. Cool the loaf upright on a wire rack for 15 minutes, then turn out onto a small heated platter. *(Note: This loaf is very delicate. To slice it, use a sharp serrated knife and a gentle sawing motion.)* Serves 8.

One Serving:

Calories	140	Protein	4 g
Total Fat	4 g	Carbohydrates	24 g
Saturated Fat	1 g	Sodium	40 mg
Cholesterol	0	Added Sugar	0
		Fiber	1 g

Polenta with Fresh Tomato Sauce

Preparation: **5 min.**
Cooking: **55 min.** (mostly unattended)

FAT SUGAR SODIUM

Polenta is an Italian cornmeal mush. Traditional recipes require the cook to stand over the pot and stir constantly, but this simpler method needs much less attention. Serve as a side dish.

5 medium-size ripe tomatoes (about 1½ pounds), peeled, cored, and quartered
1 small yellow onion, chopped fine
1 tablespoon unsalted margarine
½ teaspoon each dried basil and marjoram, crumbled
⅛ teaspoon black pepper
⅔ cup yellow cornmeal
2½ cups cold water
2 tablespoons grated Parmesan cheese

1. In a medium-size heavy saucepan over moderately low heat, cook the **tomatoes,** covered, for 10 minutes, stirring occasionally. Transfer the tomatoes and their juice to an electric blender or food processor and purée until smooth—about 1 minute.

2. Return the puréed tomatoes to the saucepan and add the **onion, margarine, basil, marjoram,** and **pepper.** Simmer, uncovered, over moderately low heat, stirring occasionally, until thickened—about 45 minutes.

3. While the sauce is cooking, combine the **cornmeal** with 1 cup of the **water** in a small bowl and set aside. Put 2 inches of water in the bottom half of a double boiler and bring to a simmer over moderate heat.

4. Pour the remaining 1½ cups of water into the top half of the double boiler, set directly over moderate heat, and bring to a boil. Stir in the cornmeal mixture and cook, stirring constantly, until it just starts to boil.

5. Set the double boiler top over the bottom, cover, and cook the polenta for 45 minutes, stirring occasionally. Transfer the polenta to a warm serving bowl, spoon the sauce over it, and sprinkle with the **cheese.** Serves 4.

One Serving:

Calories	154	Protein	4 g
Total Fat	4 g	Carbohydrates	26 g
Saturated Fat	1 g	Sodium	60 mg
Cholesterol	2 mg	Added Sugar	0
		Fiber	0

Baked Grits

This southern specialty is a good side dish with pork or chicken.

FAT SUGAR SODIUM

1	tablespoon unsalted margarine
1½	cups low-sodium chicken broth
1½	cups skim milk
⅔	cup hominy grits

¼	teaspoon salt
1	large egg
1	large egg white
⅛	teaspoon black pepper

Preparation:
5 min.
Cooking:
1 hr. 8 min. (mostly unattended)

1. Preheat the oven to 350°F. Grease a deep 1½-quart baking dish with ½ teaspoon of the **margarine** and reserve the rest. Set the dish aside.
2. In a medium-size heavy saucepan over moderately high heat, bring the **chicken broth** and 1 cup of the **milk** to a boil. Stir in the **grits** and **salt,** reduce the heat to low, and cook, stirring, about 5 minutes or until thickened. Let cool for 5 minutes.
3. In a measuring cup, whisk together the remaining milk, the **egg,** and **egg white,** then stir into the grits along with the **pepper** and remaining margarine.
4. Transfer the grits to the baking dish and bake, uncovered, for 1 hour or until golden. Serves 4.

One Serving:

Calories	186
Total Fat	5 g
Saturated Fat	1 g
Cholesterol	70 mg
Protein	9 g
Carbohydrates	26 g
Sodium	232 mg
Added Sugar	0
Fiber	0

Kasha with Onions and Noodles

Kasha is another name for toasted buckwheat. Nutritious and satisfying, it is available at most supermarkets and specialty stores. This recipe is hearty enough to serve as a main course; accompany with a green vegetable.

FAT SUGAR SODIUM

1½	tablespoons olive oil
2	medium-size yellow onions, halved and sliced thin
6	ounces bow-tie noodles or medium-size pasta shells
½	pound mushrooms, sliced thin

1	cup kasha
1	large egg, slightly beaten
¼	teaspoon salt
¼	teaspoon black pepper
3	cups hot water

Preparation:
10 min.
Cooking:
35 min.

1. Heat the **olive oil** in a heavy 12-inch skillet over moderate heat for 1 minute. Add the **onions** and cook, stirring frequently, until they start to brown—about 10 minutes.
2. Meanwhile, cook the **noodles** according to package directions, omitting the salt. Rinse with cold water, drain well, and set aside.
3. Add the **mushrooms** to the skillet and cook, stirring occasionally, for 5 minutes or until the mushrooms are lightly browned and their juices have evaporated.
4. In a small bowl, combine the **kasha** and **egg,** stirring well to coat each grain. Push the mushroom-onion mixture to one side of the skillet, add the kasha-egg mixture to the other, raise the heat to high, and stir the kasha until the grains have separated—about 4 minutes.
5. Add the **salt, pepper,** and hot **water** and stir to mix the contents of the skillet. Cover, reduce the heat to moderately low, and cook, stirring occasionally, for 15 minutes or until the kasha is tender. Stir in the cooked noodles and bring to serving temperature. Serves 4.

One Serving:

Calories	330
Total Fat	8 g
Saturated Fat	1 g
Cholesterol	69 mg
Protein	11 g
Carbohydrates	55 g
Sodium	157 mg
Added Sugar	0
Fiber	3 g

Kasha with Vegetables

Serve this as an accompaniment to beef or chicken.

FAT SUGAR SODIUM

1 tablespoon unsalted margarine
1 medium-size yellow onion, chopped
1 medium-size stalk celery, chopped
¼ pound mushrooms, sliced thin
¾ cup kasha

1 large egg
1½ cups low-sodium beef broth or water
½ cup thinly sliced water chestnuts
2 tablespoons lemon juice
½ teaspoon ground nutmeg
¼ teaspoon black pepper

Preparation:
10 min.
Cooking:
16 min.

One Serving:

Calories	141
Total Fat	5 g
Saturated Fat	1 g
Cholesterol	69 mg
Protein	5 g
Carbohydrates	21 g
Sodium	32 mg
Added Sugar	0
Fiber	1 g

1. Melt the **margarine** in a heavy 10-inch skillet over moderate heat. Add the **onion** and **celery** and cook, uncovered, for 2 to 3 minutes. Add the **mushrooms** and cook 2 to 3 minutes longer, stirring occasionally.

2. Meanwhile, using a fork, beat the **kasha** with the **egg** in a small bowl until all the grains are coated. Add to the skillet and cook, stirring constantly, for 1 to 2 minutes or until the egg is cooked.

3. Add the **beef broth,** bring to a boil, and adjust the heat so that the liquid bubbles gently; cover and cook for 10 minutes or until all the liquid is absorbed and the kasha is tender.

4. Stir in the **water chestnuts, lemon juice, nutmeg,** and **pepper,** and transfer the mixture to a serving bowl. Serves 4.

Kasha with Onions and Noodles

Bulgur Pilaf

Bulgur is the Turkish word for a cracked wheat cereal of nutty flavor and pleasantly chewy texture. Serve it as a change of pace from rice.

FAT SUGAR SODIUM

1 tablespoon unsalted margarine
1 small yellow onion, chopped fine
⅔ cup bulgur
2 cups water or low-sodium chicken broth
1 medium-size carrot, peeled and chopped fine

1 medium-size stalk celery, chopped fine
½ teaspoon dried thyme, crumbled
⅛ teaspoon black pepper

1. In a medium-size heavy saucepan, melt the **margarine** over moderate heat. Add the **onion** and cook, uncovered, until soft—about 5 minutes. Add the **bulgur** and cook, stirring, for 1 minute.
2. Add the **water, carrot, celery, thyme,** and **pepper.** Bring to a simmer, reduce the heat to low, cover, and cook for 15 minutes or until all the liquid is absorbed. Serves 4.

Preparation:
2 min.
Cooking:
23 min.

One Serving:

Calories	*144*
Total Fat	*6 g*
Saturated Fat	*1 g*
Cholesterol	*0*
Protein	*3 g*
Carbohydrates	*26 g*
Sodium	*17 mg*
Added Sugar	*0*
Fiber	*2 g*

Bulgur-Stuffed Red Peppers

½ cup bulgur
¾ cup boiling water
4 medium-size sweet red peppers
3 large plum tomatoes (about 10 ounces), peeled and chopped, or 1 cup canned low-sodium tomatoes, drained and chopped

5 cloves garlic, minced
½ cup shredded Cheddar cheese (about 2 ounces)
4 green onions, including tops, sliced
1 tablespoon minced parsley
¼ teaspoon black pepper
1 cup low-sodium chicken broth

FAT SUGAR SODIUM

1. In a heavy heat-proof bowl, combine the **bulgur** and boiling **water;** soak for about 30 minutes or until all the liquid has been absorbed.
2. Preheat the oven to 375°F. Slice the tops from the **peppers,** discarding the stems, and finely chop the tops; reserve. Scrape out the seeds and ribs, leaving the peppers intact. Cook the peppers in a large kettle of boiling unsalted water until almost tender—about 5 minutes. Drain and set aside.
3. Combine the bulgur, chopped pepper tops, **tomatoes, garlic, cheese, green onions, parsley, black pepper,** and ⅓ cup of the **chicken broth** in a medium-size bowl. Stir well to combine. Fill each pepper with ¼ of the mixture and place the stuffed peppers in an ungreased 8″x 8″x 2″ baking pan. Pour the remaining chicken broth into the bottom of the pan.
4. Cover with aluminum foil and bake for 20 minutes or until the stuffing is heated through and the peppers are tender. Serves 4.

Preparation:
35 min., including soaking of bulgur
Cooking:
25 min.

One Serving:

Calories	*234*
Total Fat	*10 g*
Saturated Fat	*6 g*
Cholesterol	*30 mg*
Protein	*11 g*
Carbohydrates	*26 g*
Sodium	*196 mg*
Added Sugar	*0*
Fiber	*3 g*

Variations:

Bulgur-Stuffed Peppers with Raisins and Nuts Omit the shredded cheese and add 3 tablespoons raisins and 3 tablespoons chopped walnuts or pecans to the stuffing. Mix well.

Bulgur-Stuffed Peppers with Vegetables Chop 1 small carrot, 1 small zucchini, and 1 small cucumber. Mix well with the stuffing and carefully mound up in the peppers.

Vegetables

Although traditionally served "on the side," vegetables are, in fact, nature's most generous source of nourishment. Leafy greens, crisp root vegetables, succulent squash, and healthful cabbage, peas, and beans—all these and more offer endless possibilities for preparation and enjoyment, as you will find in this chapter. And you can eat as much of them as you like, since they have no cholesterol and hardly any fat or sodium, and provide valuable fiber as well. Unless noted, all the recipes can be halved to serve two.

Braised Eggplant, Zucchini, and Tomatoes

Asparagus with Sesame Seeds

Preparation: **15 min.** Cooking: **9 min.** FAT SUGAR SODIUM

1½ **pounds asparagus, tough stems removed, cut into 1-inch lengths**
1½ **teaspoons unsalted margarine**
 1 **tablespoon sesame seeds**
 1 **teaspoon reduced-sodium soy sauce**
 1 **teaspoon Oriental sesame or peanut oil**
 ⅛ **teaspoon black pepper**

1. In a heavy 10-inch skillet, bring an inch of unsalted water to a boil. Add the **asparagus** and cook, covered, for 3 minutes or until just tender. Drain in a colander, rinse under cold running water to stop the cooking, and drain again. Set aside.
2. In the same saucepan, melt the **margarine** over moderate heat; add the **sesame seeds** and cook, stirring, for 3 to 4 minutes or until the seeds are golden.
3. Return the asparagus to the pan; add the **soy sauce, sesame oil,** and **pepper,** and cook, stirring, for 1 minute or until the asparagus is heated through. Serves 4.

One Serving:

Calories	57	Protein	3 g
Total Fat	4 g	Carbohydrates	4 g
Saturated Fat	1 g	Sodium	53 mg
Cholesterol	0	Added Sugar	0
		Fiber	1 g

Variation:

Sugar Snap Peas with Water Chestnuts
Substitute 1 pound Sugar Snap peas or ¾ pound snow peas for the asparagus and cook 2 to 3 minutes as directed. Substitute ¼ cup thinly sliced water chestnuts for the sesame seeds and add to the melted margarine in the saucepan along with the soy sauce, sesame oil, and black pepper. Heat for 1 minute, return the peas to the pan, and toss until heated through—about 1 minute longer.

Tip: To make sure asparagus cooks evenly, select stalks of the same thickness. To remove tough stems, break off the lower ends of the stalks as far down as they easily snap.

Baked Asparagus with Parmesan Cheese

Preparation: **10 min.** Cooking: **15 min.** FAT SUGAR SODIUM

 1 **pound asparagus, tough stems removed**
  Nonstick cooking spray
2½ **tablespoons grated Parmesan cheese**
1½ **tablespoons soft white bread crumbs**
 2 **teaspoons unsalted margarine**

1. Preheat the oven to 450°F. Arrange the **asparagus** in a 9″x 9″x 2″ baking pan that has been lightly coated with the **cooking spray.** Sprinkle with the **cheese** and **bread crumbs** and dot with the **margarine.**
2. Bake, uncovered, until the asparagus is just tender—about 15 minutes. *(Note: Baking time may vary by up to 5 minutes, depending on the thickness of the asparagus.)* Serves 4.

One Serving:

Calories	39	Protein	3 g
Total Fat	2 g	Carbohydrates	3 g
Saturated Fat	1 g	Sodium	65 mg
Cholesterol	3 mg	Added Sugar	0
		Fiber	1 g

Green Beans with Dill

Preparation: **10 min.** Cooking: **10 min.** FAT SUGAR SODIUM

 1 **pound green beans, trimmed**
1½ **teaspoons unsalted margarine**
 2 **teaspoons lemon juice**
 ⅛ **teaspoon black pepper**
 2 **tablespoons snipped fresh dill or**
  ½ **teaspoon dill weed**

1. In a large saucepan, bring an inch of unsalted water to a boil; add the **green beans** and cook, covered, for 6 to 7 minutes or until just tender. Drain in a colander, rinse under cold running water to stop the cooking, and drain again.
2. In the same saucepan, melt the **margarine** over moderate heat; return the beans to the pan and toss for 2 to 3 minutes or until heated through. Add the **lemon juice, pepper,** and **dill** and toss again. Serves 4.

One Serving:

Calories	45	Protein	2 g
Total Fat	2 g	Carbohydrates	7 g
Saturated Fat	0	Sodium	7 mg
Cholesterol	0	Added Sugar	0
		Fiber	2 g

Asparagus with Sesame Seeds (left) and *Green Beans with Pimientos* (right)

Green Beans with Pimientos

Preparation: **15 min.** Cooking: **12 min.** `FAT` `SUGAR` `SODIUM`

- 1 **pound green beans, trimmed**
- 1½ **teaspoons unsalted margarine**
- 1 **clove garlic, minced**
- 1 **jar (4 ounces) pimientos, drained and chopped**
- ⅛ **teaspoon black pepper**
- 2 **teaspoons lemon juice**
- 1 **tablespoon sliced toasted almonds**

1. In a large saucepan, bring an inch of unsalted water to a boil; add the **green beans** and cook, covered, until just tender—about 6 to 7 minutes. Drain in a colander, rinse under cold running water, and drain again. Set aside.

2. In a 10-inch nonstick skillet, melt the **margarine** over moderate heat; add the **garlic** and cook, stirring, for 1 minute. Add the beans and **pimientos** and cook, stirring often, until heated through—about 3 to 4 minutes. Stir in the **pepper** and **lemon juice** and sprinkle with the **almonds.** Serves 4.

One Serving:

Calories	60	Protein	2 g
Total Fat	2 g	Carbohydrates	9 g
Saturated Fat	0	Sodium	12 mg
Cholesterol	0	Added Sugar	0
		Fiber	2 g

Green Beans and Cherry Tomatoes

Preparation: **10 min.** Cooking: **12 min.** `FAT` `SUGAR` `SODIUM`

- 1 **pound green beans, trimmed**
- 2 **teaspoons olive oil**
- 1 **pint cherry tomatoes**
- 2 **tablespoons chopped fresh basil or 1 teaspoon dried basil, crumbled**
- 1 **tablespoon red wine vinegar**
- ¼ **teaspoon salt (optional)**

1. In a large saucepan, bring an inch of unsalted water to a boil; add the **green beans** and cook, covered, until just tender—6 to 7 minutes. Reserve 2 tablespoons of the cooking water, then drain the beans and set aside.

2. In a heavy 12-inch skillet, heat the **olive oil** over moderately high heat for 1 minute; add the **tomatoes** and cook, shaking the skillet, just until the skins of the tomatoes begin to burst—about 2 minutes. Add the **basil,** the reserved beans and cooking water, the **vinegar,** and, if you wish, the **salt.** Cook, uncovered, for 2 minutes or until the beans are heated through. Serves 4.

One Serving:

Calories	62	Protein	2 g
Total Fat	2 g	Carbohydrates	10 g
Saturated Fat	0	Sodium	10 mg
Cholesterol	0	Added Sugar	0
		Fiber	2 g

Lima Beans with Herbs

Preparation: **10 min.** Cooking: **9 min.** FAT SUGAR SODIUM

- 1 tablespoon unsalted margarine
- 2 cups lima beans (about 2 pounds, unshelled) or 1 package (10 ounces) frozen lima beans
- 1 tablespoon minced parsley
- ½ teaspoon dried marjoram, crumbled
- ⅛ teaspoon black pepper
- 2 tablespoons dry white wine or low-sodium chicken broth

In a medium-size saucepan, melt the **margarine** over moderately low heat; add the **lima beans, parsley, marjoram, pepper,** and **wine.** Cover and cook for 8 to 10 minutes or until the beans are tender. Serves 4.

One Serving:

Calories	115	Protein	4 g
Total Fat	3 g	Carbohydrates	15 g
Saturated Fat	1 g	Sodium	3 mg
Cholesterol	0	Added Sugar	0
		Fiber	3 g

Baby Lima Beans with Sour Cream and Paprika

Preparation: **15 min.** Cooking: **13 min.** FAT SUGAR SODIUM

- 2 cups fresh baby lima beans (about 2 pounds, unshelled) or 1 package (10 ounces) frozen baby lima beans
- 1 tablespoon unsalted margarine
- ⅛ teaspoon each salt and black pepper
- 3 tablespoons sour cream
- 2 tablespoons plain low-fat yogurt
- 2 tablespoons minced parsley
- 1 teaspoon paprika

1. In a large saucepan, bring an inch of unsalted water to a boil; add the **lima beans** and cook, covered, over moderate heat for 12 minutes or until tender. Drain.
2. Stir in the **margarine, salt, pepper, sour cream, yogurt, parsley,** and **paprika.** Serves 4.

One Serving:

Calories	143	Protein	6 g
Total Fat	6 g	Carbohydrates	17 g
Saturated Fat	2 g	Sodium	87 mg
Cholesterol	5 mg	Added Sugar	0
		Fiber	3 g

Yellow Wax Beans in Tomato Sauce

Preparation: **15 min.** Cooking: **26 min.** FAT SUGAR SODIUM

- 1 tablespoon olive oil
- 1 clove garlic, minced
- 1 pound yellow wax beans, trimmed
- 3 tablespoons water
- ¼ teaspoon black pepper
- 3 medium-size ripe tomatoes (about 1 pound), peeled, cored, seeded, and chopped
- 2 tablespoons chopped fresh basil or 1 teaspoon dried basil, crumbled

1. In a 12-inch skillet, heat the **olive oil** over low heat for 1 minute; add the **garlic, wax beans, water,** and **pepper,** and cook, covered, for 15 minutes, shaking the pan occasionally.
2. Add the **tomatoes** and **basil** and cook, covered, 10 minutes more. Serves 4.

One Serving:

Calories	107	Protein	3 g
Total Fat	3 g	Carbohydrates	11 g
Saturated Fat	1 g	Sodium	15 mg
Cholesterol	0	Added Sugar	0
		Fiber	2 g

Baked Beets

Preparation: **5 min.** FAT SUGAR SODIUM
Cooking: **1 hr. 6 min.** (mostly unattended)

- 6 medium-size beets (about 1½ pounds), scrubbed, with tops trimmed
- 1 tablespoon unsalted margarine
- 2 teaspoons snipped fresh dill

1. Preheat the oven to 400°F. Wrap each **beet** in aluminum foil. Place the beets on a baking sheet and bake for 1 hour or until fork-tender. Remove from the oven. When the beets have cooled, unwrap and peel off the skins. Cut into wedges.
2. In a 12-inch skillet, melt the **margarine** over moderate heat; add the beets, toss, and heat through—about 5 minutes. Sprinkle with the **dill.** Serves 4.

One Serving:

Calories	62	Protein	2 g
Total Fat	2 g	Carbohydrates	0
Saturated Fat	0	Sodium	116 mg
Cholesterol	0	Added Sugar	0
		Fiber	1 g

Yellow Wax Beans in Tomato Sauce

Sweet-and-Sour Beets

Preparation: **10 min.**
Cooking: **37 min.** (mostly unattended)

FAT SUGAR SODIUM

1½ **cups water**
 6 **medium-size beets (about 1½ pounds), scrubbed, with tops trimmed**
 ¼ **cup cider vinegar**
 2 **teaspoons sugar**
 2 **teaspoons cornstarch**
 ⅛ **teaspoon ground cloves**
 ⅛ **teaspoon black pepper**

1. In a large heavy saucepan, bring the water to a boil; add the **beets** and cook, covered, over moderate heat for 30 to 35 minutes or until tender. Drain, reserving 1 cup of the cooking water. As soon as the beets are cool enough to handle, peel them and cut them into slices ¼ inch thick.

2. To the same saucepan, add the reserved cooking water and the **vinegar.** In a small bowl, mix together the **sugar** and **cornstarch** and blend it into the saucepan liquid. Add the **cloves** and **pepper,** set the saucepan over moderately low heat, and cook, stirring, for 2 to 3 minutes or until the mixture thickens slightly and turns clear.

3. Return the beets to the saucepan and heat through—about 3 minutes. Serves 4.

Shredded Beets in Horseradish Sauce

Preparation: **20 min.** Cooking: **15 min.** FAT SUGAR SODIUM

You can serve these spicy beets either hot or cold.

 4 **medium-size beets (about 1 pound), peeled and shredded**
 2 **tablespoons water**
 ½ **cup plain low-fat yogurt**
 2 **tablespoons prepared horseradish, drained**
 2 **tablespoons snipped fresh dill or ½ teaspoon dill weed**
 ¼ **teaspoon black pepper**

1. In a medium-size saucepan over moderate heat, cook the **beets,** covered, in the **water** for 15 minutes or until tender.

2. Stir in the **yogurt, horseradish, dill,** and **pepper.** Serves 4.

One Serving:			
Calories	82	Protein	4 g
Total Fat	1 g	Carbohydrates	3 g
Saturated Fat	0	Sodium	126 mg
Cholesterol	2 mg	Added Sugar	0
		Fiber	1 g

Shredded Beets in Horseradish Sauce

One Serving:			
Calories	65	Protein	2 g
Total Fat	0	Carbohydrates	4 g
Saturated Fat	0	Sodium	82 mg
Cholesterol	0	Added Sugar	8 Cal
		Fiber	1 g

Broccoli with Peppers

Preparation: **10 min.** Cooking: **10 min.** FAT SUGAR SODIUM

- 4 teaspoons olive oil
- 1 small yellow onion, chopped fine
- 2 cloves garlic, minced
- 1 tablespoon water
- 4 cups broccoli florets (1 medium-size head)
- 1 small sweet red pepper, cored, seeded, and cut lengthwise into ½-inch strips
- 1 teaspoon dried oregano, crumbled
  Pinch red pepper flakes

1. In a heavy 12-inch skillet, heat the **olive oil** over moderate heat for 1 minute. Add the **onion, garlic, water, broccoli, red pepper, oregano,** and **red pepper flakes,** and cook, stirring, for 2 minutes.
2. Cover the skillet, reduce the heat to low, and cook 6 to 8 minutes longer, stirring often, until the broccoli is tender but still crisp. Serves 4.

One Serving:

Calories	116	*Protein*	*6 g*
Total Fat	*7 g*	*Carbohydrates*	*11 g*
Saturated Fat	*1 g*	*Sodium*	*39 mg*
Cholesterol	*0*	*Added Sugar*	*0*
		Fiber	*0*

Broccoli with Basil

Preparation: **15 min.** Cooking: **5 min.** FAT SUGAR SODIUM

- 1¾ pounds broccoli, cut into florets, with stems peeled and sliced ¼ inch thick
- 1½ cups firmly packed fresh basil or parsley
- 1 clove garlic
- 1 tablespoon pine nuts or chopped walnuts
- 1 tablespoon grated Parmesan cheese
- ¼ cup low-sodium chicken broth
- 2 teaspoons lemon juice

1. In a large saucepan, bring an inch of unsalted water to a boil; add the **broccoli** and cook, uncovered, for 4 minutes or until just tender. Drain well and transfer to a medium-size bowl.
2. In an electric blender or food processor, whirl the **basil, garlic, pine nuts, cheese,** and **chicken broth** for 20 seconds. Stir in the **lemon juice,** pour over the broccoli, and toss. Serves 4.

One Serving:

Calories	62	*Protein*	*5 g*
Total Fat	*2 g*	*Carbohydrates*	*10 g*
Saturated Fat	*0*	*Sodium*	*53 mg*
Cholesterol	*1 mg*	*Added Sugar*	*0*
		Fiber	*1 g*

Broccoli-Stuffed Tomatoes

Preparation: **20 min.** FAT SUGAR SODIUM
Cooking: **39 min.** (mostly unattended)

Here is a good way to use up leftover cooked broccoli.

- 4 medium-size firm, ripe tomatoes
- 1 teaspoon lemon juice
- ½ tablespoon unsalted margarine
- 1 small yellow onion, chopped
- ½ cup skim milk
- ¼ cup low-sodium chicken broth
- 2 tablespoons flour
- 2 tablespoons grated Parmesan cheese
- 1½ cups chopped cooked broccoli
- 1 tablespoon minced fresh basil or ½ teaspoon dried basil, crumbled
- ⅛ teaspoon black pepper
- 1 large egg white

1. Preheat the oven to 375°F. Slice the tops from the **tomatoes,** then hollow them out, leaving shells about ½ inch thick. Sprinkle the inside of each tomato with the **lemon juice** and turn upside down on paper towels to drain for 10 minutes.
2. In a heavy 10-inch skillet, melt the **margarine** over moderate heat; add the **onion** and cook, uncovered, until soft—about 5 minutes.
3. In a small bowl, whisk together the **milk, chicken broth,** and **flour.** Add to the skillet and cook, uncovered, over moderate heat, stirring frequently, for 3 minutes or until the sauce has thickened. Remove the skillet from the heat and mix in the **cheese, broccoli, basil,** and **pepper.**
4. In a small bowl, beat the **egg white** until it holds stiff peaks. Fold into the broccoli mixture. Spoon the mixture into the tomatoes, mounding it up in the center.
5. Arrange the stuffed tomatoes in an ungreased 9"x 9"x 2" baking pan; bake, uncovered, for 30 to 35 minutes or until the stuffing is puffed and golden. Serves 4.

One Serving:

Calories	99	*Protein*	*6 g*
Total Fat	*3 g*	*Carbohydrates*	*14 g*
Saturated Fat	*1 g*	*Sodium*	*95 mg*
Cholesterol	*3 mg*	*Added Sugar*	*0*
		Fiber	*3 g*

Brussels Sprouts with Lemon Sauce

Preparation: **10 min.** Cooking: **15 min.** FAT SUGAR SODIUM

- 1 **pint Brussels sprouts (about 10 ounces), trimmed**
- 1 **teaspoon sugar**
- 1 **teaspoon white vinegar**
- ½ **cup low-sodium chicken broth**
- ¼ **cup lemon juice**
- 1¼ **teaspoons cornstarch blended with 2 tablespoons cold water**
- ¼ **teaspoon ground nutmeg**

1. In a large saucepan, bring an inch of unsalted water to a boil; add the **Brussels sprouts** and cook, covered, for 10 to 12 minutes or until just tender. Drain in a colander, rinse under cold running water to stop the cooking, and drain again.

2. Meanwhile, in a medium-size saucepan over moderately high heat, boil the **sugar** and **vinegar,** swirling the pan, until the sugar is an amber color—about 2 minutes. Add the **chicken broth** and the **lemon juice** and stir in the dissolved **cornstarch** and **nutmeg.** Bring to a boil, stirring constantly, for 1 minute. Add the sprouts to the sauce; coat well. Serves 4.

One Serving:

Calories	47	Protein	3 g
Total Fat	0	Carbohydrates	10 g
Saturated Fat	0	Sodium	29 mg
Cholesterol	0	Added Sugar	4 Cal
		Fiber	4 g

Brussels Sprouts with Mustard Sauce

Preparation: **5 min.** Cooking: **13 min.** FAT SUGAR SODIUM

- 1 **pint Brussels sprouts (about 10 ounces), trimmed**
- 2 **teaspoons unsalted margarine**
- 2 **tablespoons Dijon or spicy brown mustard**
- 2 **tablespoons low-sodium beef broth**
- 1 **teaspoon lemon juice**
- ¼ **teaspoon black pepper**

1. In a medium-size saucepan, bring an inch of unsalted water to a boil; add the **Brussels sprouts** and cook, covered, for 10 to 12 minutes or until they are just tender. Drain in a

colander, rinse under cold running water to stop the cooking, and drain again. Set aside.

2. In the same saucepan, melt the **margarine** over low heat; stir in the **mustard, beef broth, lemon juice,** and **pepper** and blend until smooth—about 1 minute. Add the Brussels sprouts and coat with the mustard sauce. Serves 4.

One Serving:

Calories	54	Protein	2 g
Total Fat	3 g	Carbohydrates	7 g
Saturated Fat	0	Sodium	239 mg
Cholesterol	0	Added Sugar	0
		Fiber	4 g

Baked Cabbage Wedges with Parmesan and Bread Crumbs

Preparation: **10 min.** FAT SUGAR SODIUM
Cooking: **39 min.** (mostly unattended)

- 1 **large head cabbage (about 2 pounds), cored and cut into 8 wedges**
- 1 **cup low-sodium chicken broth**
- ¼ **cup dry white wine**
- ⅛ **teaspoon black pepper**
- ½ **tablespoon unsalted margarine**
- 2 **tablespoons fine dry bread crumbs**
- 2 **tablespoons grated Parmesan cheese**

1. Preheat the oven to 400°F. Place the **cabbage** in a shallow 2-quart flameproof casserole, add the **chicken broth, wine,** and **pepper,** and bring to a simmer, uncovered, over moderate heat. Cover, transfer to the oven, and bake for 35 to 40 minutes or until the cabbage is fork-tender.

2. Meanwhile, in a 7-inch nonstick skillet, melt the **margarine** over moderate heat; add the **bread crumbs** and cook, stirring, about 2 minutes or until the bread crumbs are lightly browned. Remove from the heat and set aside.

3. As soon as the cabbage is done, remove it from the oven and sprinkle the bread crumbs and **cheese** over the top. Increase the oven temperature to broil and place the casserole in the broiler 5 to 6 inches from the heat. Broil 1 to 2 minutes or until golden brown. Serves 4.

One Serving:

Calories	88	Protein	4 g
Total Fat	3 g	Carbohydrates	13 g
Saturated Fat	1 g	Sodium	115 mg
Cholesterol	2 mg	Added Sugar	0
		Fiber	2 g

Braised Red Cabbage with Cranberries (left) and *Stir-fried Carrots and Potatoes* (right)

Braised Red Cabbage with Cranberries

Preparation: **20 min.** Cooking: **31 min.** `FAT` `SUGAR` `SODIUM`

This vibrant red dish, scented with ginger and cloves, is ideal for Thanksgiving.

- 2 **teaspoons corn or peanut oil**
- 1 **medium-size yellow onion, chopped**
- 2 **cloves garlic, minced**
- 1 **small head red cabbage (about 1 pound), cored and sliced thin**
- 1 **cup cranberries**
- 1 **tablespoon red wine vinegar**
- 2 **teaspoons honey**
  Juice of 1 orange (about ½ cup)
- 1 **bay leaf**
- ¼ **teaspoon ground ginger**
- ⅛ **teaspoon ground cloves**

1. In a heavy 12-inch skillet, heat the **corn oil** over moderate heat for 1 minute; add the **onion** and **garlic** and cook, uncovered, until soft—about 5 minutes. Mix in the **cabbage,** cover, and cook until the cabbage is barely wilted—about 10 minutes.

2. Add the **cranberries, vinegar, honey, orange juice, bay leaf, ginger,** and **cloves;** cover and continue cooking until almost all the liquid has evaporated and the cabbage is completely wilted—about 15 minutes. If the cabbage has wilted but there is still considerable liquid left, remove the cover and raise the heat to high to boil down the liquid. Remove and discard the bay leaf. Serves 4.

One Serving:			
Calories	94	Protein	2 g
Total Fat	3 g	Carbohydrates	18 g
Saturated Fat	0	Sodium	12 mg
Cholesterol	0	Added Sugar	11 Cal
		Fiber	1 g

Curried Cabbage

Preparation: **10 min.**
Cooking: **23 min.** (mostly unattended) `FAT` `SUGAR` `SODIUM`

- 1 **small head cabbage (about 1 pound)**
- 1 **tablespoon unsalted margarine**
- 2 **teaspoons mustard seeds**
- 2 **medium-size yellow onions, sliced thin**
- 2 **teaspoons curry powder**
- ¼ **cup water**

1. Cut the **cabbage** into wedges, cut out and discard the white core, and slice each wedge ⅛ inch thick; set aside.

2. In a heavy 12-inch skillet, melt the **margarine** over moderate heat; add the **mustard seeds** and cook, covered, for 30 seconds or until they begin to sputter and pop. Add the **onions** and cook, uncovered, until soft—about 5 minutes. Stir in the **curry powder** and cook for 1 minute. Add the cabbage and **water,** cover, and cook, stirring occasionally, for 15 minutes or until the cabbage is tender. Serves 4.

One Serving:			
Calories	78	Protein	2 g
Total Fat	4 g	Carbohydrates	10 g
Saturated Fat	1 g	Sodium	22 mg
Cholesterol	0	Added Sugar	0
		Fiber	2 g

Stir-fried Carrots and Potatoes

Preparation: **15 min.** Cooking: **8 min.** FAT SUGAR SODIUM

1 **tablespoon corn oil**
4 **medium-size carrots (about ½ pound), peeled and cut into matchstick strips**
½ **cup water**
1 **large all-purpose potato, peeled and cut into matchstick strips**
⅛ **teaspoon black pepper**
1 **tablespoon snipped fresh chives or minced parsley**

1. In a 10-inch nonstick skillet, heat the **corn oil** over moderately high heat for 1 minute. Add the **carrots** and cook, stirring, for 1 minute. Stir in ¼ cup of the **water** and steam, covered, over moderate heat, shaking the pan occasionally, for 3 minutes or until the liquid has evaporated.
2. Add the **potato** and the remaining water and steam, covered, for 3 minutes or until the water has evaporated and the vegetables are just tender. Season with the **pepper** and sprinkle with the **chives**. Serves 4.

One Serving:

Calories	86	Protein	1 g
Total Fat	4 g	Carbohydrates	13 g
Saturated Fat	0	Sodium	21 mg
Cholesterol	0	Added Sugar	0
		Fiber	2 g

Carrots and Green Pepper in Cream Sauce

Preparation: **15 min.**
Cooking: **22 min.** (mostly unattended) FAT SUGAR SODIUM

1 **tablespoon unsalted margarine**
3 **green onions, chopped fine, with tops sliced and reserved**
1 **tablespoon flour**
1¼ **cups cold water**
8 **medium-size carrots (about 1 pound), peeled and sliced ¼ inch thick**
⅛ **teaspoon black pepper**
1 **medium-size sweet green pepper, cored, seeded, and chopped**
1 **tablespoon sour cream**
1 **tablespoon plain low-fat yogurt**
¼ **teaspoon lemon juice or to taste**

1. In a heavy 10-inch skillet over moderate heat, melt the **margarine;** add the **green onions** and cook, uncovered, until soft—about 5 minutes. Blend in the **flour** and cook, stirring, for 1 minute. Add the **water,** bring to a simmer, and cook, stirring constantly, for 3 minutes or until the broth has thickened.
2. Add the **carrots** and **black pepper** to the broth and cook, uncovered, for 8 to 10 minutes or until the carrots are just tender. Add the **green pepper** and cook, covered, for 3 minutes. Mix in the **sour cream, yogurt,** and **lemon juice** and return the vegetables and sauce to a simmer (do not boil or the sauce will curdle). Sprinkle with the reserved green onion tops. Serves 4.

One Serving:

Calories	93	Protein	2 g
Total Fat	4 g	Carbohydrates	14 g
Saturated Fat	1 g	Sodium	41 mg
Cholesterol	2 mg	Added Sugar	0
		Fiber	3 g

Carrots Glazed with Orange and Ginger

Preparation: **20 min.** Cooking: **11 min.** FAT SUGAR SODIUM

These carrots have a delightful tang and add interest to a meal with roast meat or poultry.

1 **tablespoon unsalted margarine**
¾ **cup orange juice**
1½ **tablespoons minced fresh ginger or 1 teaspoon ground ginger**
3 **strips orange peel, each about 2 inches long and ½ inch wide**
8 **medium-size carrots (about 1 pound), peeled and sliced ¼ inch thick**

1. Melt the **margarine** in a medium-size heavy saucepan, add the **orange juice, ginger,** and **orange peel,** and bring to a boil.
2. Add the **carrots** and adjust the heat so that the orange juice bubbles gently. Simmer, uncovered, until all the liquid has evaporated and the carrots are tender and nicely glazed—10 to 12 minutes. Serves 4.

One Serving:

Calories	92	Protein	1 g
Total Fat	3 g	Carbohydrates	10 g
Saturated Fat	1 g	Sodium	36 mg
Cholesterol	0	Added Sugar	0
		Fiber	2 g

Glazed Carrots with Five Spices

Preparation: **15 min.** Cooking: **17 min.** `FAT` `SUGAR` `SODIM`

You can serve these carrots at room temperature as well as hot.

- ¾ **cup water**
- 8 **medium-size carrots (about 1 pound), peeled and sliced diagonally ½ inch thick**
- 1 **cinnamon stick**
- ¾ **teaspoon ground cumin**
- ½ **teaspoon ground ginger**
- ¼ **teaspoon ground coriander**
- ⅛ **teaspoon cayenne pepper**
- 2 **teaspoons honey**
- 2 **teaspoons lemon juice**

1. In a heavy 10-inch skillet, bring the **water** to a boil and add the **carrots, cinnamon stick, cumin, ginger, coriander,** and **cayenne pepper.** Adjust the heat so that the liquid bubbles gently, cover, and simmer for 12 minutes.

2. Uncover, add the **honey** and **lemon juice,** raise the heat to high, and boil until all the liquid has evaporated and the carrots are just tender— about 4 minutes. Serves 4.

One Serving:			
Calories	58	Protein	1 g
Total Fat	0	Carbohydrates	14 g
Saturated Fat	0	Sodium	37 mg
Cholesterol	0	Added Sugar	8 Cal
		Fiber	2 g

Spiced Cauliflower with Tomatoes

Preparation: **18 min.** `FAT` `SUGAR` `SODIUM`
Cooking: **18 min.** (mostly unattended)

Here is a zesty vegetable that can be made hours ahead and reheated at serving time.

- 1 **small yellow onion, chopped**
- 2 **cloves garlic**
- 1½ **tablespoons minced fresh ginger or** ½ **teaspoon ground ginger**
- 1 **large ripe tomato, cored and chopped, or** 1 **can (1 pound) low-sodium tomatoes, drained and chopped**
- ¾ **teaspoon each ground cumin and coriander**
- ¼ **teaspoon ground turmeric**
- ⅛ **teaspoon each black pepper and cayenne pepper**

Spiced Cauliflower with Tomatoes (left) and *Glazed Carrots with Five Spices* (right)

½ cup water
4 cups cauliflower florets (1 medium-size head)
2 teaspoons lemon juice
2 tablespoons minced parsley

1. In an electric blender or food processor, purée the **onion, garlic, ginger,** and **tomatoes** by whirling for 10 to 15 seconds. Transfer to a heavy 12-inch skillet, add the **cumin, coriander, turmeric, black pepper, cayenne pepper,** and **water,** and bring to a boil. Adjust the heat so that the mixture bubbles gently, and simmer, uncovered, for 5 minutes.

2. Mix in the cauliflower, cover, and continue to simmer until the cauliflower is just tender— about 12 minutes. Stir in the **lemon juice** and **parsley.** Serves 4.

One Serving:

Calories	38	Protein	2 g
Total Fat	0	Carbohydrates	8 g
Saturated Fat	0	Sodium	19 mg
Cholesterol	0	Added Sugar	0
		Fiber	3 g

Cauliflower in Pimiento Sauce

Preparation: **15 min.**
Cooking: **15 min.** (mostly unattended)

The pimiento sauce enhances many other vegetables; try it with zucchini, broccoli, green beans, or potatoes.

2 teaspoons olive oil
1 medium-size yellow onion, sliced thin
2 cloves garlic, minced
2 medium-size fresh pimientos or sweet red peppers, cored, seeded, and cut into strips ¼ inch wide
¾ cup low-sodium chicken broth
4 cups cauliflower florets (1 medium-size head)
1 tablespoon minced parsley

1. Heat the **olive oil** in a heavy 10-inch skillet over moderately high heat for 1 minute. Add the **onion, garlic,** and **pimientos,** and cook, uncovered, stirring frequently, until the pimientos are tender and the onion is golden— about 12 minutes. Add the **chicken broth** and cook 2 minutes longer.

2. In an electric blender or food processor, purée the skillet mixture in 2 batches by whirling

each for 15 to 20 seconds. Return the mixture to the skillet and keep warm over low heat.

3. Meanwhile, in a large saucepan, bring an inch of unsalted water to a boil; add the cauliflower and cook, covered, for 8 minutes or until just tender. Drain and add to the skillet. Toss the cauliflower with the pimiento sauce. Sprinkle with the **parsley.** Serves 4.

One Serving:

Calories	59	Protein	2 g
Total Fat	3 g	Carbohydrates	8 g
Saturated Fat	1 g	Sodium	29 mg
Cholesterol	0	Added Sugar	0
		Fiber	2 g

Cauliflower Pudding

Preparation: **15 min.** Cooking: **36 min.** FAT SUGAR SODIUM

1 small head cauliflower (about 1¼ pounds), trimmed and chopped
1 clove garlic, minced
1½ cups chopped tomatoes or 1 can (1 pound) low-sodium tomatoes, drained and chopped
¼ teaspoon ground ginger
⅛ teaspoon black pepper
Pinch cayenne pepper
1½ tablespoons flour
½ cup plain low-fat yogurt
1½ tablespoons shredded Swiss cheese

1. In a large heavy saucepan, bring an inch of unsalted water to a boil; add the **cauliflower** and cook, covered, for 5 minutes or until barely tender. Drain.

2. Preheat the oven to 375°F. In a heavy 12-inch skillet, combine the **garlic, tomatoes, ginger, black pepper, cayenne pepper,** and cauliflower. Cook, covered, over moderate heat for 10 minutes or until the cauliflower is tender. Boil away any remaining liquid by raising the heat to high and uncovering the skillet.

3. Using an electric blender or a food processor, purée the cauliflower mixture in 3 batches for 30 seconds each. In a large bowl, stir together the **flour, yogurt, cheese,** and cauliflower. Transfer to an ungreased 9-inch pie pan and bake 20 minutes or until crusty on top. Serves 4.

One Serving:

Calories	96	Protein	7 g
Total Fat	4 g	Carbohydrates	11 g
Saturated Fat	2 g	Sodium	61 mg
Cholesterol	11 mg	Added Sugar	0
		Fiber	2 g

Cauliflower with Bread Crumbs

This simple, classic dish is sometimes called Cauliflower Polonaise. If you like, sprinkle the egg and parsley mixture on top in a decorative pattern.

FAT SUGAR SODIUM

1 medium-size head cauliflower (about 1½ pounds)
1 large hard-cooked egg white
2 tablespoons minced parsley

⅛ teaspoon black pepper
1 tablespoon unsalted margarine
2 tablespoons fine dry bread crumbs

Preparation: **10 min.**
Cooking: **21 min.**
(mostly unattended)

1. In a large heavy saucepan, bring an inch of unsalted water to a boil; add the **cauliflower** and cook, covered, over moderate heat for 20 minutes or until just tender.
2. Meanwhile, finely chop the hard-cooked **egg white** and mix it with the **parsley** and **pepper** in a small bowl; set aside.
3. In a heavy 7-inch skillet, melt the **margarine** over moderate heat; add the **bread crumbs** and cook, stirring, for 1 to 2 minutes or until golden brown. Set aside.
4. When the cauliflower is tender, drain it, transfer to a small heated platter, and sprinkle with the egg mixture and the bread crumbs. Serves 4.

One Serving:

Calories	58
Total Fat	3 g
Saturated Fat	1 g
Cholesterol	0
Protein	3 g
Carbohydrates	6 g
Sodium	46 mg
Added Sugar	0
Fiber	3 g

Celery and Artichoke Hearts in Cheese Sauce

This inviting dish can be made ahead, covered, and refrigerated until baking time. If you halve it for two, use a shallow two-cup baking dish.

FAT SUGAR SODIUM

1 package (9 ounces) frozen artichoke hearts
2 medium-size stalks celery, chopped
1 tablespoon unsalted margarine
1 small yellow onion, chopped fine
1 tablespoon flour

1 cup skim milk
½ teaspoon Dijon or spicy brown mustard
⅛ teaspoon black pepper
2 tablespoons grated Parmesan cheese
1 tablespoon fine dry bread crumbs

Preparation:
15 min.
Cooking:
35 min.

1. Preheat the oven to 400°F. In a medium-size saucepan, cook the **artichoke hearts** according to package directions, omitting the salt; drain and set aside.
2. Meanwhile, in a small heavy saucepan with enough boiling unsalted water to cover, cook the **celery,** uncovered, for 3 minutes or until just tender. Drain and set aside in a small bowl.
3. Using the same saucepan, melt the **margarine** over moderate heat; add the **onion** and cook, uncovered, until soft—about 5 minutes. Blend in the **flour** and cook over low heat, stirring, for 2 minutes. Add the **milk** and cook, stirring constantly, until the sauce has thickened slightly—about 3 minutes. Stir in the **mustard, pepper,** and **cheese,** and continue cooking and stirring over low heat another 5 minutes.
4. Spoon the artichokes and celery into an ungreased 8″x 8″x 2″ baking pan, cover with the cheese sauce, and sprinkle with the **bread crumbs.** Bake, uncovered, for 15 minutes. Increase the oven temperature to broil; transfer the pan to the broiler, about 5 to 6 inches from the heat, and broil for 1 to 2 minutes or until lightly browned. Serves 4.

One Serving:

Calories	103
Total Fat	4 g
Saturated Fat	1 g
Cholesterol	3 mg
Protein	5 g
Carbohydrates	12 g
Sodium	156 mg
Added Sugar	0
Fiber	2 g

Tip: Artichokes can turn an unappetizing gray if you cook them in a pan made from corrosive metal. Don't use aluminum or iron; do use stainless steel, enamel, or flameproof glass.

Celery and Artichoke Hearts in Cheese Sauce (left) and *Corn and Broccoli Stew* (right)

Corn and Broccoli Stew

1 slice bacon, chopped
1 small yellow onion, chopped
1 small all-purpose potato, peeled and cut into ½-inch cubes
½ cup skim milk

⅛ teaspoon black pepper
3 cups broccoli florets (1 small head)
1¼ cups fresh or frozen whole-kernel corn

Preparation: **15 min.**
Cooking: **23 min.**

One Serving:

Calories	133
Total Fat	4 g
Saturated Fat	1 g
Cholesterol	4 mg
Protein	7 g
Carbohydrates	21 g
Sodium	87 mg
Added Sugar	0
Fiber	3 g

1. In a 12-inch nonstick skillet, cook the **bacon** over low heat until it begins to brown—about 3 minutes. Add the **onion,** cover, and cook over moderately low heat for 5 minutes.

2. Add the **potato,** ¼ cup of the **milk,** and the **pepper;** cover and cook until the potato is almost tender—about 7 minutes. Add the **broccoli** and the remaining ¼ cup milk and cook, uncovered, 5 minutes longer. Add the **corn** and cook for 3 minutes or until it is heated through. Serves 4.

Corn and Lima Beans

Here is a slimmed-down version of old-fashioned succotash.

⅓ cup low-sodium chicken broth
1 cup fresh or frozen baby lima beans
1 cup fresh or frozen whole-kernel corn

¼ teaspoon sugar
⅛ teaspoon black pepper
2 tablespoons sour cream

Preparation: **5 min.**
Cooking: **11 min.**

One Serving:

Calories	105
Total Fat	3 g
Saturated Fat	1 g
Cholesterol	3 mg
Protein	5 g
Carbohydrates	18 g
Sodium	35 mg
Added Sugar	1 Cal
Fiber	3 g

1. In a small heavy saucepan, bring the **chicken broth** to a boil; add the **lima beans** and **corn** and reduce the heat to moderately low. Cover and simmer for 8 minutes or until the vegetables are just tender.

2. Add the **sugar** and **pepper** and cook for 2 to 4 minutes or until almost all the liquid has evaporated. Stir in the **sour cream** and transfer the mixture to a warm vegetable dish. Serves 4.

Corn Pudding

Preparation: **10 min.**
Cooking: **1 hr.** (mostly unattended)

FAT SUGAR SODIUM

Rather than halving for two, it's easier to make the full recipe and reheat the leftovers later.

- 1 **large egg**
- 1 **large egg white**
- 1 **cup skim milk**
- 2 **tablespoons flour**
- ¼ **teaspoon baking powder**
- ⅛ **teaspoon black pepper**
- 1⅓ **cups fresh or frozen whole-kernel corn**
- 2 **green onions, including tops, chopped fine**
- 2 **teaspoons grated Parmesan cheese**
  Nonstick cooking spray

1. Preheat the oven to 350°F. In a medium-size bowl, whisk together the **egg, egg white, milk, flour, baking powder,** and **pepper.** Stir in the **corn, green onions,** and **cheese.**

2. Coat a 9-inch pie pan with the **cooking spray,** add the corn mixture, and set the pie pan in a shallow baking pan. Add enough hot water to the baking pan to come halfway up the sides of the pie pan.

3. Bake, uncovered, for 1 to 1¼ hours or until a knife inserted in the center comes out clean and the pudding is puffed and golden. Serves 4.

One Serving:

Calories	111	Protein	7 g
Total Fat	3 g	Carbohydrates	16 g
Saturated Fat	1 g	Sodium	112 mg
Cholesterol	70 mg	Added Sugar	0
		Fiber	1 g

Braised Eggplant, Zucchini, and Tomatoes

Preparation: **20 min.**
Cooking: **43 min.** (mostly unattended)

FAT SUGAR SODIUM

If you're making this ratatouille *for two, prepare the full recipe and refrigerate the leftovers; they can be eaten hot or cold.*

- 1 **small eggplant (about ½ pound), unpeeled, cut into 1-inch cubes**
- 1 **tablespoon lemon juice**

- 1 **tablespoon olive oil**
- 1 **medium-size yellow onion, sliced thick**
- 1 **medium-size zucchini (about ½ pound), sliced ½ inch thick**
- ⅓ **cup dry white wine or water**
- 1 **large ripe tomato, peeled, cored, and chopped**
- 3 **cloves garlic, minced**
- 1 **tablespoon low-sodium tomato paste**
- ½ **teaspoon each dried thyme, basil, and marjoram, crumbled**
- 1 **large bay leaf**
- ⅛ **teaspoon black pepper**

1. Preheat the oven to 350°F. In a colander, toss the **eggplant** with the **lemon juice** and let drain for 15 minutes; pat dry on paper towels.

2. Meanwhile, in a large heavy saucepan with an ovenproof handle, heat the **olive oil** over moderate heat for 1 minute; add the **onion** and cook, uncovered, until soft—about 5 minutes. Add the eggplant and **zucchini** and cook, stirring, for 3 minutes. Pour in the **wine,** bring to a boil, and cook, uncovered, for 1 minute. Mix in the **tomato, garlic, tomato paste, thyme, basil, marjoram, bay leaf,** and **pepper.** Cover and bring to a gentle simmer—about 2 minutes.

3. Transfer the saucepan to the oven and bake for 30 minutes or until the vegetables are tender. Remove the bay leaf and serve. Serves 4.

One Serving:

Calories	79	Protein	2 g
Total Fat	4 g	Carbohydrates	11 g
Saturated Fat	0	Sodium	42 mg
Cholesterol	0	Added Sugar	0
		Fiber	2 g

Eggplant Stacks

Preparation: **10 min.** Cooking: **18 min.**   FAT SUGAR SODIUM

- 1 **medium-size eggplant (about 1 pound), unpeeled, cut into rounds ½ inch thick**
- 2 **small ripe tomatoes, cored and sliced ¼ inch thick**
- 1 **tablespoon olive oil**
- 1 **tablespoon minced fresh basil or ½ teaspoon dried basil, crumbled**
- ⅛ **teaspoon black pepper**

1. Preheat the oven to 375°F. On a nonstick baking sheet, arrange the **eggplant** slices and bake for 15 to 20 minutes or until the eggplant is fork-tender.

Mushrooms in Sour Cream–Dill Sauce (left) and *Corn Pudding* (right)

2. Increase the oven temperature to broil. Place a **tomato** slice on top of each eggplant round. Drizzle the **olive oil** over the tomatoes and sprinkle with the **basil** and **pepper.** Place the baking sheet in the broiler, 5 to 6 inches from the heat, and broil for 3 minutes or until the tomatoes are soft. Serves 4.

One Serving:			
Calories	71	Protein	2 g
Total Fat	4 g	Carbohydrates	10 g
Saturated Fat	0	Sodium	9 mg
Cholesterol	0	Added Sugar	0
		Fiber	2 g

Mushrooms in Sour Cream - Dill Sauce

Preparation: **10 min.** Cooking: **18 min.** `FAT` `SUGAR` `SODIUM`

This impressive buffet dish can be made ahead and refrigerated, but the sour cream and fresh dill should not be added until the dish is reheated.

½ **tablespoon unsalted margarine**
1 **medium-size yellow onion, chopped fine**
1 **pound small mushrooms**
¼ **cup dry white wine**
½ **cup low-sodium chicken broth**
2 **teaspoons cornstarch**
½ **teaspoon each dill weed and paprika**
2 **tablespoons sour cream**
2 **tablespoons snipped fresh dill or minced parsley**

1. In a heavy 10-inch skillet, melt the **margarine** over moderate heat; add the **onion** and cook, uncovered, until soft—about 5 minutes. Add the **mushrooms,** cover, and cook for 3 minutes; stir in the **wine** and cook, uncovered, 1 minute longer.

2. Meanwhile, in a small bowl, mix together the **chicken broth, cornstarch, dill weed,** and **paprika.** Add this mixture to the skillet and simmer, uncovered, stirring often, for 5 minutes. Raise the heat to high and cook, stirring, for 2 to 3 minutes or until the sauce has thickened.

3. Reduce the heat to low, stir in the **sour cream** and **dill,** and heat for 1 minute; be careful not to let the sauce boil or it will curdle. Serves 4.

One Serving:			
Calories	75	Protein	3 g
Total Fat	4 g	Carbohydrates	9 g
Saturated Fat	1 g	Sodium	17 mg
Cholesterol	3 mg	Added Sugar	0
		Fiber	3 g

Onions in Raisin Sauce (left) and *Vegetable-Stuffed Mushrooms* (right)

Vegetable-Stuffed Mushrooms

12 **large mushrooms
(about 1 pound)**
 1 **tablespoon unsalted margarine**
 5 **green onions, chopped fine**
 1 **medium-size stalk celery,
chopped**

 1 **small ripe tomato, cored and
chopped**
½ **teaspoon dried marjoram,
crumbled**
⅛ **teaspoon black pepper**
½ **cup soft white bread crumbs**

FAT SUGAR SODIUM

Preparation:
15 min.
Cooking:
31 min. (mostly
unattended)

1. Preheat the oven to 400°F. Wipe the **mushrooms** with a damp cloth and
twist off the stems; set the caps aside and mince the stems.
2. In a heavy 10-inch skillet, melt the **margarine** over moderate heat; add the
green onions, celery, and mushroom stems, and cook, uncovered, stirring
often, until the vegetables are soft—about 5 minutes. Add the **tomato,
marjoram,** and **pepper,** and cook, covered, 5 minutes longer. Stir in the
bread crumbs and remove the skillet from the heat.
3. Spoon the mixture into the mushroom caps, mounding it up slightly. In a
lightly greased 13″x 9″x 2″ baking pan, arrange the mushrooms in one layer.
Bake, uncovered, for 20 minutes or until lightly browned. Serves 4.

One Serving:

Calories	*81*
Total Fat	*4 g*
Saturated Fat	*1 g*
Cholesterol	*0*
Protein	*4 g*
Carbohydrates	*11 g*
Sodium	*45 mg*
Added Sugar	*0*
Fiber	*4 g*

Bermuda Onion Rings

Preparation: **10 min.** Cooking: **28 min.** `FAT` `SUGAR` `SODIUM`

2 teaspoons unsalted margarine
1 large Bermuda onion (about 1 pound), sliced 1 inch thick
1 teaspoon flour
¼ cup plain low-fat yogurt
2 teaspoons snipped fresh dill
¼ teaspoon paprika

1. In a 12-inch nonstick skillet, melt the **margarine** over low heat; add the **onion** and cook, covered, until soft and transparent—about 25 minutes.

2. Uncover, stir in the **flour,** and cook for 1 minute. Add the **yogurt, dill,** and **paprika,** and cook 1 minute longer or until just heated through. Be careful not to let the sauce boil or it will curdle. Serves 4.

One Serving:

Calories	68	Protein	2 g
Total Fat	2 g	Carbohydrates	10 g
Saturated Fat	0	Sodium	35 mg
Cholesterol	1 mg	Added Sugar	0
		Fiber	2 g

Herbed Creamed Onions

Preparation: **20 min.** Cooking: **26 min.** `FAT` `SUGAR` `SODIUM`

Nonstick cooking spray
½ tablespoon unsalted margarine
1 pound small white onions, peeled
1 cup low-sodium chicken broth
½ cup skim milk
2 tablespoons flour
¼ teaspoon each dried marjoram, rosemary, and sage, crumbled
⅛ teaspoon black pepper
1 tablespoon minced parsley

1. Coat a 10-inch nonstick skillet with the **cooking spray** and set over moderate heat for 30 seconds. Melt the **margarine** in the skillet; add the **onions** and cook, stirring, until golden—5 to 7 minutes.

2. In a small bowl, whisk together the **chicken broth, milk,** and **flour.** Add to the skillet, along with the **marjoram, rosemary, sage,** and **pepper.** Cook, stirring constantly, about 5 minutes or until the sauce has thickened. Cover and simmer over moderately low heat about 15 minutes, stirring occasionally, until the onions are tender. Sprinkle with the **parsley.** Serves 4.

One Serving:

Calories	88	Protein	4 g
Total Fat	3 g	Carbohydrates	15 g
Saturated Fat	1 g	Sodium	40 mg
Cholesterol	1 mg	Added Sugar	0
		Fiber	2 g

Onions in Raisin Sauce

Preparation: **20 min.** Cooking: **32 min.** `FAT` `SUGAR` `SODIUM`

Here is a dish that can be refrigerated for several days and reheated at serving time.

1½ teaspoons olive oil
¾ pound small white onions, peeled
2 cloves garlic, minced
⅓ cup dry white wine
1 cup low-sodium beef broth
2 tablespoons low-sodium tomato paste
2 tablespoons raisins
½ teaspoon grated orange rind
¼ teaspoon each dried basil and thyme, crumbled
⅛ teaspoon black pepper

1. In a small heavy saucepan, heat the **olive oil** over moderate heat for 1 minute; add the **onions** and cook, uncovered, stirring frequently, until they are golden—about 7 minutes.

2. Add the **garlic, wine, beef broth, tomato paste, raisins, orange rind, basil, thyme,** and **pepper,** and bring to a simmer. Cook, uncovered, stirring often, for 20 minutes or until the onions are tender.

3. Raise the heat to high and cook, stirring, until the sauce is thick—about 3 minutes. Serves 4.

One Serving:

Calories	79	Protein	2 g
Total Fat	2 g	Carbohydrates	15 g
Saturated Fat	0	Sodium	17 mg
Cholesterol	0	Added Sugar	0
		Fiber	2 g

Parsnip, Carrot, and Potato Purée

Preparation: **20 min.**
Cooking: **29 min.** (mostly unattended)

FAT SUGAR SODIUM

1½ teaspoons unsalted margarine
 1 small yellow onion, sliced thin
 2 cloves garlic, minced
 2 medium-size carrots, peeled and sliced thin
 5 medium-size parsnips (about 1 pound), peeled and sliced thin
 1 bay leaf
 1 medium-size all-purpose potato, peeled and sliced thin
1⅓ cups low-sodium chicken broth

1. In a medium-size heavy saucepan, melt the **margarine** over very low heat. Add the **onion, garlic, carrots, parsnips,** and **bay leaf;** cover and cook for 8 to 10 minutes or until the vegetables are almost tender.

2. Add the **potato** and **chicken broth** and cook, covered, over moderate heat for 20 minutes or until the potato is tender; discard the bay leaf.

3. In an electric blender or food processor, purée the vegetable mixture by whirling for 10 to 15 seconds; reheat if necessary. Serves 4.

One Serving:

Calories	136	Protein	3 g
Total Fat	4 g	Carbohydrates	27 g
Saturated Fat	1 g	Sodium	41 mg
Cholesterol	0	Added Sugar	0
		Fiber	5 g

Parsnips with Apple

Preparation: **10 min.** Cooking: **11 min.**

FAT SUGAR SODIUM

This unusual combination of vegetables goes especially well with roast pork, turkey, or chicken.

 Nonstick cooking spray
 1 tablespoon unsalted margarine
 5 medium-size parsnips (about 1 pound), peeled and sliced thin
 1 medium-size tart apple, peeled, cored, and sliced thin
¼ cup unsweetened apple juice or water
 Pinch ground cinnamon

Coat a medium-size saucepan with the **cooking spray,** add the **margarine,** and set over

moderate heat for 30 seconds. Add the **parsnips, apple, apple juice,** and **cinnamon,** and cook, covered, stirring occasionally, for 10 minutes or until tender. Serves 4.

One Serving:

Calories	125	Protein	1 g
Total Fat	3 g	Carbohydrates	24 g
Saturated Fat	1 g	Sodium	10 mg
Cholesterol	0	Added Sugar	0
		Fiber	5 g

Peas and Dumplings

Preparation: **5 min.** Cooking: **17 min.**

FAT SUGAR SODIUM

½ cup skim milk
½ cup low-sodium chicken broth
½ teaspoon mint flakes
⅛ teaspoon black pepper
⅓ cup sifted all-purpose flour
¼ teaspoon baking powder
 Pinch salt
 1 teaspoon cold unsalted margarine
 4 teaspoons ice water
1½ cups fresh green peas (about 1½ pounds unshelled) or 1 package (10 ounces) frozen green peas

1. In a medium-size saucepan, heat the **milk, chicken broth, mint,** and **pepper,** covered, until the mixture bubbles gently; simmer, covered, over low heat for 5 minutes.

2. Meanwhile, sift the **flour, baking powder,** and **salt** into a small bowl. Cut the **margarine** into tiny pieces and work them into the flour with a fork or your fingertips until the mixture resembles coarse meal. Add the **water** and stir it in with a fork to dampen the mixture.

3. Drop the dough, a teaspoonful at a time, into the simmering liquid; cover and cook for 5 minutes. Add the **peas** and simmer 5 minutes more or until the dumplings are firm. Serves 4.

One Serving:

Calories	104	Protein	5 g
Total Fat	2 g	Carbohydrates	17 g
Saturated Fat	0	Sodium	84 mg
Cholesterol	1 mg	Added Sugar	0
		Fiber	3 g

Tip: *When you buy unsalted margarine, read the label and avoid any brands that contain coconut oil. They have up to four times more saturated fat than other margarines.*

French-Style Green Peas

Preparation: **15 min.** Cooking: **15 min.** FAT SUGAR SODIUM

In many French recipes, fresh new peas are cooked with lettuce to enhance their flavor.

2 teaspoons unsalted margarine
3 green onions, sliced thin
2½ cups shredded Boston lettuce (about
  ½ large head) or other lettuce
2 cups fresh green peas (about 2 pounds
  unshelled) or 1⅓ 10-ounce packages frozen
  green peas
½ teaspoon dried marjoram, crumbled
¼ teaspoon sugar
2 teaspoons lemon juice

1. In a medium-size heavy saucepan, melt the
   margarine over moderate heat; add the **green
   onions** and cook, uncovered, until soft—about
   5 minutes.
2. Add the **lettuce,** tossing to coat with the
   margarine, and cook, covered, until wilted—
   about 4 minutes. Stir in the **peas, marjoram,**
   and **sugar;** cover and cook until the peas
   are just tender—about 5 minutes. Stir in the
   lemon juice. Serves 4.

One Serving:			
Calories	91	*Protein*	*5 g*
Total Fat	*2 g*	*Carbohydrates*	*14 g*
Saturated Fat	*0*	*Sodium*	*8 mg*
Cholesterol	*0*	*Added Sugar*	*1 Cal*
		Fiber	*4 g*

Green Pea Purée

Preparation: **15 min.** FAT SUGAR SODIUM
Cooking: **41 min.** (mostly unattended)

2 teaspoons unsalted margarine
2 green onions, sliced
1 small yellow onion, sliced
3 tablespoons dried split green peas, rinsed
1 small all-purpose potato, peeled and sliced
½ teaspoon mint flakes
¼ teaspoon sugar
1⅓ cups water
1 cup fresh green peas (about 1 pound
  unshelled) or ⅔ 10-ounce package frozen
  green peas

1. In a medium-size heavy saucepan, melt the
   margarine over moderate heat; add the **green
   onions** and **yellow onion** and cook, uncovered,
   until soft—about 5 minutes. Mix in the
   dried peas, potato, mint, sugar, and 1 cup of
   the **water;** cover and cook, stirring occasionally,
   for 30 minutes.
2. Add the **fresh peas** and the remaining water if
   the vegetables look dry; cook, covered, for 5
   minutes. Remove from the heat. In a food
   processor or electric blender, purée the mixture
   for 30 seconds or until smooth. Serves 4.

One Serving:			
Calories	104	*Protein*	*5 g*
Total Fat	*2 g*	*Carbohydrates*	*17 g*
Saturated Fat	*0*	*Sodium*	*30 mg*
Cholesterol	*0*	*Added Sugar*	*1 Cal*
		Fiber	*2 g*

Parsnips with Apple (left) and *Peas and Dumplings* (right)

Minted Peas with Orange

Preparation: **5 min.** Cooking: **9 min.** FAT SUGAR SODIUM

2 cups fresh green peas (about 2 pounds unshelled) or 1⅓ 10-ounce packages frozen green peas

2 teaspoons unsalted margarine

2 teaspoons grated orange rind

1 tablespoon minced fresh mint or ½ teaspoon mint flakes

⅛ teaspoon black pepper

1. In a small saucepan, bring an inch of unsalted water to a boil; add the **peas** and cook, covered, for 5 minutes or until tender. Drain, transfer to a bowl, and set aside.

2. Using the same saucepan, melt the **margarine** over moderately low heat; add the **orange rind** and cook, uncovered, stirring, for 1 minute. Add the **mint, pepper,** and peas; cook and stir for 2 minutes or until heated through. Serves 4.

One Serving:			
Calories	77	Protein	4 g
Total Fat	2 g	Carbohydrates	11 g
Saturated Fat	0	Sodium	3 mg
Cholesterol	0	Added Sugar	0
		Fiber	3 g

Snow Peas with Carrots and Red Pepper

Preparation: **15 min.** Cooking: **7 min.** FAT SUGAR SODIUM

Snow peas and Sugar Snaps can be used interchangeably in this recipe.

Nonstick cooking spray

1 tablespoon unsalted margarine

2 medium-size carrots, peeled and cut into matchstick strips

1 medium-size sweet red pepper, cored, seeded, and cut into matchstick strips

¾ pound snow peas or Sugar Snap peas, trimmed and strings removed

¼ teaspoon grated lemon rind

1 teaspoon lemon juice

⅛ teaspoon black pepper

1. Coat a heavy 10-inch skillet with the **cooking spray;** add the **margarine** and melt over moderate heat. Add the **carrots** and **red pepper** and cook, covered, for 3 minutes. Add the **snow**

Snow Peas with Carrots and Red Pepper (left) and *Marinated Broiled Peppers* (right)

peas, cover, and cook 3 minutes longer or until the vegetables are tender.

2. Stir in the **lemon rind, lemon juice,** and **black pepper,** and serve. Serves 4.

One Serving:

Calories	83	Protein	3 g
Total Fat	3 g	Carbohydrates	11 g
Saturated Fat	1 g	Sodium	17 mg
Cholesterol	0	Added Sugar	0
		Fiber	2 g

Sugar Snap Peas with Chives

Preparation: **10 min.** Cooking: **3 min.** FAT SUGAR SODIUM

You can substitute snow peas for the Sugar Snaps; both are at their best when prepared simply.

¾ pound Sugar Snap peas, trimmed and strings removed

1 tablespoon unsalted margarine

2 teaspoons snipped fresh chives or minced green onion

1. In a large saucepan, bring 4 cups water to a boil; add the **peas,** cover, and cook for 1 minute. Drain, transfer to a bowl, and set aside.

2. In the same saucepan, melt the **margarine** over moderate heat; add the peas and toss. Stir in the **chives** and toss again. Serves 4.

One Serving:

Calories	61	Protein	2 g
Total Fat	3 g	Carbohydrates	6 g
Saturated Fat	1 g	Sodium	37 mg
Cholesterol	0	Added Sugar	0
		Fiber	2 g

Marinated Broiled Peppers

Preparation: **5 min.,** plus 1 hr. marination Cooking: **5 min.** FAT SUGAR SODIUM

Serve these peppers with barbecued meats or as a condiment on tuna, cheese, or chicken sandwiches.

6 medium-size sweet red, green, or yellow peppers (about 2 pounds) or a combination

1 tablespoon olive oil

1 tablespoon red wine vinegar

1 clove garlic, minced

½ teaspoon dried oregano, crumbled

¼ teaspoon black pepper

1. Preheat the broiler. Place the **peppers** on the broiler pan rack and broil about 6 inches from the heat, turning 3 times, until the skins are lightly charred and blistered all over—5 to 8 minutes. Transfer the peppers to a paper bag and let steam until cool enough to handle.

2. Remove the stems, seeds, and skins of the peppers over a bowl to catch the juices. Cut the peppers into ½-inch strips and place in a serving dish. To the juices in the bowl, add the **olive oil, vinegar, garlic, oregano,** and **black pepper,** and mix together. Pour the marinade over the peppers and let them sit at room temperature for 1 hour before serving. Serves 4.

One Serving:

Calories	79	Protein	2 g
Total Fat	4 g	Carbohydrates	10 g
Saturated Fat	1 g	Sodium	6 mg
Cholesterol	0	Added Sugar	0
		Fiber	2 g

Sautéed Peppers and Tomatoes

Preparation: **15 min.** Cooking: **21 min.**   FAT SUGAR SODIUM

Serve this vegetable mixture with hamburgers or broiled fish.

1 tablespoon olive oil

3 medium-size sweet red or green peppers (about 1 pound), cored, seeded, and cut into 1-inch squares

1 large yellow onion, cut into 1-inch cubes

2 medium-size ripe tomatoes, peeled, cored, seeded, and chopped

2 tablespoons cider vinegar

2 cloves garlic, minced

1. In a heavy 12-inch skillet, heat the **olive oil** over moderate heat for 1 minute; add the **peppers** and **onion,** cover, and cook for 10 minutes.

2. Stir in the **tomatoes, vinegar,** and **garlic** and cook, covered, 10 minutes longer. Serves 4.

One Serving:

Calories	72	Protein	2 g
Total Fat	4 g	Carbohydrates	9 g
Saturated Fat	1 g	Sodium	8 mg
Cholesterol	0	Added Sugar	0
		Fiber	1 g

Danish-Style New Potatoes

Preparation: **5 min.** FAT SUGAR SODIUM
Cooking: **23 min.** (mostly unattended)

16 small new potatoes (about 1 pound), unpeeled
¼ cup water
2 teaspoons light brown sugar
½ tablespoon unsalted margarine
1 tablespoon snipped fresh dill

1. In a medium-size heavy saucepan, bring 3 cups unsalted water to a boil. Add the **potatoes** and simmer, partially covered, for 15 minutes or until the potatoes are tender. Drain, cool for 10 minutes, peel off the skins, and set aside.

2. Put the ¼ cup **water** and the **brown sugar** into a 10-inch nonstick skillet over moderate heat; bring to a simmer and cook, stirring, until the sugar has dissolved—about 2 minutes. Add the **margarine** and continue to cook, stirring, until it has melted—about 1 minute. Add the potatoes and toss until heated through—about 2 minutes longer. Sprinkle with the **dill**. Serves 4.

One Serving:

Calories	111	Protein	2 g
Total Fat	2 g	Carbohydrates	23 g
Saturated Fat	0	Sodium	8 mg
Cholesterol	0	Added Sugar	8 Cal
		Fiber	2 g

Tip: Boiled new potatoes gain an even nuttier taste and drier texture if, after draining them, you shake them in a saucepan over high heat for about one minute.

Creamy Mashed Potatoes

Preparation: **10 min.** Cooking: **15 min.** FAT SUGAR SODIUM

You can have low-fat, low-calorie mashed potatoes—try these.

3 cloves garlic, crushed
4 medium-size all-purpose potatoes (about 1 pound), peeled and sliced thin
1 bay leaf

1 tablespoon unsalted margarine
½ cup buttermilk
3 tablespoons plain low-fat yogurt

1. In a medium-size heavy saucepan, bring 3 cups unsalted water to a boil. Add the **garlic, potatoes,** and **bay leaf,** and cook, partially covered, over moderate heat for 12 minutes or until the potatoes are fork-tender. Drain, reserving 3 tablespoons of cooking water, and discard the bay leaf.

2. Transfer the potatoes to a large mixing bowl. Add the **margarine, buttermilk,** and **yogurt,** and beat in with an electric mixer. Then add just enough of the reserved water to make the potatoes creamy. Serves 4.

One Serving:

Calories	116	Protein	3 g
Total Fat	3 g	Carbohydrates	18 g
Saturated Fat	1 g	Sodium	45 mg
Cholesterol	2 mg	Added Sugar	0
		Fiber	2 g

Curried Potatoes

Preparation: **15 min.** Cooking: **19 min.** FAT SUGAR SODIUM

4 medium-size all-purpose potatoes (about 1 pound), peeled and cut into 1-inch cubes
4 teaspoons unsalted margarine
1 medium-size yellow onion, chopped
1 tablespoon curry powder

1. In a medium-size heavy saucepan, bring 3 cups unsalted water to a boil. Add the **potatoes** and cook, partially covered, over moderate heat until fork-tender—about 15 minutes.

2. Meanwhile, in a heavy 10-inch skillet, melt the **margarine** over moderate heat; add the **onion** and cook, uncovered, until soft—about 5 minutes. Stir in the **curry powder** and cook 1 minute longer.

3. As soon as the potatoes are tender, drain, add to the skillet, and cook, stirring, for 1 minute. Transfer to a heated platter. Serves 4.

One Serving:

Calories	113	Protein	2 g
Total Fat	4 g	Carbohydrates	18 g
Saturated Fat	1 g	Sodium	6 mg
Cholesterol	0	Added Sugar	0
		Fiber	2 g

Danish-Style New Potatoes (left) and *Curried Potatoes* (right)

Mashed Potatoes and Cabbage

You can substitute leftover for freshly mashed potatoes in this recipe. And you can make the dish hours ahead and refrigerate it until time to reheat.

4 medium-size all-purpose potatoes (about 1 pound), peeled and cut into 2-inch cubes

1 small head cabbage (about 1 pound), cored and sliced thin

⅓ cup skim milk
⅛ teaspoon black pepper

Preparation:
20 min.
Cooking:
50 min. (mostly unattended)

1. Preheat the oven to 400°F. In a medium-size heavy saucepan, bring 3 cups unsalted water to a boil; add the **potatoes** and cook, partially covered, over moderate heat until tender—about 20 minutes.

2. Meanwhile, in another medium-size heavy saucepan, bring 1½ cups water to a boil; add the **cabbage,** cover, and cook over moderate heat for 8 minutes or until tender. Uncover, raise the heat to high, and cook, stirring occasionally, until all the water has evaporated—about 5 minutes. Remove from the heat and set aside.

3. When the potatoes are cooked, drain and mash them. Mix the cabbage, **milk,** and **pepper** into the potatoes, and spoon the mixture into an ungreased 9"x 9"x 2" baking pan. Bake, uncovered, for 25 minutes. Increase the oven temperature to broil, transfer the pan to the broiler, about 5 to 6 inches from the heat, and broil for 1 to 2 minutes or until browned. Serves 4.

One Serving:	
Calories	102
Total Fat	0
Saturated Fat	0
Cholesterol	0
Protein	4 g
Carbohydrates	22 g
Sodium	36 mg
Added Sugar	0
Fiber	3 g

Sweet Potatoes with Apple (left) and *Twice-Baked Potatoes* (right)

Oven French Fries

Preparation: **10 min.** Cooking: **20 min.** FAT SUGAR SODIUM

- **2 large baking potatoes (about 1 pound), peeled and cut lengthwise into 8 wedges**
- **2½ teaspoons olive oil**
- **1 tablespoon malt or red wine vinegar**
- **¼ teaspoon salt (optional)**

1. Preheat the oven to 375°F. On a lightly greased baking sheet or 15½"x 10½"x 1" jelly roll pan, spread the **potatoes** in a single layer and brush lightly with 1 teaspoon of the **olive oil.**

2. Bake, uncovered, for 5 minutes. Brush with another teaspoon of the oil and bake for another 5 minutes. Brush one more time using the remaining ½ teaspoon of oil and continue baking another 10 minutes or until the potatoes are crisp, golden, and tender.

3. Before serving, sprinkle the potatoes with the **vinegar** and, if you like, the **salt.** Serves 4.

One Serving:			
		Protein	*2 g*
Calories	93	*Carbohydrates*	*15 g*
Total Fat	*3 g*	*Sodium*	*5 mg*
Saturated Fat	*0*	*Added Sugar*	*0*
Cholesterol	*0*	*Fiber*	*2 g*

Twice-Baked Potatoes

Preparation: **5 min.**
Cooking: **1 hr. 21 min.** (mostly unattended) FAT SUGAR SODIUM

These appetizing potatoes can be prepared ahead; keep covered and refrigerated until the second baking period.

- **2 large baking potatoes (about 1 pound)**
- **¼ cup buttermilk**
- **1 green onion, sliced thin**
- **1 tablespoon unsalted margarine**
- **⅛ teaspoon black pepper**
- **1 tablespoon grated Parmesan cheese**
  Pinch paprika

1. Preheat the oven to 400°F. Pierce the **potatoes** with a fork, place them in the oven, and bake for 1 hour or until fork-tender.

2. As soon as the potatoes are cool enough to handle, halve each one lengthwise and carefully scoop the pulp into a medium-size bowl. Set the shells aside. Mash the pulp with a hand masher, then beat in the **buttermilk, green onion,** half of the **margarine,** and the **pepper.** Spoon the mixture into the potato shells, score the tops with the tines of a fork to make a decorative design, and sprinkle with the **cheese** and **paprika.**

3. Arrange the stuffed potatoes in an ungreased 8"x 8"x 2" baking pan, dot with the remaining margarine, and bake, uncovered, for 20 minutes. Increase the temperature to broil, transfer the baking pan to the broiler, about 5 inches from the heat, and broil for 1 to 2 minutes or until golden brown. Serves 4.

One Serving:

Calories	122	Protein	4 g
Total Fat	3 g	Carbohydrates	20 g
Saturated Fat	1 g	Sodium	48 mg
Cholesterol	2 mg	Added Sugar	0
		Fiber	0

Sweet Potatoes with Apple

Preparation: **15 min.**   FAT SUGAR SODIUM
Cooking: **40 min.** (mostly unattended)

1 tablespoon plus 1 teaspoon unsalted margarine
3 medium-size sweet potatoes (about 1 pound), peeled and sliced ¼ inch thick
1 large sweet apple, such as Delicious, cored and sliced thin
1 tablespoon light brown sugar
Pinch ground nutmeg

1. Preheat the oven to 375°F. Grease a 9-inch pie pan with 1 teaspoon of the **margarine.** Lay the **sweet potato** and **apple** slices in the pan in a circle, alternating and overlapping the slices.

2. Mix the **brown sugar** and **nutmeg** together and sprinkle over the potatoes and apples; dot with the remaining margarine.

3. Cover the pan with aluminum foil and bake for 30 minutes. Uncover and bake 10 to 15 minutes longer or until the potatoes are tender when pierced with a fork. Serves 4.

Variation:

Sweet Potatoes with Pineapple   Prepare as directed but substitute 1 cup chopped fresh pineapple or 1 can (8 ounces) crushed pineapple, drained, for the apple. To the brown sugar–nutmeg mixture, add ½ teaspoon ground ginger.

One Serving:

Calories	169	Protein	2 g
Total Fat	4 g	Carbohydrates	43 g
Saturated Fat	1 g	Sodium	13 mg
Cholesterol	0	Added Sugar	9 Cal
		Fiber	3 g

Two-Potato Casserole

Preparation: **15 min.**   FAT SUGAR SODIUM
Cooking: **57 min.** (mostly unattended)

When cooking for two, prepare the full recipe, refrigerate the leftovers, and reheat in the oven.

Nonstick cooking spray
1 cup apple cider
¼ teaspoon salt
¼ teaspoon black pepper
⅛ teaspoon ground cloves
1 tablespoon unsalted margarine
2 medium-size sweet potatoes (about ⅔ pound), peeled and sliced ⅛ inch thick
2 medium-size baking potatoes (about ¾ pound), peeled and sliced ⅛ inch thick

1. Preheat the oven to 450°F. Coat a 1-quart ovenproof glass casserole, and a sheet of aluminum foil just large enough to cover it, with the **cooking spray;** set aside.

2. In a small heavy saucepan, bring the **apple cider, salt, pepper,** and **cloves** to a boil; cook, uncovered, until the cider has boiled down to ½ cup—about 5 minutes; set aside.

3. Melt the **margarine** in another small saucepan. On the bottom of the casserole, arrange a single layer of the **sweet potatoes,** drizzle with ½ teaspoon of the melted margarine, and spoon 1½ tablespoons of the cider over them. Cover the sweet potato layer with a layer of the **baking potatoes.** With your hands, press the potato layers firmly together. Continue to build and compress 5 more layers of the potatoes, margarine, and cider in the same fashion.

4. Place the foil directly on top of the potatoes, then place a weight, such as a heavy lid, on the foil. Bake on the lowest rack of the oven for 45 minutes. Transfer to the floor of the oven and cook for 5 minutes or until the bottom layer of potatoes is crusty and browned.

5. Cool the casserole upright on a wire rack for 3 minutes; with a spatula, gently loosen the potatoes around the edges and invert onto a heated serving platter. Serves 4.

One Serving:

Calories	171	Protein	2 g
Total Fat	3 g	Carbohydrates	34 g
Saturated Fat	1 g	Sodium	149 mg
Cholesterol	0	Added Sugar	0
		Fiber	2 g

Spinach Balls in Tomato Sauce

This recipe does not lend itself to halving for two.

FAT SUGAR SODIUM

1 tablespoon unsalted margarine

2 medium-size yellow onions, chopped fine

1 pound fresh spinach, trimmed and chopped, or 1 package (10 ounces) frozen chopped spinach, thawed and drained

4 cloves garlic, minced

1 tablespoon fine dry bread crumbs

1 teaspoon grated lemon rind

1 tablespoon grated Parmesan cheese

¼ teaspoon black pepper

1 large egg white

1 can (8 ounces) low-sodium tomato sauce

½ cup low-sodium beef broth

½ teaspoon dried basil, crumbled

Nonstick cooking spray

Preparation:
20 min., plus 15 min. refrigeration
Cooking:
45 min. (mostly unattended)

One Serving:

Calories	108
Total Fat	4 g
Saturated Fat	1 g
Cholesterol	1 mg
Protein	5 g
Carbohydrates	14 g
Sodium	138 mg
Added Sugar	0
Fiber	3 g

1. In a heavy 10-inch skillet, melt ½ tablespoon of the **margarine** over moderate heat; add half the **onions** and cook, uncovered, until soft—about 5 minutes. Add the **spinach** and half the **garlic** and cook, covered, for 2 minutes. Uncover and cook, stirring, until dry—about 2 minutes.

2. Preheat the oven to 350°F. Remove the spinach from the heat and stir in the **bread crumbs, lemon rind, cheese,** ⅛ teaspoon of the **pepper,** and the **egg white.** Using your hands, shape the mixture into 1½-inch balls. Refrigerate for 15 minutes.

3. In a small heavy saucepan, melt the remaining ½ tablespoon of margarine over moderate heat; add the remaining onion and cook, uncovered, until soft—about 5 minutes. Add the remaining garlic and pepper and the **tomato sauce, beef broth,** and **basil.** Cover and simmer over moderately low heat, stirring occasionally, for 30 minutes.

4. While the tomato sauce is cooking, coat a shallow 1-quart casserole with the **cooking spray,** add the spinach balls, and bake, uncovered, for 30 minutes. Before serving, spoon the tomato sauce over the spinach. Serves 4.

Spinach Balls in Tomato Sauce (left) and *Baked Acorn Squash with Parmesan Cheese* (right)

Sautéed Spinach with Lemon and Garlic

Preparation: **20 min.** Cooking: **10 min.** `FAT` `SUGAR` `SODIUM`

1½ **teaspoons olive oil**
1 **medium-size yellow onion, chopped fine**
1 **clove garlic, minced**
1½ **pounds fresh spinach, trimmed**
⅛ **teaspoon black pepper**
2 **teaspoons lemon juice**

1. In a large nonstick saucepan, heat the **olive oil** over moderate heat for 1 minute; add the **onion** and **garlic** and cook, uncovered, until soft—about 5 minutes. Add the **spinach,** cover, and cook, stirring often, until the spinach wilts—about 4 minutes.
2. Transfer the spinach to a warm serving dish, add the **pepper** and **lemon juice,** toss well, and serve. Serves 4.

Variation:

Spinach with Sour Cream and Nutmeg Cook the onion and garlic in 1 tablespoon unsalted margarine instead of the olive oil and brown well. Cook the spinach according to the recipe directions. Omit the lemon juice and add the black pepper, ¼ teaspoon freshly grated nutmeg, 2 tablespoons sour cream, and 1 tablespoon yogurt; toss well.

One Serving:

Calories	65	Protein	4 g
Total Fat	4 g	Carbohydrates	6 g
Saturated Fat	1 g	Sodium	98 mg
Cholesterol	0	Added Sugar	0
		Fiber	4 g

Braised Spinach

Preparation: **20 min.** Cooking: **10 min.** `FAT` `SUGAR` `SODIUM`

Collards and turnip or mustard greens can be substituted for spinach, but they require 10 to 15 minutes more cooking time.

1 **cup low-sodium chicken broth**
1 **small yellow onion, chopped**
¼ **teaspoon red pepper flakes**
1½ **pounds fresh spinach, trimmed**
2 **tablespoons white wine vinegar**

1. In a large heavy saucepan, heat the **chicken broth, onion,** and **red pepper flakes** until the broth bubbles gently; cover and simmer for 3 minutes.
2. Add the **spinach,** cover, and cook over moderate heat for 5 minutes or until the spinach has wilted. Sprinkle with the **vinegar** and toss. Serves 4.

One Serving:

Calories	35	Protein	4 g
Total Fat	1 g	Carbohydrates	5 g
Saturated Fat	0	Sodium	102 mg
Cholesterol	0	Added Sugar	0
		Fiber	3 g

Baked Acorn Squash with Parmesan Cheese

Preparation: **10 min.** Cooking: **27 min.** `FAT` `SUGAR` `SODIUM`

Nonstick cooking spray
1 **large acorn squash (about 1 pound)**
½ **tablespoon unsalted margarine**
4 **teaspoons grated Parmesan cheese**
1½ **tablespoons dry bread crumbs**

1. Preheat the oven to 400°F. Coat a baking sheet or 15½"x 10½"x 1" jelly roll pan with the **cooking spray.** Cut the **squash** in half crosswise and scoop out the seeds with a spoon. Slice the squash into rounds ¼ inch thick and arrange them in a single layer on the baking sheet. Bake the slices for 8 minutes, turn, and bake 8 minutes longer; remove from the oven and let cool.
2. Melt the **margarine** in a small skillet or saucepan. In a pie pan or on a sheet of wax paper, mix together the **cheese** and **bread crumbs.** When the squash slices are cool enough to handle, press both sides into the cheese–bread crumb mixture. Return the slices to the baking sheet and drizzle the margarine over them. Bake for 10 minutes or until the squash is tender and golden brown. Serves 4.

One Serving:

Calories	69	Protein	2 g
Total Fat	3 g	Carbohydrates	11 g
Saturated Fat	1 g	Sodium	66 mg
Cholesterol	2 mg	Added Sugar	0
		Fiber	4 g

Butternut Squash in Tomato Sauce

Preparation: **20 min.**
Cooking: **31 min.** (mostly unattended)

FAT SUGAR SODIUM

You can substitute acorn squash for the butternut squash in this recipe. When cooking for two, use a ³/₄-pound squash and an 8-ounce can of tomatoes.

½ tablespoon unsalted margarine
1 medium-size yellow onion, sliced
1 medium-size butternut squash (about 1¾ pounds), seeded, cut into 1-inch cubes and peeled
1 can (14½ ounces) low-sodium tomatoes, with their juice
2 teaspoons low-sodium tomato paste
1 teaspoon grated orange rind
1 bay leaf
½ teaspoon dried oregano, crumbled
⅛ teaspoon black pepper

1. In a heavy 10-inch nonstick skillet, melt the **margarine** over moderate heat; add the **onion** and cook, uncovered, until it is soft—about 5 minutes. Add the **squash,** cover, and cook over moderately low heat for 5 minutes.

2. In an electric blender or food processor, purée the **tomatoes** for 25 seconds. Add to the skillet along with the **tomato paste, orange rind, bay leaf, oregano,** and **pepper;** cover and bring to a simmer. Continue to let the mixture bubble gently, stirring occasionally, for 20 minutes or until the squash is tender. Remove the bay leaf. Serves 4.

One Serving:

Calories	119	Protein	3 g
Total Fat	2 g	Carbohydrates	26 g
Saturated Fat	0	Sodium	27 mg
Cholesterol	0	Added Sugar	0
		Fiber	4 g

Spaghetti Squash with Mushroom Sauce

Preparation: **15 min.** Cooking: **22 min.**   FAT SUGAR SODIUM

1 medium-size spaghetti squash (about 1½ pounds), halved lengthwise and seeded
1 tablespoon unsalted margarine
3 green onions, chopped fine
½ pound small mushrooms, quartered

½ teaspoon each dried thyme and marjoram, crumbled
⅛ teaspoon black pepper
½ cup low-sodium beef or chicken broth
1 tablespoon minced parsley

1. In a 4-quart Dutch oven, bring to a boil enough unsalted water to cover the squash. Add the **squash,** cut side up, and cook, covered, over moderate heat for 20 minutes or until the squash is fork-tender.

2. Meanwhile, in a heavy 10-inch skillet, melt the **margarine** over moderate heat; add the **green onions** and cook, uncovered, until soft— about 5 minutes. Stir in the **mushrooms, thyme, marjoram,** and **pepper;** cover and cook for 5 minutes. Add the **beef broth** and cook, uncovered, stirring occasionally, until most of the broth has evaporated—about 5 minutes.

3. As soon as the squash is done, lift it from the Dutch oven, and, with a fork, scrape the spaghetti-like strands onto a heated platter. Ladle the mushroom sauce on top, sprinkle with the **parsley,** and serve. Serves 4.

One Serving:

Calories	86	Protein	2 g
Total Fat	4 g	Carbohydrates	12 g
Saturated Fat	1 g	Sodium	25 mg
Cholesterol	0	Added Sugar	0
		Fiber	4 g

Braised Yellow Squash, Corn, and Tomatoes

Preparation: **20 min.**
Cooking: **18 min.**   FAT SUGAR SODIUM

You can substitute zucchini for the yellow squash in this summer vegetable dish.

Nonstick cooking spray
½ tablespoon unsalted margarine
1 medium-size yellow onion, sliced
2 medium-size yellow squash (about 1 pound), sliced 1 inch thick
3 medium-size ripe tomatoes (about 1 pound), peeled, cored, and chopped, or 1 can (1 pound) low-sodium tomatoes, chopped, with ¼ cup of their juice
½ cup fresh or frozen whole-kernel corn
½ teaspoon dried oregano, crumbled
⅛ teaspoon black pepper
1 clove garlic, minced
1 tablespoon minced fresh basil or parsley

1. Coat a 10-inch nonstick skillet with the **cooking spray,** add the **margarine,** and melt over moderate heat. Add the **onion** and cook, uncovered, until soft—about 5 minutes.

2. Stir in the **yellow squash, tomatoes, corn, oregano,** and **pepper** and simmer, covered, for 10 minutes or until the squash is just tender. Add the **garlic** and cook, stirring, for 2 minutes. Sprinkle with the **basil.** Serves 4.

One Serving:

Calories	85	Protein	3 g
Total Fat	3 g	Carbohydrates	15 g
Saturated Fat	0	Sodium	21 mg
Cholesterol	0	Added Sugar	0
		Fiber	3 g

Yellow Squash Casserole

FAT SUGAR SODIUM

Preparation: **12 min.**
Cooking: **43 min.** (mostly unattended)

When cooking the dish for two, make the full recipe and reheat the leftovers.

4 **medium-size yellow squash (about 2 pounds), cut into 1-inch cubes**
1 **medium-size yellow onion, chopped**
1 **tablespoon unsalted margarine**
1 **large egg white**
¾ **cup cracker crumbs**
⅛ **teaspoon each nutmeg and black pepper**
Nonstick cooking spray

1. Preheat the oven to 350°F. In a large heavy saucepan, bring the **squash** to a boil in an inch of water; add the **onion** and cook, covered, over moderately high heat for 10 minutes or until the squash is just tender.

2. Drain and coarsely mash the squash and onion. Add ½ tablespoon of the **margarine,** the **egg white,** ½ cup of the **cracker crumbs,** and the **nutmeg** and **pepper,** and stir until blended.

3. Coat a shallow 8″x 8″x 2″ baking pan with the **cooking spray.** Spoon the squash mixture into the pan and smooth the top with a spatula.

4. In a 7-inch skillet, melt the remaining margarine over low heat; add the remaining cracker crumbs, mix and toss well, and sprinkle over the squash. Bake, uncovered, for 30 minutes. Serves 4.

One Serving:

Calories	122	Protein	4 g
Total Fat	5 g	Carbohydrates	17 g
Saturated Fat	1 g	Sodium	146 mg
Cholesterol	0	Added Sugar	0
		Fiber	3 g

Braised Yellow Squash, Corn, and Tomatoes (left) *and Butternut Squash in Tomato Sauce* (right)

Zucchini and Cherry Tomatoes with Vinegar

Preparation: **10 min.** Cooking: **8 min.** FAT SUGAR SODIUM

- 1 **tablespoon olive oil**
- 2 **medium-size zucchini (about 1 pound), sliced ¼ inch thick**
- 1½ **cups small cherry tomatoes**
- 1 **clove garlic, minced**
- 1 **tablespoon cider vinegar**
- ½ **teaspoon dried basil, crumbled**
- ⅛ **teaspoon black pepper**

1. In a heavy 10-inch skillet, heat the **olive oil** over moderate heat for 1 minute; add the **zucchini** and cook, uncovered, stirring frequently, for 5 minutes.
2. Add the **cherry tomatoes, garlic, vinegar, basil,** and **pepper,** and cook, stirring, for 2 minutes or until the tomatoes are heated through. Serves 4.

One Serving:

Calories	55	Protein	2 g
Total Fat	4 g	Carbohydrates	6 g
Saturated Fat	0	Sodium	7 mg
Cholesterol	0	Added Sugar	0
		Fiber	1 g

Grated Zucchini Pancake

Squash Kebabs

Preparation: **5 min.,** plus 2 hr. marination   Cooking: **5 min.** FAT SUGAR SODIUM

- 1 **tablespoon reduced-sodium soy sauce**
- 1 **tablespoon red wine vinegar**
- 1 **tablespoon Oriental sesame or peanut oil**
- 2 **teaspoons honey**
- ¼ **teaspoon ground ginger**
- ⅛ **teaspoon hot red pepper sauce**
- 1 **small zucchini (about ¼ pound), halved lengthwise and sliced ¼ inch thick**
- 1 **small yellow squash (about ¼ pound), halved lengthwise and sliced ¼ inch thick**
- 12 **small cherry tomatoes**

1. In a large bowl, combine the **soy sauce, vinegar, sesame oil, honey, ginger,** and **red pepper sauce.** Add the **zucchini, yellow squash,** and **cherry tomatoes,** toss well, and cover with plastic wrap; let sit for 2 hours at room temperature.
2. Preheat the broiler and remove the broiler pan. Using a slotted spoon, transfer the vegetables from the marinade to a large plate. Thread the vegetables on 4 10-inch skewers, alternating the zucchini, cherry tomatoes, and yellow squash.
3. Place the skewers on the broiler pan rack and brush with the marinade. Set the broiler pan about 8 inches from the heat and broil for 5 minutes, turning the skewers 2 or 3 times and brushing each time with the marinade. Serves 4.

One Serving:

Calories	54	Protein	1 g
Total Fat	3 g	Carbohydrates	6 g
Saturated Fat	0	Sodium	159 mg
Cholesterol	0	Added Sugar	8 Cal
		Fiber	1 g

Grilled Parmesan Tomatoes

Grated Zucchini Pancake

Preparation: **20 min.** Cooking: **13 min.** FAT SUGAR SODIUM

- 1 **large zucchini (about ¾ pound), grated and squeezed dry**
- 1 **small all-purpose potato, peeled, grated, and squeezed dry**
- 3 **green onions, chopped fine**
- 2 **tablespoons flour**
- 1 **large egg, lightly beaten**
- 1 **large egg white**
- ¼ **teaspoon black pepper**
  - **Nonstick cooking spray**
- 1 **tablespoon unsalted margarine**
- 1 **tablespoon grated Parmesan cheese**

1. In a medium-size bowl, combine the **zucchini, potato, green onions, flour, egg, egg white,** and **pepper.**
2. Coat a 10-inch nonstick skillet with the **cooking spray.** Melt ½ tablespoon of the **margarine** in the skillet over moderate heat; add the zucchini mixture, shaping it into a cake with a spatula, and cook, uncovered, until golden around the edges—6 to 7 minutes.
3. Place a large plate over the skillet and invert the zucchini pancake onto it. Add the remaining margarine to the skillet, melt it over moderate heat, and slide the pancake back into the skillet. Cook, uncovered, until firm—about 5 minutes. Sprinkle with the **cheese.** Serves 4.

One Serving:			
Calories	103	Protein	5 g
Total Fat	5 g	Carbohydrates	10 g
Saturated Fat	1 g	Sodium	58 mg
Cholesterol	69 mg	Added Sugar	0
		Fiber	2 g

Grilled Parmesan Tomatoes

Preparation: **10 min.** Cooking: **3 min.** FAT SUGAR SODIUM

- 1 **tablespoon olive oil**
- 4 **medium-size ripe tomatoes (about 1⅓ pounds), cored and sliced ½ inch thick**
- 1 **clove garlic, minced**
- 2 **tablespoons minced parsley**
- ⅛ **teaspoon black pepper**
- 2 **tablespoons grated Parmesan cheese**

1. Preheat the broiler. Grease a baking sheet with 1 teaspoon of the **olive oil.** Arrange the **tomato** slices on it in a single layer.
2. In a small bowl, mix together the remaining olive oil, **garlic, parsley,** and **pepper.** Drizzle the mixture over the tomatoes and sprinkle with the **cheese.**
3. Broil 5 inches from the heat for 3 minutes or until the cheese is golden brown. Serves 4.

One Serving:			
Calories	62	Protein	2 g
Total Fat	3 g	Carbohydrates	7 g
Saturated Fat	0	Sodium	59 mg
Cholesterol	2 mg	Added Sugar	0
		Fiber	1 g

Scalloped Tomatoes

Preparation: **10 min.** FAT SUGAR SODIUM
Cooking: **32 min.** (mostly unattended)

This recipe is not suitable for halving or reheating.

- ⅓ **cup fine dry bread crumbs**
- ½ **teaspoon sugar**
- ¼ **teaspoon each dried basil and thyme, crumbled**
- ⅛ **teaspoon black pepper**
- 4 **medium-size ripe tomatoes (about 1⅓ pounds), cored and sliced**
- 2 **green onions, chopped fine**
- ½ **tablespoon unsalted margarine**

1. Preheat the oven to 350°F. In a small bowl, mix together the **bread crumbs, sugar, basil, thyme,** and **pepper.**
2. In a 9-inch nonstick pie pan, arrange a layer of **tomatoes,** sprinkle with ⅓ of the bread crumb mixture, and top with ½ of the **green onions.** Continue to layer the tomatoes in the same fashion, ending with a layer of bread crumbs.
3. Melt the **margarine** in a small saucepan or skillet and drizzle over the tomatoes; bake, uncovered, for 30 to 35 minutes or until the tomatoes are soft.
4. Increase the temperature to broil. Transfer the pie pan to the broiler, about 5 inches from the heat, and broil for 1 to 2 minutes or until the bread crumbs are golden brown. Serves 4.

One Serving:			
Calories	78	Protein	3 g
Total Fat	2 g	Carbohydrates	14 g
Saturated Fat	0	Sodium	73 mg
Cholesterol	0	Added Sugar	2 Cal
		Fiber	1 g

Turnip and Potato Purée

Preparation: **20 min.** Cooking: **36 min.** FAT SUGAR SODIUM

Try using rutabagas (yellow turnips) in this recipe for an even more interesting taste. You can turn leftovers into soup by simply thinning with low-sodium chicken broth.

2 teaspoons unsalted margarine
1 small yellow onion, sliced thin
2 cloves garlic, crushed
1 small sweet apple, such as Delicious, peeled, cored, and sliced thin
1 medium-size all-purpose potato, peeled and sliced thin
3 medium-size turnips or 1 small rutabaga (about ¾ pound), peeled and sliced thin
¼ teaspoon ground ginger
  Pinch each ground allspice and nutmeg
1⅓ cups low-sodium chicken broth

1. In a large heavy saucepan, melt the **margarine** over moderate heat; add the **onion** and **garlic** and cook, uncovered, until the onion is soft—about 5 minutes. Stir in the **apple, potato, turnips, ginger, allspice, nutmeg,** and **chicken broth;** cover and cook for 30 minutes or until the vegetables are tender.

2. In a food processor or electric blender, purée the mixture in batches, adding a little broth or water if it seems too thick. Return the purée to the saucepan and reheat if necessary. Serves 4.

One Serving:

Calories	85	Protein	2 g
Total Fat	3 g	Carbohydrates	14 g
Saturated Fat	1 g	Sodium	87 mg
Cholesterol	0	Added Sugar	0
		Fiber	3 g

Turnips Glazed with Honey and Lemon

Preparation: **15 min.** Cooking: **17 min.** FAT SUGAR SODIUM

2 large turnips or 1 medium-size rutabaga (about 1 pound), peeled and cut into ½-inch cubes
2 tablespoons honey
1 tablespoon unsalted margarine
½ teaspoon grated lemon rind
⅛ teaspoon white or black pepper

1. In a medium-size heavy saucepan over moderate heat, bring 1¼ cups unsalted water to a boil. Add the **turnips** and cook, covered, for 15 to 20 minutes or until fork-tender. Drain.

2. Add the **honey, margarine, lemon rind,** and **pepper** to the drained turnips in the saucepan. Warm, uncovered, over low heat, shaking the pan gently, for 2 to 3 minutes or until the margarine has melted and the turnips are lightly glazed. Serves 4.

Variation:

Turnips Glazed with Orange and Ginger
Substitute 2 tablespoons orange marmalade for the honey, use minced fresh ginger in place of the lemon rind, and substitute ¼ teaspoon freshly grated black pepper for the ⅛ teaspoon white pepper.

One Serving:

Calories	83	Protein	1 g
Total Fat	3 g	Carbohydrates	15 g
Saturated Fat	1 g	Sodium	62 mg
Cholesterol	0	Added Sugar	32 Cal
		Fiber	2 g

Shredded Turnips

Preparation: **12 min.** Cooking: **41 min.** FAT SUGAR SODIUM

1 tablespoon unsalted margarine
1 small yellow onion, finely chopped
4 medium-size turnips (about 1 pound), peeled and coarsely shredded
½ cup low-sodium beef or chicken broth
1 tablespoon sugar
⅛ teaspoon black pepper

1. In a heavy 10-inch skillet, melt the **margarine** over low heat. Add the **onion** and cook, uncovered, until tender and beginning to brown—about 10 minutes.

2. Stir in the **turnips, beef broth, sugar,** and **pepper;** cover and cook over moderate heat for 30 minutes or until the turnips are tender. Serves 4.

One Serving:

Calories	68	Protein	1 g
Total Fat	3 g	Carbohydrates	10 g
Saturated Fat	1 g	Sodium	63 mg
Cholesterol	0	Added Sugar	4 Cal
		Fiber	2 g

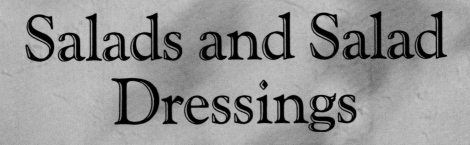

Salads and Salad Dressings

Salads aren't just for summer, and they can be much more interesting than a just a few lettuce leaves tossed with tomato wedges. The recipes in this chapter will surprise you with their variety. Most of them, like Spinach-Orange Salad, can be served as an appetizer or with the meal. Others, like Dilled Shrimp and Feta Cheese Salad, are meals in themselves. All are easily halved to serve two. You'll also find low-calorie versions of some of your favorite dressings, including Blue Cheese, Thousand Island, and Vinaigrette.

Salade Niçoise

Asparagus Vinaigrette

Preparation: **10 min.**, plus 2 hr. refrigeration   Cooking: **4 min.**

FAT SUGAR SODIUM

As the variations of this recipe show, almost any vegetable can be turned into an appetizing salad by marinating it for a few hours in a vinaigrette dressing.

1½ **pounds asparagus, tough stems removed**
2½ **teaspoons olive or vegetable oil**
¾ **teaspoon finely chopped shallot or green onion**
½ **teaspoon Dijon or spicy brown mustard**
    Pinch black pepper
1½ **teaspoons white wine vinegar or white vinegar**

1. In a heavy 12-inch skillet, bring an inch of unsalted water to a boil. Add the **asparagus** and cook, covered, for 3 minutes or until just tender. Drain, rinse under cold water to stop the cooking, and drain again.

2. In a medium-size shallow dish, combine the **olive oil, shallot, mustard,** and **pepper.** Add the cooked asparagus and toss gently to coat the spears.

3. Cover the dish and refrigerate for 2 to 3 hours, tossing occasionally. Just before serving, add the **vinegar** and toss again. Serves 4.

Variations:

Broccoli Vinaigrette   Prepare as above, substituting 2 cups broccoli florets for the asparagus. For the dressing, combine 2½ teaspoons olive or vegetable oil, ½ teaspoon grated lemon rind, and a pinch of black pepper. Just before serving, add 1½ teaspoons lemon juice and toss well.

Cauliflower Vinaigrette   Prepare as above, substituting 2 cups small cauliflower florets for the asparagus. For the dressing, combine 2½ teaspoons walnut, olive, or vegetable oil, 2¼ teaspoons orange juice, and ½ teaspoon grated orange rind. Just before serving, add 1½ teaspoons white wine vinegar and 2 teaspoons minced parsley and toss well.

Green Beans Vinaigrette   Prepare as above, substituting 2 cups trimmed green beans for the asparagus. For the dressing, combine 2½ teaspoons walnut, olive, or vegetable oil, ½ teaspoon dried thyme, and a pinch of black pepper. Just before serving, add 1½ teaspoons tarragon-flavored or white wine vinegar; toss well.

Zucchini Vinaigrette   Substitute 2 cups thinly sliced zucchini for the asparagus. For the dressing, combine 2½ teaspoons olive or vegetable oil, 1 teaspoon minced fresh ginger (or ⅛ teaspoon ground ginger), and a pinch of black pepper. Just before serving, add 1½ teaspoons balsamic or white wine vinegar and toss well.

One Serving:

Calories	46	Protein	3 g
Total Fat	3 g	Carbohydrates	4 g
Saturated Fat	0	Sodium	20 mg
Cholesterol	0	Added Sugar	0
		Fiber	1 g

Green Bean-Zucchini Salad

½ **pound green beans, trimmed and snapped in two**
2½ **teaspoons olive or vegetable oil**
1 **clove garlic, minced**
½ **teaspoon dried tarragon, crumbled**
⅛ **teaspoon black pepper**
1 **small zucchini (about ¼ pound), cut into matchstick strips**
1 **small red onion, sliced thin**
1½ **teaspoons tarragon-flavored vinegar**

1. In a small saucepan with enough boiling unsalted water to cover, cook the **green beans** until tender but still crisp—3 to 4 minutes. Drain in a colander, rinse under cold running water to stop the cooking, and drain again.

2. In a medium-size bowl, combine the **olive oil, garlic, tarragon,** and **pepper.** Add the green beans, **zucchini,** and **onion** and toss well. Cover and chill in the refrigerator for 2 to 3 hours, tossing occasionally.

3. Just before serving, add the **vinegar** and toss again. Serves 4.

FAT SUGAR SODIUM

Preparation: **25 min.**, plus 2 hr. refrigeration Cooking: **4 min.**

One Serving:

Calories	50
Total Fat	3 g
Saturated Fat	0
Cholesterol	0
Protein	1 g
Carbohydrates	6 g
Sodium	4 mg
Added Sugar	0
Fiber	2 g

Four-Bean Salad

Here is a simple salad that can be made hours in advance. Using canned beans makes the dish a snap, but for more flavor (and less sodium), cook your own.

FAT SUGAR SODIUM

2 **medium-size sweet red peppers**

¼ **pound green beans, trimmed and snapped in two**

1 **small red onion, halved and sliced thin**

1 **cup cooked and drained black beans**

1 **cup cooked and drained white beans**

1 **cup cooked and drained kidney beans**

2 **tablespoons olive oil**

2 **tablespoons lemon juice**

¼ **teaspoon black pepper**

2 **tablespoons minced parsley**

Preparation:
10 min., plus 2 hr. refrigeration
Cooking:
7 min.

One Serving:

Calories	*132*
Total Fat	*4 g*
Saturated Fat	*0*
Cholesterol	*0*
Protein	*6 g*
Carbohydrates	*19 g*
Sodium	*8 mg*
Added Sugar	*0*
Fiber	*3 g*

1. Preheat the broiler. Lay the **red peppers** on the broiler pan rack and broil 6 inches from the heat, turning them 3 times, until they are charred all over—5 to 8 minutes. Place the peppers in a paper bag, set in a bowl, and allow to cool for about 5 minutes; this will make them easy to peel.

2. Peel and core the peppers over the bowl, reserving any juice. Discard the seeds, slice the peppers lengthwise into strips ½ inch thick, and set aside.

3. In a small saucepan with enough boiling unsalted water to cover, cook the **green beans** for 2 minutes or until tender but still crisp. Drain in a colander, rinse under cold running water, and drain again.

4. In a large bowl, combine the **onion, black beans, white beans,** and **kidney beans.** Add the red peppers, their juice, and the green beans. Add the **olive oil** and **lemon juice,** sprinkle with the **black pepper** and **parsley,** and stir gently to mix. Cover and chill in the refrigerator for at least 2 hours. Serves 8.

Four-Bean Salad

Bean Sprout Salad

This crunchy salad adds an Oriental touch to a meal. Use the bacon bits labeled "real," not the imitation ones; they have better flavor and much less sodium.

FAT SUGAR SODIUM

2 cups bean sprouts
2¾ teaspoons Oriental sesame or peanut oil
1 green onion, chopped
1 teaspoon low-sodium ketchup
¾ teaspoon bacon bits
1 clove garlic, minced
½ teaspoon minced fresh ginger or pinch ground ginger

⅛ teaspoon salt
2 tablespoons chopped canned pimientos
1½ teaspoons lemon juice
1½ teaspoons rice vinegar or white wine vinegar

Preparation:
10 min., plus 2 hr. refrigeration
Cooking:
1 min.

One Serving:

Calories	53
Total Fat	4 g
Saturated Fat	1 g
Cholesterol	1 mg
Protein	2 g
Carbohydrates	4 g
Sodium	86 mg
Added Sugar	0
Fiber	2 g

1. Place the **bean sprouts** in a colander and rinse under hot tap water just until slightly limp—about 1 minute. Drain well and dry thoroughly between paper towels. Set aside.
2. In a small saucepan over low heat, combine the **sesame oil, green onion, ketchup, bacon bits, garlic, ginger,** and **salt;** cook, stirring, about 1 minute or until the mixture starts to bubble. Remove from the heat.
3. In a medium-size bowl, combine the bean sprouts and **pimiento.** Add the contents of the saucepan and toss well. Cover and chill in the refrigerator for 2 to 3 hours, tossing occasionally.
4. Just before serving, stir in the **lemon juice** and **vinegar** and toss again. Serves 4.

Sesame Broccoli Salad

FAT SUGAR SODIUM

1 tablespoon sesame seeds
1½ pounds broccoli, cut into florets, with stems peeled and coarsely chopped
1 tablespoon reduced-sodium soy sauce

2 tablespoons rice vinegar or white wine vinegar
2 teaspoons Oriental sesame or peanut oil
1 teaspoon honey

Preparation:
10 min.
Cooking:
10 min.

One Serving:

Calories	82
Total Fat	4 g
Saturated Fat	1 g
Cholesterol	0
Protein	5 g
Carbohydrates	10 g
Sodium	190 mg
Added Sugar	4 Cal
Fiber	4 g

1. To toast the **sesame seeds,** preheat the oven to 325°F. Spread the sesame seeds in a pie pan and bake, uncovered, shaking the pan frequently, until the seeds are golden—about 10 minutes. Set aside.
2. Meanwhile, bring about 2 cups unsalted water to a boil in a large heavy saucepan. Add the **broccoli,** cover, and cook for 5 minutes or until tender but still crisp. Drain in a colander, rinse under under cold running water to stop the cooking, and drain again. Transfer to a serving dish.
3. Combine the **soy sauce, vinegar, sesame oil,** and **honey.** Pour over the broccoli and toss well. Sprinkle with the sesame seeds and serve. Serves 4.

Variation:

Broccoli Salad with Garlic and Marjoram Cook the broccoli as directed, reserving 2 tablespoons of the cooking water. For the dressing, combine 4 teaspoons olive oil with the 2 tablespoons cooking water and add 2 tablespoons red wine vinegar. Add 1 minced clove garlic, 1 teaspoon minced fresh marjoram (or ½ teaspoon crumbled dried marjoram), and ¼ teaspoon black pepper. Mix well. Pour over the broccoli and toss well. Omit the sesame seeds.

Bean Sprout Salad

Pickled Beet Salad

6 medium-size beets (about 1½ pounds), scrubbed, with all but 2 inches of the tops removed, or 1 can (1 pound) beets, with ½ cup of their liquid
½ cup cider vinegar
2 teaspoons sugar
2 teaspoons prepared horseradish, drained

1 teaspoon Dijon or spicy brown mustard
6 black peppercorns
4 whole cloves
1 bay leaf
2 green onions, including tops, chopped
1 tablespoon snipped fresh dill or minced parsley

FAT SUGAR SODIUM

Preparation: **10 min.**, plus 2 hr. refrigeration
Cooking: **35 min.**

One Serving:

Calories	68
Total Fat	0
Saturated Fat	0
Cholesterol	0
Protein	2 g
Carbohydrates	5 g
Sodium	123 mg
Added Sugar	8 Cal
Fiber	1 g

1. In a large heavy saucepan, bring 2 quarts unsalted water to a boil; add the **beets** and cook, uncovered, over moderate heat for 30 to 35 minutes or until tender. Drain, reserving ½ cup of the cooking water. As soon as the beets are cool enough to handle, trim, peel, and cut into slices ¼ inch thick. Place the beets in a medium-size heatproof bowl and set aside.

2. In a small heavy saucepan over moderate heat, bring the ½ cup beet liquid and the **vinegar, sugar, horseradish, mustard, peppercorns, cloves,** and **bay leaf** to a boil. Pour the mixture over the beets and cool to room temperature. Cover and chill in the refrigerator for at least 2 hours.

3. Just before serving, remove the bay leaf, sprinkle the beets with the **green onions** and **dill,** and toss well to mix. Serves 4.

Variation:

Pickled Carrot Salad   Prepare as directed, substituting 3 cups thinly sliced cooked carrots (about 1½ pounds) for the beets. For the salad dressing, substitute 1 teaspoon each horseradish and curry powder for the 2 teaspoons horseradish.

Tip: *If you buy beets by the bunch, save the nutritious greens and cook them as you would spinach. Or tear tender young beet greens into bite-size pieces and mix with lettuce in a tossed salad.*

Sweet-and-Sour Red Cabbage and Apple Salad

Sweet-and-Sour Red Cabbage and Apple Salad

1 medium-size head red cabbage (about 1½ pounds), cored and sliced thin

1 large tart apple, peeled, cored, and cut into ½-inch cubes

1 small sweet green pepper, cored, seeded, and sliced lengthwise into strips about ¼ inch wide

1 small yellow onion, chopped fine

½ cup red wine vinegar

1 tablespoon honey

½ teaspoon caraway seeds

⅛ teaspoon each black pepper and ground cloves

1. In a large heatproof bowl, combine the **cabbage, apple, green pepper,** and **onion** and toss well to mix; set aside.

2. In a small saucepan over moderate heat, cook and stir the **vinegar, honey, caraway seeds, black pepper,** and **cloves** until the mixture just begins to boil—about 1 minute.

3. Pour the hot mixture over the salad and toss well. Let stand at room temperature for 30 minutes before serving. Serves 4.

FAT SUGAR SODIUM

Preparation: **15 min.,** plus 30 min. marination
Cooking: **1 min.**

One Serving:

Calories	77
Total Fat	*1 g*
Saturated Fat	*0*
Cholesterol	*0*
Protein	*2 g*
Carbohydrates	*21 g*
Sodium	*16 mg*
Added Sugar	*16 Cal*
Fiber	*2 g*

Creamy Yogurt Coleslaw

Here is a low-calorie version of the traditional mayonnaise-based coleslaw.

3 tablespoons plain low-fat yogurt

2 tablespoons sour cream

¾ teaspoon prepared yellow mustard

½ teaspoon sugar

½ teaspoon cider vinegar

¼ teaspoon celery seeds

⅛ teaspoon salt

⅛ teaspoon black pepper

1¾ cups coarsely shredded cabbage

¼ cup coarsely grated carrot

In a medium-size bowl, combine the **yogurt, sour cream, mustard, sugar, vinegar, celery seeds, salt,** and **pepper.** Add the **cabbage** and **carrot** and toss well to mix. Cover and chill in the refrigerator for 2 to 3 hours, tossing occasionally. Serves 4.

FAT SUGAR SODIUM

Preparation: **15 min.,** plus 2 hr. refrigeration

One Serving:

Calories	37
Total Fat	*2 g*
Saturated Fat	*1 g*
Cholesterol	*4 mg*
Protein	*1 g*
Carbohydrates	*4 g*
Sodium	*101 mg*
Added Sugar	*2 Cal*
Fiber	*1 g*

Confetti Coleslaw

A colorful combination of red and green cabbage and sweet peppers, this festive dish is easily doubled or tripled to serve at a party.

¼ **cup plain low-fat yogurt**
2 **tablespoons buttermilk**
2 **teaspoons grated yellow onion**
2 **teaspoons prepared yellow mustard**
1 **teaspoon sugar**
¼ **teaspoon caraway seeds**
¼ **teaspoon black pepper**
⅛ **teaspoon dill weed**
¾ **cup coarsely shredded green cabbage**

½ **cup coarsely shredded red cabbage**
¼ **small sweet green pepper, cored, seeded, and sliced lengthwise into ¼-inch strips**
¼ **small sweet red pepper, cored, seeded, and sliced lengthwise into ¼-inch strips**
½ **small carrot, peeled and coarsely grated**

Preparation: **15 min.**, plus 2 hr. refrigeration

One Serving:

Calories	30
Total Fat	1 g
Saturated Fat	0
Cholesterol	1 mg
Protein	2 g
Carbohydrates	5 g
Sodium	57 mg
Added Sugar	4 Cal
Fiber	0

In a large bowl, combine the **yogurt, buttermilk, onion, mustard, sugar, caraway seeds, black pepper,** and **dill weed.** Add the **green cabbage, red cabbage, green pepper, red pepper,** and **carrot;** toss well. Cover and chill in the refrigerator for 2 to 3 hours, tossing occasionally. Serves 4.

Crunchy Carrot Salad

This blend of crunchy vegetables and herbs makes a perfect summer salad. Use the sweet Nantes-type carrots, if available.

5 **medium-size carrots (about 10 ounces), peeled and cut into matchstick strips**
2½ **teaspoons olive or vegetable oil**
¼ **teaspoon each dried marjoram and thyme, crumbled**
⅛ **teaspoon dried rosemary, crumbled**
Pinch black pepper

½ **small zucchini, cut into matchstick strips**
½ **small stalk celery, cut into matchstick strips**
1 **small canned pimiento, cut into matchstick strips**
1½ **teaspoons lemon juice**

Preparation:
20 min., plus 2 hr. refrigeration
Cooking:
3 min.

One Serving:

Calories	70
Total Fat	3 g
Saturated Fat	0
Cholesterol	0
Protein	1 g
Carbohydrates	11 g
Sodium	40 mg
Added Sugar	0
Fiber	1 g

1. In a small saucepan with just enough boiling unsalted water to cover, cook the **carrots** for 2 to 3 minutes. Drain in a colander, rinse under cold running water to stop the cooking, and drain again.

2. In a medium-size bowl, combine the **olive oil, marjoram, thyme, rosemary,** and **pepper.** Add the carrots, **zucchini, celery,** and **pimiento** and toss well. Cover and chill in the refrigerator for 2 to 3 hours, tossing occasionally.

3. Just before serving, stir in the **lemon juice** and toss again. Serves 4.

Variations:

Jerusalem Artichoke Salad Substitute 3 or 4 medium-size Jerusalem artichokes (about 10 ounces), peeled and cut into matchstick strips, for the carrots. Substitute yellow squash for the zucchini and proceed as directed.

Succotash Salad Substitute 1 package (10 ounces) frozen baby limas for the carrots. Substitute 1 package (10 ounces) frozen whole-kernel corn for the zucchini. Slice the celery crosswise and proceed as directed.

Corn and Cherry Tomato Salad

¼ cup plain low-fat yogurt

2 tablespoons low-sodium ketchup

1 teaspoon prepared mustard

2 green onions, including tops, chopped

2 tablespoons snipped fresh dill or ½ teaspoon dill weed

2 cups fresh or frozen whole-kernel corn

10 cherry tomatoes, halved

1 small sweet green pepper, cored, seeded, and chopped

4 large lettuce leaves

Preparation: **12 min.**
Cooking: **3 min.**

One Serving:

Calories	92
Total Fat	*1 g*
Saturated Fat	0
Cholesterol	*1 mg*
Protein	*4 g*
Carbohydrates	*19 g*
Sodium	*49 mg*
Added Sugar	0
Fiber	*2 g*

1. Combine the **yogurt, ketchup,** and **mustard** in a large bowl; stir in the **green onions** and **dill** and set aside.

2. Bring 2 cups unsalted water to a boil in a small saucepan; add the **corn** and cook for 45 seconds or until just tender. Drain in a colander, rinse under cold running water to stop the cooking, and drain again. Add the dressing, along with the **cherry tomatoes** and **green pepper,** and toss well to mix.

3. Place the **lettuce** on plates and spoon the corn mixture on top. Serves 4.

Minted Cucumber Salad

¼ cup plain low-fat yogurt

1 tablespoon minced fresh mint or ¼ teaspoon mint flakes

1 teaspoon olive oil

¼ teaspoon sugar

⅛ teaspoon salt

⅛ teaspoon black pepper

2 large cucumbers, peeled, halved lengthwise, seeded, and sliced ¼ inch thick (about 2 cups)

Preparation: **10 min.,**
plus 2 hr. refrigeration

One Serving:

Calories	40
Total Fat	*1 g*
Saturated Fat	0
Cholesterol	*1 mg*
Protein	*2 g*
Carbohydrates	*6 g*
Sodium	*88 mg*
Added Sugar	*1 Cal*
Fiber	*1 g*

In a medium-size bowl, combine the **yogurt, mint, olive oil, sugar, salt,** and **pepper.** Add the **cucumbers** and toss well. Cover and chill in the refrigerator for 2 to 3 hours, tossing occasionally. Serves 4.

Spiced Cucumber and Sweet Red Pepper Salad

¼ cup plain low-fat yogurt

2 teaspoons Oriental sesame or peanut oil

¾ teaspoon cider vinegar

½ teaspoon minced fresh ginger or ⅛ teaspoon ground ginger

¼ teaspoon each ground cumin and coriander

1 large cucumber, peeled, halved lengthwise, seeded, and cut into matchstick strips

1 small sweet red pepper, cored, seeded, and cut into matchstick strips

Preparation: **10 min.,**
plus 2 hr. refrigeration

One Serving:

Calories	43
Total Fat	*3 g*
Saturated Fat	*1 g*
Cholesterol	*1 mg*
Protein	*1 g*
Carbohydrates	*4 g*
Sodium	*15 mg*
Added Sugar	0
Fiber	*1 g*

In a medium-size bowl, combine the **yogurt, sesame oil, vinegar, ginger, cumin,** and **coriander.** Add the **cucumber** and **red pepper** and toss well. Cover and chill in the refrigerator for 2 to 3 hours, tossing occasionally. Serves 4.

Corn and Cherry Tomato Salad

Oriental Mushroom Salad

Preparation: **6 min.,** plus 2 hr. marination

FAT SUGAR SODIUM

- 2 **teaspoons honey**
- 2 **teaspoons reduced-sodium soy sauce**
- ¼ **teaspoon ground ginger**
- 2 **teaspoons red wine vinegar**
- 2 **teaspoons Oriental sesame or peanut oil**
- 1 **clove garlic, bruised**
- ½ **pound mushrooms, sliced thin**
- 1 **small sweet red pepper, cored, seeded, and chopped**
- 2 **teaspoons minced fresh coriander or parsley**
- 1 **teaspoon toasted sesame seeds (optional)**

1. In a large bowl, whisk together the **honey, soy sauce, ginger, vinegar,** and **sesame oil.** Add the **garlic, mushrooms,** and **red pepper** and toss well. Cover and refrigerate for 2 hours.
2. Remove and discard the garlic clove. Transfer the salad to a serving platter and sprinkle with the **coriander.** Sprinkle with the **sesame seeds,** if you wish, and serve. *(Note: To toast sesame seeds, preheat the oven to 325°F. Spread the sesame seeds in a pie pan and bake, uncovered, shaking the pan frequently, until the seeds are golden—about 10 minutes.)* Serves 4.

Variation:

Mushroom Salad with Bean Sprouts   Omit the sweet red pepper. Add 3 green onions, sliced, with tops included, and ½ cup drained bean sprouts. Proceed as directed.

One Serving:			
Calories	52	Protein	2 g
Total Fat	3 g	Carbohydrates	7 g
Saturated Fat	0	Sodium	105 mg
Cholesterol	0	Added Sugar	11 Cal
		Fiber	2 g

Tip: *Because mushrooms darken quickly once they are cut, you should wait until the last minute to slice them in a salad. If you can't use them immediately, brush the cut surfaces with lemon juice or vinegar.*

Spinach-Orange Salad

German Potato Salad

4 medium-size all-purpose
  potatoes (about 1 pound)
1 slice lean bacon
1 small yellow onion, chopped
  fine
1 medium-size sweet green
  pepper, cored, seeded, and
  chopped fine
1 medium-size stalk celery,
  chopped fine

½ cup water
⅓ cup cider vinegar
1 tablespoon sugar
2 teaspoons flour
¼ teaspoon black pepper
2 large hard-cooked egg whites,
  chopped
2 tablespoons minced parsley

Preparation:
15 min.
Cooking:
22 min.

One Serving:

Calories	115
Total Fat	1 g
Saturated Fat	0
Cholesterol	1 mg
Protein	5 g
Carbohydrates	23 g
Sodium	66 mg
Added Sugar	12 Cal
Fiber	2 g

1. Place the **potatoes** in a medium-size heavy saucepan, add enough unsalted
   water to cover, and bring to a boil over moderately high heat. Cover and
   cook until the potatoes are tender—about 20 minutes.

2. Meanwhile, cook the **bacon** in a heavy 7-inch skillet over moderate heat
   until crisp and brown—3 to 4 minutes. Remove the bacon and drain on a
   paper towel; cool, then crumble and set aside.

3. When the potatoes are done, drain them and let them stand until cool
   enough to handle. Peel the potatoes, cut into ¾-inch cubes, and place in a
   large bowl. Add the **onion, green pepper,** and **celery** and set aside.

4. In a small heavy saucepan, combine the **water, vinegar, sugar, flour,** and
   black pepper; set over moderate heat and whisk until the mixture just
   comes to a boil—2 to 3 minutes.

5. Pour the hot dressing over the salad and toss well. Cool to room
   temperature, then sprinkle with the reserved bacon, the chopped **egg
   whites,** and the minced **parsley.** Serves 4.

*Tip: Always add
dressing to a potato
salad while the
potatoes are still fairly
hot; they absorb more
flavor this way.*

Spinach-Orange Salad

Preparation: **20 min.**, plus 2 hr.
refrigeration

- **2 teaspoons olive, vegetable, or hazelnut oil**
- **½ teaspoon dried marjoram, crumbled**
- **Pinch black pepper**
- **Pinch ground nutmeg**
- **½ cup coarsely chopped orange sections**
- **2 medium-size radishes, trimmed and sliced thin**
- **1 green onion, including top, chopped**
- **½ pound fresh spinach, trimmed**
- **1¼ teaspoons rice vinegar or white wine vinegar**

1. In a medium-size bowl, combine the **olive oil, marjoram, pepper,** and **nutmeg.** Add the **orange sections, radishes,** and **green onion,** and toss well. Cover and chill in the refrigerator for 2 to 3 hours, tossing occasionally.
2. Wash the **spinach,** pat it dry with paper towels, and tear it into bite-size pieces. Just before serving, add the spinach and **vinegar** to the chilled ingredients and toss well. Serves 4.

One Serving:

Calories	41	Protein	1 g
Total Fat	2 g	Carbohydrates	4 g
Saturated Fat	0	Sodium	33 mg
Cholesterol	0	Added Sugar	0
		Fiber	2 g

Wilted Spinach Salad

Preparation: **10 min.** Cooking: **6 min.**

- **1 pound fresh spinach, trimmed, or iceberg lettuce, escarole, or chicory**
- **1 slice lean bacon**
- **1 medium-size sweet red, yellow, or green pepper, cored, seeded, and sliced lengthwise into strips about ¼ inch wide**
- **1 small red onion, chopped fine**
- **1 clove garlic, minced**
- **¼ cup dry white wine**
- **¼ cup cider vinegar**
- **¼ teaspoon sugar**
- **⅛ teaspoon black pepper**

1. Wash the **spinach,** pat it dry with paper towels, and tear it into bite-size pieces. Place in a large salad bowl and set aside.

2. In a heavy 7-inch skillet over moderate heat, cook the **bacon** until crisp—3 to 4 minutes; remove the bacon and drain on a paper towel.
3. Discard all but 1 tablespoon of the bacon drippings. Add the **red pepper, onion,** and **garlic** to the hot drippings, and cook, stirring, over moderate heat for 2 minutes. Add the **wine, vinegar, sugar,** and **black pepper;** bring to a boil, then reduce the heat and simmer, uncovered, for 1 minute.
4. Pour the hot dressing over the spinach and toss well. Crumble the reserved bacon over the top and serve. Serves 4.

One Serving:

Calories	71	Protein	3 g
Total Fat	4 g	Carbohydrates	5 g
Saturated Fat	1 g	Sodium	108 mg
Cholesterol	4 mg	Added Sugar	1 Cal
		Fiber	3 g

Italian Bread and Tomato Salad

Preparation: **6 min.**, plus 2 hr. FAT SUGAR SODIUM
refrigeration

- **1½ pounds ripe plum tomatoes, cored and cut into ½-inch cubes**
- **1 small cucumber, peeled, halved lengthwise, seeded, and cut into ½-inch cubes**
- **½ small red onion, sliced thin**
- **3 tablespoons balsamic or red wine vinegar**
- **2 teaspoons olive oil**
- **2 cloves garlic, bruised**
- **3 slices stale crusty bread, each 1 inch thick and cut into 1-inch squares**
- **2 tablespoons minced fresh basil or 1 teaspoon dried basil, crumbled**

1. Place the **tomatoes, cucumber,** and **onion** in a large bowl, sprinkle with the **vinegar** and **olive oil,** and toss well to mix. Add the **garlic, bread,** and **basil,** and toss again. Cover and chill in the refrigerator for 2 hours.
2. About 20 minutes before serving, remove the salad from the refrigerator and discard the garlic. Toss well again. Serves 4.

One Serving:

Calories	120	Protein	4 g
Total Fat	3 g	Carbohydrates	21 g
Saturated Fat	0	Sodium	140 mg
Cholesterol	0	Added Sugar	0
		Fiber	1 g

Roasted Vegetable Salad

Serve this salad warm or cold. The roasted garlic has a mild, nutty taste quite different from that of raw garlic, so don't hesitate to use the entire head.

FAT SUGAR SODIUM

1 bulb (entire head) garlic
1 medium-size sweet green pepper, cored, seeded, and sliced lengthwise into strips about 1 inch wide
1 medium-size sweet red pepper, cored, seeded, and sliced lengthwise into strips about 1 inch wide
1 medium-size sweet yellow pepper, cored, seeded, and sliced lengthwise into strips about 1 inch wide
1 large yellow onion, sliced ½ inch thick

3 tablespoons olive or vegetable oil
1 teaspoon dried oregano, crumbled
½ teaspoon ground cumin
¼ teaspoon black pepper
1 medium-size ripe tomato, cored and cut into 1-inch cubes
1 tablespoon lime juice
2 tablespoons chopped parsley

Preparation:
15 min.
Cooking:
30 min. (mostly unattended)

One Serving:

Calories	*140*
Total Fat	*11 g*
Saturated Fat	*1 g*
Cholesterol	*0*
Protein	*2 g*
Carbohydrates	*11 g*
Sodium	*7 mg*
Added Sugar	*0*
Fiber	*1 g*

1. Preheat the oven to 400°F. Separate the **garlic** into individual cloves and peel. Place in an ungreased 13"x 9"x 2" baking pan along with the **green pepper, red pepper, yellow pepper, onion, olive oil, oregano, cumin,** and **black pepper.** Stir to mix.
2. Place the uncovered pan in the oven and roast the vegetables for 15 minutes, stirring 2 or 3 times. Stir in the **tomato** and roast, uncovered, 15 minutes more, again stirring 2 or 3 times.
3. Stir in the **lime juice,** transfer the vegetables to a serving dish, and sprinkle with the **parsley.** Serves 4.

Tip: The small, rose-skinned variety of garlic has the strongest flavor. Large-cloved "elephant" garlic is considerably milder.

Marinated Vegetable Salad

Use walnut oil to make this colorful salad even more special.

FAT SUGAR SODIUM

3 medium-size asparagus spears, tough stems removed, cut diagonally into 1-inch pieces
1 small yellow squash (about ¼ pound), cut diagonally into ¼-inch slices
½ cup small cauliflower florets
1 medium-size carrot, peeled and cut diagonally into ¼-inch slices

2½ teaspoons olive, vegetable, or walnut oil
1 teaspoon finely chopped shallot or green onion
½ teaspoon dried thyme, crumbled
Pinch black pepper
½ small red onion, sliced thin
1½ teaspoons balsamic or red wine vinegar

Preparation:
15 min., plus 2 hr. refrigeration
Cooking:
12 min.

One Serving:

Calories	*47*
Total Fat	*3 g*
Saturated Fat	*0*
Cholesterol	*0*
Protein	*1 g*
Carbohydrates	*5 g*
Sodium	*9 mg*
Added Sugar	*0*
Fiber	*1 g*

1. In a large saucepan, bring 2 quarts unsalted water to a boil. Add the **asparagus, squash, cauliflower,** and **carrot,** and cook for 2 minutes. Drain, rinse under cold running water to stop the cooking, and drain again.
2. In a medium-size bowl, combine the **olive oil, shallot, thyme,** and **pepper.** Add the hot vegetables and the **onion** and toss well. Cover and chill in the refrigerator for 2 to 3 hours, tossing occasionally.
3. Just before serving, stir in the **vinegar** and toss well. Serves 4.

Marinated Vegetable Salad

Greek Salad

Even though this salad has only a small amount of dressing, the combination of greens, mint, olives, and cheese makes it exceptionally flavorful.

FAT SUGAR SODIUM

½ **small head romaine lettuce**

2 **cups trimmed spinach leaves**

2 **tablespoons peeled, seeded, and chopped cucumber**

3 **tablespoons dry-curd, low-fat cottage cheese or farmer cheese**

2 **tablespoons minced fresh mint or 1½ teaspoon mint flakes**

1 **tablespoon rinsed and crumbled feta cheese**

2 **medium-size pitted ripe olives, chopped fine**

1 **teaspoon olive oil**

1 **teaspoon lemon juice**

1 **clove garlic, minced**

⅛ **teaspoon black pepper**

Preparation:
20 min.

One Serving:

Calories	*35*
Total Fat	*2 g*
Saturated Fat	*0*
Cholesterol	*2 mg*
Protein	*3 g*
Carbohydrates	*2 g*
Sodium	*54 mg*
Added Sugar	*0*
Fiber	*1 g*

1. Wash the **romaine** and **spinach** leaves, pat them dry with paper towels, and tear into bite-size pieces. Place in a large bowl with the **cucumber, cottage cheese, mint,** and **feta cheese;** set aside while preparing the dressing.

2. In a small bowl, mix the **olives, olive oil, lemon juice, garlic,** and **pepper;** whisk together until well blended. Pour the dressing over the salad, toss well, and serve. Serves 4.

Chicken Salad with Lemon and Basil

Three cups of chopped leftover roast chicken or turkey can be substituted for the chicken breasts.

FAT SUGAR SODIUM

2 cups low-sodium chicken broth

2 skinned and boned chicken breasts (about 1 pound)

¼ cup reduced-calorie mayonnaise

¼ cup plain low-fat yogurt

½ small yellow onion, chopped fine

¼ cup minced fresh basil or 1 teaspoon dried basil, crumbled

½ teaspoon finely grated lemon rind

¼ teaspoon black pepper

⅛ teaspoon sugar

6 medium-size stalks celery, chopped fine

Preparation:
25 min.
Cooking:
10 min.

One Serving:

Calories	192
Total Fat	6 g
Saturated Fat	1 g
Cholesterol	75 mg
Protein	28 g
Carbohydrates	5 g
Sodium	207 mg
Added Sugar	1 Cal
Fiber	1 g

1. In a medium-size saucepan over moderate heat, bring the **chicken broth** to a simmer. Add the **chicken** breasts, adjust the heat so that the broth bubbles gently, cover, and simmer for 10 to 12 minutes or until firm. Remove from the heat, let the breasts cool in the broth for 10 minutes, then drain, saving the broth for another use. Cut the chicken meat into bite-size pieces.

2. In a medium-size bowl, blend the **mayonnaise, yogurt, onion, basil, lemon rind, pepper,** and **sugar.** Add the chicken and **celery** and toss until well coated. Serve as a main course on lettuce leaves, or use as a sandwich filling. Serves 4.

Salade Niçoise

1 medium-size all-purpose potato

¼ pound green beans, trimmed

1 can (6½ ounces) water-packed light tuna, drained and flaked

1 small red onion, sliced thin

1 medium-size ripe tomato, cored and cut into 1-inch cubes

1 medium-size sweet green pepper, cored, seeded, and sliced lengthwise into strips about ¼ inch wide

6 medium-size pitted ripe olives, coarsely chopped

1 cup low-sodium chicken broth

¼ cup white wine vinegar

2 tablespoons lemon juice

2 tablespoons olive oil

1 clove garlic, minced

½ teaspoon Dijon or spicy brown mustard

¼ teaspoon black pepper

1 anchovy, chopped fine (optional)

1 medium-size head red-leaf or other lettuce

1 large hard-cooked egg white, chopped

FAT SUGAR SODIUM

Preparation:
20 min.
Cooking:
26 min. (mostly unattended)

One Serving:

Calories	187
Total Fat	9 g
Saturated Fat	1 g
Cholesterol	23 mg
Protein	15 g
Carbohydrates	14 g
Sodium	258 mg
Added Sugar	0
Fiber	3 g

Tip: To revive tired lettuce for a salad, soak the leaves in ice water for two minutes, then dry thoroughly with paper towels.

1. Place the **potato** in a small heavy saucepan, add enough unsalted water to cover, and bring to a boil over moderately high heat. Cover and cook until the potato is tender—about 20 minutes. Drain, then let stand until cool enough to handle. Peel the potato, cut it into ½-inch cubes, and place it in a large bowl.

2. Meanwhile, in another small heavy saucepan set over moderately high heat, cook the **green beans,** covered, in enough boiling unsalted water to cover until tender but still crisp—6 to 7 minutes; drain, rinse under cold running water to stop the cooking, and drain again. Cut the beans into 1½-inch lengths and add to the cooked potatoes along with the **tuna, onion, tomato, green pepper,** and **olives.** Toss gently to mix.

3. In a small bowl, whisk together the **chicken broth, vinegar, lemon juice, olive oil, garlic, mustard, black pepper,** and, if desired, the **anchovy.** Pour

half the dressing over the potato-tuna mixture and toss gently.

4. Wash the **lettuce,** pat it dry with paper towels, and tear the leaves into bite-size pieces. Arrange on a platter and sprinkle with 2 to 3 tablespoons of the dressing. Spoon the potato-tuna mixture on top and sprinkle with the **egg white.** Serve the remaining dressing separately. Serves 4.

Dilled Shrimp and Feta Cheese Salad

Here is a good main course for a light lunch.

FAT SUGAR SODIUM

1 pound large shrimp, shelled and deveined

3 green onions, including tops, sliced thin

½ medium-size cucumber, peeled, seeded, and chopped

1 jar (4 ounces) chopped pimientos, drained and patted dry

2 tablespoons snipped fresh dill or minced parsley

¼ cup rinsed and crumbled feta cheese (about 1 ounce)

2 tablespoons lemon juice

2 tablespoons olive oil

1 tablespoon white wine vinegar

1 teaspoon Dijon or spicy brown mustard

1 clove garlic, minced

¼ teaspoon black pepper

Preparation:
15 min.
Cooking:
7 min.

One Serving:

Calories	*193*
Total Fat	*10 g*
Saturated Fat	*2 g*
Cholesterol	*137 mg*
Protein	*21 g*
Carbohydrates	*5 g*
Sodium	*320 mg*
Added Sugar	*0*
Fiber	*0*

1. In a small heavy saucepan over moderately high heat, bring 1 quart unsalted water to a boil. Add the **shrimp** and cook, stirring, until just firm—about 2 minutes. Drain, rinse under cold running water to stop the cooking, and drain again.

2. Place the shrimp in a large bowl and add the **green onions, cucumber, pimientos, dill,** and **cheese.**

3. In a small bowl, whisk together the **lemon juice, olive oil, vinegar, mustard, garlic,** and **pepper.** Pour over the shrimp mixture and toss gently to mix. Serves 4.

Dilled Shrimp and Feta Cheese Salad

Spicy Cucumber and Fruit Salad

½ medium-size cantaloupe (about ¾ pound)

1 medium-size cucumber, peeled and sliced ¼ inch thick

½ pint strawberries, hulled and sliced ¼ inch thick

2 tablespoons lime juice

1 tablespoon vegetable oil

2 teaspoons minced hot chili peppers or ¼ teaspoon red pepper flakes

2 tablespoons chopped fresh coriander or 2 tablespoons minced parsley and ½ teaspoon ground coriander

1. With a melon baller, make 1 cup of **cantaloupe** balls. Place in a medium-size bowl, add the **cucumber** and **strawberries,** and toss.

2. Stir in the **lime juice, vegetable oil, chili peppers,** and **coriander,** and toss again. Spoon the mixture onto salad plates and serve. Serves 4.

FAT SUGAR SODIUM

Preparation: **15 min.**

One Serving:	
Calories	75
Total Fat	4 g
Saturated Fat	0
Cholesterol	0
Protein	1 g
Carbohydrates	11 g
Sodium	11 mg
Added Sugar	0
Fiber	1 g

Mixed Fruit Salad

Serve this as a lunch dish with Bran Muffins, page 240.

1 medium-size cantaloupe (about 1½ pounds), halved, seeded, sliced ¼ inch thick, and peeled

2 medium-size navel oranges, peeled and cut into ½-inch cubes

2 medium-size bananas, peeled, sliced, and sprinkled with 2 teaspoons lemon juice to prevent darkening

1 cup sliced strawberries

1 cup seedless green grapes

¾ cup plain low-fat yogurt

⅓ cup orange juice

1 tablespoon honey

1½ teaspoons grated orange rind

1 tablespoon minced fresh mint (optional)

FAT SUGAR SODIUM

Preparation: **15 min.**

One Serving:	
Calories	210
Total Fat	2 g
Saturated Fat	1 g
Cholesterol	3 mg
Protein	5 g
Carbohydrates	49 g
Sodium	40 mg
Added Sugar	12 Cal
Fiber	2 g

Citrus and Watercress Salad

1. Arrange the **cantaloupe, oranges, bananas, strawberries,** and **grapes** attractively on a large platter. Cover with plastic wrap and chill in the refrigerator until ready to serve.

2. In a small bowl, whisk together the **yogurt, orange juice, honey, orange rind,** and if you like, the **mint.** Transfer to a small pitcher and chill until ready to serve. At serving time, pass the dressing separately. Serves 4.

Waldorf Salad

3 medium-size tart apples, peeled, cored, and cut into ½-inch cubes

1 tablespoon lemon juice

1 cup seedless red or green grapes

2 medium-size stalks celery, chopped

2 medium-size green onions, chopped fine

2 tablespoons reduced-calorie mayonnaise

2 tablespoons plain low-fat yogurt

3 tablespoons apple juice

¼ teaspoon celery seeds

1 large bunch watercress (about ½ pound), stems removed

2 tablespoons chopped walnuts

FAT SUGAR SODIUM

Preparation:
20 min.

One Serving:

Calories	149
Total Fat	5 g
Saturated Fat	1 g
Cholesterol	4 mg
Protein	3 g
Carbohydrates	26 g
Sodium	82 mg
Added Sugar	0
Fiber	3 g

1. In a large bowl, toss the **apples** with the **lemon juice.** Add the **grapes, celery,** and **green onions,** and toss again.

2. In a small bowl, combine the **mayonnaise, yogurt, apple juice,** and **celery seeds,** and mix well. Spoon over the apple mixture and toss gently.

3. Wash the **watercress,** pat it dry on paper towels, and arrange it on individual salad plates. Mound the apple mixture on top, and sprinkle with the walnuts. Serves 4.

Citrus and Watercress Salad

This salad is especially good with spicy dishes, such as Curried Lamb, page 88.

6 walnut halves

1 large bunch watercress (about ½ pound), stems removed

1 large head Bibb lettuce or ½ head Boston or iceberg lettuce (about ½ pound)

2 medium-size pink grapefruits, peeled, sectioned, and seeded, with juice reserved

2 navel oranges, peeled and sectioned, with juice reserved

1 tablespoon chili sauce

1 tablespoon red wine vinegar

2 teaspoons olive oil

FAT SUGAR SODIUM

Preparation:
20 min.
Cooking:
5 min.

One Serving:

Calories	137
Total Fat	5 g
Saturated Fat	1 g
Cholesterol	0
Protein	4 g
Carbohydrates	23 g
Sodium	86 mg
Added Sugar	0
Fiber	2 g

1. Preheat the oven to 350°F. Place the **walnut** halves on an ungreased baking sheet and toast for 5 to 7 minutes in the oven. Cool, then chop coarsely.

2. Meanwhile, wash the **watercress** and **lettuce,** pat dry with paper towels, and tear into bite-size pieces. Place the **grapefruit** and **orange** sections in a large serving bowl. In a small bowl, combine the **chili sauce, vinegar, olive oil,** and 1 tablespoon each of the reserved grapefruit and orange juice; mix well. Pour the dressing over the fruit, add the watercress, lettuce, and chopped walnuts, and toss again. Serves 4.

Molded Gazpacho Salad

Here is a jelled version of the tomato-based Spanish soup. You can prepare it in a small loaf pan or in a decorative 4-cup mold.

FAT SUGAR SODIUM

2 cups low-sodium tomato juice
1 envelope unflavored gelatin
2 cloves garlic, minced
1 tablespoon red wine vinegar
¼ teaspoon hot red pepper sauce
½ medium-size sweet green pepper, cored, seeded, and chopped

½ small cucumber, peeled, halved, seeded, and chopped
½ small stalk celery, sliced
2 tablespoons chopped green onion
Lettuce leaves

Preparation:
25 min., plus 7 hr. refrigeration
Cooking:
2 min.

One Serving:

Calories	*38*
Total Fat	*0*
Saturated Fat	*0*
Cholesterol	*0*
Protein	*3 g*
Carbohydrates	*8 g*
Sodium	*31 mg*
Added Sugar	*0*
Fiber	*0*

1. Pour 1 cup of the **tomato juice** into a large heatproof bowl and sprinkle the **gelatin** over it. Let soften for 2 to 3 minutes.

2. Meanwhile, put the remaining tomato juice and the **garlic** in a small heavy saucepan and bring to a boil over moderate heat. Add to the gelatin mixture and stir until the gelatin dissolves completely. Stir in the **vinegar** and **red pepper sauce.** Chill in the refrigerator until the mixture is the consistency of unbeaten egg whites—about 1 to 1¼ hours.

3. Fold in the **green pepper, cucumber, celery,** and **green onion,** and turn into an ungreased 7½"x 3¾"x 2" loaf pan. Cover and chill for 6 hours or overnight until firm. Unmold onto a chilled platter and garnish with **lettuce leaves.** Serves 4.

Cabbage Salad Mold

Grapefruit juice gives this molded "coleslaw" a real tang.

FAT SUGAR SODIUM

2 cups grapefruit juice
1 envelope unflavored gelatin
2 tablespoons sugar
1 cup coarsely shredded green cabbage
½ cup coarsely shredded red cabbage

¼ cup shredded carrot
¼ cup coarsely chopped sweet green pepper
1½ teaspoons grated yellow onion
Lettuce leaves

Preparation:
25 min., plus 7 hr. refrigeration
Cooking:
2 min.

One Serving:

Calories	*90*
Total Fat	*0*
Saturated Fat	*0*
Cholesterol	*0*
Protein	*3 g*
Carbohydrates	*20 g*
Sodium	*10 mg*
Added Sugar	*24 Cal*
Fiber	*1 g*

1. Pour 1 cup of the **grapefruit juice** into a large heatproof bowl and sprinkle the **gelatin** over it. Let soften for 2 to 3 minutes.

2. Meanwhile, pour the remaining grapefruit juice and the **sugar** into a small heavy saucepan and bring to a boil over moderate heat, stirring occasionally to dissolve the sugar. Add to the gelatin mixture and stir until the gelatin dissolves completely. Chill in the refrigerator until the mixture is the consistency of unbeaten egg whites—about 1 to 1¼ hours.

3. Fold in the **green cabbage, red cabbage, carrot, green pepper,** and **onion,** and turn the mixture into an ungreased 4-cup decorative mold. Cover and chill for 6 hours or overnight until firm. Unmold onto a chilled platter and garnish with **lettuce leaves.** Serves 4.

Molded Gazpacho Salad

Cranberry-Pear Mold

This brilliant, deep red fruit mold makes a nice addition to the Thanksgiving table or to any autumn menu.

FAT SUGAR SODIUM

2 **cups cranberry juice cocktail**

1 **envelope unflavored gelatin**

¼ **cup cranberries, rinsed and cut in half**

2 **tablespoons sugar**

1 **medium-size pear, peeled, cored, and cut into ¾-inch cubes**

1 **tablespoon coarsely chopped pecans**

Lettuce leaves

Preparation:
20 min., plus 7 hr. refrigeration
Cooking:
2 min.

One Serving:

Calories	143
Total Fat	1 g
Saturated Fat	0
Cholesterol	0
Protein	2 g
Carbohydrates	32 g
Sodium	5 mg
Added Sugar	62 Cal
Fiber	1 g

1. Pour 1 cup of the **cranberry juice** into a large heatproof bowl and sprinkle the **gelatin** over it. Let soften for 2 to 3 minutes.

2. Meanwhile, pour the remaining cranberry juice into a small heavy saucepan and bring to a boil over moderate heat. Add to the gelatin mixture and stir until the gelatin dissolves completely. Chill in the refrigerator until the mixture is the consistency of unbeaten egg whites—about 1 to 1¼ hours.

3. While the mixture is chilling, toss the **cranberries** with the **sugar** and set aside for at least 30 minutes, tossing occasionally.

4. Just before removing the gelatin mixture from the refrigerator, place the cranberries in a large-holed strainer and shake the excess sugar from them. Fold the cranberries into the gelatin mixture along with the **pear** and **pecans;** turn into an ungreased 4-cup decorative mold. Cover and chill for 6 hours or overnight until firm. Unmold onto a chilled platter and garnish with **lettuce leaves.** Serves 4.

Savory Rice Salad

Preparation: **5 min.** Cooking: **20 min.** FAT SUGAR SODIUM

The addition of chicken makes this a main course.

1 cup long-grain rice
2 medium-size carrots, peeled and coarsely shredded
1 medium-size cucumber, peeled, halved lengthwise, seeded, and sliced ¼ inch thick
3 green onions, sliced thin
1 cup chopped cooked chicken
1 tablespoon Oriental sesame or peanut oil
1 tablespoon peanut oil
4 teaspoons rice vinegar or white wine vinegar
¼ teaspoon sugar
2 tablespoons minced fresh coriander or parsley

1. In a medium-size saucepan, cook the **rice** according to package directions, omitting the salt. Transfer to a large bowl and add the **carrots, cucumber, green onions,** and **chicken;** toss well to mix.

2. In a small bowl, whisk together the **sesame oil, peanut oil, vinegar,** and **sugar.** Pour over the rice mixture, sprinkle with the **coriander,** and toss well again. Serves 4.

One Serving:

Calories	330	Protein	14 g
Total Fat	9 g	Carbohydrates	46 g
Saturated Fat	2 g	Sodium	49 mg
Cholesterol	31 mg	Added Sugar	1 Cal
		Fiber	1 g

Summer Pasta Salad

Preparation: **10 min.** Cooking: **8 min.** FAT SUGAR SODIUM

4 ounces tiny pasta shells, elbow macaroni, or ditalini
4 teaspoons olive oil
¼ cup minced fresh basil or parsley
⅛ teaspoon black pepper
1 small red onion, chopped fine
1 medium-size cucumber, peeled, seeded, and chopped
1 large ripe tomato, cored, seeded, and cut into ½-inch cubes

1. In a large saucepan, cook the **pasta** according to package directions, omitting the salt. Drain, rinse under cold running water to stop the

cooking, and drain again. Transfer the pasta to a large bowl; add the **olive oil, basil,** and **pepper,** and toss well to mix.

2. Add the **onion, cucumber,** and **tomato,** and toss well again. Serve at room temperature. Serves 4.

One Serving:

Calories	164	Protein	4 g
Total Fat	5 g	Carbohydrates	26 g
Saturated Fat	1 g	Sodium	8 mg
Cholesterol	0	Added Sugar	0
		Fiber	1 g

Tabouleh

Preparation: **8 min.,**
plus 30 min. soaking time   FAT SUGAR SODIUM

Here is a refreshing salad of Middle Eastern origin.

1 cup bulgur
2 cups boiling water
4 teaspoons lemon juice
2 teaspoons olive oil
2 medium-size ripe tomatoes, cored, seeded, and chopped, or 1 cup canned low-sodium tomatoes, drained and chopped
¼ cup minced fresh mint or 1 tablespoon mint flakes
3 tablespoons minced parsley
½ small red onion, sliced thin
2 green onions, including tops, chopped fine
¼ teaspoon each ground coriander and cumin
⅛ teaspoon hot red pepper sauce

1. Place the **bulgur** in a large heatproof bowl and pour the boiling **water** over it. Cover and let stand for 30 minutes. Drain off any liquid that remains.

2. In another large bowl, mix the **lemon juice, olive oil, tomatoes, mint, parsley, red onion, green onions, coriander, cumin,** and **red pepper sauce.** Add the bulgur and toss well to mix. Serves 6.

One Serving:

Calories	130	Protein	3 g
Total Fat	2 g	Carbohydrates	26 g
Saturated Fat	0	Sodium	9 mg
Cholesterol	0	Added Sugar	0
		Fiber	1 g

Vinaigrette Dressing

Preparation: **5 min.** FAT SUGAR SODIUM

Use this dressing for crisp green salads. For variety, add 1 tablespoon chopped fresh dill, basil, or parsley (or 1 teaspoon dried herbs). You can also add a finely minced clove of garlic.

½ **cup low-sodium chicken broth**
2 **tablespoons olive oil**
1 **tablespoon Dijon or spicy brown mustard**
1 **teaspoon red wine vinegar**
1 **tablespoon lemon juice**

Place all the ingredients in a ½-pint screw-top jar, cover tightly, and shake vigorously to blend. Store the dressing in the refrigerator and shake well before each use. Makes ¾ cup.

One Tablespoon:

Calories	23	*Protein*	0
Total Fat	2 g	*Carbohydrates*	0
Saturated Fat	0	*Sodium*	40 mg
Cholesterol	0	*Added Sugar*	0
		Fiber	0

Italian Dressing

Preparation: **5 min.** FAT SUGAR SODIUM

½ **cup low-sodium chicken broth**
1 **clove garlic, minced**
1 **tablespoon red wine vinegar**
2 **tablespoons olive oil**
1 **tablespoon Dijon or spicy brown mustard**
½ **teaspoon each dried oregano and basil, crumbled**
½ **teaspoon paprika**
½ **teaspoon black pepper**

Place all the ingredients in a ½-pint screw-top jar, cover tightly, and shake vigorously to blend. Store the dressing in the refrigerator and shake well before each use. Makes ¾ cup.

One Tablespoon:

Calories	24	*Protein*	0
Total Fat	2 g	*Carbohydrates*	1 g
Saturated Fat	0	*Sodium*	39 mg
Cholesterol	0	*Added Sugar*	0
		Fiber	0

Tip: *Homemade oil-based dressings will keep well in the refrigerator for up to ten days; yogurt-based ones will last about a week.*

Blue Cheese Dressing

Preparation: **2 min.** FAT SUGAR SODIUM

½ **cup plain low-fat yogurt**
¼ **cup buttermilk**
¼ **cup crumbled blue cheese (about 1 ounce)**
½ **medium-size cucumber, peeled, seeded, and coarsely grated (about ½ cup)**

In a medium-size bowl, whisk together the **yogurt** and **buttermilk.** Stir in the **blue cheese** and **cucumber.** Store the dressing in a tightly covered container in the refrigerator and stir well before each use. Makes 1½ cups.

One Tablespoon:

Calories	9	*Protein*	1 g
Total Fat	0	*Carbohydrates*	1 g
Saturated Fat	0	*Sodium*	23 mg
Cholesterol	1 mg	*Added Sugar*	0
		Fiber	0

Ranch Dressing

Preparation: **4 min.,**
plus 6 hr. refrigeration FAT SUGAR SODIUM

4½ **teaspoons olive oil**
2 **teaspoons cider vinegar**
1 **teaspoon sugar**
¼ **teaspoon dried marjoram, crumbled**
⅛ **teaspoon salt**
3 **tablespoons plain low-fat yogurt**
¾ **cup buttermilk**
2 **tablespoons finely chopped yellow onion**
1 **clove garlic, minced**
2 **tablespoons minced parsley**

1. In a medium-size bowl, whisk together the **olive oil, vinegar, sugar, marjoram,** and **salt.** Whisk in the **yogurt** and **buttermilk,** then stir in the **onion, garlic** and **parsley.** Cover and chill in the refrigerator for 6 hours or overnight to thicken.

2. Whisk the dressing again before serving. Store any leftover dressing in a tightly covered jar in the refrigerator and shake well before each use. Makes 1¼ cups.

One Tablespoon:

Calories	16	*Protein*	0
Total Fat	1 g	*Carbohydrates*	1 g
Saturated Fat	0	*Sodium*	25 mg
Cholesterol	0	*Added Sugar*	1 Cal
		Fiber	0

Creamy Garlic Dressing

Preparation: **2 min.,**
plus 6 hr. refrigeration

FAT SUGAR SODIUM

1 **cup plain low-fat yogurt**
1½ **teaspoons Dijon or spicy brown mustard**
½ **teaspoon finely grated lemon rind**
⅛ **teaspoon cayenne pepper**
2 **tablespoons minced parsley**
2 **cloves garlic, crushed**

1. In a medium-size bowl, whisk together the **yogurt, mustard, lemon rind,** and **cayenne pepper.** Stir in the **parsley.** Thread the **garlic** onto a toothpick and add to the dressing. Cover and chill for 6 hours or overnight.
2. Remove the garlic and discard before serving the dressing. Store any leftover dressing in a tightly covered jar in the refrigerator and shake well before each use. Makes 1 cup.

One Tablespoon:

		Protein	*1 g*
Calories	10	*Carbohydrates*	*1 g*
Total Fat	0	*Sodium*	*24 mg*
Saturated Fat	0	*Added Sugar*	*0*
Cholesterol	*1 mg*	*Fiber*	*0*

Thousand Island Dressing

Preparation: **3 min.**

FAT SUGAR SODIUM

1 **cup plain low-fat yogurt**
3 **tablespoons chili sauce**
2 **green onions, chopped fine**
1 **tablespoon finely diced sweet green or red pepper**
1 **large hard-cooked egg white, chopped**

In a medium-size bowl, whisk together the **yogurt** and **chili sauce.** Stir in the **green onions, green pepper,** and **egg white.** Store the dressing in a tightly covered container in the refrigerator and stir before each use. Makes about 1¼ cups.

One Tablespoon:

		Protein	*1 g*
Calories	11	*Carbohydrates*	*2 g*
Total Fat	0	*Sodium*	*45 mg*
Saturated Fat	0	*Added Sugar*	*0*
Cholesterol	*1 mg*	*Fiber*	*0*

Cucumber-Yogurt Sauce

Preparation: **5 min.**

FAT SUGAR SODIUM

Serve this dressing with chicken, seafood, or tossed green salads.

1 **medium-size cucumber, peeled, seeded, and coarsely grated**
1 **medium-size tomato, peeled, cored, seeded, and chopped**
½ **cup plain low-fat yogurt**
2 **tablespoons sour cream**
2 **tablespoons minced fresh mint or 1 teaspoon mint flakes, crumbled**
2 **tablespoons minced parsley**
½ **teaspoon ground cumin**

1. Place the **cucumber** on a double thickness of paper towels. Press with the tines of a fork to remove the moisture, then transfer the cucumber to a small bowl.
2. Add the **tomato, yogurt, sour cream, mint, parsley,** and **cumin,** and mix well. Store in a tightly covered jar in the refrigerator and shake well before each use. Makes 1½ cups.

One Tablespoon:

		Protein	*0*
Calories	8	*Carbohydrates*	*1 g*
Total Fat	0	*Sodium*	*5 mg*
Saturated Fat	0	*Added Sugar*	*0*
Cholesterol	*1 mg*	*Fiber*	*0*

Honey-Yogurt Dressing

Preparation: **2 min.**

FAT SUGAR SODIUM

1 **cup plain low-fat yogurt**
2 **tablespoons plus 2 teaspoons honey**
¼ **teaspoon ground nutmeg**

In a small bowl, whisk together all the ingredients until well mixed. Store in a tightly covered jar in the refrigerator and shake well before each use. Use for fruit salads. Makes about 1 cup.

One Tablespoon:

		Protein	*1 g*
Calories	20	*Carbohydrates*	*4 g*
Total Fat	0	*Sodium*	*10 mg*
Saturated Fat	0	*Added Sugar*	*37 Cal*
Cholesterol	*1 mg*	*Fiber*	*0*

Breads

When family or friends come into a home where the aroma of freshly baked bread is in the air, they know something special is in the offing. Homemade French bread, onion-studded flatbread, whole wheat rolls, or spicy fruit-and-nut loaves can turn any meal into a culinary triumph. All of them, along with the other yeast breads and quick breads in this chapter, can be baked by even the most inexperienced cook. Whoever would have thought that eating healthily could be so wonderful!

Monkey Bread

Basic French Bread

Here is a good basic bread that is baked and steamed simultaneously; this method ensures a shiny, thin, crisp crust. The loaf has a rich, yeasty flavor, and is lower in sodium than store-bought breads.

½ ¼-ounce envelope active dry yeast
1 cup warm water (105° to 115°F)
3 cups sifted all-purpose flour

½ teaspoon salt
Nonstick cooking spray
2 tablespoons yellow or white cornmeal

Preparation:
10 min., plus 2¼ hr. rising time
Baking:
30 min.

One Slice:

Calories	80
Total Fat	0
Saturated Fat	0
Cholesterol	0
Protein	2 g
Carbohydrates	17 g
Sodium	61 mg
Added Sugar	0
Fiber	1 g

1. In a small bowl, combine the **yeast** with ½ cup of the **water.** Let stand for about 5 minutes, then stir until the yeast dissolves.

2. In the large bowl of an electric mixer, combine the **flour** and **salt.** Beat in the yeast mixture and the remaining water and continue beating until the mixture forms a ball, adding a little more flour or water as necessary until you have a workable dough.

3. Turn the dough out onto a lightly floured surface and knead until smooth and elastic—about 10 minutes. Lightly coat a large bowl with the **cooking spray,** shape the dough into a ball, place in the bowl, and turn so that the dough is coated on all sides. Cover the bowl with a clean dish towel and let the dough rise in a warm, draft-free place until doubled in bulk—about 1 hour.

4. With your fist, punch down the dough. Cover again and let the dough rise a second time until doubled in bulk—about 45 minutes.

5. Punch the dough down again and turn out onto a lightly floured surface. Let the dough rest for 5 minutes, then roll and shape it into a cylinder about 1 foot long. Coat a large baking sheet with the cooking spray and sprinkle with the **cornmeal.** Place the dough on the baking sheet, cover with the dish towel, and let it rise once more for 30 minutes.

6. Toward the end of the rising period, preheat the oven to 400°F. Fill a 13"x 9"x 2" baking pan with an inch of hot water and place it on the floor of the oven. Using a sharp knife, slash the dough ¼ inch deep down the center, then brush with water. Place the bread in the center of the oven and, using a spray bottle, spray the sides of the oven with water. Continue to spray every 5 minutes during the first 15 minutes of baking time. Bake for a total of 30 minutes or until the loaf sounds hollow when tapped. Makes 1 loaf (about 18 slices).

Tip: Always sift all-purpose flour when a recipe calls for it, even if you're using a brand that says "pre-sifted" on the label. Shipping and handling cause presifted flour to settle, costing it much of its lightness of texture. Do not sift whole wheat flour.

Basic French Bread

Country-Style Bread

1 envelope (¼ ounce) active
  dry yeast
1½ cups warm water (105° to
  115°F)
4½ cups sifted all-purpose flour
½ teaspoon salt

1 cup plus 1 teaspoon yellow or
  white cornmeal
½ cup bran
  Nonstick cooking spray

1. In a large bowl, combine the **yeast** and ¾ cup of the warm **water.** Let stand about 5 minutes, then stir until the yeast dissolves. Stir in 1 cup of the **flour,** cover the bowl with a clean dish towel, and let stand at room temperature for 24 to 48 hours.
2. Stir in another ¾ cup warm water and the **salt.** Beat in 3 cups of the remaining flour, 1 cup of the **cornmeal,** and the **bran** to make a stiff dough.
3. Turn the dough out onto a lightly floured surface and knead for 10 minutes or until it is smooth and elastic, using enough of the remaining flour to keep the dough from sticking.
4. Lightly coat a large bowl with the **cooking spray,** shape the dough into a ball, place in the bowl, and turn so that the dough is coated on all sides. Cover with a clean dish towel and let the dough rise in a warm, draft-free place until it has doubled in bulk—about 1½ hours.
5. With your fist, punch down the dough. Shape it into a ball, cover again, and let the dough rise a second time until doubled in bulk—about 1½ hours.
6. Sprinkle the remaining teaspoon of cornmeal over an ungreased baking sheet. Punch down the dough and divide in half. Shape each half into a ball and place 3 inches apart on the baking sheet. Cover with a clean dish towel and let the dough rise once more until doubled in bulk—about 1 hour.
7. Toward the end of the rising period, preheat the oven to 450°F. Using a sharp knife, slash a large X ¼ inch deep across the top of each loaf. Place the bread in the oven, reduce the temperature to 400°F, and bake for 45 minutes or until the loaves are golden brown and sound hollow when tapped. Makes 2 round loaves (about 10 slices each).

FAT **SUGAR** **SODIUM**

Preparation:
15 min., plus 28 hr.
rising time
Baking:
45 min.

One Slice:

Calories	125
Total Fat	0
Saturated Fat	0
Cholesterol	0
Protein	4 g
Carbohydrates	26 g
Sodium	56 mg
Added Sugar	0
Fiber	1 g

Tip: *You can double the life of a loaf of bread by storing it in a tightly sealed plastic bag in the refrigerator.*

229

Cottage Cheese Bread

This dense loaf is good with jam or preserves.

½ ¼-ounce envelope active dry yeast
¾ cup warm milk (105° to 115°F)
1 tablespoon honey
3 cups sifted all-purpose flour

½ teaspoon salt
½ cup low-fat cottage cheese
   Nonstick cooking spray
1 tablespoon milk

Preparation:
15 min., plus 1 hr.
40 min. rising time
Baking:
35 min.

1. In a small bowl, combine the **yeast,** warm **milk,** and **honey.** Let stand about 5 minutes or until bubbly, then stir until the yeast dissolves.
2. In a large bowl, combine the **flour** and **salt.** Add the yeast mixture and the **cottage cheese** and beat vigorously with a spoon until the dough forms a ball. Turn the dough out onto a lightly floured surface and knead for 10 minutes or until it is smooth and elastic.
3. Coat a large bowl with the **cooking spray,** shape the dough into a ball, and place in the bowl, turning so that the dough is coated on all sides. Cover the bowl with a clean dish towel and let the dough rise in a warm, draft-free place until doubled in bulk—about 1 hour.
4. Lightly coat a 9¼"x 5¼"x 2¾" loaf pan with the cooking spray. With your fist, punch down the dough. Shape it into a loaf and place in the pan, seam side down; cover with the dish towel and let the dough rise a second time until almost doubled in bulk—about 40 minutes.
5. Toward the end of the rising period, preheat the oven to 375°F. Brush the loaf with the tablespoon of **milk** and bake for 35 minutes or until it has browned and sounds hollow when tapped. Remove the loaf from the pan and cool on a wire rack before slicing. Makes 1 loaf (about 16 slices).

Variations:
Parmesan Bread   Just before shaping the dough for its second rising, knead in ⅓ cup grated Parmesan cheese, then proceed as directed.
Onion-Cheese Bread   Finely chop 1 medium-size yellow onion and squeeze it dry in a double thickness of paper towels. Just before shaping the dough for its second rising, knead in the onion, then proceed as directed.
Herb-Cheese Bread   Just before shaping the dough for its second rising, knead in ¼ cup freshly chopped dill, parsley, chives, basil, or sage, then proceed as directed.

One Slice:

Calories	95
Total Fat	1 g
Saturated Fat	0
Cholesterol	2 mg
Protein	4 g
Carbohydrates	18 g
Sodium	76 mg
Added Sugar	4 Cal
Fiber	1 g

Tip: Activating yeast with milk gives bread a soft texture. Water-activated yeast makes a chewier, crustier loaf.

Monkey Bread

Monkey bread is a loaf made up of individual rolls. To serve, simply pull off the rolls one at a time.

¾ ¼-ounce envelope active dry yeast
⅓ cup warm water (105° to 115°F)
3 cups sifted all-purpose flour
1 tablespoon sugar

½ teaspoon salt
⅔ cup warm skim milk (105° to 115°F)
   Nonstick cooking spray
3 tablespoons unsalted margarine

Preparation:
10 min., plus 1 hr.
40 min. rising time
Baking:
35 min.

1. In a small bowl, combine the **yeast** and **water.** Let stand about 5 minutes, then stir until the yeast dissolves. Meanwhile, combine the **flour, sugar,** and **salt** in a large bowl.

2. Beat the yeast mixture and **milk** into the flour mixture with a spoon; continue beating until the dough forms a ball, adding a little more flour or water if necessary. Turn the dough out onto a lightly floured surface and knead until it is smooth and elastic—about 10 minutes.

3. Coat a large bowl with the **cooking spray,** shape the dough into a ball, and place in the bowl, turning the dough so that it is coated on all sides. Cover with a clean dish towel and let the dough rise in a warm, draft-free place until doubled in bulk—about 1 hour.

4. With your fist, punch down the dough and let it rest for 5 minutes. Divide it into 24 pieces and shape each piece into a small ball.

5. Lightly coat a deep round 1½-quart baking dish with the cooking spray. In a small saucepan, melt the **margarine** over moderate heat and let it cool to room temperature. Dip the dough balls into the melted margarine and arrange in the baking dish in 3 layers. Cover with the dish towel and let rise again until the dough has risen almost to the top of the dish—about 40 minutes.

6. Toward the end of the rising period, preheat the oven to 375°F. Bake the bread for 35 minutes or until it is nicely browned and crisp. Place the baking dish on a wire rack and cool for 30 minutes. Turn the bread out by inverting the dish onto a platter and turning the bread right side up. Makes 24 rolls.

One Roll:

Calories	75
Total Fat	2 g
Saturated Fat	0
Cholesterol	0
Protein	2 g
Carbohydrates	13 g
Sodium	50 mg
Added Sugar	2 Cal
Fiber	1 g

Tip: *Use a candy thermometer to be certain that water or milk is heated to 105° to 115°F. Or judge the old-fashioned way: the temperature is right when a drop placed on the inside forearm feels comfortably warm.*

Onion Flatbread

This rich bread is ideal as a snack or as an accompaniment to soups or salads.

FAT SUGAR SODIUM

1 **envelope (¼ ounce) active dry yeast**
1 **cup warm water (105° to 115°F)**
2½ **tablespoons olive oil**
1½ **cups sifted all-purpose flour**
¼ **teaspoon salt**
  Nonstick cooking spray
1 **teaspoon dried rosemary, crumbled**
1 **small red onion, sliced thin**

1. Combine the **yeast** and **water** in a large bowl. Let stand about 5 minutes, then stir until the yeast dissolves.

2. Add 2 tablespoons of the **olive oil,** the **flour,** and **salt,** and beat well with a spoon. Turn the dough out onto a lightly floured surface and knead until it is smooth and elastic—about 10 minutes.

3. Lightly coat a large bowl with the **cooking spray,** shape the dough into a ball, place in the bowl, and turn so that the dough is coated on all sides. Cover with a clean dish towel and let the dough rise in a warm, draft-free place until doubled in bulk—about 2 hours.

4. Grease a 15"x 10"x 1" jelly roll pan with the remaining olive oil. With your fist, punch down the dough; place it on the pan and pat it out to the edges. Cover with the dish towel and let the dough rise another 30 minutes.

5. Toward the end of the rising period, preheat the oven to 400°F. Sprinkle the dough with the **rosemary.** Separate the **onion** slices into rings and scatter the rings evenly over the dough. Bake for 15 to 20 minutes or until crisp and browned. Cool and cut into 3-inch squares. Makes 15 squares.

Preparation:
20 min., plus 2½ hr. rising time
Baking:
15 min.

One Square:

Calories	72
Total Fat	3 g
Saturated Fat	0
Cholesterol	0
Protein	2 g
Carbohydrates	10 g
Sodium	37 mg
Added Sugar	0
Fiber	0

Winter Squash Bread

1 envelope (¼ ounce) active dry yeast

⅓ cup warm water (105° to 115°F)

2 tablespoons light brown sugar

2 tablespoons unsalted margarine

1 large egg, lightly beaten

1½ teaspoons grated orange rind

½ teaspoon ground cinnamon

¼ teaspoon salt

⅛ teaspoon each ground mace and cloves

½ cup mashed cooked acorn squash, butternut squash, or pumpkin

2¾ cups sifted all-purpose flour
    Nonstick cooking spray

1 large egg white, lightly beaten

FAT SUGAR SODIUM

Preparation:
15 min., plus 2¼ hr. rising time
Baking:
35 min.

One Slice:	
Calories	108
Total Fat	2 g
Saturated Fat	0
Cholesterol	17 mg
Protein	3 g
Carbohydrates	19 g
Sodium	43 mg
Added Sugar	4 Cal
Fiber	1 g

1. In a large bowl, combine the **yeast, water,** and 1 tablespoon of the **sugar.** Let stand about 5 minutes or until bubbly; stir until the yeast dissolves.

2. Meanwhile, melt the **margarine** in a small saucepan and let it cool to warm. Add the **egg, orange rind, cinnamon, salt, mace, cloves, squash,** and melted margarine to the yeast mixture; stir until thoroughly mixed. Add the **flour,** 1 cup at a time, to make a dough that is firm but not dry.

3. Turn the dough out onto a lightly floured surface and knead vigorously for 6 to 8 minutes. Coat a large bowl with the **cooking spray,** shape the dough into a ball, place in the bowl, and turn so that the dough is coated on all sides. Cover with a clean dish towel and let the dough rise in a warm, draft-free place until doubled in bulk—about 1½ hours.

4. Lightly coat a 9¼"x 5¼"x 2¾" loaf pan with the cooking spray. With your fist, punch down the dough. Knead it for 1 to 2 minutes, shape into a loaf, and place in the pan, seam side down. Cover with the dish towel and let the loaf sit until it has risen 1 inch above the rim of the pan—about 45 minutes.

5. Toward the end of the rising period, preheat the oven to 375°F. Brush the top of the loaf with the **egg white** and bake for 35 to 40 minutes or until the top is golden and the loaf sounds hollow when tapped. Makes 1 loaf (about 16 slices).

Nutty Whole Wheat Bread

This crunchy round loaf makes superb breakfast toast.

FAT SUGAR SODIUM

½ ¼-ounce envelope active dry yeast

½ cup warm milk (105° to 115°F)

4 teaspoons honey

1 cup sifted all-purpose flour

2 cups unsifted whole wheat flour

½ teaspoon salt

¼ teaspoon black pepper

1 tablespoon olive oil

½ cup warm water
    Nonstick cooking spray

3 tablespoons chopped pecans

1 tablespoon yellow or white cornmeal

1 tablespoon milk

Preparation:
20 min., plus 1 hr. 40 min. rising time
Baking:
30 min.

1. In a small bowl, combine the **yeast, milk,** and **honey.** Let stand about 5 minutes or until bubbly, then stir until the yeast dissolves.

2. In a large bowl, combine the **all-purpose flour, whole wheat flour, salt,** and **pepper.** Add the **olive oil, water,** and the yeast mixture, and beat with a spoon until the dough forms a ball. Turn the dough out onto a lightly floured

surface and knead until it is smooth and elastic—8 to 10 minutes.

3. Lightly coat a large bowl with the **cooking spray,** shape the dough into a ball, place in the bowl, and turn so that the dough is coated on all sides. Cover with a clean dish towel and let the dough rise in a warm, draft-free place until doubled in bulk—about 1 hour.

4. While the dough rises, preheat the oven to 325°F, spread the **pecans** on a baking sheet, and toast in the oven about 8 minutes. When the dough has doubled in bulk, punch it down and let it rest for 10 minutes; then knead in the pecans until they are evenly distributed.

5. Lightly coat the baking sheet with the cooking spray and sprinkle with the **cornmeal.** Shape the dough into a ball, place it on the baking sheet, and cover with the dish towel; let it rise for a second time until almost doubled in bulk—about 40 minutes.

6. Toward the end of the rising period, preheat the oven to 350°F. Brush the top of the loaf with the tablespoon of **milk.** Using a sharp knife, slash a large X ¼ inch deep across the top. Bake for 30 to 35 minutes or until the loaf sounds hollow when tapped. Makes 1 loaf (about 16 slices).

One Slice:

Calories	106
Total Fat	2 g
Saturated Fat	0
Cholesterol	1 mg
Protein	3 g
Carbohydrates	19 g
Sodium	73 mg
Added Sugar	5 Cal
Fiber	1 g

Nutty Whole Wheat Bread

Whole Wheat Dinner Rolls

These nutritious rolls take little time to make. They can be prepared ahead and frozen for future use.

1 envelope (¼ ounce) active dry yeast
¼ cup warm water (105° to 115°F)
¾ cup skim milk
1 large egg
3 tablespoons unsalted margarine, softened

1 tablespoon sugar
¼ teaspoon salt
1½ cups sifted all-purpose flour
½ cup unsifted whole wheat flour
Nonstick cooking spray

Preparation:
10 min., plus 1½ hr.
rising time
Baking:
15 min.

One Roll:

Calories	116
Total Fat	4 g
Saturated Fat	1 g
Cholesterol	23 mg
Protein	4 g
Carbohydrates	17 g
Sodium	60 mg
Added Sugar	5 Cal
Fiber	1 g

1. In a large bowl, combine the **yeast** and **water.** Let stand about 5 minutes, then stir until the yeast dissolves.

2. Add the **milk, egg, margarine, sugar,** and **salt** to the yeast mixture and beat well with a spoon. Mix in the **all-purpose flour** and **whole wheat flour.** Scrape the dough down from the sides of the bowl to form a ball. Cover with a clean dish towel and let the dough rise in a warm, draft-free place until doubled in bulk—about 1 hour.

3. Using 1 large or 2 small muffin pans, lightly coat 12 2½-inch cups with the **cooking spray.** Stir the dough down and spoon it into the muffin cups, filling them about half full. Cover loosely with the dish towel and let rise another 30 minutes.

4. Toward the end of the rising period, preheat the oven to 400°F. Bake the rolls for 15 to 20 minutes or until lightly browned. Makes 12 rolls.

Variation:
Herbed Whole Wheat Dinner Rolls   Add 1½ teaspoons dried basil, oregano, sage, or thyme to the dry ingredients and proceed as directed. Sprinkle the rolls with sesame seeds or poppy seeds, if desired.

Pretzels with Caraway Seeds

Breadsticks can also be made from this basic recipe.

1 envelope (¼ ounce) active dry yeast
¾ cup warm water (105° to 115°F)
2½ cups sifted all-purpose flour
¼ teaspoon salt

Nonstick cooking spray
1 large egg white beaten with 1 teaspoon water
2 tablespoons caraway seeds

Preparation:
10 min., plus 2 hr.
rising time
Baking:
10 min.

One Pretzel:

Calories	102
Total Fat	0
Saturated Fat	0
Cholesterol	0
Protein	3 g
Carbohydrates	21 g
Sodium	50 mg
Added Sugar	0
Fiber	1 g

1. Combine the **yeast** and **water** in a large bowl. Let stand about 5 minutes, then stir until the yeast dissolves.

2. Stir 1½ cups of the **flour** into the yeast mixture; add the **salt** and beat with a spoon until smooth. Add enough of the remaining flour to make a stiff dough. Turn the dough out onto a lightly floured surface and knead vigorously for 5 minutes.

3. Lightly coat a large bowl with the **cooking spray,** shape the dough into a ball, place in the bowl, and turn so that the dough is coated on all sides.

Cover with a clean dish towel and let the dough rise in a warm, draft-free place until doubled in bulk—about 1½ hours.

4. With your fist, punch down the dough. Divide it in half and cut each half into 6 pieces. Using the palms of your hands, roll each piece into an 18-inch strand. Twist into a pretzel shape, tucking the ends under. Lightly coat a baking sheet with the cooking spray, place the pretzels on it about 1 inch apart, and cover loosely with the dish towel. Let the pretzels rise for 30 minutes.

5. Toward the end of the rising period, preheat the oven to 400°F. Brush the pretzels with the **egg white** and sprinkle with the **caraway seeds.** Bake for 10 to 15 minutes or until browned. Makes 12 pretzels.

Variations:

Breadsticks   Preheat the oven to 350°F. Cut the dough into 36 pieces and roll each into a 6- to 8-inch length. Place on the baking sheet about ½ inch apart, cover loosely, and let rise for 30 minutes. Brush with the egg white and sprinkle with the caraway seeds. Bake for 20 minutes or until browned. Makes 36 breadsticks.

Herbed Pretzels or Breadsticks   Substitute 1 cup unsifted whole wheat flour for the all-purpose flour and knead in ½ teaspoon black pepper or 1 teaspoon dried herbs such as thyme or oregano. Substitute poppy seeds or sesame seeds for the caraway seeds.

Pretzels with Caraway Seeds

Irish Soda Bread

Irish Soda Bread

In Ireland, this bread is traditionally baked over a peat fire.

FAT SUGAR SODIUM

2 cups sifted all-purpose flour
2 cups unsifted whole wheat flour
1 teaspoon baking powder
1 teaspoon baking soda
¼ teaspoon salt
¼ cup golden raisins, chopped
2 teaspoons caraway seeds
1¼ to 1½ cups buttermilk
   Nonstick cooking spray

Preparation:
15 min.
Baking:
35 min.

1. Preheat the oven to 375°F. In a large bowl, combine the **all-purpose flour, whole wheat flour, baking powder, baking soda,** and **salt.** Stir in the **raisins** and **caraway seeds.**

2. Add enough **buttermilk** to make a dough that is firm but not dry. Turn the dough out onto a lightly floured surface and knead until it is smooth—2 to 3 minutes. Shape the dough into a round loaf and, using a sharp knife, slash a large X ¼ inch deep across the top.

3. Coat a baking sheet with the **cooking spray,** place the loaf on it, and bake for 35 to 40 minutes or until the bottom of the loaf sounds hollow when tapped. Makes 1 loaf (about 16 slices).

One Slice:

Calories	*124*
Total Fat	*1 g*
Saturated Fat	*0*
Cholesterol	*1 mg*
Protein	*5 g*
Carbohydrates	*26 g*
Sodium	*137 mg*
Added Sugar	*0*
Fiber	*2 g*

Old-Fashioned Cornbread

The variations that follow add unusual twists to this basic cornbread recipe.

Nonstick cooking spray
1 cup yellow cornmeal
¾ cup sifted all-purpose flour
2½ teaspoons baking powder
½ teaspoon sugar
¼ teaspoon salt
½ tablespoon unsalted margarine
1 cup skim milk
1 large egg

1. Preheat the oven to 400°F. Lightly coat an 8"x 8"x 2" baking pan with the **cooking spray** and set aside.
2. In a medium-size bowl, combine the **cornmeal, flour, baking powder, sugar,** and **salt;** set aside.
3. Melt the **margarine** in a small saucepan over moderate heat; pour it into a small bowl and whisk together with the **milk** and **egg.** Add to the cornmeal mixture and stir just until the dry ingredients are moistened.
4. Spoon the batter into the pan and bake for 20 minutes or until the cornbread is golden and the top springs back when touched. Cut into 9 squares and serve hot. Serves 9.

Variations:

Chive Cornbread   To the milk mixture, add 2 tablespoons minced fresh, frozen, or freeze-dried chives.
Chili Cornbread   To the dry ingredients, add 1 tablespoon chili powder.
Jalapeño Cornbread   To the milk mixture, add 2 teaspoons finely chopped jalapeño pepper.

Preparation:
10 min.
Baking:
20 min.

One Square:

Calories	116
Total Fat	2 g
Saturated Fat	0
Cholesterol	31 mg
Protein	4 g
Carbohydrates	21 g
Sodium	200 mg
Added Sugar	2 Cal
Fiber	0

Spoon Bread

This moist, puddinglike bread, long a popular dish in the South, is spooned onto dinner plates and served warm in place of potatoes.

1 cup skim milk
½ cup water
2 teaspoons sugar
¼ teaspoon salt
½ cup yellow or white cornmeal
1 large egg yolk
½ teaspoon baking powder
⅛ teaspoon cayenne pepper
3 large egg whites
Nonstick cooking spray

1. Preheat the oven to 375°F. In a large saucepan, bring the **milk, water, sugar,** and **salt** to a simmer over moderate heat. Remove from the heat, stir in the **cornmeal,** and beat the mixture with a spoon until it is thick and smooth.
2. In a small bowl, lightly beat the **egg yolk** with the **baking powder.** Add to the cornmeal mixture in the saucepan along with the **cayenne pepper.**
3. In a large bowl, beat the **egg whites** until they are stiff but not dry. Stir ¼ of the whites into the cornmeal mixture, then gently fold in the rest.
4. Coat a 1-quart baking dish with the **cooking spray** and pour in the batter. Bake for 30 to 35 minutes or until the bread is puffed and golden brown. Serve at once directly from the dish. Serves 4.

Preparation:
15 min.
Baking:
30 min.

One Serving:

Calories	61
Total Fat	2 g
Saturated Fat	0
Cholesterol	69 mg
Protein	5 g
Carbohydrates	6 g
Sodium	260 mg
Added Sugar	8 Cal
Fiber	0

Banana-Spice Loaf (left) and *Cranberry-Orange Loaf*

Prune-and-Spice Quick Bread

Here is a delectable bread that stays moist for several days.

Nonstick cooking spray	¼ **teaspoon salt**
1 **cup sifted all-purpose flour**	1 **large egg**
½ **cup unsifted whole wheat flour**	½ **cup sugar**
½ **teaspoon baking soda**	1 **cup buttermilk or sour milk**
½ **teaspoon ground cinnamon**	1 **tablespoon corn oil**
¼ **teaspoon ground nutmeg**	½ **cup chopped pitted prunes**

Preparation:
10 min.
Baking:
40 min.

One Slice:

Calories	*96*
Total Fat	*2 g*
Saturated Fat	*0*
Cholesterol	*18 mg*
Protein	*2 g*
Carbohydrates	*19 g*
Sodium	*80 mg*
Added Sugar	*23 Cal*
Fiber	*1 g*

1. Preheat the oven to 375°F. Lightly coat a 9¼"x 5¼"x 2¾" loaf pan with the **cooking spray** and set aside.

2. In a large bowl, combine the **all-purpose flour, whole wheat flour, baking soda, cinnamon, nutmeg,** and **salt;** set aside.

3. In a small bowl, combine the **egg** and **sugar** and beat well with a fork. Stir in the **buttermilk** and **corn oil.** Add to the flour mixture and stir just until the dry ingredients are moistened. Mix in the **prunes.**

4. Spoon the batter into the loaf pan and bake for 40 minutes or until a toothpick inserted in the center of the loaf comes out clean. Cool the loaf in the pan on a wire rack for 5 minutes, turn out onto the rack, and let cool completely, right side up, before slicing. Makes 1 loaf (about 16 slices).

Banana-Spice Loaf

With a few simple changes, you can make two other wholesome breads with this recipe. All can be frozen for future use.

1 **cup sifted all-purpose flour**
1 **cup unsifted whole wheat flour**
3 **tablespoons sugar**
2 **teaspoons baking soda**
1 **teaspoon each ground cinnamon and nutmeg**

¼ **cup unsalted margarine**
2 **medium-size bananas, peeled and mashed (about 1 cup)**
½ **cup buttermilk**
1 **large egg, lightly beaten**
1 **teaspoon vanilla extract**

1. Preheat the oven to 350°F. Lightly grease a 9¼"x 5¼"x 2¾" loaf pan; set aside.
2. In a large bowl, combine the **all-purpose flour, whole wheat flour, sugar, baking soda, cinnamon,** and **nutmeg;** set aside.
3. Melt the **margarine** in a small saucepan over moderate heat; pour it into a small bowl and whisk together with the **bananas, buttermilk, egg,** and **vanilla extract.** Add to the flour mixture and stir just until the dry ingredients are moistened.
4. Spoon the batter into the pan. Bake for 50 minutes or until a toothpick inserted in the center of the loaf comes out clean. Place the pan on a wire rack and cool for 10 minutes, then remove the loaf from the pan and serve warm or at room temperature. Makes 1 loaf (about 16 slices).

Variations:

Carrot-Lemon Loaf   Omit the cinnamon, nutmeg, and banana. To the buttermilk mixture, add 1 cup shredded carrots and 1½ tablespoons grated lemon rind.

Cranberry-Orange Loaf   Omit the cinnamon, nutmeg, and banana. Substitute ¼ cup orange juice for ¼ cup of the buttermilk. To the liquid mixture, add 1 cup cranberries (thawed, if frozen), halved, and 2 tablespoons grated orange rind.

Preparation:
10 min.
Baking:
50 min.

One Slice:

Calories	109
Total Fat	4 g
Saturated Fat	1 g
Cholesterol	17 mg
Protein	3 g
Carbohydrates	17 g
Sodium	116 mg
Added Sugar	9 Cal
Fiber	1 g

Yorkshire Pudding

This crisp bread, eaten with knife and fork, is traditionally served with roast beef.

1½ **tablespoons unsalted margarine, softened**
½ **cup skim milk**
1 **large egg**

½ **cup sifted all-purpose flour**
⅛ **teaspoon salt**

1. Preheat the oven to 500°F. Grease an 8"x 8"x 2" baking pan with ½ tablespoon of the **margarine** and place the pan in the oven while you prepare the pudding batter.
2. In a medium-size bowl, combine the **milk, egg, flour,** and **salt.** Using an electric mixer, beat the batter at high speed for 1 minute or until smooth.
3. In a small saucepan, melt the remaining tablespoon of margarine over moderate heat; add it to the batter and beat 30 seconds longer.
4. Pour the batter into the heated baking pan and bake, uncovered, for 20 minutes or until golden and firm (do not open the oven door during the baking period). Cut into 4 squares and serve immediately. Serves 4.

Preparation:
5 min.
Baking:
20 min.

One Serving:

Calories	121
Total Fat	6 g
Saturated Fat	1 g
Cholesterol	69 mg
Protein	4 g
Carbohydrates	13 g
Sodium	103 mg
Added Sugar	0
Fiber	0

Cream Cheese Biscuits

2 cups sifted all-purpose flour
2½ teaspoons baking powder
¼ teaspoon baking soda
¼ teaspoon salt
3 tablespoons whipped cream cheese

2 tablespoons unsalted margarine
⅔ cup skim milk
Nonstick cooking spray

Preparation:
15 min.
Baking:
12 min.

1. Preheat the oven to 425°F. In a large bowl, combine the **flour, baking powder, baking soda,** and **salt.** With a pastry blender or fork, work in the **cream cheese** and **margarine** until the mixture resembles coarse meal.
2. Stir in all but 1 tablespoon of the **milk;** the dough should be firm but not dry. Turn the dough out onto a lightly floured surface and knead 2 or 3 times or until smooth. Roll the dough out about ½ inch thick; using a 2-inch biscuit cutter dipped in flour, cut out 12 round biscuits.
3. Coat a baking sheet with the **cooking spray,** arrange the biscuits on it, and brush the tops with the remaining tablespoon of milk. Bake for 12 minutes or until the biscuits are golden. Makes 12 biscuits.

Variation:

Currant Biscuits   Add ¼ cup currants to the dry ingredients before stirring in the milk, then proceed as directed.

One Biscuit:

Calories	107
Total Fat	3 g
Saturated Fat	0
Cholesterol	3 mg
Protein	3 g
Carbohydrates	17 g
Sodium	167 mg
Added Sugar	0
Fiber	1 g

Basic Muffins

This simple all-purpose muffin recipe is followed by three suggestions for varying the flavor. The muffins can be frozen for eating later.

Nonstick cooking spray
1¾ cups sifted all-purpose flour
3 tablespoons sugar
2½ teaspoons baking powder

2 tablespoons unsalted margarine
¾ cup skim milk
1 large egg

Preparation:
10 min.
Baking:
15 min.

1. Preheat the oven to 400°F. Using 1 large or 2 small muffin pans, lightly coat 12 2½-inch cups with the **cooking spray.** *(Note: You can omit the cooking spray and use paper cupcake liners instead.)*
2. Combine the **flour, sugar,** and **baking powder** in a large bowl; set aside.
3. Melt the **margarine** in a small saucepan over moderate heat; pour it into a small bowl and whisk together with the **milk** and **egg.** Add to the flour mixture and stir just until the dry ingredients are moistened.
4. Spoon the batter into the muffin cups, filling them about half full. Bake for 15 minutes or until a toothpick inserted in the center of a muffin comes out clean. Serve warm or at room temperature. Makes 12 muffins.

Variations:

Apple-Spice Muffins   To the dry ingredients, add 1 teaspoon each ground cinnamon and nutmeg and ¼ teaspoon ground allspice. To the milk mixture, add ½ cup finely chopped peeled apple.
Berry Muffins   To the milk mixture, add ½ cup each fresh or thawed frozen dry-pack raspberries and strawberries, halved or quartered.
Bran Muffins   Reduce the flour to 1 cup and add ¾ cup bran.

One Muffin:

Calories	102
Total Fat	3 g
Saturated Fat	0
Cholesterol	23 mg
Protein	3 g
Carbohydrates	17 g
Sodium	103 mg
Added Sugar	12 Cal
Fiber	1 g

Cooking for One or Two

Although many of the recipes in this book can be reduced to serve two, the ones in this chapter were especially created as solos or duets. They are generally quick and easy to make, most require only a simple side dish to complete the meal, and all have the flavor and eye appeal missing in store-bought frozen dinners. If you like one of the dishes so much you want to serve it to company, you'll be glad to know that every recipe works fine when doubled.

Cornish Hen Glazed with Orange and Ginger

Soups

Quick Borscht

Here's a perfect summer soup served either cold or hot. With a crusty slice of dark bread and a crisp green salad, it makes a surprisingly filling lunch. If you wish, you can substitute Mock Sour Cream, page 26, for the yogurt.

FAT SUGAR SODIUM

1 can (8 ounces) low-sodium sliced beets, with their juice
1 cup low-sodium beef broth
2 tablespoons red wine vinegar
3 tablespoons plain low-fat yogurt
2 medium-size radishes, trimmed and sliced thin

1 small cucumber, peeled and sliced thin
1 green onion, including top, sliced thin
1 tablespoon snipped fresh dill or ½ teaspoon dill weed

Preparation:
5 min., plus 3 hr. refrigeration

One Serving:

Calories	*75*
Total Fat	*1 g*
Saturated Fat	*0*
Cholesterol	*1 mg*
Protein	*3 g*
Carbohydrates	*15 g*
Sodium	*76 mg*
Added Sugar	*0*
Fiber	*1 g*

1. In an electric blender or food processor, whirl the **beets** with their juice, the **beef broth,** and **vinegar** for 6 to 8 seconds or until smooth. Pour into a small glass bowl, cover with plastic wrap, and chill in the refrigerator for 3 hours or overnight.
2. When ready to serve, ladle the soup into bowls, top each portion with equal amounts of the **yogurt,** and sprinkle with the **radishes, cucumber, green onion,** and **dill.** Serves 2.

Creamy Crab Chowder

Fish fillets or other shellfish can be substituted in this simple but hearty chowder, which you can serve with a salad as a main course for two or as a first course for four. The base can be made ahead, refrigerated, and slowly reheated before the crabmeat is added.

FAT SUGAR SODIUM

1 large yellow onion, chopped
1 large all-purpose potato, peeled and chopped
1 medium-size stalk celery, sliced thin
1 medium-size carrot, peeled and sliced thin
½ teaspoon each dried thyme and basil, crumbled
1½ cups water

1 cup skim milk
2 tablespoons flour
⅛ teaspoon cayenne pepper
½ pound fresh, canned, or thawed frozen crabmeat, picked over for bits of shell and cartilage
2 tablespoons chopped parsley (optional)

Preparation:
15 min.
Cooking:
27 min.

One Serving:

Calories	*272*
Total Fat	*3 g*
Saturated Fat	*0*
Cholesterol	*115 mg*
Protein	*25 g*
Carbohydrates	*36 g*
Sodium	*309 mg*
Added Sugar	*0*
Fiber	*3 g*

1. In a medium-size heavy saucepan, combine the **onion, potato, celery, carrot, thyme, basil,** and **water.** Cook over moderate heat until the mixture bubbles gently, then simmer, uncovered, for 15 minutes.
2. In a small bowl, blend the **milk, flour,** and **cayenne pepper** until smooth. Stir into the vegetable mixture, then return to a simmer, stirring constantly, and cook 3 minutes longer. Add the **crabmeat** and cook another 5 minutes. Sprinkle each portion with **parsley,** if desired. Serves 2.

Meats
Beef Stir-fry with Mushrooms and Sweet Pepper

Nonstick cooking spray
1½ teaspoons vegetable oil
6 ounces boneless top round steak, cut across the grain into finger-size strips
1 small yellow onion, chopped
1 small sweet green pepper, cored, seeded, and sliced lengthwise into strips about ¼ inch wide
¼ pound mushrooms, sliced thin
¼ teaspoon each dried marjoram and thyme, crumbled
¼ teaspoon black pepper
¼ cup dry white wine
½ cup low-sodium beef broth
1 teaspoon cornstarch blended with 1 tablespoon cold water

FAT SUGAR SODIUM

Preparation:
15 min.
Cooking:
11 min.

One Serving:

Calories	192
Total Fat	9 g
Saturated Fat	2 g
Cholesterol	49 mg
Protein	21 g
Carbohydrates	8 g
Sodium	54 mg
Added Sugar	0
Fiber	2 g

1. Lightly coat a heavy 10-inch nonstick skillet with the **cooking spray** and set over moderately high heat; add the **vegetable oil** and heat for 30 seconds. Add the **steak** and stir-fry for 1 minute or until it is no longer pink; remove to a warm plate.

2. Add the **onion** and **green pepper** to the skillet and stir-fry for 1 minute. Mix in the **mushrooms, marjoram, thyme,** and **black pepper,** and stir-fry 2 to 3 minutes longer or until the mushrooms are golden.

3. Raise the heat to high, stir in the **wine,** and boil, uncovered, for 1 minute. Add the **beef broth** and adjust the heat so that the mixture bubbles gently; cover and simmer for 3 to 4 minutes or until the vegetables are tender but still crisp.

4. Blend in the **cornstarch** mixture and cook, stirring, until the sauce has thickened—1 to 2 minutes. Return the beef to the skillet and cook 1 minute longer or until just heated through. Serves 2.

Tip: If you buy a wok, choose a carbon steel one instead of stainless steel. Not only is it cheaper, but it's superior for stir-frying because it distributes the heat more evenly.

Beef Stir-fry with Mushrooms and Sweet Pepper

Polish Sausage and Chick Pea Casserole

You can freeze this meal-in-one casserole if you like. Do so before baking it and be sure to let it thaw 30 to 40 minutes before putting it in the oven.

1¼ cups cooked and drained chick peas

1 cup drained canned low-sodium tomatoes, chopped

1 medium-size yellow onion, chopped

1 medium-size sweet green pepper, cored, seeded, and chopped

2 ounces precooked Polish sausage (kielbasa), chopped

1 bay leaf

¼ teaspoon dried oregano, crumbled

¼ teaspoon crushed fennel seeds (optional)

Preheat the oven to 400°F. In an ungreased 8"x 8"x 2" baking dish, mix the **chick peas, tomatoes, onion, green pepper, sausage, bay leaf, oregano,** and, if you like, the **fennel seeds.** Cover tightly with aluminum foil and bake for 15 minutes. Uncover and bake 5 minutes longer or until the mixture is hot. Discard the bay leaf. Serves 2.

Preparation:
15 min.
Cooking:
20 min. (unattended)

One Serving:

Calories	327
Total Fat	11 g
Saturated Fat	3 g
Cholesterol	20 mg
Protein	17 g
Carbohydrates	42 g
Sodium	279 mg
Added Sugar	0
Fiber	9 g

Pork Chops and Rice Casserole

4 lean rib pork chops (about 1 pound), trimmed of fat

¾ teaspoon dried rosemary, crumbled

⅛ teaspoon black pepper
Nonstick cooking spray

¾ cup low-sodium beef broth

¼ cup long-grain rice

1 small yellow onion, cut into 4 thick slices

1 small ripe tomato, cored and cut into 4 thick slices

1 small sweet green pepper, cored, seeded, and cut into 4 thick rings

Preparation:
10 min.
Cooking:
53 min. (mostly unattended)

One Serving:

Calories	267
Total Fat	9 g
Saturated Fat	3 g
Cholesterol	54 mg
Protein	19 g
Carbohydrates	26 g
Sodium	47 mg
Added Sugar	0
Fiber	1 g

1. Preheat the oven to 350°F. Rub both sides of each **pork chop** with ¼ teaspoon of the **rosemary** and with the **pepper.**

2. Lightly coat a heavy 12-inch skillet with the **cooking spray** and place over moderately high heat for 1 minute. Add the chops to the skillet and brown them, uncovered, for 3 to 4 minutes on each side.

3. Transfer the pork chops to an ungreased 1-quart baking dish and add the **beef broth, rice,** and remaining rosemary. Place an **onion** slice, a **tomato** slice, and a **green pepper** ring on each chop. Cover and bake for 45 minutes or until the chops are cooked through and tender. Serves 2.

Variations:

Chicken Breasts and Rice Casserole   Prepare as directed, but substitute 1 skinned chicken breast (about ¾ pound) for the chops.

Lamb Chops and Rice Casserole   Prepare as directed, but substitute 1 lean, trimmed lamb shoulder chop (about ¾ pound) for the pork chops, reduce the beef broth to ½ cup, and add ¼ cup apple cider. In place of the onion, tomato, and green pepper, cover the chop with thinly sliced wedges from 2 cooking apples and sprinkle the top with ¼ teaspoon cinnamon and ⅛ teaspoon nutmeg.

Tip: *Don't store uncooked pork in the freezer. Because pork is served well done, it runs the risk of becoming dry when cooked; freezing will make it drier still.*

Poultry
Chicken Strips with Mustard Sauce

Preparation: **5 min.** Cooking: **6 min.** FAT SUGAR SODIUM

- 1 skinned and boned chicken breast (about ½ pound), halved and pounded to ¼-inch thickness
- ¼ teaspoon each dried sage and thyme, crumbled
- 4 teaspoons flour
- ⅛ teaspoon black pepper
- 1 tablespoon unsalted margarine
- 1 green onion, chopped fine
- ¼ cup dry white wine or vermouth
- ⅓ cup low-sodium chicken broth
- ¼ cup plain low-fat yogurt
- 2 tablespoons sour cream
- 1 teaspoon Dijon or spicy brown mustard or to taste
- 1 tablespoon minced fresh chives or parsley

1. Rub both sides of the **chicken** breast with the **sage** and **thyme,** then cut into matchstick strips. Combine 3 teaspoons of the **flour** with the **pepper** on a plate. Press the chicken strips into the mixture, coating them evenly all over and shaking off any excess.

2. In a heavy 10-inch nonstick skillet, melt the **margarine** over moderately high heat. Add the chicken and cook, stirring, for 1 to 2 minutes or until the chicken is golden; remove to a warm plate. Add the **green onion** to the skillet and stir-fry for 30 seconds. Mix in the **wine** and boil, uncovered, for 1 minute. Mix in the **chicken broth** and boil 1 minute longer.

3. In a small bowl, whisk together the **yogurt, sour cream,** the remaining teaspoon of flour, and the **mustard,** and blend into the skillet juices. Cook over moderate heat, stirring constantly, for 1 to 2 minutes or until thickened. Do not boil or the sauce will curdle.

4. Return the chicken to the skillet and cook, uncovered, 1 to 2 minutes longer or until the chicken is heated through. Sprinkle with the **chives** and serve with rice or pasta. Serves 2.

One Serving:

Calories	257	Protein	29 g
Total Fat	11 g	Carbohydrates	8 g
Saturated Fat	4 g	Sodium	224 mg
Cholesterol	74 mg	Added Sugar	0
		Fiber	0

Chinese Chicken and Vegetables

Preparation: **20 min.** Cooking: **12 min.** FAT SUGAR SODIUM

- 1½ teaspoons Oriental sesame or peanut oil
- 1 small yellow onion, sliced thin
- 1 clove garlic, minced
- 2 thin slices fresh ginger, peeled and cut into strips ⅛ inch wide, or ½ teaspoon ground ginger
- ½ skinned and boned chicken breast (about ¼ pound), pounded to ¼-inch thickness and cut into matchstick strips
- 1 medium-size carrot, peeled and sliced thin diagonally
- 1 tablespoon water
- ¼ pound snow peas, trimmed
- 1 teaspoon reduced-sodium soy sauce
- ⅛ teaspoon black pepper

1. In a heavy 10-inch nonstick skillet, heat the **sesame oil** over moderately high heat for 1 minute; add the **onion** and stir-fry for 1 minute. Mix in the **garlic** and **ginger** and stir-fry 1 minute longer.

2. Stir in the **chicken** and stir-fry for 2 minutes or until the chicken is no longer pink. Add the **carrot** and **water,** cover, and cook, stirring occasionally, for 5 minutes or until the carrot is almost tender. Mix in the **snow peas,** cover, and cook 2 to 3 minutes longer or until the chicken and vegetables are tender. Remove from the heat.

3. Stir in the **soy sauce** and **pepper.** Serve over boiled rice. Serves 1.

Variation:

Lemon Chicken with Asparagus Prepare as directed, but substitute olive oil for the sesame oil and ¼ pound asparagus spears, cut in 1-inch lengths, for the carrot and snow peas. Omit the ginger and soy sauce and add 1 tablespoon lemon juice and ½ teaspoon dried oregano. Before serving, sprinkle with 2 tablespoons grated Parmesan cheese. Accompany with noodles.

One Serving:

Calories	288	Protein	31 g
Total Fat	9 g	Carbohydrates	21 g
Saturated Fat	1 g	Sodium	308 mg
Cholesterol	66 mg	Added Sugar	0
		Fiber	4 g

Curried Chicken and Vegetables

Preparation: **20 min.** Cooking: **20 min.** FAT SUGAR SODIUM

Here is an impressive meal in one.

1 tablespoon vegetable oil
1 medium-size yellow onion, sliced
2 teaspoons curry powder
1 teaspoon ground cumin
2 cups cauliflower florets (about ¼ small head)
2 cups cubed unpeeled eggplant (about ½ small eggplant)
1 bay leaf
⅛ teaspoon cayenne pepper or to taste
1 cup low-sodium chicken broth blended with 1 tablespoon flour
3 cups thinly sliced cabbage (about ½ small head)
½ cup fresh or frozen green peas
2 cloves garlic, minced
1 tablespoon raisins
1 skinned and boned chicken breast (about ½ pound), pounded to ¼-inch thickness and cut into matchstick strips
½ cup plain low-fat yogurt
2 tablespoons minced parsley
Lemon juice to taste

1. In a large heavy saucepan, heat the **vegetable oil** over moderate heat for 1 minute; add the **onion** and cook, uncovered, until soft—about 5 minutes. Blend in the **curry powder** and **cumin** and cook, stirring, for 1 minute.

2. Add the **cauliflower, eggplant, bay leaf,** and **cayenne pepper,** and cook, stirring, 1 minute longer. Stir in the **chicken broth–flour** mixture, cover, and simmer for 3 minutes. Mix in the **cabbage, peas, garlic,** and **raisins,** cover, and simmer until the vegetables are tender but still crisp—about 6 to 8 minutes.

3. Add the **chicken** and cook, stirring constantly, 2 minutes more. Stir in the **yogurt,** 1 tablespoon of the **parsley,** and the **lemon juice,** and heat 1 to 2 minutes longer. Do not boil or the sauce will curdle. Discard the bay leaf and sprinkle with the remaining parsley. Serves 2.

One Serving:

Calories	397	Protein	38 g
Total Fat	11 g	Carbohydrates	39 g
Saturated Fat	2 g	Sodium	185 mg
Cholesterol	69 mg	Added Sugar	0
		Fiber	8 g

Cornish Hen Glazed with Orange and Ginger

Preparation: **10 min.** FAT SUGAR SODIUM
Cooking: **37 min.** (mostly unattended)

1 Cornish hen (1 to 1½ pounds), skinned
¼ teaspoon each dried sage and rosemary, crumbled
1 clove garlic, crushed
1 teaspoon minced fresh ginger or ¼ teaspoon ground ginger
¼ teaspoon black pepper
1 strip orange peel, 3 inches long and ½ inch wide
1 tablespoon olive oil
¼ cup orange juice
1 tablespoon honey
1 tablespoon red wine vinegar
2 teaspoons Dijon or spicy brown mustard
1 teaspoon grated orange rind

1. Preheat the oven to 375°F. Remove and discard all excess fat from the **hen.** Rub the body cavity with the **sage, rosemary, garlic,** ½ teaspoon of the **ginger,** and ⅛ teaspoon of the **pepper;** tuck the strip of **orange peel** inside.

2. Truss the hen, place breast side up on a rack in a shallow roasting pan, brush with the **olive oil,** and sprinkle with the remaining pepper.

3. Roast, uncovered, for 35 to 40 minutes or until a leg moves easily in the hip socket.

4. While the hen roasts, combine the **orange juice, honey, vinegar, mustard,** and remaining ginger in a small saucepan, and bring to a boil over moderately high heat. Adjust the heat so that the mixture bubbles gently and simmer, uncovered, stirring often, for 5 minutes or until the mixture is syrupy; set aside.

5. When the hen is done, transfer it to a carving board and halve lengthwise. Increase the oven temperature to broil. Return the hen to the roasting pan, breast side up, and spoon the orange and honey sauce over each half. Place in the broiler, 4 to 5 inches from the heat, and broil for 2 to 3 minutes or until the hen is golden brown. Sprinkle with the grated **orange rind** and serve. Serves 2.

One Serving:

Calories	276	Protein	24 g
Total Fat	13 g	Carbohydrates	15 g
Saturated Fat	3 g	Sodium	193 mg
Cholesterol	72 mg	Added Sugar	0
		Fiber	0

*Turkey Cutlets
with Lemon and Parsley*

*Turkey Cutlets with
Mushrooms and Sherry*

Turkey Cutlets Parmigiana

Turkey Cutlets with Lemon and Parsley

1 tablespoon flour
⅛ teaspoon salt
⅛ teaspoon black pepper
2 turkey breast cutlets (about ½ pound), each about ¼ inch thick

1½ teaspoons olive oil
1½ teaspoons unsalted margarine
1 tablespoon lemon juice
1 tablespoon minced parsley

FAT **SUGAR** **SODIUM**

Preparation:
5 min.
Cooking:
4 min.

1. Combine the **flour, salt,** and **pepper** on a plate. Press the **turkey** cutlets into the mixture, coating them evenly and shaking off any excess. Set aside.

2. In a heavy 10-inch nonstick skillet, heat the **olive oil** and **margarine** for 1 minute over moderately high heat. Add the turkey cutlets and brown for 1 to 2 minutes on each side; drain on paper towels.

3. Lower the heat to moderate and add the **lemon juice** and **parsley** to the skillet, stirring to loosen the browned bits in the pan. Return the turkey to the skillet and cook for 1 to 2 minutes or until heated through, basting often with the lemon-parsley sauce. Serves 2.

Variations:

Turkey Cutlets Parmigiana   Cook the turkey cutlets as directed. In place of the lemon juice and parsley, add 1 can (8 ounces) low-sodium tomato sauce and ½ teaspoon each crumbled dried oregano, basil, and thyme to the skillet and adjust the heat so that the sauce bubbles gently. Return the turkey to the skillet and heat for 1 minute. Sprinkle each cutlet with 1½ teaspoons shredded part-skim mozzarella cheese and ¾ teaspoon grated Parmesan cheese. Cover the skillet and cook about 1 minute longer or until the cheese melts.

Turkey Cutlets with Mushrooms and Sherry   Cook the turkey cutlets as directed. In place of the lemon juice and parsley, use an additional 1 teaspoon olive oil and ¼ pound thinly sliced mushrooms; cook over moderate heat, uncovered, for 2 to 3 minutes or until golden. Stir in ¼ cup each dry sherry and low-sodium beef broth and boil, uncovered, for 1 to 2 minutes or until almost all the liquid has evaporated and only a thick brown sauce remains. Return the turkey cutlets to the skillet, spoon the mushroom mixture on top, cover, and heat over moderate heat for 1 minute.

One Serving:

Calories	201
Total Fat	8 g
Saturated Fat	2 g
Cholesterol	70 mg
Protein	27 g
Carbohydrates	4 g
Sodium	217 mg
Added Sugar	0
Fiber	0

Tip: *Be sure to use the heaviest skillet you have when cooking poultry or veal cutlets. Because the meat cooks very quickly, it is important that the heat in the pan is evenly distributed— and the thicker the skillet, the more even the heat.*

247

Turkey-Stuffed Tortillas

2 6-inch flour tortillas
1 teaspoon vegetable oil
1 turkey breast cutlet (about ⅓ pound), about ¼ inch thick
1 teaspoon lime juice
¼ teaspoon hot red pepper sauce
2 thin slices peeled avocado (optional)

½ cup shredded iceberg lettuce
1 small ripe tomato, cored and chopped
2 thin slices yellow onion, separated into rings (optional)
2 tablespoons plain low-fat yogurt

FAT **SUGAR** **SODIUM**

Preparation:
15 min.
Cooking:
5 min.

One Serving:

Calories	236
Total Fat	7 g
Saturated Fat	1 g
Cholesterol	47 mg
Protein	21 g
Carbohydrates	22 g
Sodium	82 mg
Added Sugar	0
Fiber	1 g

1. Preheat the oven to 250°F. Wrap the **tortillas** in aluminum foil and warm them about 5 minutes in the oven.

2. Meanwhile, in a heavy 10-inch skillet, heat the **vegetable oil** over high heat for 1 minute. Add the **turkey** cutlet and cook for 2 to 3 minutes on each side or until lightly browned. Transfer the turkey to a cutting board and slice across the grain into thin strips. In a medium-size bowl, toss the turkey strips with the **lime juice** and **red pepper sauce.**

3. Place equal amounts of the turkey, **avocado,** if desired, **lettuce, tomato,** and **onion** rings in the center of each warm tortilla. Top with the **yogurt** and fold the tortilla over the filling; serve immediately. Serves 2.

Fish

Dilled Flounder with Almonds

1 tablespoon flour
⅛ teaspoon salt
⅛ teaspoon black pepper
2 flounder fillets (about 5 ounces each)
Nonstick cooking spray

1 tablespoon unsalted margarine
1 tablespoon snipped fresh dill or ¼ teaspoon dill weed
2 tablespoons slivered almonds

FAT **SUGAR** SODIUM

Preparation:
5 min.
Cooking:
7 min.

One Serving:

Calories	232
Total Fat	12 g
Saturated Fat	2 g
Cholesterol	65 mg
Protein	24 g
Carbohydrates	6 g
Sodium	243 mg
Added Sugar	0
Fiber	1 g

1. Combine the **flour, salt,** and **pepper** on a plate or a sheet of wax paper. Press the **flounder** fillets into the mixture, coating them evenly all over and shaking off any excess. Set aside.

2. Coat a heavy 10-inch nonstick skillet with the **cooking spray,** add ½ tablespoon of the **margarine,** and melt over moderate heat. Add the fish and brown for 2 to 3 minutes on each side, turning only once.

3. Transfer the fish to a warm platter, sprinkle with the **dill,** and keep warm.

4. Coat the skillet with the cooking spray again, add the remaining margarine, and melt over moderate heat. Add the **almonds** and cook, stirring, for 2 to 3 minutes or until the almonds are lightly browned. Spoon over the fish. Serves 2.

Variations:

Flounder with Basil and Pine Nuts   Substitute 1 tablespoon minced fresh basil (or ¼ teaspoon dried basil) for the dill. Substitute pine nuts for the almonds, browning as directed above.

Flounder with Parsley and Sunflower Seeds   Substitute 1 tablespoon minced fresh parsley for the dill. Substitute sunflower seeds for the almonds, browning as directed above.

Fish Fillet in Foil

Fish Fillet in Foil

Preparation: **10 min.** Cooking: **10 min.** `FAT` `SUGAR` `SODIUM`

Any white fish fillets can be prepared this way.

1 tablespoon plus 1 teaspoon unsalted
  margarine
1 large sole or snapper fillet (about 10 ounces)
2 teaspoons lemon juice
¼ teaspoon dried marjoram, crumbled
⅛ teaspoon black pepper
4 medium-size mushrooms, sliced thin
2 green onions, chopped fine
1 small ripe tomato, cored and chopped

1. Preheat the oven to 375°F. Cut a sheet of
   aluminum foil large enough to enclose the fillet.
   Lightly grease the foil with 1 teaspoon of the
   margarine. Place the **sole** fillet in the center
   and sprinkle with the **lemon juice, marjoram,**
   and **pepper.** Arange the **mushrooms, green
   onions,** and **tomato** on top and dot with the
   remaining margarine. Fold the foil over to seal.
2. Place the packet on a baking sheet and bake
   for 10 to 12 minutes. Serves 2.

One Serving:

Calories	208	Protein	25 g
Total Fat	9 g	Carbohydrates	5 g
Saturated Fat	1 g	Sodium	157 mg
Cholesterol	67 mg	Added Sugar	0
		Fiber	2 g

Tuna Patties

Preparation: **10 min.** Cooking: **7 min.** `FAT` `SUGAR` `SODIUM`

1 can (6½ ounces) water-packed light tuna,
  drained and flaked
½ cup soft fresh whole wheat bread crumbs
  (1 slice)
1 small yellow onion, chopped
⅓ cup finely chopped celery
¼ cup plain low-fat yogurt
2 tablespoons low-sodium ketchup
1 tablespoon lemon juice
¼ teaspoon black pepper
  Nonstick cooking spray
1 teaspoon unsalted margarine

1. In a medium-size bowl, mix the **tuna, bread
   crumbs, onion, celery, yogurt, ketchup, lemon
   juice,** and **pepper.** Shape into 4 thin patties
   about 3 inches in diameter.
2. Coat a heavy 10-inch nonstick skillet with the
   cooking spray, add the **margarine,** and melt
   over moderate heat. Add the patties and
   brown for 3 to 5 minutes on each side or until
   golden, turning once. Serves 2.

One Serving:

Calories	180	Protein	23 g
Total Fat	4 g	Carbohydrates	14 g
Saturated Fat	1 g	Sodium	422 mg
Cholesterol	49 mg	Added Sugar	0
		Fiber	1 g

Meatless Main and Pasta Dishes

Corn Crêpes with Spicy Tomato Sauce

5 tablespoons all-purpose flour
½ cup fresh or frozen whole-kernel corn
⅓ cup skim milk
1 tablespoon yellow cornmeal
1 tablespoon lightly beaten egg white
1 small sweet green pepper, cored, seeded, and chopped
1 small yellow onion, chopped
2 medium-size ripe tomatoes, cored, seeded, and chopped
2 cloves garlic, minced
1 teaspoon finely chopped fresh or canned green chili (optional)
2 tablespoons minced parsley
⅓ cup plain low-fat yogurt
2 tablespoons sour cream
½ teaspoon chili powder
½ teaspoon ground cumin
Nonstick cooking spray

1. In an electric blender or food processor, whirl the **flour,** ¼ cup of the **corn,** and the **milk, cornmeal,** and **egg white** for 30 seconds. Let the batter rest at room temperature for 30 minutes.
2. Meanwhile, in a medium-size bowl, mix the remaining ¼ cup corn, **green pepper, onion, tomatoes, garlic, green chili,** and 1 tablespoon of the **parsley,** and set aside.
3. In a small bowl, combine the **yogurt, sour cream, chili powder,** and **cumin** and set aside.
4. Preheat the oven to 250°F. Coat a heavy 10-inch nonstick skillet with the **cooking spray** and set over moderate heat for 30 seconds. Pour in half of the batter, swirling so that it covers the skillet bottom. Cook the crêpe for 2 to 3 minutes on each side or until crisp and golden. Ease the crêpe onto a plate and keep warm. Add another coat of cooking spray to the skillet and cook the second crêpe.
5. To assemble, divide the tomato mixture in half and spoon one part down the center of each crêpe; top with 1 tablespoon of the yogurt mixture and roll up. Spoon the rest of the yogurt mixture on top and sprinkle with the remaining parsley. Serve with a tossed green salad. Serves 2.

FAT SUGAR SODIUM

Preparation:
15 min., plus 30 min. standing time
Cooking:
9 min.

One Serving:

Calories	*242*
Total Fat	*5 g*
Saturated Fat	*2 g*
Cholesterol	*9 mg*
Protein	*10 g*
Carbohydrates	*41 g*
Sodium	*92 mg*
Added Sugar	*0*
Fiber	*3 g*

Tip: *The sharper your knife, the easier it is to cut fresh corn from the cob without losing the kernels' juices. One medium-size ear yields about ½ cup of kernels.*

French Bread Pizza

½ ½-pound loaf whole wheat French or Italian bread
1 clove garlic, cut in half
2 large ripe tomatoes, cored and chopped
½ cup shredded mozzarella cheese (about 2 ounces)
½ tablespoon olive oil
½ teaspoon dried oregano, crumbled
⅛ teaspoon black pepper
¼ cup grated Parmesan cheese

1. Preheat the broiler. Cut the **bread** in half lengthwise, then scoop out and discard the soft center. Place the bread cut side up on an ungreased baking sheet and toast in the broiler, 5 or 6 inches from the heat, for 3 or 4 minutes or until lightly browned. Remove the bread and rub with the **garlic.**
2. Meanwhile, in a small bowl, combine the **tomatoes, mozzarella cheese, olive oil, oregano,** and **pepper.** Spoon the mixture into each piece of bread and sprinkle with the **Parmesan cheese.** Broil for 3 minutes. Serves 2.

FAT SUGAR SODIUM

Preparation: **10 min.**
Cooking: **6 min.**

One Serving:

Calories	*292*
Total Fat	*12 g*
Saturated Fat	*3 g*
Cholesterol	*8 mg*
Protein	*7 g*
Carbohydrates	*17 g*
Sodium	*292 mg*
Added Sugar	*0*
Fiber	*5 g*

Black-eyed Pea Stew

Black-eyed Pea Stew

This meatless one-dish meal tastes even better the day after it is made. If you use only one portion, you can refrigerate the other one for up to three days or freeze it for a month. Top with the yogurt just before serving.

Preparation:
10 min.
Cooking:
58 min. (mostly unattended)

4 **ounces dried black-eyed peas, soaked overnight**

1 **large yellow onion, chopped fine**

2 **medium-size carrots, peeled and chopped**

2 **medium-size ripe tomatoes, peeled, cored, and chopped**

½ **teaspoon each dried savory and marjoram, crumbled**

¼ **teaspoon crushed red pepper flakes**

2 **bay leaves**

1 **cinnamon stick**

3 **cups water**

⅓ **cup fresh or frozen whole-kernel corn**

¼ **teaspoon black pepper**

⅛ **teaspoon salt**

⅔ **cup plain low-fat yogurt**

One Serving:

Calories	*363*
Total Fat	*3 g*
Saturated Fat	*1 g*
Cholesterol	*5 mg*
Protein	*21 g*
Carbohydrates	*68 g*
Sodium	*257 mg*
Added Sugar	*0*
Fiber	*3 g*

1. Drain the **black-eyed peas** and place them in a medium-size heavy saucepan together with the **onion, carrots, tomatoes, savory, marjoram, red pepper flakes, bay leaves,** and **cinnamon stick.** Add the **water,** stir to mix, place over moderately high heat, and bring to a boil—about 3 minutes. Lower the heat so that the mixture bubbles gently, partially cover, and simmer until the peas are tender—about 50 minutes.

2. Mix in the **corn, black pepper,** and **salt** and cook, uncovered, 5 minutes longer. Discard the bay leaves and cinnamon stick. Before serving, top each portion with ⅓ cup of the **yogurt.** Serves 2.

Tip: If you use canned black-eyed peas, cook them just long enough to heat through. More cooking will make them soft and mushy.

Pasta Shells with Mediterranean Vegetables

3 ounces large pasta shells

2½ teaspoons olive oil

1 medium-size yellow onion, sliced

1 clove garlic, minced

1 small sweet green pepper, cored, seeded, and cut into ¾-inch squares

1 small unpeeled eggplant (about ½ pound), cut into 1-inch cubes

1 medium-size zucchini (about ½ pound), sliced 1 inch thick

2 small ripe tomatoes, cored and cut into 1-inch cubes

3 tablespoons water

1 bay leaf

½ teaspoon each dried oregano and basil, crumbled

⅛ teaspoon black pepper

3 tablespoons grated Parmesan cheese

1. Cook the **pasta shells** according to package directions, omitting the salt. Drain, rinse under cold running water, and drain again.

2. Meanwhile, in a heavy 10-inch skillet, heat the **olive oil** over moderate heat for 1 minute; add the **onion, garlic,** and **green pepper,** and cook, uncovered, until tender but still crisp—about 3 minutes. Stir in the **eggplant, zucchini,** half the **tomatoes,** the **water, bay leaf, oregano, basil,** and **black pepper** and bring to a boil; reduce the heat, cover, and simmer for 10 minutes or until the vegetables are tender.

3. Stir in the remaining tomato, the pasta shells, and the **cheese,** and cook 1 to 2 minutes more, tossing gently until well mixed and heated through. Discard the bay leaf before serving. Serves 2.

FAT SUGAR SODIUM

Preparation:
15 min.
Cooking:
15 min.

One Serving:

Calories	325
Total Fat	9 g
Saturated Fat	2 g
Cholesterol	6 mg
Protein	13 g
Carbohydrates	51 g
Sodium	159 mg
Added Sugar	0
Fiber	5 g

Tip: *Supermarket tomatoes will ripen twice as quickly if you place them in a paper bag and close it tightly.*

Tortellini with Garden Vegetables

This recipe is endlessly versatile; substitute any vegetables you favor, and, if you like, add cooked seafood or chicken or such condiments as capers and pimientos.

5 ounces tortellini, pasta shells, penne, or elbow macaroni

1 medium-size carrot, peeled and sliced thin

½ cup fresh or frozen green peas

1 medium-size yellow squash (about ½ pound), sliced thin

1 medium-size ripe tomato, cored, seeded, and chopped

½ tablespoon unsalted margarine

⅛ teaspoon black pepper

1 tablespoon grated Parmesan cheese

1 tablespoon minced fresh chives, basil, or parsley

1. In a large heavy saucepan, bring 5 cups unsalted water to a boil over moderate heat; add the **tortellini** and **carrot** and cook, uncovered, for 3 minutes. Add the **peas** and cook 3 minutes more, stirring often. Mix in the **yellow squash** and cook, stirring, for 2 minutes or until the pasta and vegetables are just tender. Reserve ¼ cup of the cooking liquid, then drain, rinse in a colander under cold running water, and drain well again.

2. In the same saucepan, combine the reserved cooking liquid with the **tomato** and **margarine** and set over moderate heat. Return the pasta and vegetables to the saucepan and toss for 1 to 2 minutes or until the mixture is heated through. Sprinkle with the **pepper, cheese,** and **chives** and toss again. Serves 2.

FAT SUGAR SODIUM

Preparation:
10 min.
Cooking:
14 min.

One Serving:

Calories	374
Total Fat	5 g
Saturated Fat	1 g
Cholesterol	2 mg
Protein	14 g
Carbohydrates	69 g
Sodium	71 mg
Added Sugar	0
Fiber	5 g

Linguine with Tuna and Peas

Linguine with Tuna and Peas

Preparation: **5 min.** Cooking: **14 min.** [FAT] [SUGAR] [SODIUM]

- 3 ounces linguine or spaghetti
- ½ cup fresh or frozen green peas
- ¾ cup skim milk
- 1 tablespoon flour
- 1 small can (3½ ounces) water-packed light tuna, drained and flaked
- 3 tablespoons grated Parmesan cheese
- ¼ teaspoon black pepper

1. Cook the **linguine** according to package directions, omitting the salt. Drain, rinse under cold running water, and drain again.
2. Meanwhile, in a small saucepan, bring 1 cup unsalted water to a boil, add the **peas,** and cook, uncovered, for 1 minute; drain and set aside.
3. In a heavy 10-inch nonstick skillet, whisk the **milk** into the **flour** and cook, stirring constantly, over moderate heat until slightly thickened—about 2 minutes. Add the peas and cook 30 seconds longer. Add the pasta, **tuna, cheese,** and **pepper,** toss well, and heat through but do not boil—about 5 minutes. Serves 2.

One Serving:

Calories	301	Protein	23 g
Total Fat	4 g	Carbohydrates	43 g
Saturated Fat	2 g	Sodium	339 mg
Cholesterol	32 mg	Added Sugar	0
		Fiber	2 g

Salads

Chef's Salad

Preparation: **5 min.** [FAT] [SUGAR] [SODIUM]

- 1 small head Boston lettuce (about ¼ pound)
- 2 thin slices reduced-sodium ham (about 2 ounces)
- 2 thin slices cooked turkey or chicken breast (about 2 ounces)
- 2 slices low-sodium Swiss or American cheese (about 2 ounces)
- 2 thin slices red onion, separated into rings
- 1 hard-cooked egg white, coarsely chopped
- 1 medium-size ripe tomato, cored and cut into 8 wedges

1. Wash the **lettuce** and pat dry with paper towels; tear into bite-size pieces. Cut the **ham, turkey,** and **cheese** into matchstick strips.
2. Arrange equal amounts of the lettuce and **onion** rings on 2 salad plates. Top with equal portions of the ham, turkey, and cheese. Garnish with the **egg white** and the **tomato** wedges. Serve with 2 tablespoons Vinaigrette Dressing, page 225. Serves 2.

One Serving:

Calories	217	Protein	24 g
Total Fat	11 g	Carbohydrates	7 g
Saturated Fat	0	Sodium	276 mg
Cholesterol	36 mg	Added Sugar	0
		Fiber	2 g

Fruit and Cheese Salad with Orange Dressing

Here's an attractive and tasty fruit salad that makes a complete lunch in itself.

FAT SUGAR SODIUM

½ cup orange juice
2 teaspoons honey
1½ teaspoons balsamic vinegar or lemon juice
1 teaspoon cornstarch
¼ teaspoon curry powder
1 cup ¾-inch cubes fresh or canned pineapple
1 large navel orange, peeled and cut into 1-inch cubes

2 medium-size kiwis, peeled and cut into ¾-inch cubes
½ cup fresh blueberries, sorted and stemmed
4 medium-size strawberries, hulled and halved
1 cup dry-curd, low-fat cottage cheese

Preparation:
20 min., plus 30 min. refrigeration
Cooking:
3 min.

One Serving:

Calories	268
Total Fat	1 g
Saturated Fat	0
Cholesterol	5 mg
Protein	15 g
Carbohydrates	53 g
Sodium	17 mg
Added Sugar	21 Cal
Fiber	2 g

1. In a small heavy saucepan, combine the **orange juice, honey, vinegar, cornstarch,** and **curry powder.** Set over moderate heat and cook, stirring constantly, for 3 minutes or until the dressing has thickened slightly; remove from the heat. Cover with the lid and chill in the refrigerator about 30 minutes or until the dressing is cool.

2. Meanwhile, in a large bowl, mix together the **pineapple, orange, kiwis,** and **blueberries;** cover and refrigerate until serving time.

3. When ready to serve, add the **strawberries** to the bowl of fruit along with the chilled dressing and gently toss before serving on plates. Spoon **cottage cheese** onto each plate. Serves 2.

Dilled Tuna-Yogurt Salad

To make this recipe for one person, use a 3½-ounce can of tuna and halve the remaining ingredients.

FAT SUGAR SODIUM

2 tablespoons plain low-fat yogurt
2 tablespoons reduced-calorie mayonnaise
4 teaspoons snipped fresh dill or ½ teaspoon dill weed
⅛ teaspoon black pepper

1 can (6½ ounces) water-packed tuna, drained and flaked
½ cup diced celery
½ cup thinly sliced water chestnuts
1 small green onion, sliced thin
4 lettuce leaves

Preparation:
10 min.

One Serving:

Calories	190
Total Fat	6 g
Saturated Fat	1 g
Cholesterol	33 mg
Protein	23 g
Carbohydrates	12 g
Sodium	186 mg
Added Sugar	0
Fiber	1 g

1. In a medium-size bowl, combine the **yogurt, mayonnaise, dill,** and **pepper.** Add the **tuna, celery, water chestnuts,** and **green onion** and toss well.

2. Cover and chill for 1 or 2 hours, if you like, before serving on a bed of **lettuce leaves.** Serves 2.

Variation:

Dilled Salmon Salad Substitute 1 can (6½ ounces) salmon, drained and flaked, for the tuna. Reduce the celery to ¼ cup and omit the water chestnuts. Add ¼ cup chopped green pepper and 2 small radishes, sliced thin, and proceed as directed.

Breakfasts and Brown Bag Lunches

Omelets and eggs Benedict for people watching their fat and cholesterol? Yes! In this chapter you'll find ways to perform these culinary miracles, plus low-fat, low-sugar recipes for pancakes, French toast, and other old favorites. And if you're running out of inspiration for the family's brown bag meals, try the recipes starting on page 261. A marinated French bread sandwich or a salad with green peas, carrots, and mozzarella should raise those lunchtime reviews from routine to marvelous.

Scrambled Eggs Benedict

Breakfasts

Asparagus-Mushroom Omelets

1 **large egg**
5 **large egg whites**
1 **tablespoon minced fresh or freeze-dried chives**
2 **tablespoons cold water**
¼ **teaspoon black pepper**
2 **tablespoons unsalted margarine**

¼ **cup finely chopped cooked asparagus or broccoli**
¼ **cup finely chopped mushrooms**
¼ **cup finely chopped ripe tomato**
¼ **cup minced parsley**

FAT SUGAR SODIUM

Preparation:
5 min.
Cooking:
12 min.

1. In a medium-size bowl, combine the **egg, egg whites, chives, water,** and **pepper;** whisk just enough to mix lightly.
2. Melt ½ tablespoon of the **margarine** in a heavy 7-inch skillet over moderately high heat. Add ¼ each of the **asparagus** and **mushrooms** and cook, stirring, for 1 minute.
3. Add ¼ of the egg mixture (about ½ cup) and shake the skillet over the heat, stirring, for 30 seconds; then let the omelet cook, undisturbed, for 30 seconds more or until the edges and bottom are set.
4. With a spatula, either fold the omelet in half or roll it to the edge of the pan and invert it onto a heated plate. Make 3 more omelets in the same way. Top each omelet with the chopped **tomato** and sprinkle with the **parsley,** dividing the total amount evenly. Serves 4.

Variation:

Herb-Mushroom Omelet   Omit the asparagus and add 1 tablespoon minced fresh dill, oregano, basil, sage, tarragon, or chervil (or 1 teaspoon dried herb, crumbled) to the egg mixture just before cooking.

One Serving:

Calories	*98*
Total Fat	*7 g*
Saturated Fat	*1 g*
Cholesterol	*69 mg*
Protein	*6 g*
Carbohydrates	*2 g*
Sodium	*83 mg*
Added Sugar	*0*
Fiber	*1 g*

Tip: *To judge the freshness of eggs, look at their shells. Old eggs are smooth and shiny; fresh ones are rough and chalky by comparison.*

Asparagus-Mushroom Omelets

Scrambled Eggs Benedict

This has only a quarter of the cholesterol of standard Eggs Benedict. You can reduce the sodium by 200 mg if you substitute chicken or turkey for the ham.

4 **thin slices reduced-sodium ham (about ¼ pound)**	⅛ **teaspoon plus pinch black pepper**
1 **cup low-sodium chicken broth**	1 **large egg**
3 **tablespoons unsalted margarine**	4 **large egg whites**
2 **tablespoons flour**	2 **tablespoons skim milk**
1 **tablespoon lemon juice**	2 **English muffins, split**
	2 **tablespoons minced parsley**

Preparation:
8 min.
Cooking:
10 min.

One Serving:

Calories	236
Total Fat	12 g
Saturated Fat	2 g
Cholesterol	82 mg
Protein	13 g
Carbohydrates	18 g
Sodium	449 mg
Added Sugar	0
Fiber	0

1. Preheat the oven to 350°F. Wrap the **ham** slices in aluminum foil, place in the oven, and heat for 10 minutes. In a small saucepan, heat the **chicken broth** until it just starts to simmer.

2. Meanwhile, melt 2 tablespoons of the **margarine** in another small heavy saucepan over moderate heat. Add the **flour** and cook, stirring constantly, for 2 minutes. Whisk in the hot chicken broth and the **lemon juice;** bring to a simmer and cook, stirring, for 2 minutes or until the sauce has thickened. Stir in ⅛ teaspoon of the **pepper.**

3. In a small bowl, beat together the **egg, egg whites, skim milk,** and the pinch of black pepper. Melt the remaining tablespoon of margarine in a heavy 10-inch skillet over low heat, add the egg mixture, and cook, stirring often, for 4 to 5 minutes or until the eggs are set.

4. While the eggs are cooking, toast the **muffins,** then place a slice of ham on top of each one. Place ¼ of the scrambled eggs on top of each slice of ham, spoon the sauce over all, and sprinkle with the **parsley.** Serves 4.

Kedgeree

This combination of fish, rice, and hard-cooked egg is a popular breakfast and supper dish in England. It originated in India.

½ **cup brown rice**	½ **pound cod or haddock fillets, cut into ½-inch pieces**
1 **tablespoon unsalted margarine**	¼ **teaspoon black pepper**
1 **teaspoon curry powder or to taste**	2 **large hard-cooked egg whites, chopped fine**
1 **teaspoon flour**	1 **tablespoon minced parsley**
⅓ **cup low-sodium chicken broth**	

Preparation: **10 min.**
Cooking: **46 min.**
(mostly unattended)

One Serving:

Calories	170
Total Fat	4 g
Saturated Fat	1 g
Cholesterol	24 mg
Protein	14 g
Carbohydrates	19 g
Sodium	63 mg
Added Sugar	0
Fiber	2 g

1. Cook the **rice** according to package directions, omitting the salt.

2. When the rice is almost done, melt the **margarine** in a medium-size heavy saucepan over moderately low heat. Blend in the **curry powder** and cook, stirring, for 1 minute. Stir in the **flour,** add the **chicken broth,** and cook, stirring constantly, 1 to 2 minutes more or until slightly thickened.

3. Add the cooked rice to the curry mixture, along with the **cod, pepper,** and all but 1 tablespoon of the chopped **egg whites;** stir gently to mix. Heat, uncovered, over moderately low heat about 5 minutes, stirring occasionally, just until the fish is cooked through and the mixture is hot.

4. Transfer to a heated platter and sprinkle with the remaining chopped egg white and the **parsley.** Serves 4.

Swiss Health Cereal

1 cup quick-cooking rolled oats
½ cup chopped dried apricots, apples, or prunes or whole raisins
2 tablespoons chopped toasted almonds, pecans, or hazelnuts

2 tablespoons wheat germ
1 tablespoon light brown sugar
1 cup skim milk
½ cup plain low-fat yogurt
Ground cinnamon to taste

1. In a large bowl, combine the **oats, apricots, almonds, wheat germ,** and **brown sugar,** and toss well to combine. *(Note: You can store the cereal for up to a week in a tightly covered 1-pint jar; keep in a cool, dark place.)*
2. To serve, divide the cereal among 4 bowls and add ¼ cup of the **milk** to each. If you prefer crisp cereal, serve immediately; for soft cereal, let stand for 10 minutes. Top with **yogurt** and dust with **cinnamon.** Serves 4.

FAT SUGAR SODIUM

Preparation: 6 min.

One Serving:

Calories	206
Total Fat	4 g
Saturated Fat	1 g
Cholesterol	3 mg
Protein	9 g
Carbohydrates	35 g
Sodium	56 mg
Added Sugar	9 Cal
Fiber	1 g

Blueberry Breakfast Pudding

1 large egg
⅓ cup light or dark brown sugar
1 cup skim milk
1 teaspoon ground cinnamon
1 teaspoon grated lemon rind
Pinch ground nutmeg
1 teaspoon vanilla extract

6 slices whole wheat bread
Nonstick cooking spray
2 cups fresh or frozen dry-pack blueberries, sorted and stemmed
½ cup plain low-fat yogurt (optional)

1. With a fork, beat the **eggs** and **brown sugar** together in a large bowl until well blended. Stir in the **milk, cinnamon, lemon rind, nutmeg,** and **vanilla extract.** Tear the **bread** into ½-inch pieces and stir into the mixture. Cover and refrigerate for 1 hour or overnight.
2. Preheat the oven to 375°F. Lightly coat an 8″x 8″x 2″ baking pan with the **cooking spray.** Stir the **blueberries** into the bread mixture and spoon into the pan, uncovered, spreading the pudding evenly.
3. Bake for 40 minutes or until firm. Serve warm, topping each portion with 2 tablespoons of the **yogurt,** if desired. Serves 6.

FAT SUGAR SODIUM

Preparation: 10 min.
Baking: 40 min.

One Serving:

Calories	160
Total Fat	2 g
Saturated Fat	1 g
Cholesterol	47 mg
Protein	5 g
Carbohydrates	32 g
Sodium	161 mg
Added Sugar	30 Cal
Fiber	3 g

Blueberry Breakfast Pudding

Raspberry Coffee Cake

Nonstick cooking spray
1½ cups sifted all-purpose flour
3 tablespoons light or dark brown sugar
1¾ teaspoons baking powder
¼ teaspoon salt
3 tablespoons unsalted margarine

¾ cup low-fat (2% milk fat) milk
1 large egg, lightly beaten
2 teaspoons grated orange rind
½ teaspoon vanilla extract
½ cup fresh or frozen dry-pack raspberries or blueberries
2 tablespoons orange juice

FAT SUGAR SODIUM

Preparation:
5 min.
Baking:
25 min.

One Square:

Calories	148
Total Fat	5 g
Saturated Fat	1 g
Cholesterol	32 mg
Protein	3 g
Carbohydrates	22 g
Sodium	163 mg
Added Sugar	26 Cal
Fiber	1 g

1. Preheat the oven to 350°F. Lightly coat an 8"x 8"x 2" baking pan with the **cooking spray;** set aside.

2. In a large bowl, combine the **flour, brown sugar, baking powder,** and **salt.** Using a pastry blender or a fork, cut in the **margarine** until the mixture resembles coarse meal. Stir in the **milk, egg, orange rind,** and **vanilla extract,** and mix just until the dry ingredients are moistened. Spoon the batter into the baking pan.

3. In a small bowl, toss the **raspberries** with the **orange juice** and spoon on top of the batter. Bake until the coffee cake begins to shrink from the sides of the pan and a toothpick inserted in the center comes out clean—about 25 minutes. Cut into 9 squares and serve warm.

Pancakes

¾ cup sifted all-purpose flour
½ cup unsifted whole wheat flour
4 teaspoons light brown sugar
2 teaspoons baking powder
¼ teaspoon salt

1½ tablespoons unsalted margarine
1¼ cups low-fat (2% milk fat) milk
3 large egg whites
Nonstick cooking spray

FAT SUGAR SODIUM

Preparation:
5 min.
Cooking:
16 min.

One Pancake:

Calories	59
Total Fat	2 g
Saturated Fat	0
Cholesterol	2 mg
Protein	2 g
Carbohydrates	9 g
Sodium	107 mg
Added Sugar	11 Cal
Fiber	1 g

1. In a large bowl, combine the **all-purpose flour, whole wheat flour, brown sugar, baking powder,** and **salt;** set aside.

2. In a small saucepan, melt the **margarine** over moderate heat. In a small bowl, stir the margarine into the **milk,** add to the flour mixture, and stir just until the dry ingredients are moistened.

3. In another large bowl, beat the **egg whites** until they are stiff but not dry. Gently fold them into the batter.

4. Lightly coat a 12-inch nonstick skillet with the **cooking spray** and set over moderate heat. When the skillet is hot, cook the pancakes 2 at a time, using ¼ cup batter for each. Cook for 2 minutes or until bubbles form on top of the pancakes; flip, then cook about 1 minute longer or until the bottom of each pancake is golden brown. Makes 16 pancakes.

Variations:
Fruit Pancakes   After pouring the batter, top each pancake with a teaspoon of blueberries, raspberries, or a few slices of banana.
Buttermilk Pancakes   Substitute 1¼ cups buttermilk for the low-fat milk.
Cornmeal Pancakes   Substitute stone-ground yellow cornmeal for the whole wheat flour.

Tip: Overstirring the batter toughens pancakes and muffins. Stir only until the wet and dry ingredients are evenly mixed.

Jam Muffins

For variety, fill the muffins with a small square of cheese, a pitted prune, or ½ teaspoon chopped raisins instead of the jam.

FAT SUGAR SODIUM

Nonstick cooking spray
2 cups unsifted all-purpose flour
3 tablespoons sugar
1 teaspoon baking soda
¼ teaspoon salt
¼ cup unsalted margarine

1 cup buttermilk or sour milk
1 large egg, lightly beaten
¼ cup strawberry or raspberry jam

Preparation:
15 min.
Baking:
20 min.

1. Preheat the oven to 375°F. Using 1 large or 2 small muffin pans, lightly coat 12 2½-inch cups with the **cooking spray.** *(Note: You can omit the cooking spray and use paper cupcake liners instead.)*
2. In a large bowl, mix together the **flour, sugar, baking soda,** and **salt.**
3. Melt the **margarine** in a small saucepan over moderate heat. Combine in a small bowl with the **buttermilk,** then beat in the **egg** with a fork. Add the mixture to the dry ingredients, stirring only enough to moisten.
4. Spoon half the batter evenly into the muffin cups. With the back of a spoon, make a shallow indentation in the batter in each muffin cup, then spoon 1 teaspoon **jam** into each one. Top with the remaining batter, spreading to cover the filling.
5. Bake the muffins for 20 to 25 minutes or until golden brown. Serve warm. Makes 12 muffins.

One Muffin:

Calories	149
Total Fat	5 g
Saturated Fat	1 g
Cholesterol	24 mg
Protein	3 g
Carbohydrates	23 g
Sodium	187 mg
Added Sugar	12 Cal
Fiber	1 g

Tip: *Muffins bake best in humid air. Put water in any unused cups of a muffin pan.*

Orange French Toast

Try these three ways to vary ordinary French toast.

FAT SUGAR SODIUM

2 large egg whites, lightly beaten
⅔ cup skim milk
1 tablespoon grated orange rind

1 tablespoon unsalted margarine
8 thin slices whole wheat bread

Preparation:
10 min.
Cooking:
12 min.

1. In a shallow bowl or pie pan, whisk the **egg whites, milk,** and **orange rind** just until blended.
2. Melt ¼ of the **margarine** in a heavy 12-inch nonstick skillet over medium heat. Preheat the oven to 200°F.
3. Quickly dip **bread** slices in the egg mixture, turning to coat both sides well. Place in the skillet and cook about 3 minutes or until brown; turn and cook the other side about 3 minutes.
4. Prepare the remaining bread slices in the same way, adding more margarine as needed. Keep the cooked slices warm by placing them on a platter in the oven. Serves 4.

Variations:

Maple French Toast   Substitute 1 tablespoon maple extract for the grated orange rind.

Spiced French Toast   Substitute 1 teaspoon each ground cinnamon, nutmeg, and vanilla extract for the grated orange rind.

One Serving:

Calories	161
Total Fat	4 g
Saturated Fat	1 g
Cholesterol	2 mg
Protein	8 g
Carbohydrates	25 g
Sodium	289 mg
Added Sugar	0
Fiber	3 g

Mini Meat Loaves

Brown Bag Lunches
Mini Meat Loaves

If you have access to a refrigerator at work, pack these nutritious loaves for a brown bag lunch. Don't leave them unrefrigerated for more than two hours.

FAT SUGAR SODIUM

1 tablespoon unsalted margarine

2 small carrots, peeled and chopped fine

1 medium-size yellow onion, chopped fine

½ small sweet green pepper, cored, seeded, and chopped fine

½ small sweet red pepper, cored, seeded, and chopped fine

1 teaspoon dried sage, crumbled

1 large egg white, lightly beaten

1 pound lean ground turkey

1 cup soft white bread crumbs (2 slices)

⅓ cup low-sodium ketchup

2 ounces Swiss cheese, cut into ¼-inch cubes

¼ teaspoon black pepper

Preparation: **15 min.**
Cooking: **34 min.**
(mostly unattended)

One Meat Loaf:

Calories	135
Total Fat	8 g
Saturated Fat	2 g
Cholesterol	28 mg
Protein	11 g
Carbohydrates	7 g
Sodium	81 mg
Added Sugar	0
Fiber	0

1. Melt the **margarine** in a medium-size heavy saucepan over low heat. Add the **carrot, onion, green pepper, red pepper,** and **sage;** cook, covered, stirring occasionally, until the vegetables are soft—8 to 10 minutes.

2. Preheat the oven to 375°F. In a large bowl, combine the **egg white, ground turkey, bread crumbs, ketchup, cheese,** and **black pepper.** Add the cooked vegetables and mix well.

3. Place 10 2½-inch foil cupcake liners in the cups of 1 large or 2 small muffin pans. Spoon ⅓ cup of the turkey-vegetable mixture into each of the lined cups. Bake, uncovered, for 25 to 30 minutes or until the meat loaves are lightly browned and firm to the touch.

4. Cool the meat loaves in the pan upright on a wire rack for 10 minutes, then cover the pan with plastic wrap and refrigerate until ready to pack. Remove the meat loaves and wrap each one in plastic wrap or aluminum foil. Makes 10 small meat loaves.

Tip: If you prepare a brown bag lunch on a wooden cutting board, scrub down the surface first. Knicks and knife marks make an ideal breeding ground for bacteria that can cause food poisoning.

Pizza Sandwiches

These brown bag treats are good at room temperature, but you might want to heat them for three minutes in a microwave oven on low (30 percent of power) if one is handy.

1 teaspoon olive oil
1 small yellow onion, chopped fine
1 clove garlic, minced
½ cup low-sodium tomato sauce
½ teaspoon each dried oregano and basil, crumbled

¼ teaspoon dried thyme, crumbled
4 English muffins
¾ cup shredded part-skim mozzarella cheese
¼ cup grated Parmesan cheese

FAT SUGAR SODIUM

Preparation:
15 min.
Cooking:
7 min.

One Serving:

Calories	233
Total Fat	7 g
Saturated Fat	3 g
Cholesterol	16 mg
Protein	12 g
Carbohydrates	30 g
Sodium	489 mg
Added Sugar	0
Fiber	0

1. Preheat the broiler. In a small heavy saucepan, heat the **olive oil** over moderately low heat for 1 minute; add the **onion** and **garlic** and cook, uncovered, for 2 to 3 minutes. Stir in the **tomato sauce, oregano, basil,** and **thyme;** cook, stirring occasionally, for 2 minutes. Meanwhile, split and toast the **muffins.**

2. Sprinkle the 8 toasted muffin halves with half the **mozzarella cheese,** dividing it evenly. Place the muffins on the broiler pan and broil, 3 to 4 inches from the heat, for 1 to 2 minutes or just until the cheese has melted.

3. Spread 1 tablespoon of the tomato mixture on each of the muffin halves, then sprinkle with the remaining mozzarella and the **Parmesan cheese.**

4. Return the muffins to the broiler and broil 3 to 4 inches from the heat for 1 to 2 minutes or until the cheese melts. Sandwich the muffin halves together, forming 4 pizza sandwiches. Cool to room temperature, wrap in plastic wrap or aluminum foil, and refrigerate until ready to pack. Serves 4.

Stuffed Pita Sandwiches

For variety, use whole wheat pita bread or substitute other kinds of cheese.

1 tablespoon reduced-calorie mayonnaise
1 tablespoon white wine vinegar
½ teaspoon dried oregano, crumbled
¼ teaspoon paprika
⅛ teaspoon black pepper
4 slices (1 ounce each) Swiss cheese, cut into ½-inch strips

1 medium-size carrot, peeled and shredded
4 radishes, trimmed and sliced thin
4 pita breads (2 ounces each)
4 lettuce leaves
1 cup alfalfa sprouts (optional)

FAT SUGAR SODIUM

Preparation:
10 min.

One Serving:

Calories	302
Total Fat	9 g
Saturated Fat	5 g
Cholesterol	2 mg
Protein	14 g
Carbohydrates	40 g
Sodium	462 mg
Added Sugar	0
Fiber	0

1. In a medium-size bowl, blend the **mayonnaise, vinegar, oregano, paprika,** and **pepper.** Stir in the **cheese, carrot,** and **radishes.**

2. Split open the **pita breads** and insert a **lettuce leaf** in each. Spoon the cheese-vegetable mixture over the lettuce. Top with the **alfalfa sprouts,** if desired. Wrap in plastic wrap or aluminum foil. Makes 4 sandwiches.

Variation:

Stuffed Pita Sandwiches with Mushrooms   Substitute ½ medium-size stalk celery, sliced thin, for the radishes. Omit the alfalfa sprouts and top each sandwich with ¼ cup thinly sliced mushrooms.

Marinated Sandwiches

Marinated Sandwiches

This Italian specialty, called pan bagna, *gets better as it sits. It is meant to be soggy, so that its strong flavors merge.*

FAT SUGAR SODIUM

- **8 slices (¼ inch thick) crusty Italian, French, or whole wheat bread**
- **2 tablespoons olive oil**
- **2 cloves garlic, bruised**
- **2½ tablespoons red wine vinegar**
- **1 medium-size red onion, sliced thin**
- **8 medium-size pitted ripe olives, coarsely chopped**
- **2 medium-size ripe tomatoes, cored and sliced ½ inch thick**
- **1 can (6½ ounces) water-packed light tuna, drained and flaked**
- **4 tablespoons minced fresh basil or parsley**

Preparation:
3 min., plus 45 min. marination

1. Tear off 4 sheets of plastic wrap, each large enough to wrap a sandwich, and lay 2 slices of **bread** on each. Sprinkle the 8 slices with the **olive oil,** dividing it evenly, then rub the bread with the crushed **garlic;** discard the garlic. Sprinkle the bread with the **vinegar.**

2. Top each of 4 bread slices with ¼ of the **onion, olives, tomatoes, tuna,** and **basil.** Place the remaining slices, oil-and-vinegar side down, on top to make 4 sandwiches. Wrap each sandwich tightly in the plastic wrap and let sit at room temperature at least 45 minutes before eating. If packing for a picnic or brown bag lunch, refrigerate the sandwiches until ready to pack. Makes 4 sandwiches.

One Sandwich:

Calories	227
Total Fat	10 g
Saturated Fat	1 g
Cholesterol	26 mg
Protein	15 g
Carbohydrates	22 g
Sodium	375 mg
Added Sugar	0
Fiber	1 g

Muffaletto Sandwiches

Here is a slimmed-down version of the famous New Orleans hero sandwich. Refrigerate it if you can, or store no longer than two hours at room temperature. The canned roasted sweet red peppers called for in the recipe are available at most supermarkets.

FAT **SUGAR** SODIUM

1 jar (7 ounces) roasted sweet red peppers, cut into strips 1 inch wide

2 tablespoons chopped green chilies or to taste

¼ cup drained medium-size pitted green olives, chopped fine

3 large stalks celery, sliced thin

2 cloves garlic, minced

½ teaspoon dried oregano, crumbled

1 tablespoon red wine vinegar or cider vinegar

1 loaf (½ pound) French bread

¼ pound cooked turkey breast, sliced thin

2 ounces Swiss cheese, sliced thin

Preparation:
15 min., plus 1 hr. marination

One Serving:

Calories	240
Total Fat	7 g
Saturated Fat	3 g
Cholesterol	21 mg
Protein	17 g
Carbohydrates	27 g
Sodium	609 mg
Added Sugar	0
Fiber	0

1. In a medium-size bowl, combine the **roasted peppers, green chilies, olives, celery, garlic, oregano,** and **vinegar.** Mix well, cover, and refrigerate for 1 hour.

2. Halve the **bread** lengthwise, scooping out and discarding the soft center. Arrange the **turkey** and **cheese** slices on the bottom half of the bread, top with the marinated pepper-olive mixture, and cover with the top half of the bread. Cut the loaf into 4 pieces of equal size, wrap in plastic wrap or aluminum foil, and refrigerate until ready to pack in an insulated container. Makes 4 servings.

Variation:

Muffaletto with Tuna Omit the turkey and spread 1 can (6½ ounces) water-packed light tuna, drained and flaked, over the bottom half of the bread.

Tip: Bag lunches will stay fresher—and safer—if you chill them thoroughly before packing. If possible, make your sandwiches the night before and store them in the refrigerator overnight.

Crudités with Peanut Butter Dip

Here's a nutritious school lunch for children. The variations are limitless; simply use the fruits and vegetables your children like the most. To make as a snack for adults, use low-sodium, reduced-calorie peanut butter.

FAT **SUGAR** SODIUM

1 medium-size carrot, peeled and cut into matchstick strips

1 medium-size stalk celery, cut into matchstick strips

8 snow peas or green beans, trimmed

3 radishes, trimmed

½ medium-size banana, peeled

1 tablespoon peanut butter

¼ cup unsweetened apple juice

1 teaspoon lemon juice

Preparation:
10 min.

One Serving:

Calories	230
Total Fat	9 g
Saturated Fat	2 g
Cholesterol	0
Protein	7 g
Carbohydrates	35 g
Sodium	71 mg
Added Sugar	0
Fiber	3 g

1. Wrap the **carrot, celery, snow peas,** and **radishes** separately in plastic wrap or aluminum foil.

2. Place the **banana, peanut butter, apple juice,** and **lemon juice** in an electric blender or food processor. Whirl for 10 to 15 seconds or until smooth. Pour into a small plastic container, place plastic wrap directly on the surface of the mixture to prevent discoloration, and snap on the lid. Refrigerate until ready to pack. Serves 1.

Green Pea, Carrot, and Mozzarella Salad

This salad and the two that follow, all made without the usual greens that wilt, will keep in the refrigerator for several days. Spoon out the portion you need for a brown bag lunch, packing it in a lidded plastic container.

FAT SUGAR SODIUM

1 cup fresh or frozen green peas

1 medium-size carrot, peeled and chopped

½ small stalk celery, chopped

1 ounce part-skim mozzarella cheese, cut into small cubes (about ¼ cup)

2 tablespoons plus 1 teaspoon buttermilk

2 green onions, chopped fine

1 tablespoon plain low-fat yogurt

1½ teaspoons mayonnaise

½ teaspoon balsamic or red wine vinegar

½ teaspoon dried basil, crumbled

⅛ teaspoon black pepper

¼ teaspoon sugar

Preparation:
10 min.
Cooking:
6 min.

One Serving:

Calories	*80*
Total Fat	*3 g*
Saturated Fat	*1 g*
Cholesterol	*6 mg*
Protein	*5 g*
Carbohydrates	*9 g*
Sodium	*68 mg*
Added Sugar	*1 Cal*
Fiber	*2 g*

1. In a small heavy saucepan, bring an inch of unsalted water to a boil, add the **peas** and **carrot,** and cook for 5 minutes. Drain, rinse under cold running water to stop the cooking, and drain again. Place in a medium-size bowl. Add the **celery** and **cheese** and toss well to mix.

2. In a small bowl, combine the **buttermilk, green onions, yogurt, mayonnaise, vinegar, basil, pepper,** and **sugar.** Spoon over the salad and toss well. Cover and refrigerate until needed. Makes 4 servings.

Green Pea, Carrot, and Mozzarella Salad

Pasta and Broccoli Salad

1 tablespoon Oriental sesame or peanut oil

1½ teaspoons red wine vinegar

1 teaspoon dried marjoram, crumbled

1 clove garlic, minced

¼ teaspoon black pepper

1 cup broccoli florets

8 ounces elbow macaroni, fusilli, rotelle, or medium-size pasta shells

1 small sweet red pepper, cored, seeded, and cut into strips 2 inches long and ½ inch wide

1 small yellow onion, sliced thin

2 ounces Swiss cheese, cut into strips 2 inches long and ½ inch wide

1 tablespoon chopped walnuts

FAT SUGAR SODIUM

Preparation: 15 min.
Cooking: 15 min.

One Serving:

Calories	309
Total Fat	8 g
Saturated Fat	0
Cholesterol	0
Protein	12 g
Carbohydrates	46 g
Sodium	47 mg
Added Sugar	0
Fiber	2 g

1. To make the dressing, combine the **sesame oil, vinegar, marjoram, garlic,** and **black pepper** in a large heatproof bowl and whisk to mix; set aside.

2. Cook the **broccoli** for 3 minutes in a large kettle of boiling unsalted water; scoop out with a small strainer, shake to remove excess water, and add to the dressing.

3. In the same kettle of boiling water, cook the **macaroni** according to package directions, omitting the salt. Drain well and add to the broccoli, along with the **red pepper, onion, cheese,** and **walnuts.** Toss well, cover, and refrigerate until needed. Makes 4 servings.

Variations:

Pasta and Green Bean Salad   Substitute 1 cup trimmed green beans, cooked for 4 minutes, for the broccoli. Substitute toasted slivered almonds for the chopped walnuts.

Pasta and Snow Pea Salad   Substitute 1 cup trimmed snow peas, cooked for 2 minutes, for the broccoli. Substitute sunflower seeds for the chopped walnuts.

Vegetable-Cheese Salad with Artichokes

1 cup broccoli florets

1 package (9 ounces) frozen artichoke hearts

2 teaspoons olive or walnut oil

1½ teaspoons balsamic or red wine vinegar

¾ teaspoon dried tarragon, crumbled

⅛ teaspoon black pepper

6 cherry tomatoes, halved

½ cup sliced Jerusalem artichokes or water chestnuts

2 ounces part-skim mozzarella cheese, cut into ½-inch cubes

FAT SUGAR SODIUM

Preparation: **5 min.,** plus 6 hr. refrigeration
Cooking: **10 min.**

One Serving:

Calories	109
Total Fat	5 g
Saturated Fat	2 g
Cholesterol	8 mg
Protein	7 g
Carbohydrates	11 g
Sodium	105 mg
Added Sugar	0
Fiber	0

1. In a small saucepan with enough boiling unsalted water to cover, cook the **broccoli** until tender but still crisp—3 to 5 minutes. Drain in a colander, rinse under cold running water to stop the cooking, and drain again. Set aside. At the same time, cook the **artichoke hearts** according to package directions, omitting the salt; drain well and set aside.

2. In a large bowl, combine the **olive oil, vinegar, tarragon,** and **pepper.** Add the broccoli, artichoke hearts, **cherry tomatoes, Jerusalem artichokes,** and **cheese.** Toss well, cover, and refrigerate at least 6 hours before packing for a picnic or brown bag lunch. Serves 4.

Beverages

You no longer need decide between a sugar-laden drink and its chemically sweetened counterpart. In this chapter you'll find natural low-sugar, low-fat beverages for every season and occasion. In summer, try a Pineapple-Orange Cooler or Spiced Cranberry Shrub. When the weather cools, indulge in Heavenly Hot Chocolate or Mulled Apple Cider. Impress your guests with Holiday Eggnog or Ginger-Tea Punch. And when you come home in the evening, brew a pot of soothing, caffeine-free Herbal Tea.

Holiday Eggnog

Chocolate Buttermilk Drink

Preparation: **2 min.** FAT SUGAR SODIUM

Here's a tempting drink for chocolate lovers; it can be made right in the glass.

- 2 teaspoons cocoa powder (not a mix)
- 2 teaspoons sugar
- 1 cup buttermilk

In a tall glass, combine the **cocoa powder** and **sugar**; add 2 tablespoons of the **buttermilk** and stir until no lumps remain. Mix in the remaining buttermilk, stir well again, and serve. Serves 1.

One Serving:

Calories	140	Protein	9 g
Total Fat	3 g	Carbohydrates	22 g
Saturated Fat	2 g	Sodium	258 mg
Cholesterol	10 mg	Added Sugar	32 Cal
		Fiber	0

Tip: When you buy cocoa, read the label. Make sure you're getting the plain, unsweetened powder instead of the sugary, additive-laden cocoa mix that is used for making hot drinks.

Orange Buttermilk Drink

Preparation: **2 min.** FAT SUGAR SODIUM

- 1 cup buttermilk
- ½ cup orange juice
- ½ teaspoon honey
- ¼ teaspoon ground ginger

In an electric blender or food processor, combine the **buttermilk, orange juice, honey,** and **ginger,** and whirl for 1 minute or until frothy. Pour into a tall glass and serve. Serves 1.

Variation:

Pineapple Buttermilk Drink   Prepare as directed, but substitute ½ cup unsweetened pineapple juice for the orange juice and ½ teaspoon lime juice for the ground ginger.

One Serving:

Calories	166	Protein	9 g
Total Fat	2 g	Carbohydrates	28 g
Saturated Fat	1 g	Sodium	259 mg
Cholesterol	10 mg	Added Sugar	8 Cal
		Fiber	0

Cappuccino

Preparation: **1 min.** Cooking: **5 min.** FAT SUGAR SODIUM

- 6 tablespoons Italian-style espresso coffee
- 3 cups water
- ½ cup evaporated skim milk
- ½ teaspoon vanilla extract
  Ground cinnamon or cocoa powder (not a mix)

1. Place the **coffee** in the filter of a drip coffee maker. In a small heavy saucepan, bring the **water** to a boil over moderately high heat; pour the boiling water over the coffee and let it drip through—about 5 minutes. *(Note: Espresso coffee can also be made in a percolator according to the directions for that coffee maker.)*

2. In the same saucepan, heat the **milk,** uncovered, over moderate heat until it is hot—about 2 minutes—but do not let it boil.

3. Transfer the milk to the container of an electric blender, add the **vanilla extract,** and whirl at high speed for 1 minute or until foamy.

4. When the coffee is ready, pour it into 4 serving cups and top with the hot milk mixture, dividing it evenly. Sprinkle with the **cinnamon** and serve. Serves 4.

One Serving:

Calories	31	Protein	3 g
Total Fat	0	Carbohydrates	5 g
Saturated Fat	0	Sodium	41 mg
Cholesterol	1 mg	Added Sugar	0
		Fiber	0

Heavenly Hot Chocolate

Preparation: **2 min.** Cooking: **5 min.** FAT SUGAR SODIUM

Dutch-process cocoa is available in many supermarkets; because it has an intense chocolate flavor, you use less and thereby trim the calories.

- ½ cup skim milk
- ½ cup evaporated skim milk
- 1¼ teaspoons sugar
- 1 tablespoon Dutch-process cocoa powder
- 1 teaspoon water

1. In a small heavy saucepan, combine the **skim milk, evaporated skim milk,** and **sugar,** and heat, uncovered, over low heat until the milk bubbles gently—about 5 minutes.

2. Meanwhile, in an 8-ounce serving cup or mug, mix the **cocoa powder** with the **water** until it forms a thick paste.

3. When the milk is ready, slowly pour it into the cocoa paste, stirring until smooth. Serves 1.

Variations:

Mexican Hot Chocolate   Prepare as directed, but blend ¾ teaspoon ground cinnamon into the milk just before bringing it to a simmer.

Anise Hot Chocolate   Prepare as directed, but stir ⅛ teaspoon anise extract into the hot chocolate just before serving.

One Serving:

Calories	177	Protein	15 g
Total Fat	1 g	Carbohydrates	28 g
Saturated Fat	1 g	Sodium	211 mg
Cholesterol	8 mg	Added Sugar	20 Cal
		Fiber	0

Tip: *By using evaporated skim milk instead of evaporated whole milk, you can save 63 calories and 8 grams of fat per ½ cup.*

Mulled Apple Cider

Preparation: **2 min.**
Cooking: **20 min.** (mostly unattended)   FAT SUGAR SODIUM

5 **cups apple cider**
2 **cinnamon sticks, cracked**
8 **allspice berries**
6 **whole cloves**
1 **strip orange peel, about 2 inches long and ½ inch wide**
4 **thin orange slices (optional)**
4 **cinnamon sticks (optional)**

1. In a small heavy saucepan (preferably non-metallic), place the **apple cider, cinnamon sticks, allspice, cloves,** and **orange peel,** and bring to a boil over moderately high heat. Adjust the heat so that the mixture barely bubbles, cover, and simmer for 15 minutes.

2. Strain the cider mixture into 4 mugs and put an **orange slice** and **cinnamon stick** in each mug, if you like. Serves 4.

One Serving:

Calories	150	Protein	0
Total Fat	0	Carbohydrates	37 g
Saturated Fat	0	Sodium	10 mg
Cholesterol	0	Added Sugar	0
		Fiber	0

Home-Style Lemonade

Preparation: **5 min.** Cooking: **3 min.**    FAT SUGAR SODIUM

If you combine this lemonade with one recipe each of the grapefruitade, limeade, and orangeade variations that follow, you will have a terrific fruit punch that serves 16 or more.

½ **cup sugar**
2½ **cups water**
Peel of 1 lemon, cut into strips 2 inches long and ½ inch wide
12 **ice cubes**
1 **cup lemon juice**

1. In a medium-size heavy saucepan, place the **sugar, water,** and **lemon peel,** and cook, stirring, over moderate heat until the sugar dissolves—about 1 minute. Increase the heat to moderately high, bring the mixture to a boil, and cook, uncovered, for 1 minute. Remove from the heat, cover, and cool to room temperature.

2. Strain the sugar mixture into a 2-quart pitcher; remove and discard the lemon peel. Add the **ice cubes** and **lemon juice** and stir well to mix. Pour into 4 tall glasses and serve. Serves 4.

Variations:

Grapefruitade   Prepare as directed, but reduce the water to 1½ cups and substitute 2 cups unsweetened grapefruit juice for the lemon juice.

Limeade   Prepare as directed, but increase the water to 3 cups and the ice cubes to 16 and substitute lime peel for the lemon peel and 1 cup lime juice for the lemon juice.

Orangeade   Prepare as directed, but reduce the water to 1½ cups and substitute orange peel for the lemon peel and 2⅔ cups orange juice plus ½ cup lime juice for the lemon juice.

One Serving:

Calories	110	Protein	0
Total Fat	0	Carbohydrates	29 g
Saturated Fat	0	Sodium	13 mg
Cholesterol	0	Added Sugar	96 Cal
		Fiber	0

Tip: *Thin-skinned lemons yield the most juice. Avoid the kind that are spongy and pitted.*

Hot Cranberry Punch

Holiday Eggnog

Preparation: **5 min.**   FAT SUGAR SODIUM

Here's a low-calorie, fat-free, low-cholesterol eggnog that you can drink free of worry. You can double it to serve eight.

1 **can (12 ounces) evaporated skim milk, chilled**
2 **tablespoons rum or brandy or
1 teaspoon rum or brandy extract**
4 **teaspoons sugar**
2 **large egg whites
Freshly grated nutmeg or ground nutmeg**

1. In a medium-size bowl, combine the **milk, rum,** and **sugar,** stirring until the sugar dissolves.
2. In another medium-size bowl, beat the **egg whites** until they hold soft peaks, then fold into the milk mixture.
3. Ladle the eggnog into chilled punch cups or wine glasses and sprinkle each with **nutmeg.** Serves 4.

One Serving:

Calories	115	*Protein*	*9 g*
Total Fat	0	*Carbohydrates*	*15 g*
Saturated Fat	0	*Sodium*	*135 mg*
Cholesterol	*4 mg*	*Added Sugar*	*16 Cal*
		Fiber	*0*

Ginger-Tea Punch

Preparation: **2 min.** Cooking: **4 min.**   FAT SUGAR SODIUM

Here's a punch with a tang. For 24 servings, double all the ingredients; for 36, triple them.

4 **cups water**
8 **tea bags**
6 **tablespoons sugar**
2 **tablespoons minced fresh ginger or 1 teaspoon ground ginger**
2 **bottles (10 ounces each) ginger ale**

1. In a medium-size saucepan, bring the **water** to a boil over moderately high heat. Pour the boiling water into a 1-quart heatproof pitcher, add the **tea bags, sugar,** and **ginger,** and steep for 8 minutes or until the tea is as strong as desired. Remove and discard the tea bags. Cool, cover, and refrigerate until ready to serve.
2. Just before serving, strain the tea into a 3-quart pitcher or punch bowl and stir in the **ginger ale.** Serve over ice cubes in tall glasses. Serves 12.

One Serving:

Calories	44	*Protein*	*0*
Total Fat	0	*Carbohydrates*	*11 g*
Saturated Fat	0	*Sodium*	*8 mg*
Cholesterol	0	*Added Sugar*	*24 Cal*
		Fiber	*0*

Hot Cranberry Punch

Preparation: **5 min.** FAT SUGAR SODIUM
Cooking: **20 min.** (mostly unattended)

You can save 25 calories per serving by using low-calorie cranberry juice cocktail.

1 **tea bag**
1 **cup boiling water**
1 **cup cranberry juice cocktail**
3 **cups apple cider or unsweetened apple juice**
1 **cinnamon stick, cracked**
4 **whole cloves**
4 **allspice berries**
1 **strip orange peel, about 2 inches long and ½ inch wide**
4 **thin orange slices (optional)**
4 **cinnamon sticks (optional)**

1. Place the **tea bag** in a mug, add the **boiling water,** and steep for 5 minutes.
2. In a small saucepan (preferably nonmetallic), place the **cranberry juice cocktail, apple cider, cinnamon stick, cloves, allspice,** and **orange peel,** and bring to a boil over moderately high heat. Lower the heat, cover, and simmer for 15 minutes. Remove from the heat and add the tea, discarding the tea bag.
3. Strain the punch into 4 mugs and garnish each drink with an **orange slice** and **cinnamon stick,** if desired. Serves 4.

One Serving:

Calories	127	Protein	0
Total Fat	0	Carbohydrates	26 g
Saturated Fat	0	Sodium	9 mg
Cholesterol	0	Added Sugar	35 Cal
		Fiber	0

Amber Orange-Tea Punch

Preparation: **5 min.**, plus overnight FAT SUGAR SODIUM
refrigeration   Cooking: **8 min.**

2 **cups water**
4 **tea bags**
2 **cups orange juice**
2 **tablespoons sugar**
2 **cinnamon sticks, cracked**
12 **whole cloves**
2 **bottles (10 ounces each) ginger ale, chilled**

1. In a small heavy saucepan (preferably nonmetallic), bring the **water** to a boil over moderately high heat—about 2 minutes. Pour the boiling water into a 1-quart heatproof pitcher, add the **tea bags,** and steep for 8 minutes or until the tea is as strong as desired. Remove and discard the tea bags.
2. Pour 1 cup of the **orange juice** into the same saucepan and add the **sugar, cinnamon sticks,** and **cloves.** Bring to a boil, lower the heat, cover, and simmer for 5 minutes.
3. Remove the orange juice mixture from the heat and pour it into a 2-quart heatproof bowl or pitcher. Stir in the remaining orange juice and the tea, cover, and refrigerate overnight.
4. Just before serving, strain into a punch bowl or pitcher and stir in the **ginger ale.** Serves 12.

Variation:

Autumn Apple Punch   Omit the water and tea bags and substitute 1 bottle (32 ounces) unsweetened apple juice for the orange juice; reduce the sugar to 1 tablespoon.

One Serving:

Calories	46	Protein	0
Total Fat	0	Carbohydrates	11 g
Saturated Fat	0	Sodium	7 mg
Cholesterol	0	Added Sugar	31 Cal
		Fiber	0

Mocha Shake

Preparation: **2 min.**

2 **teaspoons cocoa powder (not a mix)**
1 **teaspoon sugar**
1 **teaspoon instant coffee crystals**
¼ **cup skim milk**
⅓ **cup vanilla ice milk**
2 **ice cubes**

1. In a small bowl, combine the **cocoa powder, sugar,** and **coffee.** Add the **milk** slowly, stirring until smooth.
2. Transfer the mixture to an electric blender, add the **ice milk** and **ice cubes,** and whirl for 1 minute or until frothy. Pour into a tall glass and serve. Serves 1.

One Serving:

Calories	110	Protein	5 g
Total Fat	3 g	Carbohydrates	19 g
Saturated Fat	2 g	Sodium	67 mg
Cholesterol	7 mg	Added Sugar	67 Cal
		Fiber	0

Banana Milk Shake

Preparation: **5 min.**   FAT SUGAR SODIUM

- **5 ice cubes**
- **⅓ cup skim milk**
- **½ small banana, peeled and sliced**
- **¼ teaspoon vanilla extract**
- **2 teaspoons sugar**

Place the **ice cubes** and **milk** in an electric blender and whirl for 1 minute or until smooth. Add the **banana, vanilla extract,** and **sugar,** and whirl 1 minute longer or until foamy. Pour into a tall glass and serve. Serves 1.

Variations:

Strawberry Milk Shake   Prepare as directed, but substitute 1 cup hulled and sliced strawberries for the banana.

Orange Milk Shake   Prepare as directed but reduce the ice cubes to 3 and substitute ½ cup orange juice for the banana.

Chocolate Milk Shake   Prepare as directed, but substitute 2 tablespoons cocoa powder (not a mix) for the banana and increase the vanilla extract to ½ teaspoon.

One Serving:

Calories	106	*Protein*	*3 g*
Total Fat	0	*Carbohydrates*	*23 g*
Saturated Fat	0	*Sodium*	*43 mg*
Cholesterol	*2 mg*	*Added Sugar*	*32 Cal*
		Fiber	*1 g*

Minted Grapefruit Spritzer

Preparation: **5 min.**   FAT SUGAR SODIUM

- **2½ cups unsweetened grapefruit juice**
- **3 tablespoons lemon juice**
- **4 teaspoons sugar**
- **8 sprigs mint**
- **1½ cups sodium-free seltzer water**

1. In a 1½-quart pitcher, combine the **grapefruit juice** and **lemon juice** and set aside.
2. Place 1 teaspoon **sugar** and 1 **mint sprig** in each of 4 12-ounce glasses. With the back of a spoon, crush the mint into the sugar. Fill the glasses with ice cubes, divide the grapefruit juice mixture among them, then top with

the **seltzer water.** Stir briskly to mix, add a sprig of mint to each drink, and serve. Serves 4.

One Serving:

Calories	79	*Protein*	*1 g*
Total Fat	0	*Carbohydrates*	*19 g*
Saturated Fat	0	*Sodium*	*4 mg*
Cholesterol	0	*Added Sugar*	*16 Cal*
		Fiber	*0*

Gingered Lemon-Lime Fizz

Preparation: **5 min.**   FAT SUGAR SODIUM

- **½ cup lemon juice**
- **¼ cup lime juice**
- **2 cups cold water**
- **4 teaspoons honey**
- **2 cups ginger ale**
- **4 thin lime slices (optional)**

1. In a 2-quart pitcher, combine the **lemon juice, lime juice, water,** and **honey,** and set aside.
2. Fill 4 12-ounce glasses with ice cubes, divide the lemon-lime juice mixture among them, then top with the **ginger ale.** Stir briskly and put a **lime slice,** if you like, in each drink. Serves 4.

One Serving:

Calories	74	*Protein*	*0*
Total Fat	0	*Carbohydrates*	*20 g*
Saturated Fat	0	*Sodium*	*15 mg*
Cholesterol	0	*Added Sugar*	*16 Cal*
		Fiber	*0*

Pineapple-Orange Cooler

Preparation: **5 min.**   FAT SUGAR SODIUM

- **1½ cups unsweetened pineapple juice**
- **1½ cups orange juice**
- **2 tablespoons lemon juice**
- **1¼ cups sodium-free seltzer water**
- **4 thin orange slices (optional)**

1. In a 2-quart pitcher, combine the **pineapple juice, orange juice,** and **lemon juice** and set the pitcher aside.
2. Fill 4 12-ounce glasses with ice cubes, divide the fruit juice mixture among them, then top

Gingered Lemon-Lime Fizz (left) and *Pineapple-Orange Cooler* (right)

with the **seltzer water.** Stir briskly to mix and garnish, if you like, with the **orange slices.** Serves 4.

One Serving:

Calories	96	Protein	1 g
Total Fat	0	Carbohydrates	23 g
Saturated Fat	0	Sodium	3 mg
Cholesterol	0	Added Sugar	0
		Fiber	0

Herbal Tea

Preparation: **5 min.**
Cooking: **5 min.** (unattended)　FAT SUGAR SODIUM

　5　**cups water**
　½　**cup chopped fresh mint or 2 tablespoons mint flakes**
　1　**tablespoon dried sage leaves**
　1　**tablespoon dried lemon verbena or 1 teaspoon dried tarragon leaves**

　4　**teaspoons light honey**
　4　**teaspoons lemon juice**
　4　**lemon wedges (optional)**
　4　**mint sprigs (optional)**

1. In a medium-size saucepan, bring the **water** to a boil over moderately high heat—about 5 minutes. Pour the boiling water into a warmed teapot and add the **mint, sage,** and **lemon verbena;** cover and steep for 5 minutes.

2. Strain the tea mixture into 4 cups or mugs; stir 1 teaspoon **honey** and 1 teaspoon **lemon juice** into each, and, if you like, garnish with a **lemon wedge** and a **mint sprig.** Serves 4.

One Serving:

Calories	27	Protein	0
Total Fat	0	Carbohydrates	7 g
Saturated Fat	0	Sodium	2 mg
Cholesterol	0	Added Sugar	16 Cal
		Fiber	0

Iced Apple-Mint Tea

Preparation: **5 min.** Cooking: **3 min.**　FAT SUGAR SODIUM

2½　**cups water**
　2　**tea bags**
　½　**cup chopped fresh mint or 1 tablespoon mint flakes**
　1　**strip lemon peel, about 2 inches long and ½ inch wide**
　2　**cups unsweetened apple juice or cider**
　1　**tablespoon lemon juice**
　4　**sprigs mint (optional)**

1. In a medium-size saucepan, bring the **water** to a boil over moderately high heat—about 3 minutes. Pour the boiling water into a warmed teapot and add the **tea bags, mint,** and **lemon peel;** cover and steep until cool—about 20 minutes. Remove and discard the tea bags.

2. Strain the tea into a 2-quart pitcher and stir in the **apple juice** and **lemon juice.**

3. Fill 4 12-ounce glasses with ice cubes and divide the apple-mint tea among them. Stir briskly and garnish each drink with a **mint sprig,** if you like. Serves 4.

One Serving:

Calories	62	Protein	0
Total Fat	0	Carbohydrates	15 g
Saturated Fat	0	Sodium	8 mg
Cholesterol	0	Added Sugar	0
		Fiber	0

Spiced Cranberry Shrub

Preparation: **2 min.**
Cooking: **18 min.** (mostly unattended)

FAT SUGAR SODIUM

Shrub is an old-fashioned name given to a blend of fruit juices to which an acid, such as cider or vinegar, and cold water are added.

1¼ **cups cranberry juice cocktail**
1¼ **cups unsweetened apple juice or cider**
 ¼ **cup cider vinegar**
 1 **cinnamon stick, cracked**
 2 **whole cloves**
 2 **strips lemon peel, about 2 inches long and ½ inch wide**
 2 **cups sodium-free seltzer water**
 4 **thin orange slices (optional)**

1. In a small heavy saucepan (preferably nonmetallic), place the **cranberry juice cocktail, apple juice, vinegar, cinnamon stick, cloves,** and **lemon peel,** and bring to a boil over moderately high heat. Adjust the heat so that the mixture barely bubbles, cover, and simmer for 15 minutes. Cool and strain into a 2-quart pitcher.
2. Fill 4 12-ounce glasses with ice cubes, divide the cranberry mixture among them, and top with the **seltzer water.** Stir briskly and garnish each drink with an **orange slice,** if you like. Serves 4.

One Serving:

Calories	86	Protein	0
Total Fat	0	Carbohydrates	14 g
Saturated Fat	0	Sodium	5 mg
Cholesterol	0	Added Sugar	58 Cal
		Fiber	0

Pineapple-Mint Yogurt Drink

Preparation: **1 min.**

FAT SUGAR SODIUM

Try this wholesome drink to supplement your diet as well as quench your thirst.

 1 **can (8 ounces) juice-packed crushed pineapple, with the juice**
 ½ **cup plain low-fat yogurt**
 ½ **cup skim milk**
 1 **tablespoon sugar**
 3 **tablespoons chopped fresh mint**

In an electric blender or food processor, place the **pineapple, yogurt, milk, sugar,** and **mint,** and whirl for 1 minute or until smooth and creamy. Pour into 2 tall glasses and serve. Serves 2.

Variations:

Red Berry Yogurt Drink   Prepare as directed, but substitute 1 cup fresh raspberries (or 1 cup thawed frozen dry-pack raspberries) and 1 cup fresh hulled strawberries (or 1 cup thawed frozen dry-pack strawberries) for the pineapple; reduce the skim milk to ⅓ cup and omit the mint.

Blueberry-Lemon Yogurt   Prepare as directed, but substitute 1 cup fresh stemmed and sorted blueberries (or 1 cup thawed frozen dry-pack blueberries) for the pineapple; increase the skim milk to ¾ cup, add ½ teaspoon finely grated lemon rind, and omit the mint.

One Serving:

Calories	150	Protein	6 g
Total Fat	1 g	Carbohydrates	31 g
Saturated Fat	1 g	Sodium	73 mg
Cholesterol	5 mg	Added Sugar	24 Cal
		Fiber	1 g

Garden Vegetable Juice

Preparation: **10 min.**

FAT SUGAR SODIUM

 3 **medium-size ripe tomatoes (about 1 pound), peeled, cored, seeded, and chopped**
 ½ **medium-size sweet green pepper, cored, seeded, and cut into 1-inch pieces**
 ½ **small cucumber, peeled, seeded and sliced**
 2 **teaspoons lemon juice**
 ½ **teaspoon prepared horseradish**
 2 **to 3 drops hot red pepper sauce**
 5 **ice cubes**

1. Place the **tomatoes, green pepper,** and **cucumber** in an electric blender and whirl at high speed for 1 minute or until smooth.
2. Add the **lemon juice, horseradish, red pepper sauce,** and **ice cubes,** and whirl 1 minute longer, or until smooth and frothy. Pour into tall glasses and serve. Serves 4.

One Serving:

Calories	25	Protein	1 g
Total Fat	0	Carbohydrates	6 g
Saturated Fat	0	Sodium	12 mg
Cholesterol	0	Added Sugar	0
		Fiber	1 g

Desserts

Cream Puffs filled with Make-Your-Own Chocolate Pudding, Black Forest Cake, Chocolate Meringue Drops, Apple-Raisin Crisp—these are just a few of the desserts you don't have to give up when you're eating healthily. On the following pages are many more slimmed-down, delectable versions of wickedly fattening favorites. Try a slice of Lime-Ginger Cheesecake, for example. It weighs in at only 117 calories, while a slice of ordinary cheesecake has 500 calories or more. With 24 recipes like these, you can eat right and still indulge yourself.

Black Forest Cake

Cakes and Cookies
Black Forest Cake

This impressive dessert is worth the effort; you'll find yourself asking for seconds of this low-fat, low-calorie version of the classic recipe.

FAT SUGAR SODIUM

6 tablespoons unsifted Dutch-process cocoa powder
6 tablespoons sifted cake flour
1 cup plus 2 tablespoons granulated sugar
⅛ teaspoon salt
8 large egg whites
1 teaspoon cream of tartar
1½ teaspoons vanilla extract
1 can (1 pound) water-packed pitted sour cherries, drained, with ½ cup juice reserved

2 tablespoons water
1 teaspoon unflavored gelatin
4 teaspoons light brown sugar
2 teaspoons cornstarch
½ teaspoon grated lemon rind
⅓ cup heavy cream
4 teaspoons confectioners sugar
⅓ cup ice-cold evaporated skim milk
1 teaspoon lemon juice

Preparation:
25 min.
Cooking:
27 min.

One Serving:

Calories	156
Total Fat	3 g
Saturated Fat	2 g
Cholesterol	9 mg
Protein	4 g
Carbohydrates	30 g
Sodium	71 mg
Added Sugar	84 Cal
Fiber	0

Tip: *If your cake is going to stay in the refrigerator for more than a couple of hours, construct a loose tent of aluminum foil around it. This will keep it from absorbing the odors of other foods.*

1. Preheat the oven to 375°F. Line the bottoms of 2 8-inch round layer cake pans with wax paper.

2. On a sheet of wax paper, sift together the **cocoa powder, flour,** 1 cup of the **granulated sugar,** and the **salt.** Set aside.

3. In the large bowl of an electric mixer, beat the **egg whites** at moderate speed until foamy. Add the **cream of tartar** and remaining 2 tablespoons granulated sugar, 1 at a time, and beat until the whites hold soft peaks. Increase the speed to moderately high, then add 1 teaspoon of the **vanilla extract** and beat 1 minute longer. The whites should be soft and firm, not stiff and dry.

4. With a rubber spatula, gently fold the cocoa mixture into the egg whites, about ⅓ at a time, then carefully pour the batter into the 2 cake pans, dividing it between them.

5. Bake the layers for 20 to 25 minutes or until they begin to pull away from the sides of the pans and a toothpick inserted in the centers comes out clean. Remove and cool on a wire rack upside down in the pans. When the cake layers are room temperature, loosen their sides with a metal spatula; turn them out on a work surface and remove the wax paper.

6. To prepare the filling, place the **cherries** in a bowl, saving a few for final decoration, and set aside. Place the **water** in a small saucepan and sprinkle the **gelatin** on top. Let stand for 5 minutes to soften; then set over very low heat and cook, stirring, until the gelatin dissolves—about 5 minutes. Set aside.

7. In another small saucepan, combine the **brown sugar, cornstarch,** and **lemon rind.** Slowly whisk in the reserved juice until smooth. Bring the mixture to a boil over moderate heat, stirring constantly; let boil for 1 minute. Remove from the heat, add the cherries, and mix well. Set aside.

8. In the small bowl of the electric mixer, beat the **cream** at high speed until it holds soft peaks. Add the **confectioners sugar** and the remaining vanilla extract and beat until the cream holds stiff peaks.

9. In another small bowl, combine the **evaporated skim milk** and **lemon**

juice and beat with clean beaters at high speed until very stiff; then beat in the cooled gelatin mixture and fold in the whipped cream.

10. To assemble, place 1 cake layer on a cake plate. Top with the cherry mixture, spreading it to the edge. Gently spread 1 cup of the whipped cream mixture over the cherry mixture, then place the second layer on top. Using a large pastry bag fitted with a star tip, pipe rosettes of the remaining whipped cream around the edge and in the center of the cake. Decorate with reserved cherries. Refrigerate until serving time. Serves 12.

White Cake with Seven-Minute Frosting

This light cake can be baked several days before you plan to frost and use it; be sure to wrap it well in plastic wrap and store it in a cool, dry place.

FAT SUGAR SODIUM

Nonstick cooking spray
1¾ cups sifted cake flour
2 teaspoons baking powder
⅛ teaspoon salt
5 tablespoons unsalted margarine
¾ cup sugar
1 teaspoon vanilla extract
¼ teaspoon almond extract

⅔ cup milk
3 large egg whites
For the Frosting:
¾ cup sugar
2 large egg whites
½ teaspoon cream of tartar
¼ cup cold water
2 teaspoons vanilla extract

Preparation:
15 min.
Cooking:
34 min. (mostly unattended)

One Serving:

Calories	209
Total Fat	*5 g*
Saturated Fat	*1 g*
Cholesterol	*2 mg*
Protein	*3 g*
Carbohydrates	*37 g*
Sodium	*122 mg*
Added Sugar	*96 Cal*
Fiber	*0*

1. Preheat the oven to 375°F. Coat a 9-inch springform pan with the **cooking spray** and set aside. Sift the **flour, baking powder,** and **salt** onto a piece of wax paper and set aside.

2. In the large bowl of an electric mixer, beat the **margarine** at high speed until light; reduce the speed to low and gradually add all but 2 tablespoons of the **sugar,** beating constantly. Increase the speed to high and continue beating the mixture until it is light and fluffy. Beat in the **vanilla extract** and **almond extract.**

3. Reduce the speed to low and add the sifted dry ingredients alternately with the **milk,** beginning and ending with the dry ingredients and beating after each addition just enough to combine the ingredients.

4. In the small bowl of the electric mixer, with clean beaters, beat the **egg whites** at moderate speed until foamy, then add the remaining 2 tablespoons sugar, 1 tablespoon at a time. Increase the speed to moderately high and beat until the whites hold soft peaks.

5. Stir ¼ of the egg whites into the batter, then, with a rubber spatula, fold in the balance. Spoon the batter into the pan and smooth the surface with the spatula. Bake for 25 to 30 minutes or until a toothpick inserted in the center comes out clean.

6. Place the pan upright on a wire rack and cool for 10 minutes, then turn the cake out onto the rack and cool to room temperature—about 1 hour.

7. To prepare the frosting, in the bottom half of a medium-size double boiler, bring 1 cup water to a simmer over moderate heat. In the top half of the double boiler, combine the **sugar, egg whites, cream of tartar,** and **cold water.** Set the top half over the simmering water, then beat the mixture at high speed for 6 minutes or until thick. Add the **vanilla extract** and beat 1 minute longer or until the frosting is thick enough to spread.

8. With a knife, frost the top and sides of the cake, swirling the icing into peaks and valleys. Let stand at least 2 hours before cutting. Serves 12.

Tip: Take the weather into consideration when you make cake frostings that use egg whites. High humidity makes it difficult for the frosting to thicken properly.

Lemon Angel Roll

Nonstick cooking spray
¾ **cup granulated sugar**
⅔ **cup sifted cake flour**
6 **large egg whites**
¾ **teaspoon vanilla extract**
¼ **teaspoon cream of tartar**
2 **tablespoons confectioners sugar**

For the Filling:
¼ **cup granulated sugar**
2 **tablespoons cornstarch**
1¼ **cups evaporated skim milk**
3 **tablespoons lemon juice**
1 **tablespoon grated lemon rind**

FAT SUGAR SODIUM

Preparation:
15 min.
Cooking:
23 min. (mostly unattended)

One Serving:

Calories	187
Total Fat	0
Saturated Fat	0
Cholesterol	2 mg
Protein	6 g
Carbohydrates	40 g
Sodium	85 mg
Added Sugar	103 Cal
Fiber	0

Tip: *When a recipe calls for grated lemon or orange rind, grate only the "zest," or colored part of the rind. Including the white pith can make the dish taste bitter.*

1. Preheat the oven to 300°F. Lightly coat a 15"x 10"x 1" jelly roll pan with the **cooking spray,** line the bottom with wax paper, coat again, and set aside.

2. Sift 6 tablespoons of the **granulated sugar** with the **flour** onto a piece of wax paper and set aside.

3. In the large bowl of an electric mixer, beat the **egg whites, vanilla extract,** and **cream of tartar** at moderate speed until foamy, then beat in the remaining granulated sugar, 1 tablespoon at a time. Increase the speed to moderately high and beat the whites until they hold very soft peaks. *(Note: Do not overbeat the whites or the cake will be tough.)* Sift ¼ of the flour mixture over the egg whites and, with a rubber spatula, fold in gently but thoroughly; repeat until all the flour mixture is incorporated.

4. With the spatula, spread the batter evenly in the pan and bake for 20 to 25 minutes or until the cake is pale tan and the top springs back when touched.

5. With a thin-bladed metal spatula, loosen the cake around the edges and invert immediately onto a clean dish towel that has been sprinkled with 1 tablespoon of the **confectioners sugar.** Peel off the wax paper and trim off any crisp edges. Sprinkle the cake with half the remaining confectioners sugar and, starting at a narrow end, roll it up in the towel; cool seam side down for 1 hour on a wire rack.

6. Meanwhile, prepare the filling. In a small heavy saucepan, combine the **granulated sugar** and **cornstarch.** Blend in the **milk** and **lemon juice,** set over moderate heat, and cook, stirring, for 3 minutes or until thickened and clear. Remove from the heat and stir in the **lemon rind.** Cover and cool to room temperature, whisking occasionally.

7. To fill the cake, unroll the cooled cake and remove the towel. Whisk the filling until smooth, then spread it evenly over the cake, leaving ½-inch margins all around. Reroll the cake, place it seam side down on an oblong platter, and sift the remaining confectioners sugar over it. Using a sharp serrated knife in a gentle seesaw motion, cut the roll slightly on the bias into 1-inch slices. Serves 8.

Variation:

Strawberry Angel Roll Prepare the cake as directed. For the filling, in a food processor or electric blender, whirl ½ cup sliced fresh or frozen dry-pack strawberries for 30 seconds or until smooth. In a small heavy saucepan, combine 3 tablespoons sugar and 2 tablespoons cornstarch. Blend in ¾ cup evaporated skim milk, the puréed strawberries, and 1¼ teaspoons lemon juice; set over moderate heat and cook, stirring, for 3 minutes or until thickened and clear. Remove from the heat, stir in ½ cup thinly sliced strawberries, cover, and cool to room temperature. Fill, roll, and serve the cake as directed.

Lemon Angel Roll

Raspberry-Nut Torte

FAT SUGAR SODIUM

¼ cup finely ground walnuts or almonds

7 tablespoons sugar

1 tablespoon cornstarch

4 large egg whites

⅛ teaspoon salt

⅛ teaspoon cream of tartar

¼ teaspoon almond extract

¼ cup reduced-sugar raspberry jam

Preparation:
5 min.
Baking:
35 min. (unattended)

1. Preheat the oven to 275°F. Line a baking sheet with baking parchment or aluminum foil and, using an 8-inch cake pan as a pattern, draw 2 8-inch circles on the parchment; set aside. On a sheet of wax paper, mix the **walnuts** with 1 tablespoon of the **sugar** and the **cornstarch;** also set aside.

2. In the large bowl of an electric mixer, beat the **egg whites** and **salt** at moderate speed until foamy. Add the **cream of tartar** and beat 1 minute longer. Slowly add the remaining 6 tablespoons sugar, beating constantly, then increase the speed to moderately high and beat until the whites hold stiff, glossy peaks. Beat in the **almond extract** and fold in the nut mixture.

3. Fit a pastry bag with a plain large tip and spoon in the egg white mixture, then pipe to fill in the 2 circles traced on the parchment paper. With a spatula, smooth the tops and bake the meringues until they are almost crisp but still a little sticky—about 35 minutes.

4. Set the baking sheet on a wire rack and cool the meringues to room temperature—about 1 hour. Invert and carefully peel off the baking parchment. Center 1 meringue, flat side up, on a serving plate, spread with the **raspberry jam,** then top with the remaining meringue, round side up. Cut into 6 wedges and serve. Serves 6.

One Serving:

Calories	115
Total Fat	3 g
Saturated Fat	0
Cholesterol	0
Protein	3 g
Carbohydrates	20 g
Sodium	84 mg
Added Sugar	56 Cal
Fiber	1 g

Tip: *Do not make meringue desserts in rainy or humid weather. The meringue will be soggy, not crisp.*

Chocolate Chip Cookies

Grated flecks of chocolate replace the traditional chocolate chips in this low-calorie version of America's favorite cookie.

`FAT` `SUGAR` `SODIUM`

1	cup sifted all-purpose flour
¼	cup unsifted whole wheat flour
½	teaspoon baking soda
¼	cup unsalted margarine
¼	cup granulated sugar
¼	cup firmly packed light brown sugar

1	large egg
1	large egg white
3	teaspoons vanilla extract
1	square (1 ounce) semisweet chocolate, grated fine

Preparation:
10 min.
Baking:
8 min.

One Cookie:

Calories	45
Total Fat	2 g
Saturated Fat	0
Cholesterol	8 mg
Protein	1 g
Carbohydrates	6 g
Sodium	15 mg
Added Sugar	17 Cal
Fiber	0 g

1. Preheat the oven to 375°F. In a small bowl, combine the **all-purpose flour, whole wheat flour,** and **baking soda** and set aside.
2. In the large bowl of an electric mixer, beat the **margarine, granulated sugar,** and **brown sugar** at moderately low speed for 2 minutes or until smooth and creamy; then beat in the **egg, egg white,** and **vanilla extract.**
3. Using a wooden spoon, mix in the dry ingredients and the grated **chocolate.**
4. Drop the dough by rounded teaspoonfuls onto ungreased baking sheets, spacing the cookies about 2 inches apart. Bake for 8 to 10 minutes or until lightly browned around the edges. Remove immediately to wire racks to cool. Makes about 36 cookies.

Chocolate Chip Meringue Drops

It's hard to believe that these tempting cookies are so low in calories.

`FAT` `SUGAR` `SODIUM`

2	large egg whites
½	cup sugar
1	teaspoon vanilla extract
3	tablespoons cocoa powder (not a mix)

½	cup semisweet chocolate chips (½ 6-ounce package)

Preparation:
8 min.
Baking:
1 hr. (unattended)

One Cookie:

Calories	23
Total Fat	1 g
Saturated Fat	0
Cholesterol	0
Protein	0
Carbohydrates	4 g
Sodium	3 mg
Added Sugar	10 Cal
Fiber	0

1. Preheat the oven to 250°F. Line 2 baking sheets with baking parchment or aluminum foil and set aside.
2. In the large bowl of an electric mixer, beat the **egg whites** at moderately high speed until they hold stiff peaks. Beat in the **sugar,** 1 tablespoon at a time, then beat in the **vanilla extract.** Reduce the speed to low and beat in the **cocoa powder.** With a rubber spatula, fold in the **chocolate chips.**
3. Drop the mixture by rounded teaspoonfuls onto the baking sheets, spacing the cookies 1 inch apart, and bake for 1 hour. Turn off the oven and dry the cookies in the oven 2 hours longer. Remove them and store in an airtight container. Makes about 40 cookies.

Variation:

Chocolate Nut Meringue Drops Prepare as directed, substituting ½ cup coarsely chopped pecans or walnuts for the chocolate chips and adding a pinch each of ground cinnamon and nutmeg to the beaten egg whites.

Lemon Squares

FAT SUGAR SODIUM

Nonstick cooking spray
1 **cup plus 4½ teaspoons sifted
    all-purpose flour**
⅓ **cup plus 1 tablespoon sifted
    confectioners sugar**
½ **teaspoon baking powder**
¼ **cup cold unsalted margarine,
    cut into bits**

2 **tablespoons ice water**
1 **large egg**
1 **large egg white**
⅔ **cup granulated sugar**
¼ **cup lemon juice**
1 **teaspoon grated lemon rind**
⅛ **teaspoon salt**

Preparation:
15 min.
Baking:
45 min. (unattended)

One Square:

Calories	*103*
Total Fat	*3 g*
Saturated Fat	*1 g*
Cholesterol	*17 mg*
Protein	*1 g*
Carbohydrates	*17 g*
Sodium	*39 mg*
Added Sugar	*67 Cal*
Fiber	*0*

1. Preheat the oven to 375°F. Coat an 8″x 8″x 2″ baking pan with the **cooking spray** and set aside.

2. In a medium-size mixing bowl, combine the 1 cup **flour,** the ⅓ cup **confectioners sugar,** and ¼ teaspoon of the **baking powder.** Using a fork or pastry blender, cut in the **margarine** until the mixture resembles coarse meal. Sprinkle with the ice **water** and mix just until a small lump of dough pinched between the fingers holds together.

3. Pat the dough evenly over the bottom of the pan and bake for 20 minutes.

4. Meanwhile, in the small bowl of an electric mixer, beat the **egg, egg white, granulated sugar,** and **lemon juice** at moderate speed for 2 minutes or until the mixture is light and smooth. Whisk in the remaining 4½ teaspoons flour, the **lemon rind,** the remaining ¼ teaspoon baking powder, and the **salt.**

5. When the dough has finished baking, quickly remove the pan from the oven and pour the lemon mixture over it. Immediately return it to the oven, and bake for 25 minutes or until the lemon topping has set.

6. Place the pan upright on a wire rack and cool to room temperature—about 1 hour. Cut into squares and sift the remaining 1 tablespoon **confectioners sugar** over the top before removing from the pan. Makes 16 squares.

Chocolate Chip Meringue Drops

Oatmeal Wafers

1½ **cups rolled oats**
½ **cup sifted all-purpose flour**
¼ **cup firmly packed light brown sugar**
½ **teaspoon ground cinnamon**

⅛ **teaspoon salt**
½ **cup unsalted margarine**
1 **tablespoon maple syrup**

Preparation:
5 min.
Cooking:
9 min.

1. Preheat the oven to 375°F. Lightly grease 2 baking sheets and set aside. In a medium-size bowl, mix the **oats, flour, brown sugar, cinnamon,** and **salt** and set aside.
2. In a small saucepan or skillet, melt the **margarine** over moderate heat. Add the margarine and **maple syrup** to the dry ingredients and mix well.
3. Drop the dough by teaspoonfuls onto the baking sheets, spacing the cookies about 2 inches apart. Bake for 8 minutes or until lightly browned. Remove the cookies from the oven and let them harden on the baking sheets for 2 minutes before transferring to wire racks to cool. Makes 40 cookies.

One Cookie:

Calories	44
Total Fat	2 g
Saturated Fat	0
Cholesterol	0
Protein	1 g
Carbohydrates	5 g
Sodium	8 mg
Added Sugar	5 Cal
Fiber	0

Fruit Desserts

Apple-Raisin Crisp

3 **medium-size firm cooking apples, peeled, cored, and sliced**
1 **tablespoon lemon juice**
½ **cup raisins**
¼ **cup plus 2 tablespoons firmly packed dark brown sugar**

2½ **teaspoons ground cinnamon**
2½ **slices whole wheat bread, finely crumbled**
2 **tablespoons unsalted margarine**

Preparation:
15 min.
Cooking:
46 min. (mostly unattended)

1. Preheat the oven to 300°F. In a large bowl, toss the **apples** with the **lemon juice, raisins,** the ¼ cup **brown sugar,** and 1½ teaspoons of the **cinnamon.** Spoon the mixture into an ungreased 9-inch pie pan and set aside.
2. To prepare the topping, spread the **bread crumbs** on a 15"x 10"x 1" jelly roll pan and bake, stirring occasionally, for 15 minutes or until dry. Remove the crumbs from the oven and transfer to a small bowl. In a small skillet or saucepan, melt the **margarine** over low heat. Add it to the crumbs along with the remaining 2 tablespoons brown sugar and the remaining 1 teaspoon cinnamon and mix well. Increase the oven temperature to 375°F.
3. Sprinkle the crumb topping over the apples and bake for 30 minutes or until bubbly. *(Note: If, after 10 minutes, the topping is browning too fast, cover loosely with aluminum foil.)* Cool the crisp slightly before serving. Serves 8.

One Serving:

Calories	138
Total Fat	3 g
Saturated Fat	1 g
Cholesterol	0
Protein	1 g
Carbohydrates	28 g
Sodium	43 mg
Added Sugar	48 Cal
Fiber	2 g

Variations:

Ginger-Peach Crisp Prepare as directed, but substitute 4 cups sliced, peeled, and pitted peaches for the apples; omit the raisins, but add ¾ teaspoon ground ginger. Spoon the mixture into the pie pan and set aside. Instead of the topping called for, toss 1½ cups gingersnap crumbs (about 36 gingersnaps) with 1 tablespoon dark brown sugar, ¾ teaspoon ground ginger, and 2 tablespoons melted margarine. Sprinkle over the peaches and bake as directed.

Blueberry-Lemon Crisp Prepare as directed, but substitute 4 cups blueberries for the apples and use golden raisins; omit the lemon juice and

Ginger-Peach Crisp

Apple-Raisin Crisp

Blueberry-Lemon Crisp

cinnamon and add 1 tablespoon grated lemon rind and 1 teaspoon ground nutmeg. Spoon the mixture into the pie pan and set aside. For the topping, substitute 1½ cups melba toast crumbs tossed with 3 tablespoons dark brown sugar, ¾ teaspoon grated lemon rind, ¾ teaspoon ground nutmeg, and 2 tablespoons melted margarine. Sprinkle over the berries and bake as directed.

Blueberry Cobbler

FAT SUGAR SODIUM

Nonstick cooking spray
1½ **cups fresh blueberries, stemmed and sorted, or 1½ cups thawed frozen dry-pack blueberries**
1 **tablespoon orange-flavored liqueur, such as Cointreau (optional)**
2 **tablespoons plus 2 teaspoons granulated sugar**

⅔ **cup skim milk**
⅓ **cup sifted all-purpose flour**
1 **large egg**
1 **teaspoon grated orange rind**
2 **teaspoons vanilla extract**
¼ **teaspoon ground cinnamon**
1 **tablespoon confectioners sugar (optional)**

Preparation:
8 min., plus 30 min. standing time
Baking:
1 hr. (unattended)

One Serving:

Calories	137
Total Fat	2 g
Saturated Fat	0
Cholesterol	69 mg
Protein	4 g
Carbohydrates	28 g
Sodium	42 mg
Added Sugar	40 Cal
Fiber	2 g

1. Preheat the oven to 350°F. Coat a 6-cup shallow baking dish with the **cooking spray** and set aside.
2. In a medium-size bowl, toss the **blueberries** with the **orange-flavored liqueur,** if desired, and 1 teaspoon of the **granulated sugar,** and let stand, uncovered, at room temperature for 30 minutes.
3. In an electric blender or food processor, combine 2 tablespoons of the granulated sugar and the **milk, flour, egg, orange rind, vanilla extract,** and **cinnamon** by whirling for 5 seconds or until smooth.
4. Spoon the blueberries into the baking dish, pour the batter evenly over them, then sprinkle with the remaining 1 teaspoon granulated sugar.
5. Bake for 1 hour or until puffy and golden. Sprinkle with the **confectioners sugar,** if desired, before serving. Serves 4.

Strawberry Chiffon Charlotte

Strawberry Chiffon Charlotte

Here's a spectacular low-cal dessert that can be prepared in stages. You can make the meringue ladyfingers up to a week in advance, if you want, and store them in an airtight container.

FAT **SUGAR** **SODIUM**

Nonstick cooking spray
2 large egg yolks
¾ cup sifted confectioners sugar
½ teaspoon vanilla extract
5 large egg whites
⅛ teaspoon salt
½ cup sifted cake flour
1 envelope unflavored gelatin

¼ cup cold water
1 pint strawberries, hulled
1 tablespoon lemon juice
1 tablespoon kirsch or cassis (optional)
1 cup plain low-fat yogurt
½ cup superfine sugar
12 whole strawberries, hulled

Preparation:
20 min., plus 4 hr. refrigeration
Cooking:
12 min.

One Serving:

Calories	*166*
Total Fat	*2 g*
Saturated Fat	*1 g*
Cholesterol	*70 mg*
Protein	*6 g*
Carbohydrates	*32 g*
Sodium	*92 mg*
Added Sugar	*84 Cal*
Fiber	*1 g*

1. Preheat the oven to 325°F. Coat 2 baking sheets with the **cooking spray** and set aside. Also coat an 8½"x 4½"x 2½" loaf pan, line the bottom and sides with wax paper, and set aside.

2. In the large bowl of an electric mixer, beat the **egg yolks** at moderate speed until thick and pale, then add ¼ cup of the **confectioners sugar**, 1 tablespoon at a time. Increase the speed to high and beat the yolks until they are the consistency of mayonnaise. Beat in the **vanilla extract.**

3. In a medium-size bowl, with clean beaters, beat 3 of the **egg whites** and

the **salt** at moderate speed until foamy. Add 2 tablespoons of the remaining confectioners sugar, 1 tablespoon at a time, then increase the speed to moderately high and beat until the whites hold stiff peaks.

4. In a small bowl, combine another 2 tablespoons of the confectioners sugar with the **flour.** With a rubber spatula, alternately fold the flour mixture and the beaten egg whites into the yolk mixture a little at a time, beginning and ending with the flour mixture.

5. Spoon the mixture into a pastry bag fitted with a ½-inch plain tip and pipe 4-inch long ladyfinger strips on the baking sheets, spacing the strips about 2 inches apart. Sift another 2 tablespoons of the confectioners sugar over the strips and bake for 12 to 15 minutes or until pale golden. Cool for 5 minutes on the baking sheets, then transfer the ladyfingers to wire racks and cool completely—about 30 minutes.

6. To line the loaf pan, arrange some of the ladyfingers over the bottom of the pan, then stand additional ladyfingers around the sides, trimming them to fit snugly and reserving any leftovers. Set the pan aside.

7. In a small bowl, soften the **gelatin** in the **water** for 5 minutes; then set the bowl in a pan of hot water and stir until the gelatin dissolves.

8. In an electric blender or food processor, whirl the pint of **strawberries** for 1 minute, then strain into a large bowl; stir in the gelatin mixture, **lemon juice,** and, if desired, the **kirsch.** Fold in the **yogurt.**

9. In the small bowl of the electric mixer, beat the 2 remaining egg whites at moderate speed until foamy. Add the **superfine sugar,** 1 tablespoon at a time, then increase the speed to moderately high and beat until the whites hold stiff peaks. With a rubber spatula, fold ¼ of the beaten whites into the strawberry mixture, then gently but thoroughly fold in the balance. Spoon the strawberry mixture into the ladyfinger-lined pan, smoothing the top, and crumble any remaining ladyfingers on top. Cover with plastic wrap and refrigerate at least 4 hours or overnight.

10. To serve, cover the pan with a small oblong platter and invert the charlotte onto it. Garnish with the **whole strawberries,** slicing some of them, if you wish, then sift the remaining 2 tablespoons confectioners sugar on top. Serves 8.

Pies, Pastries, and Puddings
Deep-Dish Peach Pie

FAT SUGAR SODIUM

Preparation: **10 min.**
Baking: **30 min.**

8 medium-size firm ripe peaches, peeled, pitted, and sliced ½ inch thick	½ teaspoon ground cinnamon
¼ cup plus 4 teaspoons firmly packed light brown sugar	⅛ teaspoon ground nutmeg
	2 tablespoons flour
	1 tablespoon unsalted margarine, softened

One Serving:

Calories	*149*
Total Fat	*2 g*
Saturated Fat	*1 g*
Cholesterol	*0*
Protein	*2 g*
Carbohydrates	*34 g*
Sodium	*4 mg*
Added Sugar	*47 Cal*
Fiber	*2 g*

1. Preheat the oven to 375°F. In an ungreased 1-quart baking dish or soufflé dish, place the **peaches,** the ¼ cup **brown sugar,** the **cinnamon,** and **nutmeg,** and stir together.

2. In a small bowl, blend the remaining brown sugar with the **flour** and **margarine** and sprinkle evenly over the peaches.

3. Bake for 30 minutes or until the peaches are tender. Serve warm or cold, topped, if you like, with Mock Whipped Cream, page 27. Serves 6.

Ginger-Pumpkin Chiffon Pie

Nonstick cooking spray
1 teaspoon unsalted margarine
¼ cup fine gingersnap crumbs (about 6 gingersnaps)
½ cup sugar
1 cup evaporated skim milk
1 envelope unflavored gelatin

1¼ teaspoons ground ginger
1 large egg yolk
1 can (1 pound) solid-pack pumpkin
3 large egg whites
¼ teaspoon cream of tartar

FAT SUGAR SODIUM

Preparation:
15 min., plus 8 hr.
20 min. refrigeration
Cooking:
8 min.

One Serving:

Calories	137
Total Fat	2 g
Saturated Fat	1 g
Cholesterol	38 mg
Protein	6 g
Carbohydrates	25 g
Sodium	92 mg
Added Sugar	55 Cal
Fiber	1 g

1. Lightly coat the bottom and sides of a 9-inch pie pan with the **cooking spray.** In a small saucepan, melt the **margarine** over low heat. Remove from the heat and mix in the **gingersnap crumbs.** Transfer the crumb mixture to the pie pan and press evenly over the bottom and sides; lightly pat to make the crumbs stick. Refrigerate while you prepare the filling.

2. In a small saucepan, combine ¼ cup of the **sugar** and ¼ cup of the **milk;** sprinkle the **gelatin** and **ginger** evenly over the surface and let soften for 5 minutes. Set the saucepan over moderately low heat and cook, stirring, for 5 to 6 minutes or until the gelatin and sugar dissolve. Remove from the heat.

3. In a small bowl, beat the **egg yolk** and remaining milk together, then slowly whisk in the hot gelatin mixture. Transfer the mixture back to the saucepan, set over low heat, and cook, stirring, for 2 to 3 minutes or until slightly thickened; be careful not to boil or the mixture will curdle.

4. Transfer the filling to a large bowl, blend in the **pumpkin,** cover, and refrigerate for 20 to 30 minutes, stirring occasionally, until the mixture mounds slightly when dropped from a spoon.

5. In the large bowl of an electric mixer, beat the **egg whites** and **cream of tartar** at moderate speed until foamy; slowly add the remaining ¼ cup sugar and beat at moderately high speed until the whites hold soft peaks.

6. With a rubber spatula, fold the egg whites into the pumpkin mixture and spoon into the crust. Refrigerate at least 8 hours before serving. Serves 8.

Blueberry-Peach Tarts

You can store the meringue shells for about a week in an airtight container.

FAT SUGAR SODIUM

3 large egg whites
⅛ teaspoon salt
⅛ teaspoon cream of tartar
¾ cup superfine sugar
½ teaspoon vanilla extract
1 cup fresh blueberries, stemmed and sorted, or 1 cup thawed frozen dry-pack blueberries

3 medium-size firm ripe peaches, peeled, pitted, and sliced
1 tablespoon lemon juice
2 teaspoons granulated sugar
1 teaspoon grated lemon rind

Preparation:
20 min., plus 1 hr. refrigeration
Baking:
1 hr.

One Serving:

Calories	153
Total Fat	0
Saturated Fat	0
Cholesterol	0
Protein	2 g
Carbohydrates	37 g
Sodium	73 mg
Added Sugar	51 Cal
Fiber	1 g

1. Preheat the oven to 250°F. Line a baking sheet with baking parchment or wax paper. Using a 3-inch biscuit cutter as a pattern, draw 6 3-inch circles about 2 inches apart on the parchment; set the sheet aside.

2. In the large bowl of an electric mixer, beat the **egg whites** and **salt** at moderate speed until foamy. Add the **cream of tartar** and beat until the whites hold soft peaks. Beat in the **superfine sugar,** 1 tablespoon at a time, then increase the speed to moderately high and continue to beat until the whites are glossy and hold stiff peaks. Beat in the **vanilla extract.**

3. Fit a pastry bag with a ¼-inch star tip, spoon in the egg whites, then pipe to fill in the circles on the parchment until about ⅓ inch thick. Pipe stars, just touching one another, around the edges to form borders 2 inches high.

4. Bake the meringues for 1 hour, then turn off the oven and let them dry in the oven for 2 to 3 hours. *(Note: The meringues can be stored at this point.)*

5. About 1 hour before serving, in a medium-size bowl, toss the **blueberries** with the **peaches, lemon juice, granulated sugar,** and **lemon rind.** Cover and refrigerate for 1 hour. Just before serving, spoon the fruit into the meringues, dividing the total amount evenly. Serves 6.

Cream Puffs and Eclairs

FAT SUGAR SODIUM

Nonstick cooking spray
1 cup water
5 tablespoons unsalted margarine
½ cup sifted all-purpose flour
¼ cup cornstarch
3 large eggs

Preparation:
2 min.
Cooking:
40 min. (mostly unattended)

1. Preheat the oven to 400°F. Lightly coat a baking sheet with the **cooking spray** and set aside.

2. In a medium-size heavy saucepan, bring the **water** and **margarine** to a boil, uncovered, over moderately high heat—about 1 minute. Meanwhile, in a small bowl, combine the **flour** and **cornstarch** and quickly add—all at once—to the boiling mixture. Stir briskly with a wooden spoon until the mixture forms a ball around the spoon and does not cling to the sides of the pan. Remove from the heat and cool for 2 minutes, then add the **eggs,** one at a time, beating well after each addition, until the dough is smooth and glossy.

3. To shape cream puffs, drop the dough by heaping tablespoonfuls onto the baking sheet, spacing the puffs about 2 inches apart. To shape eclairs, shape the dough into narrow rectangles about 3½ inches long (it's easiest to do this by piping the dough through a pastry bag fitted with a large plain tip).

4. Bake the puffs or eclairs for 10 minutes, then reduce the heat to 350°F and bake 25 minutes longer or until the puffs are firm. Transfer to wire racks and cool to room temperature—about 1 hour.

5. To fill, slice the puffs in half horizontally, spoon a tablespoon of Make-Your-Own Chocolate Pudding, page 289, or another low-calorie filling into the bottoms, and replace the tops. Makes 15 large cream puffs or eclairs.

One Serving:

Calories	*72*
Total Fat	*5 g*
Saturated Fat	*1 g*
Cholesterol	*55 mg*
Protein	*2 g*
Carbohydrates	*5 g*
Sodium	*14 mg*
Added Sugar	*0*
Fiber	*0*

Cream Puffs and Eclairs

Lime-Ginger Cheesecake

Nonstick cooking spray
1 tablespoon unsalted margarine
4 zwieback toasts, crumbled fine, or 3 tablespoons fine dry bread crumbs
½ cup plus 1 teaspoon loosely packed light brown sugar
1½ teaspoons grated lime rind

1 teaspoon ground ginger
3 tablespoons lime juice
2 envelopes unflavored gelatin
2 cups part-skim ricotta cheese
1 cup plain low-fat yogurt
½ cup skim milk
1 large egg yolk

FAT **SUGAR** **SODIUM**

Preparation:
10 min., plus 5 hr. refrigeration
Cooking:
6 min.

One Serving:

Calories	117
Total Fat	5 g
Saturated Fat	2 g
Cholesterol	35 mg
Protein	7 g
Carbohydrates	12 g
Sodium	73 mg
Added Sugar	24 Cal
Fiber	0

1. Coat an 8-inch springform pan with the **cooking spray** and set aside. In a small saucepan or skillet, melt the **margarine** over low heat. Remove from the heat and mix in the **zwieback crumbs,** 1 teaspoon of the **brown sugar,** ½ teaspoon of the **lime rind,** and ¼ teaspoon of the **ginger.** Press the mixture evenly over the bottom of the springform pan and refrigerate while you prepare the filling.

2. Place the **lime juice** in a small heatproof glass measuring cup, sprinkle the **gelatin** on top, and let stand at room temperature until softened—about 5 minutes. In a small shallow saucepan, bring about 1 cup water to a simmer over moderately high heat. Place the measuring cup in the gently bubbling water, adjust the heat to low, and stir until the gelatin dissolves completely—about 4 minutes. Remove from the heat and set aside.

3. In an electric blender or food processor, combine the **ricotta cheese, yogurt,** remaining ½ cup brown sugar, and the **milk,** and whirl until smooth—about 1 minute. Add the **egg yolk,** the remaining 1 teaspoon lime rind, and the remaining ¾ teaspoon ginger, and whirl about 1 minute to blend. Add the cooled gelatin mixture and whirl 15 seconds longer.

4. Gently pour the cheese mixture over the crust in the springform pan and refrigerate at least 5 hours or until set. Serves 12.

No-Sugar Fruit Pudding

Here's a sugar-free version of the famous English dessert summer pudding, which calls for a variety of fresh berries in season.

½ tablespoon unsalted margarine
8 thin slices firm white bread, crusts removed
3 cups fresh raspberries or 1 package (12 ounces) frozen dry-pack raspberries

1 can (4 ounces) juice-packed crushed pineapple, drained, with ⅓ cup of the juice reserved

FAT **SUGAR** **SODIUM**

Preparation:
10 min.
Cooking:
6 min.

One Serving:

Calories	172
Total Fat	3 g
Saturated Fat	1 g
Cholesterol	1 mg
Protein	4 g
Carbohydrates	33 g
Sodium	183 mg
Added Sugar	0
Fiber	5 g

1. Grease a 4-cup mold with the **margarine** and line the bottom and sides with 7 slices of the **bread,** overlapping them slightly.

2. In a medium-size heavy saucepan, bring the **raspberries, pineapple,** and reserved juice to a boil, uncovered, over moderately high heat—about 2 minutes. Lower the heat so that the mixture bubbles gently, and simmer, uncovered, for 4 minutes.

3. Spoon the fruit mixture into the mold and top with the remaining slice of bread. Cover with a round of wax paper, then place a weight, such as a plate weighted down with cans of food, on top. Refrigerate overnight.

4. To serve, loosen with a thin-bladed metal spatula and invert onto a serving plate. Serve plain or with Mock Whipped Cream, page 27. Serves 4.

Make-Your-Own Chocolate Pudding

FAT SUGAR SODIUM

1 square (1 ounce) unsweetened chocolate

2 cups skim milk

⅓ cup sugar

3 tablespoons cornstarch

1 teaspoon vanilla extract

Preparation: **1 min.,** plus 3 hr. refrigeration
Cooking: **23 min.**

1. In the bottom half of a medium-size double boiler, bring about 1 cup water to a simmer over moderate heat—about 2 minutes. Place the **chocolate** in the top half of the double boiler and melt it over the gently bubbling water in the bottom half—about 2 minutes. Stir in 1¾ cups of the **milk** and the **sugar,** cover, and heat for 3 minutes or until the milk is very hot.

2. In a measuring cup, blend the **cornstarch** with the remaining milk; stir into the hot chocolate mixture. Cook, stirring constantly, until the mixture has thickened and is smooth—about 1 minute. Cover and cook 15 minutes longer; then mix in the **vanilla extract.**

3. Spoon the pudding into serving bowls, cover with plastic wrap, and refrigerate at least 3 hours before serving. Serves 4.

One Serving:

Calories	*168*
Total Fat	*4 g*
Saturated Fat	*2 g*
Cholesterol	*2 mg*
Protein	*5 g*
Carbohydrates	*30 g*
Sodium	*64 mg*
Added Sugar	*64 Cal*
Fiber	*0*

No-Sugar Fruit Pudding

Lemon Soufflé

⅓ cup granulated sugar
4½ teaspoons cornstarch
½ cup skim milk
1 large egg yolk
2 tablespoons lemon juice

1 teaspoon grated lemon rind
½ teaspoon vanilla extract
4 large egg whites
1 tablespoon confectioners sugar (optional)

FAT SUGAR **SODIUM**

Preparation:
10 min.
Cooking:
33 min. (mostly unattended)

1. Preheat the oven to 350°F. In a small heavy saucepan, combine the **granulated sugar** and **cornstarch** and slowly stir in the **milk.** Set over moderate heat and cook, stirring, until the mixture comes to a boil—about 2 minutes; cook, stirring, 30 seconds longer. Remove from the heat.
2. Mix 2 tablespoons of the hot milk mixture into the **egg yolk,** then stir the egg mixture back into the pan. Add the **lemon juice, lemon rind,** and **vanilla extract,** and mix thoroughly. Transfer to a medium-size heatproof bowl and cool to room temperature—about 1 hour—stirring occasionally to prevent a skin from forming on the surface.
3. In a large bowl, beat the **egg whites** at moderately high speed until they hold soft peaks. With a rubber spatula, fold the whites into the cooled lemon mixture. Spoon into a 1-quart soufflé or baking dish. Bake, uncovered, for 30 to 35 minutes or until the soufflé is puffy and lightly browned. Sift the **confectioners sugar** on top, if desired, and serve immediately. Serves 6.

One Serving:

Calories	78
Total Fat	*1 g*
Saturated Fat	0
Cholesterol	*46 mg*
Protein	*3 g*
Carbohydrates	*14 g*
Sodium	*47 mg*
Added Sugar	*38 Cal*
Fiber	0

Variation:

Orange Soufflé Prepare as directed, but substitute Grand Marnier or another orange liqueur for the lemon juice and 1½ teaspoons grated orange rind for the lemon rind. Omit the vanilla extract.

Frozen Desserts and Sauces

Fresh Peach Ice

½ cup sugar
1 cup water
3 cups peeled and sliced peaches (about 4 large ripe peaches)

2 tablespoons lemon or lime juice

FAT SUGAR **SODIUM**

Preparation:
20 min., plus 11 hr. refrigeration
Cooking:
5 min.

1. In a small heavy saucepan, combine the **sugar** and **water** and cook over low heat, uncovered, for 5 minutes or until the sugar dissolves. Cool the syrup for 30 minutes, then refrigerate, covered, for 4 hours.
2. In an electric blender or food processor, whirl the **peaches** for 1 minute. Add the syrup and **lemon juice** and whirl for 30 seconds or until blended.
3. Freeze in an ice cream freezer following manufacturer's directions, then proceed to Step 5, or freeze in a 13"x 9"x 2" pan until firm—about 3 hours.
4. Remove the pan from the freezer. Break the ice into chunks and transfer to the large bowl of an electric mixer. Beat at high speed until light and fluffy.
5. Spoon into a ½-gallon freezer container, cover, and freeze at least 4 hours before serving. Serves 12.

One Serving:

Calories	51
Total Fat	0
Saturated Fat	0
Cholesterol	0
Protein	0
Carbohydrates	*13 g*
Sodium	*1 mg*
Added Sugar	*32 Cal*
Fiber	0

Variation:

Fresh Melon Ice Prepare as directed, but substitute 3 cups peeled and seeded cantaloupe or watermelon chunks for the peaches.

Chocolate-Berry Crunch Parfait

Chocolate-Berry Crunch Parfait

Preparation: **20 min.,**
plus 2 hr. refrigeration

`FAT` `SUGAR` `SODIUM`

This parfait is pleasantly tart and has a nice crunch from the wheat germ. If you must strictly watch your sugar intake, use the sugar substitute.

2 cups fresh or thawed frozen dry-pack raspberries
2 tablespoons sugar or 1 packet sugar substitute (or to taste)
2 cups plain low-fat yogurt
2 tablespoons cocoa powder (not a mix)
4 teaspoons wheat germ
4 sprigs mint (optional)

1. In a medium-size bowl, combine the **raspberries** with 1 tablespoon of the **sugar** and set aside.

2. In another medium-size bowl, combine the **yogurt, cocoa powder,** and remaining 1 tablespoon sugar, whisking until smooth and creamy.

3. Spoon ¼ cup of the yogurt mixture into each of 4 8-ounce parfait glasses, top with ¼ cup of the raspberries, then sprinkle with ½ teaspoon of the **wheat germ.** Make 3 more layers, ending with the yogurt. Refrigerate for 2 to 3 hours before serving. Garnish, if you like, with **mint.** Serves 4.

One Serving:			
Calories	106	Protein	5 g
Total Fat	2 g	Carbohydrates	20 g
Saturated Fat	1 g	Sodium	40 mg
Cholesterol	3 mg	Added Sugar	24 Cal
		Fiber	3 g

Frozen Berry Yogurt

Preparation: **20 min.,** FAT SUGAR SODIUM
plus 5 hr. refrigeration

- 1 **teaspoon unflavored gelatin**
- ¼ **cup skim milk**
- 3 **cups fresh blueberries, raspberries, or strawberries, hulled or stemmed, or 3 cups thawed frozen dry-pack berries**
- 2 **tablespoons sugar or 2 packets sugar substitute (or to taste)**
- 2 **teaspoons lemon juice**
- ⅔ **cup plain low-fat yogurt**

1. In a heatproof bowl, soften the **gelatin** in the **milk** for 5 minutes; set the bowl in a pan of hot water and stir until the gelatin dissolves.
2. Place the **berries** and **sugar** in a food processor and whirl for 60 seconds to purée; strain the purée into a medium-size bowl, and mix in the **lemon juice, yogurt,** and gelatin mixture.
3. Transfer to a freezer or ice cube tray, cover with plastic wrap, and freeze until almost set—1 to 1½ hours. Whirl the partially frozen yogurt in the food processor for 1 minute or until smooth. Return to the freezer tray and freeze for 4 hours or until just firm. Serves 4.

One Serving:

Calories	117	Protein	4 g
Total Fat	1 g	Carbohydrates	25 g
Saturated Fat	0	Sodium	42 mg
Cholesterol	3 mg	Added Sugar	24 Cal
		Fiber	3 g

Lemon Sauce

Preparation: **5 min.** Cooking: **3 min.** FAT SUGAR SODIUM

- ½ **cup sugar**
- 2 **tablespoons cornstarch**
- 1¼ **cups water**
- ¼ **cup lemon juice**
- ½ **teaspoon grated lemon rind**

1. In a small heavy saucepan, combine the **sugar** and **cornstarch** and gradually whisk in the **water** and **lemon juice.** Set over moderate heat, cover, and bring to a boil; immediately reduce the heat to low and cook, stirring constantly, until the sauce has thickened and is clear—about 2 to 3 minutes.
2. Remove from the heat, cool, and stir in the **lemon rind.** Store, tightly covered, in the refrigerator for up to 1 week. Makes 1½ cups.

Variations:

Lemon-Raisin Sauce Prepare as directed, adding 2 tablespoons raisins at the end.
Orange Sauce Prepare as directed, but use 1½ cups orange juice instead of the water and lemon juice, and substitute orange rind for the lemon rind.
Fresh Ginger Sauce In a 2-cup glass measuring cup, mix 1½ cups boiling water and 1 tablespoon minced fresh ginger; cool to room temperature and use in place of the water in the original recipe. Proceed as directed for the Lemon Sauce, but reduce the lemon juice to 1 teaspoon and the lemon rind to ¼ teaspoon.

One Tablespoon:

Calories	19	Protein	0
Total Fat	0	Carbohydrates	5 g
Saturated Fat	0	Sodium	1 mg
Cholesterol	0	Added Sugar	4 Cal
		Fiber	0

Chocolate Sauce

Preparation: **3 min.** Cooking: **3 min.** FAT SUGAR SODIUM

- 2 **tablespoons sugar**
- 1 **tablespoon cornstarch**
- ½ **cup skim milk**
- ½ **cup evaporated skim milk**
- 1 **square (1 ounce) semisweet chocolate, grated**
- ½ **teaspoon vanilla extract**

1. In a small heavy saucepan, combine the **sugar** and **cornstarch** and slowly add the **skim milk** and **evaporated skim milk.** Blend until smooth, then set over moderate heat and cook, stirring constantly, for 3 to 5 minutes or until thickened and smooth.
2. Transfer to a small bowl, stir in the **chocolate** and **vanilla extract,** and stir until the chocolate is melted. Cover and cool before serving. Makes about 1 cup.

Variations:

Mocha Sauce Prepare as directed, but add 2 teaspoons instant coffee crystals to the sugar-cornstarch mixture.
Chocolate-Orange Sauce Prepare as directed, but stir 1 teaspoon finely grated orange rind into the sauce along with the vanilla extract.

One Tablespoon:

Calories	26	Protein	1 g
Total Fat	1 g	Carbohydrates	4 g
Saturated Fat	0	Sodium	13 mg
Cholesterol	0	Added Sugar	7 Cal
		Fiber	0

Index

A

Additives, 15
Alcohol, 9
Alfredo-style noodles, 161
Amber orange-tea punch, 271
Anise hot chocolate, 269
Appetizers, 38–48
  barley-vegetable loaf with yogurt-dill sauce, 133
  black bean dip, 38
  cheese blini, 45
  cherry tomatoes stuffed with shrimp, 44
  chick pea snack, 48
  chilled cheese fingers, 41
  cold spiced shrimp, 130
  crispy mushroom chips, 48
  crunchy popcorn mix, 48
  deviled shrimp, 40–41
  herbed cottage cheese dip, 38
  lemony Chinese chicken morsels, 39
  marinated fresh vegetables, 48
  peppery chicken wings, 40
  potted turkey spread, 39
  roasted garlic dip, 38
  sardine-rice bundles, 44
  southwestern-style guacamole, 39
  spicy stuffed eggs, 41
  spinach soufflé squares, 46
  spinach-stuffed mushrooms, 43
  super nachos, 42
  tangy cheese-stuffed new potatoes, 43
  tortellini with spinach pesto dip, 46
  tuna-stuffed cucumbers, 44
  zucchini, carrot, and onion quiche, 47
Apple(s)
  -carrot soup, 56–57
  chicken with cabbage and, 104
  cider, mulled, 269
  -mint tea, iced, 273
  pancakes, 32
  parsnips with, 190
  punch, autumn, 271
  -raisin crisp, 282
  and red cabbage salad, sweet-and-sour, 210
  -spice muffins, 240
  sweet potatoes with, 197
  Waldorf salad, 221
  –wild rice stuffing, Cornish game hens with, 116
Apricot(s)
  chicken, sweet-and-sour, 100
  curried brown rice with, 168
  roast chicken stuffed with rice and, 92
Arteriosclerosis, 8

Artichoke(s)
  chicken, and rice casserole, 102
  hearts and celery in cheese sauce, 184
  -stuffed peppers with lemon sauce, 134
  vegetable-cheese salad with, 266
Asparagus
  baked, with Parmesan cheese, 174
  brown rice with egg and, 167
  herbs and spices for, 17
  lemon chicken with, 245
  marinated vegetable salad, 216
  -mushroom omelets, 256
  with sesame seeds, 174
  soup, cream of, 55
  spaghetti with pecans and, 158
  stir-fried lamb, sweet red pepper and, 88
  vinaigrette, 206
Autumn apple punch, 271

B

Bad foods, list of, 12
Baked
  acorn squash with Parmesan cheese, 199
  asparagus with Parmesan cheese, 174
  beans on dark bread, 132
  beets, 176
  cabbage wedges with Parmesan and bread crumbs, 179
  grits, 170
  macaroni and cheese, 156
  tuna-stuffed tomatoes, 126
  ziti with mozzarella, 155
Banana(s)
  milk shake, 272
  mixed fruit salad, 220–221
  -spice loaf, 239
Barbecue(d)
  chicken thighs, tangy, 104
  seasoning mix, 29
Barley
  -mushroom soup, 58
  -vegetable loaf with yogurt-dill sauce, 133
Basil
  broccoli with, 178
  -tomato paste, beef stew with, 70
Bean(s), black
  cold roast pork with fruit and, 78
  dip, 38
  four-bean salad, 207
  and rice, 138
  soup, hearty, 56
  vegetarian chili with rice, 141

Bean(s), dried, herbs and spices for, 17
Bean(s), green
  and cherry tomatoes, 175
  with dill, 174
  four-bean salad, 207
  herbs and spices for, 17
  lamb, and carrot stew, 87
  and pasta salad, 266
  with pimientos, 175
  salade Niçoise, 218
  vinaigrette, 206
  -zucchini salad, 206
Bean(s), kidney
  four-bean salad, 207
  and rice, Italian-style, 164
Bean(s), lima
  baby, with sour cream and paprika, 176
  and corn, 185
  with herbs, 176
  herbs and spices for, 17
  succotash salad, 211
Bean(s), pink, cornmeal pizza with, 149
Bean(s), pinto
  baked, on dark bread, 132
  vegetarian chili with rice, 141
Bean(s), white
  four-bean salad, 207
  sauce, spinach ring with, 136
  yellow squash, and tomato stew, 143
Bean(s), yellow wax, in tomato sauce, 176
Bean sprout(s)
  mushroom salad with, 213
  salad, 208
Béarnaise sauce, mock, 32–33
Beef
  chili con carne, 75
  easy red and green pepper steak, 68
  grilled Oriental steak, 69
  hamburgers Lindstrom, 75
  herbs and spices for, 17
  Mexican sliced steak, 70
  minute steaks with pimientos and mushrooms, 67
  old German sauerbraten, 65
  picadillo platter, 72
  quick steak pizzaiola, 67
  roast sirloin with black peppercorn crust, 64
  roll with chili sauce, 66
  savory macaroni and, 73
  sliced, with romaine, cucumber, and tomatoes, 69
  spaghetti with meat and tomato sauce, 159
  spinach and rice loaf with mushroom sauce, 73
  steak parsley, 68
  stew with basil-tomato paste, 70
  stir-fry with mushrooms and sweet pepper, 243
  Swedish meatballs, 74

Beef *(contd.)*
  Yankee pot roast, 64
  zucchini and tomato kebabs, 71
Beer mustard, 36
Beet(s)
  baked, 176
  hamburgers Lindstrom, 75
  herbs and spices for, 17
  quick borscht, 242
  salad, pickled, 209
  shredded, in horseradish sauce, 177
  sweet-and-sour, 177
Bermuda onion rings, 189
Beverages, 268–274
  amber orange-tea punch, 271
  banana milk shake, 272
  cappuccino, 268
  chocolate buttermilk drink, 268
  garden vegetable juice, 274
  gingered lemon-lime fizz, 272
  ginger-tea punch, 269
  heavenly hot chocolate, 268–269
  herbal tea, 273
  holiday eggnog, 269
  home-style lemonade, 269
  hot cranberry punch, 271
  iced apple-mint tea, 273
  minted grapefruit spritzer, 272
  mocha shake, 271
  mulled apple cider, 269
  orange buttermilk drink, 268
  pineapple-mint yogurt drink, 274
  pineapple-orange cooler, 272–273
  spiced cranberry shrub, 274
BHA and BHT, 15
Biscuits, cream cheese, 240
Black bean(s)
  cold roast pork with fruit and, 78
  dip, 38
  four-bean salad, 207
  and rice, 138
  soup, hearty, 56
  vegetarian chili with rice, 141
Black-eyed pea stew, 251
Black Forest cake, 276–277
Blini, cheese, 45
Blueberry(ies)
  breakfast pudding, 258
  cobbler, 283
  coffee cake, 259
  frozen berry yogurt, 292
  -lemon crisp, 282–283
  -lemon yogurt, 274
  -peach tarts, 286–287
Blue cheese
  dressing, 225
  peppery chicken wings, 40
Bluefish, wine-poached, with onion and dill, 118

Borscht, quick, 242
Braised
    eggplant, zucchini, and
        tomatoes, 186
    red cabbage with
        cranberries, 180
    spinach, 199
    whole chicken with green
        onion stuffing, 93
    yellow squash, corn, and
        tomatoes, 200–201
Bran, 13
    muffins, 240
Bread(s), 228–240
    banana-spice loaf, 239
    basic French, 228
    basic muffins, 240
    carrot-lemon, 239
    cottage cheese, 230
    country-style, 229
    cranberry-orange, 239
    cream cheese biscuits,
        240
    Irish soda, 236
    jam muffins, 260
    monkey, 230–231
    nutty whole wheat,
        232–233
    old-fashioned corn-, 237
    onion flat-, 231
    orange quick, 31
    **pretzels with caraway
        seeds, 234–235**
    prune-and-spice quick, 238
    quick, mix, 31
    raspberry coffee cake, 259
    spiced wheat germ muffins,
        31
    spoon, 237
    whole wheat dinner rolls,
        234
    winter squash, 232
    Yorkshire pudding, 239
Breakfasts, 256–260
    apple pancakes, 32
    basic muffins, 240
    blueberry breakfast
        pudding, 258
    cheese blini, 45
    jam muffins, 260
    kedgeree, 257
    menus for, 23–24
    nutty whole wheat bread,
        232–233
    orange French toast, 260
    pancakes, 259
    raspberry coffee cake, 259
    scrambled eggs Benedict,
        257
    spiced wheat germ muffins,
        31
    Swiss health cereal, 258
Broccoli
    with basil, 178
    **brown rice with egg and,
        167**
    -Cheddar soufflé, 144
    and corn stew, 185
    herbs and spices for, 17
    and pasta salad, 266
    **pasta with, in sweet
        tomato sauce, 160**
    with peppers, 178
    sauce, pasta with, 157
    sesame salad, 208
    -stuffed tomatoes, 178
    vinaigrette, 206

Broiled
    chicken with vinegar and
        honey, 93
    garlic-stuffed Cornish
        game hens, 116
    **lamb chops with herbs,
        86**
    salmon with sweet red
        pepper sauce, 120
Broth, low-sodium chicken,
    34
Brown bag lunches, 261–266
    **crudités with peanut
        butter dip, 264**
    green pea, carrot, and
        mozzarella salad, 265
    marinated sandwiches, 263
    mini meat loaves, 261
    muffaletto sandwiches, 264
    **pasta and broccoli salad,
        266**
    pizza sandwiches, 262
    stuffed pita sandwiches,
        262
    **vegetable-cheese salad
        with artichokes, 266**
Brunswick stew, 94
Brussels sprouts
    herbs and spices for, 17
    with lemon sauce, 179
    with mustard sauce, 179
Buckwheat
    **kasha with onions and
        noodles, 170**
    kasha with vegetables, 171
Bulgur
    pilaf, 172
    **-stuffed red peppers,
        172**
    tabouleh, 224
Burritos, chicken, 103
Buttermilk
    chocolate drink, 268
    orange drink, 268
    pancakes, 259
    salad dressing mix, 28
Butternut squash
    soup, golden, 61
    in tomato sauce, 200

C

Cabbage
    braised red, with
        cranberries, 180
    chicken with apples and,
        104
    confetti coleslaw, 211
    creamy yogurt coleslaw,
        210
    curried, 180
    herbs and spices for, 17
    mashed potatoes and, 195
    -noodle casserole, 132
    red, and apple salad,
        sweet-and-sour, 210
    salad mold, 222
    wedges with Parmesan and
        bread crumbs, baked, 179
Cake
    Black Forest, 276–277
    lemon angel roll, 278

Cake (contd.)
    white, with seven-minute
        frosting, 277
California seafood medley, 127
Calories, 19–20
Cancer, 7, 13–14
**Cannelloni with ricotta and
    peas, 153**
Cantaloupe
    fresh melon ice, 290
    mixed fruit salad,
        220–221
    spicy cucumber and fruit
        salad, 220
Cappuccino, 268
Carbohydrates, 8, 11, 13
    guidelines for, 20
Caribbean lime chicken, 105
Carrot(s)
    -apple soup, 56–57
    creamy yogurt coleslaw,
        210
    glazed with five spices,
        182
    glazed with orange and
        ginger, 181
    green pea, and mozzarella
        salad, 265
    and green pepper in cream
        sauce, 181
    herbs and spices for, 17
    lamb, and green bean stew,
        87
    -lemon loaf, 239
    parsnip, and potato purée,
        190
    salad, crunchy, 211
    salad, pickled, 209
    snow peas with red pepper
        and, 192–193
    stir-fried potatoes and,
        181
    and wild rice loaf, 169
    zucchini, and onion quiche,
        47
Casseroles
    cabbage-noodle, 132
    **chicken, artichoke, and
        rice, 102**
    chicken pot pie, 96
    deviled tuna pot pie, 125
    **easy cheese and potato
        pie, 145**
    easy ham, green pea, and
        noodle, 85
    Mexicali pork chop, 81
    **Polish sausage and chick
        pea, 244**
    pork and red cabbage, 82
    pork chops and rice, 244
    **seven-vegetable, with
        couscous crust, 137**
    **Spanish-style vegetable,
        143**
    two-cheese, 146
    two-potato, 197
    yellow squash, 201
Cauliflower
    with bread crumbs, 184
    herbs and spices for, 17
    marinated vegetable salad,
        216
    in pimiento sauce, 183
    pudding, 183
    **spiced, with tomatoes,
        182–183**
    vinaigrette, 206

Celery and artichoke hearts
    in cheese sauce, 184
Cereal, Swiss health, 258
Cheddar cheese
    -broccoli soufflé, 144
    fish rarebit, 121
    Welsh rarebit, 148
Cheese
    baked asparagus with
        Parmesan, 174
    baked macaroni and, 156
    blini, 45
    blue, dressing, 225
    bread, cottage, 230
    broccoli-Cheddar soufflé,
        144
    and corn pudding, Mexican,
        146
    cream, biscuits, 240
    eggplant lasagne, 134
    enchiladas, zesty, 145
    feta, and shrimp salad,
        dilled, 219
    fingers, chilled, 41
    fish rarebit, 121
    and fruit salad with
        orange dressing, 254
    Greek salad, 217
    herbed cottage, dip, 38
    hot roast pork and
        tortilla sandwiches, 77
    mozzarella, green pea, and
        carrot salad, 265
    **pasta, and tomato pie,
        159**
    peppery chicken wings, 40
    pizza sandwiches, 262
    **and potato pie, easy,
        145**
    ricotta, zucchini filled
        with spinach and, 137
    roasted garlic dip, 38
    sauce, celery and
        artichoke hearts in, 184
    soup, 55
    soup, quick, 33
    spicy lasagne roll-ups,
        152
    **spinach soufflé squares,
        46**
    **-stuffed chicken Kiev,
        110**
    -stuffed new potatoes,
        tangy, 43
    super nachos, 42
    turkey cutlets parmigiana,
        247
    two-, casserole, 146
    **-vegetable salad with
        artichokes, 266**
    Welsh rarebit, 148
    whole wheat pizza with
        green peppers, 150
Cheesecake, lime-ginger, 288
Chef's salad, 253
**Cherry tomatoes stuffed
    with shrimp, 44**
Chicken
    **artichoke, and rice
        casserole, 102**
    biriyani, 95
    braised whole, with green
        onion stuffing, 93
    **breasts and rice
        casserole, 244**
    breasts Dijon, 106
    breasts Parmesan, 110

*Recipes in **bold** type are extra low in fat, sugar, and sodium.*

Chicken *(contd.)*
  breasts with lemon and capers, 108
  broiled, with vinegar and honey, 93
  broth, low-sodium, 34
  Brunswick stew, 94
  burritos, 103
  with cabbage and apples, 104
  Caribbean lime, 105
  chef's salad, 253
  chili con carne, 75
  Chinese vegetables and, 245
  consommé, homestyle, 50
  country captain, 101
  Creole, 107
  curried vegetables and, 246
  cutlets, 30
  -escarole soup, 50
  with fresh tomato sauce, 109
  fricassee, 98
  gardener's style, 103
  with green sauce, 92
  gumbo, 52
  with herb dumplings, 99
  herbs and spices for, 17
  jambalaya, 164–165
  Kiev, cheese-stuffed, 110
  Laredo, 100
  morsels, lemony Chinese, 39
  and mushrooms in foil, 109
  oven-fried, 98
  pot pie, 96
  Provençal, 106
  roast, stuffed with rice and apricots, 92
  salad with lemon and basil, 218
  seasoned crumb mix for pork or, 30
  slices with ham, 112
  with snow peas and peanut sauce, 95
  soup with mint, 52
  spicy lasagne roll-ups, 152
  strips with mustard sauce, 245
  sweet-and-sour apricot, 100
  tandoori, 97
  tetrazzini with spaghetti squash, 97
  thighs, tangy barbecued, 104
  tortellini with garden vegetables, 252
  wings, peppery, 40
Chick pea(s)
  macaroni with tomatoes and, 155
  patties in pita pockets, 148
  and Polish sausage casserole, 244
  pork stew with, 83
  snack, 48
  sweet and spicy vegetable stew, 142
  vegetarian chili with rice, 141

Chili
  con carne, 75
  sauce, beef roll with, 66
  seasoning mix, 29
  vegetarian, with rice, 141
Chinese dishes. *See* Oriental dishes.
Chive vichyssoise, 59
Chocolate
  -berry crunch parfait, 291
  Black Forest cake, 276–277
  buttermilk drink, 268
  chip cookies, 280
  chip meringue drops, 280
  heavenly hot, 268–269
  milk shake, 272
  mocha shake, 271
  -orange sauce, 292
  pudding, make-your-own, 289
  sauce, 292
Cholesterol, 15
  arteriosclerosis and, 8
  blood, lowering, 8, 12
  cutting down on, 9, 16
  fat and, 8, 10
  guidelines for, 20–21
Chowder
  corn, 57
  crab, 242
  spicy tomato-fish, 52
Cider, mulled apple, 269
Citrus and watercress salad, 221
Coffee
  cappuccino, 268
  mocha shake, 271
Coffee cake, raspberry, 259
Coleslaw
  confetti, 211
  creamy yogurt, 210
Colon cancer, 7, 13–14
Company dinner menus, 22
Complementary proteins, 11, 16
Condiments
  Dijon mustard, 36
  hamburger relish, 35
  ketchup, 36
  onion relish, 34–35
  salsa, 36
  three-pepper relish, 34
Confetti coleslaw, 211
Consommé, homestyle chicken, 50
Cookies
  chocolate chip, 280
  chocolate chip meringue drops, 280
  oatmeal wafers, 282
Cooking for one or two, 242–254
  asparagus-mushroom omelets, 256
  beef stir-fry with mushrooms and sweet pepper, 243
  black-eyed pea stew, 251
  chef's salad, 253
  chicken strips with mustard sauce, 245
  Chinese chicken and vegetables, 245
  corn crêpes with spicy tomato sauce, 250
  Cornish hen glazed with orange and ginger, 246

Cooking for one or two *(contd.)*
  crab chowder, 242
  curried chicken and vegetables, 246
  dilled tuna-yogurt salad, 254
  fish fillet in foil, 249
  French bread pizza, 250
  fruit and cheese salad with orange dressing, 254
  linguine with tuna and peas, 253
  menus for, 24
  pasta shells with Mediterranean vegetables, 252
  Polish sausage and chick pea casserole, 244
  pork chops and rice casserole, 244
  quick borscht, 242
  tortellini with garden vegetables, 252
  tuna patties, 149
  turkey cutlets with lemon and parsley, 247
Cooking the healthful way, 16–19
Corn
  braised yellow squash, tomatoes and, 200–201
  and broccoli stew, 185
  and cheese pudding, Mexican, 146
  and cherry tomato salad, 212
  chowder, 57
  crêpes with spicy tomato sauce, 250
  herbs and spices for, 17
  and lima beans, 185
  pudding, 186
  succotash salad, 211
Cornbread, old-fashioned, 237
Cornish game hen(s)
  broiled garlic-stuffed, 116
  glazed with orange and ginger, 246
  with wild rice–apple stuffing, 116
Cornmeal
  pancakes, 259
  pizza with pink beans, 149
  polenta with fresh tomato sauce, 169
  spoon bread, 237
Cottage cheese
  baked macaroni and, 156
  blini, 45
  bread, 230
  dip, herbed, 38
  and fruit salad with orange dressing, 254
  Greek salad, 217
  spinach crêpes with tomato sauce, 135
  spinach soufflé squares, 46
  -stuffed new potatoes, tangy, 43
Country captain, 101
Country-style bread, 229

Crab
  chowder, 242
  deviled, 129
  and pasta salad, 162
Cranberry(ies)
  braised red cabbage with, 180
  -orange loaf, 239
  -pear mold, 223
  punch, hot, 271
  shrub, spiced, 274
Cream cheese biscuits, 240
Cream of vegetable soup, 55
Cream puffs and eclairs, 287
Crème fraîche, mock, 27
Creole dishes
  chicken, 107
  seafood gumbo, 128
Crêpes
  corn, with spicy tomato sauce, 250
  spinach, with tomato sauce, 135
Crispy mushroom chips, 48
Crudités with peanut butter dip, 264
Crunchy carrot salad, 211
Crunchy popcorn mix, 48
Cucumber(s)
  -dill sauce, salmon with, 119
  and fruit salad, spicy, 220
  salad, minted, 212
  sliced beef with romaine, tomatoes, and, 69
  soup, cold, 57
  and sweet red pepper salad, spiced, 212
  tuna-stuffed, 44
  -yogurt sauce, 226
Currant biscuits, 240
Curry, curried
  brown rice with apricots, 168
  cabbage, 180
  chicken and vegetables, 246
  lamb, 88
  mulligatawny soup, 51
  potatoes, 194
  tuna and fruit, cold, 124
  vegetable, with yogurt sauce, 141
  vichyssoise, 59

D

Dairy products, 9, 16
Danish-style new potatoes, 194
Deep-dish peach pie, 285
Desserts, 276–292
  apple-raisin crisp, 282
  Black Forest cake, 276–277
  blueberry cobbler, 283
  blueberry-peach tarts, 286–287
  chocolate-berry crunch parfait, 291
  chocolate chip cookies, 280
  chocolate chip meringue drops, 280

*Recipes in **bold** type are extra low in fat, sugar, and sodium.*

Desserts *(contd.)*
  cream puffs and eclairs, 287
  deep-dish peach pie, 285
  fresh peach ice, 290
  frozen berry yogurt, 292
  ginger-pumpkin chiffon pie, 286
  lemon angel roll, 278
  lemon soufflé, 290
  lemon squares, 281
  lime-ginger cheesecake, 288
  make-your-own chocolate pudding, 289
  no-sugar fruit pudding, 288
  oatmeal wafers, 282
  raspberry-nut torte, 279
  strawberry chiffon charlotte, 284–285
  white cake with seven-minute frosting, 277
Deviled
  crab, 129
  shrimp, 40–41
  tuna pot pie, 125
Diabetes, 10
Dietary guidelines, 9
Diets, 10
Dijon mustard, 36
Dill(ed)
  -cucumber sauce, salmon with, 119
  green beans with, 174
  rice with lemon and, 166
  shrimp and feta cheese salad, 219
  -sour cream sauce, mushrooms in, 187
  tuna-yogurt salad, 254
  wine-poached bluefish with onion and, 118
Dining out, 18
Dip
  black bean, 38
  herbed cottage cheese, 38
  peanut butter, crudités with, 264
  roasted garlic, 38
Dumplings
  herb, chicken with, 99
  peas and, 190

E

East Indian dishes
  beef, zucchini, and tomato kebabs, 71
  chicken biriyani, 95
  kedgeree, 97
  mulligatawny soup, 51
  spiced pork chops, 80
  tandoori chicken, 97
  See also Curry, curried.
Eclairs and cream puffs, 287
Egg(s)
  asparagus-mushroom omelets, 256
  Benedict, scrambled, 257
  broccoli-Cheddar soufflé, 144
  brown rice with asparagus and, 167
  herbs and spices for, 17

Egg(s) *(contd.)*
  kedgeree, 257
  spicy stuffed, 41
  zucchini frittata, 147
Eggnog, holiday, 269
Eggplant
  braised zucchini, tomatoes, and, 186
  herbs and spices for, 17
  lasagne, 134
  soup, roasted, 58
  stacks, 186–187
Enchiladas, zesty cheese, 145
Escarole-chicken soup, 50
Exercise, 8, 11

F

Family dinner menus, 22
Fats, 7, 8–10
  cancer and, 7
  cholesterol and, 8, 10
  cutting down on, 7, 9, 16, 18
  food labels and, 15
  guidelines for, 10, 20
  heart disease and, 8
  sources of, 8–10
Fiber, 7, 9, 13–14
  guidelines for, 21
First courses, 44–48
  cheese blini, 45
  cherry tomatoes stuffed with shrimp, 44
  marinated fresh vegetables, 48
  sardine-rice bundles, 44
  southwestern-style guacamole, 39
  spinach soufflé squares, 46
  tortellini with spinach pesto dip, 46
  tuna-stuffed cucumbers, 44
  zucchini, carrot, and onion quiche, 47
Fish, 118–128
  baked tuna-stuffed tomatoes, 126
  broiled salmon steaks with radish-yogurt sauce, 124
  broiled salmon with sweet red pepper sauce, 120
  California seafood medley, 127
  chowder, 242
  chowder, spicy tomato-, 52
  cold curried tuna and fruit, 124
  deviled tuna pot pie, 125
  fillet in foil, 249
  fisherman's baked shells, 154
  flounder and vegetables sealed in silver, 120
  with fresh tomato sauce, 109
  gingery grilled swordfish steaks, 123
  herbs and spices for, 17
  kedgeree, 257
  lemony baked stuffed whiting, 119

Fish *(contd.)*
  linguine with tuna and peas, 253
  linguine with tuna-caper sauce, 157
  marinated sandwiches, 263
  muffaletto with tuna, 264
  Omega-3 in, 10, 18
  rarebit, 121
  salmon loaf with green pea sauce, 127
  salmon with cucumber-dill sauce, 119
  sardine-rice bundles, 44
  savory salmon patties, 126
  seafood gumbo, 128
  sesame sole, 122
  stuffed fillets with nutmeg sauce, 123
  tortellini with garden vegetables, 252
  tuna patties, 249
  tuna-stuffed cucumbers, 44
  wine-poached bluefish with onion and dill, 118
  See also Shellfish.
Flounder and vegetables sealed in silver, 120
Food labels, 9, 15
Foods
  good and bad, list of, 12
  storing, 19
Four-bean salad, 207
French bread pizza, 250
French fries, oven, 196
French-style green peas, 191
French toast, 260
Fresh peach ice, 290
Frozen berry yogurt, 292
Fruit
  and cheese salad with orange dressing, 254
  cold curried tuna and, 124
  cold roast pork with black beans and, 78
  pancakes, 259
  salad, mixed, 220–221
  See also specific kinds of fruit.
Fusilli with parsley-mushroom sauce, 161

G

Garden-fresh vegetable soup, 54
Garden vegetable juice, 274
Garlic
  dip, roasted, 38
  dressing, creamy, 226
  -stuffed Cornish game hens, broiled, 116
Garlicky white bean dip, 38
Gazpacho
  refreshing red, 62
  salad, molded, 222
German dishes
  chicken with cabbage and apples, 104
  homemade noodles, 163
  potato salad, 214
  sauerbraten, 65

Ginger(ed)
  carrots glazed with orange and, 181
  lemon-lime fizz, 272
  -lime cheesecake, 288
  -peach crisp, 282
  -pumpkin chiffon pie, 286
  sauce, fresh, 292
  -tea punch, 269
Gingery grilled swordfish steaks, 123
Glazed
  carrots with five spices, 182
  turkey breast with sweet potato stuffing, 111
Golden butternut squash soup, 61
Good foods, list of, 12
Grains, 164–172
  baked grits, 170
  brown rice with asparagus and egg, 167
  brown rice with poppy seed sauce, 166
  bulgur pilaf, 172
  bulgur-stuffed red peppers, 172
  curried brown rice and apricots, 168
  easy nutted brown rice, 168
  Italian-style rice and beans, 164
  jambalaya, 164–165
  kasha with onions and noodles, 170
  kasha with vegetables, 171
  noodles and rice, 164
  polenta with fresh tomato sauce, 169
  rice and green peas, 166
  rice with lemon and dill, 166
  spinach-rice mold, 165
  wild rice and carrot loaf, 169
Grapefruit(s)
  citrus and watercress salad, 221
  cold roast pork with black beans and fruit, 78
  spritzer, minted, 272
Grapefruitade, 269
Grated zucchini pancake, 203
Gravy, 33
Greek salad, 217
Green bean(s)
  and cherry tomatoes, 175
  with dill, 174
  four-bean salad, 207
  herbs and spices for, 17
  lamb, and carrot stew, 87
  and pasta salad, 266
  with pimientos, 175
  salade Niçoise, 218
  vinaigrette, 206
  -zucchini salad, 206
Green gazpacho, 62
Green German noodles, 163
Grits, baked, 170
Guacamole, southwestern-style, 39
Gumbo
  chicken, 52
  seafood, 128

H

Ham
  green pea, and noodle
    casserole, easy, 85
  scrambled eggs Benedict,
    257
  turkey slices with, 112
  and vegetable loaf, spicy, 85
Hamburger(s)
  Lindstrom, 75
  relish, 35
Heart attacks, 14
Heart disease, 7, 10
  fat and, 8
Heavenly hot chocolate,
  268–269
Height/weight tables, 10
Herb(ed)
  -cheese bread, 230
  cottage cheese dip, 38
  creamed onions, 189
  -mushroom omelet, 256
  mustard, 36
  noodles, 163
  salad dressing mix, 28
  veal with summer squash,
    90
Herbal tea, 273
Herbs and spices, 17, 19
High blood pressure
  (hypertension), 10, 14
Holiday eggnog, 269
Hollandaise sauce, mock, 32
Homemade German noodles,
  163
Homestyle chicken consommé,
  50
Home-style lemonade, 269
Hominy grits, 170
Honey-yogurt dressing, 226
Hors d'oeuvres, 38–43
  black bean dip, 38
  chilled cheese fingers, 41
  deviled shrimp, 40–41
  herbed cottage cheese dip,
    38
  lemony Chinese chicken
    morsels, 39
  peppery chicken wings, 40
  potted turkey spread, 39
  roasted garlic dip, 38
  **southwestern-style
    guacamole, 39**
  spicy stuffed eggs, 41
  **spinach-stuffed
    mushrooms, 43**
  super nachos, 42
  tangy cheese-stuffed new
    potatoes, 43
Horseradish sauce, shredded
  beets in, 177
Hypertension (high blood
  pressure), 10, 14

I

Iced apple-mint tea, 273
Indian dishes. *See* East
  Indian dishes.
Intestinal disorders, 7, 13
Irish soda bread, 236
Italian dishes
  bread and tomato salad, 215

Italian dishes *(contd.)*
  dressing, 225
  eggplant lasagne, 134
  polenta with fresh tomato
    sauce, 169
  rice and green peas, 166
  spaghetti squash, 140
  -style rice and beans, 164
  veal shanks, 89
  See also Pasta.

J

Jambalaya, 164–165
Jam muffins, 260
Jellied consommé, 50
Jerusalem artichoke salad,
  211

K

Kale and potato soup, 60–61
Kasha
  **with onions and noodles,
    170**
  with vegetables, 171
Kebabs
  **beef, zucchini, and
    tomato, 71**
  pork on skewers, savory
    broiled, 82
  squash, 202
Kedgeree, 257
Ketchup, 36
Kidney beans
  four-bean salad, 207
  **and rice, Italian-style,
    164**
Kidney problems, 11, 14

L

Labels, food, 9, 15
Lamb
  carrot, and green bean
    stew, 87
  **chops and rice casserole,
    244**
  **chops with herbs,
    broiled, 86**
  curried, 88
  herbs and spices for, 17
  stir-fried asparagus,
    sweet red pepper, and, 88
  **stuffed leg of, with
    orange gravy, 86**
Lasagne
  eggplant, 134
  roll-ups, spicy, 152
  **zucchini, mushroom, and
    pimiento, 153**
Lemon(y)
  angel roll, 278
  baked stuffed whiting, 119
  -blueberry crisp, 282–283
  -blueberry yogurt, 274
  -carrot loaf, 239
  chicken with asparagus,
    245
  Chinese chicken morsels,
    39
  -lime fizz, gingered, 272

Lemon(y) *(contd.)*
  -raisin sauce, 292
  sauce, 292
  soufflé, 290
  squares, 281
  veal cutlets with sage
    and, 89
Lemonade, home-style, 269
Lentil(s)
  **stew, hearty low-calorie,
    138**
  **vegetarian chili with
    rice, 141**
Lettuce
  chef's salad, 253
  French-style green peas,
    191
  Greek salad, 217
  picadillo platter, 72
  salad, wilted, 215
Lima beans
  baby, with sour cream and
    paprika, 176
  and corn, 185
  with herbs, 176
  herbs and spices for, 17
  succotash salad, 211
Lime
  chicken, Caribbean, 105
  fizz, gingered lemon-, 272
  -ginger cheesecake, 288
Limeade, 269
Linguine
  with tuna and peas, 253
  **with tuna-caper sauce,
    157**
  **with white clam sauce,
    156**
Loin of pork with vegetable
  stuffing, 77
Low-calorie dinner menus, 23
Low-sodium chicken broth, 34
Lunches
  menus for, 23
  See also Brown bag lunches.

M

Macaroni
  baked cheese and, 156
  **with chick peas and
    tomatoes, 155**
  savory beef and, 73
Main dishes
  **Alfredo-style noodles,
    161**
  apple pancakes, 32
  artichoke-stuffed peppers
    with lemon sauce, 134
  **asparagus-mushroom
    omelets, 256**
  baked beans on dark bread,
    132
  baked macaroni and cheese,
    156
  baked tuna-stuffed
    tomatoes, 126
  **baked ziti with
    mozzarella, 155**
  **barley-vegetable loaf
    with yogurt-dill sauce, 133**
  **beef, zucchini, and
    tomato kebabs, 71**
  beef roll with chili
    sauce, 66

Main dishes *(contd.)*
  **beef stir-fry with mushrooms
    and sweet pepper, 243**
  **beef stew with basil-
    tomato paste, 70**
  **black beans and rice,
    138**
  black-eyed pea stew, 251
  braised whole chicken with
    green onion stuffing, 93
  broccoli-Cheddar soufflé,
    144
  broiled chicken with
    vinegar and honey, 93
  broiled garlic-stuffed
    Cornish game hens, 116
  **broiled lamb chops with
    herbs, 86**
  broiled salmon steaks with
    radish-yogurt sauce, 124
  broiled salmon with sweet
    red pepper sauce, 120
  **brown rice with asparagus
    and egg, 167**
  Brunswick stew, 94
  **bulgur-stuffed red
    peppers, 172**
  cabbage-noodle casserole,
    132
  California seafood medley,
    127
  **cannelloni with ricotta
    and peas, 153**
  Caribbean lime chicken, 105
  **casserole of pork and red
    cabbage, 82**
  cheese blini, 45
  **cheese-stuffed chicken
    Kiev, 110**
  chef's salad, 253
  **chicken, artichoke, and
    rice casserole, 102**
  **chicken and mushrooms in
    foil, 109**
  chicken biriyani, 95
  chicken breasts Dijon, 106
  chicken breasts Parmesan,
    110
  **chicken breasts with
    lemon and capers, 108**
  chicken burritos, 103
  chicken Creole, 107
  chicken-escarole soup, 50
  chicken fricassee, 98
  **chicken gardener's style,
    103**
  chicken gumbo, 52
  chicken Laredo, 100
  chicken pot pie, 96
  chicken Provençal, 106
  chicken soup with mint, 52
  **chicken strips with
    mustard sauce, 245**
  chicken tetrazzini with
    spaghetti squash, 97
  chicken with cabbage and
    apples, 104
  **chicken with fresh tomato
    sauce, 109**
  **chicken with green sauce,
    92**
  chicken with herb
    dumplings, 99
  chicken with snow peas and
    peanut sauce, 95
  chick pea patties in pita
    pockets, 148

*Recipes in **bold** type are extra low in fat, sugar, and sodium.*

Main dishes *(contd.)*
chili con carne, 75
Chinese chicken and
vegetables, 245
cold curried tuna and
fruit, 124
**cold roast pork with
black beans and fruit,
78**
cold spiced shrimp, 130
**corn crêpes with spicy
tomato sauce, 250**
**Cornish game hens with
wild rice–apple
stuffing, 116**
Cornish hen glazed with
orange and ginger, 246
**cornmeal pizza with pink
beans, 149**
country captain, 101
crab and pasta salad, 162
crab chowder, 242
**curried chicken and
vegetables, 246**
curried lamb, 88
deviled crab, 129
deviled tuna pot pie, 125
dilled shrimp and feta
cheese salad, 219
**dilled tuna-yogurt salad,
254**
**easy cheese and potato
pie, 145**
easy red and green pepper
steak, 68
eggplant lasagne, 134
**fisherman's baked shells,
154**
fish fillet in foil, 249
fish rarebit, 121
**flounder and vegetables
sealed in silver, 120**
French bread pizza, 250
fruit and cheese salad
with orange dressing,
254
**fusilli with parsley-
mushroom sauce, 161**
**gingery grilled swordfish
steaks, 123**
**glazed turkey breast with
sweet potato stuffing,
111**
green pea, carrot, and
mozzarella salad, 265
grilled Oriental steak, 69
ham, green pea, and noodle
casserole, easy, 85
ham and vegetable loaf,
spicy, 85
hamburgers Lindstrom, 75
**hearty low-calorie lentil
stew, 138**
herbed veal with summer
squash, 90
hot roast pork and
tortilla sandwiches, 77
hot vegetable hero, 150
Indian-spiced pork chops, 80
**Italian-style rice and
beans, 164**
jambalaya, 164–165
**kasha with onions and
noodles, 170**
kedgeree, 257
lamb, carrot, and green
bean stew, 87

Main dishes *(contd.)*
lemony baked stuffed
whiting, 119
linguine with tuna and
peas, 253
linguine with tuna-caper
sauce, 157
**linguine with white clam
sauce, 156**
loin of pork with
vegetable stuffing, 77
**macaroni with chick peas
and tomatoes, 155**
maple-glazed pork roast,
76
marinated sandwiches, 263
Mexican corn and cheese
pudding, 146
Mexican sliced steak, 70
minestrone, 53
mini meat loaves, 261
**minute steaks with
pimientos and mushrooms,
67**
muffaletto sandwiches, 264
mulligatawny soup, 51
old German sauerbraten, 65
orange French toast, 260
oven-fried chicken, 98
pancakes, 259
**pasta, cheese, and tomato
pie, 159**
**pasta and broccoli salad,
266**
**pasta shells with
Mediterranean
vegetables, 252**
**pasta with broccoli in
sweet tomato sauce, 160**
**pasta with spinach sauce,
157**
picadillo platter, 72
pizza sandwiches, 262
**Polish sausage and chick
pea casserole, 244**
pork balls in tomato-
orange sauce, 84
**pork chop casserole,
Mexicali, 81**
**pork chops and rice
casserole, 244**
pork scaloppine with honey
mustard, 79
**pork stew with chick
peas, 83**
pork stir-fry with five
vegetables, 80
potato and kale soup,
60–61
quick borscht, 242
quick steak pizzaiola, 67
roast chicken stuffed with
rice and apricots, 92
roast sirloin with black
peppercorn crust, 64
salmon loaf with green pea
sauce, 127
salmon with cucumber-dill
sauce, 119
savory broiled pork on
skewers, 82
**savory macaroni and beef,
73**
savory rice salad, 224
savory salmon patties, 126
scallops marinated in
orange and fennel, 129

Main dishes *(contd.)*
scrambled eggs Benedict,
257
seafood gumbo, 128
sesame sole, 122
**seven-vegetable casserole
with couscous crust,
137**
sliced beef with romaine,
cucumber, and tomatoes,
69
spaghetti squash Italian
style, 140
**spaghetti with asparagus
and pecans, 158**
**spaghetti with meat and
tomato sauce, 159**
**Spanish-style vegetable
casserole, 143**
spicy lasagne roll-ups, 152
**spinach and rice loaf
with mushroom sauce, 73**
spinach crêpes with tomato
sauce, 135
spinach-rice mold, 165
spinach ring with white
bean sauce, 136
split pea and potato soup,
60
steak parsley, 68
stir-fried lamb,
asparagus, and sweet red
pepper, 88
stir-fried lobster,
mushrooms, and snow
peas, 130
**stuffed fish fillets with
nutmeg sauce, 123**
**stuffed leg of lamb with
orange gravy, 86**
stuffed pita sandwiches,
262
Swedish meatballs, 74
sweet-and-sour apricot
chicken, 100
**sweet and spicy vegetable
stew, 142**
tandoori chicken, 97
tangy barbecued chicken
thighs, 104
tarragon turkey loaf, 114
**tofu stir-fry with rice,
139**
**tortellini with garden
vegetables, 252**
tuna patties, 249
turkey balsamico, 115
turkey cutlets with lemon
and parsley, 247
**turkey scaloppine with
sherried cream, 113**
turkey slices with ham,
112
turkey–sour cream patties,
114–115
turkey-vegetable soufflé,
112
two-cheese casserole, 146
veal and mushroom
paprikash with yogurt,
90
veal cutlets with lemon
and sage, 89
**veal shanks Italian
style, 89**
**vegetable-cheese salad
with artichokes, 266**

Main dishes *(contd.)*
**vegetable curry with
yogurt sauce, 141**
vegetable lo mein, 142
**vegetarian chili with
rice, 141**
Welsh rarebit, 148
**white bean, yellow squash,
and tomato stew, 143**
whole wheat pizza with
green peppers, 150
**wine-poached bluefish
with onion and dill,
118**
Yankee pot roast, 64
zesty cheese enchiladas,
145
**zucchini, mushroom, and
pimiento lasagne, 153**
zucchini filled with
spinach and ricotta, 137
zucchini frittata, 147
Make-your-own chocolate
pudding, 289
Maple
French toast, 260
-glazed pork roast, 76
Marinated
broiled peppers, 193
fresh vegetables, 48
sandwiches, 263
vegetable salad, 216
**Mashed potatoes and
cabbage, 195**
Mayonnaise, mock, 26
Meals-in-one, 24
Meatless main dishes,
132–150
**Alfredo-style noodles,
161**
artichoke-stuffed peppers
with lemon sauce, 134
baked beans on dark bread,
132
baked macaroni and cheese,
156
**baked ziti with
mozzarella, 155**
**barley-vegetable loaf
with yogurt-dill sauce,
133**
black beans and rice, 138
black-eyed pea stew, 251
broccoli-Cheddar soufflé,
144
**brown rice with asparagus
and egg, 167**
cabbage-noodle casserole,
132
**cannelloni with ricotta
and peas, 153**
chick pea patties in pita
pockets, 148
complementary proteins in,
11, 16
**corn crêpes with spicy
tomato sauce, 250**
**cornmeal pizza with pink
beans, 149**
**easy cheese and potato
pie, 145**
eggplant lasagne, 134
French bread pizza, 250
**fusilli with parsley-
mushroom sauce, 161**
**hearty low-calorie lentil
stew, 138**

Meatless main dishes *(contd.)*
  hot vegetable hero, 150
  Italian-style rice and beans, 164
  kasha with onions and noodles, 170
  macaroni with chick peas and tomatoes, 155
  Mexican corn and cheese pudding, 146
  pasta, cheese, and tomato pie, 159
  pasta with broccoli in sweet tomato sauce, 160
  seven-vegetable casserole with couscous crust, 137
  spaghetti squash Italian style, 140
  spaghetti with asparagus and pecans, 158
  Spanish-style vegetable casserole, 143
  spinach crêpes with tomato sauce, 135
  spinach ring with white bean sauce, 136
  sweet and spicy vegetable stew, 142
  tofu stir-fry with rice, 139
  two-cheese casserole, 146
  vegetable curry with yogurt sauce, 141
  vegetable lo mein, 142
  vegetarian chili with rice, 141
  Welsh rarebit, 148
  white bean, yellow squash, and tomato stew, 143
  whole wheat pizza with green peppers, 150
  zesty cheese enchiladas, 145
  zucchini, pimiento, and mushroom lasagne, 153
  zucchini filled with spinach and ricotta, 137
  zucchini frittata, 147
Meats, 64–90
  beef, zucchini, and tomato kebabs, 71
  beef roll with chili sauce, 66
  beef sauté with mushrooms and sweet pepper, 243
  beef stew with basil-tomato paste, 70
  broiled lamb chops with herbs, 86
  buying, 16
  casserole of pork and red cabbage, 82
  chili con carne, 75
  cold roast pork with black beans and fruit, 78
  curried lamb, 88
  easy ham, green pea, and noodle casserole, 85
  easy red and green pepper steak, 68
  grilled Oriental steak, 69
  hamburgers Lindstrom, 75
  herbed veal with summer squash, 90
  hot roast pork and tortilla sandwiches, 77

Meats *(contd.)*
  Indian-spiced pork chops, 80
  lamb, carrot, and green bean stew, 87
  loin of pork with vegetable stuffing, 77
  maple-glazed pork roast, 76
  Mexicali pork chop casserole, 81
  Mexican sliced steak, 70
  minute steaks with pimientos and mushrooms, 67
  old German sauerbraten, 65
  picadillo platter, 72
  Polish sausage and chick pea casserole, 244
  pork balls in tomato-orange sauce, 84
  pork chops and rice casserole, 244
  pork scaloppine with honey mustard, 79
  pork stew with chick peas, 83
  pork stir-fry with five vegetables, 80
  pork with roasted peppers, 79
  quick steak pizzaiola, 67
  roast sirloin with black peppercorn crust, 64
  savory broiled pork on skewers, 82
  savory macaroni and beef, 73
  sliced beef with romaine, cucumber, and tomatoes, 69
  spicy ham and vegetable loaf, 85
  spinach and rice loaf with mushroom sauce, 73
  steak parsley, 68
  stir-fried lamb, asparagus, and sweet red pepper, 88
  stuffed leg of lamb with orange gravy, 86
  Swedish meatballs, 74
  veal and mushroom paprikash with yogurt, 90
  veal cutlets with lemon and sage, 89
  veal shanks Italian style, 89
  Yankee pot roast, 64
Menus, suggested, 22–24
Mexican dishes
  chicken burritos, 103
  chili con carne, 75
  corn and cheese pudding, 146
  hot chocolate, 269
  hot roast pork and tortilla sandwiches, 77
  pork chop casserole, 81
  sliced steak, 70
  super nachos, 42
  zesty cheese enchiladas, 145
Middle Eastern dishes
  chick pea patties in pita pockets, 148
  tabouleh, 224
Milk, 16

Milk shakes
  banana, 272
  mocha, 271
Minerals, 7, 14, 19
Minestrone, 53
Mini meat loaves, 261
Mint(ed)
  chicken soup with, 52
  cucumber salad, 212
  grapefruit spritzer, 272
  peas with orange, 192
  tea, iced apple-, 273
  yogurt drink, pineapple-, 274
Mixed fruit salad, 220–221
Mixes
  barbecue seasoning, 29
  basic white sauce, 33
  buttermilk salad dressing, 28
  chili seasoning, 29
  herb salad dressing, 28
  quick bread, 31
  seasoned crumb, for chicken or pork, 30
  spaghetti sauce seasoning, 29
  taco seasoning, 30
  yogurt salad dressing, 28
Mocha
  sauce, 292
  shake, 271
Mock
  crème fraîche, 27
  hollandaise sauce, 32
  mayonnaise, 26
  sour cream, 26
  whipped cream, 27
Molded gazpacho salad, 222
Monkey bread, 230
Monosodium glutamate (MSG), 15
Mozzarella
  baked ziti with, 155
  eggplant lasagne, 134
  green pea, and carrot salad, 265
  -stuffed chicken Kiev, 110
  super nachos, 42
  turkey cutlets parmigiana, 247
  -vegetable salad with artichokes, 266
  whole wheat pizza with green peppers, 150
  zesty cheese enchiladas, 145
MSG (monosodium glutamate), 15
Muffaletto sandwiches, 264
Muffins
  basic, 240
  jam, 260
  spiced wheat germ, 31
Mulled apple cider, 269
Mulligatawny soup, 51
Mushroom(s)
  -asparagus omelets, 256
  -barley soup, 58
  beef stir-fry with sweet pepper and, 243
  chicken and, in foil, 109
  chips, crispy, 48
  herbs and spices for, 17

Mushroom(s) *(contd.)*
  minute steaks with pimientos and, 67
  noodles with, 161
  -parsley sauce, fusilli with, 161
  pork stew with chick peas, 83
  salad, Oriental, 213
  sauce, spaghetti squash with, 200
  sauce, spinach and rice loaf with, 73
  soup, cream of, 55
  soup, quick cream of, 33
  in sour cream–dill sauce, 187
  spinach-stuffed, 43
  stir-fried lobster, snow peas and, 130
  stuffed pita sandwiches with, 262
  turkey cutlets with sherry and, 247
  and veal paprikash with yogurt, 90
  vegetable-stuffed, 188
  zucchini, and pimiento lasagne, 153
Mustard
  chicken breasts Dijon, 106
  Dijon, 36
  pork scaloppine with honey, 79
  sauce, Brussels sprouts with, 179
  sauce, chicken strips with, 245

N

Nachos, super, 42
Nitrites, 15
Noodle(s)
  Alfredo-style, 161
  -cabbage casserole, 132
  ham, and green pea casserole, easy, 85
  homemade German, 163
  kasha with onions and, 170
  and rice, 164
  sesame, 163
  See also Pasta.
No-sugar fruit pudding, 288
Nut(s)
  easy nutted brown rice, 168
  meringue drops, chocolate, 280
  spaghetti with asparagus and pecans, 158
  torte, raspberry-, 279
Nutty whole wheat bread, 232–233

O

Oatmeal wafers, 282
Old-fashioned cornbread, 237
Old German sauerbraten, 65
Omega-3 fatty acids, 10, 18
One- or two-person meals. *See* Cooking for one or two.

*Recipes in **bold** type are extra low in fat, sugar, and sodium.*

Onion(s)
-cheese bread, 230
flatbread, 231
herbed creamed, 189
kasha with noodles and, 170
in raisin sauce, 189
relish, 34–35
rings, Bermuda, 189
soup, hearty French, 59
stuffing, green, braised whole chicken with, 93
zucchini, and carrot quiche, 47
Orange(s)
buttermilk drink, 268
carrots glazed with ginger and, 181
-chocolate sauce, 292
citrus and watercress salad, 221
cold curried tuna and fruit, 124
cold roast pork with black beans and fruit, 78
-cranberry loaf, 239
French toast, 260
gravy, stuffed leg of lamb with, 86
milk shake, 272
minted peas with, 192
mixed fruit salad, 220–221
-pineapple cooler, 272–273
quick bread, 31
sauce, 292
soufflé, 290
-spinach salad, 215
-tea punch, amber, 271
-tomato sauce, pork balls in, 84
Orangeade, 269
Oriental dishes
bean sprout salad, 208
chicken with snow peas and peanut sauce, 95
Chinese chicken and vegetables, 245
mushroom salad, 213
pork stir-fry with five vegetables, 80
steak, grilled, 69
tofu stir-fry with rice, 139
vegetable lo mein, 142
Oven French fries, 196
Oven-fried chicken, 98

P

Pancakes, 259
apple, 32
cheese blini, 45
corn crêpes with spicy tomato sauce, 250
grated zucchini, 203
spinach crêpes with tomato sauce, 135
Parmesan bread, 230
Parsley
-mushroom sauce, fusilli with, 161
-rice mold, 165

Parsnip(s)
with apple, 190
carrot, and potato purée, 190
Pasta, 152–164
Alfredo-style noodles, 161
baked macaroni and cheese, 156
baked ziti with mozzarella, 155
with broccoli in sweet tomato sauce, 160
and broccoli salad, 266
cannelloni with ricotta and peas, 153
cheese, and tomato pie, 159
and crab salad, 162
fisherman's baked shells, 154
kasha with onions and noodles, 170
linguine with tuna and peas, 253
linguine with tuna-caper sauce, 157
linguine with white clam sauce, 156
macaroni with chick peas and tomatoes, 155
pork with roasted peppers, 79
shells with Mediterranean vegetables, 252
spaghetti with asparagus and pecans, 158
spaghetti with meat and tomato sauce, 159
spicy lasagne roll-ups, 152
with spinach sauce, 157
summer salad, 224
tortellini with garden vegetables, 252
tortellini with spinach pesto dip, 46
zucchini, mushroom, and pimiento lasagne, 153
See also Noodles.
Pea(s), green
cannelloni with ricotta and, 153
carrot, and mozzarella salad, 265
and dumplings, 190
French-style, 191
ham, and noodle casserole, easy, 85
herbs and spices for, 17
linguine with tuna and, 253
minted, with orange, 192
purée, 191
and rice, 166
sauce, salmon loaf with, 127
Pea(s), snow and Sugar Snap
with carrots and red pepper, 192–193
chicken with peanut sauce and, 95
Chinese chicken and vegetables, 245
with chives, 193
and pasta salad, 266
stir-fried lobster, mushrooms, and, 130
with water chestnuts, 174
Pea, split, and potato soup, 60

Peach
-blueberry tarts, 286–287
-ginger crisp, 282
ice, fresh, 290
pie, deep-dish, 285
Peanut butter dip, crudités with, 264
Peanut sauce, chicken with snow peas and, 95
Pear-cranberry mold, 223
Pecan(s)
chocolate nut meringue drops, 280
easy nutted brown rice, 168
nutty whole wheat bread, 232–233
spaghetti with asparagus and, 158
Pepper(s)
artichoke-stuffed, with lemon sauce, 134
broccoli with, 178
bulgur-stuffed red, 172
cauliflower in pimiento sauce, 183
confetti coleslaw, 211
four-bean salad, 207
green, and carrots in cream sauce, 181
green, whole wheat pizza with, 150
herbs and spices for, 17
marinated broiled, 193
picadillo platter, 72
pork with roasted, 79
red, snow peas with carrots and, 192–193
relish, three-, 34
roasted vegetable salad, 216
steak, easy red and green, 68
sweet, beef stir-fry with mushrooms and, 243
sweet red, and cucumber salad, spiced, 212
sweet red, sauce, broiled salmon with, 120
sweet red, stir-fried lamb, asparagus and, 88
and tomatoes, sautéed, 193
Peppery chicken wings, 40
Picadillo platter, 72
Pickled beet salad, 209
Pie
ginger-pumpkin chiffon, 286
peach, deep-dish, 285
Pimiento(s)
green beans with, 175
minute steaks with mushrooms and, 67
sauce, cauliflower in, 183
zucchini, and mushroom lasagne, 153
Pineapple
buttermilk drink, 268
cold curried tuna and fruit, 124
-mint yogurt drink, 274
no-sugar fruit pudding, 288
-orange cooler, 272–273
sweet potatoes with, 197

Pink beans, cornmeal pizza with, 149
Pinto beans
baked, on dark bread, 132
vegetarian chili with, 141
Pita
pockets, chick pea patties in, 148
sandwiches, stuffed, 262
Pizza
cornmeal, with pink beans, 149
French bread, 250
sandwiches, 262
whole wheat, with green peppers, 150
Polenta with fresh tomato sauce, 169
Polish sausage and chick pea casserole, 244
Polysorbates, 15
Popcorn mix, crunchy, 48
Poppy seed
noodles, 163
sauce, brown rice with, 166
Pork
balls in tomato-orange sauce, 84
with cabbage and apples, 104
casserole of red cabbage and, 82
chop casserole, Mexicali, 81
chops, 30
chops, Indian-spiced, 80
chops and rice casserole, 244
cold roast, with black beans and fruit, 78
herbs and spices for, 17
hot roast, and tortilla sandwiches, 77
loin of, with vegetable stuffing, 77
roast, maple-glazed, 76
with roasted peppers, 79
savory broiled, on skewers, 82
scaloppine with honey mustard, 79
seasoned crumb mix for chicken or, 30
stew with chick peas, 83
stir-fry with five vegetables, 80
See also Ham.
Potato(es)
casserole, two-, 197
and cheese pie, easy, 145
chive vichyssoise, 59
creamy mashed, 194
curried, 194
herbs and spices for, 17
and kale soup, 60–61
mashed, and cabbage, 195
new, Danish-style, 194
oven French fries, 196
parsnip, and carrot purée, 190
salad, German, 214
savory salmon patties, 126
and split pea soup, 60
stir-fried carrots and, 181

Potato(es) *(contd.)*
 tangy cheese-stuffed, 43
 and turnip purée, 204
 twice-baked, 196–197
Pot pie
 chicken, 96
 deviled tuna, 125
Pot roast
 old German sauerbraten, 65
 Yankee, 64
Potted turkey spread, 39
Poultry, 92–116
 braised whole chicken with
  green onion stuffing, 93
 broiled chicken with
  vinegar and honey, 93
 broiled garlic-stuffed
  Cornish game hens, 116
 Brunswick stew, 94
 Caribbean lime chicken, 105
 **cheese-stuffed chicken
  Kiev, 110**
 **chicken, artichoke, and
  rice casserole, 102**
 chicken and mushrooms in
  foil, 109
 chicken biriyani, 95
 chicken breasts Dijon, 106
 chicken breasts Parmesan,
  110
 **chicken breasts with
  lemon and capers, 108**
 chicken burritos, 103
 chicken Creole, 107
 chicken fricassee, 98
 **chicken gardener's style,
  103**
 chicken Laredo, 100
 chicken pot pie, 96
 chicken Provençal, 106
 **chicken strips with
  mustard sauce, 245**
 chicken tetrazzini with
  spaghetti squash, 97
 chicken with cabbage and
  apples, 104
 **chicken with fresh tomato
  sauce, 109**
 **chicken with green sauce,
  92**
 chicken with herb
  dumplings, 99
 chicken with snow peas and
  peanut sauce, 95
 Chinese chicken and
  vegetables, 245
 **Cornish game hens with
  wild rice–apple
  stuffing, 116**
 Cornish hen glazed with
  orange and ginger, 246
 **curried chicken and
  vegetables, 246**
 **glazed turkey breast with
  sweet potato stuffing,
  111**
 oven-fried chicken, 98
 roast chicken stuffed with
  rice and apricots, 92
 sweet-and-sour apricot
  chicken, 100
 tandoori chicken, 97
 tangy barbecued chicken
  thighs, 104
 tarragon turkey loaf, 114
 turkey balsamico, 115

Poultry *(contd.)*
 turkey cutlets with lemon
  and parsley, 247
 **turkey scaloppine with
  sherried cream, 113**
 turkey slices with ham,
  112
 turkey–sour cream patties,
  114
 turkey-vegetable soufflé,
  112
**Pretzels with caraway
  seeds, 234–235**
Protein, 8, 11, 13
 complementary, 11, 16
 guidelines for, 20
 requirements for, 11
 sources of, 9
Prune-and-spice quick bread,
  238
Pudding
 blueberry breakfast, 258
 chocolate, make-your-own,
  289
 no-sugar fruit, 288
Pumpkin
 chiffon pie, ginger-, 286
 herbs and spices for, 17
 winter squash bread, 232
Punch
 amber orange-tea, 271
 ginger-tea, 269
 hot cranberry, 271

Q

Quiche, zucchini, carrot, and
  onion, 47
Quick bread
 mix, 31
 orange, 31
 prune-and-spice, 238

R

Raisin
 -apple crisp, 282
 -lemon sauce, 292
 sauce, onions in, 189
Ranch dressing, 225
Rarebit
 fish, 121
 Welsh, 148
Raspberry(ies)
 chocolate-berry crunch
  parfait, 291
 coffee cake, 259
 frozen berry yogurt, 292
 no-sugar fruit pudding, 288
 -nut torte, 279
 red berry yogurt drink, 274
 -strawberry muffins, 240
Refreshing red gazpacho, 62
Relish
 hamburger, 35
 onion, 34–35
 three-pepper, 34
Restaurants, 18
Rice
 **and beans, Italian-style,
  164**

Rice *(contd.)*
 black beans and, 138
 **brown, with asparagus and
  egg, 167**
 brown, with poppy seed
  sauce, 166
 **chicken, and artichoke
  casserole, 102**
 curried brown, with
  apricots, 168
 easy nutted brown, 168
 and green peas, 166
 herbs and spices for, 17
 kedgeree, 257
 with lemon and dill, 166
 and noodles, 164
 **and pork chops casserole,
  244**
 roast chicken stuffed with
  apricots and, 92
 salad, savory, 224
 -sardine bundles, 44
 **and spinach loaf with
  mushroom sauce, 73**
 -spinach mold, 165
 tofu stir-fry with, 139
 **vegetarian chili with,
  141**
 wild, and carrot loaf, 169
 **wild rice–apple stuffing,
  Cornish game hens with,
  116**
Ricotta
 **cannelloni with peas and,
  153**
 chilled cheese fingers, 41
 roasted garlic dip, 38
 zesty cheese enchiladas,
  145
 zucchini filled with
  spinach and, 137
Roast
 chicken stuffed with rice
  and apricots, 92
 old German sauerbraten, 65
 pork, maple-glazed, 76
 sirloin with black
  peppercorn crust, 64
 Yankee pot, 64
Roasted
 eggplant soup, 58
 garlic dip, 38
 vegetable salad, 216
Rolls
 monkey bread, 230–231
 whole wheat dinner, 234
Russian dishes
 **cheese-stuffed chicken
  Kiev, 110**
 quick borscht, 242

S

Salad dressings
 blue cheese, 225
 creamy garlic, 226
 **cucumber-yogurt sauce,
  226**
 honey-yogurt, 226
 Italian, 225
 mixes for, 28
 ranch, 225
 Thousand Island, 226
 vinaigrette, 225

Salads, 206–226
 asparagus vinaigrette, 206
 bean sprout, 208
 cabbage mold, 222
 chef's, 253
 chicken, with lemon and
  basil, 218
 citrus and watercress, 221
 **cold roast pork with
  black beans and fruit,
  78**
 confetti coleslaw, 211
 **corn and cherry tomato,
  212**
 cranberry-pear mold, 223
 creamy yogurt coleslaw,
  210
 crunchy carrot, 211
 dilled shrimp and feta
  cheese, 219
 dilled tuna-yogurt, 254
 four-bean, 207
 fruit and cheese, with
  orange dressing, 254
 German potato, 214
 Greek, 217
 green bean-zucchini, 206
 green pea, carrot, and
  mozzarella, 265
 Italian bread and tomato,
  215
 marinated vegetable, 216
 minted cucumber, 212
 mixed fruit, 220–221
 molded gazpacho, 222
 Niçoise, 218
 Oriental mushroom, 213
 pasta and broccoli, 266
 pickled beet, 209
 roasted vegetable, 216
 savory rice, 224
 sesame broccoli, 208
 spiced cucumber and sweet
  red pepper, 212
 spicy cucumber and fruit,
  220
 spinach-orange, 215
 summer pasta, 224
 sweet-and-sour red cabbage
  and apple, 210
 tabouleh, 224
 **vegetable-cheese, with
  artichokes, 266**
 Waldorf, 221
 wilted spinach, 215
Salmon
 broiled, with sweet red
  pepper sauce, 120
 with cucumber-dill sauce,
  119
 loaf with green pea sauce,
  127
 patties, savory, 126
 salad, dilled, 254
Salsa, 36
Salt. *See* Sodium.
Sandwiches
 ham and vegetable loaf,
  spicy, 85
 hot roast pork and
  tortilla, 77
 hot vegetable hero, 150
 marinated, 263
 muffaletta, 264
 pizza, 262
 stuffed pita, 262
Sardine-rice bundles, 44

*Recipes in **bold** type are extra low in fat, sugar, and sodium.*   **301**

Sauce
  basic white, mix, 33
  chocolate, 292
  cucumber-yogurt, 226
  lemon, 292
  mock hollandaise, 32
  **pork with roasted
    peppers, 79**
  spaghetti, seasoning mix,
    27
  tomato-orange, pork balls
    in, 84
Sauerbraten, old German, 65
Sautéed
  peppers and tomatoes, 193
  spinach with lemon and
    garlic, 199
Savory salt substitute, 26
Scalloped tomatoes, 203
Scallops marinated in orange
  and fennel, 129
Scrambled eggs Benedict,
  257
Seafood gumbo, 128
Seasoning mixes
  barbecue, 29
  chili, 29
  crumb, for chicken or
    pork, 30
  spaghetti sauce, 29
  taco, 30
Seasonings, 17, 19
Sesame
  broccoli salad, 208
  noodles, 163
  seeds, asparagus with, 174
  sole, 122
**Seven-vegetable casserole
  with couscous crust,
  137**
Shellfish, 127–130
  California seafood medley,
    127
  **cherry tomatoes stuffed
    with shrimp, 44**
  chowder, 242
  cold spiced shrimp, 130
  crab and pasta salad, 162
  deviled crab, 129
  deviled shrimp, 40–41
  dilled shrimp and feta
    cheese salad, 219
  herbs and spices for, 17
  linguine with white clam
    sauce, 156
  Omega-3 in, 10, 18
  scallops marinated in
    orange and fennel, 129
  seafood gumbo, 128
  stir-fried lobster,
    mushrooms, and snow
    peas, 130
Shredded beets in
  horseradish sauce, 177
Shredded turnips, 204
Shrimp
  **cherry tomatoes stuffed
    with, 44**
  cold spiced, 130
  deviled, 40–41
  and feta cheese salad,
    dilled, 219
Snack(s)
  chick pea, 48
  **crispy mushroom chips,
    48**
  crunchy popcorn mix, 48

Snow pea(s)
  **brown rice with asparagus
    and egg, 167**
  with carrots and red
    pepper, 192–193
  chicken with peanut sauce
    and, 95
  Chinese chicken and
    vegetables, 245
  and pasta salad, 266
  stir-fried lobster,
    mushrooms, and, 130
  with water chestnuts, 174
Sodium, 18
  cutting down on, 9, 14,
    16–19
  food labels and, 15
  guidelines for, 21
  high blood pressure and,
    14
  substitutes for, 14, 17,
    19, 26
Sodium nitrite, 15
Soufflé
  broccoli-Cheddar, 144
  lemon, 290
  squares, spinach, 46
  turkey-vegetable, 112
Soups, 50–62
  carrot-apple, 56–57
  chicken, with mint, 52
  chicken-escarole, 50
  chicken gumbo, 52
  chive vichyssoise, 59
  cold cucumber, 57
  corn chowder, 57
  crab chowder, 242
  cream of vegetable, 55
  creamy chilled tomato, 62
  garden-fresh vegetable, 54
  golden butternut squash,
    61
  hearty black bean, 56
  hearty French onion, 59
  homestyle chicken
    consommé, 50
  minestrone, 53
  mulligatawny, 51
  mushroom-barley, 58
  potato and kale, 60–61
  quick borscht, 242
  quick cheese, 33
  quick cream of mushroom,
    33
  refreshing red gazpacho,
    62
  roasted eggplant, 58
  spicy tomato-fish chowder,
    52
  split pea and potato, 60
  squash, yellow, 61
  turnip and potato purée,
    204
Sour cream, mock, 26
**Southwestern-style
  guacamole, 39**
Spaghetti
  **with asparagus and
    pecans, 158**
  **with meat and tomato
    sauce, 159**
  pork balls in tomato-
    orange sauce, 84
  sauce seasoning mix, 29
  See also Pasta.
Spaghetti squash
  chicken tetrazzini with, 97

Spaghetti squash *(contd.)*
  Italian style, 140
  with mushroom sauce, 200
  pork balls in tomato-
    orange sauce, 84
**Spanish-style vegetable
  casserole, 143**
Spiced
  **cauliflower with
    tomatoes, 182**
  cranberry shrub, 274
  cucumber and sweet red
    pepper salad, 212
  French toast, 260
  wheat germ muffins, 31
Spicy
  cucumber and fruit salad,
    220
  ham and vegetable loaf, 85
  lasagne roll-ups, 152
  stuffed eggs, 41
  tomato-fish chowder, 52
Spinach
  balls in tomato sauce, 198
  braised, 199
  -chicken soup, 50
  crêpes with tomato sauce,
    135
  Greek salad, 217
  herbs and spices for, 17
  orange salad, 215
  pesto dip, tortellini
    with, 46
  **and rice loaf with
    mushroom sauce, 73**
  -rice mold, 165
  ring with white bean
    sauce, 136
  salad, wilted, 215
  sauce, pasta with, 157
  sautéed, with lemon and
    garlic, 199
  soufflé squares, 46
  soup, cream of, 55
  spicy lasagne roll-ups,
    152
  -stuffed mushrooms, 43
  zucchini filled with
    ricotta and, 137
Split pea and potato soup,
  60
Spoonbread, 237
Squash, spaghetti
  chicken tetrazzini with, 97
  Italian style, 140
  with mushroom sauce, 200
  pork balls in tomato-
    orange sauce, 84
Squash, summer
  braised corn, tomatoes,
    and, 200–201
  casserole, 201
  herbed veal with, 90
  herbs and spices for, 17
  kebabs, 202
  marinated vegetable salad,
    216
  soup, 61
  **white bean, and tomato
    stew, 143**
  See also Zucchini.
Squash, winter
  baked acorn, with Parmesan
    cheese, 199
  bread, 232
  **butternut, in tomato
    sauce, 200**

Squash, winter *(contd.)*
  golden butternut soup, 61
  herbs and spices for, 17
Starch, 9
Steak(s)
  **beef, zucchini, and
    tomato kebabs, 71**
  beef roll with chili
    sauce, 66
  easy red and green pepper,
    68
  grilled Oriental, 69
  Mexican sliced, 70
  **minute, with pimientos
    and mushrooms, 67**
  parsley, 68
  pizzaiola, quick, 67
  roast sirloin with black
    peppercorn crust, 64
  sliced beef with romaine,
    cucumber, and tomatoes,
    69
Stew
  **beef, with basil-tomato
    paste, 70**
  black-eyed pea, 251
  Brunswick, 94
  corn and broccoli, 185
  lamb, carrot, and green
    bean, 87
  **lentil, hearty low-
    calorie, 138**
  **pork, with chick peas,
    83**
  **sweet and spicy
    vegetable, 142**
  **white bean, yellow squash,
    and tomato, 143**
Stir-fry(ied)
  **beef with mushrooms and
    sweet pepper, 243**
  carrots and potatoes, 181
  lamb, asparagus, and sweet
    red pepper, 88
  lobster, mushrooms, and
    snow peas, 130
  pork with five vegetables,
    80
  tofu, with rice, 139
Storing foods, 19
Strawberry(ies)
  angel roll, 278
  chiffon charlotte,
    284–285
  frozen berry yogurt, 292
  milk shake, 272
  mixed fruit salad,
    220–221
  -raspberry muffins, 240
  red berry yogurt drink,
    274
  spicy cucumber and fruit
    salad, 220
Strokes, 7, 8, 14
Stuffed
  fish fillets with nutmeg
    sauce, 123
  **leg of lamb with orange
    gravy, 86**
  pita sandwiches, 262
Substitutes, 26–36
  **barbecue seasoning mix,
    27**
  **basic white sauce mix,
    33**
  buttermilk salad dressing
    mix, 28

Substitutes *(contd.)*
chili seasoning mix, 27
Dijon mustard, 36
hamburger relish, 35
herb salad dressing mix, 28
ketchup, 36
low-sodium chicken broth, 34
mock crème fraîche, 27
mock hollandaise sauce, 32
mock mayonnaise, 26
mock sour cream, 26
mock whipped cream, 27
onion relish, 34–35
quick bread mix, 31
salsa, 36
salt, commercial, 14
savory salt, 26
seasoned crumb mix for chicken or pork, 30
spaghetti sauce seasoning mix, 27
taco seasoning mix, 30
three-pepper relish, 34
yogurt salad dressing mix, 28
Succotash salad, 211
Sugar, 13
cutting down on, 9, 18, 19
food labels and, 15
guidelines for, 20, 21
Sugar Snap peas. *See* Pea(s), Snow and Sugar Snap.
Sulfites, 15
Summer pasta salad, 224
Summer squash
braised corn, tomatoes, and, 200–201
casserole, 201
herbed veal with, 90
herbs and spices for, 17
kebabs, 202
marinated vegetable salad, 216
soup, 61
white bean, and tomato stew, 143
See also Zucchini.
Super nachos, 42
Suppers, 23
Swedish meatballs, 74
Sweet-and-Sour
apricot chicken, 100
beets, 177
red cabbage and apple salad, 210
Sweet and spicy vegetable stew, 142
Sweet potato(es)
with apple, 197
herbs and spices for, 17
stuffing, glazed turkey breast with, 111
two-potato casserole, 197
Swiss health cereal, 258
Symbols in recipes, 21

T

Tabouleh, 224
Taco seasoning mix, 30
Tandoori chicken, 97
Tarragon turkey loaf, 114
Tarts, blueberry-peach, 286–287

Tea
herbal, 273
iced apple-mint, 273
punch, amber orange-, 271
punch, ginger-, 269
Thousand Island dressing, 226
Three-pepper relish, 34
Tofu
stir-fry with rice, 139
vegetable lo mein, 142
Tomato(es)
baked tuna-stuffed, 126
-basil paste, beef stew with, 70
beef, and zucchini kebabs, 71
braised eggplant, zucchini, and, 186
braised yellow squash, corn and, 200–201
and bread salad, Italian, 215
broccoli-stuffed, 178
cherry, and corn salad, 212
cherry, and zucchini with vinegar, 202
cherry, green beans and, 175
cherry, stuffed with shrimp, 44
consommé Madrilène, 50
-fish chowder, spicy, 52
grilled Parmesan, 203
herbs and spices for, 17
jambalaya, 164–165
ketchup, 36
macaroni with chick peas and, 155
molded gazpacho salad, 222
-orange sauce, pork balls in, 84
pasta, and cheese pie, 159
and peppers, sautéed, 193
picadillo platter, 72
quick steak pizzaiola, 67
salsa, 36
sauce, spinach crêpes with, 135
scalloped, 203
sliced beef with romaine, cucumber, and, 69
soup, creamy chilled, 62
spiced cauliflower with, 182–183
white bean, and yellow squash stew, 143
Tomato sauce
butternut squash in, 200
fresh, chicken with, 109
fresh, polenta with, 169
spaghetti with meat and, 159
spicy, corn crêpes with, 250
spinach balls in, 198
sweet, pasta with broccoli in, 161
yellow wax beans in, 176
Tortellini
with garden vegetables, 252
with spinach pesto dip, 46

Tuna
-caper sauce, linguine with, 157
fisherman's baked shells, 154
and fruit, cold curried, 124
linguine with peas and, 253
marinated sandwiches, 263
muffaletto with, 264
patties, 249
pot pie, deviled, 125
salade Niçoise, 218
-stuffed cucumbers, 44
-stuffed tomatoes, baked, 126
-yogurt salad, dilled, 254
Turkey
balsamico, 115
biriyani, 95
breast, glazed, with sweet potato stuffing, 111
chef's salad, 253
cutlets with lemon and parsley, 247
with fresh tomato sauce, 109
gumbo, 52
herbs and spices for, 17
jambalaya, 164–165
mini meat loaves, 261
potted spread, 39
salad with lemon and basil, 218
scaloppine with sherried cream, 113
slices with ham, 112
–sour cream patties, 114–115
tarragon loaf, 114
-vegetable soufflé, 112
Turnip(s)
glazed with honey and lemon, 204
herbs and spices for, 17
and potato purée, 204
shredded, 204
Twice-baked potatoes, 196–197
Two-cheese casserole, 146
Two-potato casserole, 197

V

Veal
cutlets with lemon and sage, 89
herbed, with summer squash, 90
herbs and spices for, 17
and mushroom paprikash with yogurt, 90
shanks Italian style, 89
Swedish meatballs, 74
Vegetable(s), 172–204
asparagus with sesame seeds, 174

Vegetable(s) *(contd.)*
baby lima beans with sour cream and paprika, 176
baked acorn squash with Parmesan cheese, 199
baked asparagus with Parmesan cheese, 174
baked beets, 176
baked cabbage wedges with Parmesan and bread crumbs, 179
-barley loaf with yogurt-dill sauce, 133
Bermuda onion rings, 189
braised eggplant, zucchini, and tomatoes, 186
braised red cabbage with cranberries, 180
braised spinach, 199
braised yellow squash, corn, and tomatoes, 200–201
broccoli-stuffed tomatoes, 178
broccoli with basil, 178
broccoli with peppers, 178
Brussels sprouts with lemon sauce, 179
Brussels sprouts with mustard sauce, 179
butternut squash in tomato sauce, 200
carrots and green pepper in cream sauce, 181
carrots glazed with orange and ginger, 181
casserole, Spanish-style, 143
cauliflower in pimiento sauce, 183
cauliflower pudding, 183
cauliflower with bread crumbs, 184
celery and artichoke hearts in cheese sauce, 184
-cheese salad with artichokes, 266
consommé, 50
cooking, 19
corn and broccoli stew, 185
corn and lima beans, 185
corn pudding, 186
creamy mashed potatoes, 194
crudités with peanut butter dip, 264
curried cabbage, 180
curried potatoes, 194
curry with yogurt sauce, 141
Danish-style new potatoes, 194
eggplant stacks, 186–187
French-style green peas, 191
garden, tortellini with, 252
glazed carrots with five spices, 182
grated zucchini pancake, 203

*Recipes in **bold** type are extra low in fat, sugar, and sodium.*

Vegetable(s) *(contd.)*
green beans and cherry tomatoes, 175
green beans with dill, 174
green beans with pimientos, 175
green pea purée, 191
grilled Parmesan tomatoes, 203
and ham loaf, spicy, 85
herbed creamed onions, 189
hero, hot, 150
juice, garden, 274
kasha with, 171
lima beans with herbs, 176
lo mein, 142
marinated broiled peppers, 193
marinated fresh, 48
mashed potatoes and cabbage, 195
Mediterranean, pasta shells with, 252
minted peas with orange, 192
mushrooms in sour cream–dill sauce, 187
onions in raisin sauce, 189
oven French fries, 196
parsnip, carrot, and potato purée, 190
parsnips with apple, 190
peas and dumplings, 190
salad, marinated, 216
salad, roasted, 216
salade Niçoise, 218
sautéed peppers and tomatoes, 193
sautéed spinach with lemon and garlic, 199
scalloped tomatoes, 203
seven-, casserole with couscous crust, 137

Vegetable(s) *(contd.)*
shredded beets in horseradish sauce, 177
shredded turnips, 204
snow peas with carrots and red peppers, 192–193
spaghetti squash with mushroom sauce, 200
spiced cauliflower with tomatoes, 182–183
spinach balls in tomato sauce, 198
squash kebabs, 202
stew, sweet and spicy, 142
stir-fried carrots and potatoes, 181
-stuffed mushrooms, 188, 188
Sugar Snap peas with chives, 193
Sugar Snap peas with water chestnuts, 174
sweet-and-sour beets, 177
sweet potatoes with apple, 197
tofu stir-fry with rice, 139
turnip and potato purée, 204
turnips glazed with honey and lemon, 204
twice-baked potatoes, 196–197
two-potato casserole, 197
yellow squash casserole, 201
yellow wax beans in tomato sauce, 176
zucchini and cherry tomatoes with vinegar, 202
Vegetarian meals, 11, 16
See also Meatless main dishes.
Vinaigrette dressing, 225
herbal, 28
Vitamins, 7, 8, 19

W

Waldorf salad, 221
Walnut(s)
chocolate nut meringue drops
easy nutted brown rice, 168
raspberry-nut torte, 279
Water chestnuts, Sugar Snap peas with, 174
Watercress
and citrus salad, 221
soup, cream of, 55
Weight, losing, 10–11
Welsh rarebit, 148
Wheat germ muffins, spiced, 31
Whipped cream, mock, 27
White bean(s)
four-bean salad, 207
sauce, spinach ring with, 136
yellow squash, and tomato stew, 143
White cake with seven-minute frosting, 277
White sauce mix, basic, 33
Whiting, lemony baked stuffed, 119
Whole-grain mustard, 36
Whole wheat
bread, nutty, 232–233
dinner rolls, 234
pizza with green peppers, 150
Wild rice
and carrot loaf, 169
–apple stuffing, Cornish game hens with, 116
Wilted spinach salad, 215
Wine-poached bluefish with onion and dill, 118
Winter squash
baked acorn, with Parmesan cheese, 199
bread, 232
butternut, in tomato sauce, 200

Winter squash *(contd.)*
golden butternut soup, 61
herbs and spices for, 17

Y

Yankee pot roast, 64
Yellow wax beans in tomato sauce, 176
Yogurt
-cucumber sauce, 226
drink, pineapple-mint, 274
frozen berry, 292
-honey dressing, 226
salad dressing mix, 28
sauce, vegetable curry with, 141
Yorkshire pudding, 239

Z

Zesty cheese enchiladas, 145
Zucchini
beef, and tomato kebabs, 71
braised eggplant, tomatoes, and, 186
brown rice with egg and, 167
carrot, and onion quiche, 47
and cherry tomatoes with vinegar, 202
filled with spinach and ricotta, 137
frittata, 147
-green bean salad, 206
herbed veal with summer squash, 90
mushroom, and pimiento lasagne, 153
pancake, grated, 203
scallops marinated in orange and fennel, 129
vinaigrette, 206
See also Summer squash.

*Recipes in **bold** type are extra low in fat, sugar, and sodium.*